Essentials of Conservation Biology

To Margaret, Daniel, William, and Jasper

Table of Contents

PART ONE
Major Issues That Define the Discipline

PART TWO
Valuing Biodiversity

PART FOUR
Conservation at the Population and Species Levels

PART FIVE
Practical Applications

Preface

When the first edition of *Essentials of Conservation Biology* appeared in 1993, conservation biology as a distinct field of study was less than a decade old. The years leading up to the decision to write what would become the first comprehensive textbook of conservation biology were exciting, filled with new ideas, fascinating scientific developments, and original and novel research, much of it published in the fledgling Society for Conservation Biology's journal *Conservation Biology*. The publication of *Essentials* was received with enthusiasm, and its success helped to spur continued growth within the discipline. The five years that have passed since the first edition have seen the development of a new maturity in conservation biology—a change that has heavily influenced the revisions made to this second edition.

In 1993, conservation biology was still a rapidly expanding field of study. Journal articles and books covering a staggering variety of subjects appeared at a furious pace, yet many of them served to highlight the amount of knowledge that practitioners of this discipline still lacked. Allied fields such as restoration ecology, environmental ethics, and ecological economics were in their infancy; data on important ecological issues such as threats to amphibian species were scarce and sketchy. Hence, the first edition of *Essentials* opened a window onto many subjects, but in certain cases could not explore them in depth—the information simply wasn't readily available at the time.

Five years later, however, many of these topics have become well defined, and the new edition reflects these developments. Conservation biologists have filled in many of the gaps that were present in the field five years ago while simultaneously opening up new avenues for scientific exploration, which keep the discipline vibrant and growing. For example, the first edition sidebar about amphibian declines was based upon a few scattered reports indicating that researchers in different parts of the world were observing a growing problem. In the past five years, this subject has met a veritable explosion of research interest: it has been the subject of many books, several international symposia, and large numbers of articles in both the scientific and popular media. Similar progress has been made in many other areas, such as the breeding of endangered animals and the exploration of the deep sea. Unexpected and new species of plants and animals continue to be identified, including an entirely new phylum, the Cycliophora.

Yet some of the most significant achievements of the discipline are found outside of the realm of research. Many prominent scientists have taken the call to activism to heart and have made productive efforts to create a strong international movement supporting the conservation of biological diversity. The 1992 Rio Conference and related international agreements such as the Convention on Biological Diversity are in part products of conservation biologists' striving to raise popular awareness of and concern for the threats to biological diversity. One of the greatest challenges ahead lies in finding ways to link sustainable development with the protection of biological diversity. In many cases this will involve forging cooperative agreements among conservation biologists, government officials, local people, and the business community.

In keeping with this approach, and with the assistance of the staff at Sinauer Associates, I have attempted to make conservation biology as accessible as possible to a wider audience. In 1995, Sinauer published an abridged version of the first edition, called *A Primer of Conservation Biology*. The *Primer* was intended to reach students in short or non-science courses, as well as being more attractive to a popular audience than a standard college textbook. At the same time, I embarked on an effort to reach an international audience by seeking out colleagues in other countries to translate both books for non-English-speaking students. The first of these translations, *Naturschutzbiologie*, was published in Germany by Spektrum in 1995, and a Chinese translation followed not long after. As new editions were proposed by other interested colleagues, it became clear that the best way to make the material accessible was to include case studies of species, conservation issues, laws, and customs from those regions that are of more immediate relevance to the intended readers.

In the past three years, regionally adapted translations of *Essentials* and the *Primer* have been published in Japanese (with Hiromi Kobori) and Indonesian (with Jatna Supriatna and others). Korean, French, Spanish, and Portuguese editions are planned for the near future. The MacArthur foundation, which funded the Indonesian edition, has also agreed to sponsor adapted editions for Vietnam and China. Like many of my colleagues, I feel that it is crucial that conservation biology develop as a discipline with a global scope; these translation projects represent my own efforts to contribute to that development.

Acknowledgments

Individual chapters or groups of chapters in this edition were reviewed by Tom Ankersen, B. Beehler, Katrina Brandon, Cutler Cleveland, Lisa Delissio, Donald Falk, Nick Gotelli, Devra Kleiman, Bruce Pavlik, Kent Redford, Craig Shafer, John Silander, Dan Simberloff, Phil Tabas, Lou Toth, Joan Walker, and Garrison Wilkes.

The new and updated boxes and case studies of specific topics are crucial to the book, and many people offered specialized input that helped make them current: Susan Alberts, W. H. Allen, George Archibald, Jonathan Atwood, Vadim Birstein, Andrew Blaustein, Vernon Bleich, Tim Clark, Tom Cade, Paul Cox, James Dietz, James Estes, Michelle Frankel, Tim Gerrodotte, J. Gosselink, Gary Jacobson, Frances James, Margaret Kinnard, Ronald Lamberson, Tom Ledig, Lloyd Loope, Dale Lewis, David Maehr, Joseph Makarewicz, Lynn McGuire, Don Melnick, Charles Munn, Peter Neuenschwander, Tim O'Brien, Dave Pearson, Joseph Pechmann, M. Phillips, Tim Power, Pascal Raevel, Lisa Sorenson, T. Spies, Margaret Stewart, Don Waller, M. S. Warren, J. Weir, E. B. Welch, Kent Whaley, and David Whitacre.

Phil Cafaro, April Algaier Stern, and Elizabeth Platt were the principal research assistants for the project, providing valuable criticism of early drafts and revising the boxes. Daniel Tsyvine, Jennifer Smith, Linus Chen, Tigga Kingston, and Amy Lerner assisted in proofreading and putting together the bibliography. Judith Fuhring helped immensely in obtaining many of the dramatic new photographs that appear in this edition. Andy Sinauer, Carol Wigg, and Jeff Johnson of Sinauer Associates did a great job of turning the manuscript into a book.

And finally, special thanks are due to Kamaljit Bawa, Les Kaufman, and Margaret Primack for their constant encouragement. I would also like to express my thanks to Boston University for providing me with the excellent facilities and environment that made this project possible, and to the many Boston University students who have taken the conservation biology course over the years. Their suggestions, feedback, and enthusiasm have helped me find new ways to present this topic.

Richard Primack
Boston University, March 1998

PART ONE

Major Issues That Define the Discipline

CHAPTER 2

What Is Biological Diversity?

THE PROTECTION OF biological diversity is central to conservation biology, but the phrase "biological diversity" can have different meanings. The World Wildlife Fund (1989) defines it as "the millions of plants, animals, and microorganisms, the genes they contain, and the intricate ecosystems they help build into the living environment." By this definition, biological diversity must be considered on three levels:

1. *Species diversity.* All the species on Earth, including bacteria and protists as well as the species of the multicellular kingdoms (plants, fungi, and animals).
2. *Genetic diversity.* The genetic variation within species, both among geographically separated populations and among individuals within single populations.
3. *Community diversity.* The different biological communities and their associations with the physical environment ("the ecosystem") (Figure 2.1).

All these levels of biological diversity are necessary for the continued survival of species and natural communities, and all are important to people. Species diversity represents the entire range of evolutionary and ecological adaptations of species to particular environments. The diversity of species provides people with resources and resource alter-

Genetic diversity in a rabbit population

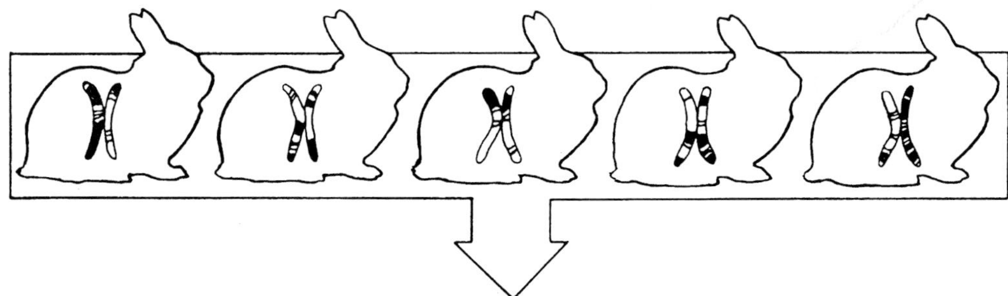

Species diversity in a prairie ecosystem

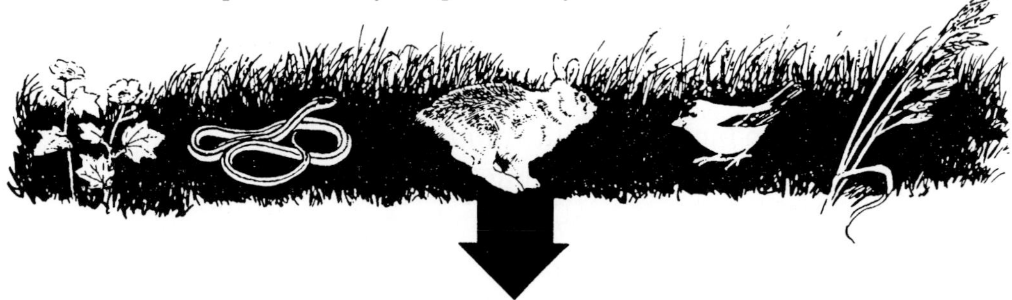

Community and ecosystem diversity across an entire region

Figure 2.1 Biological diversity includes genetic diversity (the genetic variation found within each species), species diversity (the range of species in a given ecosystem), and community/ecosystem diversity (the variety of habitat types and ecosystem processes extending over a given region). (From Temple 1991; drawing by T. Sayre.)

The origination of new species is normally a slow process, taking place over hundreds, if not thousands, of generations. The evolution of new genera and families is an even slower process, lasting hundreds of thousands, or even millions, of years. However, there are mechanisms whereby new species can arise in just one generation without geographical separation. Unusual, unequal divisions of chromosome sets in plant reproduction may result in offspring with extra sets of chromosomes; these offspring are known as **polyploids**. Polyploid individuals may be morphologically and physiologically different from their parents and, if they are well suited to the environment, may form a new species within the range of the parent species.

Even though new species are arising all the time, the present rate of species extinction is probably more than 1000 times faster than the rate of speciation. The situation is actually worse than this grim statistic suggests. First, the rate of speciation may actually be slowing down because so much of the Earth's surface has been taken over for human use and no longer supports evolving biological communities. As habitats decline, fewer populations of each species exist, and thus there are fewer opportunities for evolution. Many of the existing protected areas and national parks may be too small to allow the process of speciation to occur (Figure 2.3). Second, many of the species threatened with extinction are the sole remaining representatives of their genus or

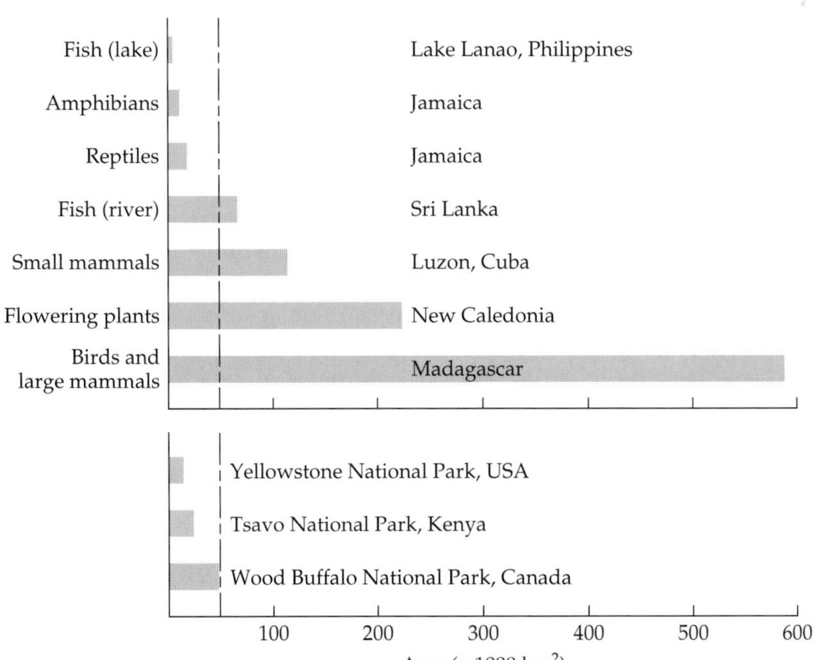

Figure 2.3 Certain groups of organisms apparently need a minimum area in order to undergo the process of speciation (upper graph). For example, for small mammals, the smallest islands (Cuba and Luzon) on which a single species is known to have given rise to two species are 100,000 km^2. Even the largest national parks (lower graph) are probably too small to allow for the evolution of new species of flowering plants, birds, or mammals, although they might be large enough for the continued evolution of fishes, amphibians, and reptiles. (After Soulé 1980.)

family; examples include the coelacanth (*Latimeria chalumnae*), a fish found in the Indian Ocean, and the giant panda (*Ailuropoda melanoleuca*) in China. The extinction of taxonomically unique species representing ancient lineages is not balanced by the appearance of new species.

Genetic Diversity

At each level of biological diversity—species, genetic, and community—conservation biologists study the mechanisms that alter or maintain diversity. Genetic diversity within a species is often affected by the reproductive behavior of individuals within populations (Tamarin 1996). A **population** is a group of individuals that mate with one another and produce offspring; a species may include one or more separate populations. A population may consist of only a few individuals or millions of individuals, providing that the individuals actually produce offspring. A single individual of a sexual species would not constitute a population. Neither does a group of individuals that cannot reproduce; for example, the last 10 dusky seaside sparrows (*Ammodramus maritimus nigrescens*) did not constitute a true population because all of them were males.

Individuals within a population usually are genetically different from one another. Genetic variation arises because individuals have slightly different forms of their **genes**, the units of the chromosomes that code for specific proteins. These different forms of a gene are known as **alleles**, and the differences originally arise through **mutations**—changes that occur in the deoxyribonucleic acid (DNA) that constitutes an individual's chromosomes. The various alleles of a gene may affect the development and physiology of an individual organism. Crop breeders and animal breeders take advantage of this genetic variation to breed higher yielding, pest-resistant strains of domesticated species such as wheat, corn, cattle, and poultry.

Genetic variation increases when offspring receive unique combinations of genes and chromosomes from their parents via the **recombination** of genes that occurs during sexual reproduction. Genes are exchanged between chromosomes, and new combinations are created when chromosomes from two parents combine to form a genetically unique offspring. Although mutations provide the basic material for genetic variation, the ability of sexually reproducing species to randomly rearrange alleles in different combinations dramatically increases the potential for genetic variation.

The total array of genes and alleles in a population is the **gene pool** of the population, while the particular combination of alleles that any individual possesses is its **genotype**. The **phenotype** of an individual represents the morphological, physiological, anatomical, and biochemical characteristics of the individual that result from the expression of its genotype in a particular environment (Figure 2.4). Some characteristics of humans, such as the amount of body fat and tooth decay, are strikingly influenced by the environment, while other characteristics, such as eye color, blood type, and forms of certain enzymes, are determined predominantly by an individual's genotype.

Sometimes individuals that differ genetically also differ in ways related to their survival or ability to reproduce, such as their ability to tolerate cold, their resistance to disease, or the speed at which they can run away from danger. If individuals with certain alleles are better able to survive and produce offspring than individuals without these alleles, then **gene frequencies** in the population will change in subsequent generations. This phenomenon is called **natural selection**.

The amount of genetic variability in a population is determined by both the number of genes that have more than one allele (**polymorphic genes**) and the number of alleles for each polymorphic gene. The existence of a polymorphic gene allows some individuals in the population to be **heterozygous** for the gene, that is, to receive a different allele of the gene from each parent. This genetic variation allows species to adapt to a changing environment. Rare species usually have less genetic variation than widespread species and, consequently, are more vulnerable to extinction when environmental conditions change. However, there are examples of plant species with little or no genetic variation that are surviving quite well.

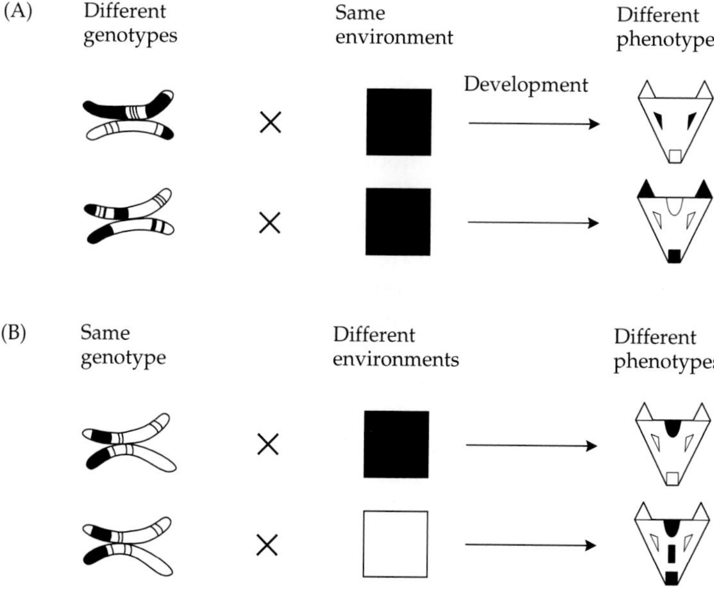

Figure 2.4 The physical, physiological, and biochemical characteristics of an individual—its *phenotype*—are determined by its genotype and by the environment (e.g., hot vs. cold climate; abundant vs. scarce food) in which the individual lives. (After Alcock 1993.)

In a wide variety of plant and animal populations it has been demonstrated that individuals that are heterozygous have greater **fitness** than comparable individuals that are homozygous; i.e., heterozygous individuals have greater growth, survival, and reproduction rates (Allendorf and Leary 1986). The reasons for this appear to be that (1) having two different forms of an enzyme gives the individual greater flexibility in dealing with life's challenges, and (2) nonfunctional or harmful alleles received from one parent are masked by the functioning alleles received from the other parent. This phenomenon of increased fitness in highly heterozygous individuals, also referred to as **hybrid vigor**, is widely known in domestic animals.

Populations of a species may be genetically different from one another in their relative frequencies of alleles and even the types of allele forms for particular genes. These genetic differences may result from adaptation of each population to its local environment or simple random chance. Unique populations of a species, particularly those found at the edges of a species range, are considered an important component of biological diversity and worth protecting.

Although most mating occurs within populations, individuals occasionally move from one population to another, allowing the transfer of new alleles and genetic combinations between populations. This genetic transfer is referred to as **gene flow**. Natural gene flow between populations is sometimes interrupted by human activities, causing a reduction in the genetic variation in each population. The importance of genetic variability to conservation biology is discussed at length in Chapters 11 and 12.

Genetic variation also occurs within domesticated plants and animals. In traditional societies, people preserved new plant forms that were well suited to their needs. Through generations of this process of **artificial selection**, varieties of species were developed that were productive and adapted to local conditions of soil, climate, and crop pests. This process has accelerated in modern agriculture, with scientific breeding programs that manipulate genetic variation to meet present human needs. Without genetic variation, improvements in agriculture would be more difficult. Advanced techniques of biotechnology allow even more precise use of genetic variation. Thousands of varieties of crops, such as rice, potatoes, and corn, have been incorporated into the breeding programs of modern agriculture. Among animals, the huge numbers of breeds of domestic dogs, cats, chickens, cattle, sheep, and pigs are evidence of the ability of artificial selection to alter gene pools for the benefit of people (Figure 2.5). Genetic variation is also maintained in specialized collections of species used in scientific research, such as *Drosophila* fruit fly stocks used in genetic research; the tiny, fast-growing *Arabidopsis* mustard plants that are used in plant research; and mice used in physiological and medical research.

Mayr, E. 1991. *One Long Argument: Charles Darwin and the Genesis of Modern Evolutionary Thought*. Harvard University Press, Cambridge, MA. Darwin has had a dominant influence on modern biology.

Odum, E. P. 1997. *Ecology: A Bridge Between Science and Society*. Sinauer Associates, Sunderland, MA. A classic brief text with updated examples.

Pimm, S. L. 1991. *The Balance of Nature*. University of Chicago Press, Chicago. An advanced text on the principles of community organization and their application.

Power, M., D. Tilman, J. A. Estes, B. A. Menge et al. 1996. Challenges in the quest for keystones. *BioScience* 46: 609–620. An excellent review article, with strong coverage of theory and examples.

Ricklefs, R. E. 1994. *The Economy of Nature*, 3rd Edition. W. H. Freeman and Co., New York. A well-written textbook on the basic principles of ecology.

Standley, L. A. 1992. Taxonomic issues in rare species protection. *Rhodora* 94: 218–242. A discussion of how taxonomic problems can complicate efforts at legal protection of rare species.

Tamarin, R. H. 1996. *Principles of Genetics*, 5th Edition. Wm. C. Brown, Dubuque, IA. A good background text for learning the principles of population and molecular genetics.

CHAPTER 3

Where Is the World's Biological Diversity Found?

THE MOST SPECIES-RICH environments appear to be tropical rain forests, coral reefs, the deep sea, and large tropical lakes (WCMC 1992; Heywood 1995). Tropical dry habitats—shrublands, grasslands, and deserts—also have an abundance of species (Mares 1992), as do temperate shrublands with Mediterranean climates such as South Africa, southern California, southwestern Australia, Chile, and the countries of the Mediterranean Basin (Cowling et al. 1996).

The diversity of the tropical rain forests is due primarily to the great abundance of animal species in a single class: the insects. In coral reefs and the deep sea, diversity is spread over a much broader range of phyla and classes. These marine systems contain representatives of 28 of the 33 animal phyla that exist today; 13 of these phyla exist *only* in the marine environment (Grassle et al. 1991). (In contrast, only one phylum is found exclusively in the terrestrial environment, and no phylum is restricted to the freshwater environment.) Four marine phyla are found only in symbiotic association with other species. Diversity in the deep sea may be due to the great age, enormous area, isolation of certain seas by intervening land masses, and stability of the environment, as well as specialization on particular sediment types (Ray et al. 1991; Etter and Grassle 1992; Waller 1996). However, this traditional view of the "unchanging" sea is being reevaluated as a result of evidence showing decreased deep-sea biodiversity during postglacial episodes (Rex 1997).

The great diversity of fishes and other species in large tropical lakes is a result of rapid evolutionary radiation in a series of isolated, productive habitats (Kaufman 1992).

Patterns of diversity are known primarily through the efforts of taxonomists who have methodically collected organisms from all areas of the world, but they are known only in broad outline for many groups of organisms. For example, 80% of the beetle species collected in a study in Panama were new to science, even though Panama is one of the best-known areas of the tropics (Erwin 1983; May 1992).

Almost all groups of organisms show an increase in species diversity toward the tropics. For example, Costa Rica has 205 species of mammals while France has only 93, despite the fact that the two countries have roughly the same land area (Table 3.1). The contrast is particularly striking for trees and other flowering plants: ten hectares of forest in Amazonian Peru or Brazil might have 300 or more tree species, whereas an equivalent forest in temperate Europe or the United States would probably contain 30 species or less. In the case of tiger beetles (Cicindelidae), a widespread and well-known insect family, major tropical regions of the world have over 300 species, while

TABLE 3.1 ***Number of mammal species in selected tropical and temperate countries paired for comparable size***

Tropical country	Area (1000 km^2)	Number of mammal species	Temperate country	Area (1000 km^2)	Number of mammal species
Brazil	8456	394	Canada	9220	139
Zaire	2268	415	Argentina	2737	258
Mexico	1909	439	Algeria	2382	92
Indonesia	1812	515	Iran	1636	140
Colombia	1039	359	South Africa	1221	247
Venezuela	882	288	Chile	748	91
Costa Rica	511	205	France	550	93
Philippines	298	166	United Kingdom	242	50
Rwanda	25	151	Belgium	40	58

Source: Data from WRI 1994

temperate regions have less than 150 species (Pearson and Cassola 1992). Within a given continent, the number of species increases toward the equator (Figure 3.1).

Attempts are being made to use particular groups of species as indicators of overall species diversity, so that locations of high species diversity can be rapidly identified (Prendergast et al. 1993; Williams 1994; Beccaloni and Gaston 1995). In general, there is a rough correspondence in the distribution of species richness between different groups of organisms. For example, in Africa, concentrations of birds, amphibians, and mammal species are found in the same general areas: southern African shrubland, West African tropical forests and rivers, the Great Lakes region, and the Ethiopian highlands (Figure 3.2) (Bibby et al. 1992). Each group of living organisms may reach its greatest species richness in a different part of the world due to historical circumstances or the suitability of the site to its needs. More work is needed on this topic of correlated patterns of species richness and distribution before definitive conclusions can be reached (Currie 1991).

Patterns of diversity in terrestrial species are paralleled by patterns in marine species, again with an increase in species diversity toward the tropics. For example, the Great Barrier Reef off the eastern coast of Australia has 50 genera of reef-building coral at its northern end where it approaches the tropics, but only 10 genera at its southern end, farthest away from the tropics (Stehli and Wells 1971). In the case of sea squirts (tunicates), only 103 species are known to exist in the Arctic, but over 600 species have been identified in tropical waters (Fischer 1960).

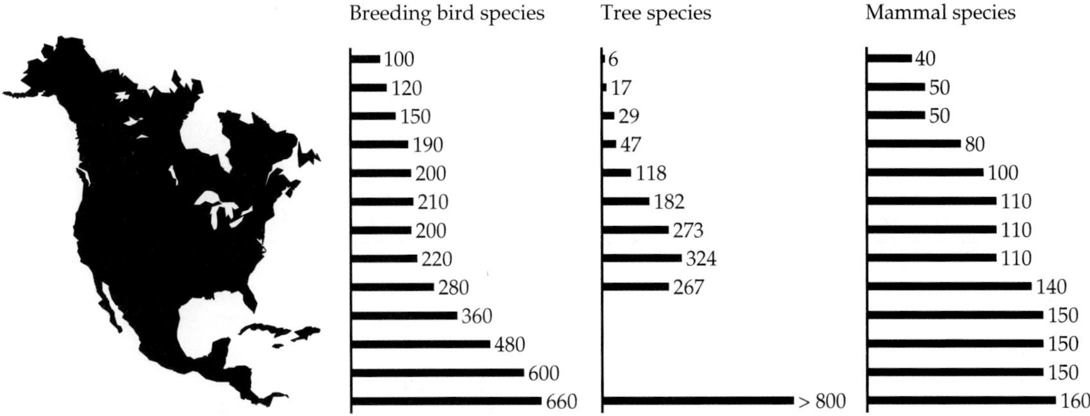

Figure 3.1 In North America, as in all the continents, the numbers of bird, tree, and mammal species increase toward the tropics. The numbers of species indicated in the bar graphs correspond to latitude in the map at left. Tree species diversity is not available for some lower latitudes. (From Briggs 1995.)

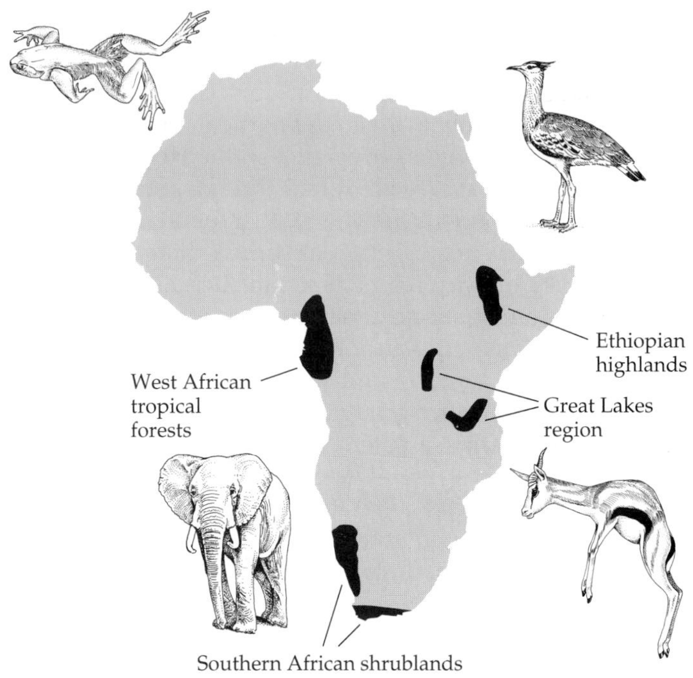

Figure 3.2 In Africa, concentrations of species of birds, amphibians, and mammals are found in the same general areas: the Ethiopian highlands, the African Great Lakes, West African tropical rain forests, and in the Mediterranean climate of southern Africa's shrublands. (Map after Bibby et al. 1992.)

These increases in richness of coastal species toward the tropics are paralleled by increases in planktonic species, such as foraminiferans, and increases in deep-sea species (Buzas and Culver 1991).

Local variation in topography, climate, and environment also affects patterns of species richness (Diamond 1988a; Currie 1991; Huston 1994). In terrestrial communities, species richness tends to increase with decreasing elevation, increasing solar radiation, and increasing precipitation. The lower richness of plants and animals in Africa, in comparison with South America and Asia, may be due to a combination of lower rainfall, smaller total area, and greater human impact. Even within tropical Africa itself, areas of low rainfall in the Sahel have fewer species than forested areas with higher rainfall to the south. However, the extensive savannah areas of East and Central Africa have a richness and abundance of antelopes and other ungulate grazers not found on other continents. The greatest abundance of mammal species may occur at intermediate levels of precipitation rather than in the wettest or driest habitats (Western 1989; Mares 1992). Strong, seasonal temperature fluctuations are another factor associated with large numbers of species in tropical communities (Scheiner and Rey-Benayas 1994). In the marine environment, species diversity apparently decreases with increasing depth, though the diversity of the deep sea is still poorly known.

Species richness can be greater where complex topography provides more environmental variation and allows genetic isolation, local adaptation, and speciation to occur. For example, a sedentary species occupying a series of isolated mountain peaks in the Andes may eventually evolve into several different species, each adapted to its local mountain environment. A similar process could happen in a fish that occupies a large drainage system that becomes divided into several smaller systems. Geologically complex areas can produce a variety of soil conditions with very sharp boundaries between them, leading to multiple communities and species adapted to one soil type or another. The greatest species richness in open ocean communities exists where waters from different biological communities overlap, but the locations of these boundary areas are often unstable over time (Angel 1993).

In temperate communities, great diversity is found among plant species in southwestern Australia, South Africa, California, Chile, and the Mediterranean Basin, all of which are characterized by a climate of moist winters and hot, dry summers. The shrub and herb communities in these areas are apparently rich in species due to their combination of considerable geological age, complexity of site conditions, and severe environmental conditions. The frequency of fire in these areas also may favor rapid speciation (Cowling et al. 1996).

Historical factors are also important in defining patterns of species richness; areas that are geologically older have more species than younger areas. For example, coral species richness is several times greater in the Indian and West Pacific Oceans than in the Atlantic Ocean, which is geologically younger (Figure 3.3). More than 50 genera of coral exist in many of the Indo-Pacific areas, but only about 20

Figure 3.3 Global distribution of the coral reef biome. (After Wells and Hanna 1992.)

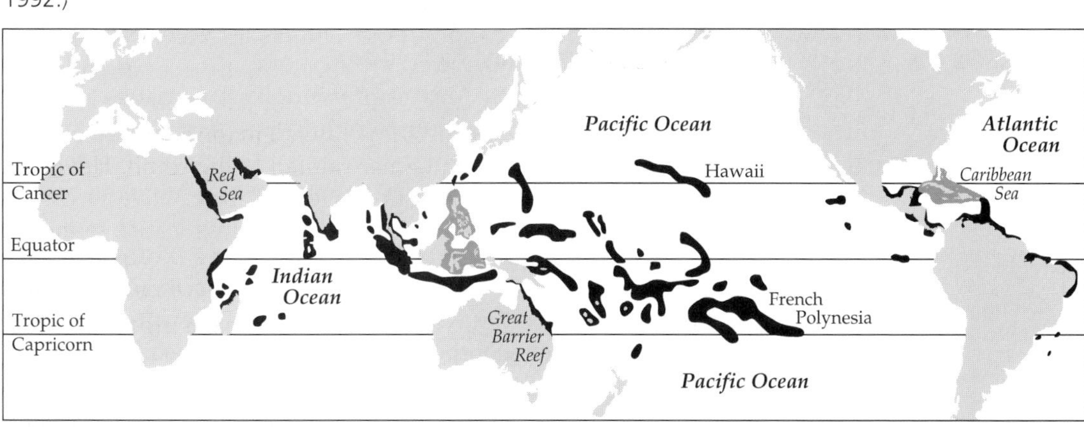

genera occur in the Caribbean Sea and adjacent Atlantic Ocean. Areas that are geologically older have had more time to receive species from other parts of the world and more time for existing species to undergo adaptive speciation in response to local conditions.

Why Are There So Many Species in the Tropics?

There is ample evidence demonstrating that tropical environments possess the greatest species diversity. Many theories have been advanced to explain this (Connell and Orias 1964; Pianka 1966). The following are some of the most reasonable theories.

1. Tropical communities are more stable than temperate communities, which have had to move in response to periods of glaciation. This greater age has allowed the processes of evolution and speciation, in response to local conditions, to occur uninterrupted in tropical communities. A longer period of evolution has allowed a greater degree of specialization and local adaptation to occur in tropical areas. Species of tropical areas have smaller north-to-south ranges on average than do temperate species. Many tropical species are quite specialized in their habitat requirements and reproductive behaviors. The greater diversity of plant species in the tropics has promoted the evolution of large numbers of insect species that feed on particular plant species or even particular parts of plants.
2. The warm temperatures and high humidity in many tropical areas provide favorable conditions for the growth and survival of many species. In contrast, species living in temperate zones must have physiological mechanisms that allow them to tolerate the cold and freezing conditions found there. These species may also have specialized behaviors, such as dormancy, hibernation, or migration, to help them survive the winter. The inability of many groups of plants and animals to live outside the tropics suggests that these adaptations are not easily evolved.
3. Tropical species may face greater pressure from parasites and disease because there is no winter to reduce pest populations. Ever-present populations of these parasites prevent any single species or group of species from dominating communities, creating an opportunity for numerous species to coexist at low individual densities. In many ways, the biology of the tropics is the biology of rare species. In contrast, temperate zone species may face reduced parasite pressure because the winter cold reduces their populations, allowing one or a few competitively superior species to dominate the community and exclude many other, less competitive species.
4. Among plant species, rates of outcrossing (interbreeding with other individuals of the same species, as opposed to self-pollination)

appear to be higher in tropical plant species than in temperate ones (Bawa 1992). Higher rates of outcrossing may lead to higher levels of genetic variability (see Chapter 11), local adaptation, and speciation. Speciation also may have been accelerated in tropical areas during cooler, drier glacial periods when rain forests were restricted in area and divided into many, smaller patches, each evolving their own distinctive species.

5. Tropical regions receive more solar energy over the course of a year than temperate regions. As a result, many tropical communities have a higher rate of productivity than temperate communities, in terms of the number of kilograms of living material (biomass) produced each year per hectare of habitat. This high productivity results in a greater resource base that can support a wider range of species. The drawback to this hypothesis, however, is that there is only a loose correlation between productivity and species diversity, and some highly diverse communities occur in habitats with intermediate productivity.

Tropical Rain Forests

Even though the world's tropical forests occupy only 7% of the land area, they contain over half of the world's species (Caulfield 1985; Whitmore 1990). This estimate is based on limited sampling of insects and other arthropods, groups that are thought to contain the majority of the world's species (Figure 3.4). Estimates of the number of undescribed insect species in tropical forests range from 5 million to 30 million (May 1992). If the 30 million figure is correct, it would mean that insects found in tropical forests may constitute over 90% of the world's species. Information on other groups, such as plants and birds, is much more accurate. For flowering plants, gymnosperms, and ferns, about 86,000 species occur in tropical America; 38,000 species occur in tropical Africa and Madagascar; and 45,000 species occur in tropical Asia, including New Guinea and tropical Australia (Brenan 1978; Reid and Miller 1989). This total is about two-thirds of the estimated 250,000 plant species believed to exist worldwide. More than 100,000 of these plant species are found in tropical forests (Myers 1980).

About 30% of the world's bird species—1300 species in the American tropics, 400 species in tropical Africa, and 900 in tropical Asia—depend on tropical forests (A. Diamond 1985). This figure is probably an underestimate, since it does not include species (such as migrant birds) that are only partially dependent upon tropical forests, nor does it reflect the high concentrations of tropical forest birds living in restricted habitats, such as islands, that may be more vulnerable to habitat loss. In forested islands such as New Guinea, 78% of the nonmarine birds depend on the forest for their survival.

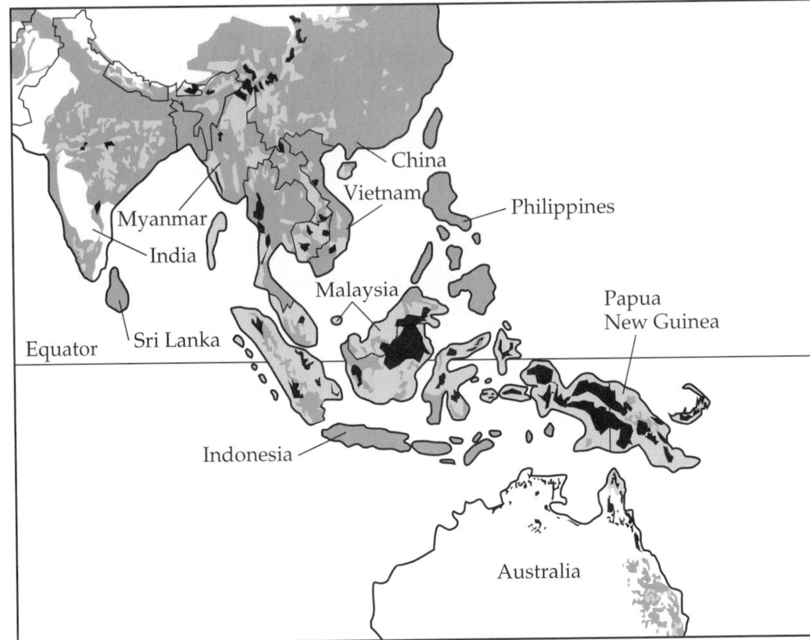

Figure 3.4 Tropical rain forests are found predominantly in wet, equatorial regions of America, Africa, and Asia. Eight thousand years ago, tropical forests covered the entire shaded area, but human activities have resulted in the loss of a great deal of forest cover, shown in the darkest shade. In the lighter shaded area forests remain, but are secondary forests that have grown back following cutting; plantation forests such as rubber and teak; or forests degraded by logging and fuelwood collection. Only in the regions shown in black are there still blocks of intact natural tropical forest large enough to support all of their biodiversity. (After Bryant et al. 1997.)

Coral Reefs

Colonies of tiny coral animals build the large coral reef ecosystems that are the marine equivalent of tropical rain forests in their species richness and complexity (Figure 3.5). One explanation for this richness is the high primary productivity of coral reefs, which produce 2500 grams of biomass per square meter per year in comparison with 125 $g/m^2/yr$ in the open ocean. The clarity of the water in the reef ecosystem allows sunlight to penetrate deeply so that high levels of photosynthesis occur in the algae living mutualistically inside the coral. Extensive niche specialization among coral species and adaptations to varying levels of disturbance may also account for high species richness.

The world's largest coral reef is Australia's Great Barrier Reef, with an area of 349,000 km^2. The Great Barrier Reef contains over 300 species of coral, 1500 species of fish, 4000 species of mollusks, and 5 species of turtles, and provides breeding sites for some 252 species of birds (IUCN/UNEP 1988). The Great Barrier Reef contains about 8% of the world's fish species, even though it occupies only 0.1% of its ocean surface area (Goldman and Talbot 1976). The Great Barrier Reef is part of the rich Indo–West Pacific region. The greater diversity of species in the Indo–West Pacific region in contrast to other areas is illustrated by the more than 2000 fish species found in the Philippine Islands in contrast with 448 species in the mid-Pacific Hawaiian

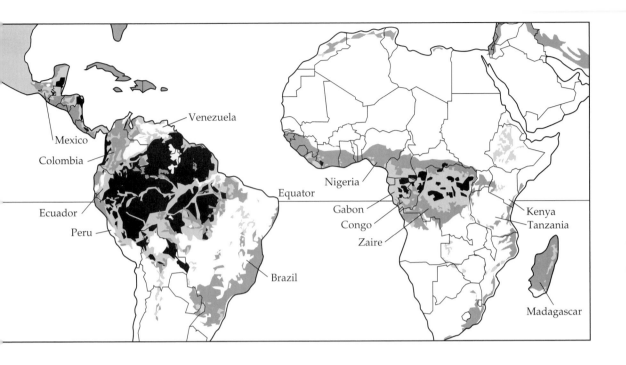

Venezuela
Mexico
Colombia
Nigeria
Equator
Ecuador
Gabon
Kenya
Congo
Tanzania
Peru
Zaire
Brazil
Madagascar

Figure 3.5 Coral reefs in tropical waters are built up from the skeletons of billions of tiny individual animals. The intricate coral landscapes create a habitat for many other marine species, such as these snapper and goatfish shoaling on the Great Astrolabe Reef, Fiji. (Photograph © Simon Jennings.)

Islands and around 500 species in the Bahama Islands. By comparison, the number of marine fishes in temperate areas is low; the mid-Atlantic seaboard of North America has only 250 fish species and the Mediterranean has fewer than 400 species (Briggs 1974).

One notable difference between tropical forest species and coral reef species is that, unlike many forest species that have restricted distributions, very few coral reef species show such patterns of narrow distribution (Vernon 1986). Species of the coral reefs are apparently adapted to disperse widely in the ocean at the juvenile stage so that they are found over a wide area. Only isolated islands, such as Hawaii, have numerous endemic species (i.e., species found there and nowhere else); fully 20% of Hawaiian coral species are endemic to the area (Hourigan and Reese 1987). Because coral reef species are more widely distributed, they may be less prone to extinction by the destruction of a single locality than are rain forest species. However, this assertion may be a taxonomic bias, since coral reef species are not as well known as terrestrial species; further research may reveal many locally distributed species. As tropical reefs become damaged by human activity, the possibility that such species of restricted range might be lost is cause for serious concern.

How Many Species Exist Worldwide?

A strategy for conserving biological diversity must be based on a firm grasp of the numbers of species that exist in the world today and how those species are distributed (Figure 3.6A) (Heywood 1995). While certain groups of organisms, such as birds, mammals, and temperate flowering plants, are relatively well known, a small but steady number of new species in these groups are being discovered each year. Since 1991, six new species of primate have been found in Brazil, and more will probably be found if scientists keep looking for them (Morell 1996). Sometimes new species are discovered when further research, often involving the techniques of molecular systematics, reveals that what was originally thought to be a single species with a number of geographically distinct populations is really two or more species. In groups such as insects, spiders, mites, nematodes, and fungi, the number of described species is still increasing at the rate of 1% to 2% per year (May 1992). Huge numbers of species in these groups, mostly in tropical areas but also in the temperate zone, have yet to be discovered and described (Figure 3.6B). At the present time, about 1.5 million species have been described in total. It is certain that at least twice this number of species remain undescribed, primarily in the tropics, leading to an estimate that there are about 5 million species in the world.

Two of the most remarkable discoveries of new species in the present century involve "living fossils"—species known from the fossil

ery when one considers that the plants in this park were thought to be well known to botanists. The location of these trees is being kept secret while efforts are made to propagate them from seeds and cuttings.

The coelacanth and the Wollemi pine had been overlooked because their sole remaining habitats were located in out-of-the-way places. Both species came quickly to the attention of biologists because they are conspicuous—that is, they are easily seen with the naked eye and are clearly distinct from other species. Inconspicuous organisms, including small rodents, most insects, and microorganisms, are much less likely to be observed by chance outside their natural habitats, as the coelacanth was, or even within their native environments. Many inconspicuous species that live in remote habitats will not be found and catalogued unless biologists go in search of them. This factor delays a thorough understanding of the full extent of biological diversity because inconspicuous species constitute the majority of species on Earth.

Large institutions often undertake biological surveys of entire countries or regions, which may involve decades of specimen collection in the field, identification of known species, descriptions of new species, and, finally, publication of the results so others may use the information. Two such examples are the massive Flora of North America Project, based at the Missouri Botanical Garden, and the Flora Malesiana in the Indo-Pacific region, organized by the Rijksherbarium in Leiden, the Netherlands.

Scientists determine the identity and numbers of species present in an area by a thorough collection of specimens over an extended time, followed by a careful examination of this material in a museum. For example, a team from the Natural History Museum of London collected over one million beetles from a 500-hectare lowland rain forest in the Dumoga-Bone National Park on Sulawesi, Indonesia, in 1985. This effort led to an initial list of 3488 species, large numbers of which were previously unknown to science. Subsequent museum work allowed the identification of 1000 more species, with as many as 2000 remaining species to be identified over the coming years and decades.

The most diverse group of organisms appears to be the insects, with about 750,000 species described already, or about half the world's species (see Figure 3.6A). If the number of insect species can be estimated accurately, then it may be possible to determine the total number of species in the world. Recent studies in tropical America have attempted to sample entire insect communities using insecticidal fogging of whole trees (Figure 3.8) (Erwin 1982). These studies have revealed an extremely rich and largely undescribed insect fauna in the canopies of these trees (Wilson 1991). Sampling of trees at localities across the Amazon further suggests that these insect communities are frequently localized in distribution.

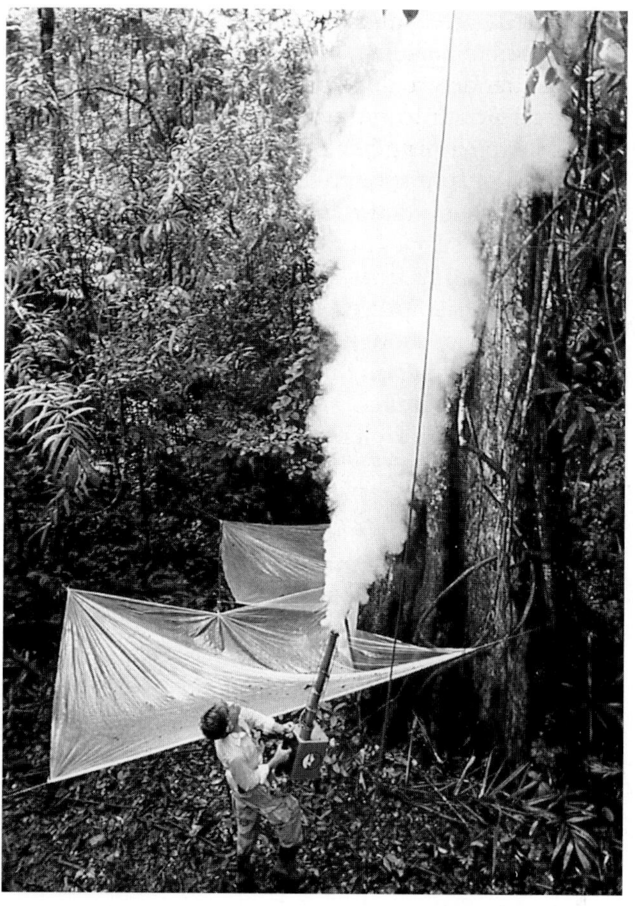

Figure 3.8 A researcher uses insecticidal fog to sample the vast number of insect species in the canopy of a tropical forest. (Photograph © Mark Moffett/Minden Pictures.)

On the basis of this evidence, Erwin (1982) has attempted to estimate the number of insect species in the world. He reasons as follows: In Panama, 1200 species of beetles were collected from the canopy of a single tree species, *Luehea seemannii*. About 800 of these beetles were herbivorous. He estimated that 20% of these herbivorous beetles (160 species) are specialist feeders on this tree species. Since beetles represent 40% of all insect species, there may be a total of 400 species of specialized insects that feed in the canopy of each tree species. Erwin estimated that canopy species represent only about two-thirds of the insect species on the tree, suggesting that there are 600 insect species specializing on each plant species. Since there are about 50,000 species of tropical woody plants, there may be as many as 30 million species of insects.

Each step in the calculation leading to the estimate of 30 million species is so speculative that many knowledgeable scientists do not accept it and keep to the earlier figure of about 5 million total species (Gaston 1991). The number of insect species specializing on each plant species may be as much as 10 times too high, leading to an estimate of only 3 million species. However, Erwin's work is very significant in calling attention to large numbers of undescribed species, developing a new approach to estimating insect numbers, and emphasizing the relationships among plant and animal species.

Another approach to estimating biological diversity involves developing "rules" for determining how many species are involved in biological relationships (May 1992). For example, in Britain and Europe there are about six times more fungus species than plant species. If this general ratio is applicable throughout the world, there may be as many as 1.6 million fungus species, in addition to the estimated 270,000 plant species worldwide. Since only 69,000 species of fungi have been described so far, it is possible that there are over 1.5 million species of fungi waiting to be discovered, most of them in the tropics (Hawksworth 1991a,b).

Yet another approach could be to assume that each species of plant or insect, which together form the majority of currently known species, has at least one species of specialized bacteria, protist, nematode, and virus; hence the estimates of the number of species should be multiplied by five—bringing it to 25 million, using traditional estimates, or to 150 million species if one accepts Erwin's estimates. Perhaps biological communities have a number of common species that can be readily assessed and used to estimate the number of rare species that are harder to find. Developing such preliminary approaches might allow ecological estimates to be made of the number of species in communities before more rigorous work is completed.

Inconspicuous species have not received their proper share of taxonomic attention. For example, mites and nematodes in the soil are small and hard to study. These groups also could number in the hundreds of thousands of species if they were properly studied. Now that the role of nematode species (roundworms) as parasites of agricultural plants has been demonstrated, scientists have dramatically increased their efforts to collect and describe these minute animals. Consequently, the catalogue of this one group of organisms has grown from the 80 nematode species known in 1860 to around 20,000 species known today. Most of the described nematode species are known from northwest European coastal regions, with specialists estimating that there may be as many as 100 million species waiting to be described (Boucher and Lambshead 1995). The number of trained specialists is the limiting factor in unlocking the diversity of this enormous group of species, as it is with so many other taxonomic groups.

Bacteria are also very poorly known (Hawksworth and Richie 1993). Only about 4,000 species of bacteria are recognized by microbiologists because of the difficulty in growing and identifying specimens. However, recent work analyzing bacterial DNA hints that there may be more than 4000 species in a single gram of soil and an equally

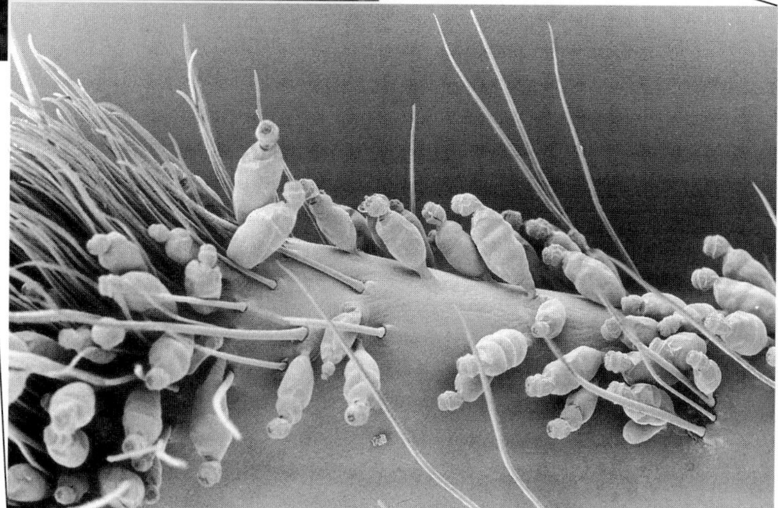

Figure 3.9 A new phylum, the Cyclio-phora, was first described in 1995. The phylum contains one vase-shaped species, *Symbion pandora* (around 40 of which are shown below), which attaches itself on the mouthparts of the Norway lobster, *Nephrops norve-gicus* (inset). (Photographs courtesy of Reinhardt Kris-tensen, University of Copenhagen.)

large number of different species from marine sediments (Giovannoni et al. 1990; Ward et al. 1990).

A lack of collecting has hampered our knowledge especially of the species richness in the marine environment (Grassle 1991). The marine environment appears to be a great frontier of biological diversity, with huge numbers of species and even entire communities still unknown. An entirely new animal phylum, the Loricifera, was described in 1983 based on specimens from the deep sea (Kristensen 1983), and another new phylum, the Cycliophora, was first described in 1995 based on tiny, ciliate creatures found on the mouthparts of the Norway lobster (Figure 3.9) (Funch and Kristensen 1995). Undoubtedly, more species, genera, families, orders, classes, and phyla (and perhaps even king-doms!) are waiting to be discovered. For the sake of discussion later in this book, 10 million will be assumed as a reasonable estimate of the total number of biological species worldwide.

Recently Discovered Communities

Entire biological communities are still being discovered, often in localities that are extremely remote and inaccessible. Often these communities consist of inconspicuous species, such as bacteria, protists, and small invertebrates, that have escaped the attention of earlier taxonomists. These communities may occur in highly specialized habitats that were not previously explored. As a result of specialized exploration techniques, particularly in the deep sea and the forest canopy, these communities are being discovered and investigated, often with considerable public attention. Some recently discovered communities include:

- Diverse communities of animals, particularly insects, that are adapted to living in the canopies of tropical trees and rarely, if ever, descend to the ground (Wilson 1991; Moffat 1994). The use of technical climbing equipment, canopy towers and walkways, and tall cranes are opening this habitat up to exploration (Figure 3.10).
- A remote, mountainous rain forest reserve on the border between Vietnam and Laos was only recently surveyed by biologists. To their amazement, they discovered three mammal species new to science, now known as the giant muntjac, the Vu Quang ox, and the slow-running deer (Linden 1994).
- The floor of the deep sea, which remains almost entirely unexplored due to the technical difficulties of transporting equipment and peo-

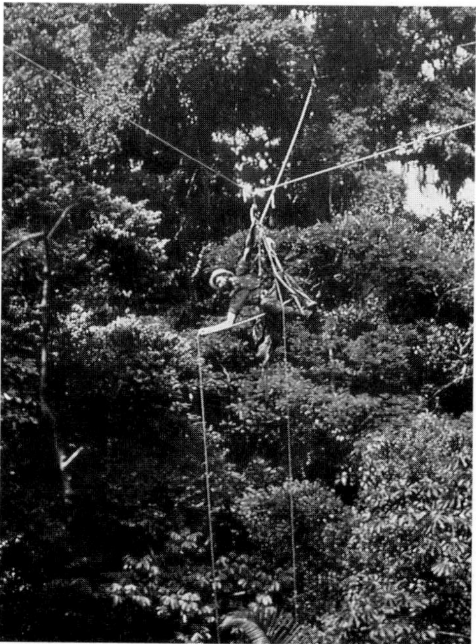

Figure 3.10 Biologists are gaining access to the diverse world of the rain forest canopy by using techniques borrowed from technical rock climbing. (Photographs courtesy of Nalini Nadkarni.)

Box 5 **Conserving a World Unknown: Hydrothermal Vents and Oil Plumes**

Biologists are aware that many species exist that have not been adequately studied and described, a fact that frequently hampers conservation. In recent years, it has become apparent that there are entire communities that remain undiscovered in the more remote parts of the Earth. The biota of deep-sea hydrothermal vents, discovered only recently with the invention of technology that enables scientists to photograph and collect specimens from depths of over 2000 meters (Jannasch and Motti 1985; Grassle 1985; Gage and Tyler 1991), demonstrates that species, genera, and even families of organisms exist about which scientists know nothing. Such organisms pose a significant problem for conservationists: how does one go about conserving undiscovered or barely known species and communities?

Hydrothermal vents are temporary underwater openings in the Earth's crust. Heat and minerals escape from these vents and support a profusion of species in the deepest parts of the ocean. Communities of large animals such as clams, crabs, fishes, and tube worms (also known as pogonophorans) derive their energy from chemosynthetic microorganisms, which are the primary producers of the vent ecosystem. The vents themselves are short-lived, spanning a few decades at most; however, the communities supported by these vents are thought to have evolved over the past 200 million years or more. Until deep-sea submersibles were developed in the 1970s, scientists were completely unaware of the communities that live around the vents. Since 1979, however, when the submersible *Alvin* was first used to examine the vents around the Galápagos Rift in the Pacific Ocean, nearly 20 new families of animals—not including microorganisms—have been described (Lutz and Haymon 1994). As investigation of deep-sea vents continues, more families will certainly be discovered, encompassing many new genera and species.

Like many terrestrial communities, hydrothermal communities vary according to differences in their local environment. Distribution of hydrothermal communities is dependent upon the character of the vents, including the temperature, chemical composition, and flow pattern of hydrothermal fluid issuing from the vents. Scientists studying hydrothermal species may work for decades, yet only acquire minimal knowledge of the dynamics of these communities because of the unique nature of the study sites: the vents are ephemeral, sometimes existing for only a few years, and inaccessible; they can be reached only with the use of expensive, specialized equipment.

Petroleum seep communities, another little-known ecosystem, like the assemblages at hydrothermal vents, exist at ocean depths far below the reach of sunlight. In this case, the initial source of energy comes from petrochemicals—oil—seeping from cracks in the ocean floor (Schneider 1995). Some of the same species that congregate around hydrothermal and petroleum-seep vents may also colonize the carcasses of large fish and marine mammals, such as whales, which sink to the bottom of the ocean floor; these unpredictable bonanzas of organic matter may provide crucial stepping stones for organisms to disperse among widely scattered hydrothermal vents and petroleum seeps.

Hampered by the inaccessibility of the sites and the cost of investigation, biologists nevertheless need to think ahead to conservation problems that

---

ple under high water pressure, has unique communities of bacteria and animals that grow around deep-sea geothermal vents (Box 5). Undescribed, active bacteria have even been found in marine sediments 500 m below the seafloor, where they undoubtedly play a major chemical and energetic role in this vast ecosystem (Tunnicliffe 1992; Parkes et al. 1994).

- Diverse bacterial communities exist 2.8 km deep in the Earth's crust, at densities ranging from 100 to 100 million bacteria per gram of might face these species in the future. Industrial pollutants, for example, have damaged ocean species in shallower waters and in theory could harm these communities as well. Deep-sea oil rigs could pump dry oil seeps and cause local extinctions (Schneider 1995). As whale and fish stocks decline, the corresponding decrease in carcasses on the sea bottom may remove a critical resource necessary for the dispersal and maintenance of certain populations. How would conservationists respond to such a situation?

Though as yet these problems are strictly hypothetical, they illustrate a frustrating aspect of conservation biology: too little is known about too many species and ecosystems to develop and implement specific measures that might prevent future extinctions. As time passes, new species, genera, and families continue to be added to the list of known organisms living on the Earth, but many others are lost before they are even discovered. How does conservation biology account for species and perhaps whole communities that are still unknown but are nonetheless in need of conservation? Experience has shown that a specific conservation program created in ignorance of a species' behavior and biological needs can sometimes be worse than no program at all. Do we develop conservation programs despite our lack of information and hope for the best? Or do we continue our studies in the hope that the time lost will not prove fatal to the species? At this stage, there is only one definitive statement that can address these dilemmas: we know that restricting pollution has broadly positive effects on natural communities, so pollution abatement programs may offer the best conservation strategy in these situations, even when the biological communities are not thoroughly understood.

Part of a hydrothermal vent community. Large tube worms (*Riftia pachyptila*) dominate the ecosystem. Crabs and mussels also make their home here. The energy and nutrients that support this community are derived from the hydrogen sulfide and minerals emitted by volcanic vents. (Photograph by E. Kristoff/National Geographic Image Collection.)

rock. Molecular genetic techniques have revealed these communities to be composed of numerous species, each with their own characteristic DNA (Fredrickson and Onstott 1996). Crucial limiting factors in such extreme environments are the availability of water, space, and an energy source. These communities are being actively investigated as a source of novel chemicals, for their potential usefulness in degrading toxic chemicals, and for insight into whether life could exist on other planets.

The Need for More Taxonomists

A major problem the scientific community faces in describing and cataloguing the biological diversity of the world is the lack of trained taxonomists able to take on the job (Raven and Wilson 1992). At the present time, there are only about 1500 taxonomists in the world who are competent to work with tropical species, and many of them are based in temperate countries. Unfortunately, this number is declining rather than increasing. When academic taxonomists retire, universities have a tendency to either close the position due to financial difficulties or replace the retiring biologist with a nontaxonomist. Many members of the younger generation of taxonomists are so preoccupied with the mathematical theories of numerical taxonomy and the technology of molecular systematics that they are not interested in or capable of continuing the great tradition of cataloguing the world's biological treasures. At least a fivefold increase in the number of field taxonomists focused primarily on describing and identifying tropical and marine species is needed to complete the task of describing the world's biological diversity before it is too late (Gaston 1994). Much of this effort should be directed to lesser known groups, such as fungi, bacteria, and invertebrates. One possible solution is for museums and conservation projects in the developing world to train talented local people in the basic elements of collecting and cataloguing; the amount of materials available to university- and museum-based taxonomists would thus increase and a record of which species exist in which locations could be preserved and maintained. Natural history societies and clubs that combine professional and amateur naturalists can also play a valuable role in assisting these efforts and in exposing the general public and student groups to the issues and excitement of biological diversity.

Summary

1. In general, species richness is greatest in tropical rain forests, coral reefs, tropical lakes, the deep sea, and shrublands with a Mediterranean climate. In terrestrial habitats, species richness tends to be greatest at lower elevations and in areas with abundant rainfall. Areas that are geologically old and topographically complex also tend to have more species.

2. Tropical rain forests occupy only 7% of the Earth's land area, yet they are estimated to contain most of the Earth's species. The great majority of these species are insects not yet described by scientists. Coral reef communities are also rich in species, with many of the species widely distributed. The deep sea also appears to be rich in species, but is still not adequately explored.

3. About 1.5 million species have been described and at least twice that number of species remain to be described. Estimates of the total number of species range from 5 to 120 million, with 10 million species a reasonable working estimate given present knowledge.

4. While conspicuous groups, such as flowering plants, mammals, and birds, are reasonably well known to science, other inconspicuous groups, particularly insects, bacteria, and fungi, have not been thoroughly studied. Recent attempts to collect all of the insects in the tropical forest canopy have yielded mostly undescribed species, suggesting that far more species exist than previously suspected.

5. New biological communities are still being discovered, especially in the deep sea and the forest canopy. For example, spectacular communities that occupy deep-sea hydrothermal vents and oil seeps are a recent discovery. There is a vital need for more taxonomic scientists to study, classify, and help protect the world's biological diversity before it is lost.

For Discussion

1. If taxonomists are so important to documenting and protecting biological diversity, why are their numbers declining instead of increasing? How could societal and scientific priorities be readjusted to reverse this trend? Is the ability to identify and classify species a skill that every conservation biologist should possess?

2. Develop arguments for both low and very high estimates of the total number of species in particular groups, such as bacteria, fungi, or nematodes. Read more about groups that you don't know well. Why is it important to identify and name all the species in a particular group?

3. What are the factors promoting species richness? Why is biological diversity diminished in particular environments? Why aren't species able to overcome these limitations and undergo the process of speciation?

4. Recent findings suggest that life may have existed on Mars and that bacteria actually flourish in rocks deep under the Earth's surface. Speculate, as wildly as you can, about where to search for previously unsuspected species, communities, or novel life forms.

Suggested Readings

Boucher, G. and P. J. D. Lambshead. 1995. Ecological biodiversity of marine nematodes in samples from temperate, tropical, and deep-sea regions. *Conservation Biology* 9: 1594–1605. Biologists grapple with deciding how many tiny little worm species there are in the world.

Bryant, D., D. Nielson and L. Tangley. 1997. *The Last Frontier Forests: Ecosystems and Economies on the Edge*. World Resources Institute, Washington, D.C. Authoritative report on the status and future of primary forests.

Caulfield, C. 1985. *In the Rainforest*. Alfred A. Knopf, New York. A popular account of the issues in rain forest conservation.

Cowling, R. M., P. W. Rundel et al. 1996. Plant diversity in Mediterranean climate regions. *Trends in Ecology and Evolution* 11: 362–366. A succinct review of patterns of species richness in these communities and threats to their continued existence.

Fredrickson, J. K. and T. C. Onstatt. 1996. Microbes deep inside the Earth. *Scientific American* 275 (October): 68–73. Exciting new finds of bacterial communities deep inside the Earth's rocky crust.

Gage, J. D. and P. A. Tyler. 1991. *Deep-Sea Biology: A Natural History of Organisms at the Deep Seafloor*. Cambridge University Press, Cambridge. Covers a wide range of organisms and issues.

Hawksworth, D. L. and J. M. Richie (eds.). 1993. *Biodiversity and Biosystematic Priorities: Microorganisms and Invertebrates*. CAB International, Wallingford, U.K. Focuses on less known groups of species.

Heywood, V. H. 1995. *Global Biodiversity Assessment*. Cambridge University Press, Cambridge. This massive book comprehensively treats the subject, with chapters by leading scientists and a huge bibliography.

Huston, M. A. 1994. *Biological Diversity: The Coexistence of Species on Changing Landscapes*. Cambridge University Press, Cambridge. Extensive review of the patterns and theories of biological diversity.

May, R. M. 1992. How many species inhabit the Earth? *Scientific American* 267 (October): 42–48. Excellent review of the arguments for different estimates of the number of species.

Pearson, D. L. and F. Cassola. 1992. Worldwide species richness patterns of tiger beetles (Coleoptera: Cicindelidae). Indicator taxon for biodiversity and conservation studies. *Conservation Biology* 6: 376–391. Case study of the geographic patterns of species distribution, with applications for pinpointing species concentrations.

Raven, P. and E. O. Wilson 1992. A 50-year plan for biodiversity surveys. *Science* 258: 1099–1100. A clear statement of the need for a comprehensive survey of the world's biodiversity.

Ray, G. C., J. F. Grassle and contributors. 1991. Marine biological diversity. *BioScience* 41: 453–465. An overview of marine biodiversity, with many other related articles in the same issue.

Waller, G. (ed.). 1996. *Sealife: A Guide to the Marine Environment*. Smithsonian Institution Press, Washington, D.C. This is the book to start with if you want to learn about the marine environment in depth.

Whitmore, T. C. 1990. *An Introduction to Tropical Rain Forests*. Clarendon Press, Oxford. An authoritative short presentation by a leading scientist.

Wilson, E. O. 1991. Rain forest canopy: The high frontier. *National Geographic* 180 (December): 78–107. An authoritative and vivid account of diversity in the forest canopy.

PART TWO

Valuing Biodiversity

CHAPTER 4

What Is the Value of Biological Diversity?

DECISIONS ON PROTECTING species, communities, and genetic variation often come down to arguments over money: How much will it cost? And how much is it worth? The economic value of something is generally accepted as the amount of money people are willing to pay for it. This is only one possible way of assigning value to things, even biological diversity. Ethical, aesthetic, scientific, and educational methods are available as well. However, economic valuation is currently the principal method used by government and corporate officials in making major policy decisions. When the loss of biological diversity is perceived to cost money, perhaps governments and corporations will act to protect it. A major problem with standard economics is that it tends to undervalue natural resources; thus, the costs of environmental damage have been ignored, the depletion of natural resource stocks disregarded, and the future value of resources discounted.

Ecological Economics

Ecological economics, a major new discipline that integrates valuations of biological diversity in economic terms and includes ecology, environmental science, and public policy, has been developing to remedy this shortsighted perspective (Barbeir et al. 1994; Costanza et al. 1996; Krishnan et al. 1996). Conservation biologists are using the methodology and vocabulary of ecological economics in their arguments for the protection of diversity because government and corporate officials are more readily convinced of the need to protect biological diversity when there is an economic incentive. Governments need to allocate their resources in the most efficient manner possible, and a well-considered argument, based on economic grounds, for the conservation of biological diversity will often effectively support arguments based on biological, ethical, and emotional grounds.

Before the trend of the loss of biological diversity can be reversed, its fundamental causes must be understood. What factors induce humans to act in a destructive manner? Usually, environmental degradation and species loss occur as a by-product of human economic activities. Forests are logged for revenue from timber sales. Species are hunted for personal consumption, sale, and sport. Marginal land is converted into cropland because people have nowhere else to farm. Species transported accidentally by commercial vessels or purposefully by people are introduced onto new islands and continents without any consideration for the resulting environmental devastation. Because the underlying cause of environmental damage is so often economic in nature, the solution must incorporate economic principles as well.

An understanding of a few fundamental economic principles will clarify why people treat the environment in what appears to be a shortsighted, wasteful manner. One of the most universally accepted tenets of modern economic thought is that a voluntary transaction takes place only when it is beneficial to the parties involved. For example, a baker who sells his loaves for 50 dollars will find few customers. Likewise, a customer who is willing to pay only 5 cents for a loaf will soon go hungry. Only when a mutually agreeable price is set that benefits both parties will the transaction occur. Adam Smith, an eighteenth-century philosopher whose ideas are the foundation of much modern economic thought, wrote, "It is not upon the benevolence of the butcher, the baker, or the brewer that we eat our daily bread, but upon his own self-interest" (Smith 1909). All parties involved in an exchange expect to improve their own situation. The sum of each individual acting in his or her self-interest results in society as a whole becoming more prosperous. Smith referred to an "invisible hand" guiding the market, turning selfish, uncoordinated actions into increased prosperity and relative social harmony.

There is a notable exception to Smith's principle of free exchange benefiting society that directly applies to environmental issues. It is generally assumed that the costs and benefits of free exchange are accepted and borne by the participants in the transaction. In some cases, however, associated costs are suffered or benefits enjoyed by individuals not directly involved in the exchange. These hidden costs or benefits are known as **externalities**. Perhaps the most notable and frequently overlooked externality is the environmental damage that occurs as a consequence of human economic activity, such as dumping industrial sewage into a river. In this example, the indirect costs, or externalities, of the activity are degraded drinking water, fewer fish safe to eat, and the loss of many species unable to survive in the polluted river. Where externalities exist, the market fails to benefit society as a whole. **Market failure** results in the misallocation of resources that allows individuals or businesses to benefit at the expense of society. As a result, the society becomes less prosperous from certain economic activities, not more prosperous.

The fundamental challenge facing the conservation biologist is to ensure that all the costs of economic behavior, as well as the benefits, are understood. Companies or individuals involved in production that results in ecological damage generally do not bear the full cost of their activities. For example, the company owning an oil refinery that emits toxic fumes benefits from the sale of fuel, as does the consumer of the product. Yet the hidden costs of this transaction—increased respiratory disease, decreased visibility, and a polluted environment—are distributed throughout society. Understanding this imbalance is central to understanding market failure: the wide distribution of the economic cost, combined with the concentrated benefit to a small group, creates an economic–ecological conflict.

Assigning Value to Biological Diversity

Natural resources such as clean air, clean water, soil quality, rare species, and even scenic beauty are considered to be **common property resources** owned by society at large. These resources usually are not assigned a monetary value. People, industries, and governments using and damaging these resources without paying more than a minimal cost, sometimes paying nothing at all, create a market failure situation described as **the tragedy of the commons** (Hardin 1968, 1985). In the more complete systems of "green" accounting being developed, such as National Resource Accounting, the use of common property resources is included as part of the internal cost of doing business instead of being regarded as an externality.

When people and organizations must pay for their actions, they will be much more likely to stop or minimize damaging the environment

(Repetto 1990b, 1992; Arrow et al. 1995). Some suggestions for bringing this about include higher taxes on fossil fuels, penalties for inefficient energy use and pollution, and mandatory recycling programs. Severe financial penalties for damaging biological diversity could be developed so that industries would be careful to protect the natural world.

The emerging field of ecological economics has begun to strengthen the conservation movement by assigning monetary values to species, communities, and ecosystems (McNeely 1988; McNeely et al. 1990; Perrings 1995). Initial efforts have been simplistic, in many cases, due to the difficulties of assigning economic values to variables such as the amelioration of drastic climate change and the future use of presently unused species (Daly and Cobb 1989; Daily 1997). The hidden costs of environmental degradation that occur during income-producing activities, such as logging, agriculture, and commercial fishing, make it hard to determine the real value of natural resources (Repetto 1992). Economists are still looking for appropriate methods to determine the long-term costs associated with the disruption of a biological community by economic activity.

Cost–Benefit Analysis

Ecological economists evaluate large projects using **environmental impact assessments,** which consider the present and future effects of the projects on the environment. The environment is often broadly defined to include not only harvestable natural resources, but also air and water quality, the lives of local people, and endangered species. In its most comprehensive form, **cost–benefit analysis** compares the values gained against the costs of the project (Hanley and Splash 1994; Perrings 1995). For example, during feasibility studies for a large logging operation that will remove a forest, monetary values could be assigned to the cost of replacing naturally occurring resources (e.g., game meat, medicinal plants, wild foods) and compared with the products of human activity (in this case, forestry or agriculture). Alternatively, the cost of restoring the community or resource to its original condition after it is destroyed may be calculated. These different strategies are likely to have very different costs and produce very different results.

In one cost–benefit analysis, the competing uses of the terrestrial and marine environments in Bacuit Bay, Palawan, Philippines were compared (Table 4.1). While logging provided more revenues than tourism and fishing when all three activities occurred at the same time, logging had strong negative impacts on the fishing industry and tourism through the high levels of sedimentation that kill coral communities and the fish that depend on them. In the alternative option, in which the forests are protected through a ban on logging, the fisheries and tourist industries provided more revenue than when all three industries operate together (Hogson and Dixon 1988).

TABLE 4.1 **Cost–benefit analysis of two development options in Bacuit Bay, Palawan, Philippines**

Source of revenue	Amount of revenue generated[a] Option 1: Logging banned[b]	Option 2: Logging continues until timber depleted[c]	10-Year comparison[d]
Tourism	$25	$ 6	+19
Fisheries	$17	$ 9	+ 8
Logging	$ 0	$10	–10
Total revenue	$42	$25	+17

Source: Data from Hodson and Dixon 1988.

[a] Revenues are in millions of dollars over a 10-year period.

[b] In Option 1, tourism and fisheries are major sustainable industries.

[c] In Option 2, logging substantially decreases the revenues from tourism and fisheries. Timber completely depleted after 5 years.

[d] Overall, over a 10-year period, a ban on logging (Option 1) results in 68% more revenue ($17 million) than all three activities together (Option 2).

In theory, if the analysis shows that a project is profitable, it should go forward, while if the project is unprofitable, it should be stopped. In practice, cost–benefit analyses are notoriously difficult to calculate because benefits and costs are hard to assign and change over time. For example, when a new paper mill is being constructed in a forested area, it is difficult to project the future price of paper, the profitability of the industry, the future need for clean water, and the value of other plant and animal species in the forests being harvested. In the past, natural resources being used or damaged by large projects were either ignored in environmental impact assessments or were grossly undervalued.

Natural Resource Loss and the Gross Domestic Product

Recent attempts have been made to include the loss of natural resources in calculations of gross domestic product (GDP) and other indices of national productivity (Daly and Cobb 1989; Repetto 1992). The problem with the GDP is that it measures economic activity in a country without accounting for all the costs. Nonsustainable and unproductive activities (including overfishing of coastal waters and poorly managed strip-mining) cause the GDP to increase, even though these activities may be destructive to a country's long-term economic well-being. In actuality, the economic costs associated with environmental damage can be considerable and often offset the gains attained through agricultural and industrial development.

In Costa Rica, for example, the value of the forests destroyed during the 1980s greatly exceeded the income produced from forest products, so that the forestry sector actually represented a drain on the wealth of the country. Similarly, the costs associated with soil erosion decreased the value of agriculture by 17%. In the United States, one controversial estimate shows that soil erosion costs the economy $44 billion every year in direct damage to agricultural lands and indirect damage to waterways and to human and animal health (Pimental et al. 1995). For the entire world, this cost is estimated to approach $400 billion per year. Even if these controversial estimates are eventually revised downward, the costs of soil erosion are enormous by any standard—and all such costs are underappreciated.

By not including environmental costs and the loss of natural resources, many countries that appear to be achieving impressive economic gains actually may be on the verge of economic collapse. Unregulated national fisheries are classic examples of the need to monitor assets. Increased investment in fishing fleets may result in higher catches and impressive profits, but gradually leads to the overharvesting and destruction of one commercial species after another and, eventually, to the collapse of the entire industry.

The hidden costs that can be associated with superficial economic gains are effectively demonstrated by the case of the *Exxon Valdez* oil spill in Alaska in 1989. The spill cost billions of dollars to clean up, damaged the environment, and wasted 11 million gallons of oil, yet the event was recorded as a net economic gain because expenditures associated with the cleanup increased the U.S. gross domestic product and provided employment for cleanup crews hired throughout the United States. Without consideration of the hidden environmental costs and long-term damage to natural resources, a disaster like the *Valdez* spill is easily misrepresented as economically beneficial.

Another attempt to account for natural resource depletion, pollution, and income distribution in measures of national productivity has been the development of the Index of Sustainable Economic Welfare (ISEW) (Daly and Cobb 1989). This method includes factors such as the loss of farmlands, the filling in of wetlands, the impacts of acid rain, and the effects of pollution on human health. Using the ISEW, the U.S. economy apparently did not improve during the period from 1956 to 1986, even though the standard GDP index showed a dramatic gain. While a measure such as the ISEW is still in a preliminary stage, its early use suggests that many modern economies are achieving their growth only through the nonsustainable consumption of natural resources. As these resources run out, the economies on which they are based may be seriously disrupted.

Many conservationists would argue that any attempt to place a strictly monetary value on biological diversity is inappropriate and potentially corrupting, since many aspects of the natural world are unique and thus truly priceless (Ehrenfeld 1989). Supporters of this position point out that there is no way to put a value on the wonder

values are further divided into **consumptive use value** for goods that are consumed locally, and **productive use value** for products that are sold in markets.

Consumptive Use Value

Goods such as fuelwood and game that are consumed locally and do not appear in the national and international marketplace are assigned consumptive use value. People living close to the land often derive a considerable proportion of the goods they require for their livelihood from the surrounding environment. These goods do not appear in the GDP of countries because they are neither bought nor sold. However, if rural people are unable to obtain these products, as might occur following environmental degradation, overexploitation of natural resources, or even creation of a protected reserve, their standard of living will decline, possibly to the point where, unable to subsist, they are forced to relocate.

Studies of traditional societies in the developing world show how extensively these people use their natural environment to supply fuel, vegetables, fruit, meat, medicine, cordage, and building materials (Figure 4.1) (Myers 1983; Balick and Cox 1996). One study of Amazonian Indians found that about half of the species of rain forest trees in the area were used for some specific product other than fuel (Prance et al. 1987; Dobson 1995). About 80% of the world's population still relies principally on traditional medicines derived from plants and animals as their primary source of treatment (Farnsworth 1988). More than 5000 species are used for medicinal purposes in China, while 2000 species are used in the Amazon basin (Schultes and Raffauf 1990; WRI/IUCN/UNEP 1992).

One of the most crucial requirements of rural people is protein, which they obtain by hunting wild animals for meat. In many areas of Africa, wild meat constitutes a significant portion of the protein in the average person's diet—about 40% in Botswana and about 75% in the Democratic Republic of Congo (formerly Zaire) (Myers 1988b). In Nigeria, over 100,000 tons of giant rats (*Cricetomys* sp.) are consumed each year, while in Botswana over 3 million kg of springhare (*Pedetes capensis*) are eaten per year. This wild meat includes not only birds, mammals, and fish, but adult insects, snails, caterpillars, and grubs. In certain areas of Africa, insects may constitute the majority of the dietary protein and supply critical vitamins. In areas along coasts, rivers, and lakes, wild fish represent an important source of protein. Throughout the world, 100 million tons of fish, mainly wild species, are harvested each year. Much of this catch is consumed locally.

Consumptive use value can be assigned to a product by considering how much people would have to pay to buy equivalent products in the market if their local sources were no longer available. One example of this approach was an attempt to estimate the number of wild

(A)

(B)

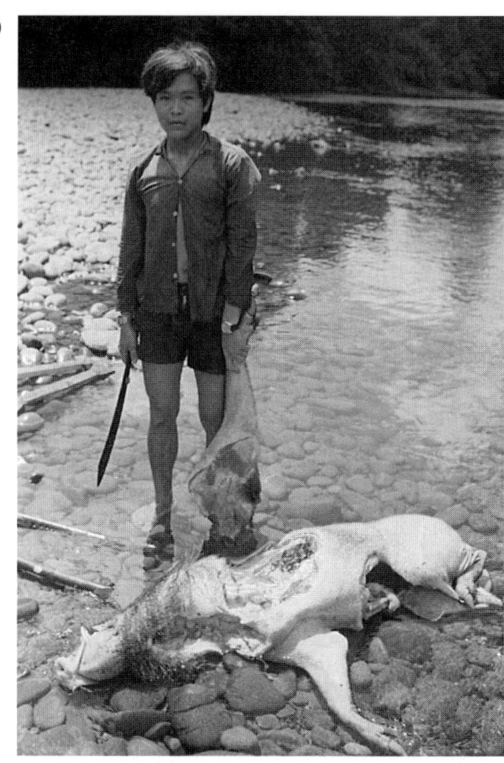

Figure 4.1 (A) A wide variety of plants and other natural products are used in Chinese medicine. (Photograph by Catherine Pringle/Biological Photo Service.) (B) Wild animals, such as this wild pig, provide people with a crucial source of protein in many areas of the world. (Photograph by Richard Primack.)

pigs harvested by native hunters in Sarawak, East Malaysia. The study involved counting the number of shotgun shells used in rural areas and interviewing hunters (Figure 4.1B). This pioneering (and somewhat controversial) study estimated that the consumptive value of the wild pig meat was approximately $40 million per year (Caldecott 1988). In many cases local people do not have the money to buy products in the market. When the local resource is depleted, they are forced into rural poverty, or they migrate to urban centers.

Consumptive value can also be assigned to fuel used for heating and cooking, which is gathered from forests and shrublands (Figure 4.2). In countries such as Nepal, Tanzania, and Malawi, most primary energy comes from fuelwood and animal dung. The value of these fuels can be determined by considering how much people would have to pay for kerosene or other fuels if they were unable to obtain fuel from their environment. In many areas of the world, rural people have consumed all local fuel sources but do not have the money to buy fuel. This situation, the "poor man's energy crisis," forces the poor to walk great distances to obtain fuel and leads to ever-widening circles of deforestation.

Figure 4.2
One of the most important natural products required by local people is fuelwood, particularly in Africa and southern Asia. Here a woman in Burkina Faso gathers kindling. (World Bank Photo by Yosef Hadar, © IBRD.)

In the past, people developed systems of extracting resources from the natural environment in ways that prevented overuse of renewable resources (Gadgil and Guha 1992). Certain species of wild fruit trees could never be cut down; the breeding season of the year was taboo for hunting; families owned hunting territories that other families were not allowed to enter. These systems were organized at the village and tribal level and were enforced through strong social pressures. For example, traditional Sherpa villages in Nepal had the custom of "shingo nava," in which men were elected to be forest guards. These men determined how much fuelwood people could collect and what trees could be cut and so protected the common resource. People violating the village rules were made to pay fines, which were used for village activities.

Most of these traditional conservation systems have broken down as cash economies have developed. People now frequently sell natural resources in town markets for money. As social controls break down at the village level, the villagers, as well as outsiders, begin to extract local resources in a destructive and nonsustainable manner, resulting in "the tragedy of the commons" (Hardin 1968), in which an individual obtains the benefits of the resource, while the cost is spread throughout the village. As the resources become depleted, many villagers are forced to pay high prices in the towns for many of the products that they formerly obtained free from their natural environment.

Although dependency on local natural products is primarily associated with the developing world, there are rural areas of the United States, Canada, and other developed countries where hundreds of thousands of people are dependent on fuelwood for heating and on wild game for meat. Many of these people would be unable to survive if they had to buy these necessities.

Productive Use Value

Products that are harvested from the wild and sold in both national and international commercial markets are assigned productive use value. Standard economic methods value these products at the price paid at the first point of sale minus the costs incurred up to that point, rather than the final retail cost of the products. But what may appear to be minor natural products may actually be the bases of major manufactured products. For example, bark from the wild cascara (*Rhamnus purshiana*) gathered in the western United States is the major ingredient in certain brands of laxatives. The purchase price of the bark is about $1 million, but the final retail price of the medicine is $75 million (Prescott-Allen and Prescott-Allen 1986).

The productive use value of natural resources is significant, even in industrial nations. The Prescott-Allens calculated that 4.5% of the U.S. gross domestic product depends in some way on wild species, an amount averaging about $87 billion per year. The percentage would be far higher for developing countries that have less industry and a higher percentage of the population living in rural areas.

The range of products obtained from the natural environment and then sold in the marketplace is enormous, but the major ones are fuelwood, construction timber, fish and shellfish, medicinal plants, wild fruits and vegetables, wild meat and skins, fibers, rattan, honey, beeswax, natural dyes, seaweed, animal fodder, natural perfumes, and plant gums and resins (Perrings 1995; Radmer 1996; Baskin 1997).

FOREST PRODUCTS Timber is among the most significant products obtained from natural environments, with a value of over $75 billion per year (Reid and Miller 1989). Timber products from the forests of tropical countries are being exported at a rapid rate to earn foreign currency, to provide capital for industrialization, and to pay foreign debt. In tropical countries such as Indonesia and Malaysia, timber products earn billions of dollars per year (Primack and Lovejoy 1995) (Figure 4.3A).

(A)

(B)

Figure 4.3 (A) The timber industry is a major source of revenue in many tropical countries. Here "monkey puzzle" trees—a species with a very narrow distribution pattern—are harvested in Chile. (Photograph by Alejandro Frid/Biological Photo Service.) (B) Nontimber products are often important in local and national economies. Many rural people supplement their incomes by gathering natural forest products to sell in local markets. Here a Land Dayak family in Sarawak (Malaysia) sells wild honey and edible wild fruits. (Photograph by R. Primack.)

Nonwood products from forests, including game, fruits, gums and resins, rattan, and medicinal plants, also have a great productive use value (Figure 4.3B). For example, the value of nontimber forest products exported by Indonesia is about $200 million per year, and in India, nontimber products account for 63% of the total foreign exchange (Gupta and Guleria 1982). These nontimber products are sometimes erroneously called "minor forest products," while in reality they are very important economically.

Although many countries focus on logging and timber exports, other forest products may be much more valuable. Researchers compared the productive values of Amazonian tropical rain forests that are being logged with those that are sustainably harvested for fruits and latex (Peters et al. 1989). For a species-rich rain forest in the Peruvian Amazon 30 km from Iquitos, the net productive value of the forest was calculated at $490 per ha when used for timber production, compared to $6330 per ha when used for fruit and latex production. The greatest value in a single year can be realized by harvesting and selling timber, but then no more timber can be harvested for decades. According to these calculations, the greatest long-term value comes from gathering fruit and latex, which can be brought to market and sold every year. The economic value of the land for cattle ranching is less than half that of collecting rain forest products. In this analysis, the net benefit of selective logging is also surprisingly low because of the damage it does to latex- and fruit-producing trees.

This method of valuation assumes that there are stable markets for these nontimber forest products. Other analyses do not show such high values for these nontimber products (Perrings 1995). Admittedly, the profitability of harvesting fruits declines dramatically with increasing distances from large towns, and the prices of these products may fall if more people bring the products to market (Godoy et al. 1993). However, when the added value of harvesting wildlife and plants for food, medicine, and other products is included, maintaining and utilizing natural communities may be more productive than intensive logging, converting the forest into commercial plantations, or establishing cattle ranches (Panayotou and Ashton 1992; Daily 1997). Careful harvesting of trees in ways that minimize damage to the surrounding biological community and soil, combined with the gathering of nontimber products, may be a profitable approach that justifies maintaining the land in forest.

ECOSYSTEM PRODUCTION The large ecosystems of the world have enormous productive value. Extensive rangelands provide fodder for sheep, cattle, and other domestic grazers. Coastal areas, the open ocean, rivers, and large lakes produce vast quantities of seaweed, shellfish, and fish that are harvested for human use. The incidental preservation of species diversity that occurs when communities are sustainably harvested adds further value to activities that are not destructive.

PROVIDING NEW STOCK Many species have great productive use value in their ability to provide founder stock for industry and agriculture and for the genetic improvement of agricultural crops. These uses differ from the traditional approach of continuous harvesting from the wild. Wild species of plants and animals that are currently harvested on a local scale can be grown on plantations and ranches, and some may be cultured in laboratories. The wild populations provide the initial breeding stock for these colonies and are a source of material for genetic improvement of the species. In the case of crop plants, a wild species or variety might have a special gene that confers pest resistance or increased yield. This gene needs to be obtained from the wild only once; the gene then can be incorporated into the breeding stock of the crop species and stored in gene banks. The continued genetic improvement of cultivated plants is necessary not only for increased yield, but also to guard against pesticide-resistant insects and more virulent strains of fungi, viruses, and bacteria (Baskin 1997).

Catastrophic crop failures often can be directly linked to low genetic variability: the 1846 potato blight in Ireland, the 1922 wheat failure in the Soviet Union, and the 1984 outbreak of citrus canker in Florida were all related to low genetic variability among crop plants (Plucknett et al. 1987). To overcome this problem, new, resistant varieties of agricultural species are constantly being substituted for susceptible varieties. The source of resistance often comes from genes obtained from wild relatives of crop plants, and from local varieties of the domestic species grown by traditional farmers.

Development of new crop varieties can have a noticeable economic impact. Genetic improvements in U.S. crops were responsible for increasing the value of the harvest by an average of $1 billion per year from 1930 to 1980 (OTA 1987). Genetic improvements of rice and wheat varieties during the "Green Revolution" increased harvests in Asia by an estimated $3.5 billion per year (WCMC 1992). Genes for high sugar content and large fruit size from wild tomatoes from Peru have been transferred into domestic varieties of tomatoes, resulting in an enhanced value of $80 million to the industry (Iltis 1988). The discovery of a wild perennial relative of corn in the Mexican state of Jalisco is potentially worth billions of dollars to modern agriculture because it could lead to the development of a high-yielding perennial corn crop, thus eliminating the need for annual plowing and planting.

BIOLOGICAL PEST CONTROL Wild species can also be used as **biological control agents** (Van Driesche and Bellows 1996). Biologists have sometimes controlled exotic, noxious species by searching the pest species' original habitat for a control species that limits its population (Box 7). This control species can be brought to the new locality, where it can be released to act as a biological control agent.

A classic example of biological control is the case of the prickly pear cactus (*Opuntia inermis*), a South American species introduced into Australia for use as a hedgerow plant. The cactus spread out of control and took over millions of hectares of rangeland. In the prickly pear's native habitat, the larvae of a particular moth species (*Cactoblastis cactorum*) feeds on this cactus. The moth was successfully introduced into Australia, where it has reduced the cactus to comparative rarity. Thus pristine habitats can be of great value as reservoirs of natural pest control agents.

THE NATURAL PHARMACY The natural world is an important source of new medicines. One outstanding example of such a species is the rose periwinkle (*Catharanthus roseus*) from Madagascar. Two potent drugs derived from this plant are effective in treating Hodgkin's disease, leukemia, and other blood cancers. Treatment using these drugs has increased the survival rate of childhood leukemia from 10% to 90%. How many more such valuable plants will be discovered in the years ahead—and how many will go extinct before they are discovered?

Box 7 Cassava Mealybugs: A Biocontrol Success Story

"These fields are planted mostly with *ajes*. The Indians sow little shoots, from which small roots grow that look like carrots. They serve this as bread, by grating and kneading it, then baking it in the fire." So wrote Christopher Columbus in his journal for Sunday, December 16, 1492, in the first European report of a new world food crop: cassava (*Manihot esculenta*) (Sokolow 1992). In the following century Portuguese traders introduced the edible root to the Congo region of Africa. From there it spread throughout equatorial Africa, eventually becoming a staple of subsistence agriculture from Senegal to Madagascar.

In the early 1970s, an agricultural scientist transporting a new variety of cassava from South America to Africa inadvertently introduced a new pest into the Congo: the cassava mealybug (*Phenacoccus manihoti*) (Beard 1991; Stevens 1993). Previously unknown to science, the cassava mealybug feeds on cassava plants and lays its eggs at their growing tips, weakening and denuding them. As the mealybug spread through West Africa, infested cassava fields lost 80% to 90% of their productivity; losses were estimated at $2 billion per year. Pesticides eliminated very few of the insects because mealybugs are protected by a waxy secretion that repels toxins. Spreading at a rate of 300 km per year, the bugs quickly infested the cassava growing region—an area one and a half times the size of the continental United States. With 200 million Africans depending on cassava for a large portion of their daily calories, there was imminent danger of widespread famine.

When more conventional control techniques failed, the International Institute of Tropical Agriculture (IITA), in collaboration with other institutions, began work on a biological control program that would rely on the natural predators of the mealybug. But because the mealybug was a newly discovered species, the scientists initially did not know where to turn to find its natural predators. Although investigators suspected that the cassava mealybug was an exotic species from the New World, it had only been described from cassava fields in Africa. The search was on to find the bug in the wild.

At first the search focused on the Caribbean and northern South America. Investigators believed they had identified the mealybug in its natural habitat in the 1970s, and they discovered two parasitoid insects that preyed on the Caribbean mealybugs. Surprisingly, when released in African fields, the parasitoids had no effect on the African mealybugs; it was discovered several years later that the Caribbean mealybug was a different species than the one from Africa. Parasitoids (parasites that eventually consume their hosts) are often extremely host-specific. Although the two mealybug species are closely related, the parasitoids that preyed on the Caribbean mealybug would not accept as prey the cousin of their normal host (Herren and Neuenschwander 1991).

Several years later, the real culprit was identified in a field in Paraguay, thousands of miles from the home of the Caribbean mealybug. This Paraguayan mealybug was found in traditional cassava fields in low, irregular concentrations: several natural enemies kept its numbers low. It is also possible that local cassava varieties may have developed a resistance to the mealybug that the African varieties had not had the time to develop.

Researchers began a series of tests to determine which insects would be successful biological control agents. First, they tested parasitoids for host specificity—whether the parasitoid fed and bred solely on its host, dying out if its host died out. This factor was important, because mealybug parasites that fed on other animals, such as honeybees, might become pests themselves, destroying beneficial species or altering natural ecosystems. So researchers tested these parasitoids' interest in other African insects. Parasitoids that showed a tendency to attack other insects were rejected.

One very promising parasite was the wasp *Aponagyrus (Epidinocarsis) lopezi*, which laid its own eggs in mealybug eggs, destroying them. *A. lopezi* has no common name, only a scientific name, for the very good reason that these wasps are extremely small: they are only about 10 times the size of the period at the end of this sentence. Although small, they have a large effect on cassava mealybugs, and subsequent tests showed that they attacked *only* cassava mealybugs and did not eat other plant or animal species. *A. lopezi* was approved by an international agency for field tests as a biological control agent.

The results were a smashing success. Although the wasps did not wipe out the mealybugs, they greatly limited their numbers. Losses to cassava crops were reduced by 95%, an impressive achievement. The wasps bred quickly and dispersed well: 10 months after one experimental release, *A. lopezi* had spread throughout most cassava fields within a radius of 15 kilometers. Farmers got free biological control of mealybugs, without the dangers of pesticide poisoning and pollution to the surrounding environment.

As long as mealybugs remained in an area, the wasps did too, keeping mealybug numbers and their damage down. Armed with evidence of this success, the IITA won $20 million from international aid donors to fund a multiyear program of wasp releases and follow-up studies. Facilities were developed for raising 250,000 wasps per week. Developing a technique for successfully releasing wasps from airplanes helped facilitate the release program. Today *A. lopezi* is found almost everywhere that cassava mealybugs are found in Africa. The tiny wasp has saved hundreds of millions of dollars in crop losses in some of the world's poorest countries, perhaps averting famine as well.

The success of the campaign against the cassava mealybug convinced national governments and international aid donors of the usefulness of biological control efforts. Today the IITA has expanded its biological control programs to fight a number of important tropical pests, including corn borers, and cowpea and banana pests. Such efforts continue worldwide.

Cassava mealybugs caused extensive damage to cassava plants (below) across a wide area of Africa. Scientists found a tiny wasp (right) that lays its eggs in the mealybug's larvae, providing an effective means of biological control. (Photographs courtesy of D. V. Neuenschwander, FAO.)

The IITA search for a biological control agent for the cassava mealybug depended on the patient efforts of scientists and nonscientists from around the world. Bug hunting in South America, lab analysis and testing in England, field testing and release in Africa, and strong international funding were all necessary elements. Most important, biological control was possible because biological diversity had been preserved. Because cassava strains had been preserved in their area of origin in Paraguay, the cassava mealybug had also been preserved with its full complement of predators. If these fields had been intensively managed using pesticides or converted to other uses, the wasp predators of the cassava mealybug might have gone extinct and been unavailable as biological control agents. Instead, parasitoid wasps can now be used to protect human food crops in an ecologically sensible way. This project has become one of the best documented biological control successes and serves as a beacon for new efforts to protect food crops and wild species.

Even in the case of medicines that are now produced synthetically by chemists, many of the original structures were first discovered in a wild species used in traditional medicine (Figure 4.4). Extracts of willow tree bark (*Salix* sp.) were used by the ancient Greeks and by tribes of Native Americans to treat pain, leading to the discovery of acetylsalicylic acid—the painkilling ingredient in modern aspirin, one of the most widely taken and important medicines. Similarly, the use of coca (*Erythoxylum coca*) by natives of the Andean highlands eventually led to synthetic derivatives such as novocaine and xylocaine, commonly used as local anesthetics in dentistry and surgery. Many other important medicines were first identified in animals. Poisonous animals such as rattlesnakes, bees, and cone snails have been especially rich sources of chemicals with valuable medical and biological applications (Tangley 1996; Carte 1996).

All of the 20 most frequently used pharmaceuticals in the United States are based on chemicals first identified in natural products; these drugs have a combined sales value of $6 billion per year. Twenty-five percent of the prescriptions filled in the United States contain active ingredients derived from plants, and many of the most important antibi-

Figure 4.4 Antonio Cue of Belize carries on the traditions of his Mayan ancestors as he prepares useful medicines from plants that are growing in the local area. He is now working with scientists to determine if chemicals in these plants can be developed for use in modern medicine. (Photograph courtesy of M. J. Balick.)

Figure 4.5 Taxonomists at INBio are sorting and classifying Costa Rica's rich array of species. In the offices shown here many species of plants and insects are cataloged. (Photograph by Steve Winter.)

otics, such as penicillin and tetracycline, are derived from fungi and other microorganisms (Eisner 1991; Dobson 1995). Most recently, the fungus-derived drug cyclosporine has proved to be a crucial element in the success of heart and kidney transplants.

The biological communities of the world are being continually searched for new plants, animals, fungi, and microorganisms that can be used to fight human diseases (Cox and Balick 1994; Balick et al. 1996; Grifo and Rosenthal 1997). These searches are generally carried out by government research institutes and pharmaceutical companies. In 1987, the U.S. National Cancer Institute initiated an $8 million program to test extracts of thousands of wild species for their effectiveness in controlling cancer cells and the AIDS virus. To facilitate the search for new medicines and to profit financially from new products, the Costa Rican government established the National Biodiversity Institute (INBio) to collect biological products and supply samples to drug companies (Figure 4.5). The Merck Company has signed an agreement to pay INBio $1 million for the right to screen samples and will pay royalties to INBio on any commercial products that result from the research. Expected royalties are difficult to calculate, but one estimate suggests a figure of $4.8 million per new drug developed (Reid et al. 1993). Another approach has been to target traditional medicinal plants and other natural products for screening, often in collaboration with local healers. Programs such as these provide financial incentives for countries to protect their natural resources and the knowledge of biodiversity possessed by indigenous inhabitants.

Summary

1. Standard economics tends to ignore the costs of environmental damage and the depletion of natural resources. The new field of ecological economics is developing methods for valuing biological diversity and, in the process, is providing arguments for its protection. While some conservation biologists would argue that biological diversity is priceless and should not be assigned economic values, economic justification for biological diversity will play an increasingly important role in debates on the use of natural resources.

2. Many countries that show annual increases in gross domestic product may actually have stagnant or even declining economies when the depletion of natural resources and damage to the environment are included in the calculations. More large development projects are being analyzed through environmental impact assessments and cost–benefit analyses before being approved.

3. A number of methods have been developed to assign economic value to biological diversity. In one method, resources are divided between direct values, which are assigned to products harvested by people, and indirect values, which are assigned to benefits provided by biological diversity that do not involve harvesting or destroying the resource.

4. Direct values can be further divided into consumptive use value and productive use value. Consumptive use value is assigned to products that are consumed locally, such as fuelwood, wild meat, fruits and vegetables, medicinal plants, and building materials. These goods can be valued by determining how much money people would have to pay for them if they were unavailable in the wild. When these wild products become unavailable, the living standard of people that depend on them declines. Productive use value is assigned to products harvested in the wild and sold in markets, such as commercial timber, fish and shellfish, and wild meat. Species collected in the wild have great productive use value in their ability to provide new founder stock for domestic species and for the genetic improvement of agricultural crops. Agriculturalists also look to new species to provide biologically based pest control. Wild species are also a major source of new medicines.

For Discussion

1. Choose a recent large development project, such as a dam, sewage treatment plant, or housing development, and learn all you can about it. Estimate the costs and benefits of this project in terms of biological diversity, economic prosperity, and human health. Who pays the costs and who receives the benefits? Consider other projects carried out in the past and determine their impact on the surrounding biological and human communities.

2. How do traditional societies use and value biological diversity? What is the relative importance of biological diversity and knowledge of biodiversity in both traditional and modern societies?

3. Suppose a medicinal plant used by traditional people in a remote area in Indonesia is investigated by a European pharmaceutical company and found to have huge potential as a new cancer medicine. Who will profit from the sale of this medicine under current practices? Can you suggest alternative methods to distribute the profits in a way that would be more equitable and would increase the possibility of preserving Indonesia's biological diversity?

Suggested Readings

Balick, M. J. and P. A. Cox. 1996. *Plants, People and Culture: The Science of Ethnobotany*. Scientific American Library, New York. Fascinating story of traditional use of plants, filled with anecdotes and beautifully illustrated.

Balick, M. J., E. Elisabetsky and S. A. Laird (eds.). 1996. *Medicinal Resources of the Tropical Forest: Biodiversity and Its Importance to Human Health*. Columbia University Press, New York. Tropical forests are an important source of new medicines.

Barbier, E. B., J. C. Burgess and C. Folke. 1994. *Paradise Lost? The Ecological Economics of Biodiversity*. Earthscan Publications, London. A clear introduction to this new field.

Baskin, Y. 1997. *The Work of Nature: How the Diversity of Life Sustains Us*. Island Press, Washington, D.C. Excellent semipopular account of the many benefits of preserving biological diversity.

Carte, B. K. 1996. Biomedical potential of marine natural products. *BioScience* 46: 271–286. Describes search for valuable new chemicals in marine organisms, from bacteria to mollusks.

Costanza, R., O. Segura and J. Martinez-Alier. 1996. *Getting Down to Earth: Practical Applications of Ecological Economics*. Island Press, Washington, D.C. Leading authorities apply ecological economics to the issues of environmental health and sustainability.

Daily, G. C. (ed.). 1997. *Nature's Services: Societal Dependence on Ecosystem Services*. Island Press, Washington, D.C. Clear explanations of why maintaining species and ecosystems is critical to human societies.

Dobson, A. 1995. Biodiversity and human health. *Trends in Ecology and Evolution* 10: 390–391. Preserving the natural worlds is critical to the future of human health; an excellent short article.

Grifo, F. and J. Rosenthal (eds.). 1997. *Biodiversity and human health*. Island Press, Washington, D. C. For a wide variety of reasons, maintaining human health and well-being depends on protecting biological diversity.

Krishnan, R., J. M. Harris and N. R. Goodman (eds.). 1995. *A Survey of Ecological Economics*. Island Press, Washington, D.C. Summaries of 95 key papers.

McNeely, J. A. 1988. *Economics and Biological Diversity: Developing and Using Economic Incentives to Conserve Biological Resources*. IUCN, Gland, Switzerland. Case studies are used to demonstrate the economic justifications for preserving biodiversity.

Perrings, C. 1995. Economic values of biodiversity. In *Global Biodiversity Assessment*, pp. 823–914. V. H. Heywood (ed.). Cambridge University Press, Cambridge. Outstanding summary of ecological economics, with numerous examples.

Peters, C. M., A. H. Gentry and R. Mendelsohn. 1989. Valuation of a tropical forest in Peruvian Amazonia. *Nature* 339: 655–656. This groundbreaking but controversial study drew attention to the great economic potential of managed rain forests.

Prescott-Allen, C. and R. Prescott-Allen. 1986. *The First Resource: Wild Species in the North American Economy*. Yale University Press, New Haven, CT. An innovative examination of the economic importance of wild species to a modern economy.

Primack, R. B. and T. E. Lovejoy (eds.). 1995. *Ecology, Conservation and Management of Southeast Asian Rainforests*. Yale University Press, New Haven, CT. Timber products play a crucial role in the economic development of this region.

Reid, W. V. and K. R. Miller. 1989. *Keeping Options Alive: The Scientific Basis for Conserving Biodiversity*. World Resources Institute, Washington, D.C. An excellent summary of conservation biology with a strong emphasis on ecological economics.

Reid, W. V., S. A. Laird, R. G. Elmez et al. (eds.). 1993. *Biodiversity Prospecting*. World Resources Institute, Washington, D.C. Licensing agreements between species-rich countries and international biotechnology corporations may provide economic incentives to investigate and protect biodiversity.

CHAPTER 5

Indirect Economic Values

ASPECTS OF BIOLOGICAL diversity that provide economic benefits without being harvested and destroyed during use are assigned indirect use values. Because ecological benefits are not goods or services in the usual economic sense, they do not appear in the statistics of national economies such as the gross domestic product (GDP). However, they are crucial to the continued availability of the natural products on which economies depend. For example, mountain forests prevent soil erosion and flooding, which could damage human settlements and farmlands in nearby lowland areas; coastal estuaries provide rich harvests of fish and shellfish worth billions of dollars annually, and, during severe storms, they protect human coastal developments worth billions more. In thinking about the indirect use values of ecosystems, consider this summary of the consequences of deforestation (F. H. Bormann 1976):

> We must find replacements for wood products, build erosion control works, enlarge reservoirs, upgrade air pollution control technology, install flood control works, improve water purification plants, increase air conditioning, and provide new recreational facilities. These substitutes represent an enormous tax burden, a drain on the world's supply of natural resources, and an increased stress on the natural system that remains.

Nonconsumptive Use Value

Biological communities provide a great variety of environmental services that are not used for consumption. **Nonconsumptive use value** is sometimes relatively easy to calculate, as in the case of the value of wild insects that pollinate crop plants. About 150 species of crop plants in the United States require insect pollination of their flowers. Many of these species are currently pollinated primarily by wild insects (Buchmann and Nabhan 1996). The value of these pollinators could be assigned by calculating either how much the crop currently increases in value through the actions of the wild insects or how much value the wild insects will have in the near future as they take over the pollination role of domestic honeybees, whose populations are declining due to disease, pests, and low honey prices.

Economists are just beginning to calculate the value of ecosystem services at regional and global levels (Table 5.1) (Chichilnisky 1996). These calculations are still at a preliminary stage, but they suggest that the value of ecosystem services is enormous, around $32 trillion per year, greatly exceeding the direct use value of biological diversity

TABLE 5.1 ***Estimated value of the world's ecosystems using ecological economics***

Ecosystem[a]	Total area (millions of hectares)	Annual local value (dollars/ hectare/year)	Annual global value (trillion dollars/year)
Coastal	3,102	4,052	12.6
Open ocean	33,200	252	8.4
Wetlands	330	14,785	4.9
Tropical forests	1,900	2,007	3.8
Lakes, rivers	200	8,498	1.7
Other forests	2,955	302	0.9
Grasslands	3,898	232	0.9
Cropland	1,400	92	0.1

Source: Costanza et al. 1997

[a] Desert, tundra, urban, and ice/rock ecosystems not included.

(Costanza et al. 1997). Because this amount is greater than the global gross national product of $18 billion, the point can be made that human societies are totally dependent on natural ecosystems and would not persist if these ecosystem services were permanently degraded or destroyed. The most important ecosystem services not accounted for in the current market system are waste treatment and nutrient retention provided by wetlands and coastal areas, totaling $18 trillion per year. Using a different approach, Pimentel et al. (1997) came up with a much lower estimate for the global value of biodiversity, $3 trillion per year, indicating that much more work needs to be done on this topic. Biodiversity has been estimated to be worth $70 billion per year for Canada (Mosquin et al. 1995) and $319 billion per year for the U.S.A. (Pimentel et al. 1997). The following is a discussion of some of the general benefits, derived from conserving biological diversity, that do not appear on the typical balance sheets of environmental impact assessments or in national GDPs.

Ecosystem Productivity

The photosynthetic capacity of plants and algae allows the energy of the sun to be captured in living tissue. The energy stored in plants is sometimes harvested by humans directly as fuelwood, fodder, and wild foods. This plant material is also the starting point for the innumerable food chains that lead to all of the animal products that are harvested by people. Approximately 40% of the productivity of the terrestrial environment is dominated by human needs for natural resources (Vitousek 1994). The destruction of the vegetation in an area through overgrazing by domestic animals, overharvesting of timber, or frequent fires will destroy the system's ability to make use of solar energy, and eventually lead to the loss of production of plant biomass and the deterioration of the animal community (including humans) that lives at that site.

Likewise, coastal estuaries are areas of rapid plant and algal growth that provide the starting point for food chains leading to commercial stocks of fish and shellfish (see Table 5.1). The U.S. National Marine Fisheries Service estimated that damage to coastal estuaries has cost the United States more than $200 million per year in lost productive value of commercial fish and shellfish and in lost nonconsumptive value of fish caught for sport (McNeely et al. 1990). Even when degraded or damaged ecosystems are rebuilt or restored at great expense, they often do not function as well as before and almost certainly do not contain their original species composition or species richness.

Scientists are actively investigating how the loss of species from biological communities affect ecosystem processes, such as the total growth of plants and the ability of plants to absorb atmospheric carbon dioxide (CO_2) (Johnson et al. 1996; Baskin 1997). This question was addressed experimentally at a grassland in Minnesota in which either 1, 2, 6, 8, 12, or 24 species were grown on 3 m × 3 m plots (Tilman et al. 1996). The growth of plant material and uptake of soil nutrients such as nitrogen was greater in plots with more species, clearly demonstrating the importance of species diversity to productivity (Figure 5.1). These results were further supported by similar observations of nearby native grasslands. Plots with a greater diversity of species also showed increased ability to withstand drought.

We know that species diversity is being reduced in major ecosystems as a result of human activities. At what point will the productivity of these ecosystems decline as well? We need to know the answer to this question before world forestry, ranching, agriculture, and fishing industries become critically affected by the consequences of species declines. It is a pretty safe bet that ecosystems with greater diversity of species will be better able to adapt to the altered weather conditions associated with rising CO_2 levels and global climate change.

Protecting Water and Soil Resources

Biological communities are of vital importance in protecting watersheds, buffering ecosystems against extremes of flood and drought, and maintaining water quality (Ehrlich and Mooney 1983; Likens 1991; Power et al. 1996). Plant foliage and dead leaves intercept the rain and reduce its impact on the soil, and plant roots and soil organisms aerate the soil, increasing its capacity to absorb water. This increased water-holding capacity reduces the flooding that otherwise occurs after heavy rains and allows a slow release of water for days and weeks after the rains have ceased.

When vegetation is disturbed by logging, farming, and other human activities, the rates of soil erosion and even occurrences of landslides

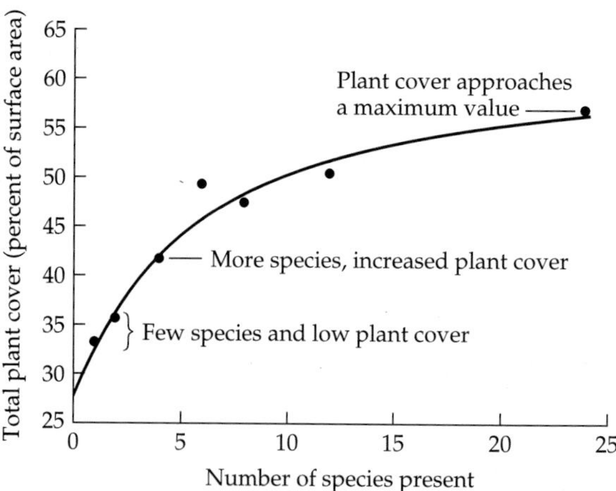

Figure 5.1 Varying numbers of prairie plant species were grown in experimental plots. The plots with the most species had the greatest overall amount of growth, as measured by the total plant cover (the percentage of the total surface area occupied by plants) and plant productivity (the total dry weight of plants on the plot). (After Tilman et al. 1996.)

In many areas of the developing world, people settle near natural water sources to obtain water for drinking, washing, and irrigation. As hydrological cycles are disrupted by deforestation, soil erosion, and dam projects, and as water quality deteriorates due to pollution, people are increasingly unable to obtain their water needs from natural systems. The cost of boiling water, buying bottled water, or building new wells, rain catchment systems, water treatment plants, pipes, and water pumps gives some measure of the consumptive value of water from surface sources. Increases in waterborne disease and intestinal ailments and subsequent lost days of work that occur as water quality declines add to estimates of the economic value of water and the natural systems that provide it.

The need to protect water supplies led New York City to agree to pay $1 billion to rural counties in New York state to maintain forests on the watersheds surrounding its reservoirs. This was a good investment, because water treatment plants doing the same job would have cost $8 to $9 billion (McKibben 1996).

Climate Regulation

Plant communities are important in moderating local, regional, and probably global climate conditions (Nobre et al. 1991; Clark 1992). At the local level, trees provide shade and transpire water, which reduces the local temperature in hot weather. This cooling effect reduces the need for fans and air conditioners, and increases the comfort and work efficiency of people. Trees are also locally important as windbreaks for agricultural fields and homes, and in reducing heat loss from buildings in cold weather.

At the regional level, transpiration from plants recycles rainwater back into the atmosphere so that it can return as rain. At the global level, loss of vegetation from large forested regions of the world such as the Amazon Basin and West Africa may result in reduction of average annual rainfall (Fearnside 1990). In both terrestrial and aquatic environments, plant growth is tied into the carbon cycle. A reduction in plant life results in reduced uptake of carbon dioxide, contributing to rising carbon dioxide levels that lead to global warming. And plants are the chief source of the oxygen in our atmosphere that all animals, including people, require for respiration.

Waste Treatment and Nutrient Retention

Toxic materials from farms, human settlements, and industries generally make their way (if not released directly) into aquatic communities such as swamps, lakes, rivers, tidal marshes, mangroves, floodplains, estuaries, the coastal shelf, and the open ocean. These biological communities are capable of breaking down and immobilizing toxic pollutants, such as heavy metals, pesticides, and sewage, that have been released into the environment by human activities (Odum 1997). Fungi and bacteria are particularly important in this role. When these ecosystems are damaged and degraded, expensive pollution controls must be installed and operated to assume these functions. Waste treatment by these biological communities is estimated to be valued at around $2.4 trillion per year (Costanza et al. 1997).

Aquatic biological communities also play an important role in processing and storing the large amount of nutrients that enter the ecosystem as sewage or agricultural run-off, so that these nutrients can be taken up by photosynthetic organisms. These communities also provide a matrix for the bacteria that fix atmospheric nitrogen. These roles in nutrient processing and retention have an estimated value of $15.9 trillion per year, with most of the total accounted for by coastal marine areas.

An excellent example of the value of an ecosystem is provided by the New York Bight, a 2000 square-mile (5200 km^2) bay at the mouth of the Hudson River. The New York Bight provides a free sewage disposal system into which the waste produced by 20 million people in the New York metropolitan area is dumped (Young et al. 1985). Until recently, the Bight was able to break down and absorb this onslaught of sewage because of the high degree of bacterial activity and tidal mixing in the area. However, the Bight is now showing signs of stress—fish die-offs and beach contamination—that suggest the system is overloaded. The system is being further strained by progressive filling in and development of real estate on the coastal estuaries and marshes, which are essential in the breakdown and assimilation process. As the New York Bight becomes overwhelmed and damaged by a combination of sewage overload and coastal development, an alternative waste disposal system of massive waste treatment facilities and giant landfills will have to be developed at a cost of tens of billions of dollars.

Species Relationships

Many of the species harvested by people for their productive use value depend on other wild species for their continued existence. For example, the wild game and fish harvested by people are dependent on wild insects and plants for their food. A decline in insect and plant populations will result in a decline in animal harvests. Thus, a decline in a wild species of little immediate value to humans may result in a corresponding decline in a harvested species that is economically important. Crop plants also benefit from birds and predatory insects, such as praying mantises, which feed on pest insect species that attack the crops (Pimentel et al. 1997). Many useful wild plant species depend on fruit-eating animals, such as bats and birds, to act as seed dispersers (see Box 4 in Chapter 2).

Option Value

A species' potential to provide an economic benefit to human society at some point in the future is its **option value**. As the needs of society change, so must the methods of satisfying those needs. The solution often lies in previously untapped animal or plant species. Health agencies and pharmaceutical companies are making a major effort to collect and screen species for compounds that have the ability to fight cancer, AIDS, and other human diseases (Plotkin 1993; Reid et al. 1993; Eisner and Beiring 1994; Davis 1995). The discovery of a potent anticancer chemical in the Pacific yew (*Taxus brevifolia*), a tree native to North American old-growth forests, is only the most recent discovery in this search. Another example is the ginkgo tree (*Ginkgo biloba*), a species that occurs in the wild in a few isolated localities in China. During the last 20 years, an industry valued at $500 million a year has developed around the cultivation of the ginkgo tree (Figure 5.6) and the manufacture of medicines made from its leaves, which are widely used in Europe and Asia to treat circulatory problems, including strokes (Del Tredici 1991). The search for valuable natural products is wide-ranging: entomologists search for insects that can be used as biological control agents; microbiologists search for bacteria that can assist in biochemical manufacturing processes; and wildlife biologists search for species that can potentially produce animal protein more efficiently and with less environmental damage than existing domestic species.

The growing biotechnology industry is finding new ways to reduce pollution, to develop alternative industrial processes, and to fight diseases threatening human health. In some cases, newly discovered or well-known species have been found to have exactly those properties needed to deal with a significant human problem. Innovative techniques in molecular biology are allowing unique, valuable genes found in one species to be transferred to another species. If biological diversity is reduced, the ability of scientists to locate and utilize a broad range of species also will be reduced.

Some of the most promising new species being investigated by industrial scientists are the bacteria that live in extreme environments, such as deep-sea thermal vents and hot springs. Bacteria that thrive in unusual chemical and physical environments can often be adapted to special industrial applications of considerable economic value. One of the most important techniques developed by the multibillion dollar biotechnology industry, the polymerase chain reaction (PCR) for multiplying copies of DNA, depends on an enzyme that is stable at high temperatures. This enzyme was originally derived from a bacterium (*Thermus aquaticus*) endemic to natural hot springs in Yellowstone National Park. The companies Hoffman-LaRoche and Perkin-Elmer, owners of the PCR patents, are earning $200 million per year from this technology (Chester 1996).

Figure 5.6 (A) Ginkgo trees are preserved in the wild in the Tian Mu Shan forest reserve in China; no other wild populations exist. This species is the basis of a pharmaceutical business worth hundreds of millions of dollars each year. (B) Because of the valuable medicines made from their leaves, ginkgo trees are now cultivated as a crop. Each year the woody stems sprout new shoots and branches, which are harvested. (Photographs by Peter Del Tredici, Arnold Arboretum of Harvard University.)

An exciting development in the search for valuable bacteria species is the $43 million DEEPSTAR (Deep-Sea Environment Exploration Program: Suboceanic Terrane Animalcule Retrieval) project in Japan (Myers and Anderson 1992). The project includes plans to build manned vessels capable of exploring the oceans at a depth of 6500 meters, find new bacteria, and then culture the bacteria in the laboratory at pressures up to 1000 atmospheres. The leader of the project, Koki Horikoshi, has a long career of searching for unusual bacteria. In his previous "Superbugs" project, Horikoshi investigated bacteria in high pH (alkaline) environments and isolated an enzyme that could digest cellulose. This enzyme was found to be effective in removing dirt from cotton clothing and is now an ingredient in the best-selling brand of laundry detergent in Japan. The race is on to discover other microbial systems of economic value.

The option value of species could be determined by examining the impact on the world economy of wild species only recently utilized by humans. Consider a hypothetical example: If, during the last 20 years, newly discovered uses of 100 previously unused plant species accounted for $100 billion of new economic activity in terms of increased agriculture, new industrial products, and improved medicines, and there are presently 250,000 unused plant species, then a rough calculation might demonstrate that each presently unused plant species has the potential to provide an average of $400,000 worth of benefits to the world economy in the next 20 years. These types of calculations are now at a very preliminary stage, and they assume, for the sake of convenience, that the average value of a species can be determined.

While most species may have little or no direct economic value, and probably will not have any in the immediate future, a small proportion may have enormous potential value to supply medical treatments, to support a new industry, or to prevent the collapse of a major agricultural crop. If just one of these species became extinct before it was discovered, it would be a tremendous loss to the global economy, even if the majority of the world's species were preserved. As Aldo Leopold commented (1953):

> If the biota, in the course of aeons, has built something we like but do not understand, then who but a fool would discard seemingly useless parts? To keep every cog and wheel is the first precaution of intelligent tinkering.

The diversity of the world's species can be compared to a manual on how to keep the Earth running effectively. The loss of a species is like tearing a page out of the manual. If we ever need the information from that page in the manual to save ourselves and the Earth's other species, the information will be irretrievably lost.

A question currently being debated among conservation biologists, governments, environmental economists, and corporations is, "Who owns the commercial development rights to the world's biological diversity?" In the past, species were freely collected from wherever they occurred (often in the developing world) by corporations (almost always headquartered in the developed world). Whatever these corporations found useful in the species was then processed and sold at a profit. Countries in the developing world now frequently demand a share in the commercial activities that are dependent on the biological diversity contained within their borders. Writing treaties and developing procedures to guarantee participation in this process will be a major diplomatic challenge in the coming years.

Existence Value

Many people throughout the world care about wildlife and plants and are concerned for their protection. This concern may be associated with a desire to someday visit the habitat of a unique species and see it in the wild; alternatively, concerned individuals may not expect, need, or even desire to see these species personally or experience the wilderness in which they live. In either case, these individuals recognize an **existence value** in wild nature. Particular species, the so-called "charismatic megafauna" such as pandas, whales, lions, elephants, bison, manatees, and many birds, elicit strong responses in people (Figure 5.7). People place value on wildlife and wild lands in a direct way by joining and contributing billions of dollars each year to conservation organizations that protect species. In the United States, $2.3 billion was contributed in 1990 to environmental wildlife organizations, with The Nature Conservancy, the World Wildlife Fund, Ducks Unlimited, and the Sierra Club topping the list (WCMC 1992). Citizens also show their concerns by directing their governments to spend money on conservation programs and to purchase land for habitat and landscape protection. For example, the government of the United States has spent more than $20 million to protect a single rare species, the California condor (*Gymnogyps californianus*). The citizens of the United States have indicated in surveys that they are willing to spend around $19 per person per year (around $5 billion per year in total) to protect a national symbol, the bald eagle (*Haliaeetus leucocephalus*), a bird whose populations have suffered significant declines (Figure 5.8) (Perrings 1995).

Existence value can be attached to biological communities, such as tropical rain forests and coral reefs, and to areas of scenic beauty. Growing numbers of people and organizations contribute large sums of money annually to ensure the continuing existence of these habitats.

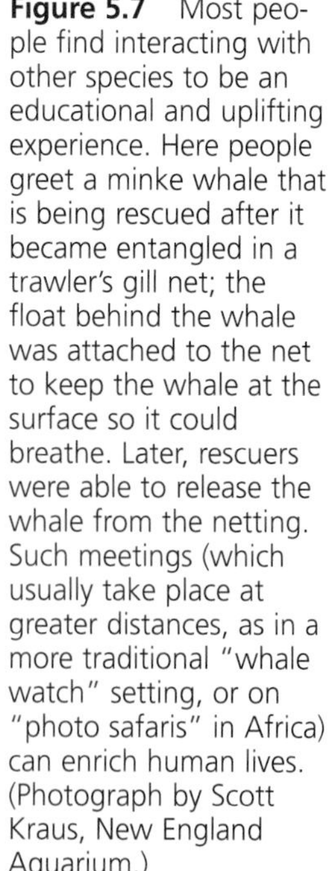

Figure 5.7 Most people find interacting with other species to be an educational and uplifting experience. Here people greet a minke whale that is being rescued after it became entangled in a trawler's gill net; the float behind the whale was attached to the net to keep the whale at the surface so it could breathe. Later, rescuers were able to release the whale from the netting. Such meetings (which usually take place at greater distances, as in a more traditional "whale watch" setting, or on "photo safaris" in Africa) can enrich human lives. (Photograph by Scott Kraus, New England Aquarium.)

Figure 5.8 The bald eagle is a symbol of the United States. Many people have indicated a willingness to pay to protect its continued existence. (Photograph by Jessie Cohen, National Zoological Park.)

In Costa Rica, 91% of respondents said they would be willing to pay higher prices for water and electricity, if the money was used to protect environmental quality and biological diversity (Holl et al. 1995). In a survey relating to the spectacular, scenic Grand Canyon, which has been marred in recent years by sulphur dioxide air pollution from a nearby power plant, U.S. citizens indicated that they would be willing to pay $1.30 to $2.50 per household per year to have improved pollution control equipment installed at the power plant—an amount that translates into well over $100 million per year (Nash 1991). Another survey, taken over a period of several years, showed steadily increasing numbers of U.S. citizens approving of the statement that "environmental improvements must be made, regardless of the cost" (Figure 5.9) (Ruckleshaus 1989). Current surveys continue to show that the public places a high value on environmental protection.

The money spent to protect biological diversity, particularly in the developed countries of the world, is in the order of hundreds of millions, if not billions, of dollars per year. This sum represents the existence value of species and communities—the amount that people are willing to pay to prevent species from going extinct and habitats from being destroyed. At present, existence value is not extended, in many people's perceptions, to include the full range of the world's species, particularly insects and other invertebrates (Kellert 1996). Although a few species, such as the monarch butterfly (*Danaus plexippus*) and the

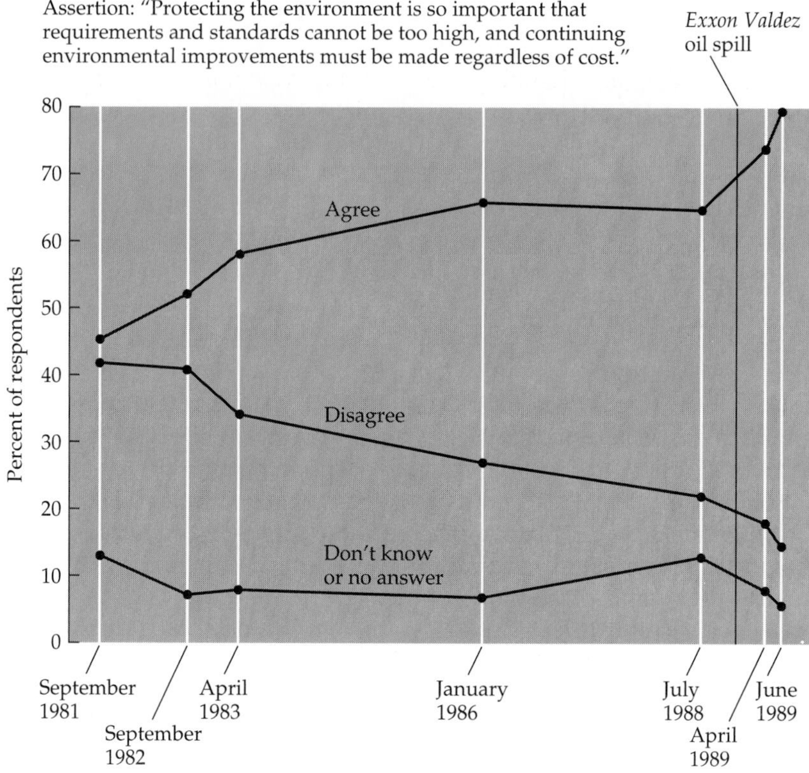

Figure 5.9 Increasingly, people throughout the world are unwilling to tolerate damage to the natural environment. In the United States, New York *Times*/CBS polls have been tracking public attitudes since 1981. People were asked to respond to the statement, "Protecting the environment is so important that requirements and standards cannot be too high, and continuing environmental improvements must be made regardless of cost." The final polls shown here were taken just after the tanker *Exxon Valdez* spilled 11 million gallons of oil onto Alaska's coastline. (From Ruckleshaus 1989.)

American burying beetle (*Nicrophorus americanus*), receive protection and attention, people are indifferent to most invertebrate species. Perhaps this will change in the near future, as the public becomes better educated on the subject of biological diversity.

Concluding Comments on Ecological Economics

In the more complete systems of accounting being developed by ecological economics, the use of common property resources, such as water, air, species, and biological communities, are included in the cost of doing business instead of being left out of the accounting process (Repetto 1992; Levin 1996; Daily 1997). When people and businesses have to pay for their actions, perhaps they will stop damaging the environment, or at least become much more careful. These accounting models are thus a positive development. However, their use can be viewed as acceptance of the present world economic system, with only minor changes. Some environmental thinkers advocate much stronger changes in the present economic system, which is responsible for pollution, environmental degradation, and species extinctions at unprecedented rates.

Perhaps the most damning aspect of this system is the unnecessary overconsumption of resources by a minority of the world's citizens while a majority of people face poverty. Given a world economic system in which millions of children die each year from disease, malnutrition, warfare, crime, and other factors strongly correlated with poverty, and in which thousands of unique species go extinct each year due to habitat destruction, do we need to make minor adjustments or major structural changes? An alternative approach to protecting biological diversity and improving the human situation would be to dramatically lower the consumption of resources in the developed world, reduce the need to exploit natural resources, and greatly increase the value placed on the natural environment and biological diversity, as described in the next chapter. Some suggestions for bringing this about include stabilization or reduction of the number of people in the world, higher taxes on fossil fuels, penalties for inefficient energy use and pollution, and mandatory recycling programs. Restrictions could be placed on trade, so that only those products derived from sustainable activities could be bought or sold on national and international markets; endangered species are already governed by such treaties, and certification of products is increasing in the international trade in wood products. Debts of developing countries could be reduced or dismissed and investment redirected to activities that provide the most benefits to the greatest number of people in poverty. Finally, financial penalties for damaging biological diversity could be established and made so severe that industries would be forced to protect the natural world.

Summary

1. Indirect values can be assigned to aspects of biological diversity that provide economic benefit to people but are not harvested or damaged during use. A major group of indirect values are the nonconsumptive use values of ecosystems. These include ecosystem productivity (important as the starting point for all food chains), protection of water resources and soils, the enhancement of commercial crops by wild species, and regulation of local, regional, and global climates.

2. Biological diversity features prominently in the growing recreation and ecotourism industry. The number of people involved in nature recreation and the amount of money spent on such activities are surprisingly large. In many countries, particularly in the developing world, ecotourism represents one of the major sources of foreign income. Even in industrialized countries, the economy in areas around national parks is increasingly dominated by the recreation industry. Educational materials and the mass media draw heavily on themes of biological diversity and create materials of considerable value.

3. Biological diversity also has an option value in terms of its potential to provide future benefits to human society, such as new medicines, biological con-

trol agents, and new crops. The biotechnology industry is developing innovative techniques to take advantage of new chemicals and physiological properties found in the living world.

4. People are often willing to pay money in the form of taxes and voluntary contributions to ensure the continued existence of unique species, biological communities, and landscapes; this amount represents the existence value of biological diversity.

5. The economic valuation of biological diversity provides one possible method for justifying increased protection of species and communities. However, assigning economic value to wild species perhaps assumes a willingness to accept the present system with only minor changes. Given a world in which there is an unequal distribution of resources, terrible poverty, war, disease, and thousands of species going extinct each year, people need to ask, "Do we need minor adjustments to the present economic system or major structural changes?"

For Discussion

1. Consider the natural resources people use where you live. Can you place an economic value on those resources? If you can't think of any products harvested directly, consider basic ecosystem services such as flood control, fresh water, and soil retention.

2. Ask people how much money they spend on nature-related activities. Also ask them how much they would be willing to spend each year to protect well-known species, such as bald eagles, grizzly bears, and songbirds; to save a rare, endangered freshwater mussel; and to protect water quality and forest health. Multiply the average values by the number of people in your city, your country, or the world to obtain estimates as to how much these components of biological diversity are worth. Is this an accurate method for gauging the economic value of biodiversity? How might you improve this simple methodology?

3. Imagine that the only known population of a dragonfly species will be destroyed unless money can be raised to purchase the pond where it lives and the surrounding land. How much is this species worth? Consider different methods for assigning a monetary value to this species and compare the different outcomes. Which method is best?

Suggested Readings

Buchmann, S. L. and G. P. Nabhan 1998. *The Forgotten Pollinators.* Island Press, Washington, D. C. Wild pollinators are crucial to agricultural production as described in this wonderful book.

Chester, C. C. 1996. Controversy over Yellowstone's biological resources. *Environment* 38(6): 10–15, 34–6. The national parks of the United States are potential sources of species with great economic value, but who owns the rights to use these species and what are the applicable laws?

Chichilnisky, G. 1996. The economic value of the Earth's resources. *Trends in Ecology and Evolution* 11: 135–140. Effective summary of key points of ecological economics.

Costanza, R., R. d'Arge, R. de Gros, S. Farber et al. 1997. The value of the world's ecosystem services and natural capital. *Nature* 387: 253–260. High-profile article by top ecological economists estimates the total ecosystem services as worth around $32 trillion a year.

Davis, W. 1995. *One River: Exploration and Discoveries in the Amazon Rainforest.* Simon & Schuster, New York. True-life adventure story about ethnobotanists' search in the Amazon for valuable plant species.

Ehrlich, P. R. and H. A. Mooney. 1983. Extinction, substitution and ecosystem services. *BioScience* 33: 248–254. Outstanding brief review of the value of ecosystem functions.

Johnson, K. H., K. A. Vogt, H. J. Clark et al. 1996. Biodiversity and the productivity and stability of ecosystems. *Trends in Ecology and Evolution* 11: 372–377. Excellent review of the theories and evidence linking biodiversity and productivity.

Levin, S. A. 1996. Economic growth and environmental quality. *Ecological Applications* 6: 12. Special issue of the journal devoted to discussion of environmental quality.

McKibben, B. 1996. What good is a forest? *Audubon* 98 (3): 54–65. Eloquent statement of the great value of forests, and the need to protect them.

McNeely, J. A., K. R. Miller, W. V. Reid et al. 1990. *Conserving the World's Biological Diversity.* IUCN, World Resources Institute, CI, WWF-US, the World Bank, Gland, Switzerland, and Washington, D.C. Outstanding summary of the value of biodiversity and strategies for preservation.

Mosquin, T., P. G. Whiting and D. E. McAllister. 1995. *Canada's Biodiversity: The Value of Life, Its Status, Economic Benefits, Conservation Costs and Unmet Needs.* Canadian Museum of Nature, Ottawa. Biodiversity provides $70 billion to Canada's economy, as described in this fascinating book.

Pimentel, D., C. Wilson, C. McCallum et al. 1997. Economic and environmental benefits of diversity. *BioScience* 47: 747–757. Creative preliminary calculations of the value of biodiversity to the U.S. and world economies.

Plotkin, M. J. 1993. *Tales of a Shaman's Apprentice.* Viking/Penguin, New York. Vivid account of ethnobotanical exploration and efforts to preserve medical knowledge.

Power, T. M. 1991. Ecosystem preservation and the economy in the Greater Yellowstone area. *Conservation Biology* 5: 395–404. Ecosystem preservation and recreational benefits are surprisingly important.

Repetto, R. 1992. Accounting for environmental assets. *Scientific American* 266 (June): 94–100. Environmental degradation decreases national wealth.

Whelan, T. (ed.). 1991. *Nature Tourism: Managing for the Environment.* Island Press, Washington, D.C. Case histories of successful ecotourism projects, and overviews of important questions.

CHAPTER 6

Ethical Values

THE NEW DISCIPLINE of ecological economics is a positive change influencing the growth of conservation biology. Still, reliance upon ecological economics arguably implies a willingness to accept the present world economic system and the values it enshrines as it is, with only minor changes (Daly and Cobb 1989; Sagoff 1990). Although economic arguments can be advanced to justify the protection of biological diversity, there are also strong ethical arguments for doing so (Naess 1989; Rolston 1994). Economic arguments often are assumed to be more objective or more convincing, but ethical arguments have foundations in the value systems of most religions and philosophies and can be readily understood by the general public (Hargrove 1986). They may appeal to a general respect for life, a reverence for nature or specific aspects of nature, a sense of the beauty, fragility, uniqueness, or antiquity of the living world, or a belief in divine creation.

Many traditional cultures have successfully coexisted with rich local flora and fauna for hundreds of years because their societal ethics encourage personal responsibility and thoughtful use of resources. People in these societies feel duty-bound to respect wild animals and plants even as they harvest them or "borrow" their habitat for human purposes. Traditional beliefs treat rivers, mountains, and other ecosystems as sacred places to be approached with reverence and an appreciation for what they are, rather than for what human beings can make of them (Callicott 1994).

Even in Western industrial societies, ethical arguments can and do convince people to conserve biodiversity. For example, in the United States the rights of species are strongly protected under the Endangered Species Act, and a judge ruling in a major court decision stated "that Congress intended endangered species to be afforded the highest of priorities" (Rolston 1988). The justification for this protection is the "esthetic, ecological, educational, historical, recreational and scientific value" of species. Significantly, economic value is not included in this legal rationale, and economic interests are explicitly stated to be of secondary importance when protecting species from extinction. According to the law, profits and economic values must be reconsidered, and sometimes set aside, when their pursuit threatens to extinguish a species. The law does allow economic values to prevail in some cases, but only if a so-called "God squad" of senior government officials rules that these economic concerns are of overriding national interest.

Economic arguments by themselves provide a basis for valuing species, but they can also provide grounds for extinguishing them or for saving one species and not another. In conventional economic terms, a species with low population numbers, limited geographical range, of small physical size or unattractive appearance, of no immediate use to people, and having no relationship to any species of economic importance will be given a low value. Such qualities may characterize a substantial proportion of the world's species, particularly insects and other invertebrates, fungi, nonflowering plants, bacteria, and protists. Halting profitable developments or making costly attempts to preserve these species may not have any obvious economic justification. In some circumstances, economic justification could exist for destroying an endangered species, particularly organisms that cause disease or that attack crop plants. Still, many people would argue that the conscious destruction of a natural species is morally wrong, even if it is economically profitable. Ethical arguments for preserving biological diversity appeal to the nobler instincts of people. All known human societies have made decisions based on both ethical and economic values. Decisions about slavery and child labor are two such issues. If modern society adopted values that strongly supported preservation of the natural environment and maintenance of biological diversity, we could expect to see lower

human needs (Ferry 1995). They argue that humans have a value beyond all other species' value, because only we are fully conscious, rational, and moral beings, and unless our actions affect other people, directly or indirectly, any treatment of the natural world is morally acceptable. Many writers, especially those arguing from the perspective of animal rights, have difficulty with assigning rights to *species* (Regan 1992). Singer (1979), for one, argues that "species as such are not conscious entities and so do not have interests above and beyond the interest of individual animals that are members of a species." However, Rolston (1994) counters that on both biological and ethical grounds, species, rather than individual organisms, are the appropriate targets of conservation efforts. All individuals eventually die; it is the species that continues, evolves, and sometimes forms new species. In a sense, individuals are temporary representatives of species.

It might seem strange to assign rights of existence and legal protection to nonhuman species, when they lack the self-awareness that is usually associated with the morality of rights and duties. However, whether or not we allow them "rights," species carry great value as the repositories of the accumulated experience and history of millions of previous life forms through their continuous, evolutionary adaptation to a changing environment. The premature extinction of a species due to human activities destroys this history and natural process, and could be regarded as a "superkilling" (Rolston 1989) because it kills future generations of the species and eliminates the processes of evolution and speciation.

This focus on species challenges the modern Western ethical tradition of individualism. But the preservation of biodiversity seems to demand that the needs of endangered species take precedence over the needs of individuals. For example, the U.S. National Park Service killed hundreds of rabbits on Santa Barbara Island to protect a few plants of the endangered species Santa Barbara live-forever (*Dudleya traskiae*); in this case, one endangered species was judged to be more valuable than hundreds of individual animals of a common species (Figure 6.1). Similarly, hundreds of weedy, exotic plants might have to be destroyed, if they were overtopping and outcompeting a few individuals of a rare, native species.

STEWARDSHIP IS A COVENANT WITH GOD Many religious adherents find it wrong to allow the destruction of species, because they are God's creation. If God created the world, then presumably the species God created have value. Within the Jewish and Christian traditions, human responsibility for protecting animal species is explicitly described in the Bible as part of the covenant with God. The Book of Genesis describes the creation of the Earth's biological diversity as a divine act, after which "God saw that it was good" and "blessed them." In the story of Noah's Ark, God commanded Noah to save two of *all* species, not just the ones

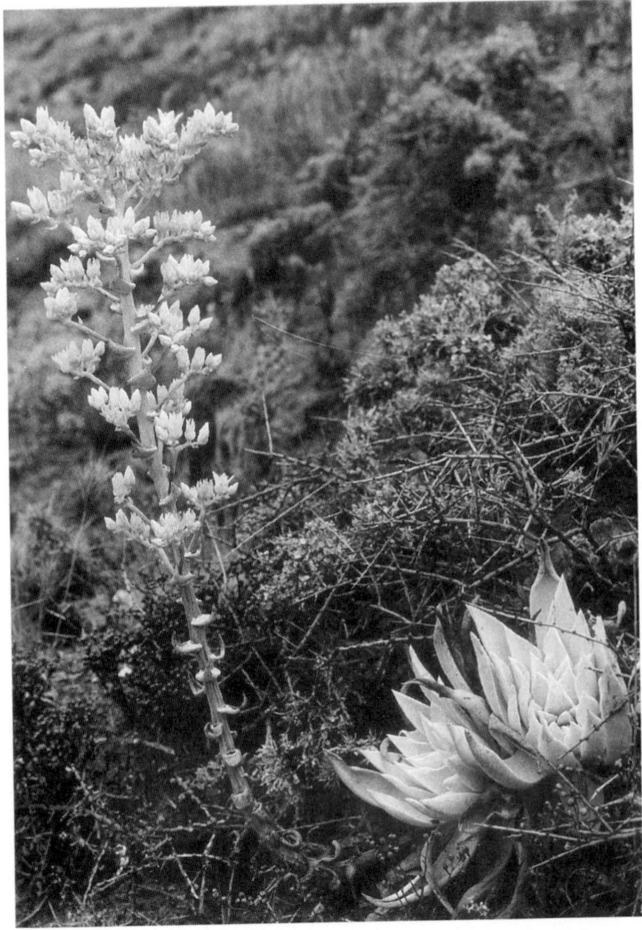

Figure 6.1 Government agencies judged the continued existence of the endangered plant Santa Barbara live-forever (*Dudleya traskiae*; the tall plant at left) to be more valuable than the common rabbits on its island home. The rabbits, which fed on the plant's fleshy leaves (shown at the bottom right), were killed to stop their destruction of this fragile plant species. (National Park Service Photograph.)

human beings found useful. God provided detailed instructions for building the ark, an early species rescue project, saying "Keep them alive with you." After the flood subsided, the animals were released to repopulate the Earth. This story can be interpreted as an early awareness of the importance of biological diversity and the initiation of a species preservation plan. The prophet Muhammad, founder of Islam, continued this theme of human responsibility, saying, "The world is green and beautiful and God has appointed you as His stewards over it. He sees how you acquit yourselves." This belief in the value of God's creation supports a **stewardship argument** for preserving biodiversity: human beings have been given dominion over God's creation, and must preserve what they have been given, not destroy it (Box 10).

Other religious traditions also support the preservation of nonhuman nature (Callicott and Ames 1989; Callicott 1994). For example, Hinduism locates divinity in certain animals, and recognizes a basic

Box 10 **Mighty Multitudes of Microbes: Not To Be Ignored!**

They're out there, and there are billions of them. They occupy cities, suburbs, countrysides, and forests; they're equally at home in spiffy high-rise hotels, filthy shanty towns, and barren deserts. They live in hospitals, restaurants, parks, theaters, and your digestive tract, as well as on mountaintops, in rain forests, and on seashores. They can be found swimming in the ocean's depths and warming themselves near volcanoes—they may even exist on Mars. The living world's quintessential jet-setters, we find them everywhere we look—or we would, if we could see at the microscopic level. Fortunately for the peace of mind of most people, we can't, so the billions of microbes that inhabit our world go unnoticed. Out of sight and out of mind, except when we're bothered by a cold or have gone too long without cleaning out the vegetable drawer in the refrigerator.

The word "microbe" is a catchall for thousands of species of bacteria, yeasts, protozoa, fungi, and the bacteria-like species in the primitive kingdom Archaea.* A handful of soil can contain thousands, millions, even billions of each of these different types of microbes, except for the Archaea, which at present are known only from extreme environments such as deep-sea thermal vents, coal deposits, highly salty environments, and hot springs (see Box 5). Few people realize how utterly essential these invisible critters are to our day-to-day existence. When we think of them, we tend to look upon microbes as nuisances that pose a potential threat to our health—hence the proliferation of antibacterial soaps and antibiotic sprays on supermarket shelves.

In truth, most microbes either actively help us live our lives or at the very least do little harm. Those microbes that do harm us—pathogens ranging from the annoying fungus that causes athlete's foot to the deadly viruses and protozoa that cause killer diseases such as AIDS and malaria—are fairly few in number when compared to the total range of microbes present in the world. On the other hand, we literally couldn't live without some of them. Microbes play a vital role in the production of foods such as bread, cheese, vinegar, yogurt, soy sauce, and tofu, and alcoholic beverages such as beer and wine. Bacteria in our gastrointestinal tract help break down the food we eat (Canby 1993). A few species of bacteria perform the vital biochemical function of transforming nitrogen gas from the atmosphere into a form that plants can take up from the soil as a nutrient. Such "fixed" nitrogen is essential for plant growth. Bacteria and fungi in the soil also aid in the decomposition of organic wastes, freeing up more nutrients for plants to use as they grow. In short, without bacteria, there would be no plants—and thus no food or oxygen available for the animal kingdom, including humans.

In recent years, scientists have begun to appreciate that these organisms are important not only to

Bacteria can be genetically engineered to "eat" crude oil. In this laboratory simulation of an oil spill (left), adapted bacteria added to the spill (top, right) quickly reduce the area of the damaging pollutant (bottom right). (Photographs by Charles O'Rear.)

*The term "microbes" also encompasses viruses, which are fragments of genetic material surrounded by a protective protein coat that can invade the cells of other species and make copies of themselves. Viruses are not generally considered to be living, independent organisms.

Box 10 (Continued)

sustain life as we know it, but also to assist in the conservation of threatened species. Some microbes have uses that may ultimately help reduce environmental pollution and habitat degradation. For instance, a major cause of the decline of many insect and bird species is the presence of harmful compounds in sprays used to control agricultural pests and pathogens. These chemicals harm important nonpest species either by killing them outright or by interfering with their ability to forage and reproduce; at the same time, many pests and pathogens have grown resistant to the compounds (NRC, 1996). As pesticides have become less effective, agronomists have begun turning to microbial solutions to pest problems. Important species include the bacterial species *Bacillus thuringiensis*, which produces a toxin that kills some insect pests, and *Agrobacterium radiobacter*, which controls a bacterial pathogen that attacks several important fruit and flower species. Using microbes as biological controls is advantageous for two important reasons: First, they tend to be highly specific in terms of what organisms they will attack, so that unlike chemicals, they are likely to harm only a narrow range of species. Though a microbe that causes disease in cabbage moth caterpillars could not be used, for instance, in an area also inhabited by an endangered butterfly, it could be used elsewhere without concern that it would harm beneficial insects such as bees or dragonflies. A second advantage is that, like the pathogens they attack, microbes are capable of mutating into many different varieties. Unlike chemical pesticides, a microbe can be genetically altered to counteract the mutations of the pathogen; thus, although the pest species might become resistant to one strain of the bacterium used for biological control, additional strains can be developed to counteract the resistance. The process has been observed in medicine: penicillin, once a "wonder drug" derived from a fungal mold and used for curing bacterial infections, is now used less commonly because many bacteria have become resistant to this antibiotic drug. Doctors now frequently prescribe synthetic variants of penicillin or other antibiotics.

In addition to replacing harmful chemicals with microbes, bioengineering has allowed us to "train" microbes to perform tasks that are not feasible using technological means. For example, bacteria engineered to attack pollutants such as cyanide, crude oil, and creosote are used more and more often in cleaning up toxic waste sites (Canby 1993). This use of microbes may become an important factor in reclaiming damaged habitat, possibly an essential component of future conservation efforts. It seems strangely ironic that the simplest, "lowest" life forms on Earth should be in a position to address problems created by the most complex and "highest" life form, humankind.

Yet even as microbes supply a potential means to solve significant conservation problems, the feared smallpox virus is presenting one of the knottiest ethical dilemmas in conservation biology. Since the dawn of civilization in the Old World, smallpox has been a familiar and deadly companion to human communities. Many adult inhabitants of the modern industrial world literally bear the scars of this microbe in the form of the small, round smallpox inoculation mark that for decades was given to children in an effort to wipe out this deadly disease. In the late 1970s, this effort was successful: the last known case of smallpox occurred in 1978, the result of careless handling of a lab sample. Because the virus apparently is no longer present in the natural world and vaccinations are no longer being given, an epidemic could occur if the virus were to be accidentally or deliberately released. For this reason, the World Health Organization has recommended repeatedly that the two remaining stocks of the virus—one at the Centers for Disease Control in Atlanta and the other at the Institute for Viral Preparations in Moscow—be destroyed (Joklik 1993). For medical practitioners, this recommendation represents the last logical step in eliminating a hazard that has decimated human populations for millennia. The argument for preserving the virus has several compelling practical components. For instance, the means by which the smallpox virus is able to evade the immune system is still unknown. Although the genetic material in the virus has been thoroughly studied and sequenced, the mechanisms of transmission have not, and it is unlikely that they can be determined using anything other than the live virus. However, aside from its potential utility in medical research, there is an important ethical consideration that must be considered by conservation biologists: do we have the right to destroy a species that has the potential to destroy human populations? A deliberate decision to obliterate a species could set a disturbing precedent for the elimination of "undesirable" species.

kinship between humans and other beings (including the transmigration of souls from one species to another). A primary ethical concept in Hinduism and other Indian religions, such as Jainism and Buddhism, is *ahimsa*—avoiding unnecessary harm to life. In attempting to live this ideal, many religious people become vegetarians and live as simply as possible. Of course, religions sometimes articulate views that put human beings at the center of creation, supporting a domineering attitude toward nature. Since many people base their ethical values on a religious faith, the development of religious arguments in support of conservation might be effective in motivating people to conserve biodiversity (Nash 1991; Oelschlaeger 1994).

ALL SPECIES ARE INTERDEPENDENT Species interact in complex ways in natural communities. The loss of one species may have far-reaching consequences for other members of the community: other species may become extinct in response, or the entire community may become destabilized as the result of cascades of species extinctions (Box 11). As we learn more about global processes, we are finding out that many chemical and physical characteristics of the atmosphere, the climate, and the ocean are linked to biological processes in a self-regulating manner. For these reasons, if we value some parts of nature, we should protect all of nature. Even if we only value human beings, our instincts toward self-preservation should impel us to preserve biodiversity. When the natural world prospers, we prosper. We see countless examples of how people suffer when the natural world is harmed in the form of widespread human health problems, such as asthma and cancer, that can be caused or aggravated by environmental pollution.

In a colorful metaphor, Ehrlich and Ehrlich (1981) imagine that species are rivets holding together the Earthship, which carries all species, including humans, in its travel through time. Species going extinct are like rivets popping out of the structure. While lost species may be more or less important, when enough species go extinct, the Earthship will crash, and humans will be harmed as well. Myers (1979) developed a similar metaphor, "the sinking ark," for the extinction of species. These two metaphors, in which the species (as rivets) prevent the Earthship-ark from crashing (or sinking) represent a new twist on the original Bible story, in which Noah built an ark at God's instruction to preserve each species; rather than people saving biodiversity, biodiversity is seen as the salvation of people.

PEOPLE HAVE A DUTY TO THEIR NEIGHBORS Humans must be careful to minimize damage to their natural environment because such damage not only harms other species, it harms people as well. Much of the pollution and environmental degradation that occurs is unnecessary and could be minimized with better planning. Our duty to other humans requires us to live within sustainable limits (Norton 1991; Luper-Foy

Box 11 Sharks: An Unpopular Animal in Decline

Of the many plants and animals threatened by human exploitation, one of the least loved is the shark. Public perception of these animals is based almost entirely upon news reports of attacks upon humans (attacks that are actually much rarer than one might imagine; Manire and Gruber 1990) and gruesome media images (e.g., the movie *Jaws*), which portray sharks as merciless, indiscriminate killers. For most people, a shark is little more than a terrifying triangular fin and a mouthful of very sharp teeth. For conservationists concerned with rapidly dwindling shark populations worldwide, the shark's bad reputation is a public relations nightmare.

When we contrast the 10 people per year killed by sharks with the estimated 100 million sharks per year killed by people, it is clear that people are the more dangerous species (Lemonick 1997). Sharks actually help people far more than they harm people. Shark's liver oil was an important source of vitamin A, until it was synthesized in 1947; shark's liver oil is also highly effective at shrinking human hemorrhoids, and is widely used in medicines for that purpose. The immune system of sharks is being intensively studied to learn the secret of why sharks have an unusually low incidence of cancer, even when experimentally exposed to known carcinogens. The chemical squalamine found in the internal organs of dogfish has the ability to inhibit the growth of certain brain tumors in humans. With their grace and power in the water and their ability to provide new medical benefits to people, it would seem that sharks would be more appreciated by the public, along with whales, manatees, seals, and otters.

The single quality that redeems these animals in the public eye is not one which encourages conservation: sharks are a popular item on menus in Chinese restaurants. Shark fishing has become a booming business in the past decade. In Asia, shark-fin soup is a delicacy that has created high demand for several species of shark; shark fins may bring up to $44 per kg (Waters 1992). The cruel and wasteful practice called "finning," in which a captured shark is flung back into the water to die after its fins are amputated, has spurred some public sympathy for sharks and has led to call for banning the practice. A more serious problem, however, is the tendency for sharks to become "by-catches" of commercial fishing using drift gill nets. More than half of the annual shark kills are related to accidental gill net catches; sharks caught in this manner are usually simply discarded.

High shark mortality has conservationists concerned for several reasons. Sharks mature very slowly, have long reproductive cycles, and produce only a few young at a time. Fishes such as salmon (which have also been overharvested) can recover rapidly because of the large numbers of offspring they produce annually; sharks do not have this capability. A second problem is that harvesting of sharks by commercial and private fishing concerns is largely unregulated. Sharks are increasingly harvested for their meat, often used in fish-and-chips. Sharks are also targeted by sport fishermen because of their size and fierce reputation. A few countries, notably the U.S.A., Australia, New Zealand, and Canada, have enacted legislation to stem shark losses including banning finning, but major contrib-

1992). This goal can be achieved by people in the industrialized countries taking strong actions to reduce their excessive and disproportionate consumption of natural resources.

Technology and social policy should be directed toward using natural resources in the most efficient manner possible to minimize human demands on the environment. For example, if water is recycled or used more efficiently, we will not disrupt as many hydrological cycles, and aquatic plants and animal communities are less likely to be destroyed. Or, if selective logging is practiced carefully, there will be far less soil erosion, flooding, and unnecessary destruction of forests.

utors to commercial shark fishing either see no need for action or are delaying proposed regulations. Recent government-imposed 50% reductions of the total catch of coastal sharks caught in United States waters are a step in the right direction, but catch limits may still be too high to let vulnerable species recover to their original numbers.

Finally, the decimation of shark populations is occurring at a time when very little is known about more than a handful of individual species. Though more than 350 species of sharks exist, management proposals often treat all sharks as a single entity because, lacking specific information, management by species is not possible. Species that have been studied, including the lemon shark (*Negaprion brevirostris*), have demonstrated a precipitous decrease in numbers of young observed in the past five years.

The decline of shark populations is a matter for concern in and of itself, but it is also an important factor in a larger problem. Sharks are among the most important predators in marine ecosystems; they feed upon a variety of organisms and are distributed throughout oceans, seas, and lakes worldwide. Terrestrial ecologists have already observed the benefits of predation for prey populations and the problems that occur when predators are removed from an ecosystem. The decline of sharks could have a significant, and possibly catastrophic, cascade effect upon marine ecosystems, allowing unwanted species to rapidly increase in numbers. Ironically, sharks have fulfilled their role for some 400 million years, making them one of the longest-lived groups of organisms on the planet; yet their future depends upon a change in human attitudes and perceptions. Conservationists have their work cut out for them. They must persuade world governments to look beyond the shark's terrifying aspect and act to preserve this diverse group of species that is a vital to the health of the world's oceans.

Shark fishing in Florida. The sharks are caught by vacationers on a pleasure cruise, displayed for photographs, and then discarded. (Photograph © Paige Chichester.)

PEOPLE HAVE A RESPONSIBILITY TO FUTURE GENERATIONS If in our daily living we degrade the natural resources of the Earth and cause species to become extinct, future generations will pay the price in terms of a lower standard of living and quality of life. Rolston (1995) predicts, "[I]t is safe to say that in the decades ahead, the quality of life will decline in proportion to the loss of biotic diversity, though it is often thought that one must sacrifice biotic diversity to improve human life." Imagine that we are borrowing the Earth from future generations who expect to get it back in good condition. As species are lost, children are deprived of one of their most exciting experiences in growing up—the wonder of seeing "new" animals and plants in the wild.

RESPECT FOR HUMAN LIFE AND HUMAN DIVERSITY IS COMPATIBLE WITH A RESPECT FOR BIOLOGICAL DIVERSITY Some people worry that recognizing an intrinsic value in nature requires devaluing human beings. But a respect for human life and human diversity is compatible with a respect for biological diversity (Kellert and Wilson 1993; Kelly 1994). People will be more likely to accept their responsibility for protecting biological diversity when citizens of all countries have full political rights, a secure livelihood, and an awareness of environmental issues (Nickel and Viola 1994). Some of the most exciting developments in conservation biology involve supporting the economic development of disadvantaged rural people in ways that are linked to the protection of biological diversity. Helping poor people establish sustainable plots of cash crops and achieve a degree of economic independence sometimes reduces the need to overharvest wild species. Working with indigenous people to establish legal title to their land gives them the means to protect the biological communities in which they live.

Human maturity leads naturally to self-restraint and a respect for others. Environmentalists have argued that the further maturation of the human species will involve an "identification with all life forms" and "the acknowledgment of the intrinsic value of these forms" (Naess 1986) in an expanding circle of moral obligations, moving outward from oneself to include duty to relatives, the social group, all humanity, animals, all species, the ecosystem, and ultimately the whole Earth (Figure 6.2). Actions taken to protect species and biological communities should, whenever possible, benefit people as well. Conservation biologists need to be sensitive to the public perception that they care more about birds, turtles, or nature generally than they do about people.

Some people argue that recognizing an intrinsic value in nature leads to absurdity. Because we must use nature, they say, we cannot recognize its intrinsic value which, by definition, would limit the ways in which we use it. Even people who are sympathetic to environmentalism and appreciate wild nature often resist granting its intrinsic value. Recognizing intrinsic value demands a lot from us: if nature is wonderful and complex, as science and our own experience tells us it is, how can we go on using it? We must do so to survive. But the world is already filled with rules limiting our actions; adding another layer of rules to our already rule-burdened lives is tiresome. When lifestyles depend to a large extent on an ecologically destructive economic system, many despair of changing it, and give up trying to live in an environmentally responsible manner.

However, despite these legitimate concerns, effective action to protect biological diversity is both possible and desirable. First, it is possible to use natural resources in a respectful and limited way: it is neces-

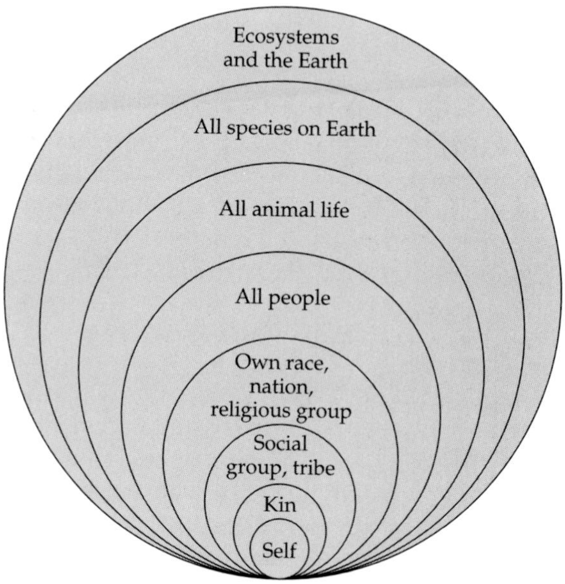

Figure 6.2 An ethical sequence in which the individual extends concern outward beyond the self to progressively more inclusive levels. (From Noss 1992.)

sary to use nature, but not all use of nature is necessary. Second, while no one likes more rules, growing up and living moral lives involves recognizing our duty to others. If nature does in fact have intrinsic value, we should respect that value—whether doing so is convenient or not.

Enlightened Self-Interest: Biodiversity and Human Excellence

Economic arguments stress that preserving biological diversity is in our material self-interest. Ethical arguments based on the intrinsic value of wild nature and our duty to others stress that we should act altruistically toward nature; that is, regardless of our own material self-interest, we should treat nature respectfully. A second ethical argument appeals to our enlightened self-interest, arguing that preserving biodiversity and developing our knowledge of it will make us better and happier people (Naess 1989; Rolston 1988a, 1994; Kellert 1996).

MATERIAL SELF-INTEREST: PROTECTING OUR LIFE-SUPPORT AND ECONOMY

It cannot be repeated too often that biological diversity preserves our basic life-support systems of food production, water supply, oxygen replenishment, waste disposal, soil conservation, and more. People will be healthier and more productive in a clean, intact environment. We depend on this and should value it. Similarly, biodiversity allows us to create tremendous economic wealth, directly and indirectly, as detailed in Chapters 4 and 5.

AESTHETIC AND RECREATIONAL ENJOYMENT. Nearly everyone enjoys wildlife and landscapes aesthetically, and joy makes our lives good lives. The beauty of a field of wildflowers in Glacier National Park or a migrating warbler on a spring morning in a city park enriches the lives of people who appreciate them. For many people, a high quality of life involves experiencing nature in an undisturbed setting. Simply reading about species or seeing them in museums, gardens, and zoos will not suffice. Hiking, canoeing, and mountain climbing are physically, intellectually, and emotionally satisfying. People spend tens of billions of dollars annually in these pursuits, proof enough of their value.

ARTISTIC AND LITERARY EXPRESSION Throughout history, poets, writers, painters, and musicians of all cultures have drawn inspiration from wild nature (Leopold 1949; Burks 1994; Abrams 1996). Nature provides countless forms and symbols for painters and sculptors to render and interpret (Figure 6.3). Poets have often found their greatest inspiration in either wild nature or pastoral countrysides. Preserving biological diversity preserves possibilities for all artists. It also allows those of us who appreciate such creativity access to those sources and experiences that often inspire great artists. A loss in biological diversity could very well limit the creative energies of people in the future and thus restrict the development of human culture. For instance, if many species of whales, butterflies, and orchids go extinct in the next few decades,

Figure 6.3 Rare wildflowers and butterflies are the inspiration for botanical sculptor Patrick O'Hara. In his studio in western Ireland, O'Hara molds, sculpts, and paints delicate porcelain scenes from nature that inspire an appreciation of conservation in a worldwide audience. (Photograph courtesy of Patrick O'Hara.)

whole sets of imagery will be lost to the direct experience of future generations of artists.

SCIENTIFIC KNOWLEDGE Science and the growth of knowledge of nature are among humanity's greatest achievements. This knowledge is facilitated by the preservation of wild nature. Wild areas allow the study of natural ecological interactions. Wild species preserve the record of evolution. Young people are inspired to become scientists by personal contacts with wild nature, and those who do not become professional scientists can take a basic knowledge of science and apply it to an understanding of their own local fields, forests, and streams (Orr 1994).

Two of the central mysteries in the world of science are how life originated and how the diversity of life found on Earth today came about. Thousands of biologists are working on these problems and are coming ever closer to the answers. Recent discoveries of bacteria deep in the Earth's crust and the ancient Wollemi pine in Australia (see Figure 3.7) are important recent developments in this exciting story. New techniques of molecular biology allow greater insight into the relationships of living species as well as some extinct species known from fossils. However, when species become extinct, important clues are lost, and the mystery becomes harder to solve. If the Wollemi pine had been destroyed by logging activity, we would have missed this amazing insight into the origin of early plant life. If *Homo sapiens'* closest living relatives, the great apes, disappear from the wild, we will lose important clues regarding human physical and social evolution.

HISTORICAL UNDERSTANDING Knowing nature, both scientifically and by personal experience, is a key to self-knowledge and an understanding of human history (Thomashow 1996). In walking the landscapes our ancestors walked, we gain insight into how they experienced the world, at a slower pace and without mechanized aids. People often forget, or don't realize, just how recently mankind has moved to ultrafast transportation, fully illuminated cities that shut out the night, and other aspects of modern life. We need to preserve natural areas in order to develop our historical imaginations.

RELIGIOUS INSPIRATION Many religions have traditions of "wandering in the wilderness" in order to commune with God or with spirits. Moses, Isaiah, Jesus, and St. Francis of Assisi, from the Western tradition, all sought out the solitude of wilderness. Being in nature allows us to clear and focus our minds and, sometimes, experience the transcendent. When we are surrounded by the artifacts of civilization, our minds stay fully focused on human purposes and our everyday lives. Religion probably would not disappear from a totally tamed human environment, but perhaps it would become diluted for many.

Deep Ecology

Recognition of both the economic value and the intrinsic value of biological diversity leads to new limits to acceptable human action. This can make it seem like conservation is simply a neverending list of "thou shalt nots," but many environmentalists believe that an understanding of our true self-interest would lead to a different conclusion (Naess 1989):

> The crisis of life conditions on Earth could help us choose a new path with new criteria for progress, efficiency, and rational action. ... The ideological change is mainly that of appreciating life quality rather than adhering to a high standard of living.

In the past two hundred years, the industrial revolution with its accompanying technological advances and social changes has generated tremendous material wealth in spite of the world's great ethical and religious traditions that have always downplayed the importance of wealth in living a good life. For many in the developed world, heaping up further wealth at the expense of life quality makes little sense (Thoreau 1971; McPhee 1971; Shi 1985). Similarly, the continued loss of biodiversity and taming of the natural landscape will not improve people's lives. What is being lost is unique and increasingly more precious as monetary wealth increases and opportunities to experience nature diminish. Human happiness and human development require preserving our remaining biodiversity, not sacrificing it for increased individual or corporate wealth.

During the twentieth century, ecologists, nature writers, and philosophers have increasingly articulated an appreciation of nature and spoken of the need for changes in human lifestyles in order to protect it (Gore 1992; List 1992; Warren 1996). Paul Sears, recognizing that a true belief in the value of nature would lead to a questioning of destructive practices common in modern society and often taken for granted, called ecology a "subversive science." In the 1960s and 1970s, Paul Ehrlich and Barry Commoner demonstrated that professional biologists and academics can use their knowledge of environmental issues to create and lead political movements to protect species and ecosystems. Commoner even ran for President in 1980. Environmental political movements, such as these and the Green political parties in Europe, and activist conservation organizations such as Greenpeace and EarthFirst! now appear throughout the world.

One well-developed environmental philosophy that supports this activism is known as **deep ecology** (Sessions 1987). Deep ecology builds on the basic premise of biocentric equality, which expresses "the intuition . . . that all things in the biosphere have an equal right to live and blossom and to reach their own individual forms of unfolding" (Devall and Sessions 1985). Humans have a right to live and thrive, as do the

Callicott, J. B. 1994. *Earth's Insights: A Multicultural Survey of Ecological Ethics from the Mediterranean Basin to the Australian Outback.* University of California Press, Berkeley, CA. Comparison of the environmental ethics of major world religions, including conceptions of nature and the value given to nonhuman beings.

Environmental Ethics. Leading journal in the field. Website with home page and bibliography: http://www.cep.unt.edu/ISEE.html.

Gore, A. 1992. *Earth in the Balance: Ecology and the Human Spirit.* Houghton Mifflin, Boston. A popular account of the need to establish a better balance between development and the environment, written by the U.S. Vice President.

Hargrove, E. C. (ed.). 1986. *Religion and the Environmental Crisis.* University of Georgia Press, Athens. What religious traditions have to say about conservation and environmental issues.

Kellert, S. R. 1996. *The Value of Life: Biological Diversity and Human Society.* Island Press/Shearwater Books, Washington, D.C. Insightful examination of people's attitudes toward biological diversity, as affected by class, ethnicity, sex, and nationality; also, eloquent statement of the importance of biodiversity to human happiness.

Kellert, S. R. and E. O. Wilson (eds.). 1993. *The Biophilia Hypothesis.* Island Press, Washington, D.C. Discussion of inherent biological reasons for valuing and cherishing nature.

Leopold, A. 1949. *A Sand County Almanac: And Sketches Here And There.* Oxford University Press, New York. Beautifully written work by one of the twentieth century's leading conservationists on the need for establishing a better balance between people and the natural world.

List, P. C. (ed.). 1992. *Radical Environmentalism: Philosophy and Tactics.* Wadsworth Publishing, Belmont, CA. Activist organizations and radical philosophical positions challenge mainstream environmentalists and provoke debate.

McPhee, J. 1971. *Encounters with the Archdruid.* Farrar, Straus, and Giroux, New York. Unique book describing an exchange of ideas between the leader of the Sierra Club and real estate developers and mining engineers during wilderness backpacking trips.

Naess, A. 1989. *Ecology, Community, and Lifestyle: Outline of an Ecosophy.* Cambridge University Press, Cambridge. Good explanation of, and argument for, deep ecology by a leading proponent.

Nash, J. A. 1991. *Loving Nature: Ecological Integrity and Christian Responsibility.* Abington, Nashville. Relationship of Western religions to preservation of nature.

Rolston III, H. 1994. *Conserving Natural Value.* Columbia University Press, New York. In this and other works listed in the bibliography, a leading environmental philosopher lays out the ethical arguments for preserving biological diversity.

Shi, D. E. 1985. *The Simple Life: Plain Living and High Thinking.* Oxford University Press, New York. Traces the many ways Americans have pursued the ideal of simple yet rich living, from the Puritans and Quakers to Thoreau and modern back-to-the land philosophies.

Thoreau, H. D. 1971. *Walden.* Princeton University Press, Princeton, N.J. Classic statement of love of nature, the unimportance of material possessions, and the pursuit of self-realization.

VanDeVeer, D. and C. Pierce. 1994. *The Environmental Ethics and Policy Book: Philosophy, Ecology, Economics.* Wadsworth Publishing Company, Belmont, CA. Excellent collection of essays by well-known authors; suitable for supplementary reading or advanced course.

Warren, K. J. (ed.). 1996. *Ecological Feminist Philosophies*. Indiana University Press, Bloomington. Scholars pursue the connections between feminism and environmentalism.

PART THREE

Threats to Biological Diversity

White Mountains paintbrush

CHAPTER 7

Extinction

WE LIVE AT A HISTORIC MOMENT, a time in which the world's biological diversity is being rapidly destroyed. The present geological period has more species than any other period, yet the current rate of extinction of species is greater now than at any time in the past. Ecosystems and communities are being degraded and destroyed, and species are being driven to extinction. The species that persist are losing genetic variation as the number of individuals in populations shrinks, unique populations and subspecies are destroyed, and remaining populations become increasingly isolated from one another.

The cause of this loss of biological diversity at all levels is the range of human activity that alters and destroys natural habitats to suit human needs. At present, approximately 40% of the net primary productivity of the terrestrial environment—roughly 25% of the total primary productivity of the world—is used or wasted in some way by people (Vitousek 1994). Genetic variation is being lost even in domesticated species, such as wheat, corn, rice, chickens, cattle, and pigs, as farmers abandon traditional agriculture. In the United States, about 97% of the vegetable varieties that were once cultivated are now extinct (Cherfas 1993). In tropical countries, farmers are abandoning their local varieties in favor of high-yielding varieties for commercial sale (Altieri and Anderson 1992). This loss of variability among food plants and animals, and its implications for world agriculture, are discussed further in Chapters 14 and 20.

The most serious aspect of environmental damage is the extinction of species. Communities can be degraded and reduced in area, but as long as all of the original species survive, communities retain the potential to recover. Similarly, genetic variation within a species is reduced when population size drops, but species can regain genetic variation through mutation, natural selection, and recombination. However, once a species is eliminated, the unique genetic information contained in its DNA and the special combination of characters that it possesses are forever lost—its populations cannot be restored, the communities that it inhabited are impoverished, and its potential value to humans will never be realized.

The word "extinct" has many nuances and can vary somewhat depending on the context. A species is considered *extinct* when no member of the species remains alive anywhere in the world: "Bachman's warbler is extinct" (Figure 7.1). If individuals of a species remain alive only in captivity or in other human-controlled situations, the species is said to be *extinct in the wild*. "The Franklin tree is extinct in the wild but grows well under cultivation." In both of these situations the species also would be considered to be *globally extinct*. A species is considered to be *locally extinct* when it is no longer found in an area it once inhabited but is still found elsewhere in the wild: "The gray wolf once occurred throughout North America; it is now locally extinct in Massachusetts." Some conservation biologists speak of a species being *ecologically extinct* if it persists at such reduced numbers that its effects on the other species in its community are negligible: "So few tigers remain in the wild that their impact on prey populations is insignificant." In order to successfully maintain species, conservation biologists must identify the human activities that affect the stability of populations and drive species to extinction.

Past Rates of Extinction

The diversity of species found on the Earth has been increasing since life first originated. This increase has not been steady, rather it has been characterized by periods of high rates of speciation followed by periods of minimal change and episodes of mass extinction (Sepkoski and

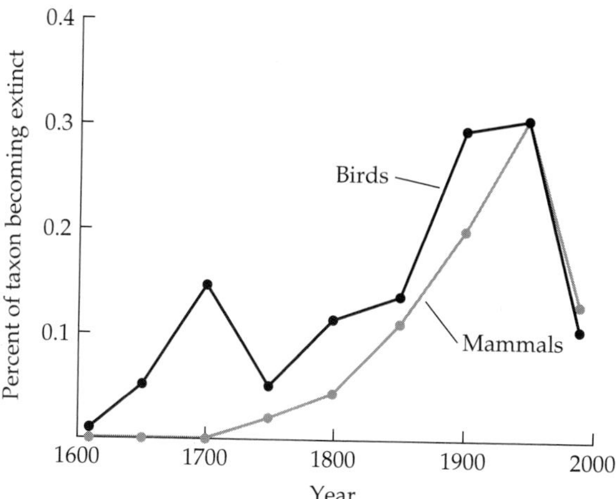

Figure 7.4 Extinction rates for birds and mammals have been steadily increasing, with the most dramatic increase occurring within the last 150 years. (Smith et al. 1993.)

shown in Table 7.1. These estimates indicate, for example, that about 85 species of mammals and 113 species of birds have become extinct since the year 1600, representing 2.1% of known mammal species and 1.3% of known birds* (Reid and Miller 1989; Smith et al. 1993; Heywood 1995). While these numbers may not seem alarming initially, the trend of these extinction rates is on the rise, with the majority of extinctions occurring in the last 150 years (Figure 7.4). The extinction rate for birds and mammals was about one species every decade during the period from 1600 to 1700, but it rose to one species every year during the period from 1850 to 1950, and four species per year between 1986 and 1990. This increase in the rate of species extinction indicates the seriousness of the threat to biological diversity.

Some evidence suggests a decline in the extinction rates for birds and mammals during the past few decades. This may be due in part to recent efforts to save species from extinction, but also can be attributed to a procedure adopted by international organizations to list a species as extinct only when it has not been seen for 50 years. Many species not yet technically extinct have been decimated by human activities and persist only in very low numbers. These species may be considered "ecologically extinct," in that they no longer play a role in their communities. The future of many such species is doubtful.

About 11% of the world's remaining bird species are threatened with extinction; the same percentage holds for mammal species. Table

---

*Only around 72 species of insects are known to have gone extinct, roughly 0.001% of the number of species in this taxon. However, this extremely low reported extinction rate is principally due to the poor state of our knowledge of this large group; many species may have gone extinct without scientists ever having been aware they existed.

TABLE 7.2 **Numbers of species threatened with extinction in major groups of animals and plants, and some key families and orders**

Group	Approximate number of species	Number of species threatened with extinction	Percentage of species threatened with extinction
VERTEBRATE ANIMALS			
Fishes	24,000	452	2
Amphibians	3,000	59	2
Reptiles	6,000	167	3
Boidae (constrictor snakes)	17[a]	9	53
Varanidae (monitor lizards)	29[a]	11	38
Iguanidae (iguanas)	25[a]	17	68
Birds	9,500	1,029	11
Anseriformes (waterfowl)	109[a]	36	33
Psittaciformes (parrots)	302[a]	118	39
Mammals	4,500	505	11
Marsupialia (marsupials)	179[a]	86	48
Canidae (wolves)	34[a]	13	38
Cervidae (deer)	14[a]	11	79
PLANTS			
Gymnosperms	758	242	32
Angiosperms (flowering plants)	240,000	21,895	9
Palmae (palms)	2,820	925	33

Source: Data from Smith et al. 1993 and Mace 1994.
[a] Number of species for which information is available.

7.2 shows certain animal groups for which the danger is even more severe, such as the family of lizards known as iguanas (Mace 1994). The threat to some freshwater fishes and mollusks may be equally severe (Williams and Nowak 1993). Plant species are also at risk, with gymnosperms (conifers, ginkgos, and cycads) and palms among the especially vulnerable groups.

What is the natural rate of extinction in the absence of human influence? Natural background extinction rates can be estimated by looking at the fossil record. In the fossil record, an individual species lasts about one to 10 million years before it goes extinct or evolves into a new species (Raup 1979). Since there are perhaps 10 million species on the Earth today, it would be predicted that one to ten of the world's species would be lost per year as a result of natural extinction. These estimates are derived from studies of wide-ranging marine animals, so they may be lower than natural extinction rates for species of narrow distribution, which are more vulnerable to habitat disturbance; how-

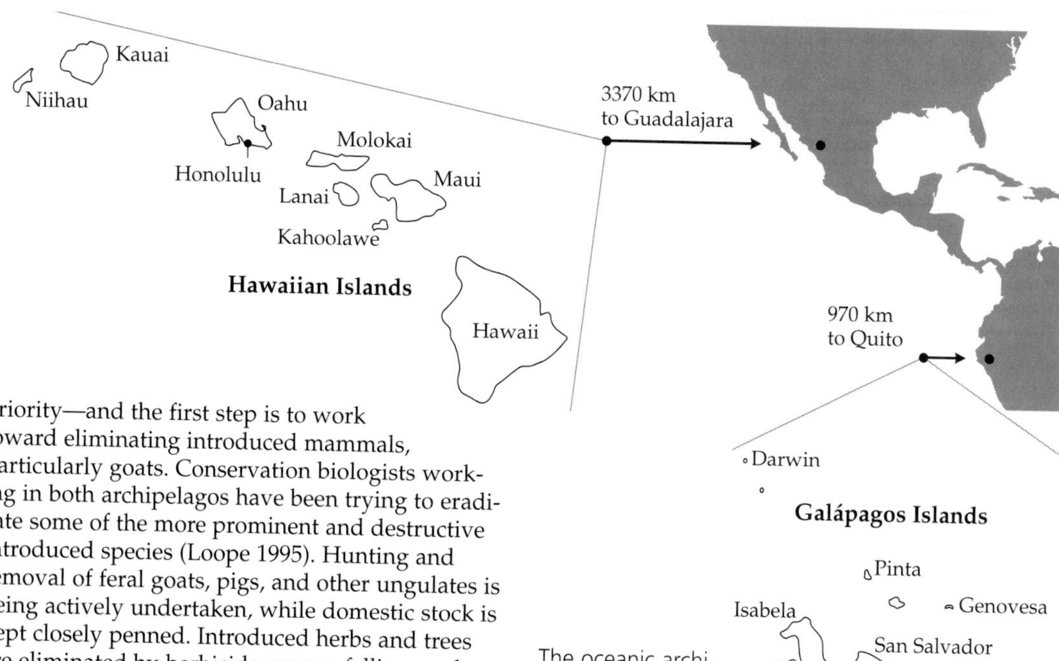

priority—and the first step is to work toward eliminating introduced mammals, particularly goats. Conservation biologists working in both archipelagos have been trying to eradicate some of the more prominent and destructive introduced species (Loope 1995). Hunting and removal of feral goats, pigs, and other ungulates is being actively undertaken, while domestic stock is kept closely penned. Introduced herbs and trees are eliminated by herbicide sprays, felling, and burning. Over 75% of the management costs for Hawaii's protected areas are spent on the control of exotic species (Holt 1996). These measures are sometimes effective against larger species. For example, when rat populations were controlled on Santa Cruz and Floreana in the Galápagos, nesting success of dark-rumped petrels increased from 0%–7% to 67%–72% (Powell and Gibbs 1995). Where pigs and other large animals have been eliminated from montane forests, the native species have recovered (Stone and Loope 1996). Control of exotic insects and other invertebrates and many herbaceous weeds is often far more difficult. Now that the problem of exotic species has been identified, the respective governments and conservation organizations are actively managing areas of the islands to protect and enlarge the original biological communities that remain.

The oceanic archipelagos of Hawaii and the Galápagos have unique, rich, and severely threatened endemic biotas.

plant species are endemic to the islands. About 10% of these endemic species have become extinct, and 40% of the remaining endemics are at risk (Davis et al. 1986). In Madagascar, 80% of the plant species are endemic and threatened with extinction (WRI 1994). About 80% of Madagascar's land has been altered or destroyed by human activity, possibly leading to almost half of the endemic species being lost. To protect this rich natural heritage, Madagascar is moving toward setting up national parks, but only 1.5% of the island has been preserved so far.

A similar pattern can be found on other islands. The colonization of New Zealand by Polynesians in 1000 A.D. led to hunting, deforestation, and the introduction of dogs and rats. Before the arrival of Europeans, all 13 species of the giant flightless moa birds were extinct, along with 16 other endemic bird species.

European colonization of islands has sometimes been more destructive than colonization by other peoples because European colonization includes greater amounts of clearing and the wholesale introduction of non-native species. For instance, between 1840 and 1880, more than 60 species of vertebrates, particularly grazing animals, such as sheep, were deliberately introduced into Australia, where they displaced native species and altered many communities. An extreme example of the extent of the introduction of non-native species are the over 1,200 species of insects that have been brought into the United States. In the 1500s, the first European visitors to the Mascarene Islands (Mauritius, Reunion, and Rodrigues) released monkeys and pigs. These animals, and subsequent colonization by Dutch settlers, led to the extinction of the dodo bird, 19 other species of birds, and 8 species of reptiles. The impact of introduced predators on island species is highlighted by the example of the flightless Stephen Island wren, a bird that was endemic to a tiny island off New Zealand. Every Stephen Island wren on the island was killed by a single cat belonging to the lighthouse keeper (Diamond 1984)—even one introduced predator can eliminate an entire species.

The vulnerability of island species is further illustrated when comparing the number of species that have gone extinct in mainland areas, on islands, and in the oceans from 1600 to the present (see Table 7.1). Of the 726 species of animals and plants known to have gone extinct, 351 (about half of the total) were island species, even though islands represent only a small fraction of the Earth's surface (Smith et al. 1993).

Extinction Rates in Water

In contrast with the large number of terrestrial species that have gone extinct, only five species—four marine mammals and one limpet—are known to have gone extinct in the world's vast oceans during historic times. This calculation is almost certainly an underestimate, since marine species are not as well known as terrestrial species, but it may reflect greater resiliency of marine species in response to disturbance. The significance of these losses may be greater than the numbers suggest, however. Many marine mammals are top predators, and their loss could have a major impact on marine communities. Some marine species are the sole species of their genus, family, or even order. The extinction of even a few marine species can possibly represent a serious loss to global biological diversity.

Also in contrast to terrestrial extinctions, the majority of freshwater fish extinctions have occurred in mainland areas rather than on islands because of the vastly greater number of species in mainland waters (Box 13). In a survey of the rich freshwater fish fauna of the Malay Peninsula, only 122 of the 266 species of fish known to exist on the basis of earlier collections could still be found (Mohsin and Ambak 1983). In North America, over one-third of freshwater fish species are in danger of extinction (Moyle and Leidy 1992). The fish of California are particularly vulnerable because of the scarcity of water and intense development—7% of California's 115 types of native fish are already extinct and 56% are in danger of extinction (Moyle 1995). Large numbers of fish and aquatic invertebrates, such as mollusks, are in danger of extinction in the southeastern United States because of dams, pollution, invasion of alien species, and general habitat damage (Figure 7.7).

Island Biogeography and Modern Extinction Rates

Studies of island communities have led to general rules on the distribution of biological diversity, synthesized as the **island biogeography model** by MacArthur and Wilson (1967). The central observation that this model was built to explain is the **species–area relationship**: islands with large areas have more species than islands with smaller

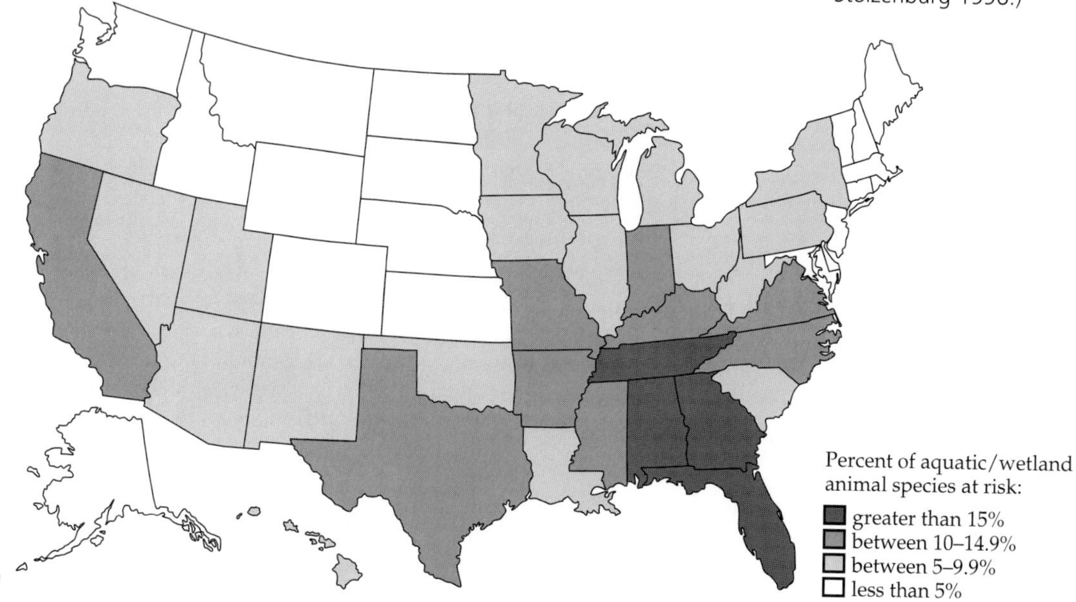

Figure 7.7 Dams, polluted runoff from industry and agriculture, introduced species, and habitat destruction threaten as many as 23% of the aquatic species in the United States, including dozens of species of freshwater mussels, fish, and crayfish. The species of the southeastern section of the country are most at risk. (After Stolzenburg 1996.)

Box 13 **Conserving Endemic Fish in Lake Victoria**

The extinction of individual species usually does not take place in isolation; too frequently, a species is lost in conjunction with many other component species of a damaged ecosystem. Ecological changes affecting single species can have a domino effect upon other organisms, leading to catastrophic transformation of the entire ecosystem. This principle is illustrated by the recent, devastating changes in the ecology of Lake Victoria in East Africa. The lake, which is surrounded by Kenya, Tanzania, and Uganda, is one of the world's largest freshwater ecosystems. Until the early 1980s, it was also one of the most diverse in number of fish species. Prior to that time, Lake Victoria had over 400 endemic species of fish in its waters (Kaufman and Cohen 1993; Goldschmidt 1996). At present, however, only one native species and two introduced species inhabit the lake in significant numbers; all of the remaining species are threatened, endangered, or extinct.

The rapid losses of the endemic species has been correlated with an abrupt increase in the population of a single species of fish: the Nile perch, *Lates nilotica*, which was introduced into Lake Victoria in 1954 to create a new food resource for the fishing industry, with more serious attempts in the 1960s. Based solely on this information, one might conclude that the Nile perch either consumed or outcompeted the native fishes, and was thus responsible for the recent losses. Such a conclusion, however, is only partially correct. While the Nile perch has played a role in the decline of endemic fishes in the lake, subtle ecological forces have also contributed to the losses.

The introduction of the Nile perch apparently did not have a significant impact upon the Lake Victoria fish population until decades after its introduction. In 1978, Nile perch constituted less than 2% of the lake's annual fishing harvest. By 1986, however, this species was nearly 80% of the total catch (Kaufman 1992). The endemic species were virtually gone from the lake, and the Nile perch had undergone an abrupt population explosion. While the perch was a prime consumer of many of the smaller native fish species, the ascendancy of the Nile perch was more than simply a case of an introduced species running amok.

One clue that other factors were contributing to native fish losses was the change in the occurrence of algal blooms in the lake's shallower waters. Algal blooms had been observed at intervals throughout the lake's history, but the frequency of these events increased noticeably in the early 1980s, at the same time that the perch population explosion took place. Increases in algae are often associated with decreased oxygen levels in the lower depths of large bodies of water, which in turn makes the water less habitable for algae-eating fish. Prior to 1978, Lake Victoria had fairly high oxygen levels at all depths; because of these aerobic conditions, fish were able to survive even in the deepest waters of the lake, which in some places exceeds 60 meters in depth. Studies done in 1989–1992 revealed that Lake Victoria had severely depleted oxygen levels at depths below 25 meters, and was in the process of becoming anoxic—that is, completely lacking in oxygen, below a certain depth (Kaufman 1992). The anoxic conditions effectively reduced the available habitat within the lake; fish species that preferred the deeper regions of the lake may have died out as a result, either because they could not adapt to the different conditions of shallower water or because they were unable to escape shallow-water predators such as the Nile perch. The mystery does not end there, however; algal blooms had occurred before, without this devastating effect upon the native fauna. Why did the mass extinctions occur this time?

The answer is probably a combination of factors. Initial high population levels of some native species in the 1960s and 1970s probably were related to high inputs of nutrients from agricultural runoff, sewage from towns and villages, and other anthropogenic sources. The majority of these endemic species were haplochromine cichlids, which fed on the algae and other lake flora and fauna that increased because of the nutrient inputs. However, overfishing and predation by a rapidly expanding Nile perch population between 1978 and 1984 contributed to a rapid decline in

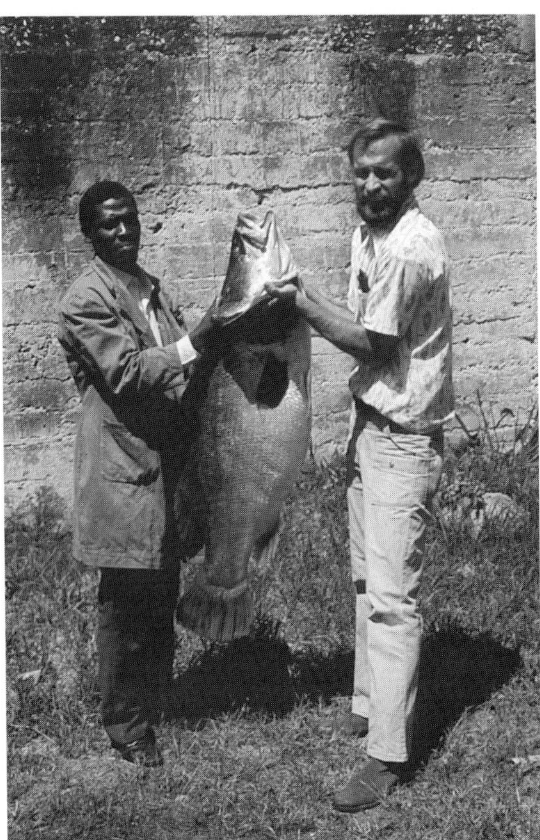

Lates niloticus—the Nile perch—was introduced into Lake Victoria as a food source in the 1950s and 1960s. It became a major factor in the eradication of the lake's rich cichlid fish fauna. (Photograph by John N. Rinne.)

native fish species diversity and abundance; as the cichlids decreased in numbers, the excess nutrients and reduced herbivory encouraged frequent algal blooms, which exacerbated the process of eutrophication. The lack of oxygen in the lower depths of the lake drove the remaining native fish to shallower waters, where they were more vulnerable to fishing nets and ever-increasing numbers of Nile perch—and as the perch increased, the cycle continued in a downward spiral: fewer cichlids led to increased algal blooms, leading to decreased oxygen in deep water, which then further reduced the remaining cichlids.

In 1990, the situation was compounded by the appearance and explosive spread of water hyacinth in Lake Victoria. Water hyacinth (*Eichornia crassipes*) is a floating water weed from South America, often introduced for its flowers, which are beautiful in small doses. Unfortunately this weed is extremely fecund under eutrophic conditions such as those that prevail in today's Lake Victoria. Now entire bays and inlets are covered by thick mats of hyacinth, choking breeding and nursery areas for the important tilapia fishery, and swamping the littoral habitats so important to the haplochromine cichlids. Property owners, fishermen, ferry boat operators, lakeside residents, and, of course, politicians are now all up in arms about this singular and highly visible problem.

Restoration of the once-diverse Lake Victoria ecosystem is one of the most challenging problems facing conservation biologists today. Captive breeding and restocking the endangered cichlids will not work unless some method of restoring damaged ecosystem processes is first developed. Transforming a eutrophic tropical lake of this size has never been attempted. If scientists are somehow successful in restoring oxygen levels, they must then deal with the different factors that contributed to the problem in the first place: excessive inputs of nutrients from human activity, overharvesting by fisheries, and the presence of the Nile perch. Recently, the World Bank and other donors joined forces to fund efforts by the three nations that border the lake to do just that. In this project, called the Lake Victoria Environmental Management Programme, funds are earmarked to deal with the different factors that contribute to the underlying problems.

There are many signs of hope. Overfishing of Nile perch has been followed by local resurgence in a few of the indigenous haplochromine species and even some native food fishes. There is evidence that restrictions on the Nile perch fishery that are in the best interests of that industry will also help to restore native fishes. Finally, the three countries have agreed that it is desirable to restore a multi-species fishery rather than try to perpetuate the boom–bust cycles of Nile perch.

areas (Figure 7.8). This rule makes intuitive sense because large islands will tend to have a greater variety of local environments and community types than small islands. Also, large islands allow greater geographic isolation and a larger number of populations per species, increasing the likelihood of speciation and decreasing the probability of local extinction of newly evolved as well as recently arrived species. The species–area relationship can be accurately summarized by the empirical formula:

$$S = CA^Z$$

where S is the number of species on an island, A is the area of the island, and C and Z are constants. The exponent Z determines the slope of the curve. The values for C and Z will depend on the types of islands being compared (tropical versus temperate, dry versus wet, etc.) and the types of species involved (birds versus reptiles, etc.) (Simberloff 1986). Z values are typically around 0.25, with a range from 0.15 to 0.35 (Connor and McCoy 1979). Island species of restricted ranges, such as reptiles and amphibians, tend to have Z values near 0.35, while widespread mainland species tend to have Z values closer to 0.15. Values of C will be high in groups that are high in species numbers, such as insects, and low in groups that are low in species numbers, such as birds.

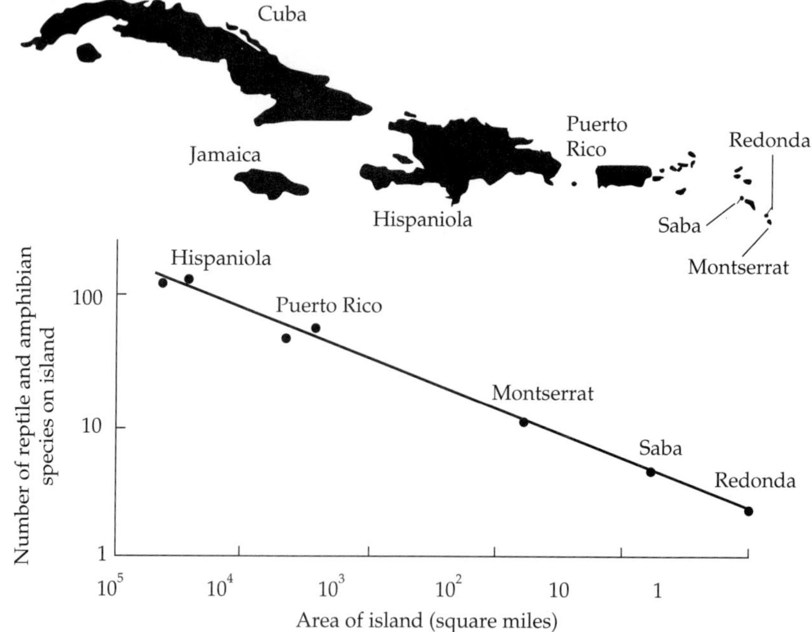

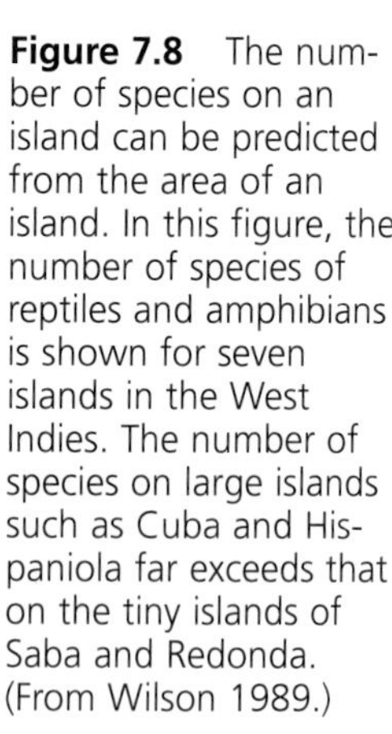
Figure 7.8 The number of species on an island can be predicted from the area of an island. In this figure, the number of species of reptiles and amphibians is shown for seven islands in the West Indies. The number of species on large islands such as Cuba and Hispaniola far exceeds that on the tiny islands of Saba and Redonda. (From Wilson 1989.)

For numerous groups of plants and animals, this general island biogeography model has been found to give a reasonably good fit to the observed richness of species, explaining about half of the variation in numbers of species. Imagine the simplest situation, in which $C = 1$ and $Z = 0.25$, for raptorial birds on a hypothetical archipelago:

$$S = (1)A^{0.25}$$

Islands of 10, 100, 1000, and 10,000 km^2 in area would be predicted to have 2, 3, 6, and 10 species, respectively. It is important to note that a tenfold increase in island area does not result in a tenfold increase in the number of species; with this equation, each tenfold increase in island area increases the number of species by a factor of approximately 2.

The model has been empirically validated to the point of acceptance by most biologists (Quammen 1996). In their classic text, MacArthur and Wilson (1967) hypothesized that the number of species occurring on an island represents a dynamic equilibrium between the arrival of new species (and also the evolution of new species) and the extinction rate of existing species. Starting with an unoccupied island, the number of species will increase over time, since more species will be arriving than are going extinct, until the rates of extinction and immigration are balanced (Figure 7.9). The extinction rate will be lower on large islands than small islands because large islands have greater habitat

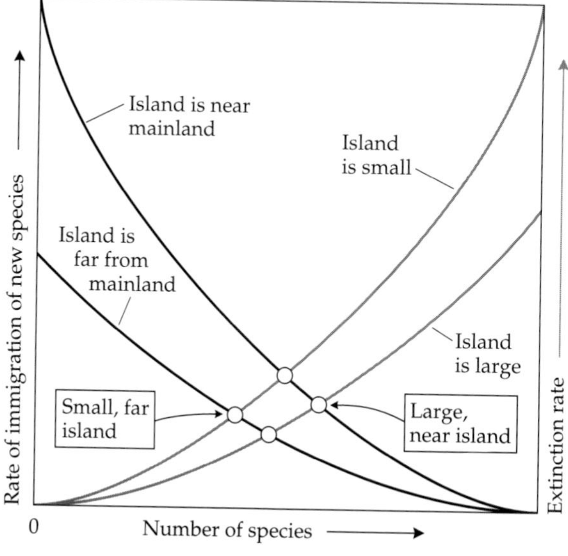

Figure 7.9 The island biogeography model describes the relationship between the rates of colonization and extinction of islands. The immigration rate (black curves) on unoccupied islands is initially high, as species with good dispersal abilities rapidly take advantage of the available open habitats. The immigration rate slows as the number of species increases and sites become occupied. The extinction rate (gray curves) *increases* with the number of species on the island; the more species on an island the greater the likelihood that a species will go extinct at any time interval. Colonization rates will be highest for islands near a mainland population source, since species can disperse over shorter distances more easily than longer ones. Extinction rates are highest on small islands, where both population sizes and habitat diversity are low. The number of species present on an island reaches an equilibrium when the colonization rate equals the extinction rate (circles). The equilibrium number of species is greatest on large islands near the mainland, and lowest on small islands far from the mainland. (After MacArthur and Wilson 1967.)

diversity and a greater number of populations. The rate of immigration of new species will be higher for islands near to the mainland than for islands farther away, since mainland species are able to disperse to near islands more easily than to distant islands. The model predicts that for any group of organisms, such as birds or trees, the number of species found on large islands near a continent will be greater than that on small islands far from a continent.

Species–area relationships have been used to predict the number and percentage of species that would become extinct if habitats were destroyed (Simberloff 1986, 1992). The calculation assumes that, if an island has a certain number of species, reducing the area of natural habitat on the island would result in the island being able to support only a number of species corresponding to that on a smaller island (Figure 7.10). This model has been extended to national parks and nature reserves that are surrounded by damaged habitat. The reserves can be viewed as **habitat islands** in an inhospitable "sea" of unsuitable habitat. The model predicts that when 50% of an island (or habitat island) is destroyed, approximately 10% of the species occurring on the island will be eliminated. If these species are endemic to an area, they will become extinct. When 90% of the habitat is destroyed, 50% of the species will be lost; and when 99% of the habitat is gone, about 75% of the original species will be lost.

Predictions of extinction rates based on habitat loss vary considerably, because each species–area relationship is unique. Because insects and plants in tropical forests account for the great majority of the

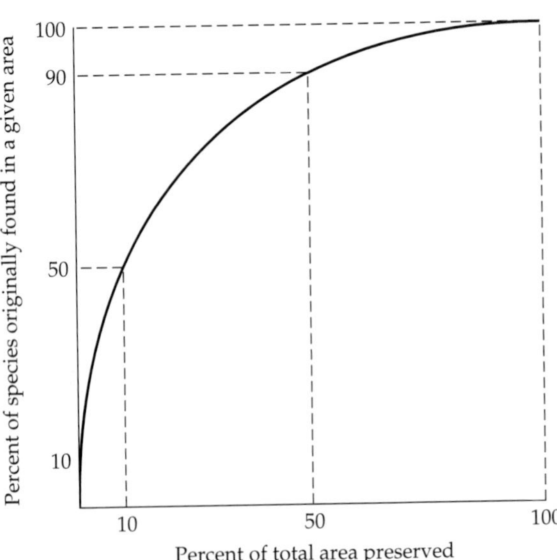

Figure 7.10 The number of species present in an area increases asymptotically to a maximum value. As a result, if the area of habitat is reduced by 50%, the number of original endemic species going extinct may be 10%; if the habitat is reduced by 90%, the number of endemic species going extinct may be 50%. The shape of the curve is different for each region of the world and each group of species, but it gives a general indication of the impact of habitat destruction on species extinction and the persistence of species in the remaining habitat.

world's species, estimates of present and future rates of species extinction in rain forests gives an approximation of global rates of extinction. At present rates of deforestation, 15% of the plant species in the Neotropics are predicted to become extinct between 1986 and 2000, and 12% of Amazon bird species are predicted to go extinct (Simberloff 1986a). If deforestation continues until all of the forests are cut down, except those in national parks and other protected areas, about two-thirds of all plant and bird species will be driven to extinction.

In the past, rates of deforestation have been more rapid in the Old World Tropics—Africa, Madagascar, Asia and the Pacific region—than in the Neotropics, resulting in a loss of between 10%–25% of the original species. Losses of rain forest species are predicted to be 7%–17% during the period from 1990 to 2020 in Asia and the Pacific region due to the combination of rapid population growth, increasing economic development, and a huge timber industry (Reid and Miller 1989).

Using the conservative estimate that 1% of the world's rain forests is being destroyed each year, Wilson (1989) estimated that 0.2%–0.3% of all species—20,000 to 30,000 species if based on a total of 10 million species—would be lost per year, or 68 species per day, with 3 species lost each hour. Over the 10-year period from 1993 to 2003, approximately 250,000 species would become extinct. Other methods applied to the rates of extinction in tropical rain forests estimate a loss of between 2% and 11% of the world's species per decade (Reid and Miller 1989; Reid 1992; Koopowitz et al. 1994). The variation in rates is caused by different estimates of the rate of deforestation, different values for the species–area curves, and different mathematical approaches. Extinction rates might in fact be higher because the highest rates of deforestation are occurring in countries with large concentrations of rare species, and large forest areas are increasingly being fragmented by roads and development projects (Balmford and Long 1994). Extinction rates might be lowered if species-rich areas were targeted for conservation. Regardless of which figure is the most accurate, all of these estimates indicate that tens of thousands, if not hundreds of thousands, of species are headed for extinction within the next 50 years (Kaufman and Mallory 1993; Schmidt 1997). These rates of species extinction are without precedent since the great mass extinction of the Cretaceous period 65 million years ago.

These estimates make a number of assumptions and generalizations in calculating species extinction rates, which may limit the validity of this approach (Reid 1992; Simberloff 1992). First, all of these estimates are based on typical values for the species–area curves. Groups of species with broad geographical ranges, such as marine animals and temperate tree species, will tend to have lower rates of extinction than species of narrow geographic distribution, such as island birds and freshwater fish. Second, the models assume that all endemic species are eliminated from areas that have been largely cleared of forest. It is possible that many species can survive in isolated patches of forest and recolonize secondary forest that develops on abandoned land. A few primary forest species may also be capable of surviving in plantations and managed forests. Adaptation to managed forests is likely to be particularly significant in Asian forests that are being selectively logged on a large scale. Third, the species–area models assume that areas of habitat are eliminated at random. In fact, areas of species richness are sometimes targeted for species conservation efforts and national park status. As a result, a greater percentage of species may be protected than is assumed in the species–area models. And fourth, the degree of habitat fragmentation may affect extinction rates. If remaining areas of land are divided into very small parcels or crossed by roads, then wide-ranging species or species requiring large population sizes may be unable to maintain themselves. Also, hunting, clearing land for agriculture, and the introduction of exotic species may increase in fragmented forests, leading to the further loss of species.

Another approach to estimating extinction rates uses information on projected declines in habitat, numbers of populations, and the geographical range of well-known individual species (Mace 1995). This approach uses empirical information to give a more accurate estimate of extinction rates for a smaller number of species. Applied to 725 threatened vertebrate species, this method predicts that some 15 to 20 species will go extinct over the next 100 years. Extinction rates are expected to be much higher in certain groups; within 100 years it is likely that half of the 29 threatened species in the deer family (Cervidae) will be extinct, as will 3 of the world's 10 threatened hornbill species (Bucerotidae).

The time required for a given species to go extinct following a reduction in area or fragmentation of its range is a vital question in conservation biology, and the island biogeography model makes no prediction as to how long it will take. Although the pace of extinction is increasing, there is little current evidence that the mass extinctions predicted 10 years ago are actually occurring today (Whitmore and Sayer 1992; Lawton and May 1995). For many species, a few individuals might persist for years or decades, and even reproduce, but their ultimate fate is extinction (Adams and Carwardine 1990; Tilman et al. 1994; Loehle and Li 1996). For woody plants in particular, individuals can persist for hundreds of years. Species that are doomed to extinction following habitat destruction have been called "the living dead" or "committed to extinction." Though technically the species is not extinct while these individuals live, the population is no longer reproductively viable, hence the species' future is limited to the lifespans of the remaining individuals (Gentry 1986; Janzen 1986). Evidence from forest fragments and parks indicates that, following the destruction of the surrounding habitat, species diversity of vertebrates may actually show a temporary increase as animals flee into the few remaining

2. Why should conservation biologists, or anyone else, care if species go locally extinct if they are still found somewhere else?

3. If 50% of the species present today go extinct within the next 200 years, what is your estimate of how long it would take for the process of speciation to replace the lost number of species?

Suggested Readings

Adams, D. and M. Carwardine. 1990. *Last Chance to See*. Harmony Books, New York. A light but poignant account of the threat of imminent extinction facing many well-known species.

Goldschmidt, T. 1996. *Darwin's Dreampond: Drama in Lake Victoria*. MIT Press, Cambridge, MA. Personal account of working with an amazing group of fish—and then watching them go extinct.

Janzen, D. H. 1986. The eternal external threat. In *Conservation Biology: The Science of Scarcity and Diversity*, pp. 286–330. M. E. Soulé, (ed.). Sinauer Associates, Sunderland, MA. A superb essay on the causes of tropical extinctions, with vivid natural history examples.

Kaufman, L. and K. Mallory (eds.). 1993. *The Last Extinction*, 2nd Edition. The MIT Press (in cooperation with the New England Aquarium), Cambridge, MA. Essays on the threats faced by groups of species, with a particularly strong treatment of marine examples.

Lawton, J. H. and R. M. May (eds.). 1995. *Extinction Rates*. Oxford University Press, Oxford. Superb short volume with leading authorities.

Leakey, R. and R. Lewin. 1996. *The Sixth Extinction: Patterns of Life and the Future of Humankind*. Doubleday, New York. Popular account of the mass extinctions by an anthropologist and a science writer.

Loope, L. L., O. Hamman and C. P. Stone. 1988. Comparative conservation biology of oceanic archipelagoes: Hawaii and the Galápagos. *Bioscience* 38: 272–282. This article and others in the same issue give an outstanding overview of these two archipelagos.

MacArthur, R. H. and E. O. Wilson. 1967. *The Theory of Island Biogeography*. Princeton University Press, Princeton, NJ. This classic text outlining the island biogeography model has been highly influential in shaping modern conservation biology.

Quammen, D. 1996. *The Song of the Dodo: Island Biogeography in an Age of Extinctions*. Scribner, New York. Popular account of early and modern explorations, and of island biogeography theory.

Raup, D. M. 1992. *Extinction: Bad Genes or Bad Luck*. Norton, New York. Clearly written overview of extinction, with an emphasis on geological processes.

Schmidt, K. 1997. Life on the brink. *Earth* (April): 26–33. Popular account of the extinction crisis, incorporating comments from leading scientists.

Simberloff, D. 1986. Are we on the verge of a mass extinction in tropical rain forests? In *Dynamics of Extinction*, pp. 165–180. D. K. Elliott (ed.). John Wiley & Sons, New York. A demonstration of the application of the island biogeography model to calculate extinction rates.

Smith, F. D. M., R. M. May, R. Pellew, T. H. Johnson and K. R. Walter. 1993. How much do we know about the current extinction rate? *Trends in Ecology and Evolution* 8: 375–378. Excellent short summary with analysis by taxonomic groups and geographical regions.

Whitmore, T. C. and J. A. Sayer. 1992. *Tropical Deforestation and Species Extinction*. Chapman and Hall, London. Critical evaluation of predictions of species loss.

Wilson, E. O. 1989. Threats to biodiversity. *Scientific American* 261: 108–116. How extinction rates are increasing due to human activities.

World Conservation Monitoring Centre. 1992. *Global Biodiversity 1992: Status of Earth's Living Resources*. World Resources Institute, Washington, D.C. Shows the status of species and communities.

These three contrasting components of rarity can be applied to the entire range of species or to the distribution and abundance of species in a particular place. In a study of 160 plant species in the British Isles, one of the biologically best-known areas of the world, Rabinowitz et al. (1986) used these three components of rarity in various combinations to designate eight categories of species (Table 8.1). Under this system, species of wide geographical distribution, broad habitat specificity, and large local population size, such as lamb's quarters (*Chenopodium album*), a weed that prefers disturbed ground, would be considered a classic common species. In contrast, a species with a narrow geographical range, restricted habitat specificity, and small population size, such as the alpine lily (*Lloydia serotina*), would be considered a classic rare species. There are also species categories that combine elements of rarity and abundance, such as the Scottish bird's-eye primrose (*Primula scotica*), which has a narrow geographical range, a broad habitat specificity, and sometimes large populations; or the knotroot bristlegrass (*Setaria geniculata*), which has a broad geographic distribution, broad habitat specificity, but always occurs in small populations.

In analyzing these patterns of rarity and commonness, the most striking finding is that 149 out of the 160 plant species studied in Britain have large populations at least somewhere in their ranges. This stands in apparent contradiction to the observations of community ecologists who found that, at a local scale, there tend to be only a few common species but many rare species. These contrasting observations can be reconciled, because even though most species will have large local populations somewhere in their range, each species will be rare at the majority of sites that it occupies.

TABLE 8.1 **Categories of rarity for 160 plant species in the British Isles based on geographical distribution, habitat specificity, and local population size**[a]

	Geographical distribution	
Local population size	**Wide**	**Narrow**
	Broad habitat specificity	
Somewhere large	58 spp.	6 spp.
Always small	2 spp.	0 spp.
	Restricted habitat specificity	
Somewhere large	71 spp.	14 spp.
Always small	6 spp.	3 spp.

Source: After Rabinowitz et al. 1986.

[a] Based on the three criteria, 58 species are common; 3 species are rare by all criteria; and the remaining 99 species exhibit some traits of rarity.

Most rare plant species in the British Isles (71 out of 102 species) have a wide range, are habitat specialists, and have large populations at least somewhere. The next largest group of rare species (14 species) are geographically restricted habitat specialists that have large populations at least somewhere. Small numbers of species occupy the other categories of Table 8.1, with one exception: there appears to be no species with a narrow geographical range, broad habitat specificity, and always small populations.

This system of classification highlights priorities for conservation. Species with a narrow geographical range and specific habitat requirements that are always found in small populations require immediate habitat protection and, possibly, habitat management to maintain their few, fragile populations. This also applies, to a somewhat lesser degree, to species with larger populations. However, where species have a narrow geographical distribution but a broad habitat specificity, experiments in which individuals are transported to unoccupied but apparently suitable localities to create new populations may be a strategy worth considering (see Chapter 13), since these species may have been unable to disperse outside of their narrow geographical area. This suggestion is supported by a further study showing that plant species with poor dispersal abilities (no adaptation for long-distance dispersal) tend to have more aggregated populations in contrast to species with good dispersal ability (light, wind-dispersed seeds, or seeds dispersed by mammals and birds), which tend to have more widely dispersed populations (Quinn et al. 1994). Species with broad geographical ranges are less susceptible to extinction and less likely to need rescue efforts, since they tend to have more extant populations and more opportunities to colonize potentially suitable sites.

Which Species Are Most Vulnerable?

When environments are damaged by human activity, the population sizes of many species will be reduced, and some species will become extinct. Some species must be carefully monitored and managed in conservation efforts (Box 14). Ecologists have observed that particular categories of species are most vulnerable to extinction (Terborgh 1974; Pimm et al. 1988; Gittleman 1994).

- *Species with a very narrow geographical range.* Some species occur at only one or a few sites in a restricted geographical range, and if that whole range is affected by human activity, the species may become extinct. Bird species on oceanic islands are good examples of species with restricted ranges that have become extinct or are in danger of extinction (Grant and Grant 1997); many fish species confined to a single lake or a single watershed have also disappeared (Figure 8.2).

live longer than smaller species. Also, in Neotropical forest mammals, large body size tends to be correlated with a wider geographic distribution and less vulnerability to habitat destruction in one place (Arita et al. 1990).

- *Species that are not effective dispersers.* Environmental changes prompt species to adapt, either behaviorally or physiologically, to the new conditions of their habitat. Species unable to adapt to changing environments must either migrate to more suitable habitat or face extinction. The rapid pace of human-induced changes often prevents adaptation, leaving migration as the only alternative. Species that are unable to cross roads, farmlands, and disturbed habitats are doomed to extinction as their original habitat becomes affected by pollution, exotic species, and global climate change. In particular, many animal species in isolated forest fragments are unwilling or unable to cross pastures and colonize unoccupied areas of forest (Lovejoy et al. 1986). Dispersal is important in the aquatic environment as well, where dams, point sources of pollution, channelization, and sedimentation can limit movement. Limited ability to disperse, as well as more specialized habitat requirements, may explain why in the United States 68% of the freshwater fauna of mussels and snails are extinct or threatened with extinction in contrast to some 40% of freshwater fish species (which have the ability to swim actively) and around 20% of dragonfly species (which can fly between the aquatic sites needed by their larval stages (Stein and Flack 1997).

  The importance of dispersal in preventing extinction is illustrated by two studies from Australia. The first, a detailed analysis of the vertebrates of Western Australia, revealed that modern extinctions were almost exclusively confined to nonflying mammals, with few extinctions recorded in birds and bats (Burbidge and McKenzie 1989). Among the birds, species that are unable to fly or are poor fliers showed the greatest tendency for extinction. In the second study, which examined 16 non-flying mammal species in Queensland rain forests, the most important characteristic determining the ability of species to survive in isolated forest fragments was their ability to use, feed on, and move through the intervening matrix of secondary vegetation (Laurance 1991a). While large-bodied, long-lived, low-fecundity species initially appeared to be more vulnerable to extinction, this effect disappeared when the abundance of individual species in secondary vegetation was included in the analysis. This study highlights the importance of maintaining secondary vegetation to the survival of primary forest species.

- *Seasonal migrants.* Species that migrate seasonally depend on two or more distinct habitat types. If either one of these habitat types is damaged, the species may be unable to persist. The billion songbirds of 120 species that migrate each year between the northern U.S. and the American tropics depend on suitable habitat in both locations to survive and breed (see Figure 7.1). Also, if barriers to dispersal are created between the needed habitats by roads, fences, or dams, a species may be unable to complete its life cycle. Salmon species that are blocked by dams from swimming up rivers and spawning are a striking example of this problem. Many animal species migrate among habitats in search of food, often along elevational and moisture gradients. Herds of wild pigs, grazing ungulates, frugivorous vertebrates, and insectivorous birds are all examples of these. If these species are unable to migrate and thus are confined to one habitat type, they may not survive, or, if they do survive, they may be unable to accumulate the nutritional reserves needed to reproduce. Species that cross international barriers represent a special problem, in that conservation efforts have to be coordinated by more than one country. Imagine the difficulties of the tiny flock of Siberian cranes (*Grus leucogeranus*) that must migrate 4800 km from Russia to India, crossing 6 highly militarized, tense international borders.

- *Species with little genetic variability.* Genetic variability within a population can sometimes allow a species to adapt to a changing environment (see Chapters 2 and 11). Species with little or no genetic variability may have a greater tendency to become extinct when a new disease, a new predator, or some other change occurs in the environment, but there is little evidence to support this hypothesis. For example, extremely low genetic variability is considered to be a contributing factor to the lack of disease resistance in the cheetah (*Acinonyx jubatus*) (O'Brien and Evermann 1988), though environmental factors may be the predominant reason for the decline of this species (Caro and Laurenson 1994). Investigating the relationships among genetic variability, population persistence, and extinction is a crucial area for conservation biology in the future.
- *Species with specialized niche requirements.* Once a habitat is altered, the environment may no longer be suitable for specialized species. For example, wetland plants that require very specific and regular changes in water level may be rapidly eliminated when human activity affects the hydrology of an area. Soil arthropods and herbaceous plants may be eliminated when introduced livestock intensively graze native grasslands and, in the process, alter competitive relationships, change nutrient dynamics, and compact the soil. Species with highly specific dietary requirements are also at risk. There are species of mites that feed only on the feathers of a single bird species. If the bird species goes extinct, so do its associated feather mite species.

Some species are confined to a single unusual habitat type that is scattered and rare across the landscape. Examples are found in vernal pools in California, granite outcrops in the southeastern United States, and isolated high mountains in the northeastern United States. Commenting on the Sheffield flora, Hodgson (1986) said, "Most of the differences between common and rare species in the Sheffield region may be interpreted in terms of the availability of suitable habitats within the region, with common species occupying common, and rare species less common, habitats." These examples illustrate the importance of habitat preservation in the conservation of species with a narrow range.

- *Species that are characteristically found in stable, pristine environments.* Many species are found in environments where disturbance is minimal, such as in old stands of tropical rain forests and the interiors of rich temperate deciduous forests. When these forests are logged, grazed, burned, and otherwise altered, many native species are unable to tolerate the changed microclimatic conditions (more light, less moisture, greater temperature variation) and influx of exotic species. Also, species of stable environments tend to delay reproduction to an advanced age and produce only a few young. Following one or more episodes of habitat disturbance, such species are often unable to rebuild their populations fast enough to avoid extinction. When the environment is altered by air and water pollution, species unable to adapt to the destabilized physical and chemical environment will be eliminated from the community (Box 15). Coral reef species and freshwater invertebrates, such as crayfish, mussels, and snails, often cannot survive when their environments receive large inputs of sediment and sewage from human activities.
- *Species that form permanent or temporary aggregations.* Species that group together in specific places are highly vulnerable to local extinction. For example, bats forage widely, but typically roost together in particular caves. Hunters entering these caves during the day can rapidly harvest every individual in the population. Herds of bison, flocks of passenger pigeons, and schools of fish all represent aggregations that have been exploited and completely harvested by people. Temporary aggregations include schools of salmon and alewife moving up rivers to spawn; nets across rivers can catch virtually every fish and eliminate a species in a few days. Overly efficient harvesting of wild fruits from a cluster of neighboring trees for commercial markets can eliminate the seedlings that will grow into the next generation. Even though sea turtles may swim across vast stretches of ocean, egg collectors and hunters on a few narrow nesting beaches can threaten a species with extinction. Many species of social animals may be unable to persist when their

Box 15 **Why Are Frogs and Toads Croaking?**

At the First World Congress on Herpetology in 1989 in Canterbury, England, casual findings began to take on a disturbing significance: scientists from around the world were seeing a decline in amphibian populations (Phillips 1990). A workshop to address this possibility, hastily put together in 1990, confirmed that evidence existed for widespread population crashes among numerous amphibian species. Species that had been common less than two decades ago were becoming rare, some to the point of near extinction. Although many scientists had only anecdotal evidence for the population crisis and explanations for the phenomenon were speculative, reports from the United States, Central America, the Amazon Basin, the Andes, Europe, and Australia repeated similar themes: habitat destruction and pollution were contributing to the rapid declines of many species.

Amphibians may be particularly vulnerable to human disturbance because many species require two separate habitats, aquatic and terrestrial, to complete their life cycles. If either habitat is damaged, the species will not be able to reproduce. Amphibians, like many other taxa, are also sensitive to a number of global environmental problems, including climate changes, increased ultraviolet radiation, habitat fragmentation, chemical pollution, and acid rain (see Chapter 9). The latter two factors may be particularly dangerous to these animals: chemical pollution can easily penetrate the thin epidermis characteristic of amphibians, while slight decreases in pH can destroy eggs and tadpoles.

Subsequent studies attempted to pinpoint a cause for the apparent global decline. The main explanation continues to be loss of habitat, particularly wetlands; the number of farm ponds, a favorite habitat for amphibians in Britain, has declined by 70% over the last 100 years. Research on the natterjack toad (*Bufo calamita*) in England, one of the most intensively studied amphibians, also supported the acidification hypothesis. Ponds that had formerly supported significant populations of the species had become gradually more acid, a change that greatly increases the mortality of eggs and young toads (Beebee 1996). An increase in heavy metals and soot particles was associated with the acidification, indicating that the process was most likely related to industrial activities.

However, species in relatively undisturbed, protected areas elsewhere in the world also exhibited declines. Introduced predatory fish, drought, epidemic disease, unusual climatic events, and increased ultraviolet radiation due to a decrease in the protective ozone layer were subsequently blamed for the decline of individual species (Blaustein and Wake 1995; Drost and Fellers 1996; Laurance et al. 1996).

The most surprising result of all these studies is that scientists are no longer sure that all amphibian species really are declining on a global scale. What may appear to be a drastic decline in one population over the course of a few years may actually be a normal response to environmental variability. Because so little is known about amphibian population dynamics, it is difficult for a short-term study to distinguish between an ominous decline and a natural fluctuation in numbers. A number of long-term studies turned up no consistent increase or decrease in amphibian populations. In those few populations in which a signifi-

Studies of the natterjack toad (*Bufo calamita*) and its habitat in England pointed to pollution and acidification of pondwater as a cause for the decline in numbers of this species. (Photograph by Richard Griffiths.)

cant, long-term reduction in numbers has been documented, no single factor can account for all the declines.

Much of the initial hubbub over amphibian declines occurred because amphibians are commonly perceived as being more sensitive to environmental disturbance and could thus serve as an "indicator species" to give early warning of environmental damage. Few hard data exist to support this perception, however. Although amphibian populations certainly have been affected in many areas by habitat degradation and destruction, it is unclear whether or not they have been affected disproportionately. Recent surveys suggest that around 25% of the world's amphibians are threatened with extinction; while this figure is cause for concern, it is the same as the figure for mammals (25%), lower than fishes (34%), and only slightly higher than reptiles (20%) (IUCN 1996). Premature warnings about an amphibian crisis run the risk of drawing attention and resources away from other species that are at greater risk (Pechmann et al. 1994). The drama over amphibian populations highlights one of the dilemmas of conservation biology: balancing the need to act with the need to know more.

population size falls below a certain number; they may be unable to forage, mate, or defend themselves. Such species may be more vulnerable to habitat destruction than asocial species in which individuals are widely dispersed.

- *Species that have evolved in isolation and have not had prior contact with people.* As we discussed in relation to islands in Chapter 7, species that have experienced prior human disturbance and persisted have a greater chance of surviving than species encountering people, along with their associated animals and plants, for the first time (see Figure 7.6) (Balmford 1996). The rate of recent bird extinction is far lower on Pacific islands colonized in the past by Polynesians than on islands not colonized by Polynesians (Pimm et al. 1995). Similarly, Western Australia, which has only recently experienced intense human impact, has a modern extinction rate for plant species 10 times higher than the Mediterranean region, which has a long history of heavy human impact (Greuter 1995).
- *Species that are hunted or harvested by people.* Overharvesting can rapidly reduce the population size of a species (see Chapter 10). If hunting and harvesting are not regulated, either by law or by local customs, the species can be driven to extinction. Utility has often been the prelude to extinction.

Characteristics of extinction-prone species are not independent; rather they group together into categories of characteristics. As an example, species with a specialized diet tend to have low population densities—both characteristics of extinction-prone species. The characteristics often vary among groups because of peculiarities of natural history; for example, butterflies differ from jellyfish and cacti in characters associated with vulnerability to extinction. By identifying characteristics of extinction-prone species, conservation biologists can anticipate the need for managing populations of vulnerable species. Those species most vulnerable to extinction may have the full range of characteristics, as Ehrenfeld (1970) imagined:

> [A] large predator with a narrow habitat tolerance, long gestation period, and few young per litter [is] hunted for a natural product and/or for sport, but is not subject to efficient game management. It has a restricted distribution but travels across international boundaries. It is intolerant of man, reproduces in aggregates, and has nonadaptive behavioral idiosyncrasies. Although there is probably no such animal, this model, with one or two exceptions, comes very close to being a description of a polar bear.

Conservation Categories

To mark the status of rare and endangered species for conservation purposes, the International Union for the Conservation of Nature (IUCN) and the World Conservation Monitoring Centre (WCMC) established 10 conservation categories (IUCN 1994a, 1996); species in categories 3, 4, and 5 are considered to be threatened with extinction. These categories have proved to be useful at the national and international level by directing attention toward species of special concern and identifying species threatened with extinction for protection through international agreements, such as the Convention on International Trade in Endangered Species (CITES), and through published Red Data Books and Red Lists of threatened species.

1. *Extinct*. A species (or other taxa, such as subspecies or varieties) that is no longer known to exist. Exhaustive and repeated searches of localities where the species was once found, and of other possible sites, have failed to detect the species.

2. *Extinct in the wild*. The species exists only in cultivation, in captivity, or as a naturalized population well outside its original range. Searches of its known localities have failed to detect the species.

3. *Critically endangered*. Species that have an extremely high risk of going extinct in the wild in the immediate future. Of particular concern are species whose numbers of individuals have been declining and are reduced to the point where survival of the species is unlikely if present trends continue.

4. *Endangered*. Species that have a high risk of extinction in the wild in the near future, and may become critically endangered.

5. *Vulnerable*. Species that have a high risk of extinction in the wild in

the medium-term future, and may become endangered.

6. *Conservation-dependent*. The species is not currently threatened, but is dependent on a conservation program, without which the species would be threatened with extinction.
7. *Near threatened*. The species is close to qualifying as vulnerable, but is not currently considered threatened.
8. *Least concern*. The species is not considered near threatened or threatened.
9. *Data deficient*. Inadequate information exists to determine the risk of extinction for the species. In many cases, species have not been seen for years, or decades, because no biologists have made the effort to look for them. More information is required before the species can be assigned to a threat category.
10. *Not evaluated*. The species has not yet been assessed for its threat category.

Given the legal restrictions that accompany these assignments, with resulting financial implications to landowners, corporations, and governments, definitions needed to be clarified to prevent arguments over the meaning of each category. To correct this situation, the IUCN recently issued refined and more quantitative definitions in a three-level system of classification based on the probability of extinction (Mace and Lande 1991; IUCN 1994a, 1996):

1. *Critically endangered* species have a 50% or greater probability of extinction within 10 years or 3 generations, whichever is longer.
2. *Endangered* species have a 20% probability of extinction within 20 years or 5 generations.
3. *Vulnerable* species have a 10% or greater probability of extinction within 100 years.

Assignment of categories depends on having at least one of the following types of information:

1. Observable decline in numbers of individuals.
2. The geographical area occupied by the species, and the number of populations.
3. The total number of individuals alive, and the number of breeding individuals.
4. The expected decline in the numbers of individuals if current and projected trends in population decline or habitat destruction continue.

5. The probability of the species going extinct in a certain number of years or generations.

The most serious problem with the old IUCN system was that the criteria were subjective. With greater numbers of people and organizations involved in assigning and evaluating threat categories, there was the potential for species to be arbitrarily assigned to particular categories. The new criteria for assigning categories are based on the developing methods of population viability analysis (see Chapter 12) and focus particularly on population trends and habitat condition. For example, a critical species has at least one of the following characteristics: total population size less than 250 individuals or less than 50 breeding individuals; population has declined by 80% or more over the last 10 years or 3 generations; a more than 25% decline in population numbers is expected within 3 years or one generation; or the overall extinction probability is greater than 50% in 10 years or 3 generations. Species can also be assigned critical status as a result of restricted range of the species (less than 100 km^2 at a single location), observed or predicted habitat loss, ecological imbalance, or commercial exploitation. The use of habitat loss in assigning categories is particularly useful for species that are poorly known biologically, such as many tropical insect species; species can be listed as threatened if their habitat is being destroyed.

The advantage of the revised system is that it provides a standard, quantitative method of classification by which decisions can be reviewed and evaluated by other scientists, according to accepted quantitative criteria and using whatever information is available. However, this method can also become arbitrary, if decisions have to be made with insufficient data. Gathering the data needed for this approach could be too expensive and time consuming, particularly in developing countries and in rapidly changing situations. Regardless of these limitations, the new system of species classification is a distinct improvement and will assist attempts to protect species.

Using the IUCN categories, the World Conservation Monitoring Centre (WCMC) has evaluated and described the threats to about 60,000 plant and 5000 animal species in its series of Red Data Books and Red Lists (IUCN 1990, 1996). As can be seen from the sample shown in Table 8.2, the great majority of the species on these lists are plants, reflecting the recent trend of listing plant species in threatened habitats. However, there are also numerous listed species of fish (700), amphibians (100), reptiles (200), mollusks (900), insects (500), inland water crustaceans (400), birds (1100), and mammals (1100). All bird species have been evaluated using the IUCN system because these species are well known, but the levels of evaluation are lower for mammals (50%), reptiles (20%), amphibians (10%), and fish (5%) (Vincent

TABLE 8.2 ***Percentage of species in some temperate countries that are threatened with global extinction***

	Mammals		Birds		Reptiles		Amphibians		Plants	
Country	Number of species	Percent threatened[a]	Number of species	Percent threatened[a]	Number of species	Percent threatened[a]	Number of species	Percent threatened[a]	Number of species	Percent threatened[a]
Argentina	255	10.2	927	1.9	204	3.4	124	0.8	9,000	1.7
Canada	163	4.9	434	1.6	32	3.1	40	0	3,220	0.3
Japan	186	4.8	632	3.0	85	2.4	58	1.7	4,022	9.8
South Africa	279	7.2	774	1.7	299	1.0	95	1.1	23,000	5.0
United States[b]	367	10.3	1,090	6.1	368	4.6	222	6.3	20,000	8.5

Source: Data from WRI/IIED 1988; WCMC 1992.
[a] Threatened species include those in the current IUCN categories critically endangered, endangered, and vulnerable.
[b] Includes Pacific and Caribbean islands.

and Hall 1996). The evaluation of insects and other invertebrates, fungi, and microorganisms are even less adequate.

The IUCN system has been applied to specific geographical areas as a way of highlighting conservation priorities. Malaysia provides an example (Kiew 1991):

- Of 2830 tree species in peninsular Malaysia, 511 species are considered threatened.
- A large number of Malaysian herb species are endemic to single localities, such as mountaintops, streams, waterfalls, or limestone outcrops. These species are threatened with extinction if their habitat is destroyed.
- All 5 species of sea turtles in Malaysia are considered threatened due to a combination of habitat loss, egg collecting, hunting, pollution of marine waters, unregulated tourism, and entanglement in fishing nets.
- Thirty-five Malaysian bird species are listed as threatened, and many more species have experienced population declines associated with habitat destruction.
- More than 80% of Malaysian Borneo's primate species are under some threat, due to a combination of habitat destruction and hunting pressure.

To help focus attention on the threatened species most in need of immediate conservation efforts, the IUCN has begun to issue lists of the world's most threatened plants and animals. These lists include species of unique conservation value. Among the animals are the kagu

(*Rhynochetos jubatus*), a rare flightless bird that is the symbol of New Caledonia; the kouprey (*Bos sauveli*), a primitive wild ox from Southeast Asia that has been hunted to near extinction; and the Orinoco River crocodile (*Crocodylus intermedius*), which has been decimated by illegal trade in hides. The plant list includes the giant *Rafflesia* of Sumatran rain forests, which produces a flower about 1 m across, and the African violet (*Saintpaulia ionantha*), the most common houseplant in the world, but only known in the wild from a few plants in fragments of mountain forest in central Tanzania.

In Switzerland, efforts are being made to identify those threatened (or Red List) species that are responding to conservation efforts (Gigon et al. 1998). Species included in this "Blue List" have stable populations or are increasing in abundance. The method identifies species for which nature conservation and environmental protection techniques are known but have not been fully applied. The Blue List approach highlights successful conservation efforts and suggests further projects that might succeed (Figure 8.3).

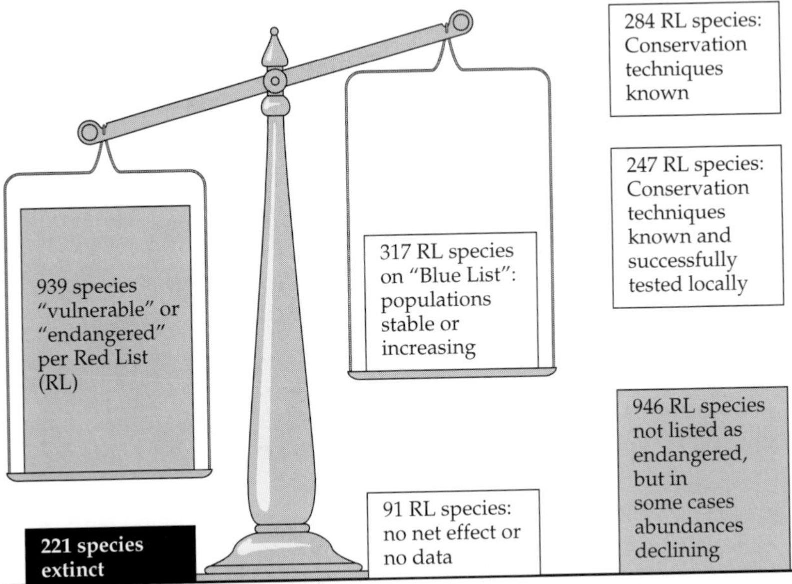

Figure 8.3 An innovative approach being developed in three Swiss cantons to evaluate the current status of the 2106 species of plants and animals (filled boxes) currently on the Red List of endangered and extinct species. Of these, 317 species have been identified as stable or increasing in abundance, thanks to conservation and protection measures; these species form a "Blue List" of recovering species. Protection and conservation techniques have been locally tested and successful for 247 species; these species are future candidates for the Blue List. An additional 284 species could be helped with known conservation and environmental protection techniques. The goal is to shift the balance as the Blue List lengthens. (After Gigon et al. 1997.)

A program similar to the efforts of the IUCN and WCMC is the network of Natural Heritage Data Centers that covers all 50 of the United States, 3 provinces in Canada, and 14 Latin American countries (Jenkins 1996). This program, strongly supported by The Nature Conservancy, gathers, organizes, and manages information on the occurrence of more than 35,000 species and 7000 subspecies, as well as biological communities, referred to as elements of conservation interest. Elements are given status ranks based on a series of standard criteria: number of remaining populations or occurrences, number of individuals remaining (for species) or aerial extent (for communities), number of protected sites, degree of threat, and innate vulnerability of the species or community. On the basis of these criteria, elements are assigned an imperilment rank from 1 to 5, from critically imperiled to demonstrably secure, on a global, national, and regional basis. Species are also classified as X (extinct), H (known historically with searches for them going on), and unknown (uninvestigated elements).

The Nature Conservancy approach has been applied in detail to the species of the United States. The results, given by Stein and Flack in the *Species Report Card: The State of U.S. Plants and Animals* (1997), demonstrate that aquatic species groups, including freshwater mussels, crayfish, amphibians, and fish, are in greater danger of extinction than well-known groups of insects and vertebrates (Figure 8.4).

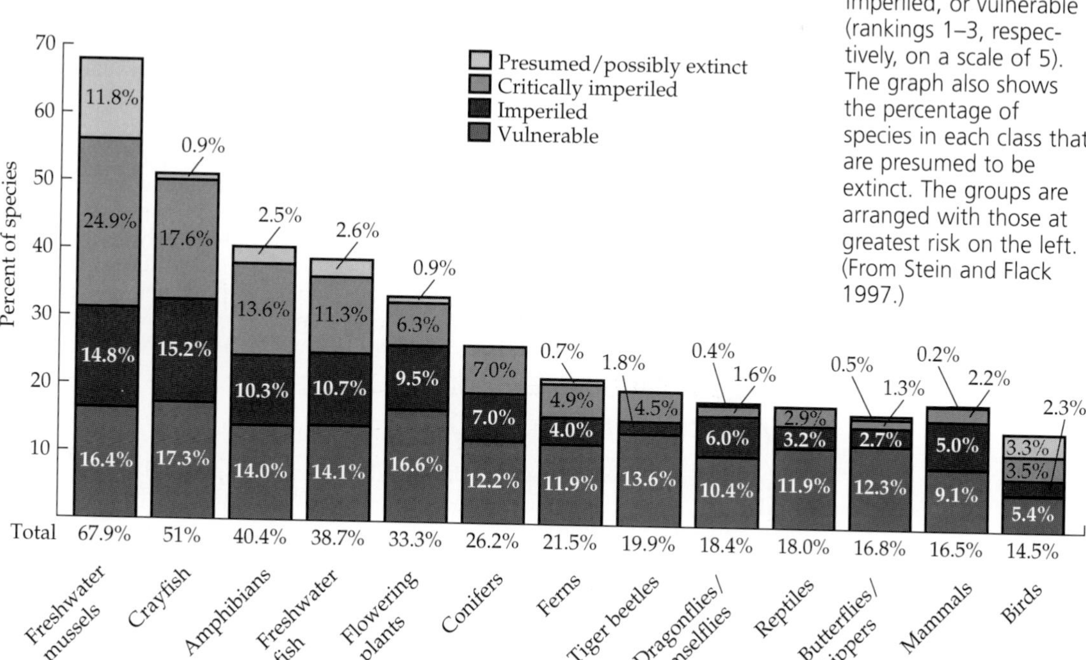

Figure 8.4 Some species groups studied in the United States and ranked according to criteria endorsed by the Nature Conservancy as critically imperiled, imperiled, or vulnerable (rankings 1–3, respectively, on a scale of 5). The graph also shows the percentage of species in each class that are presumed to be extinct. The groups are arranged with those at greatest risk on the left. (From Stein and Flack 1997.)

Freshwater mussels are by far the most endangered species group, with 11.8% of these species presumed to be extinct already and almost 25% critically imperiled. Land plants are intermediate in degree of endangerment.

This system has proved to be extremely successful and useful in organizing between 300,000 to 400,000 records of occurrence. Regional data centers are maintained by hundreds of staff and are consulted approximately 200,000 times a year for information to assist protection efforts on behalf of endangered species, environmental impact reports, scientific research, and land use decisions. Organizing vast amounts of conservation information is an expensive, labor-intensive activity, but it is a crucial component of conservation efforts. We need to know what species and biological communities are in danger and where they occur in order to protect them.

Summary

1. A species can be considered rare if it has one of these three characteristics: it occupies a narrow geographical range; it only occupies one or a few specialized habitats; or it is always found in small populations. Isolated habitats such as islands, lakes, and mountaintops often have many locally endemic species with narrow distributions.

2. Species most vulnerable to extinction have particular characteristics, such as very narrow range, one or only a few populations, small population size, declining population size, and economic value leading to overexploitation. Additional characteristics include: low population density, requirement of a large home range, large body size, low rate of population increase, poor dispersal ability, necessary migration among different habitats, little genetic variability, specialized niche requirements, a need for a stable environment, or typically found in large aggregations. An extinction-prone species may display several of these characteristics.

3. To highlight the status of species for conservation purposes, the International Union for the Conservation of Nature (IUCN) has established 10 conservation categories, including the three categories of threat: critically endangered, endangered, and vulnerable. This system of classification is now widely used to evaluate the status of species and establish conservation priorities. Designation of conservation categories depends on having quantitative information on species, such as number of individuals alive in the wild, number of extant populations, trends in population size, and predicted future threats to the species.

For Discussion

1. Learn about a well-known endangered species, such as the bald eagle, the koala bear, the right whale, or the cheetah. Why are these particular species vulnerable to extinction?

2. Develop an imaginary animal, recently discovered, that is extraordinarily vulnerable to extinction. Give your species a whole range of characteristics that make it vulnerable; then, consider what could be done to protect it. Give your species a hypothetical set of population characteristics, population history, and

geographic range. Then apply the recently developed IUCN system to the species to determine its conservation category.

3. Using information from a book, monograph, or knowledgeable biologist, apply Rabinowitz et al.'s (1986) classification of rarity to some group of plants or animals. Does it give you any new insight?

Suggested Readings

Balmford, A. 1996. Extinction filters and current resilience: The significance of past selection pressures for conservation biology. *Trends in Ecology and Evolution* 11: 193–196. Current extinction rates are highest for groups of species encountering people for the first time.

Blaustein, A. R. and D. B. Wake. 1995. The puzzle of declining amphibian populations. *Scientific American*. 274 (4): 52–57. Summary of the evidence and theories.

Diamond, J. M. 1987. Extant unless proven extinct? Or, extinct unless proven extant? *Conservation Biology* 1: 77–81. Determining the status of rare species in areas not regularly visited by biologists should be a priority.

Grant, P. R. and B. R. Grant. 1997. The rarest of Darwin's finches. *Conservation Biology* 11: 119–126. The mangrove finch has only a few small populations in a specialized habitat and now faces threats from human activity.

IUCN. 1996. *1996 IUCN Red List of Threatened Animals*. IUCN, Gland, Switzerland. Evaluation of 5205 animal species using new quantitative criteria plus a wealth of other information.

Jenkins, R. E. 1996. Natural Heritage Data Center Network: Managing information for managing biodiversity. In *Biodiversity in Managed Landscapes*. R. C. Szaro and D. W. Johnston (eds.). Oxford University Press, Oxford. Explanation of successful system for keeping track of 35,000 species.

Laurance, W. F. 1991. Ecological correlates of extinction proneness in Australasian tropical rain forest mammals. *Conservation Biology* 5: 79–89. Excellent case study with statistical analysis.

Mace, G. M. 1995. Classification of threatened species and its role in conservation planning. In *Extinction Rates*, pp. 197–213, J. Lawton and R. M. May (eds). Oxford University Press, Oxford. A more objective and quantitative approach for assessing the threats to species.

Miller, B., R. P. Reading and S. Forrest. 1996. *Prairie Night: Black-Footed Ferrets and the Recovery of Endangered Species*. Smithsonian Institution Press, Washington, D.C. An insider's look at an intensive recovery effort.

Rabinowitz, D., S. Cairnes and T. Dillon. 1986. Seven forms of rarity and their frequency in the flora of the British Isles. In *Conservation Biology: The Science of Scarcity and Diversity*, pp. 182–204. M. E. Soulé (ed.). Sinauer Associates, Sunderland, MA. An influential paper describing patterns of rarity and their significance to conservation.

Stein, B. A. and S. R. Flack. 1997. *Species Report Card: The State of U.S. Plants and Animals*. The Nature Conservancy, Arlington, VA. The Nature Conservancy approach applied to the relatively well known U.S. biota.

Terborgh, J. 1974. Preservation of natural diversity: The problem of extinction-prone species. *BioScience* 24: 715–722. Why certain species are more vulnerable than others to extinction.

Vincent, A. C. J. 1996. The threatened status of marine fishes. *Trends in Ecology and Evolution* 11: 360–361. Brief overview highlighting the lack of information on the status of most marine fishes.

ically rich nations, Zimbabwe and the Democratic Republic of Congo (formerly Zaire), are relatively better off, still having about half of their forests, although it is too soon to say whether the recent civil war in the latter country has affected its wildlife population. Present rates of deforestation vary considerably among countries, with particularly high annual rates of 1.5%–2% for such tropical countries as Vietnam, Paraguay, Mexico, Côte d'Ivoire, and Costa Rica (Figure 9.3). In the Mediterranean region, which has been densely populated by people for thousands of years, only 10% of the original forest cover remains.

For many important wildlife species, the majority of habitat in their original range has been destroyed, and very little of the remaining habitat is protected. For certain Asian primates, such as the Javan gibbon, more than 95% of the original habitat has been destroyed, and some of these species are protected on less than 2% of their original range (IUCN/UNEP 1986a). The orangutan, a great ape that lives in Sumatra and Borneo, has lost 63% of its range and is protected in only 2% of its range.

Threatened Rain Forests

The destruction of tropical rain forests has come to be synonymous with the loss of species. Tropical moist forests occupy 7% of the Earth's

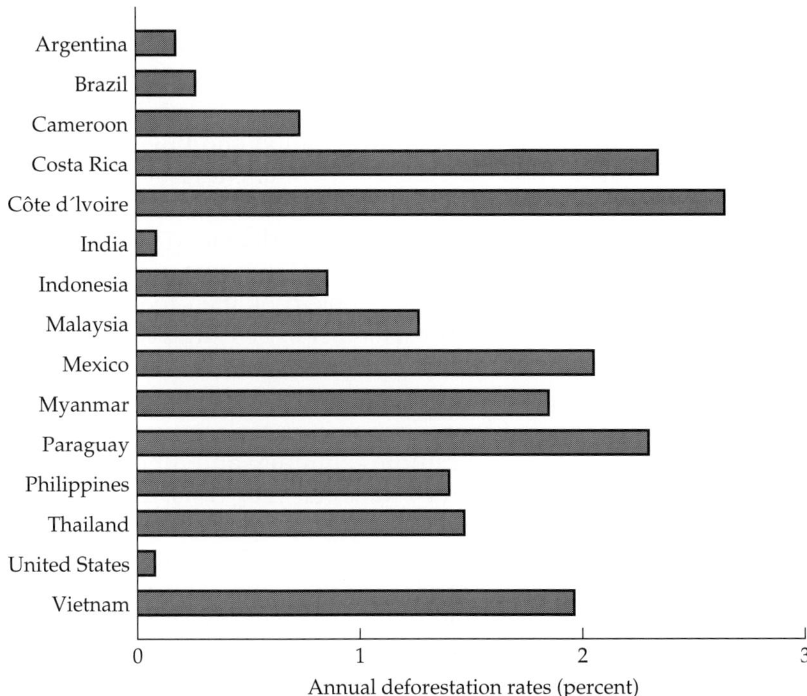

Figure 9.3 Huge amounts of habitat are lost each year as the world's forests are cut down. These estimates for annual deforestation rates (percentage of current forest cover lost each year) are based on data accumulated in 1980 and 1990 by the Food and Agriculture Organization (FAO) of the United Nations. (After Groom and Schumaker 1993.)

land surface, but they are estimated to contain over 50% of its species (Myers 1986). These evergreen to partly evergreen forests occur in frost-free areas below about 1800 m in altitude and have at least 100 mm (4 inches) of rain per month in most years. These forests are characterized by a great richness of species and a complexity of species interaction and specialization unparalleled in any other community. The original extent of tropical rain forests and related moist forests has been estimated at 16 million km^2, based on current patterns of rainfall and temperature (Myers 1984, 1986, 1991b; Sayer and Whitmore 1991). A combination of ground surveys, airplane photos, and remote-sensing data from satellites showed that in 1982 only 9.5 million km^2 remained, an area about equal in size to the continental United States. Another census in 1991 showed a loss of another 2.8 million km^2 during this 9-year period. At the present time, as much as 140,000 km^2 of rain forest are being lost per year, an area larger than the state of Tennessee or the country of Guatemala, with almost half completely destroyed and the remainder degraded to the point that the species composition and ecosystem processes of the community are greatly altered (see Figure 3.4). Tropical forest ecosystems are easily degraded because the soils are often thin and nutrient-poor, and they erode readily in heavy rainfall. At present, there is considerable discussion in the scientific literature about the original extent and current area of tropical forests as well as rates of deforestation. Despite the difficulty in obtaining accurate numbers, a general consensus exists that tropical deforestation rates are alarmingly high and are growing.

On a global scale, about 86,000 km^2 per year (61%) of rain forest destruction results from small-scale cultivation of crops by poor farmers, most of whom have been shifted to the agricultural frontier to practice temporary farming out of desperation and poverty (Myers 1991). Some of this land is converted to permanent farm plantations and pastures, but much of the area returns to secondary forest following shifting cultivation. Included here is land degraded each year for fuelwood production, mostly to supply local villagers with wood for cooking fires. More than two billion people cook their food with firewood, so their impact is significant. Another 29,000 km^2 per year (21%) is destroyed through commercial logging in clear-cutting and selective logging operations. Around 15,000 km^2 per year (11%) is cleared for cattle ranches (Figure 9.4). Clearing for cash-crop plantations (oil palm, cocoa, rubber, etc.) plus road building, mining, and other activities account for about another 10,000 km^2 per year (7%). The relative importance of these enterprises varies by geographical region; logging is a significant activity in tropical Asia and America, cattle ranching is most prominent in tropical America, and farming is more important for the rapidly expanding population in tropical Africa (Kummer and Turner 1994; Rudel and Roper 1996; Bawa and Dayanandan 1997).

(A)

(B)

(C)

Figure 9.4 Rain forest displacement for agricultural purposes. (A) Swidden agriculture in northwest Amazonia; gardens are hewn from the forest with slash-and-burn techniques. Indigenous peoples have used such farming practices for centuries. However, when large numbers of people must eke out a living from the land, rain forest destruction is vast. (Photograph by Paul Patmore.) (B) Rice paddies take over rain forest in southwestern India. (Photograph by R. Primack.) (C) Again in Amazonia, forest land is burned to clear it for cattle pasture. Huge amounts of forest acreage are destroyed in this manner. (Photograph from The Woods Hole Research Center.)

Extending the projection reveals that, at the current rate of loss, there will be virtually no tropical forest left after the year 2040, except in the relatively small protected areas. The situation is actually more grim than these projections indicate because the world's population is still increasing, and poverty is on the rise in many developing tropical countries, putting ever greater demands on the dwindling supply of rain forest.

The destruction of tropical rain forests is caused frequently by demand in industrialized countries for cheap agricultural products, such as rubber, palm oil, cocoa, and beef, and for low-cost wood products. During the 1980s, Costa Rica had one of the world's highest rates of deforestation as a result of the conversion of rain forests into cattle ranches (Downing et al. 1992). Much of the beef produced on these ranches was sold to the United States and other developed countries to produce inexpensive hamburgers. Adverse publicity resulting from this "hamburger connection," followed by consumer boycotts, led major restaurant chains in the United States to stop buying tropical beef from these ranches. Even though deforestation continued in Costa Rica, the boycott was important in making people aware of the international connections promoting deforestation.

Another well-documented linkage involves the forests of Thailand and the livestock industry of the Netherlands. The Dutch import large quantities of tapioca (made from cassava), palm-kernel cake, and other tropical products to use as cattle feed. In order to supply this market, farmers in Thailand had increased their cultivation of cassava and other fodder plants from 100,000 ha in 1965 to 1 million ha by the mid-1980s. Fully 25% of the deforestation in northeastern Thailand can be related to land clearing by the half-million families involved in cassava cultivation. What seems on the surface to be a minor Dutch import to supply a minor domestic industry in fact has major environmental consequences (Netherlands National Committee for the IUCN 1988). A priority for conservation biology is to help provide the information, programs, and public awareness that will allow the greatest amount of rain forest to persist once the present cycle of destruction ends.

The stories of four locations illustrate how rapid and serious rain forest destruction can be.

RONDONIA This state in Amazonian Brazil was almost entirely covered by primary forest as late as 1975, with only 1200 km^2 cleared out of a total area of 243,000 km^2 (Myers 1986; Fearnside 1990, 1996). In the 1970s, the Brazilian government built part of the trans-Amazon highway through Rondonia, including a network of lateral roads leading away from the highway into the forest. The government also provided lucrative tax subsidies to allow corporations to establish cattle ranches in the region and encouraged poor, landless people from coastal states to migrate to Rondonia with offers of free land. These incentives were necessary because the soils of the Amazon region are low in mineral nutrients, and the new pastures and farmlands are usually unproductive and unprofitable. During this land rush, 10,000 km^2 of the forest was cleared by 1982, and an additional 6000 km^2 was cleared by 1985 (Figure 9.5). By the late 1980s, the population of the state was growing at 15.8% per year, with deforestation increasing 37% per year. These rates of growth and deforestation are phenomenally high compared to

(A)

(B)

Figure 9.5 (A) A satellite photo of a new highway through the Amazon rain forest in Rondonia; the area shown covers about 24,500 km^2. Note the lateral roads that provide access into the forest. (B) With access to the interior and lucrative tax subsidies from the government, a Rondonian "land rush" resulted in massive deforestation as 16,000 km^2 were cleared over the space of a few years in the 1980s. (Photographs from The Woods Hole Research Center.)

most other parts of the world, whether industrial or developing. International protests against this environmental damage led the government to reduce its subsidies of the cattle industry. Reduced subsidies and a general economic recession has somewhat decreased the rate of deforestation during the early 1990's. However, massive damage has already been done, and the rate of deforestation has begun to increase again as the result of unusually dry weather in 1997 and 1998, which facilitated land clearing and burning.

MADAGASCAR The moist forests of Madagascar, with their rich heritage of endemic species, originally covered 112,000 km^2. By 1985, they had been reduced to 38,000 km^2 by a combination of shifting cultivation, cattle grazing, and fire. The present rate of deforestation is about 1100 km^2 per year, which means that by the year 2020 there may be no moist forests left on Madagascar, except in the 1.5% of the island under protection (Myers 1986; Green and Sussman 1990). Because Madagascar is the only place where lemurs, a type of primate, occur in the wild, the loss of Madagascar's forests will result in the global extinction of many lemur species (Box 16).

ATLANTIC COAST OF BRAZIL Another area with high endemism is the Atlantic coast forest of northern Brazil. Fully half of its tree species are endemic to the area, and the region supports a number of rare and endangered animals, including the golden lion tamarin (*Leontopithecus rosalia*) (see Box 23 in Chapter 13). In recent decades, the Atlantic coast of Brazil has been almost entirely cleared for sugarcane, coffee, and cocoa production; less than 9% of the original forest remains (Myers 1986). The remaining forest is not in one large block but is divided into isolated fragments that may be unable to support long-term viable populations of many wide-ranging species. The single largest patch is only 7000 km^2 and is highly disturbed in places. Only 3000 km^2 of forest are included in protected areas, and many species in this region are at severe risk of extinction (Brooks and Balmford 1996).

COASTAL ECUADOR The coastal region of Ecuador originally was covered by a rich forest filled with endemic species. It was minimally disturbed by human activity until 1960. At that time, roads were developed and forests cleared to establish human settlements and oil palm plantations. One of the last surviving fragments is the 1.7 km^2 Rio Palenque Science Reserve. This tiny conservation area has 1025 recorded plant species of which 25% are not known to occur anywhere else (Gentry 1986). More than 100 undescribed plant species have been recorded at this site. Many of these species are known only from a single individual plant and are doomed to certain extinction.

Centinella, an isolated ridge 8 kilometers east of Rio Palenque, was formerly covered by a cloud forest. Despite the small area of the ridge

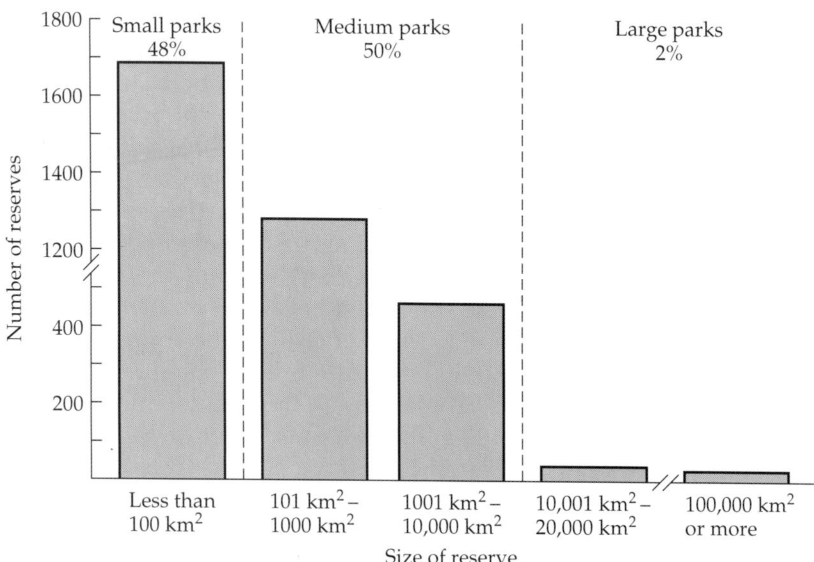

Figure 9.13 Almost one-half of the world's national parks and protected areas are less than 100 km^2, and 98% of the parks are less than 10,000 km^2. (Data from IUCN 1982.)

open landscape. Fences may prevent the natural migration of large grazing animals, such as wildebeest or bison, forcing them to overgraze an unsuitable habitat, eventually leading to starvation of the animals and degradation of the habitat.

Barriers to dispersal can also restrict the ability of widely scattered species to find mates, leading to a loss of reproductive potential for many animal species. Plants also may have reduced seed production if butterflies and bees are less able to migrate among habitat fragments to pollinate flowers.

Third, habitat fragmentation may precipitate population decline and extinction by dividing an existing widespread population into two or more subpopulations in a restricted area. These smaller populations are then more vulnerable to inbreeding depression, genetic drift, and other problems associated with small population size (see Chapter 11). While a large area may support a single large population, it is possible that none of the smaller subpopulations are sufficiently large to persist for a long period.

Edge Effects

Habitat fragmentation also changes the microenvironment at the fragment edge. Some of the more important edge effects include microclimatic changes in light, temperature, wind, humidity, and incidence of fire (Schelhas and Greenberg 1996; Laurance and Bierregaard 1997). Each of these edge effects can have a significant impact upon the vitality and composition of the species in the fragment:

MICROCLIMATE CHANGES Sunlight is absorbed and reflected by the layers of leaves, particularly in forest communities and other communities with a dense plant cover. In forests, often less than 1% of the light energy may reach the forest floor. The forest canopy buffers the microclimate of the forest floor, keeping the forest floor relatively cool, moist, and shaded during the day, reducing air movement, and trapping heat during the night. When the forest is cleared, these effects are removed. As the forest floor is exposed to direct sunlight, the ground becomes much hotter during the day, and without the canopy to reduce heat and moisture loss, the forest floor is also much colder at night and generally less humid. These effects will be strongest at the edge of the habitat fragment and decrease toward the interior of the fragment. In studies of Amazonian forest fragments, microclimate effects were evident up to 100 m into the forest interior. Since species of plants and animals are often precisely adapted to temperature, humidity, and light levels, changes in these factors will eliminate many species from forest fragments. Shade-tolerant wildflower species of the temperate forest, late-successional tree species of the tropical forest, and humidity-sensitive animals, like amphibians, often are rapidly eliminated by habitat fragmentation because of altered

(A)

Figure 9.14 (A) Forest clearing for pasture in Brazil results in sharp edges that change the rain forest microclimate. (Photograph by R. Bierregaard.) (B) Various effects of habitat fragmentation, as measured from the edge into the interior of an Amazon rain forest fragment. For example, disturbance-adapted butterflies migrate 250 m into the forest from an edge, and the relative humidity of the air is lowered within 100 m of the forest edge. (After Laurance and Bierregaard 1997.)

environmental conditions, leading to a shift in the species composition of the community.

The habitat edge is usually the most altered region of the fragment (Figure 9.14). Edges may have very high daytime temperatures, when the angle of the sun is low, and very cold night temperatures due to the lack of buffering by other vegetation. However, a dense tangle of vines and fast-growing pioneer species grow up at the forest edge in response to these altered conditions and often create a barrier that reduces the effects of environmental disturbance on the interior of the fragment. In this sense, the forest edge plays an important role in preserving the composition of the forest fragment, but in the process the species composition of the forest edge is dramatically altered, and the area occupied by forest interior species is further reduced. Over time, the forest edge may be occupied by species of plants and animals different from those found in the forest interior.

Wind changes can have a significant effect in fragmented forest habitats. In an intact forest, wind velocity is substantially reduced by the tree canopies; the wind moves strongly over the forest but is reduced to a gentle breeze within the forest. When a habitat is fragmented, the wind is able to enter the habitat and move through the forest. The impact of wind will be greatest at the forest edge, which is subject to the full force of the wind, but the effects on air movement may be felt over a considerable distance as well, particularly in flat terrain. The

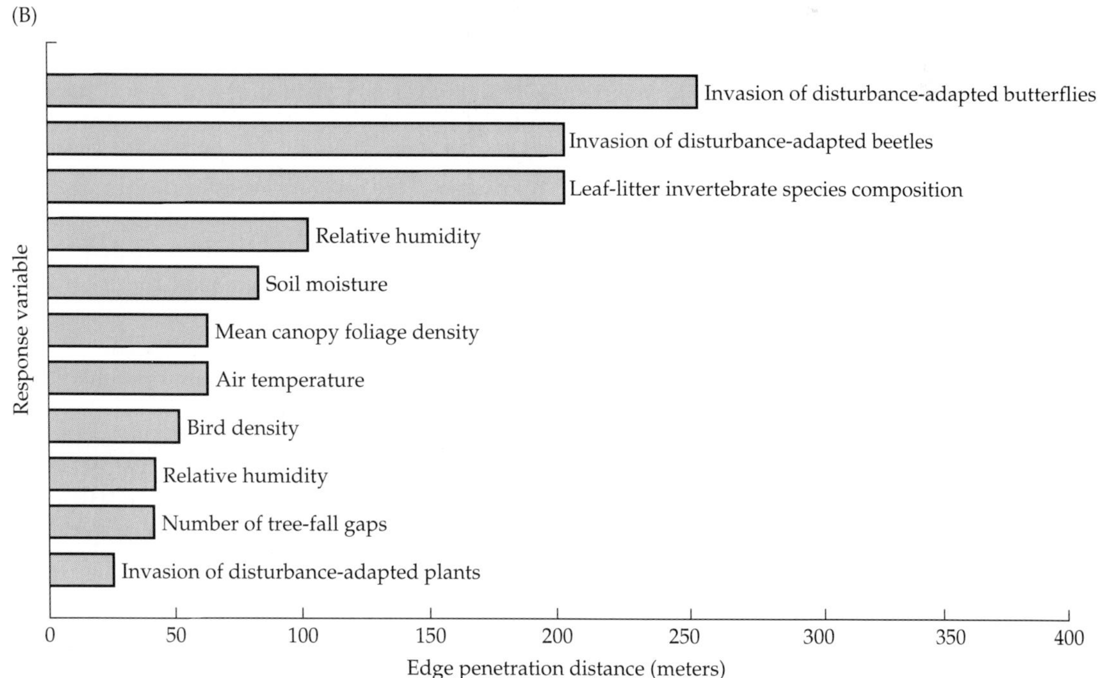

increased wind and air turbulence directly damages vegetation, particularly at the forest edge. Trees that have grown up in the forest interior with minimal wind stress will have leaves and branches stripped off by the wind or may be blown down (Laurance 1991b, 1994; Essen 1994). Increased wind also leads to increased drying of the soil, lower air humidity, and higher water loss from leaf surfaces. This increased water stress may kill many forest interior plant species. The overall result of wind effects may be to kill the trees along the forest edge, which will then be occupied by a new suite of species better adapted to the new conditions. While such effects are most evident within 200 m of the forest edge, increased forest damage was noted up to 500 m inside forest margins of Australian rain forests.

INCREASED INCIDENCE OF FIRE Increased wind, lower humidity, and higher temperatures make fires more likely. Fires may spread into habitat fragments from nearby agricultural fields that are being burned regularly, as in sugarcane harvesting, or from the irregular activities of farmers practicing slash-and-burn agriculture. Forest fragments may be particularly susceptible to fire damage when wood has accumulated on the edge of the forest where trees died or were blown down by the wind. In Indonesian Borneo, several million hectares of tropical moist forest burned during an unusual dry period in 1982 and 1983, and forests are again burning in 1997 and 1998; a combination of forest fragmentation from farming and selective logging, the accumulation of brush after selective logging, and human-caused fires contributed to the extent of this environmental disaster (Leighton and Wirawan 1986).

INTERSPECIFIC INTERACTION Habitat fragmentation increases the vulnerability of the fragment to invasion by exotic and native pest species. The forest edge represents a high-energy, high-nutrient, disturbed environment in which many pest species of plants and animals can increase in numbers and then disperse into the interior of the fragment (Janzen 1983; Paton 1994). For example, the seeds of wind-dispersed plants may be blown great distances into the interior of the fragment and then colonize open, sunny areas where trees and shrubs have recently died, either from natural causes or because of the newly altered growing conditions. Light-loving butterflies from open habitats may migrate up to 250 m into the forest interior.

Omnivorous native animals, such as raccoons, skunks, and blue jays, may increase in population size along forest edges, where they can eat foods of both undisturbed and disturbed habitats (Yahner 1988). These aggressive feeders seek out the nests of interior forest birds, often preventing successful reproduction for many bird species hundreds of meters from the nearest forest edge (see Box 17). Nest-parasitizing cowbirds, which live in fields and edge habitats, use habitat areas. In line with the lower beetle populations, dung decomposed at a lower rate in small forest fragments.

There are several reasons why beetle populations might be lower in small forest fragments. First, primates, birds, and other vertebrate species that the beetles depend on as sources of dung and carrion are at lower densities in small forest fragments, thus there is a decreased food resource for the beetles. Second, the microclimate in small forest fragments is hotter and drier than in continuous forest and may no longer be suitable for beetle larvae development. Finally, many beetle species are at low density in isolated forest fragments and may be eliminated by ordinary random fluctuations in population size. If clear-cut areas act as barriers to dispersal, then isolated forest fragments may be cut off from colonization from nearby forested areas.

This study demonstrates that dung beetles are significantly affected by forest fragmentation. It also suggests that a reduction in beetle populations can have a widespread effect on community interactions and ecosystem processes.

THE FLATTENED MUSK TURTLE The existence of numerous geographically separate drainage systems in the southeastern United States has led to the evolution of a rich endemic fauna of mollusks, fish, and other aquatic species. Habitat modification caused by channelization, dam construction, chemical spills, siltation following construction and strip mining, and sewage discharge has made large areas of these stream systems uninhabitable for the native fauna (Moyle and Leidy 1992). The flattened musk turtle (*Stenotherus depressus*) is an endemic species of the Southeast, confined to river channels in the Warrior River Basin of central Alabama (Dodd 1990). This species is of special concern because it is protected by the U.S. Endangered Species Act. An extensive survey of the turtle revealed that its populations occupy only 7% of its original range; it is now confined to a series of isolated populations that are bounded by habitat rendered unsuitable to migration by human activities and physical barriers. Many of the remaining populations appear to be vulnerable to local extinction due to disease, failure to breed (as shown by an absence of juveniles), removal of old logs from rivers that are needed by the turtles for basking, and collecting of turtles by people. This combination of threats to isolated populations and the lack of opportunities for migration and recolonization suggest that the flattened musk turtle is in danger of extinction.

Habitat Degradation and Pollution

Even when a habitat is unaffected by overt destruction or fragmentation, the communities and species in that habitat can be profoundly affected by human activities. Biological communities can be damaged and species driven to extinction by external factors that do not change the structure of dominant plants in the community, so that the damage is not immediately apparent. For example, in temperate deciduous forests, physical degradation of a habitat might be caused by frequent, uncontrolled ground fires; these fires might not kill the mature trees, but the rich perennial wildflower community and insect fauna on the forest floor would gradually become impoverished. Keeping too many cattle in grassland communities gradually changes the biological community, often eliminating many native species and favoring exotic species that can tolerate grazing. Frequent boating and diving among coral reefs degrade the community, as fragile species are crushed by divers' flippers, boat hulls, and anchors. The most subtle form of environmental degradation is pollution, commonly caused by pesticides, sewage, fertilizers from agricultural fields, industrial chemicals and wastes, emissions from factories and automobiles, and sediment deposits from eroded hillsides. The general effects of pollution on water quality, air quality, and even the global climate are cause for great concern, not only because of the threats to biological diversity, but also their effects on human health. Sometimes, as in the case of the massive oil spills and the 500 oil well fires set at the end of the Persian Gulf War, environmental pollution is highly visible and dramatic (Figure 9.17).

Pesticide Pollution

The dangers of pesticides were brought to the world's attention in 1962 by Rachel Carson's influential book, *Silent Spring*. Carson described a process known as **biomagnification** through which DDT (dichloro-

Figure 9.17 Although it causes extensive damage to ecological communities over widespread areas, air pollution is often subtle and easy for humans to ignore. The massive air pollution generated by oil well fires set during the 1991 war in the Persian Gulf was a more conspicuous example of this constant threat. (Photograph © Reuters/Bettmann.)

along with pest species. At the same time, mosquitoes and other targeted insects evolved resistance to the chemicals, so that ever larger doses of DDT were required to suppress the insect populations. Recognition of this situation in the 1970s led many industrialized countries to ban the use of DDT and other stable pesticides. The ban eventually allowed the partial recovery of many bird populations, most notably peregrine falcons, ospreys, and bald eagles (Cade et al. 1988; Porteous 1992). Nevertheless, the continuing use of these classes of chemicals in other countries is still cause for concern, not only for endangered animal species, but also for the potential long-term effects on people, particularly the workers who handle these chemicals in the field and the consumers of agricultural products treated with these chemicals. These chemicals are widely dispersed in the air and water and can harm plants, animals, and people living far from where the chemicals are actually applied. In addition, these chemicals persist in the environment of countries that outlawed them decades ago, where they have a detrimental effect on the reproductive systems of aquatic vertebrates (McLachlan and Arnold 1996).

Water Pollution

Water pollution has serious consequences for human populations: it destroys important food sources and contaminates drinking water with chemicals that can cause immediate and long-term harm to human health. In the broader picture, water pollution often severely damages aquatic communities (Figure 9.18) (Moyle and Leidy 1992). Rivers,

Figure 9.18 Chemicals and other waste products from a pulp mill gush from pipes into the Exploits River in Newfoundland. Industrial wastes are a major source of water pollution. (Photograph by J. N. A. Lott, McMaster U./Biological Photo Service.)

lakes, and oceans are used as open sewers for industrial wastes and residential sewage. Pesticides, herbicides, oil products, heavy metals (such as mercury, lead, and zinc), detergents, and industrial wastes directly kill organisms living in aquatic environments. Even if the organisms are not killed outright, these chemicals can make the aquatic environment so inhospitable that species can no longer thrive (Figure 9.19). In contrast to a dump in the terrestrial environment, which has primarily local effects, toxic wastes in aquatic environments diffuse over a wide area. Toxic chemicals, even at very low levels, can be concentrated to lethal levels by aquatic organisms. Many aquatic environments are naturally low in essential minerals, such as nitrates and phosphates, and aquatic species have adapted to the natural absence of minerals by developing the ability to process large volumes of water and concentrate these minerals. When these species process polluted water, they concentrate toxic chemicals along with the essential minerals, which eventually poisons the plant or animal. Species that feed upon these aquatic species ingest these concentrations of toxic chemicals.

Figure 9.19 Aquatic habitats such as rivers, lakes, estuaries, and the open ocean are used as dumping grounds for sewage, garbage, and industrial wastes—to the detriment of biological communities. (After Eales 1992.)

birds, particularly raptors, leading to a decline in populations. Water pollution by petroleum products, sewage, and industrial wastes can kill species outright or gradually eliminate them. Increased sediment loads caused by soil erosion and excess nutrient inputs from sewage are particularly harmful to some aquatic communities, often by changing the species composition of the community. Acid rain, high ozone levels at ground level, and airborne toxic metals are aspects of air pollution that damage communities.

5. Global climate patterns may change within the coming century because of the large amounts of carbon dioxide and other greenhouse gases produced by human activities such as burning fossil fuels. Predicted temperature increases could be so rapid during the next century that many species will be unable to adjust their ranges and will go extinct. Low-lying coastal communities may be submerged by seawater if polar ice caps start to melt. Conservation biologists need to monitor these changes and take action when species cannot adapt to climate change.

For Discussion

1. Human population increase is sometimes blamed for the loss of biological diversity. Is this a valid assumption? What other factors are responsible, and how do we weigh their relative importance?

2. Excessive consumption of resources by people in developed countries is a major cause of the loss of biological diversity. An alternative is to "live simply, so that others may simply live," or to "live as if life mattered." Consider the absolute minimum of food, shelter, clothing, and energy that you and your family need to survive and compare it with what you now use. Would you be willing to change your lifestyle to preserve the environment and help others?

3. What can an individual citizen do to improve the environment and conserve biodiversity? Consider the options from doing no harm to becoming actively involved.

4. Consider the most damaged and the most pristine habitats near where you live. Why have some been preserved and others allowed to degrade?

5. Examine maps of parks and nature reserves. Have these areas been fragmented by roads, power lines, and other human activities? How has fragmentation affected the average fragment size, the area of interior habitat, and the total length of edge? Analyze the effects of adding new roads or eliminating existing roads and developments from the parks and consider their biological, legal, political, and economic implications.

Suggested Reading

Allan, T. and A. Warren (eds.). 1993. *Deserts, the Encroaching Wilderness: A World Conservation Atlas*. Oxford University Press, London. Beautiful book with clear description of desert ecology.

Bierregaard, R. O., T. E. Lovejoy, V. Kapos, A. A. Dos Santos and R. W. Hutchings. 1992. The biological dynamics of tropical rainforest fragments. *BioScience* 42: 859–866. A summary of extensive long-term study of rain forest fragmentation in Brazil, in a special issue on conservation and community ecology.

Birkeland, C. (ed.). 1997. *The Life and Death of Coral Reefs*. Chapman and Hall, New York. Extensive background on this important ecosystem, including discussion of the threats that confront it.

BioScience. May 1994. A special issue of this journal that focuses on global patterns of land use change, with articles on Amazonia, Southeast Asia, and Africa.

BirdLife International. 1997. *Climate Change and Wildlife*. A summary of an international workshop at the National Center for Atmospheric Research, Boulder, Colorado, published by BirdLife International, Bedfordshire, U.K. An excellent summary of recent research findings.

Carson, R. 1962. *Silent Spring*. Reprint, Penguin, Harmondsworth, England, 1982. This book describing the harmful effects of pesticides on birds created heightened public awareness when it was first published.

Dugan, P. 1993. *Wetlands in Danger: A World Conservation Atlas*. Oxford University Press, New York. Beautifully illustrated book.

Edwards, M. 1994. Pollution in the former USSR: Lethal legacy. *National Geographic* 1994 (August): 70–98. Appalling, graphic examples of environmental neglect harming people and the environment.

Gates, D. M. 1993. *Climate Change and Its Biological Consequences*. Sinauer Associates, Inc., Sunderland, MA. A clear and thorough description of both past and predicted climate changes and their effects.

Homer-Dixon, T. F., J. H. Boutwell and G. W. Rathjens. 1993. Environmental change and violent conflict. *Scientific American* 268: 38–45. Outlines the relationships between population growth, environmental degradation, and conflict.

Intergovernmental Panel on Climate Change (IPCC). 1996. *Climate Change 1995: The Science of Climate Change*. World Meteorological Organization and United Nations Environmental Programme. A comprehensive presentation of the current state of our knowledge.

Karl, T., N. Nicholls and J. Gregory. 1997. The Coming Climate. *Scientific American* 276: 78–83. Global climate change will affect the weather in diverse ways.

Laurance , W. F. and R. O. Bierregaard, Jr. (eds.). 1997. *Tropical Forest Remnants: Ecology, Management and Conservation of Fragmented Communities*. The University of Chicago Press, Chicago. Comprehensive treatment of habitat fragmentation.

Meyer, W. B. 1996. *Human Impact on the Earth*. Cambridge University Press, Cambridge. Balanced survey of changes in the environment caused by human activity; written in clear, nontechnical language.

Meyer, W. B. and B. L. Turner (eds.). 1994. *Changes in Land Use and Land Cover: A Global Perspective*. Cambridge University Press, New York. Human impact is described for major ecosystems.

Reed, R. A., J. Johnson-Barnard and W. L. Baker. 1996. Fragmentation of a forested Rocky Mountain landscape, 1950–1993. *Biological Conservation* 75: 267–277. Case study presenting methods for analyzing quantitative trends in fragmentation.

Schelhas, J. and R. Greenberg (eds.). 1996. *Forest Patches in Tropical Landscapes*. Island Press, Washington, D.C. Results of ecological and management studies of our increasingly fragmented landscape.

Terborgh, J. 1992. Why American songbirds are vanishing. *Scientific American* 264: 98–104. A variety of theories are examined in light of recent evidence.

1992); as the total area of habitat available to such animals decreases, fights and injuries become more frequent, lowering the animals' resistance to disease. Plant populations are similarly affected by fragmentation and degradation. Changes in plant microenvironments caused by fragmentation, stress caused by air pollution, and direct injury occurring during logging or other human activities directly leads to increased levels of disease in plant populations (Gilbert and Hubbell 1996). Aquatic species also exhibit increased levels of disease due to water pollution, injury, and unusual environmental perturbations (Kushmaro et al. 1996).

Third, in many conservation areas and zoos, species may come into contact with other species that they would rarely or never encounter in the wild, so that infections spread from one species to another (MacDonald 1996). Once infected with exotic diseases, such captive animals cannot be returned to the wild without threatening the entire wild population. Captive Arabian oryx infected with bluetongue virus of domestic livestock and orangutans affected by human tuberculosis could not be reintroduced into the wild as planned for fear of infecting free-ranging animals. The spread of diseases can move very rapidly between captive species kept in crowded conditions. An outbreak of herpes virus spread across the captive colony at the International Crane Federation, killing cranes belonging to several rare species. The outbreak was apparently related to a high density of birds in the colony (Docherty and Romaine 1983).

As areas are fragmented and human activities affect the landscape, disease can spread from domestic animals into wild populations. A species that is common and fairly resistant to a parasite can act as a reservoir for the disease, which can then infect a population of a highly susceptible species. At Tanzania's Serengeti National Park, at least 25% of the lions have recently been killed by canine distemper, a viral disease apparently contracted from one or more of the 30,000 domestic dogs living near the park (Morell 1994). For endangered species, such outbreaks can do phenomenal harm: the last population of black-footed ferrets known to occur in the wild (see Box 14 in Chapter 8) was destroyed by the canine distemper virus. Sometimes disease transmission occurs even under seemingly controlled circumstances. For example, the Mauritius pink pigeon (*Columba mayeri*), endangered in the wild, is being bred in captivity at the Rio Grande Zoo. Because this species often abandons its eggs, domestic pigeons were used as foster mothers. Unfortunately, the pink pigeon chicks died after about one week due to infection by the herpes virus carried by the otherwise healthy domestic pigeons (Figure 10.10). Infected humans have been responsible for directly transmitting tuberculosis, measles, and influenza to orangutans, colobus monkeys, ferrets, and other animals (Thorne and Williams 1988).

Figure 10.10 Chicks of the endangered Mauritius pink pigeon (*Columba mayeri*), here being raised in a captive breeding colony, are highly susceptible to viruses carried by apparently healthy domestic pigeons. (Photograph © NYZS/The Wildlife Conservation Society.)

Diseases transmitted to new parts of the world can decimate common species: North American chestnut trees (*Castanea dentata*), once common throughout the eastern United States, have been virtually obliterated by an ascomycete fungus carried by Chinese chestnut trees imported to New York City. Fungal diseases are also eliminating elm trees (*Ulmus americana*) and flowering dogwoods (*Cornus florida*) from these forests (Figure 10.11). Introduced diseases have particularly powerful adverse effects on endemic island species. An important factor in the decline and extinction of many endemic Hawaiian birds is the introduction of the mosquito *Culex quinquefasciatus* and the malaria protozoan *Plasmodium relictum capistranode*.

An outbreak of disease is often the final result of a complex series of factors that have affected a population. Forester (1971) described the conditions that led to outbreaks of the lungworm-pneumonia disease in bighorn sheep: "poor range conditions, resulting in overcrowding and malnutrition, inclement weather, multiple parasitism, increase in the rate of transmission of protostrongylid lungworms due to conditions favoring the survival of the intermediate hosts and larvae of the lungworm, and secondary invasion by bacteria, resulting in pneumonia."

The Implications of Exotic Species and Diseases for Human Health

The spread of exotic species and disease-causing organisms has direct implications for humans as well. Not only do exotic killer bees and fire ants that are spreading in the New World displace the native insect down. Even when a species is not completely eliminated by overexploitation, the population size may be so low that the species is unable to recover.

2. Humans have deliberately and accidentally moved thousands of plant and animal species to new regions of the world. Island species are most vulnerable to exotic species: introduced grazers overgraze the native plants; introduced predators eat defenseless island animals; and introduced plants often outcompete native plants and dominate the vegetation of an area. Aquatic communities throughout the world are often dramatically altered by the introduction of exotic fish and other exotic species, either accidentally or with the intention of enhancing commercial and sport fishing.

3. Human activities may increase the incidence of disease in wild species. The levels of disease and parasites often increase when animals are confined to a nature reserve or a habitat fragment rather than being able to disperse over a wide area. Also, animals are more susceptible to infection when they are weak and under stress. Animals held in captivity in zoos are prone to higher levels of disease, which sometimes spreads between related species of animals; if diseased captive animals are returned to the wild, they may spread the disease to the wild population.

4. Species may be threatened by a combination of factors, all of which must be addressed in a comprehensive conservation plan.

For Discussion

1. Learn about one endangered species in detail. What is the full range of immediate threats to this species? How do these immediate threats connect to larger social, economic, political, and legal issues?

2. Control of exotic pests may involve searching for parasites of that pest within its original range and releasing this parasite to control the pest at the new location. For example, attempts are currently underway to control exotic purple loosestrife in North America by releasing a European beetle species that eats the plant in its home area. What if this biological control agent begins to attack native species rather than its intended host? How might such a consequence be avoided? Consider the issues involved in a decision to institute a biological control program.

3. Why is it so difficult to regulate the fishing industry in many places and maintain a sustainable level of harvesting? Consider fishing, hunting, logging, and other harvesting activities in your region. Are these well managed? Try to calculate what the sustainable harvest levels of these resources would be, and how such harvesting levels could best be monitored and enforced.

4. Develop a verbal or computer model of how disease spreads in a population. The rate of spread could be determined by the density of the host, the percentage of host individuals infected, the rate of transmission of the disease, and the effects of the disease on the host's survival and rate of reproduction. How will an increase in the density of the host—caused by crowding in zoos or nature reserves, or an inability to migrate due to habitat fragmentation—affect the percentage of individuals that are infected and the overall population size?

Suggested Readings

Drake, J. A. and 6 others (eds.). 1989. *Biological Invasions: A Global Perspective.* John Wiley & Sons, Chichester. The impact of invasions on a wide range of ecosystems.

Fitzgerald, S. 1989. *International Wildlife Trade: Whose Business Is It?* World Wildlife Fund, Washington, D.C. Clearly written account of legal and illegal wildlife trade, covering terrestrial and aquatic species, and both plants and animals.

Fitzgibbon, C. D., H. Mogaka and J. H. Fanshawe. 1995. Subsistence hunting in Arabuko-Sokoke Forest, Kenya, and its effects on mammal populations. *Conservation Biology* 9: 1116–1126. Case study of methods to measure harvesting intensity and to determine if harvesting levels are sustainable.

Freese, C. H. (ed.). 1997. *Harvesting Wild Species: Implications for Biodiversity Conservation.* Johns Hopkins University Press, Baltimore. Case histories of projects that link harvesting of natural resources with economic development.

Hemley, G. (ed.). 1994. *International Wildlife Trade: A CITES Sourcebook.* Island Press, Washington, D.C. Legal and illegal trade in wildlife is surprisingly large.

Jones, R. F. 1990. Farewell to Africa. *Audubon* 92: 50–104. An excellent extended essay on the problems faced by wildlife in Africa.

Ludwig D., R. Hilborn and C. Walters. 1993. Uncertainty, resource exploitation, and conservation: Lessons from history. *Science* 260: 17, 36. Good, short explanation of why commercial exploitation so often destroys its resource base.

McCallum, H. and A. Dobson. 1995. Detecting disease and parasite threats to endangered species and ecosystems. *Trends in Ecology and Evolution* 10: 190–194. Disease needs to be dealt with by endangered species management.

Matthiessen, P. 1959. *Wildlife in America.* Viking Press, New York. Popular account of threats to America's wildlife with a strong emphasis on historical events.

Mowat, F. 1984. *Sea of Slaughter.* McClelland and Stewart, Toronto. Account of overexploitation by an outstanding Canadian author.

Safina, C. 1993. Bluefin tuna in the West Atlantic: Negligent management and the making of an endangered species. *Conservation Biology* 7: 229-234. The difficulties of implementing an effective international policy on tuna.

Scott, M. E. 1988. The impact of infection and disease on animal populations: Implications for conservation biology. *Conservation Biology* 2: 40–56. An excellent review article.

Simberloff, D., D. C. Schmitz and T. C. Brown (eds.). 1997. *Strangers in Paradise: Impact and Management of Nonindigenous Species in Florida.* Island Press, Washington, D.C. Exotic species are a major threat to Florida's biodiversity, and removing them is difficult and expensive.

Taylor, V. J. and N. Dunstone (eds.). 1996. *The Exploitation of Mammal Populations.* Chapman and Hall, London. Experts attempt to determine if sustainable harvesting is possible, with excellent case studies.

Vincent, A. 1994. The improbable seahorse. *National Geographic* 186(4): 126–140. The males get pregnant, but that does not save this unique and beautiful group of fish from overexploitation. Also, see the well-done "Nova" video.

Vitousek, P. M., C. M. D'Antonio, L. L. Loope and R. Westerbrooks. 1996. Biological invasions as global environmental change. *American Scientist* 84: 468–478. Excellent review article describing impact of exotic species on ecosystems, human health, and the economy.

Webster, D. 1997. The looting and smuggling and fencing and hoarding of impossibly precious, feathered and scaly wild things. *The New York Times Magazine,* February 16, 1997, pp. 26–33, 48–49, 53, 61. Personal investigation of this $10 billion black market, focusing on Madagascar.

PART FOUR

Conservation at the Population and Species Levels

CHAPTER 11

Problems of Small Populations

NO POPULATION TRULY lasts forever. Changing climate, succession, disease, and a range of rare events ultimately leads every population to the same fate: extinction. The real questions are whether a population goes extinct sooner rather than later, what factors cause the extinction, and whether other populations of the same species will continue elsewhere. Will a population of African lions last for more than 1000 years and go extinct only after a change in climate, or will the population go extinct after 10 years due to hunting by humans and introduced disease? Will individual lions from the original population start new populations in currently unoccupied habitat, or has all potential lion habitat disappeared because of new human settlements?

The extinction of species as a result of human activities is now occurring roughly 1000 times faster than the natural rate of extinction—far more rapidly than new species can evolve. Because an endangered species may consist of just a few populations, or even a single population, protecting populations is the key to preserving species; it is often the few remaining populations of a rare species that are targeted for conservation efforts. In order to successfully maintain species under the restricted conditions imposed by human activities, conservation biologists must determine the stability of populations under certain circumstances. Will a population of an endangered species persist or even increase in a nature reserve? Is the species in rapid decline, and does it require special attention to prevent it from going extinct?

Many national parks and wildlife sanctuaries have been created to protect "charismatic" megafauna such as lions, tigers, rhinos, bison, and bears, which are important national symbols and attractions for the tourist industry. However, designating the habitats in which these species live as protected areas may not be enough to stop their decline and extinction, even when they are legally protected. Sanctuaries generally are created after most populations of the threatened species have been severely reduced by loss, degradation, and fragmentation of habitat or by overharvesting. Under these circumstances, a species tends to dwindle rapidly toward extinction. Also, individuals outside park boundaries remain unprotected and at risk. What, then, is the best strategy for protecting the few remaining populations of an endangered species?

An adequate conservation plan for an endangered species requires the preservation of as many individuals as possible within the greatest possible area. To accomplish this, the planners, land managers, politicians, and wildlife biologists who are trying to protect species from extinction with limited funds at their disposal need specific guidelines (Schonewald-Cox et al. 1983; Lande 1995). Since these are generally unavailable, planners often must proceed without a firm understanding of the range and habitat requirements of a species. For example, how much long-leaf pine habitat does the red-cockaded woodpecker require? Is it necessary to protect 50, 500, 5000, 50,000, or more individuals to ensure the survival of the species? Furthermore, planners must reconcile conflicting demands on finite resources—a problem vividly demonstrated in the owls vs. jobs debate over conservation of the northern spotted owl, an endangered species that occupies valuable old-growth timber stands in the Pacific Northwest.

Minimum Viable Populations

In a ground-breaking paper, Shaffer (1981) defined the number of individuals necessary to ensure the long-term survival of a species as the **minimum viable population**, or **MVP**: "A minimum viable population for any given species in any given habitat is the smallest isolated population having a 99% chance of remaining extant for 1000 years despite the foreseeable effects of demographic, environmental, and genetic stochasticity, and natural catastrophes." In other words, MVP is the smallest population size that can be predicted to have a very high chance of persisting for the foreseeable future. Shaffer emphasized the tentative nature of this definition, saying that the survival probabilities could be set at 95%, 99%, or any other percentage, and that the time frame might similarly be adjusted, for example, to 100 years or 500 years. The key point is that the minimum viable population size allows a quantitative estimate to be made of how large a population must be to assure long-term survival.

Shaffer (1981) compares MVP protection efforts to flood control. It is not sufficient to use average annual rainfall as a guideline when planning flood control systems and regulating building on wetlands. We recognize the need to plan for severe flooding, which may occur only once every 50 years. In protecting natural systems, we understand that certain catastrophic events, such as hurricanes, earthquakes, forest fires, volcanic eruptions, epidemics, and die-offs of food items, may occur at even longer intervals. To plan for the long-term protection of endangered species, we not only have to provide for their survival in average years, but also in exceptionally harsh years. For instance, in drought years animals may need to migrate well beyond their normal ranges to obtain drinking water.

An accurate estimate of the minimum viable population size for a particular species may require a detailed demographic study of the population and an analysis of its environment. This can be expensive and require months or even years of research (Soulé 1990; Thomas 1990). For vertebrates, some biologists have suggested that protecting at least 500 to 5000 individuals would adequately preserve genetic variability and would allow a minimum number of individuals to survive in catastrophic years and return to former levels (Lande 1988, 1995). For species with extremely variable population sizes, such as certain invertebrates and annual plants, it has been suggested that protecting a population of about 10,000 individuals would generally be an effective strategy.

Once a minimum viable population size has been established for a species, the **minimum dynamic area (MDA)**—the area of suitable habitat necessary for maintaining the minimum viable population—can be estimated by studying the home-range size of individuals and colonies of endangered species (Thiollay 1989). It has been estimated that reserves of 100 to 1,000 km^2 are needed to maintain many small mammal populations (Schonewald-Cox 1983). To preserve populations of grizzly bears (*Ursus arctos horribilis*) in Canada, the areas needed are enormous: 49,000 km^2 for 50 individuals, and 2,420,000 km^2 for 1000 individuals (Noss 1992).

One of the best-documented cases of minimum viable population size comes from a study of the persistence of 120 bighorn sheep (*Ovis canadensis*) populations in the deserts of the southwestern United States (Berger 1990). Some of these populations have been followed for 70 years. The striking observation was that 100% of the populations with fewer than 50 individuals went extinct within 50 years, while virtually all of the populations with more than 100 individuals persisted within the same time period (Figure 11.1). No single cause was evident for most of the populations that died out; rather a wide variety of factors appears responsible for the extinctions. For bighorn sheep the minimum population size is at least 100 individuals, and populations below 50 cannot maintain their numbers even in the short term.

Field evidence from long-term studies of birds on the Channel Islands between England and France supports the fact that large pop-

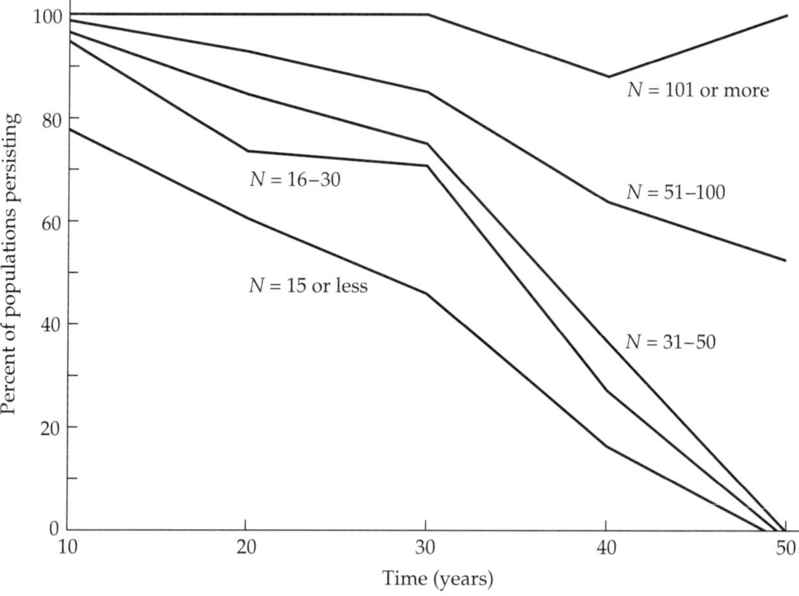

Figure 11.1 The relationship between the size of a population of bighorn sheep and the percentage of populations that persist over time. The numbers on the graph indicate population size (*N*); almost all populations with more than 100 sheep persisted beyond 50 years, while populations with fewer than 50 individuals died out within 50 years. (After Berger 1990; photograph by Mark Primack.)

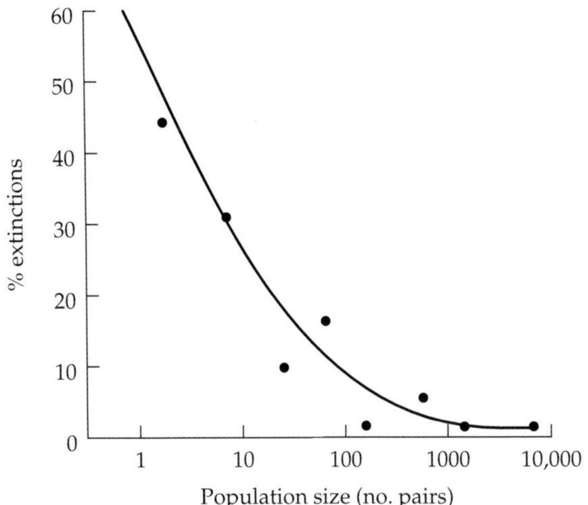

Figure 11.2 Extinction rates of bird species on the Channel Islands. Each dot represents the extinction percentage of all the species in that population size class; extinction rate decreases as the size of the population increases. Populations with less than 10 breeding pairs had an overall 39% probability of extinction over 80 years; populations of between 10 and 100 pairs averaged around 10% probability of extinction, and populations of over 100 pairs had a very low probability of extinction. (From Jones and Diamond 1976.)

ulations are needed to ensure population persistence; only bird populations with more than 100 breeding pairs had a greater than 90% chance of surviving for 80 years (Figure 11.2). There is no need, however, to give up entirely on small populations: many populations of birds apparently have survived for 80 years with 10 or fewer breeding pairs, and northern elephant seals have recovered to a population of 30,000 individuals after being reduced by hunting to only about 20 individuals (Bonnell and Selander 1974).

Exceptions notwithstanding, large populations are needed to protect most species, and species with small populations are in real danger of going extinct. Small populations are subject to rapid decline in numbers and local extinction for three main reasons:

1. Loss of genetic variability and related problems of inbreeding depression and genetic drift.
2. Demographic fluctuations due to random variations in birth and death rates.
3. Environmental fluctuations due to variation in predation, competition, disease, and food supply; and natural catastrophes that occur at irregular intervals, such as fires, floods, volcanic eruptions, storms, or droughts.

Loss of Genetic Variability

A population's ability to adapt to a changing environment depends on **genetic variability,** which occurs as a result of individuals having different forms of the same genes; each form of a gene is known as an

allele. Some individuals show **heterozygosity**; that is, they possess two alleles (one inherited from each parent) of the same gene. Within a population, the frequency of a given allele can range from common to very rare. New alleles arise in a population either by random mutations or through the migration of individuals from other populations, as described in Chapter 2.

In small populations, allele frequencies may change from one generation to the next simply because of chance—that is, which individuals survive to sexual maturity, mate, and leave offspring. This process is known as **genetic drift**. When an allele occurs at a low frequency in a small population, it has a significant probability of being lost in each generation. For example, if a rare allele occurs in 5% of all the genes present (the "gene pool") in a population of 1000 individuals, then 100 copies of the allele are present (1000 individuals × 2 copies per individual × 0.05 allele frequency), and the allele will probably remain in the population for many generations. However, in a population of 10 individuals, only one copy of the allele is present (10 individuals × 2 copies per individual × 0.05 allele frequency) and it is possible that the rare allele will be lost from the population in the next generation.

Considering the general case of an isolated population in which there are two alleles of each gene in the gene pool, Wright (1931) proposed a formula to express the proportion of original heterozygosity remaining after each generation (H) for a population of breeding adults (N_e):*

$$H = 1 - \frac{1}{2N_e}$$

According to this equation, a population of 50 breeding individuals would have 99% of its original heterozygosity after 1 generation:

$$H = 1 - \frac{1}{100} = 1.00 - 0.01 = 0.99$$

The proportion of heterozygosity remaining after t generations (H_t) is equal to

$$H_t = H^t$$

For our population of 50 animals, then, H = 98% after 2 generations (0.99 × 0.99), 97% after 3 generations, and 90% after 10 generations. A population of 10 individuals would have 95% of its original heterozygosity after 1 generation, 90% after 2 generations, 86% after 3 generations, and 60% after 10 generations (Figure 11.3).

---

*N_e, the "effective population size," is discussed in detail beginning on page 291.

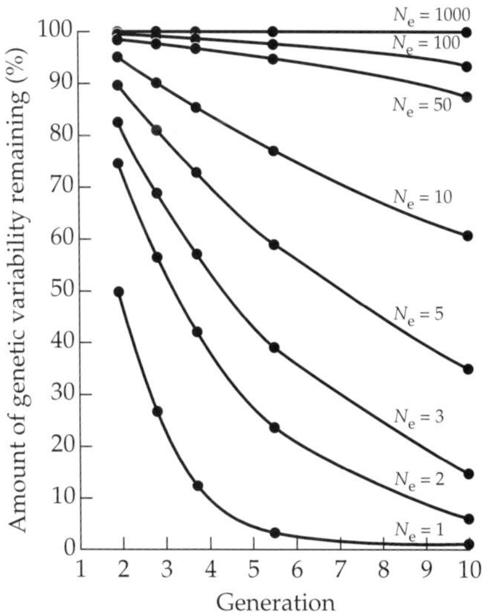

Figure 11.3 Genetic variability is lost randomly over time through genetic drift. This graph shows the average percentage of genetic variability remaining after 10 generations in theoretical populations of various effective population sizes (N_e). After 10 generations, there is a loss of genetic variability of approximately 40% with a population size of 10, 65% with a population size of 5, and 95% with a population size of 2. (From Meffe and Carroll 1997.)

The migration of individuals among populations and the natural mutation of genes tend to increase the amount of genetic variability within the population and balance the effects of genetic drift. The mutation rates found in nature—about 1 in 1000 to 1 in 10,000 per gene per generation—may make up for the random loss of alleles in large populations, but they are insignificant in countering genetic drift in small populations of 100 individuals or less. However, even a low frequency of movement of individuals between populations minimizes the loss of genetic variability associated with small population size (Figure 11.4) (Lacy 1987). If even one or two immigrants arrive each generation, in an isolated population of about 100 individuals the impact of genetic drift will be greatly reduced. With 4–10 migrants per generation from nearby populations, the effects of genetic drift are negligible (Mills and Allendorf 1996). Gene flow from neighboring populations appears to be the major factor preventing the loss of genetic variability in small populations of Galápagos finches (Grant and Grant 1992).

In addition to theories and simulations, field data also show that lower effective population size leads to a more rapid loss of alleles from the population. For example, the wind-pollinated dioecious conifer *Halocarpus bidwillii* of New Zealand naturally occurs in discrete populations in subalpine habitats. Protein electrophoresis was used to examine genetic variation in populations ranging from 10 to 400,000 individuals. There was a strong correlation between population size and genetic variation—large populations had the greatest levels of heterozygosity, percent polymorphic genes, and mean number of alleles per gene (Figure 11.5) (Billington 1991). Populations smaller than 8000

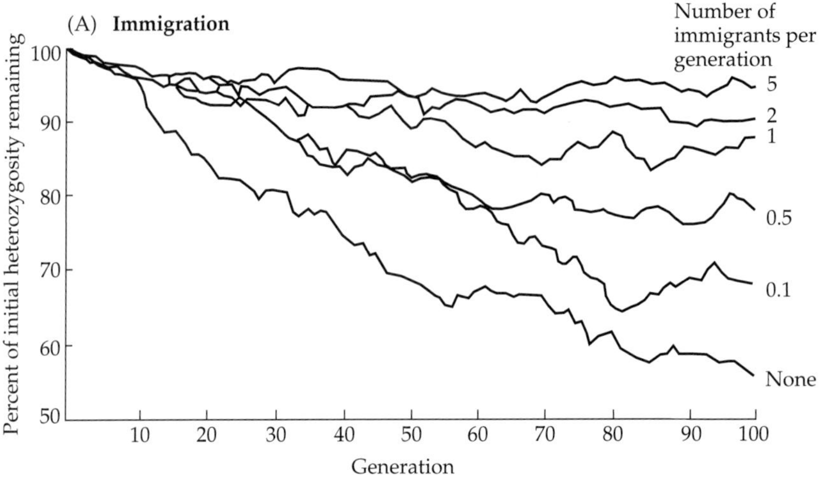

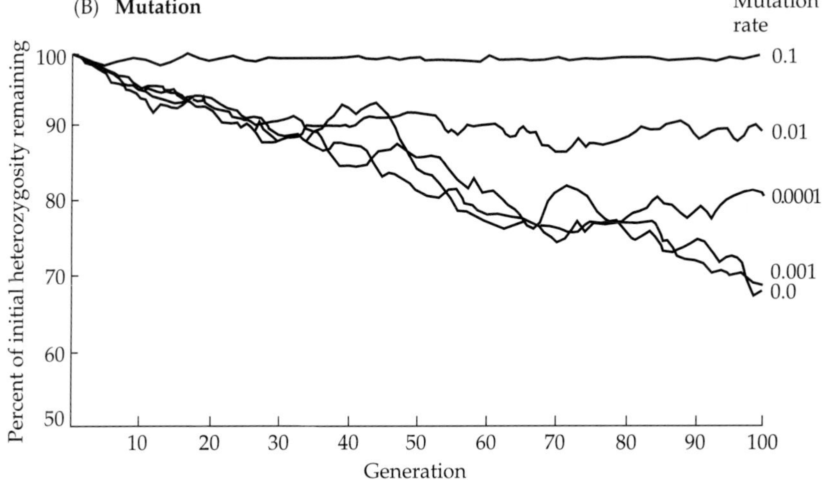

Figure 11.4 The effects of immigration and mutation on genetic variability in 25 simulated populations of size N_e = 120 individuals over 100 generations. (A) In an isolated population of 120 individuals, even low rates of immigration from a larger source population prevent the loss of heterozygosity from genetic drift. In the model, an immigration rate as low as 0.1 (1 immigrant per 10 generations) increases the level of heterozygosity, while genetic drift is negligible with an immigration rate of 1. (B) It is more difficult for mutation to counteract genetic drift. In the model, the mutation rate *m* must be 1% per gene per generation (*m* = 0.01) or greater to affect the level of heterozygosity. Since this mutation rate is far higher than what is observed in natural populations, mutation appears to play a minimal role in maintaining genetic variability in small populations. (From Lacy 1987.)

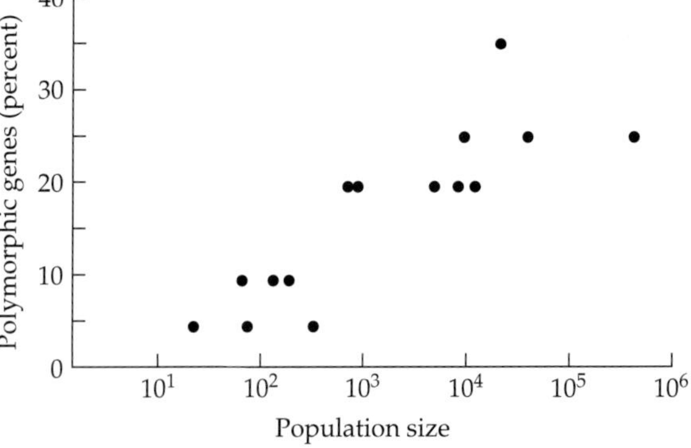

Figure 11.5 The level of genetic variability is directly correlated with population size in populations of a New Zealand coniferous shrub, *Halocarpus bidwillii.* This pattern holds true for the percentage of genes that are polymorphic as well as for the mean number of alleles per gene and the level of heterozygosity. (From Billlington 1991.)

individuals appeared to suffer a loss of genetic variation, with the lowest variation in the smallest populations.

A recent review of studies of genetic variation in plants and animals found that large populations had more genetic variation than small populations in 22 out of 23 species (Frankham 1996). Genetic variation was also lower for endangered species and species with narrow ranges than for nonthreatened species and species with wide ranges. In some cases, entire species lacked genetic variation. An extensive review of genetic variation in plants showed that only 8 of 113 plant species had no genetic variation and these often had very limited ranges (Hamrick et al. 1979).

Consequences of Reduced Genetic Variability

Small populations subjected to genetic drift have greater susceptibility to a number of deleterious genetic effects, such as inbreeding depression, and loss of evolutionary flexibility, and may also be susceptible to outbreeding depression. These factors may contribute to a decline in population size and a greater probability of extinction (Ellstrand and Elam 1993; Thornhill 1993; Loeschcke et al. 1994; Avise and Hamrick 1996).

INBREEDING DEPRESSION A variety of mechanisms prevent inbreeding, mating among close relatives, in most natural populations. In large populations of most animal species, individuals do not normally mate with close relatives. They often disperse from their place of birth or are inhibited from mating with relatives through unique individual odors or other sensory cues. In many plants, a variety of morphological and physiological mechanisms encourage cross-pollination and prevent self-pollination. In some cases, particularly when population size is small and no other mates are available, these mechanisms fail to prevent inbreeding. Mating among parents and their offspring, siblings, and cousins, and self-fertilization in hermaphroditic species may result in inbreeding depression, which is characterized by higher mortality of offspring, fewer offspring, or offspring that are weak, sterile, or have low mating success (Ralls et al. 1988).

For example, plants of the scarlet gilia (*Ipomopis aggregata*) that come from populations with fewer than 100 individuals produce smaller seeds with a lower rate of seed germination and exhibit greater susceptibility to environmental stress than do plants from larger populations (Figure 11.6) (Heschel and Paige 1995). Symptoms associated with inbreeding depression and loss of genetic variation are reduced when plants from small populations are cross-pollinated by hand with pollen from plants from large populations (Jiménez et al. 1994; Keller et al. 1994). A small (less than 40 adults) isolated population of adders (*Vipera berus*) in Sweden had a variety of symptoms of inbreeding depression: small litter size, high proportion of deformed and stillborn

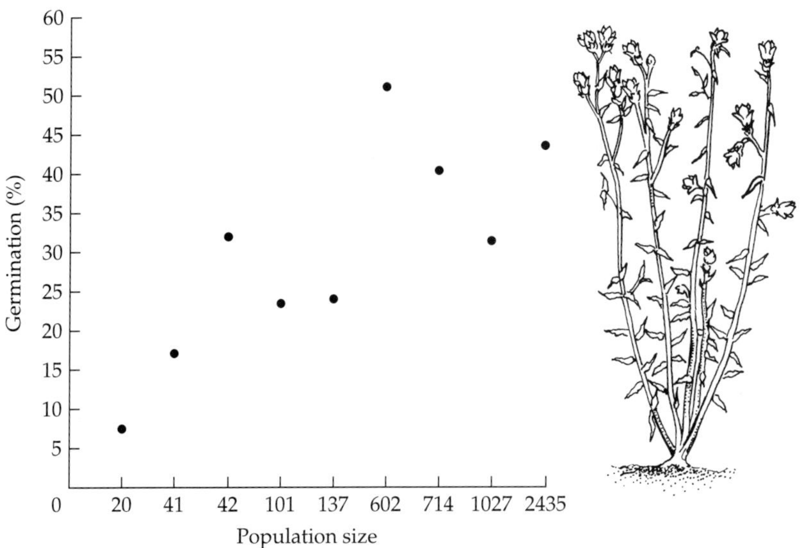

Figure 11.6 Seed germination in populations of the scarlet gilia (*Ipomopsis aggregata*) from montane Arizona is lower in small populations (fewer than 150 individuals) in comparison to larger populations. Seed germination is strongly reduced in the smallest populations. Populations are arranged from smallest to largest. (After Heschel and Paige 1995.)

offspring, and a low degree of genetic heterozygosity (Madsen et al. 1996). When adult males from other areas were introduced into the population, offspring viability increased, suggesting that the effects of inbreeding had been reduced.

The most plausible explanation for inbreeding depression is that it allows the expression of harmful alleles as homozygotes (Barrett and Kohn 1991). **Outcrossing**—mating between individuals that are not closely related—not only increases the level of heterozygosity in a population but also allows many rare but harmful recessive alleles that arise by mutation to accumulate unexpressed in populations; as long as these alleles are rare, the function of the gene will be performed by the more common dominant allele of the gene. When the population size of an outcrossing species declines, close relatives may be forced to inbreed because no other mates are available. This allows rare, harmful recessive alleles to become exposed in the homozygous form, resulting in damage to the offspring. However, certain plant species, particularly weeds, are able to self-fertilize without any loss of fitness. In these species, harmful recessive genes must have already been lost from the population.

Evidence for the existence of inbreeding depression comes from studies of human populations, captive animal populations, and cultivated plants (Darwin 1876; Charlesworth and Charlesworth 1987). In a wide range of captive mammal populations, matings among close relatives, such as parent-offspring mating and sibling mating, resulted on average in offspring with a 33% higher mortality rate than in nonin-

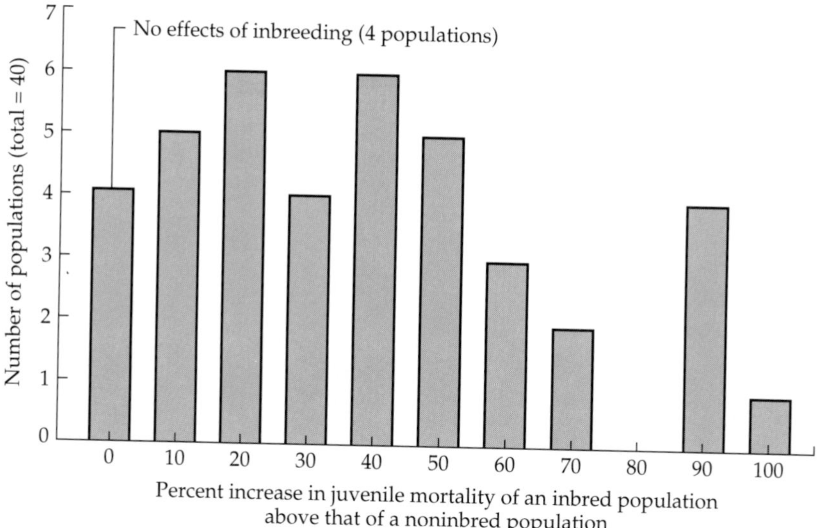

Figure 11.7 A high degree of inbreeding (such as matings between mother and son, father and daughter, brother and sister) results in a "cost of inbreeding." In the above data, based on a survey of 40 inbred mammal populations, the cost is expressed as a percentage of increase in juvenile mortality above the juvenile mortality of outbreeding animals of the same species. (From Ralls et al. 1988.)

bred animals (Figure 11.7) (Ralls et al. 1986, 1988). Inbreeding depression can be a severe problem in small captive populations in zoos and domestic livestock breeding programs. The effects of inbreeding in the wild are just now being investigated, and appear to be significant (Barrett and Kohn 1991). In writing about the tendency of species to avoid breeding with close relatives, Charles Darwin (1868) commented: "That any evil directly follows from the closest inbreeding has been denied by many persons; but rarely by any practical breeder; and never, as far as I know, by anyone who has largely bred animals which propagate their kind quickly."

The variety of genetic factors that affect small populations is illustrated by studies of gray wolves on Isle Royale, Canada (Wayne et al. 1991). A pair of wolves established a population on Isle Royale in Lake Superior around 1949. The population had increased to about 50 individuals in 1980 but had dropped to only about 14 by 1990, with many females not breeding and few pups sighted. Decreased availability of food, the effects of canine provirus disease, and a loss of genetic variation have been posited as possible explanations for the population decline. Loss of genetic variation and heterozygosity seems to be the most likely explanation: there have only been 2–3 breeding pairs of wolves for 5–7 generations, which predicts (applying the equations presented earlier) a 39%–65% loss of genetic variation. Genetic studies demonstrate that the island population has lost 50% of its variation in comparison with mainland populations. The wolves of Isle Royale are as genetically similar to each other as siblings and are probably descended from a single mother. These genetic findings suggest that inbreeding depression and an unwillingness of close relatives to mate could explain the decline in population size.

OUTBREEDING DEPRESSION Individuals of different species rarely mate in the wild; there are strong ecological, behavioral, physiological, and morphological isolating mechanisms that ensure mating only happens between individuals of the same species. However, when a species is rare or its habitat is damaged, **outbreeding**—mating between individuals of different species—may occur. Individuals unable to find mates within their own species may mate with an individual of a related species. The resulting offspring are often weak or sterile due to **outbreeding depression**: the lack of compatibility of the chromosomes and enzyme systems inherited from their different parents (Templeton 1986; Thornhill 1993). To use an example from artificial selection, domestic horses and donkeys are commonly bred to produce mules. Although mules are not physically weak (on the contrary, they are quite strong, which is why humans find them useful), they are almost always sterile.

Outbreeding depression can also result from matings between different subspecies, or even matings between divergent genotypes or populations of the same species. In such cases, the hybrid offspring are unlikely to have the precise mixture of genes that allows individuals to survive and reproduce successfully in a particular set of local conditions. For example, when the ibex (*Capra ibex*) population of Slovakia went extinct, ibex from Austria, Turkey, and the Sinai were brought in to start a new population. These different subspecies mated and produced hybrids that bore their young in the harsh conditions of winter rather than in the spring, and consequently had a low survival rate. Outbreeding depression caused by the pairing of individuals from the extremes of the species' geographic range meant failure for the experiment.

Outbreeding depression may be significant in plants, where the arrival of pollen onto the receptive stigma of the flower is to some degree a matter of the chance movement of pollen by wind, insects, or other pollen vector. A rare plant species growing near to a closely related common species may be overwhelmed by the pollen of the common species (Ellstrand 1992). The offspring of such hybridization events are often either sterile or poorly adapted to the environment of the parent species.

Even when the hybrids are not sterile, the genetic identity of the rare species becomes lost as its small gene pool is mixed into the much larger gene pool of the common species. The seriousness of this threat is illustrated by the fact that more than 90% of California's threatened and endangered plants occur in close proximity to other species in the same genus with which the rare plants could possibly hybridize. Outbreeding depression can also take place in gardens when individuals from different parts of a species' range are grown next to each other and are cross-pollinated, producing hybrid seed.

LOSS OF EVOLUTIONARY FLEXIBILITY Rare alleles and unusual combinations of alleles that confer no immediate advantages may be uniquely suited for a future set of environmental conditions. Loss of genetic variability in a small population may limit its ability to respond to new conditions and long-term changes in the environment, such as pollution, new diseases, and global climate change (Allendorf and Leary 1986; Falk and Holsinger 1991). A small population is less likely than a large population to possess the genetic variation necessary for adaptation to long-term environmental changes and so will be more likely to go extinct. For example, in many plant populations a small percentage of individuals have alleles that promote tolerance for high concentrations of toxic metals such as zinc and lead, even when these metals are not present (Antonovics 1976). If toxic metals become abundant in the environment due to pollution from nearby mining and smelting operations, individuals with these alleles will grow, survive, and reproduce better than typical individuals; consequently, frequency of these alleles in the population increases dramatically. However, if the population is small and the genotypes for metal tolerance are not present, the population could go extinct.

Effective Population Size

How many individuals are needed to maintain genetic variability? Franklin (1980) suggested that 50 reproductive individuals might be the minimum number necessary to avoid inbreeding depression. This figure is based on the practical experience of animal breeders, which indicates that animal stocks can be maintained with a loss of 2%–3% of heterozygosity per generation. Wright's formula (see page 284) shows that a population of 50 individuals will lose only 1% of its heterozygosity per generation, which would be erring on the safe side. However, because this figure is based on work with domestic animals, its applicability to the wide range of wild species is uncertain. Using data on mutation rates in *Drosophila* fruit flies, Franklin also suggested that in populations of 500 reproductive individuals, the rate of new genetic variability arising through mutation might balance the variability being lost due to small population size. This range of values has been referred to as the **50/500 rule**: isolated populations need to have at least 50 individuals and preferably 500 individuals to maintain genetic variability. This rule has been questioned by Lande (1995), who suggests that mutation rates may be lower than previously reported. If he is correct, then at least 5000 reproductive individuals must be protected to maintain the genetic variability and long-term survival of a population. A better rule of thumb may be to protect as many individuals of rare and endangered species as possible to maximize their chance of survival.

The 50/500 rule is often difficult to apply because it assumes that all individuals within a population have an equal probability of mating and having offspring. However, many individuals do not produce offspring due to factors that prevent some animals from finding mates, such as age, poor health, sterility, malnutrition, small body size, and social structures. Because of these factors, the **effective population size** (N_e) of breeding individuals is often substantially smaller than the actual population size (N). Because the rate of loss of genetic variability is based on the *effective* population size, the loss of genetic variability can be quite severe even in a large population (Kimura and Crow 1963; Lande and Barrowclough 1987; Nunney and Elam 1994). For example, a population of 1000 alligators has only 10 animals, 5 males and 5 females, that are old enough and healthy enough to breed, and each animal has the same number of offspring; therefore the effective population size is 10, not 1000. A smaller than expected effective population size can exist when there is an unequal sex ratio, variation in reproductive output, or population fluctuations and bottlenecks.

Unequal Sex Ratio

A population may consist of unequal numbers of males and females due to chance, selective mortality, or the harvesting of only one sex by people. If, for example, a population of a monogamous (one male and one female form a long-lasting pair bond) goose species consists of 20 males and 6 females, only 12 individuals, 6 males and 6 females, will be mating. In this case, the effective population size is 12, not 26. In other animal species, social systems may prevent many individuals from mating even though they are physiologically capable of doing so. Among elephant seals, for example, a single dominant male usually controls a large group of females and prevents other males from mating with them (Figure 11.8), whereas among African wild dogs the dominant female in the pack may bear all of the pups.

The effect of unequal numbers of breeding males and females on N_e can be described by the formula

$$N_e = \frac{4N_m N_f}{N_m + N_f}$$

where N_m and N_f are the numbers of breeding males and breeding females, respectively, in the population. In general, as the sex ratio of breeding individuals becomes increasingly unequal, the ratio of the effective population size to the number of breeding individuals (N_e/N) also goes down (Figure 11.9). Only a few individuals of one sex are making a disproportionately large contribution to the genetic makeup

Figure 11.8 A single male elephant seal (the larger animal with the extended snout, seen roaring in the center of the photograph) controls large numbers of females; thus the effective population size is reduced because only one male is providing genetic input. (Photograph by Frank S. Balthis.)

of the next generation, rather than the equal contribution found in monogamous mating systems. For example, consider a population of seals that contains 6 breeding males and 150 breeding females, with each male mating with 25 females. The calculation demonstrates that the effective population size is actually 23, not 156, because of the relatively few males involved in mating:

$$N_e = \frac{(4)(6)(150)}{(6+150)} = \frac{3600}{156} = 23$$

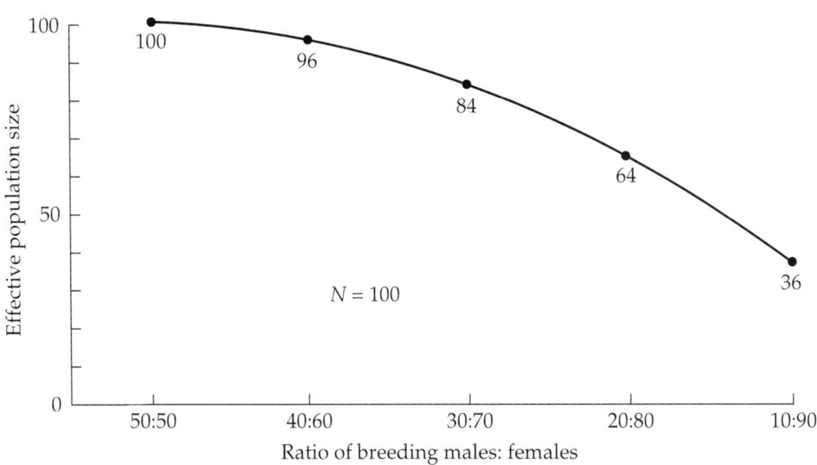

Figure 11.9 The effective population size (N_e) declines when the number of males and females in a breeding population of 100 individuals is increasingly unequal. N_e is 100 when 50 males and 50 females breed, but only 36 when 10 males and 90 females breed.

Variation in Reproductive Output

In many species the number of offspring varies substantially among individuals. This phenomenon is particularly true in plants, where some individuals may produce a few seeds while others produce thousands of seeds. Unequal production of offspring leads to a substantial reduction in N_e because a few individuals in the present generation will be disproportionately represented in the gene pool of the next generation. In general, when the variation in reproductive output is high, the effective population size is lower than the actual population size. For a variety of species, Crow and Morton (1955) estimated that variation in offspring number reduces effective population size by a factor of 60%–85%. In many annual plant populations that consist of large numbers of tiny plants producing one or a few seeds and a few gigantic individuals producing thousands of seeds, N_e could be reduced even more.

Population Fluctuations and Bottlenecks

In some species, population size varies dramatically from generation to generation. Particularly good examples of this are checkerspot butterflies in California (Murphy et al. 1990), annual plants, and amphibians. In extreme fluctuations, the effective population size is somewhere between the lowest and the highest number of individuals. The effective population size can be calculated over a period of *t* years using the number of individuals (*N*) breeding in any one year:

$$N_e = t/(1/N_1 + 1/N_2 + \ldots + 1/N_t)$$

Consider a butterfly population, monitored for 5 years, that has 10, 20, 100, 20, and 10 breeding individuals in the successive five years. In this case

$$N_e = 5/(1/10 + 1/20 + 1/100 + 1/20 + 1/10) = 5/(31/100) = 5(100/31) = 16.1$$

The effective population size over the course of 5 years is above the lowest population level of 10 but well below the maximum number of 100 and the arithmetic average population size of 32.

The effective population size tends to be determined by the years with the smallest numbers. A single year of drastically reduced population numbers will substantially lower the value of *N*. This principle applies to a phenomenon known as a **population bottleneck**. When a population is greatly reduced in size, rare alleles in the population will be lost if no individuals possessing those alleles survive and reproduce (Carson 1983; Barrett and Kohn 1991). With fewer alleles present and a decline in heterozygosity, the overall fitness of the individuals in the population may decline. A special category of bottleneck, known as the

among individuals within populations and among populations (Lesica et al. 1988). This lack of variation is thought to be due to fluctuations in population size and a tendency for flowers to self-fertilize. A similar lack of genetic variation is apparent in four populations of the rare Furbish's lousewort (*Pedicularis furbishiae*), an endemic plant of Maine (Menges 1990). In this case, the lack of genetic variation is attributed to genetic bottlenecks resulting from a series of temporary populations established on river banks after colonization by a few seeds.

It should be noted that population bottlenecks do not always lead to greatly reduced heterozygosity. If the population expands rapidly in size after a temporary bottleneck, average heterozygosity in the population may be restored even though the number of alleles present is severely reduced (Nei et al. 1975; Allendorf and Leary 1986). An example of this phenomenon is the high level of heterozygosity found in the greater one-horned rhinoceros (*Rhinoceros unicornis*) in Nepal, even after the population passed through a bottleneck (Figure 11.13; Box 20). Population size declined from 800 individuals in Chitwan National Park to less than 100 individuals; fewer than 30 were breeding. As a result of strict protection of the species by park guards, the population recovered to 400 individuals (Dinerstein and McCracken 1990).

These examples demonstrate that the effective population size is often substantially less than the total number of individuals in the population, especially when there is a combination of factors such as fluctuating population size and population bottlenecks, numerous nonreproductive individuals, and an unequal sex ratio. A review of a wide range of wildlife studies revealed that the average effective population size was only 11% of total population size; that is, a population of 300 animals, seemingly large enough to maintain the population, might only have an effective population size of 33, indicating that it is in serious danger of extinction (Frankham 1996). As a field example, the threatened winter run of chinook salmon (*Oncorhynchus*

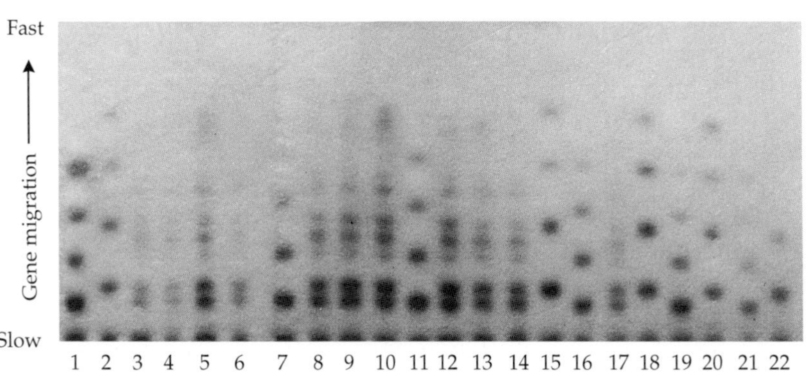

Figure 11.13 Starch gel electrophoresis reveals that the population of greater one-horned rhinoceros (*Rhinoceros unicornis*) at Chitwan National Park in Nepal shows high levels of genetic variation. This technique is based on the fact that the proteins (in this case, an enzyme called LDH) produced by different alleles of a gene migrate at different rates across an electrically charged starch gel plate, appearing as bands at different distances from the starting point at the bottom of the gel. Each column represents one individual animal. Note that animals 10 and 11, for example, have bands at different positions, indicating that these two individuals are genetically different from each other for the enzyme LDH. (From Dinerstein and McCracken 1990.)

Box 20 Rhino Species in Asia and Africa: Genetic Diversity and Habitat Loss

In recent decades, conservationists have focused extraordinary effort on restoring the numbers of rhinoceros in parts of their original ranges. The task is monumental: the five species of rhinoceros that inhabit Asia and Africa, all critically endangered, represent ancient and unusual adaptations for survival. Habitat destruction and poaching represent serious threats to the three species of the Asian forests, while the illegal killing of rhinos for their horns is the main problem for the two African species. Rhino losses are so severe that it is estimated that fewer than 11,000 individuals of all five species survive today. These species only exist in a tiny fraction of their former range. The most numerous of the five is the white rhinoceros, *Ceratotherium simum*; this species numbers approximately 5700 wild animals, although there are fewer than 50 individuals of the distinctive northern subspecies. The rarest species—the elusive Javan rhinoceros, *Rhinoceros sondaicus*—is thought to number around 57 animals on the island of Java and another 8 to 12 in Vietnam. The population decline of each species is alarming enough, but the problem is apparently exacerbated by the fact that many of the remaining animals live in very small, isolated populations. The black rhino, *Diceros bicornis*, for example, numbers about 2400, but these individuals are in approximately 75 small, widely separated subgroups (Ashley et al. 1990). The existing populations of the Sumatran rhino (*Dicerhinus sumatrensis*) are all less than 100 individuals (Caughley and Gunn 1996), with the total species count under 500. Some biologists fear that these small populations may not be viable as a result of inbreeding depression, genetic diseases resulting from matings among closely related individuals.

The question of genetic viability in rhino populations is not as simple as it first appears. Genetic diversity varies greatly among rhino species. Studies of the greater one-horned, or Indian, rhinoceros (*Rhinoceros unicornis*) in Nepal indicate that despite its small total population—an estimated 1500 animals—the genetic diversity of this species is extremely high (see Figure 11.13), contradicting the common assumption that small populations automatically have low heterozygosity. The combination of long generation times and high individual mobility may have allowed the Indian rhino to maintain its genetic variability despite passing through a population bottleneck (Dinerstein and McCracken 1990). In contrast, six living subspecies of the black rhinoceros are known to exist, representing adaptations to local environmental conditions throughout the species' range. Certain of these subspecies appear to have very low genetic variability; in three cases, *D. bicornis brucii, D. bicornis longipes,* and *D. bicornis chobiensis*, only a few dozen animals remain to represent these variants (Ashley et al. 1990).

On the basis of genetic viability alone, one might assume that the Indian rhino has the advantage over the black rhino and is more likely to survive. However, the Indian rhino faces a different and possibly more deadly threat: habitat loss. Though no immediate threat of inbreeding exists for the Indian rhino, the critical pressure upon this species' range since the nineteenth century has reduced its numbers dramatically, from possibly tens of thousands of animals to less than 1000 by the 1960s (Dinerstein and McCracken 1990). The geographic range of this animal, originally covering northern India, Pakistan, southern Nepal, Burma, and Bangladesh, has been almost completely taken over by human settlement. Indian rhino populations in parks and sanctuaries have increased dramatically and are genetically healthy; however, the species will always be limited to these small, heavily-guarded remnant habitats, with no opportunity to return to its former range or numbers.

In contrast, much of the range of the black rhino in Africa is still open and is not likely to be subject to human encroachment at any time in the near future. A degree of heterozygosity could be maintained in the species by bringing all black rhinos together in a single breeding population, or by moving individuals between populations. If the black rhino population is managed for genetic

Each of the five rhinoceros species currently occupies only a tiny fraction of its former range, but their level of endangerment and their situations vary greatly. (From Caughley and Gunn 1996.)

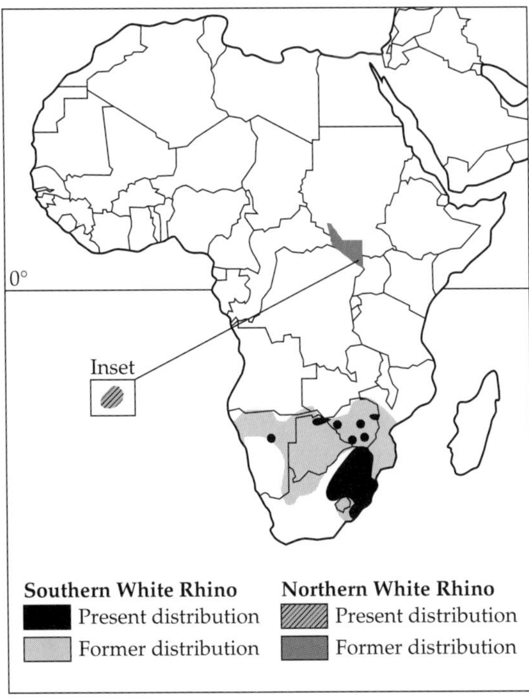
0°
Inset
Southern White Rhino
Present distribution
Former distribution
Northern White Rhino
Present distribution
Former distribution

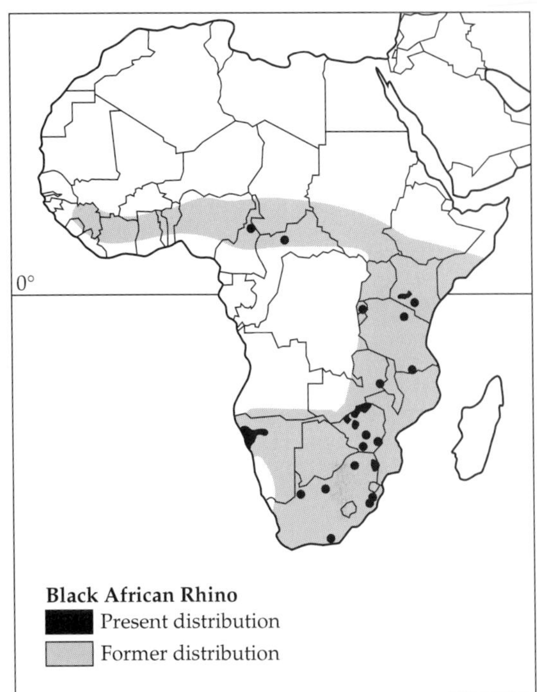
0°
Black African Rhino
Present distribution
Former distribution

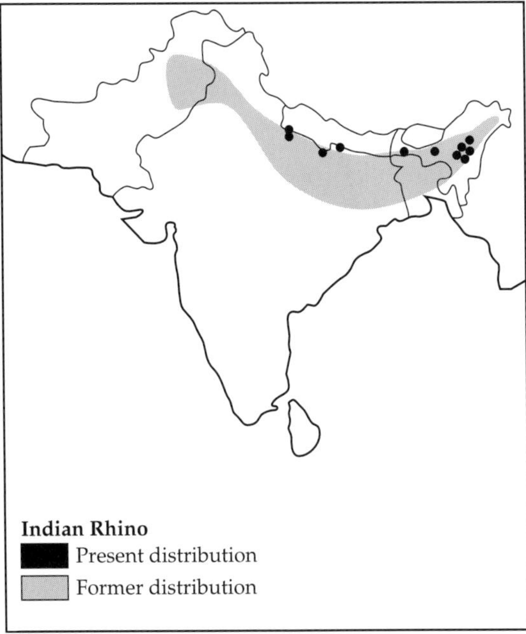
Indian Rhino
Present distribution
Former distribution

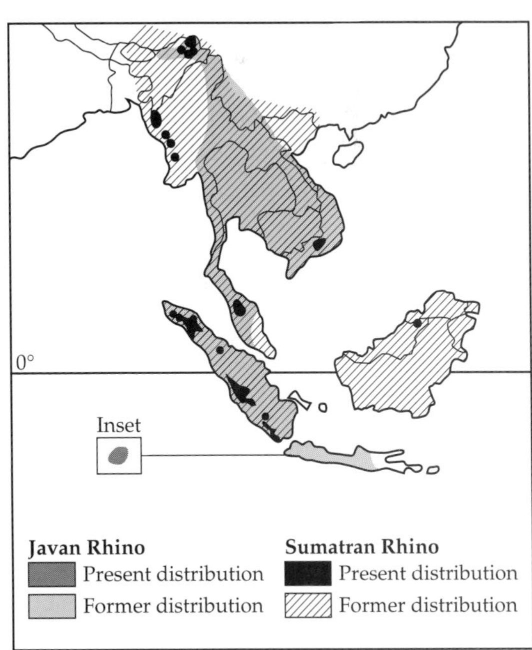
0°
Inset
Javan Rhino
Present distribution
Former distribution
Sumatran Rhino
Present distribution
Former distribution

Box 21 (continued)

diversity in this manner, it is conceivable that this species could be fully restored to its original numbers and much of its range. Yet the problem of microenvironmental adaptations remains: by placing black rhinos from a number of different locations together in a sanctuary to increase genetic diversity in the species, would the rhinos risk losing adaptive differences that might prove crucial to the survival of local subspecies? Analysis of mitochondrial DNA in populations of black rhinos (Ashley et al. 1990) indicates that in certain populations the relationship between most individuals is so close that the need to diversify the black rhino population outweighs any possible costs. Maintaining genetic diversity is contingent upon controlling outside threats to the breeding population, including illegal poaching for their horns. Optimal park conditions must also be maintained to ensure that all adult individuals reproduce.

Genetic analysis is also useful for decisions on the conservation of the Sumatran rhinoceros, numbering less than 400 individuals and found in scattered populations in four separate regions: eastern Sumatra, western Sumatra, Peninsular Malaysia, and Borneo. Analysis of mitochondrial DNA from blood and hair samples showed that the Borneo population represented a distinct lineage from the other three populations, which were genetically similar. The recommendation is that the Borneo rhinos be treated as a separate population for breeding and conservation purposes, whereas the other three populations could be managed as one conservation unit (Morales et al. 1997).

Conservation of rhinos is therefore a task that must be tailored to the specific circumstances of particular species and populations. The different species face a number of challenges with a variety of possible solutions. For species threatened with habitat loss, such as the Indian rhino, sanctuaries and habitat preservation may be the most important methods of preserving the species. Others, such as the black rhino, may require management to increase genetic diversity, including breeding programs and protection of the remnant populations. The rarest species, the Sumatran and Javan rhinos, may require a combination of approaches. They need habitat protection because both of these Asian species are under severe pressure from logging and conversion of forest to agricultural land, and they need breeding programs to increase and maintain genetic diversity. For each of these rhinos, there is no single, all-encompassing answer; the problems and circumstances of conserving the species must be evaluated individually.

---

tshawytscha) in the Sacramento River has about 2000 adults in the mating population, but only 85 in the effective population size (Bartley et al. 1992). The disparity was attributed to unequal breeding success, as only a small number of adults produced most of the offspring. A similarly low effective population size (of only 132) was noted in a commercial salmon hatchery, even when up to 10,000 fish were present in the spawning population. Both wild and hatchery-raised fish populations apparently have effective population sizes well below the adult population size and are in danger of losing significant amounts of genetic variability. Hatchery managers have recognized that more adults must be used in breeding programs, more tanks must be used to subdivide the population, and progeny from different parents must be maintained. The small and declining number of salmon in this wild run combined with the low effective population size make it likely that this salmon population will be lost in the near future (Hedrick et al. 1995).

One way to estimate effective population size is by measuring the loss of heterozygosity over time in repeatedly censused populations. The rationale for this approach is that the rate of loss of heterozygosity over time due to genetic drift is directly correlated to N_e. This approach was used to examine eight large captive populations of *Drosophila melanogaster* flies using a technique for evaluating the number of variable alleles (Briscoe et al. 1992). All eight populations had been maintained separately with a population size of about 5000 individuals for between 8 and 365 generations. Despite the large population size, N_e varied between 185 and 253—only about 4% of the population size. Like the chinook salmon, the effective population size is severely reduced, presumably because of unequal breeding success; possibly a few males mated with the majority of reproductive females, and a small proportion of highly fertile females may have laid most of the eggs. These results suggest that merely maintaining large population sizes may be insufficient to prevent the loss of genetic variation in both wild and captive populations. In the case of captive populations, genetic variation may be effectively maintained by controlling breeding, perhaps by subdividing the population and allowing limited migration.

Demographic Variation

In an ideal, stable environment, a population would increase until it reached the carrying capacity (*K*) of the environment. At this point the average birth rate (*b*) per individual would equal the average death rate (*d*), and there would be no net change in population size. In any real population, individuals do not usually produce the average number of offspring, but might leave no offspring, somewhat fewer than the average, or more than the average. For example, in an ideal, stable giant panda population, each female would produce an average of two surviving offspring in her lifetime, but field studies show that rates of reproduction among individual females vary widely around that number. However, as long as population size is large, the average birth rate provides an accurate description of the population. Similarly, the average death rate in a population can be determined only by examining large numbers of individuals.

Population size may fluctuate over time because of changes in the environment or other factors without ever approaching a stable value. In general, once population size drops below about 50 individuals, individual variation in birth and death rates begins to cause the population size to fluctuate randomly up or down (Gilpin and Soulé 1986; Menges 1992). If population size fluctuates downward in any one year, due to a higher than average number of deaths or a lower than average number of births, the resulting smaller population will be even more susceptible to demographic fluctuations in subsequent years. Random fluctuations upward in population size are eventually bound by the carrying capacity of the environment, and the population again may fluctuate downward. Consequently, once a population becomes small because of habitat destruction and fragmentation, demographic variation, also known as **demographic stochasticity**, becomes important and the population has a higher probability of going extinct due to chance alone (Richter-Dyn and Goel 1972; Lacy and Lindenmayer 1995). Species with highly variable birth and death rates, such as annual plants and short-lived insects, may be particularly susceptible to demographic stochasticity. The chance of extinction is also greater in species that have low birth rates, such as elephants, because these species take longer to recover from chance reductions in population size.

As a simple example, imagine a population of three hermaphroditic individuals that live for one year, need to find a mate, reproduce, and then die. Assume that each individual has a 33% probability of producing 0, 1, or 2 offspring, resulting in an average birth rate of 1 per individual; in this instance, there is theoretically a stable population. However, when these individuals reproduce, there is a 1-in-27 chance ($0.33 \times 0.33 \times 0.33$) that no offspring will be produced in the next generation and that the population will go extinct. Consider also that there is a 1-in-9 chance that only 1 offspring will be produced in the next generation ($0.33 \times 0.33 \times 0.33 \times 3$); because this individual will not be able to find a mate, the population will be doomed to extinction in the next generation. There is also a 22% chance that the population will decline to 2 individuals in the next generation. Thus, random variation in birth rates can lead to demographic stochasticity and extinction in small populations. Similarly, random fluctuations in the death rate can lead to fluctuations in population size. When populations are small, random high mortality in one year might eliminate the population altogether.

When populations drop below a critical number, there are possible deviations from an equal sex ratio and a declining birth rate. For example, imagine a population of 4 birds that includes 2 mating pairs of males and females, in which each female produces an average of 2 surviving offspring in her lifetime. In the next generation, there is a 1-in-8 chance that only male or only female birds will be produced, in which case no eggs will be laid to produce the following generation. There is a 50% (8-in-16) chance that there will be either 3 males and 1 female or 3 females and 1 male in the next generation, in which case only 1 pair of birds will mate and the population will decline. Though these are hypothetical situations, examples from nature illustrate this point. The last 5 surviving individuals of the extinct dusky sparrow (*Ammodramus maritimus nigrescens*) were all males, so there was no opportunity to establish a captive breeding program. In Illinois, the last 3 individuals of the rare lakeside daisy (*Hymenoxys acaulis* var. *glabra*) remaining in the state are unable to produce viable seeds when cross-pollinated among themselves because they belong to the same self-infertile mating type (De Mauro 1993). Pollen has to be brought in from Ohio plants in order for the Illinois plants to produce seeds.

In many animal species, small populations may be unstable due to the inability of the social structure to function once the population falls below a certain size; this is known as the **Allee effect**. Herds of grazing mammals and flocks of birds may be unable to find food and defend themselves against attack when numbers fall below a certain level. Animals that hunt in packs, such as wild dogs and lions, may need a certain number of individuals to hunt effectively. Many animal species that live in widely dispersed populations, such as bears, whales, spiders, and eagles, may be unable to find mates once the population density drops below a certain point. In this case, the average birth rate will decline, making the population size even smaller and worsening the problem. In plant species, as population size decreases, the distance between plants increases; pollinating animals may not visit more than one of the isolated, scattered plants, resulting in the loss of seed production (Bawa 1990). This combination of random fluctuations in demographic characteristics, unequal sex ratios, disruption of social behavior, and decreased population density contributes to instabilities in population size, which often leads to local extinction.

Environmental Variation and Catastrophes

Random variation in the biological and physical environment, also known as **environmental stochasticity**, can also cause variation in the population size of a species. For example, the population of an endangered rabbit species might be affected by fluctuations in the population of a deer species that eats the same types of plants, fluctuations in the population of a fox species that feeds on the rabbits, and fluctuations in the populations of parasites and disease-causing organisms affecting the rabbits. Variation in the physical environment might also strongly influence the rabbit populations—rainfall during an average year might encourage plant growth and allow the population to increase, while dry years might limit plant growth and cause rabbits to starve. Environmental stochasticity affects all individuals in the population, unlike demographic stochasticity, which causes variation among individuals within the population.

Natural catastrophes such as droughts, storms, earthquakes, and fires occurring at unpredictable intervals and cyclical die-offs of the surrounding biological community can cause dramatic fluctuations in population levels. Natural catastrophes can kill part of a population or even eliminate an entire population from an area. Numerous examples exist of die-offs in populations of large mammals; in many cases 70%–90% of the population dies (Young 1994). Even though the probability of a natural catastrophe in any one year is low, over the course of decades and centuries, natural catastrophes have a high likelihood of occurring.

As an example of environmental variation, imagine a rabbit population of 100 individuals in which the average birth rate is 0.2 and an average of 20 rabbits are eaten each year by foxes. On average, the population will maintain its numbers at exactly 100 individuals, with 20 rabbits born each year and 20 rabbits eaten each year. However, if there are three successive years in which the foxes eat 40 rabbits per year, the population size will decline to 80 rabbits, 56 rabbits, and 27 rabbits in years 1, 2, and 3, respectively. If there are then three years of no fox predation, the rabbit population will increase to 32, 38, and 46 individuals in years 4, 5, and 6. Even though the same average rate of predation occurred over this six-year period, by introducing variation in year-to-year predation rates the rabbit population size declined by 50%. At a population size of 46 individuals, the rabbit population will go rapidly extinct when subjected to the average rate of 20 rabbits eaten by foxes per year.

Modeling efforts by Menges (1992) and others have shown that random environmental variation is generally more important than random demographic variation in increasing the probability of extinction in populations of small to moderate size. Environmental variation can substantially increase the risk of extinction even in populations showing positive population growth under the assumption of a stable environment (Mangel and Tier 1994). In general, introducing environmental variation into population models, in effect making them more realistic, results in populations with lower growth rates, lower population sizes, and higher probabilities of extinction. Menges (1992) introduced environmental variation into models of plant populations that had been developed by field ecologists working with palms. Considering only demographic variation and before the inclusion of environmental variation, these plant models suggested that the minimum viable population size, the number of individuals needed to give the population a 95% probability of persisting for 100 years, was about 140 mature individuals (Figure 11.14). When moderate environmental variation was included, however, the minimum viable population size increased to 380 individuals, making protection of the species more difficult.

Extinction Vortices

The smaller a population becomes, the more vulnerable it is to further demographic variation, environmental variation, and genetic factors that tend to reduce population size even more and drive the popula-

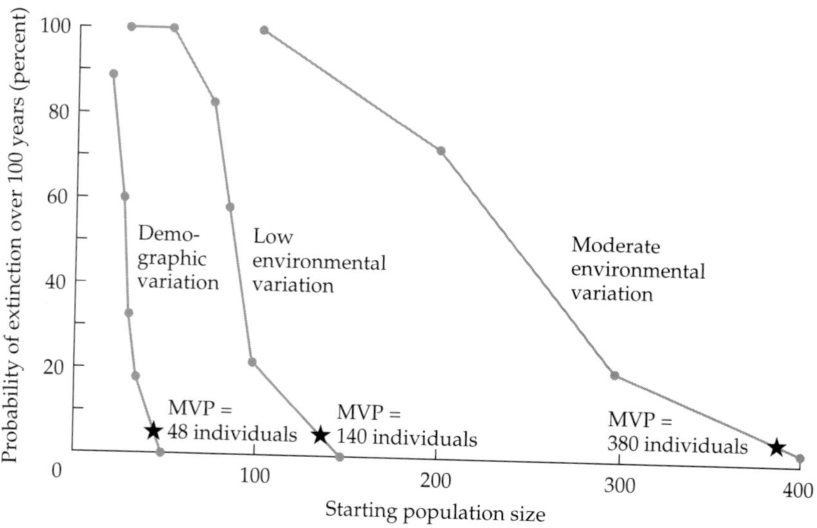

Figure 11.14 The effects of demographic variation, low environmental variation, and moderate environmental variation on the probablility of extinction of a population of the Mexican palm, *Astrocaryum mexicanum.* (In this study, the minimum viable population size, shown as stars, was defined as the population size at which there is a less than 5% chance of the population going extinct within 100 years.) (From Menges 1992; data from Pinero et al. 1984.)

tion to extinction. This tendency of small populations to decline toward extinction has been likened to a vortex: a whirling mass of gas or liquid spiraling inward; the closer it gets to the center, the faster it moves. At the center of an **extinction vortex** is oblivion: the permanent disappearance of the species. Once caught in such a vortex, it is difficult for a species to resist the pull toward extinction (Gilpin and Soulé 1986).

For example, a natural catastrophe, a new disease, or human disturbance could reduce a large population to a small size. This small population could then suffer from inbreeding depression with an associated lowered juvenile survival rate. This increased death rate could result in an even lower population size and more inbreeding. Similarly, demographic variation will often reduce population size, resulting in even greater demographic fluctuations and, once again, a greater probability of extinction.

These three forces—environmental variation, demographic variation, and loss of genetic variability—act together so that a decline in population size caused by one factor will increase the vulnerability of the population to the other two factors (Figure 11.15). For example, a decrease in orangutan population size caused by forest fragmentation may cause inbreeding depression, decreasing population size; decreased population size may then disrupt the social structure and the ability to find mates, leading to an even lower population size; the smaller population is then more vulnerable to further population reduction and eventual extinction caused by unusual environmental events. The drought, forest fires, and dense smoke cover in Borneo and

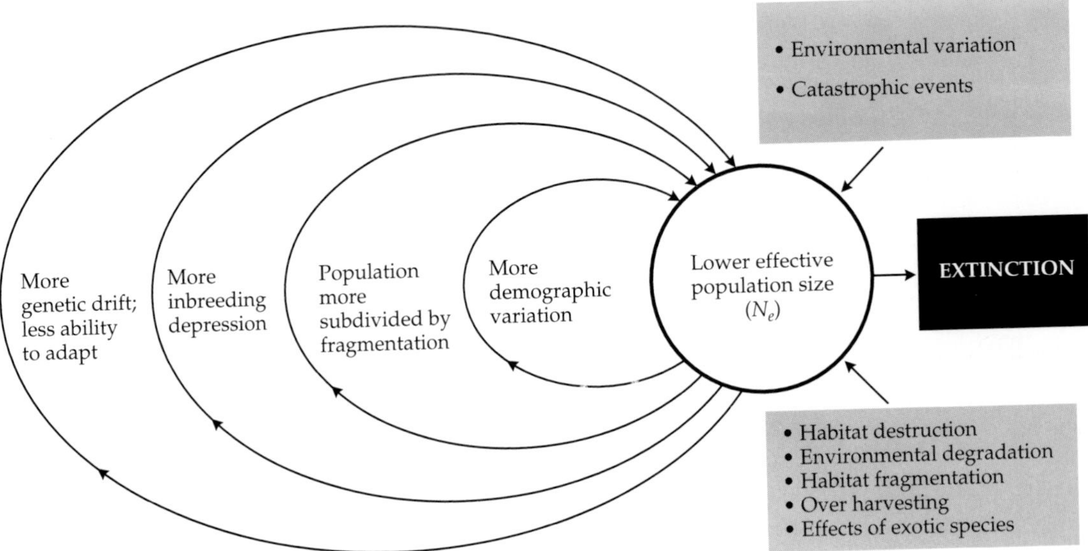

Figure 11.15 Extinction vortices progressively lower population size, leading to local extinctions of species. Once a population drops below a certain size, it enters a vortex, in which the factors that affect small populations tend to drive its size progressively lower. (After Gilpin and Soulé 1986 and Guerrant 1992.)

Sumatra in 1997 are the type of environmental events that drive small populations to extinction.

Once a population has declined to a small size, it will probably go extinct unless unusual and highly favorable conditions allow the population size to increase. Such populations require a careful program of population and habitat management to reduce demographic and environmental variation, and so minimize the effects of small population size.

Summary

1. Biologists have observed that small populations have a greater tendency to go extinct than large populations. Small populations are subject to a rapid extinction for three main reasons: loss of genetic variability, demographic fluctuations, and environmental variation or natural catastrophes.

2. As a population becomes smaller, it tends to lose genetic variability just by chance, a process known as genetic drift, leading to inbreeding depression and a lack of evolutionary flexibility. Experience with captive animals suggests that isolated populations should have at least 50 to 500 breeding individuals to maintain genetic variability, though 5000 individuals is preferable in wild populations.

3. The key to protecting small populations is the determination of effective population size based on the number of individuals that are actually producing offspring. The calculated effective population size is often much lower than simply the number of living individuals because (1) many individuals are not reproducing; (2) there may be an unequal sex ratio; (3) there may be variation among individuals in number of offspring produced; and (4) populations may show large fluctuations in size over time.

4. Variations in reproductive and mortality rates can cause small populations to fluctuate randomly in size, leading to extinction. Environmental variation can also cause random fluctuations in population size, with infrequent natural catastrophes sometimes causing major reductions.

5. Once a population's size has been reduced, it is even more vulnerable to random fluctuations in size and eventual extinction. The combined effects of demographic variation, environmental variation, and loss of genetic variability on small populations create an extinction vortex that tends to accelerate the drive to extinction.

For Discussion

1. Imagine a species that has four populations, consisting of 4, 10, 40, and 100 individuals. Using Wright's formula, calculate the loss in heterozygosity over 1, 2, 5, and 10 generations for each population. Calculate the effective population size for each population, assuming that there are equal numbers of males and females; then calculate assuming different proportions of males and females. Allow the population size of each group to fluctuate wildly around its average value. Calculate how this affects the loss of heterozygosity and the effective population size.

2. Construct a simple population model of a rare squirrel that has a stable population size (see page 304); then add environmental variation (such as severe winter storms or predation) and demographic variation (number of offspring produced per squirrel per year) and determine whether the population would be able to persist over time. Use the methods shown in the text, computer simulations, or random number generators (flipping coins is the easiest).

3. Find out about species that are currently endangered in the wild. How are they or how might they be affected by the problems of small populations? Address genetic, physiological, behavioral, and ecological aspects, as appropriate.

Suggested Readings

Avise, J. C. and J. L. Hamrick (eds.). 1996. *Conservation Genetics: Case Histories from Nature*. Chapman and Hall, New York. Leading experts present current knowledge of genetics for many groups of organisms.

Barrett, S. C. H. and J. R. Kohn. 1991. Genetic and evolutionary consequences of small population size in plants: Implications for conservation. In *Genetics and Conservation of Rare Plants,* D. A. Falk and K. E. Holsinger (eds.), pp. 3–30. Oxford University Press, New York. Excellent review of the genetics of small populations with numerous references to plant studies.

Berger, J. 1990. Persistence of different-sized populations: An empirical assessment of rapid extinctions in bighorn sheep. *Conservation Biology* 4: 91–98. A fine case study.

Caughley, G. and A. Gunn. 1996. *Conservation Biology in Theory and Practice.* Blackwell Science, Cambridge, MA. Strong presentation emphasizing quantitative analyses of vertebrate populations.

Falk, D. A. and K. E. Holsinger (eds.). 1991. *Genetics and Conservation of Rare Plants.* Oxford University Press, New York. Conservation efforts involving plants require some special considerations.

Frankham, R. 1996. Relationships of genetic variation to population size in wildlife. *Conservation Biology* 10: 1500–1508. Concise summary and literature review of 10 hypotheses.

Franklin, I. R. 1980. Evolutionary change in small populations. In *Conservation Biology: An Evolutionary-Ecological Perspective*, M. E. Soulé and B. A. Wilcox (eds.), pp. 135–149. Sinauer Associates, Sunderland, MA. Seminal paper outlining the problems of small populations.

Gilpin, M. E. and M. E. Soulé. 1986. Minimum viable populations: Processes of species extinction. In *Conservation Biology: The Science of Scarcity and Diversity*, M. E. Soulé (ed.), pp. 19–34. Sinauer Associates, Sunderland, MA. Excellent summary of the extinction vortices facing small populations.

Lacy, R. C. 1987. Loss of genetic diversity from managed populations: Interacting effects of drift, mutation, immigration, selection, and population subdivision. *Conservation Biology* 1: 143–158. Clearly presented simulations of various realistic scenarios.

Loeschcke, V., J. Tomiuk and S. K. Jain (eds.). 1994. *Conservation Genetics*. Birkhauser Verlag, Basel. The current state of knowledge in this important field.

Menges, E. S. 1992. Stochastic modeling of extinction in plant populations. In *Conservation Biology: The Theory and Practice of Nature Conservation, Preservation and Management*, P. L. Fiedler and S. K. Jain (eds.), pp. 253–275. Chapman and Hall, New York. Clear presentation of extinction models.

Packer, C. 1992. Captives in the wild. *National Geographic* 181 (4): 122–136. The story of Ngorongoro Crater lions. Natural history and genetics combined.

Ralls, K., P. H. Harvey and A. M. Lyles. 1986. Inbreeding in natural populations of birds and mammals. In *Conservation Biology: The Science of Scarcity and Diversity*, M. Soulé (ed.), pp. 35–56. Sinauer Associates, Sunderland, MA. Summarizes the evidence for inbreeding depression.

Schonewald-Cox, C. M., S. M. Chambers, B. MacBryde and L. Thomas (eds.). 1983. *Genetics and Conservation: A Reference for Managing Wild Animal and Plant Populations*. Benjamin/Cummings, Menlo Park, CA. Excellent set of early papers on the genetic problems of small populations.

Shaffer, M. L. 1981. Minimum population sizes for species conservation. *BioScience* 31 (2): 131–134. A key paper.

Soulé, M. E. (ed.). 1990. *Viable Populations for Conservation*. Cambridge University Press, Cambridge. Leading authorities discuss the problems of small populations.

Thornhill, N. W. (ed.) 1993. *The Natural History of Inbreeding and Outbreeding*. University of Chicago Press, Chicago. Field studies demonstrate that species avoid mating with close relatives.

CHAPTER 12

Applied Population Biology

HOW CAN CONSERVATION biologists determine whether a specific plan to manage an endangered or rare species has a good chance of succeeding? The ability of a species to persist in a protected area can often be predicted using standard methods of population biology and the newly developed mathematics of population viability analysis. These techniques can be used to estimate the minimum viable population (MVP) size, the smallest number of individuals needed to maintain a long-term population. Even without human disturbance, a population of any species can be stable, increasing, decreasing, or fluctuating in numbers of individuals. In general, widespread human disturbance destabilizes populations of native species, often sending them into sharp decline.

The key to protecting and managing a rare or endangered species is to have a firm grasp of the ecology of the species, its distinctive characteristics (sometimes called its

natural history), and the status of its populations and the dynamic processes that affect population size and distribution (its **population biology**). With more information concerning a rare species' natural history, land managers are able to more effectively maintain the species and identify factors that place it at risk of extinction.

The following categories of ecological questions elicit answers that provide important information for the implementation of effective population-level conservation efforts (Gilpin and Soulé 1986). For most species, only a few of these questions can be answered without further investigation. Yet management decisions may have to be made before this information is available or while it is being gathered.

- *Environment*. What are the habitat types where the species is found, and how much area is there of each? How variable is the environment in time and space? How frequently is the environment affected by catastrophic disturbance? How have human activities affected the environment?
- *Distribution*. Where is the species found in its habitat? Are individuals clustered together, distributed at random, or spaced out regularly? Do individuals of this species move and migrate among habitats or to different geographical areas over the course of a day or over a year? How efficient is the species at colonizing new habitats? How have human activities affected the distribution of the species?
- *Biotic interactions*. What types of food and other resources does the species need and how does it obtain them? What other species compete with it for these resources? What predators or parasites affect its population size? How have human activities altered the relationships among species in the community?
- *Morphology*. What does the species look like? What are its shape, size, color, surface texture, and the function of its parts? How does the morphology of the species change over its geographical range? Do all of the individuals in the population look the same? How does the shape of its body parts relate to their function and help the species to survive in its environment? How large are new offspring, and are they different in appearance from adults?
- *Physiology*. How much food, water, minerals, and other necessities does an individual need to survive, grow, and reproduce? How efficient is an individual at using its resources? How vulnerable is the species to extremes of climate, such as heat, cold, wind, and rain? When does the species reproduce, and what are its special requirements during reproduction?
- *Demography*. What is the current population size, and what was it in the past? Are the numbers of individuals stable, increasing, or decreasing? Does the population have a mixture of adults and juveniles, indicating that recruitment of new individuals is occurring?

- *Behavior.* How do the actions of an individual allow it to survive in its environment? How do individuals in a population mate and produce offspring? In what ways do individuals of a species interact, cooperatively or competitively?
- *Genetics.* How much variation occurs in morphological and physiological characteristics? How much of this variation is genetically controlled? What percentage of the genes are variable? How many alleles does the population have for each variable gene?

Gathering Ecological Information

The basic information needed for an effort to conserve a species or determine its status can be obtained from three major sources: published literature, unpublished literature, and fieldwork.

PUBLISHED LITERATURE Other people may have studied the same rare species (or a related species) or have investigated a habitat type. Library indices such as *BioSys, Biological Abstracts,* and *The Zoological Record* are often accessible by computer and provide easy access to a variety of books, articles, and reports. Sometimes sections of the library will have related material shelved together, so finding one book leads to others. Asking biologists and naturalists for ideas on references is another way to locate published materials. Checking indices of newspapers, magazines, and popular journals is also an effective strategy because results of important scientific research often appear first in the popular news media and are sometimes more clearly summarized there than in the professional journals.

Once one key reference is obtained, the bibliography often can be used to discover useful earlier references. *Science Citation Index*, available in many libraries, is a valuable tool for tracing the literature forward in time; for example, most of the recent scientific papers on the Hawaiian monk seal can be located by looking at the current *Science Citation Index* for the name W. K. Kenyon, who wrote several important papers about the Hawaiian monk seal between 1959 and 1981.

UNPUBLISHED LITERATURE A considerable amount of information on conservation biology is contained in unpublished reports by individuals, government agencies, and conservation organizations such as national and regional forest and park departments, government fisheries and wildlife agencies, The Nature Conservancy, the International Union for the Conservation of Nature, and the World Wildlife Fund. This so-called "gray literature" is sometimes cited in published literature or mentioned by leading authorities in conversations, lectures, or articles. For example, the unpublished series of Tropical Forest Action

Plans contains some of the most comprehensive sources of information on conservation in tropical countries. Often a report known through word of mouth can be obtained through direct contact with the author. In addition, conservation organizations are able sometimes to supply additional reports not found in the published literature. (A list of information sources is found in the Appendix.)

Scientific materials are increasingly available via the Internet on the World Wide Web, which is rapidly becoming a crucial research tool. At its best, the Internet can provide immediate access to high-quality, authoritative, current reports.

FIELDWORK The natural history of species usually must be learned through careful observations in the field. Fieldwork is necessary because only a tiny percentage of the world's species have been studied, and the ecology of a species often changes from one place to another. Only in the field can the conservation status of a species be determined, as well as its relationships to the biological and physical environment. Fieldwork for species such as the polar bear, the humpback whale, or tropical trees can be time-consuming, expensive, and physically arduous, but it is crucial for developing conservation plans for endangered species and exhilarating and deeply satisfying, as well. There is a long tradition, particularly in Britain, of dedicated amateurs conducting excellent studies of species in their immediate surroundings with minimal equipment and financial support. While much natural history information can be obtained through careful observation, many of the techniques are complicated and are best learned by studying under the supervision of an expert or reading manuals (Rabinowitz 1993; Heyer et al. 1994; Kricher 1998; Wilson and Cole 1998).

The need for natural history information is highlighted by a report on the conservation of the red panda, *Ailurus fulgens* (Figure 12.1). Despite the attractive appearance of this species, its unique taxonomic status within the mammals, and the threat of extinction over much of its Himalayan range, there was virtually no information about the field biology of the red panda until a study was conducted at Lantang National Park in Nepal (Yonzon and Hunter 1991). This study showed that the red panda is a specialist on fir-jhapra bamboo forests between 2800 and 3900 m, a habitat rare within the park. The population is probably less than 40 in the park and divided into at least 4 subpopulations. Red pandas produce only one cub per year, and these cubs suffer from a high mortality rate, mostly caused by human activities such as cattle grazing. The red panda has a low-quality diet consisting mainly of bamboo leaves, seasonally supplemented with fruits and mushrooms. This combination of natural history and population information demonstrates that the precarious existence of the red panda in the Himalayas is due to its specialized habitat requirements, low den-

tion and was focusing full time on "active conservation." Both her methods and her dismissal of science were criticized by some, but others saw her efforts as essential, even heroic, steps in salvaging a population at the brink of extinction. Under such conditions, her supporters argued, detailed scientific study is beside the point. The well-known zoologist George Schaller believes Fossey had her priorities in order: "When you have any kind of rare species, the first priority is to work for its protection. Science is necessarily secondary" (Morell 1986).

The contributions of these three scientists are, appropriately, threefold. First, they have created an astonishing body of knowledge on species that are our closest relatives. Second, they have made the international community aware of the dangerous plight of these species and have taken prominent, active, and self-sacrificing stands on behalf of the apes. Finally, they provide role models for young women, scientists, and students worldwide, inspiring them to enrich the scientific world with their own contributions.

Monitoring has a long history in temperate countries, particularly Britain (Goldsmith 1991), and plays an increasingly important role in conservation biology. In North America, the Breeding Bird Survey has been censusing bird abundance at approximately 1000 transects over the past 30 years, and this information is now being used to determine the stability of migrant songbird populations over time (James et al. 1996). Some of the most elaborate projects involve establishing permanent research plots in tropical forests, such as the 50-ha site at Barro Colorado Island in Panama, to monitor changes in species and communities (Condit et al. 1992). The Barro Colorado studies have shown that many tropical tree and bird species are more dynamic in numbers than had previously been suspected, suggesting that estimates of the minimum viable population size may need to be revised upward.

Monitoring studies are increasing dramatically as government agencies and conservation agencies have become more concerned with protecting rare and endangered species (Goldsmith 1991; Heywood 1995). Some of these studies are mandated by law as part of management efforts. A review of projects monitoring rare and endangered plants in the United States showed a phenomenal increase in the number of research projects initiated from 1974 to 1984; only one project was initiated from 1974 to 1976, whereas more than 120 projects were initiated from 1982 to 1984 (Palmer 1987). A follow-up study would almost certainly show an even greater increase of projects in the 1990s.

The most common types of monitoring conducted were inventories (40%) and population demographic studies (40%), with survey studies somewhat less frequently used (20%). Statistical analyses of monitoring studies often require special care since many of the studies were not designed with the conservation of species in mind (Eberhardt and Thomas 1991; Usher 1991).

INVENTORIES An **inventory** is a count of the number of individuals present in a population and is an inexpensive and straightforward method for conservation purposes. By repeating an inventory over successive time intervals, it can be determined whether the population is stable, increasing, or decreasing in numbers. An inventory of the only population of sweet bay magnolia (*Magnolia virginiana*) in Massachusetts (Primack et al. 1986) might answer such questions as: How many plants exist at present? Is the population stable in numbers during the period for which inventory records exist? Has the population increased during the last 15 years, when the overstory pine trees were cut to increase light levels? Are the plants fruiting, and are any seedlings present? Inventories of a community can be conducted to determine what species are currently present in a locality; a comparison of current occurrences with past inventories can highlight species that have been lost. Inventories conducted over a wide area can help to determine the range of a species and its areas of local abundance. Inventories taken over time can highlight changes in the range of species.

The most extensive inventories have been carried out in the British Isles by a large number of local amateur naturalists supervised by professional societies. The most detailed mapping efforts have involved plants, lichens, and birds, with presence or absence recorded in a mosaic of 10-km squares covering the British Isles. The Biological Records Centre (BRC) at Monks Wood Experimental Station maintains and analyzes the 4.5 million distribution records, which contain information on 16,000 species. One component of these efforts involved the Botanical Society in the British Isles Monitoring Scheme, in which the British Isles were intensively surveyed in 1987–1988 by 1600 volunteers, who collected one million records of all plant species occurrences on a 10-km square grid (Rich and Woodruff 1996). When the 1987–1988 data was compared with a detailed survey from 1930–1960, it was found that numerous species of grasslands, heathlands, and aquatic and swamp habitats had declined in frequency, while introduced weed species had increased (Figure 12.3).

SURVEYS A **survey** of a population involves using a repeatable sampling method to estimate the number of individuals or the density of a species in part of a community. An area can be divided into sampling segments and the number of individuals in certain segments counted. These counts can then be used to estimate the actual population size. For example, the number of Venus's-flytrap plants (*Dionaea muscipula*) can be counted in a series of 100 m × 2 m transects through a North Carolina savannah to establish the overall density of plants and then estimate the total population size in the 10,000 m^2 area. If there are an average of 30 plants in each of four such transects, the density would be 30 plants per 200 m^2, so in a total area of 10,000 m^2 the population

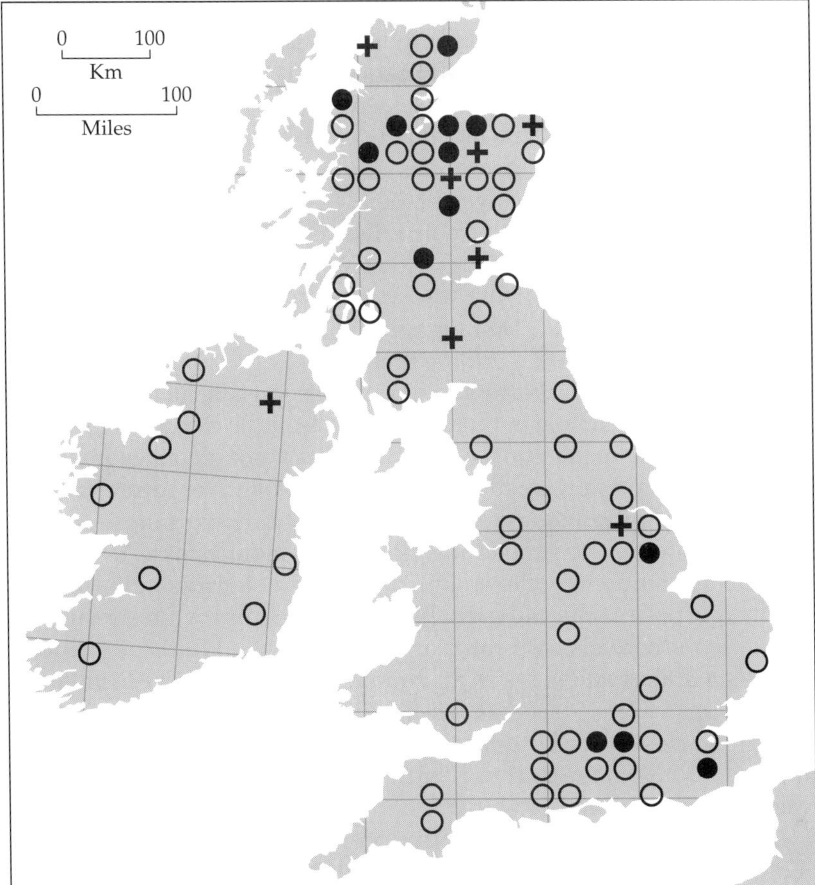

Figure 12.3 The British Isles Monitoring Scheme for *Gnaphalium sylvaticum,* the woodland cudweed. Large numbers of populations present in 1930–1960 were no longer present in 1987–1988 (open circles), particularly in Ireland and England. Many populations in Scotland persisted during this interval (black dots), and there were few new populations (crosses). (From Rich and Woodruff 1996.)

estimate would be 1500 plants. Similar methods can be used for different species in a variety of ecosystems; for instance, the number of crown-of-thorns starfish can be counted in a series of 10 m × 10 m quadrats to estimate the total starfish population on a coral reef. The number of bats caught in mist nets per hour or the density of a particular crustacean species per liter of seawater can also be counted.

Survey methods are used when a population is very large or its range is extensive. Although these methods are time-consuming, they are a methodical and repeatable way to examine a population and determine whether it is changing in size. Survey methods are particularly valuable when there are stages in the life cycle that are inconspicuous, tiny, or hidden, such as the seedling stages of many plants or the larval stages of aquatic invertebrates (Hutchings 1991). In the case of the Venus's-flytrap population, a series of small, 50 cm × 50 cm quadrats could be carefully censused to determine the density of tiny seedlings on the ground. Soil samples could be taken at fixed survey points and examined in the laboratory to determine the density of seeds expressed as the number of seeds per cubic cm of soil. Disadvantages of survey methods are that they may be expensive (chartering a vessel to sample deep-sea species), technically difficult (identifying poorly known immature stages in the life cycle), and inaccurate (sampling may miss or include infrequent aggregations of species). This is particularly true in the marine environment (Grassle 1991).

DEMOGRAPHIC STUDIES **Demographic studies** follow known individuals in a population to determine their rates of growth, reproduction, and survival. Individuals of all ages and sizes must be included in such a study. Either the whole population or a subsample can be followed. In a complete population study, all individuals are counted, aged if possible, measured for size, sexed, and tagged or marked for future identification; their position on the site is mapped, and tissue samples sometimes are collected for genetic analysis. The techniques used to conduct a population study vary depending on the characteristics of the species and the purpose of the study. Each discipline has its own technique for following individuals over time; ornithologists band birds' legs, mammalogists often attach tags to an animal's ear, and botanists nail aluminum tags to trees (see Goldsmith 1991). Information from demographic studies can be used in life history formulae to calculate the rate of population change and to identify critical stages in the life cycle (Menges 1986; Caswell 1989; Tuljapurkar and Caswell 1997).

Demographic studies provide the most information of any monitoring method and, when analyzed thoroughly, suggest ways in which a site can be managed to ensure population persistence. The disadvantages of demographic studies are that they are often time-consuming, expensive, and require repeated visits and a knowledge of the species' life history. For the Venus's-flytrap population, demographic data gathered over time can be used to predict whether the population will be present at different future dates and what the population size will be. If the population is predicted to go extinct, estimates can be made of the extent to which the survival and reproductive rates need to be increased through site management to maintain or enlarge the population. Populations showing a pattern of decline and populations predicted to decline in the future are cause for special concern and action to prevent their extinction.

Demographic studies can provide information on the age structure of a population. A stable population typically has an age distribution with a characteristic ratio of juveniles, young adults, and older adults. The absence or low representation of any age class, particularly of juveniles, may indicate that the population is in danger of declining. Conversely, a large number of juveniles and young adults may indicate that the population is stable or even expanding. However, it is difficult to determine the age of individuals for species such as plants, fungi, and colonial invertebrates. A small individual may be either young or slow-growing and old; a large individual may be either old or unusually fast-growing but young. For these species, the distribution of size classes is often taken as an approximate indicator of population stability, but this needs to be confirmed by following individuals over time to determine rates of growth and mortality. It is significant that for many long-lived species, such as trees, the establishment of new individuals in the population is an episodic event, with many years of low reproduction and an occasional year with abundant reproduction. Careful analysis of long-term data on changes in the population over time is needed in order to distinguish short-term fluctuations from long-term trends.

In general, populations are stable when the growth rate is zero, that is, when the average birth rate equals the average death rate. While a population with an average growth rate of zero is expected to be stable over time and a growth rate above zero should lead to an expanding population, random variation in population growth rates in different years can lead to population decline and extinction even with a positive average growth rate (see Chapter 11).

Demographic studies can also indicate the spatial characteristics of a species, which might be very important to maintaining the vitality of separate populations. The number of populations of the species, movement among populations, and the stability of these populations in space and time are all important considerations. This is particularly true for species that occur in an aggregate of temporary or fluctuating populations linked by migration, known as a **metapopulation**. Demographic studies can identify the core sites that support large, fairly permanent populations and supply colonists to temporary satellite areas. (Metapopulations are discussed in detail later in the chapter.)

Reproductive characteristics of populations—such as sex ratio, mating structure, percentage of breeding adults, and monogamous or polygamous mating systems—will also affect the success of conservation strategies and should be thoroughly analyzed. For example, a strategy to increase genetic diversity in a highly inbred population such as the lions of Ngorongoro Crater (see Chapter 11) might include introducing individuals from outside this population to mate with the inbred animals. If the "migrant" individuals do not fit into the social dynamics of the group, they may not breed and may even be driven out or killed by the native population.

Finally, demographic studies can supply clues to the maximum carrying capacity of the environment. These studies are important in determining how large a population the environment can support before it deteriorates and the population declines. Nature reserves may have abnormally large populations of certain species due to the recent loss of adjoining habitat or the inability of individuals to disperse from the nature reserve. Due to limited available space, many nature reserves are expected to support large populations over long periods of time. Data that help define the maximum carrying capacity of the reserves are crucial to preventing population and environmental stress, particularly in circumstances where natural population control mechanisms such as predators have been eliminated by humans.

Monitoring: Some Case Studies

A few case studies provide an overview of how the various monitoring techniques have been used in the field.

- *Butterflies.* Long-term trends in the abundance of butterfly species in the Netherlands were analyzed using an inventory of 230,000 butterfly records from 1901 to 1986 (van Swaay 1990). Of 63 species analyzed, 29 species (46%) have declined in abundance or gone extinct. Most of the species that have declined in this century occupied nutrient-poor grasslands that now have largely been converted to agriculture. Because these declining species overwinter as larvae and produce only one generation a year, they are vulnerable to land-use changes.

  In Britain, butterfly inventories have been carried out on a grid of 2 km × 2 km squares covering Hertfordshire County (Thomas and Abery 1995). This amazingly detailed study documents a surprisingly high rate of local extinction—66.9% of the 2-km squares occupied by particular species before 1970 had no current population of that species.

- *Hawaiian monk seals.* Population inventories of the Hawaiian monk seal (*Monachus schauinslandi*) on the beach at Kure Atoll have documented a decline from almost 100 adults in the 1950s to less than 14 in the late 1960s (Figure 12.4) (Gerrodette and Gilmartin 1990). The number of pups similarly declined during this period. On the basis of these trends, the Hawaiian monk seal was declared an endangered species in 1976 under the U.S. Endangered Species Act, and conservation efforts were implemented that reversed the trend for some populations.

- *The griffon vulture.* A severe decline in the population of the griffon vulture (*Gyps fulvus*) in northern Spain during the 1950s and 1960s led to strict protection of the species and its nesting sites, as well as banning the use of strychnine to kill pest animals (which were then eaten by griffon vultures). Repeated inventories have shown a steady recovery of the species in northern Spain from 282 breeding pairs in 23 colonies during 1969 to 1975, to 1097 breeding pairs in 46 colonies by 1989 (Donázar and Fernández 1990).

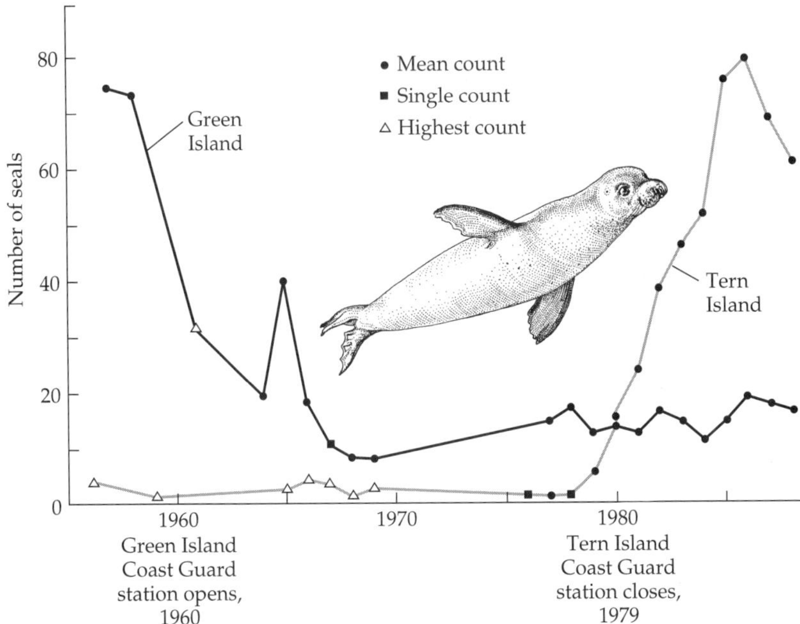

Figure 12.4 Inventories of Hawaiian monk seal populations on Green Island, Kure Atoll (black trace) and on Tern Island, French Frigate shoals (shaded trace) revealed that this species was in danger of extinction. Population counts were plotted from either a single count, the mean of several counts, or the maximum of several counts. Note the effect on seal populations of the Coast Guard stations on the islands. (After Gerrodette and Gilmartin 1990.)

- *Marine mollusks in South Africa.* In Transkeii, South Africa, coastal people collect and eat marine mollusks such as the brown mussel, the abalone, and the turban shell to supplement their diet (Lasiak 1991). To determine whether traditional collecting methods are likely to deplete shellfish populations, the frequency and size distribution of mollusks in protected and exploited rocky areas was compared in a survey. Even though collection depleted the adult populations in exploited areas, they were quickly replaced by larvae, probably due to immigration from nearby protected areas and adjacent, inaccessible subtidal areas.
- *The early spider orchid.* This orchid (*Ophrys sphegodes*) has shown a substantial decline in range during the past 50 years in Britain. A 9-year demographic study showed that the plants were unusually short-lived for perennial orchids, with only half of the individuals surviving beyond two years (Hutchings 1987). This short half-life makes the species unusually vulnerable to unfavorable habitat changes. In one population in which the species was declining in numbers, demographic analysis highlighted soil damage by cattle grazing as the primary cause of decline. A change in land management to sheep grazing (sheep grazing causes less soil damage than cattle grazing) and allowing the sheep to graze only when the orchids are not flowering and fruiting has enabled the population to make a substantial recovery.

Population Viability Analysis

Determining whether a species has the ability to persist in an environment requires **population viability analysis** (PVA), an extension of demographic analysis (Shaffer 1991; Boyce 1992; Akçakaya 1994; Ruggiero et al. 1994; Akçakaya et al. 1997). Population viability analysis can be thought of as risk assessment, using mathematical and statistical methods to predict the probability that a population or a species will go extinct at some point in the future. By looking at the range of a species' requirements and the resources available in its environment, vulnerable stages in the natural history of the species can be identified. PVA can be useful in considering the effects of habitat loss, habitat fragmentation, and habitat deterioration of a rare species. An important part of PVA is estimating how management efforts such as reducing (or increasing) hunting or increasing (or decreasing) the area of protected habitat will affect the probability of extinction. Population viability analysis may be particularly useful when investigating species characterized by populations that fluctuate widely in size.

Although PVA is still developing as an approach for examining species persistence and does not yet have a standard methodology or statistical framework (Burgman et al. 1993; Lacy and Lindemayer 1995), its goals of systematically and comprehensively examining species data are natural extensions of population biology, natural history research, and demographic studies. In this sense, the comprehensive research efforts made already to help manage populations of rare species such as the black-footed ferret, Furbish's lousewort, and the Florida panther can be considered the forerunners of PVA.

Using statistics to predict future trends in population sizes and the effects of human activities must be used with caution and a large dose of common sense (Harcourt 1995). The results of some models can often change dramatically with different model assumptions and slight changes in parameters. If the PVA approach can be developed to the point at which accurate predictions can be made concerning the ability of a rare species to survive in its current environment under different management strategies, it will become a central part of conservation strategies. Indeed, attempts to utilize population viability analysis as part of practical conservation efforts have already begun.

- *The crested mangabey.* One of the most thorough examples of PVA, combining both genetic and demographic analyses, is a study of the Tana River crested mangabey (*Cercocebus galeritus galeritus*), an endangered primate confined to the floodplain forests in a nature reserve along the Tana River in eastern Kenya (Figure 12.5) (Kinnaird and O'Brien 1991). As its habitat has been reduced in area and fragmented by agricultural activities and natural changes in the river's course in the last 15–20 years, the species has experienced a decline

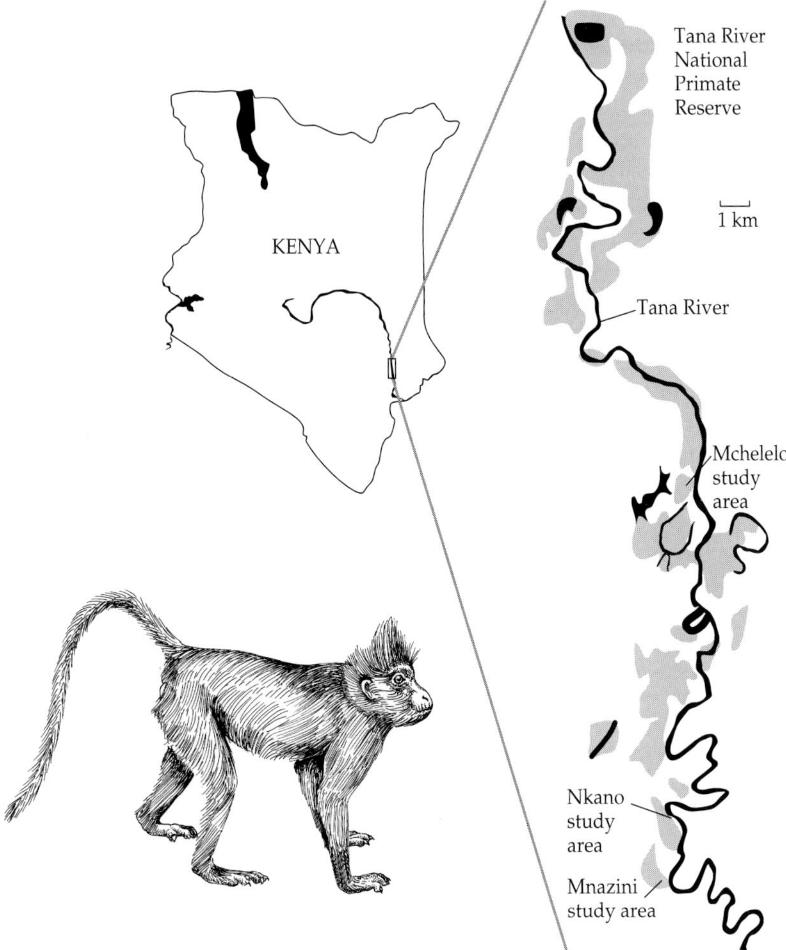

Figure 12.5 The Tana River National Primate Reserve, Kenya; remaining forested patches along the river are shaded gray. The Tana River crested mangabey occurs only in this region of East Africa and is increasingly endangered by forest fragmentation and human encroachment on its habitat. (From Kinnaird and O'Brien 1991.)

in overall population size of about 50%, as well as a decline in the number of groups. While the number of mangabeys in 1989 was about 700 individuals, the effective population size is only about 100, due to the large proportion of nonreproductive individuals and the variation in number of offspring produced by different individuals. With such a low effective population size, the mangabey is in danger of losing significant amounts of its genetic variation. To maintain an effective population size of 500 individuals—a number considered sufficient by some population geneticists to maintain genetic variability—a population of about 5000 mangabeys would have to be maintained. In addition, a demographic analysis of the population suggests that in the current situation, the probability of the population going extinct over the next 100 years is 40%. To ensure that the population has a 95% probability of persisting for 100 years, based on demographic factors alone, the population size would have to be almost 8000 individuals.

Both the genetic and the demographic analyses suggest that the long-term future of the present mangabey population is bleak. Given the restricted range and habitat of the species and the growing human population in the area, increasing the population size to 5000 to 8000 individuals is probably unrealistic. A management plan that combines increasing the area of protected forests, enrichment planting of existing forests to increase mangabey food plants, and establishment of corridors to facilitate movement between forest fragments might increase the survival probability of the Tana River crested mangabey.

- *Grizzly bears.* The grizzly bear (*Ursus arctos horribilis*) is an important symbol that seems (for many people) to capture the essence of North American wilderness. Efforts are being made to maintain populations in at least four areas of the western United States. Grizzlies present special management problems in national parks, since they are large (up to 1800 kg) and extremely powerful. Grizzly bears will attack and even kill humans who wander too close and violate the animal's "security zone," which may extend up to 100 m in radius for a mother with a cub.

  PVAs of grizzly bears have been made using estimates of environmental and demographic stochasticity. These models predict that grizzly populations must have at least 50 to 90 animals to be viable, defined in this case as a 95% chance of persisting for 100 years (Knight and Eberhardt 1985). Because of the wide-ranging nature of grizzly bears, even the largest national parks in the United States may be too small to maintain long-term populations of the species. Across its range, many of the small isolated populations of grizzly bears will go extinct, particularly due to mating failure at low population density, inbreeding depression, and genetic drift, unless gene flow is encouraged by facilitating movement of individual bears among populations (Allendorf and Servheen 1986). Efforts being made by the park managers to increase the park population will reduce this probability of extinction.

- *African elephants.* Conservation efforts on behalf of the African elephant (*Loxodonta africana*) have taken on international importance because of the species' precipitous decline in numbers and its symbolic importance as a representative of wildlife throughout the world. A population viability analysis of elephant populations in semiarid land at Tsavo National Park in Kenya indicated that a minimum reserve size of 2500 km^2 is needed to attain a greater than 99%

lowing three examples demonstrate how the metapopulation approach has proved to be more useful in understanding and managing species than a single-population description.

- *California mountain sheep.* Mountain sheep in the desert of southeastern California exhibit the shifting mosaic of populations best described as a metapopulation. Sheep have been observed migrating between mountain ranges and occupying previously unpopulated sites, while mountains that previously had sheep populations are now unoccupied (Figure 12.8).
- *Furbish's lousewort.* The endemic Furbish's lousewort (*Pedicularis furbishiae)* occurs along a 200-km stretch of the St. John's River in northern Maine and New Brunswick, Canada, subject to periodic flooding (Menges 1990). Flooding often destroys some existing populations of this herb species, but also creates exposed riverbank conditions suitable for establishing new populations. These populations eventually decline as the growth of shrubs and trees shade out the lousewort plants. Studies of any single population would give an incomplete picture of the species, because the current populations are short-lived. Dispersal of seeds from existing populations to newly exposed soil suitable for colonization is a feature of the species. The metapop-

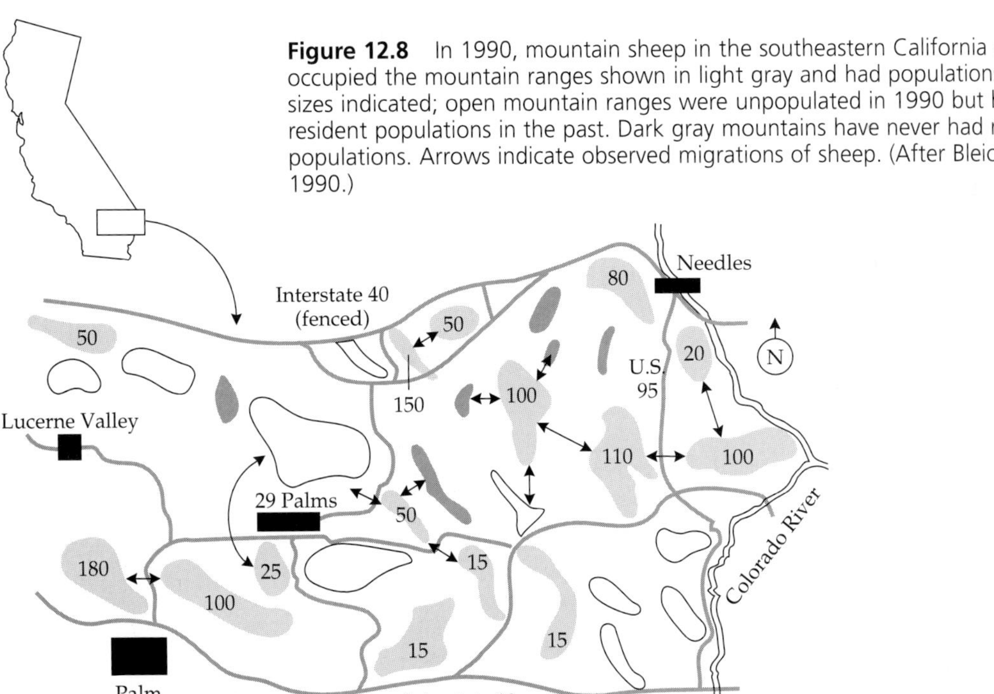

Figure 12.8 In 1990, mountain sheep in the southeastern California desert occupied the mountain ranges shown in light gray and had populations of the sizes indicated; open mountain ranges were unpopulated in 1990 but have had resident populations in the past. Dark gray mountains have never had resident populations. Arrows indicate observed migrations of sheep. (After Bleich et al. 1990.)

ulation is really the appropriate unit of study, and the watershed is the appropriate unit of management.

- *The European nuthatch.*This songbird (*Sitta europaea*) occupies fragments of forest ranging in area from 0.3 to 30 ha within the agricultural landscapes of western Europe (Verboom et al. 1991). Populations are dynamic in any one fragment, but populations in small fragments are more prone to extinction than populations in larger and better-quality fragments. The colonization rate of unoccupied forest fragments depends on the density of nuthatches in the surrounding forest patches.
- *Checkerspot butterflies.* These butterflies (*Euphydryas* spp.) have been studied extensively in California (Ehrlich and Murphy 1987; Murphy et al. 1990). Individual butterfly populations often become extinct, but dispersal and colonization of unoccupied habitat allow the species to survive in most years (Figure 12.9). Environmental stochasticity and a lack of habitat variation at a particular site often cause extinction in local populations. The largest and most persistent populations are found in large areas that have both moist north-facing slopes and warmer south-facing slopes. Butterflies migrating out from these core populations often colonize the unoccupied satellite areas.

In metapopulation situations, destruction of the habitat of one central, core population might result in the extinction of numerous smaller populations that depend on the core population for periodic colonization. Also, human disturbances that inhibit migration, such as fences, roads, and dams, might reduce the rate of migration among habitat patches and so reduce the probability of recolonization after local extinction. Habitat fragmentation resulting from these and other

Figure 12.9 Studies of the bay checkerspot butterfly (*Euphydryas editha bayensis*) have been used to demonstrate the metapopulation approach. Core populations of this species colonize unoccupied satellite areas during favorable years. (Photograph courtesy of Dennis Murphy, Stanford University.)

human activities sometimes has the effect of changing a large, continuous population into a metapopulation in which small, temporary populations occupy habitat fragments. When population size within each fragment is small and the rate of migration among fragments is low, populations within each fragment will gradually go extinct and recolonization will not occur (Lacy and Lindenmayer 1995; Lindenmayer and Lacy 1995).

Metapopulation models highlight the dynamic nature of population processes and show how the elimination of a few core populations or reducing the potential for migration could lead to the local extinction of a species over a much wider area. Effective management of a species often requires an understanding of these metapopulation dynamics and a restoration of lost habitat and dispersal routes (Hanski et al. 1996).

Long-Term Monitoring of Species and Ecosystems

The long-term monitoring of ecosystem processes (such as temperature, rainfall, humidity, soil acidity, water quality, discharge rates of streams, and soil erosion), communities (species present, percent vegetative cover, amount of biomass present at each trophic level, etc.), and population numbers (number of individuals present of particular species in populations and metapopulations of particular concern) is necessary to protect biological diversity, because it is difficult to distinguish normal year-to-year fluctuations from long-term trends (Magnuson 1990; Primack 1992).

For example, many amphibian, insect, and annual plant populations are highly variable from year to year, so many years of data are required to determine whether a particular species is actually declining in abundance over time or merely experiencing a number of low population years that are in accord with its regular pattern of variation. In one instance, a salamander species that initially appeared to be very rare on the basis of several years of low breeding numbers turned out to be quite common in a favorable year for breeding (Pechmann et al. 1991). In another instance, 40 years of observation populations of two flamingo species (*Phoenicopterus ruber*, the greater flamingo, and *Phoeniconaias minor*, the lesser flamingo) in southern Africa revealed that large numbers of chicks fledged only in years with high rainfall (Figure 12.10). However, the number of chicks fledging in the current populations is much lower than in the past, indicating that the species may be heading toward local extinction (Simmons 1996).

Another challenge to understanding change is the fact that effects may lag for many years behind their initial causes. For example, acid rain and other components of air pollution may weaken and kill trees over a period of decades, increasing the amount of soil erosion into

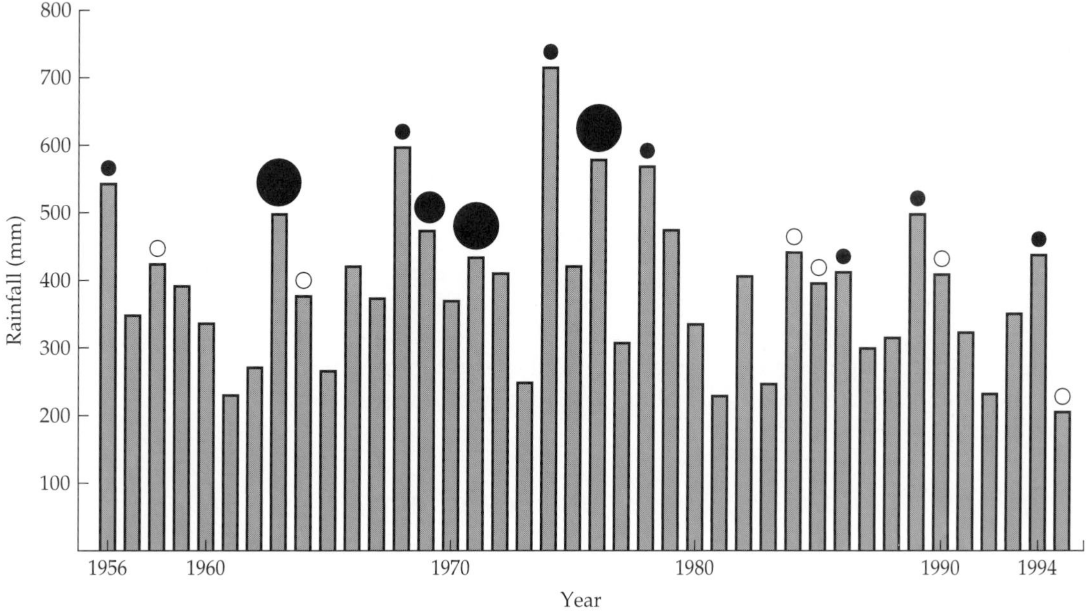

Figure 12.10 The bars show rainfall data from Etosha National Park for the years 1956–1995. The circles indicate that flamingo breeding events happened in those years. Open circles indicate failed breeding events: eggs were laid but no chicks hatched. The small, medium, and large black circles indicate, respectively, fewer than 100 chicks hatched, hundreds of chicks hatched, and thousands of chicks hatched. The last large hatching occurred in 1976. (From Simmons 1996.)

adjacent streams and ultimately making the aquatic environment unsuitable for the larvae of certain rare insect species. In this case, the cause (air pollution) may have occurred decades before the effect (insect decline) is detectable.

Acid rain, global climate change, vegetation succession, nitrogen deposition, and invasion of exotic species are all examples of processes often hidden from our short-term perspective that cause long-term changes in biological communities. Some long-term records are available from weather stations, annual census counts of birds, forestry plots, water authorities, and old photographs of vegetation, but the number of long-term monitoring efforts for biological communities is inadequate for most conservation purposes. To remedy this situation, many scientific research stations have begun to implement programs for monitoring ecological change over the course of decades and centuries. One program is the system of 172 Long-Term Ecological Research (LTER) sites established by the U.S. National Science Foundation (Figure 12.11) (Swanson and Sparks 1990). Other programs involve the United Nations Man and the Biosphere system of Biosphere Reserves and the increasing number of community-level permanent research plots being established in tropical forests (see Chapter 20) (Dallmeier 1992; Primack 1992).

A major purpose of these sites is to gather essential data on ecosys-

	Years	Research scales	Physical events	Biological phenomena
10^5	100 Millennia			Evolution of species
10^4	10 Millennia	Paleoecology and limnology ↓	Continental glaciation	Bog succession Forest community migration
10^3	Millennium		Climate change	Species invasion Forest succession
LTER 10^2	Century		Forest fires CO_2-induced climate warming	Cultural eutrophication
LTER 10^1	Decade			Population cycles
LTER 10^0	Year		Sun spot cycle El Niño events Prairie fires	Prairie succession Annual plants Seasonal migration
LTER 10^{-1}	Month	↑	Lake turnover Ocean upwelling	Plankton succession
10^{-2}	Day	Most ecology	Storms Daily light cycle	Algal blooms Daily movements
10^{-3}	Hour		Tides	

Figure 12.11 The Long-Term Ecological Research (LTER) program focuses on time scales ranging from years to centuries in order to understand changes in the structure, function, and processes of biological communities that are not apparent from short-term observations. (From Magnuson 1990.)

tem functions and biological communities that can be used to monitor changes in natural communities. Monitoring in these studies allows managers to determine if the goals of their projects are being achieved, or if adjustments have to made in the management plans. Increasingly, monitoring of biological diversity is being combined with the monitoring of social and economic characteristics of the same system, in recognition of the importance of people in conservation (Kremen et al. 1994; Bawa and Menon 1997). For example, the World Wildlife Fund's Biodiversity Conservation Network Program brings together biologists, social scientists, government officials, and local leaders to develop comprehensive monitoring programs for conservation projects. Such monitoring provides an early warning system for disruption or decline of ecosystem functions and the social systems of humans that depend on it. Magnuson (1990) has expressed the need as follows:

> In the absence of the temporal context provided by long-term research, serious misjudgments can occur not only in our attempts to understand and predict change in the world around us, but also in our attempts to manage our environment. Although serious accidents in an instant of mismanagement can be envisioned that might cause the end of Spaceship Earth (sensu Fuller 1970), destruction is even more likely to occur at a ponderous pace in the secrecy of the invisible present.

Summary

1. The key to protecting and managing a rare or endangered species is having a firm grasp of its ecology and its distinctive characteristics, sometimes called its natural history. The essential knowledge covers the species' environment, distribution, biotic interactions, morphology, physiology, demography, behavior, and genetics. This information can be obtained from the published and unpublished literature, or from fieldwork. Long-term monitoring of a species in the field can reveal temporal changes in population size and help to distinguish short-term fluctuations from long-term decline. Monitoring involves counting the population size and, in more complete studies, following individuals over time. Demographic studies are particularly valuable in calculating the long-term stability of populations.

2. Population viability analysis (PVA) uses demographic, genetic, environmental, and natural catastrophe data to estimate the probability of a population persisting in an environment. This analysis may determine the minimum viable population size, sometimes defined as the minimum population size necessary to give the population a 99% chance of persisting for 100 years. Population viability analysis is still developing needed methodologies and statistical techniques, but it shows considerable promise.

3. Many species of ephemeral habitats are characterized by metapopulations made up of a shifting mosaic of temporary populations that are linked by some degree of migration. In other species, the metapopulation may be characterized by one or more core populations with relatively stable numbers and several satellite areas with unstable, temporary populations.

4. Long-term monitoring efforts are now being developed throughout the world to follow changes in populations and communities over the course of decades and centuries. These programs will provide an early warning system for damage to species, communities, and ecosystem functions.

For Discussion

1. Read the paper on Tana River mangabey by Kinnaird and O'Brien (1991) or another population viability analysis study. What are the strengths and weaknesses of PVA?

2. Construct models of various metapopulations, using Figure 12.7 as a starting point. The simplest model would be an infinitely large core population that continuously sends out colonists to a satellite population that is regularly destroyed by a catastrophic event such as a hurricane. Then include random variation in the frequency of hurricanes (destroying the population on average once every 4 years) and rate of colonization (sending out colonists on average once every 4 years). How realistic are such models?

3. Construct your own population viability analysis of an endangered toad species. This species formerly occupied many large islands, but now occupies only one small, isolated island in the middle of the Atlantic Ocean. There are presently 10 toads on the island, and the island can support a maximum of 20 toads. In the spring, males and females form mating pairs, and each pair can produce 0, 1, 2, 3, 4, or 5 offspring, all of which survive and reach maturity the following year (for example, flip 5 coins for each mated pair; the number of heads is the number of offspring). Individuals not mated because of uneven sex ratios do not breed. After breeding, the toads die. The sex of the offspring

is assigned at random (for example, flip a coin for each animal with heads for males and tails for females, or use a random number generator or simulation software such as STELLA).

Run 10 population simulations for 10 generations each and chart population size over time. What percentage of populations go extinct? Try making the conditions more severe by lowering the island's carrying capacity to 15 (or even 10) or by imposing a 50% mortality on offspring every third year due to an introduced rat. Examine the impact of supplying extra food to the toads, allowing more offspring to be produced per breeding pair. Make different variants of this basic model, corresponding to different ecological, genetic, and life history constraints. Use a computer program if possible.

Example: *A 2-year simulation for the island toad*

Year 1 (Initial Population = 10)

Toads alive in spring	Sex (assigned at random)	Number of the breeding pair	Number of offspring
1	M	1	0
2	F	2	4
3	M	3	3
4	M	4	1
5	F		
6	F		
7	M		
8	F		
9	F		
10	F		
Population size 10		4 pairs	8

Year 2

Toads alive in spring	Sex (assigned at random)	Number of the breeding pair	Number of offspring
1	M	1	4
2	F	2	1
3	M	3	2
4	F		
5	M		
6	M		
7	M		
8	F		
Population size 8		3 pairs	7

Suggested Readings

Akçakaya, H. R. 1994. *RAMAS/GIS: Linking Landscape Data with Population Viability Analysis* (Version 1.0). Applied Biomathematics, Setauket, NY. Software that can be used to teach, demonstrate, and analyze mathematical aspects of conservation biology at the population and landscape levels.

Akçakaya, H. R., M. A. Burgman and L. R. Ginzburg. 1997. *Applied Population Ecology: Using RAMAS Ecoloab*. Applied Biomathematics, Setauket, NY. Quantitative principles of population biology are applied to conservation biology, using the Ecolab software.

Boyce, M. S. 1992. Population viability analysis. *Annual Review of Ecology and Systematics* 23: 481–506. Review of developments in this field.

Burgman, M. A., S. Ferson and H. R. Akçakaya. 1993. *Risk Assessment in Conservation Biology*. Chapman and Hall, London. Thorough, well-written text on population viability analysis for the serious student.

Fossey, D. 1990. *Gorillas in the Mist*. Houghton Mifflin, Boston. Read the book, then watch the movie. Was she courageous or crazy?

Galdikas, B. 1995. *Reflections of Eden: My Years with the Orangutans of Borneo*. Little-Brown, Boston. A personal approach to conservation by an unusual person.

Goldsmith, B. (ed.). 1991. *Monitoring for Conservation and Ecology*. Chapman and Hall, New York. Purpose and methods of conservation monitoring, clearly explained.

Hanski, I., A. Moilanen and M. Gyllenberg. 1996. Minimum viable metapopulation size. *American Naturalist* 147: 527–541. The applicability of metapopulation theory to conservation strategies. Also check out other articles by Hanski.

Kinnaird, M. F. and T. G. O'Brien. 1991. Viable populations for an endangered forest primate, the Tana River crested mangabey (*Cercocebus galeritus galeritus*). *Conservation Biology* 5: 203–213. Excellent case study demonstrating application of population viability analysis.

Kricher, J. 1998. *A Neotropical Companion*. Princeton University Press, Princeton, NJ. A good place to begin learning tropical natural history.

Lacy, R. C. and D. B. Lindenmayer. 1995. A simulation study of the impacts of population subdivision on the mountain brushtail possum *Trichosurus caninus* Ogilby (Phalangeridae: Marsupialia) in South-eastern Australia. II. Loss of genetic variation within and between populations. *Biological Conservation* 73: 131–142. This article and others in this issue give excellent examples of population viability analysis and metapopulation models.

Magnuson, J. J. 1990. Long-term ecological research and the invisible present. *BioScience* 40: 495–501. Long-term research provides important insights not apparent in short-term studies.

McCullough, D. R. (ed.). 1996. *Metapopulations and Wildlife Conservation*. Island Press, Washington, D. C. Case studies of important vertebrate species.

Murphy, D. D., K. E. Freas and S. B. Weiss. 1990. An environment-metapopulation approach to population viability analysis for a threatened invertebrate. *Conservation Biology* 4: 41–51. Excellent introduction to the metapopulation concept.

Primack, R. B. and P. Hall. 1992. Biodiversity and forest change in Malaysian Borneo. *BioScience* 42: 829–837. The conservation, policy, and management implications of tropical community studies. See other monitoring studies in the same issue.

Rich, T. C. G. and E. R. Woodruff. 1996. Changes in the vascular plant floras of England and Scotland between 1930–1960 and 1987–1988; the BSBI monitoring scheme. *Biological Conservation* 75: 217–229. Monitoring with an astonishing degree of precision.

Schemske, D. W., B. C. Husband, M. H. Ruckelshaus, C. Goodwillie, I. M. Parker and J. M. Bishop. 1994. Evaluating approaches to the conservation of rare and endangered plants. *Ecology* 75: 584–606. Monitoring populations is crucial to the evaluation of conservation efforts.

Tuljapurkar, S. and H. Caswell (eds.). 1997. *Structured-Population Models in Marine, Terrestrial, and Freshwater Systems*. International Thompson Publishing, Florence, KY. An advanced treatment of demographic analysis.

Wilson, D. E. and R. F. Cole. 1998. *Measuring and Monitoring Biological Diversity: Standard Methods for Mammals*. Smithsonian Institution Press, Washington, D.C. The latest in a series explaining standard methods for gathering, analyzing, and presenting field data.

CHAPTER 13

Establishing New Populations

RATHER THAN PASSIVELY observing endangered species decline toward extinction, many conservation biologists are developing approaches to save these species. Some exciting conservation methods involve establishing new wild and semiwild populations of rare and endangered species and increasing the size of existing populations. These important new approaches allow species living only in captivity or in small, isolated populations to regain their ecological and evolutionary roles within the biological community. Widely dispersed populations in the wild may be less likely to be destroyed by catastrophes (such as earthquakes, hurricanes, disease, epidemics, or war) than confined captive populations or isolated populations occupying only a small area. Furthermore, increasing the number and size of populations for a species will generally reduce the probability of its extinction. Many species benefit from the complementary approaches of establishing new populations in the wild and captive breeding programs.

Reestablishment programs are unlikely to be effective, however, unless the factors leading to the decline of the original wild populations are clearly understood and eliminated, or at least controlled (Kleiman 1989; Gipps 1991; Bowles and Whelan 1994). For example, bird species have been eliminated from Pacific islands because of predation by the introduced brown snake (see Figure 10.5). In a successful reestablishment program, the snake has to be removed from the island, or the nests have to be protected from the snake in some way. Alternatively, the birds could be introduced onto another island where there are no snakes. If a marine turtle species is hunted to near extinction in the wild by local villagers, its eggs collected for food, and its nesting beaches damaged by development, these social and economic issues must be addressed as an integral part of the reestablishment program. Simply releasing captive-bred turtle hatchlings into the wild without discussions with local people would produce the same crisis (Frazer 1992). A crucial initial step in establishing new populations is to locate suitable unoccupied sites for the species or to create new sites.

Three basic approaches have been used to establish new populations of animals and plants. A **reintroduction program** involves releasing captive-bred or wild-collected individuals into an ecologically suitable site within their historic range where the species no longer occurs. The principal objective of a reintroduction program is to create a new population in its original environment. For example, a recently implemented plan to reintroduce gray wolves into Yellowstone National Park aims to restore the equilibrium of predators and herbivores that existed prior to human intervention in the region (Box 22). Frequently, individuals are released near the site where they or their ancestors were collected to ensure genetic adaptation to their environment. Individuals are also sometimes released elsewhere within the range of the species when a new protected area has been established, when an existing population is under a new threat and will no longer be able to survive in its present location, or when natural or artificial barriers to the normal dispersal tendencies of the species exist.

Unfortunately, some confusion exists about the terms denoting the reintroduction of populations. These programs sometimes are called "reestablishments" or "restorations." Another term, "translocation," usually refers to moving individuals from a location where they are about to be destroyed to another site that often provides a greater degree of protection.

There are two other distinct types of release programs. An **augmentation program** involves releasing individuals into an existing population to increase its size and gene pool. These released individuals may be raised in captivity or may be wild individuals collected elsewhere.

Box 22 **Wolves Return to a Cold Welcome**

When conservationists speak of saving endangered animal species, the creatures that come to mind are usually those whose very existence hangs in the balance. Species such as the California condor, with only around 120 remaining individuals, or the giant panda, whose numbers are estimated at less than 1100, receive most of the headlines because of the immediacy of the threat. The ultimate goal of conservation, however, is to restore ecosystems to their previous balanced, functional state.

Until recently, Yellowstone National Park was an ecosystem out of balance, largely due to the systematic extermination of gray wolf (*Canis lupus*) populations in the late 1800s and early 1900s. Wolves were believed to pose a threat to the herds of elk and other game animals inhabiting the park. The result of their extinction was a burgeoning population of elk and other herbivores, which damaged vegetation and starved during times of scarcity. When the U.S. Fish and Wildlife Service proposed in 1987 that the gray wolf be reintroduced into Yellowstone National Park and surrounding government lands, opposition erupted immediately. Ranchers in Montana, Wyoming, and Idaho argued that wolves would destroy livestock and possibly endanger humans as well (Fischer 1995). Hunters objected that wolves would reduce the supply of game animals, and logging and mining companies were concerned that the presence of a protected species would limit their ability to utilize resources on federal lands. Underpinning their objections is the argument that the wolf, with an estimated population of 50,000 in Canada alone, is in no immediate danger of extinction. Furthermore, wolves have been steadily recolonizing the northern states, including Wisconsin and Michigan.

From a biological perspective, however, the wolf is necessary to restore ecological balance in Yellowstone. Wolves may be able to maintain the health of the elk herds by removing older, sick, and weak animals and keeping population levels below the environmental carrying capacity. Without these predators, herbivore herds become so dense that hundreds can starve in a winter. Releasing wolves into the park and carefully documenting their effect on elk behavior and numbers allows these ideas to be tested.

Academic debate about the impact of releasing wolves in Yellowstone has now become concrete. Two complete wolf packs, as well as a few individuals, have been transferred from Canada to the park. The wolves were held in a large pens for

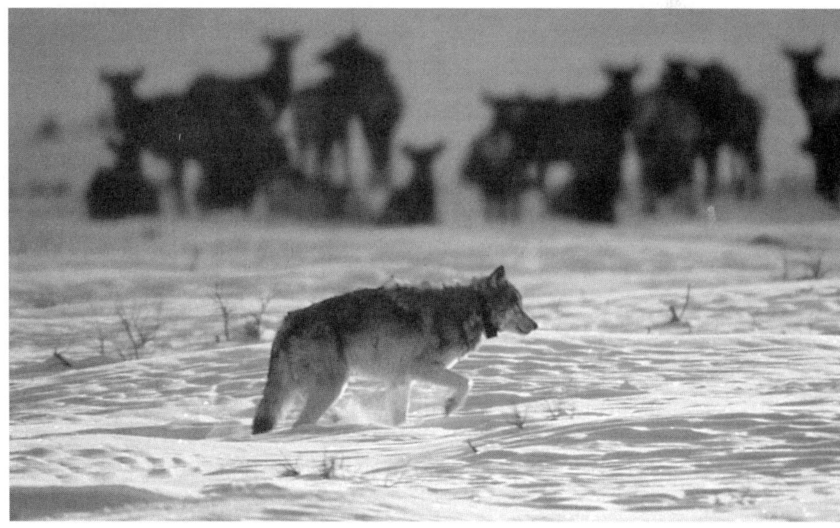

A gray wolf stalks an elk herd in Yellowstone National Park. As a result of the wolves' presence, elk have changed their behavior, congregating in dense herds and becoming more alert to danger. (Photograph by Bill Campbell.)

Box 22 (continued)

several weeks to adapt to their surroundings before being released in 1995 and 1996. The wolves adapted well to the park, hunting prey and producing pups. As of January 1998, a total of 90 free-ranging wolves have formed 9 packs, and most reside almost exclusively within the park. Because of the good health of the animals, there are large numbers of pups and an expanding wolf population.

The wolves' activities are reshaping the ecological structure of the park. Elk are congregating in larger herds, and wolves have been seen fighting grizzly bears. The availability of carrion from wolf kills is affecting the dynamics of scavengers from grizzlies to carrion beetles. Perhaps most importantly, wolves are having an impact on coyotes, which were the top predators in the absence of a wolf population. Wolves are killing coyotes and their pups, forcing them to change their denning behavior and driving them out of some areas. This may directly benefit ranchers, as coyotes are known to attack livestock. As one of the major attractions of Yellowstone National Park, wolves are having a positive economic impact as the featured subject of books and souvenirs sold to park visitors.

Fears that wolves would kill large numbers of livestock remain largely unfounded. No livestock were killed in 1995, and only 12 sheep had been killed as of September 1996—a tiny number considering the scale of the project. An organization called Defenders of Wildlife has assumed responsibility for compensating ranchers for verified wolf kills, but reactions by ranchers in the areas surrounding Yellowstone remain mixed. Wolves that attack livestock on private land have been captured, held for a period in the pens, and then released onto government lands. Wolves suspected of killing livestock have also been shot. As the wolf population grows, however, so will the potential for depredations beyond park boundaries and for further conflict with ranchers.

The controversy surrounding the reestablishment of the wolf in Yellowstone reflects a dilemma central to conservation biology: how to balance environmental needs with human demands. When the survival of a species is at risk, conservationists have an urgency to their arguments that tips the balance in favor of the environment. In the case of the wolf, however, the problem is not so clear-cut. People directly affected by the reestablishment are unwilling to accommodate the wolf without a compelling reason; restoring ecological equilibrium does not yet rank so high in their minds.

An **introduction program** involves moving animals and plants to areas suitable for the species outside their historic range (Conant 1988). This approach may be appropriate when the environment within the known range of a species has deteriorated to the point where the species can no longer survive there, or when reintroduction is impossible because the factor causing the original decline is still present. Again, these may be captive-bred or wild-collected individuals.

The introduction of a species to new sites needs to be carefully thought out in order to ensure that the species does not damage its new ecosystem or harm populations of any local endangered species. Care must be taken that released individuals have not acquired any diseases while in captivity that could spread to and decimate wild populations. Also, a species may adapt genetically to its new environment so that the original gene pool is not actually being preserved.

New populations can be established using different approaches and experimental treatments that give insight into why the species declined in the first place. For example, an experiment involving establishing two new populations of a rare antelope species might involve either giving supplemental food and water to one group of animals while they learn about their new habitat or, alternatively, *not* giving extra food and water to the second group of animals. An example with plants might involve planting individuals either into a habitat from which competing plants have been removed or into an intact, unmodified habitat. By carefully monitoring such experiments, existing management techniques can be evaluated and new techniques developed. These management techniques can then be applied to better manage existing natural populations of the species.

Behaviors of Released Animals

To be successful, reintroduction and introduction programs must address the behaviors of animals that are being released (Kleiman 1989; Olney et al. 1994; Curio 1996; Clemmons and Buchholz 1997). When social animals, particularly mammals and some bird species, grow up in the wild, they learn from other members of their population—particularly their parents—about their environment and how to interact with other members of their species. In the wild, these social animals learn how to search their environment for food and how to capture, gather, and consume food. For carnivores such as lions and wild dogs, hunting techniques are complex, subtle, and require considerable teamwork. Herbivores like hornbills and gibbons must learn seasonal migration patterns that cover a wide area to obtain the variety of food items necessary to stay alive and reproduce. The knowledge of how to find and recognize food is often taught in family groups, and many species have distinctive cues or rituals that must be performed to attract a mate.

When mammals and birds are raised in captivity, their environment is limited to a cage or pens, so exploration is unnecessary. Searching for food and learning about new food sources is not needed, since the same food items come day after day on schedule. Social behavior may become highly distorted when animals are raised alone or in unnatural social groupings (i.e., single-gender or single-age groups). In such cases, animals may lack the skills to survive in their natural environment and the social skills necessary to cooperatively find food, sense danger, find mating partners, and raise young.

To overcome these behavioral problems, captive-raised mammals and birds may require extensive training before and after release into the environment (McLean et al. 1996). They must learn how to find food and shelter, avoid predators, and interact in social groups. Training techniques have been developed for several mammals and a few

Figure 13.1 Captive golden lion tamarins learn skills needed for life in the wild, in this case, the animals must find food inside a complicated puzzle box. (Photograph by Jessie Cohen, National Zoological Park, Smithsonian Institution.)

birds. Captive chimps, for instance, have been taught how to use twigs to feed on termites and to build nests in captivity. Red wolves are taught how to kill live prey. Golden lion tamarins are given complex food boxes to gain skill at opening wild fruit (Figure 13.1). Captive animals are taught to fear potential predators by being frightened in some way when a dummy predator is shown.

Social interaction is one of the most difficult behaviors to teach captive-bred mammals and birds, because for most species the subtleties of social behavior are poorly understood. Nevertheless, some successful attempts have been made to socialize captive-bred mammals. Wild individuals sometimes are used as "instructors" for the captive individuals of the same species. For instance, wild-bred golden lion tamarins may be paired with captive-bred tamarins to form social groups. They are then released together, in the hope that the captive-bred tamarins will learn from the wild ones (Box 23). In other cases, humans mimic the appearance and behavior of the wild species. This method is particularly important when dealing with very young animals. For example, captive-bred condor hatchlings were originally unable to learn the behaviors of their wild relatives because they had imprinted on their human keepers. Newly hatched condors are now fed with condor puppets and kept from the sight of visitors so they learn to identify with their own species rather than a foster species or humans (Box 24).

When captive-bred animals are released into the wild, they sometimes join existing social groups or mate with wild animals and so gain some knowledge of their environment. The development of social rela-

Box 23 **The Golden Lion Tamarin**

The fiery red-orange fur and playful mannerisms of the golden lion tamarin (*Leontopithecus rosalia*) have made it the darling of the pet and zoo industry. The charm of this small primate could not save it from a precipitous decline in numbers, however, as its Atlantic coastal rain forest habitat in Brazil became fragmented or disappeared altogether as a result of human activities. By the early 1970s, there were estimated to be fewer than 500 golden lion tamarins left in the wild in small isolated populations, and fewer than 75 in zoos around the world. After considerable research on captive husbandry and behavior, increased numbers of breeding golden lion tamarins in zoos made them an excellent choice for reintroduction efforts. In addition, their charisma made them an excellent flagship species to promote regional conservation (Dietz et al. 1994).

Valuable lessons were learned from the failure of initial release efforts. Captive-born tamarins lacked the skills necessary to forage, avoid predators, navigate, and interact socially with other golden lion tamarins. Most tamarins released in the first two years were lost to predators or disease, or were simply unable to find their way back to their social groups. Virtually no reproduction took place. In addition, many factors that had contributed to their decline, such as human predation, still existed. The Golden Lion Tamarin Conservation Program, coordinated by the National Zoological Park and Smithsonian Institution, issued a mission statement that addressed the many facets involved in promoting regional conservation. Their stated goals included maximizing the probability of golden lion tamarin survival in the wild, increasing public awareness and involvement in conservation efforts, and coordinating efforts with other conservation programs. The long-term goal of the project is to establish 20,000 ha of protected habitat with a self-sustaining population of 2000 golden lion tamarins.

Reintroduction of golden lion tamarins is a complex undertaking. First, biologists must ensure that the captive population has the ability to find food, shelter, and mates before removing individuals for release into the wild; without training, they may be unable to fit into either their habitat or the arena of tamarin social behavior. Second, the genetic diversity and reproductive potential of the captive population must be maintained. Finally, the survival of reintroduced tamarins depends upon the elimination or reduction of those factors that originally led to their decline in the wild.

Reintroduction efforts have addressed each of these concerns. A biennial review keeps track of the captive populations of the golden lion tamarin, monitors infant mortality, and makes recommendations for which animals should be mated to maintain genetic diversity (Ballou 1995). Animals are released into areas that contain suitable habitat but no longer contain golden lion tamarin populations. Early in the program, captive animals were taught survival skills before release, given free-ranging experience in forests to learn how to locomote on natural vegetation and presented food in a variety of boxes and compartments that required the tamarins to exercise persistence and dexterity (see Figure 13.1). Success rates following release were very low, however. Now, captive tamarins are released only after being given free-ranging experience in outdoor forest areas in zoos to learn how to move around in natural vegetation. They are fed at feeding stations for their first 18 months in the wild (a "soft release") while they learn to forage and move through the forest on their own (Kleiman

The logo used for the Poço das Antas Biological Reserve in Brazil was designed to increase public awareness of the Golden Lion Tamarin Project. (From Kleiman 1989.)

Box 23 (continued)

1989). Wild tamarin "teachers" are also used; captive-born animals paired and released together with wild-caught tamarins acquire survival skills much more quickly than captive animals released without a tutor. As reintroduction techniques improved, so did the success rate. The free-ranging tamarins began to reproduce, and the young born in the wild learned to find food and orient even more quickly than their captive-born parents.

Brazil's Poço das Antas Biological Reserve was the first site for the reintroduction effort, but initial losses made it clear that additional public support was necessary. Over 20% of tamarin disappearances were due to human activity, primarily poaching. Through public service announcements on radio and television, educational programs in public schools, production of audiovisual materials, and other methods biologists and educators increased public awareness not only of the plight of the tamarin, but also of broader conservation efforts centered around the reserve. The tamarin, an animal with an attractive and charismatic appearance, provided a focal point for garnering public support for the reserve and appears on the logo of the reserve and the conservation program. Landlords whose past activities have damaged unprotected forest lands are encouraged by these educational programs, as well as by direct discussions with biologists, to find alternative uses for their land that will not degrade the forest. As a result, public awareness of the plight of the tamarins has increased significantly. Thirteen privately owned ranches adjoining the reserve have even agreed to become partners in the project, increasing the area of protected habitat by 43%.

Between 1984 and 1996, 147 golden lion tamarins were released, most on private lands. Only 22 of the original animals were surviving as of December 1996. However, a total of 268 infants had been born to released tamarins, of which 176 survived. The proportion of the reintroduced population that was born in the wild is now over 88% and continues to rise (Beck and Martins 1995). The high reproductive rate and the ability of wild-born young to survive suggests that the reintroduced tamarin population is well on its way to becoming self-sustaining. Tamarins from this program now comprise about 28% of the total protected wild population, which still, however, numbers fewer than 800 individuals. Most importantly, the reintroduced tamarins are a source of pride to landowners who have them in their forests. When asked "What would you show a newcomer?" local people once answered "Nothing. All we have here is forest" (Dietz et al. 1994). Conservation and education efforts are ensuring that the local people will know that they have much, much more in their environment.

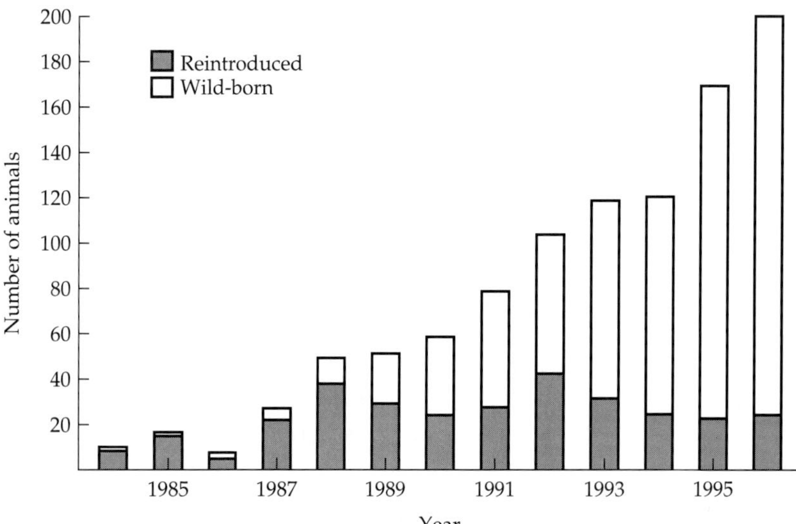

The proportion of the tamarin population that was born in the wild to reintroduced animals is close to 90%. This seems to indicate a successful program and a population that could soon become self-sustaining. (From Beck and Martins 1995.)

Figure 13.2 The Arabian oryx (*Oryx leucoryx*), almost extinct in the wild, is being reintroduced to places in its former range, such as Oman. (Photograph by Ron Garrison, San Diego Zoo.)

tion of the last remaining fragments of the Atlantic coastal forest (Box 23). In Oman, captive-bred Arabian oryx were successfully reintroduced into desert areas, creating an important national symbol and a source of employment for the local Bedouins who run the program (Figure 13.2) (Stanley-Price 1989).

Establishment programs for common game species have always been widespread and have contributed a great deal of knowledge for the development of new programs for threatened and endangered species. A detailed study examined 198 bird and mammal establishment programs conducted between 1973 and 1986 and supported a number of significant generalizations (Griffith et al. 1989):

1. Success was greater for game species (86%) than for threatened, endangered, and sensitive species (44%).
2. Success was greater for releases in excellent quality habitat (84%) than in poor quality habitat (38%).
3. Success was greater in the core of the historic range (78%) than at the periphery of and outside the historic range (48%).

4. Success was greater with wild-caught (75%) than with captive-reared animals (38%).
5. Success was greater for herbivores (77%) than for carnivores (48%).

For these bird and mammal species, the probability of establishing a new population increased with the number of animals being released up to about 100. Releasing more than 100 animals did not further enhance the probability of success. These results were confirmed by a subsequent update and reanalysis of the data in 1993 (Wolf et al. 1996).

A second survey of reintroduction projects (Beck et al. 1994) used a more restricted definition of reintroduction: the release of captive-born animals within the historic range of the species. A program was judged a success if there was a self-maintaining population of 500 individuals. Using this restricted and more appropriate definition, only 16 out of 145 reintroduction projects were judged successful—a dramatically lower rate of success than the earlier survey. According to this new study, the key to success involves releasing large numbers of animals over many years. A survey of more than 400 releases of short-lived fish species into wild habitats of the western United States showed a success rate of around 26%, though incomplete information on many species made compiling and evaluating the results extremely difficult (Hendrick and Brooks 1991). Reintroductions and translocations of endangered amphibians and reptiles appear to have an extremely low rate of success, perhaps due to highly specialized habitat requirements (Dodd and Seigel 1991).

Clearly, monitoring ongoing programs is crucial in determining whether efforts to establish new populations are achieving their stated goals. Key elements of monitoring involve determining if released individuals survive and establish a breeding population and then following that population over time to see if it increases in numbers of individuals and geographical range. Monitoring may need to be carried out over many years, even decades, because many reintroductions that initially appear successful eventually fail. For example, a reintroduction of topminnows into a stream in the western United States resulted in a large, viable population; however, a flood eliminated the population after 10 years (Minckley 1995). Also, the results of monitoring need to be published in scientific journals, so that successful methods can be incorporated into new reintroduction efforts.

Case Studies

Case studies illustrate the courses species reintroductions can follow.

- *Red wolves.* Red wolves (*Canis rufus*) have been reestablished in the Alligator River National Wildlife Refuge in northeastern North Carolina through the release of 42 captive-born animals. Survival of adults is about 50% after 3 years, and 23 pups have been born. Animals in the program have established packs and survive by hunting deer and raccoons and eating carrion (Phillips and Henry 1992). The Red Wolf Recovery Program appears to be successful.

- *Kemp's Ridley sea turtles.* Attempts have been made to stop the rapid decline of Kemp's Ridley sea turtles (*Lepidochelys kempii*) by collecting wild eggs from a Mexican beach, raising the hatchlings in captivity, and releasing them in the wild. Despite having released 18,000 "headstarted" hatchlings over a 14-year period, no turtles have been observed returning to Gulf of Mexico beaches to breed. Protecting beaches from turtle poaching and requiring turtle-excluders on the nets of commercial fishing boats will probably be the most important elements in protecting this endangered species (Taubes 1992).
- *Otters.* Eleven wild-caught otters (*Lutra lutra*) and 25 captive-bred otters were fitted with radio transmitters and reintroduced into an area in Sweden. The survival rate after one year was 79% for wild-caught animals and 42% for captive animals (Sjoåsen 1996).
- *The kakapo.* The kakapo (*Strigops habraptilus*) is not only the largest parrot species in the world, it is also flightless, nocturnal, and solitary. The New Zealand kakapo was believed extinct due to introduced mammalian predators, but two small populations were discovered in the late 1970s. These populations were declining in numbers, requiring urgent action to save the species. Sixty-five kakapos were collected in the wild and released on four offshore islands that lack most predators (Lloyd and Powlesland 1994). The kakapos did not initially form nests, probably due to inadequate food sources. Subsequent supplemental feeding with apples and sweet potatoes has allowed the birds to breed. Unfortunately, chick survival is still low, making the long-term success of the project uncertain.
- *Big Bend gambusia.* The Big Bend gambusia (*Gambusia gaigei*) was originally known from a single spring in Texas, which dried up in 1954 and eliminated the one known population. The fish was then discovered one year later in an artificial pond. A combination of captive breeding and releases into new artificial ponds helped the species survive a series of droughts and invasions by exotic fish. In 1983 the species was reestablished in its original spring, and the natural flow of the spring is now mandated under the management plan for this protected species (Minckley 1995).
- *Coral reefs.* Coral reefs on the Pacific coast of Costa Rica have been destroyed in places by human activities and natural disturbances. Experimental attempts at restoration have involved attaching live pieces of coral from nearby living reefs onto the dead reef. Survival of these transplants is high, and there is a large increase of new colonies (Guzman 1991).

- *St. Catherine's Island.* St. Catherine's Island is a 14,000-acre conservation area off the Georgia coast, managed for conservation, research, and education by a private foundation in cooperation with the Wildlife Conservation Society and the American Museum of Natural History. The native coastal vegetation provides habitat for native wildlife such as alligators, wild turkeys, white ibises, and wood storks. In addition, nonnative endangered animals that do not thrive in captivity or need large areas for social interactions have been introduced to establish breeding populations. Some of these are the red-fronted macaw (*Ara rubrogenys*), known only from one valley in Bolivia, and the gopher tortoise (*Gopherus polyphemus*), which is increasingly rare in the wild. A captive group of 12 Madagascar ring-tailed lemurs (*Lemus catta*) was released in 1985; this group has survived and grown to number 31 individuals with the birth of many new lemur infants in the wild.

Establishment of New Plant Populations

Methods used to establish new populations of rare and endangered plant species are fundamentally different from those used to establish terrestrial vertebrate animal species and are still in the early stages of development (Falk et al. 1996). Animals can disperse to new locations and actively seek out the most suitable microsite conditions. In the case of plants, seeds are dispersed to new sites by agents such as wind, animals, water, or the actions of conservation biologists (Primack and Miao 1992). Alternatively, either wild-collected or greenhouse-grown adults can be planted at the site to bypass the vulnerable seedling stage. Once a seed lands on the ground or an adult is planted at a site, it is unable to move, even if a suitable microsite exists just a few meters away. The immediate microsite is crucial for plant survival—if the environmental conditions are in any way too sunny, too shady, too wet, or too dry, either the seed will not germinate, or the resulting plant will die. Plants are also vulnerable to predation by insects and other animals, fungi, and nematodes. Disturbance in the form of fire or blowdowns may also be necessary for seedling establishment in many species; therefore, a site may be suitable for seedling establishment only once every several years. Careful site selection is thus critical in plant reintroductions; otherwise, plants will not be able to survive and flower. However, just as with animal reintroductions, identifying the factors causing the original decline in the plant species is critical for success. For example, in California many rare native annuals are being outcompeted by introduced annual grasses. Developing management techniques to control or eliminate these grasses is an essential part of the reintroduction process (Guerrant and Pavlik 1998).

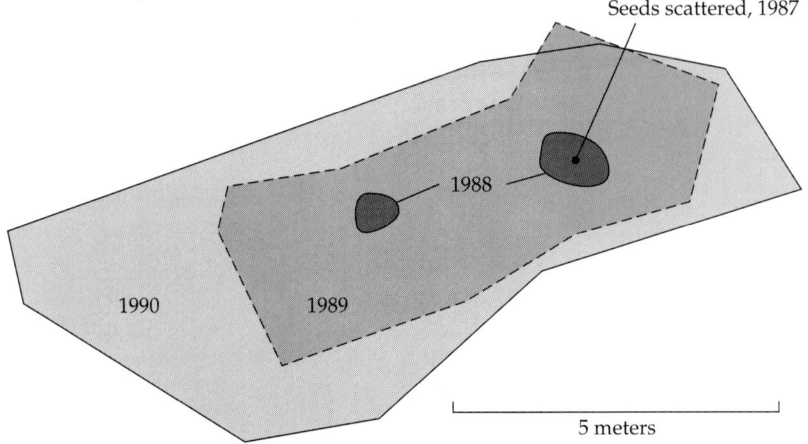

Figure 13.3 Sometimes a new plant population can be established by the introduction of seeds. In September 1987, 100 seeds of *Impatiens capensis*, an annual species of jewelweed, were introduced into an unoccupied site in Hammond Woods, near Boston, Massachusetts. The seeds were scattered within a meter of a stake (black dot). In 1988, two groups of plants separated by several meters had established themselves (darkest gray areas). The populations continued to expand, as shown by the limits in 1989 (dashed lines) and 1990 (solid lines). By 1994, population size had reached to more than 10,000 individuals and had spread 30 meters. (After Primack and Miao 1992.)

Plant populations typically fail to establish from introduced seeds at most sites that appear to be suitable for them. In one study, large numbers of seeds of six species of annual plants were planted at 48 apparently suitable sites (Primack 1996). Of these 48 attempts, new populations persisted for 2 years at only 5 sites, and for 6 years at only 1 site. At this apparently successful site, the population had increased to more than 10,000 individuals and had spread 30 m around the margins of a marshy pond (Figure 13.3). Subsequent attempts to establish new populations of 35 species of perennial herbs by sowing seeds at 173 apparently suitable sites had an even lower rate of success, highlighting the difficulties of establishing new plant populations. No seedlings at all were seen at 167 of the 173 sites, and no individuals at all were seen for 32 of the 35 species.

To increase their chances of success, botanists often germinate seeds in controlled environments and grow the young plants in protected conditions (Figure 13.4). Only after the plants are past the fragile seedling stage will they be transplanted into the field. Planting has to be executed using the techniques appropriate to the species (planting depth, watering, time of day, time of year, site preparation, etc.) to ensure survival. Transplanted seedlings and adults often flower and fruit much sooner than plants growing from seed sown in a wild field, which increases the potential for seed dispersal and formation of a second generation of plants.

While transplanting seedlings and adults has a better chance of ensuring that the species survives at a new location, it does not perfectly mimic a natural process, and the new population often fails to produce seed and form the next generation. Plant ecologists are currently trying to work out new techniques to overcome these difficul-

Figure 13.4 Seedlings of rare plant species being grown on a greenhouse bench. These seedling were subsequently planted in the wild. (Photograph by R. Primack.)

ties, such as fencing to exclude animals, removal of some of the existing vegetation to reduce competition, controlled burning, planting nurse plants in arid regions, and adding mineral nutrient (Figure 13.5). Keys to success seem to be using as many sites as possible, using as many seeds or adult transplants as possible, and reintroducing species over several successive years at the same site (Primack and Drayton 1997). Reintroductions require careful monitoring of the numbers of

Figure 13.5 A variety of methods are being investigated to create new populations of rare wildflower species on U.S. Forest Service land in South Carolina. Seeds are being planted in a pine forest from which the oak understory has been removed. The wire cages will be placed over some plantings to determine if herbivory is an important factor in plant establishment. (Photograph by R. Primack.)

seedlings and adults to determine if the project is a success. A successful project would be one in which there was a self-maintaining or even growing population with subsequent generations of plants replacing the reintroduced individuals.

Case Studies

Several case studies illustrate some successful plant species reintroductions.

- The large-flowered fiddleneck (*Amsickia grandiflora*) is an annual plant from northern California and has a narrow range. The species is in decline because livestock grazing and fire suppression—both human introductions—have favored exotic grasses over native plants. Experimental reintroductions of the fiddleneck were combined with different management treatments, including grass-specific herbicides and burning (Guerrant and Pavlik 1998). Management techniques that proved successful on the experimental populations were then applied to a declining natural population, resulting in a major increase in plant numbers (Figure 13.6).
- The endemic Clanwilliam cedar (*Widdringtonia cedarbergensis*) of South Africa has been declining in numbers due to its vulnerability to intense wild fires (Mustart et al. 1995). Along with moving toward a controlled fire regime of frequent, low-intensity fires, which the cedars often survive, an active program of population augmentation using seeds and seedlings is being carried out. In general, the survival of planted seedlings has been higher than sown seeds, and seedlings have done best when they were planted in the shade.

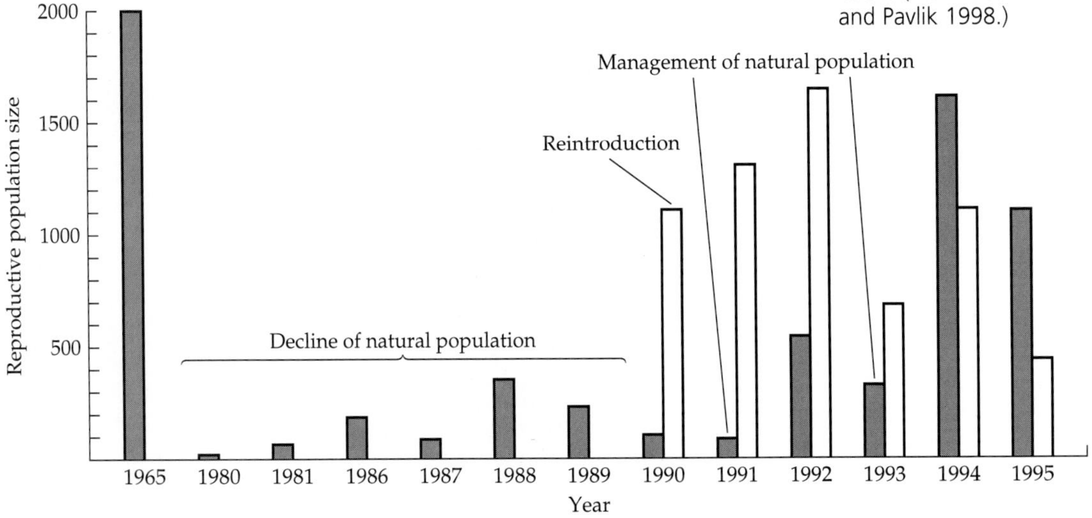

Figure 13.6 A natural population (shown as dark gray bars) of *Amsickia grandiflora*, an endangered annual plant of northern California, was in severe decline during the 1980s as a result of competition with exotic annual grasses. A reintroduction was carried out at a second site, starting in 1990 (white bars), combined with various management treatments to eliminate exotics. Successful treatments were then applied to the natural population in 1991 and 1993, with major increases in plant numbers seen in 1992 and 1994. (From Guerrant and Pavlik 1998.)

- Knowlton's cactus (*Pediocactus knowltonii*) is a tiny, perennial cactus known only from one narrow hilltop location in northwestern New Mexico (Figure 13.7). Despite the fact that the site is now owned by The Nature Conservancy, this threatened species remains vulnerable to human disturbance from oil and gas exploration, livestock grazing, and removal of plants by collectors. To reduce the possibility of extinction, two nearby, comparable sites were selected for introductions. At one site, 150 individuals grown from cuttings were planted and watered. After 7 years, 70% of the plants are still alive, with about half of them flowering and fruiting. After 5 years, only 8 seedlings had been produced from 408 seeds sown at the same site (Cully 1996).
- The perennial lakeside daisy *Hymenoxys acaulis* var. *glabra* is only known from one, declining population in Illinois with fewer than 30 plants (De Mauro 1993). The remaining plants were all of the same mating type and were unable to produce seed. Mating between garden-grown Illinois plants and plants from outside the state produced seeds that were germinated in a greenhouse from which large numbers of genetically diverse, reproductively fertile plants were obtained.

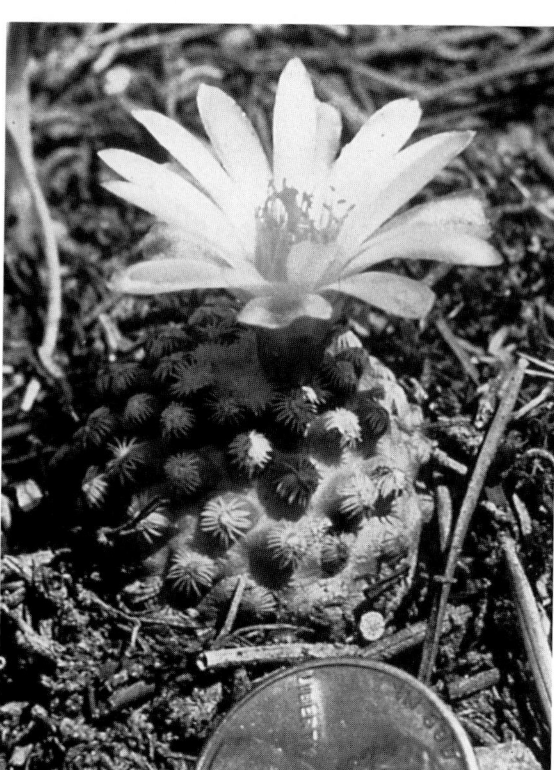

Figure 13.7 Knowlton's cactus (*Pediocactus knowltonii*) growing in New Mexico. The coin shown for scale is 1.9 cm (0.75 in) in diameter. (Photograph courtesy of The Nature Conservancy.)

Over 2000 seedlings were planted at two Illinois nature reserves over several years. While mortality was sometimes high, more than 500 plants became established, and many of these have flowered, set seed, and begun a new generation of seedlings.

Reestablishment Programs and the Law

Reintroduction, introduction, and augmentation programs will increase in the coming years as the biological diversity crisis eliminates more species and populations from the wild. Many of the reintroduction programs for endangered species will be mandated by official recovery plans set up by national governments (Tear et al. 1993). However, programs and research increasingly are being affected by endangered species legislation that restricts the possession and use of endangered species (Minckley 1995; Reinartz 1995; Falk et al. 1996). If government officials rigidly apply these laws to scientific research programs, which certainly was not the intent of the legislation, the creative insights and new approaches coming out of these programs could be stifled (Ralls and Brownell 1989).

Projects to establish experimental populations have sometimes been delayed for more than 5 years while waiting for government approval. New scientific information is central to establishment programs and other conservation efforts. Government officials who block reasonable scientific projects may be doing a disservice to the organisms they are trying to protect. The potential harm to endangered species caused by carefully planned scientific research is relatively insignificant when compared with the actual massive loss of biological diversity being caused by habitat destruction and fragmentation, pollution, and overexploitation. Conservation biologists must be able to explain the benefits of their research programs in a way that government officials and the general public can understand and address the legitimate concerns of those groups (Farnsworth and Rosovsky 1993).

Experimental populations of rare and endangered species successfully created by introduction and reintroduction programs are given various degrees of legal protection (Falk and Olwell 1992). The U.S. Endangered Species Act recognizes two categories of experimental populations: "Experimental, essential" populations are regarded as critical to the survival of endangered species and are as rigidly protected as naturally occurring populations. "Experimental, nonessential" populations are not considered essential to the survival of a species and are not protected under the Act. Designating populations as nonessential means that local landowners are not limited by the provisions of the Act and may not oppose the creation of an experimental population.

Legislators, environmental engineers, and scientists alike must understand that the establishment of new populations through reintroduction programs in no way reduces the need to protect the original populations of the endangered species. These original populations are more likely to have the most complete gene pool of the species and the most intact interactions with other members of the biological community.

In many cases, proposals are made to compensate for damaging habitats or eradicating populations of endangered species by creating new habitat or new populations elsewhere. This is generally referred to as **mitigation**. Mitigation is often directed at legally protected species and habitats such as wetlands. Proposals to establish new populations of endangered species merely for the convenience and profit of developers should be regarded with considerable skepticism. Given the poor success of most attempts to create new populations of rare species, protection of existing populations of rare species should be given the highest priority. While the replacement and restoration of damaged habitat such as wetlands may be a good thing, artificially created wetlands are generally neither as biologically rich nor as functionally useful as natural wetlands (in terms of water storage capacity, ability to break down sewage and human pollutants, etc.). Here again, claims to be able to mitigate the loss of biodiversity are usually exaggerated.

Summary

1. New populations of rare and endangered species can be established in the wild using either captive-raised or wild-caught animals. Reintroduction involves releasing individuals within the historic range of the species; introduction involves release of individuals at a site outside of the historic range of the species; augmentation involves releasing individuals into an existing population to increase population size and genetic variability.

2. Mammals and birds raised in captivity may lack the skills needed to survive in the wild. Some species require social and behavioral training before release, and some degree of maintenance after release. Establishment of a new population of rare bird and mammal species is enhanced when the release occurs in excellent habitat within the historic range of the species and when using large numbers (up to 100) of wild-caught animals.

3. Reintroduction of plant species requires a different approach because of their specialized environmental requirements and inability to move. Reintroduction efforts involving plants appear to have a lower chance of success than attempts with mammals and birds. Current research focuses on improving site selection and habitat management, and determining which age of plant (seed, seedling, or adult) is best to use.

4. Newly created populations of endangered species are sometimes given legal status as "experimental" populations. Conservation biologists involved in establishing new populations of endangered species must be careful that their efforts do not weaken the legal protection currently given to natural populations of those species. Similarly, they must educate the public about the limits and uncertainties of reintroduction efforts, which should never become an excuse for allowing a species to decline to the point of extinction.

For Discussion

1. How do you judge whether a reintroduction project is successful? Develop simple and then increasingly detailed criteria to evaluate a project's success. Use demographic, environmental, and genetic factors in your evaluation.

2. Design reintroduction projects involving a rodent species, an annual plant species, and a marine mollusk. What similarities and what differences would you expect in working with these three species?

3. Does our increasing ability to create new populations of rare and endangered species mean that we do not have to be concerned with protecting the known sites where these species occur? What are the costs and benefits of reintroduction programs?

4. Many endangered plant species are currently being propagated by commercial growers and botanical gardens and then sold (as both plants and seeds) to government agencies, conservation organizations, garden clubs, and the general public, who then in effect create new populations of these legally protected species (Reinartz 1995). There is little or no regulation of these sales or the subsequent planting out of the plants. What do you see as the advantages and disadvantages of this widespread activity? Should the propagation and planting of legally protected species be more closely regulated by the government?

Suggested Readings

Beck, B. B., L. G. Rapport, M. Stanley Price and A. Wilson. 1994. Reintroduction of captive-born animals. In *Creative Conservation: Interactive Management of Wild and Captive Animals*, P. J. Olney, G. M. Mace and A. T. Feistner (eds.), pp. 265–286. Chapman and Hall, London. Critical analysis of animal reintroduction programs.

Bowles, M. L. and C. J. Whelan (eds.). 1994. *Restoration of Endangered Species: Conceptual Issues, Planning, and Implementation*. Cambridge University Press, Cambridge. Good mixture of case studies, reviews, and analysis.

Clemmons, J. R. and R. Buchholz (eds.). 1997. *Behavioral Approaches to Conservation in the Wild*. Cambridge University Press, New York. Conservation projects need to pay careful attention to animal behavior and to adjust management practices accordingly.

Falk, D. A., C. I. Millar and M. Olwell (eds.). 1996. *Restoring Diversity: Strategies for Reintroduction of Endangered Plants*. Island Press, Washington, D.C. Policy, biology, legal issues, and case studies.

Farnsworth, E. J. and J. Rosovsky. 1996. The ethics of ecological field experimentation. *Conservation Biology* 7: 463–472. Ecologists need to be able to justify their research to the government and the public, and follow relevant regulations and laws.

Fischer, H. 1995. *Wolf Wars: The Remarkable Inside Story of the Restoration of Wolves to Yellowstone*. Falcon Press, Helena, MT. Political, legal, and economic issues play a surprisingly important role in reintroduction programs, as this high-profile case study demonstrates.

Frazer, N. B. 1992. Sea turtle conservation and halfway technology. *Conservation Biology* 6: 179–184. Attempts to help endangered species must first deal with the human activities leading to population declines.

Gipps, J. H. W. (ed.) 1991. *Beyond Captive Breeding: Reintroducing Endangered Species through Captive Breeding*. Zoological Society of London Symposium 62. Clarendon Press, Oxford. Essays on reintroduction by leading authorities.

Griffith, B., J. M. Scott, J. W. Carpenter and C. Reed. 1989. Translocation as a species conservation tool: Status and strategy. *Science* 245: 477–480. Analysis of 198 establishment programs.

Kleiman, D. G. 1989. Reintroduction of captive mammals for conservation. *BioScience* 39: 152–161. Outstanding outline of mammal reintroduction efforts, with many examples.

Minckley, W. L. 1995. Translocation as a tool for conserving imperiled fishes: Experiences in western United States. *Biological Conservation* 72: 297–309. Review of freshwater fish releases; also see other articles on fish conservation in this issue.

Olney, P. J. S., G. M. Mace and A. T. C. Feistner (eds.). 1994. *Creative Conservation: Interactive Management of Wild and Captive Animals.* Chapman and Hall, London. Captive breeding is needed to save species from extinction, but reintroduction should be the eventual goal.

Primack, R. and B. Drayton. 1997. The experimental ecology of reintroduction. *Plant Talk* 11 (Oct.): 25–28. Investigation of the best methods for plant reintroduction, in a wonderful new publication available from P.O. Box 65226, Tucson, AZ 85728-5226.

Primack, R. B. and S. L. Miao. 1992. Dispersal can limit local plant distribution. *Conservation Biology* 6: 513–519. The special requirements of plant reintroduction efforts.

Reading, R. P. and S. R. Kellert. 1993. Attitudes toward a proposed reintroduction of black-footed ferrets (*Mustela nigripes*). *Conservation Biology* 7: 569–580. The public needs to be educated about and convinced of the value of reintroductions.

Reinartz, J. A. 1995. Planting state-listed endangered and threatened plants. *Conservation Biology* 9: 771–781. Legal and moral issues involved in selling and planting of endangered species.

Stanley-Price, M. R. 1989. *Animal Re-introductions: The Arabian Oryx in Oman.* Cambridge University Press, Cambridge, England. History of a successful example of reintroduction.

CHAPTER 14

Ex Situ Conservation Strategies

THE BEST STRATEGY for the long-term protection of biological diversity is the preservation of natural communities and populations in the wild, known as π or **on-site preservation**. Only in natural communities are species able to continue their process of evolutionary adaptation to a changing environment. Further, only populations in the wild typically are large enough to prevent the loss of genetic variability through genetic drift. However, in the face of increasing human activities, in situ preservation is not currently a viable option for many rare species. Species may decline and go extinct in the wild for any of the reasons already discussed: genetic erosion and inbreeding, demographic and environmental variability, insufficient habitat, deteriorating habitat quality, competition from exotic species, disease, and excessive hunting and collecting.

If a remnant population is too small to maintain the species, or if the remaining individuals are found outside of protected areas, then in situ preservation may not be effective. It is likely that the only way species in such circumstances can be prevented from going extinct is to temporarily maintain individuals in artificial conditions under human supervision (Kleiman et al. 1996). This strategy is known as **ex situ** or **off-site preservation**. Already a number of species that are extinct in the wild survive in captive colonies, such as the Père David's deer (*Elaphurus davidianus*) and Przewalski's horse (*Equus caballus przewalski*) (Figure 14.1). The beautiful Franklin tree (see Figure 7.1) grows only in cultivation and is no longer found in the wild. The long-term goal of many ex situ conservation programs is the eventual establishment of new populations in the wild, once sufficient numbers of individuals and a suitable habitat are available.

(A)

Figure 14.1 (A) Père David's deer (*Elaphurus davidanus*) has been extinct in the wild since about 1200 B.C. The species remained only in managed hunting reserves kept by Chinese royalty. (B) Przewalski's horse (*Equus caballus przewalski*) does well in captivity but is now probably extinct in the wild. This species was once abundant in Central Asia and is the last living species of wild horse. Animals are now being reintroduced into grassland habitats. (Photographs by Jessie Cohen, National Zoological Park, Smithsonian Institution.)

(B)

Ex situ facilities for animal preservation include zoos, game farms, aquaria, and private breeders, while plants are maintained in botanical gardens, arboreta, and seed banks. An intermediate strategy that combines elements of both ex situ and in situ preservation is the monitoring and management of populations of rare and endangered species in small, protected areas; such populations are still somewhat wild, but human intervention may be necessary occasionally to prevent population decline.

Ex situ and in situ conservation are complementary strategies (Robinson 1992). Individuals from ex situ populations can be periodically released into the wild to augment in situ conservation efforts. Research on captive populations can provide insight into the basic biology of the species and suggest new conservation strategies for in situ populations. Long-term, viable ex situ populations can also reduce the need to collect individuals from the wild for display and research. Finally, captive-bred individuals on display can help to educate the public about the need to preserve the species and so protect other members of the species in the wild. In situ preservation of species, in turn, is vital to the survival of species that are difficult to maintain in captivity, as well as to the continued ability of zoos, aquaria, and botanical gardens to display species. The number of people visiting zoos is enormous; in the United States alone, over 120 million people visit zoos every year (Figure 14.2).

Figure 14.2 Modern zoos offer educational opportunities to the public as well as serving as sanctuaries for the animals. These visitors to the Bronx Zoo are observing prairie dogs in a surrounding that lets them imitate the animals' behavior. (Photograph by Michael K. Nichols/ National Geographic Image Collection.)

Ex situ conservation is not cheap: the cost of maintaining African elephants and black rhinos in zoos is 50 times greater than protecting the same number of individuals in East African national parks (Leader-Williams 1990); the cost of maintaining U.S. zoos is around $1 billion per year. Nevertheless, ex situ conservation strategies are an important part of an integrated conservation strategy to protect endangered species.

Ex situ conservation efforts have certain basic limitations in comparison with in situ preservation (Snyder et al. 1996):

- *Population size.* To prevent genetic drift, ex situ populations of at least several hundred individuals need to be maintained. No one zoo can maintain such large numbers of any of the larger animals, and only a few vertebrate species can be maintained in captivity at such numbers globally. In botanical gardens, only one or a few individuals of most species typically are maintained, especially in the case of trees.
- *Adaptation.* Ex situ populations may undergo genetic adaptation to their artificial environment. For example, animal species kept in captivity for several generations may exhibit changes in mouthparts and digestive enzymes due to the diet of zoo food; when the animals from this altered population are returned to the wild, they may have difficulty eating their natural diet.
- *Learning skills.* Individuals in ex situ populations may be ignorant of their natural environment and unable to survive in the wild. For example, captive-bred animals may no longer recognize wild foods as edible or be able to locate water sources if they are released back into the wild. This problem is most likely to occur among social mammals and birds in which juveniles learn survival skills and locations of critical resources from adult members of the population. Migratory animals will not know where or when to migrate.
- *Genetic variability.* Ex situ populations may represent only a limited portion of the gene pool of the species. For example, a captive population started using individuals collected from a warm lowland site may be unable to adapt physiologically to colder highland sites formerly occupied by the species.
- *Continuity.* Ex situ conservation efforts require a continuous supply of funds and a steady institutional policy. While this is also true to some extent for in situ conservation efforts, interruption of care in a zoo, aquarium, or greenhouse lasting only days or weeks can result in considerable losses of both individuals and species. Frozen and chilled collections of sperm, eggs, tissues, and seeds are particularly vulnerable to the loss of electric power. The breakup of the former Soviet Union, the deterioration of the Russian economy, and civil wars in its outlying states provide abundant examples of how rapidly conditions can shift in a country. Zoos are not going to be able to maintain their animal collections under such circumstances.

- *Concentration.* Because ex situ conservation efforts are sometimes concentrated in one relatively small place, there is a danger of an entire population of an endangered species being destroyed by a catastrophe such as fire, hurricane, or epidemic.
- *Surplus animals.* Some species breed *too* easily in captivity. What should be done with surplus animals in captivity that no other zoo wants and that have no chance of surviving in the wild? This ethical issue must be addressed: the welfare of any animal taken into human custody is the responsibility of its captors, so it may be unacceptable to kill or sell an individual animal, particularly when each animal in a highly threatened species might represent a key component of the species' future survival.

In spite of these limitations, ex situ conservation strategies may prove to be the best, perhaps the only alternative when in situ preservation of a species is difficult or impossible. As Michael Soulé says, "There are no hopeless cases, only people without hope and expensive cases" (Soulé 1987).

Zoos

Zoos have traditionally focused on large vertebrates—especially mammals—since these species are of greatest interest to the general public. The emphasis on "charismatic" megafauna such as pandas, giraffes, and elephants tends to ignore the enormous threats against the huge numbers of insects and other invertebrates that comprise most of the world's animal species. However, these animals do energize public opinion for conservation purposes. The world's two thousand zoos and aquaria are increasingly incorporating ecological themes and the threats to endangered species in their public displays and research programs as part of the World Zoo Conservation Strategy (Robinson 1992; Tarpy 1993; Olney and Ellis 1995). Educational programs at zoos, articles written about zoo programs, and zoo field projects all direct public attention to animals and habitats of conservation significance. If, for example, the general public becomes interested in protecting giant pandas after seeing them in zoos and reading about them, then money may be donated, pressure may be exerted on governments, and eventually mountains in China may be set aside as protected areas (Box 25). At the same time, thousands of other plant and animal species occupying these environments will be protected.

Zoos, along with affiliated universities, government wildlife departments, and conservation organizations, presently maintain over 700,000 individuals of terrestrial vertebrates, representing 3000 species of mammals, birds, reptiles, and amphibians (Conway 1988). While this number of captive animals may seem impressive, it is trivial in comparison to the numbers of domestic cats, dogs, and fish kept by people as pets.

Box 25 **Love Alone Cannot Save the Giant Panda**

The giant panda (*Ailuropoda melanoleuca*) is one of the most familiar endangered species in the world. It is so well known and so beloved by millions of people that its image is the symbol for the World Wide Fund for Nature (also known as the World Wildlife Fund), a prominent international conservation organization. Nevertheless, the panda's future is in jeopardy. As with many endangered species, human pressure on the panda's habitat is the most significant threat to its survival (Schaller 1993). Moreover, human pressure appears to exacerbate some of the unusual traits of the panda's physical and behavioral makeup that make this species particularly vulnerable to extinction.

One of the more bizarre features of panda biology is the species' diet of bamboo. Pandas are related to carnivores, so they lack many of the anatomical adaptations, such as elongated digestive tracts, that enable herbivores to use plant foods efficiently. Most herbivores have symbiotic bacteria in their digestive systems that help break down cellulose, further improving digestive efficiency; pandas lack these organisms. Consequently, pandas must eat continually to obtain sufficient nutrients to survive.

To further complicate matters, pandas periodically must change their behavior in response to cyclical bamboo die-offs. Bamboo species reproduce in long-term cycles of anywhere from 15 to over 100 years; typically, all individuals in a given species within a certain area will produce flowers and seeds in a single season, then die. Two to three years are generally required before new seedlings appear. Though in a certain place pandas may prefer one particular species of bamboo above all others, during die-off events they switch to other species. Frequently, this change requires that they migrate from the high-altitude regions they prefer to lowland areas, especially on those uncommon occasions when two or three bamboo species flower simultaneously. The bamboo die-offs trigger conflict between the needs of the pandas and human populations. Pandas are solitary and shy; they will not go into the human-populated lowland areas. Cut off from the lowland regions by humans, pandas have no recourse when bamboo die-offs occur. In the 1970s, when three species of bamboo flowered simultaneously, at least 138 pandas starved—almost 14% of the estimated panda population.

Following this catastrophe, in 1983 the Chinese government instituted a policy of searching for starving pandas during bamboo die-offs. The policy is not without its drawbacks. "Rescued" animals, many of which were captured unnecessarily, frequently ended up in zoos, depleting the wild population further. Zoos around the world compete for exhibition animals and offer large sums for them. Giant pandas put on display are rarely given the opportunity or the environment necessary for captive breeding.

Among the most beloved of all endangered species, the panda has become a symbol of conservation efforts. (Photograph by Jessie Cohen, National Zoological Park, Smithsonian Institution.)

Attempts to establish a self-sustaining captive breeding population have been unsuccessful. Giant pandas are extremely selective in choosing mates, and pandas paired by zoos often prove incompatible, or the zoos do not provide the pandas with enough time or enough choices. Artificial insemination has been used to circumvent the pandas' choosiness, but even so, its success has been limited—giant pandas rarely give birth to live young, and live young often do not survive more than a few days. Between 1963, when China first began to breed captive pandas, and 1989, only 90 cubs were born; only 37 survived for more than 6 months. The birth of 11 pandas in captivity in China in 1992 is a hopeful sign that some of these problems can be overcome; however, the population is still not expanding significantly. For captive breeding to benefit the wild population, captive-bred individuals must eventually be released back into the wild or at least used to raise public interest and funds needed for in situ conservation of wild giant pandas.

Some of the difficulties encountered in breeding pandas are a consequence of panda physiology and imperfect management techniques. Females go into heat only once every year, and are fertile for only two or three days. The problem of bringing a female and her mate into mating readiness at the same time remains unresolved. Cubs are born singly or in pairs and are remarkably small and helpless, weighing just four ounces. A panda female usually raises only one cub at a time, even if she gives birth to two live cubs. Moreover, the 3–5 month pregnancy is followed by 5 months of nursing, and, since the female does not generally go into heat again immediately after she stops nursing, she misses a year's breeding season. Thus the rate of population growth is very slow even under the best conditions. Young pandas are dependent on their mothers for up to 22 months after birth, so injury, sickness, or death of the mother may mean the loss of the cub as well. Would-be panda breeders worldwide are still attempting to find out why captive pandas frequently do not mate or, in the case of many females, do not even come into heat.

Fragmentation is another problem for the long-term success of the species. The remaining wild pandas number around 1000 individuals and are scattered in about 25 small populations over a very large geographical area. As a result, the receptive females may be unable to find mates and small populations may suffer from inbreeding depression. Poaching pandas for their skins is another problem that has become increasingly common despite stiff penalties, including death, imposed by the Chinese government.

The Chinese government has put significant financial resources into setting aside more habitat for the remaining wild pandas, but it will not be easy for the reserves to withstand the pressure of China's immense human population. The pandas need forest, bamboo, and protection from poachers—difficult resources to provide. Time will tell whether they will get what they need.

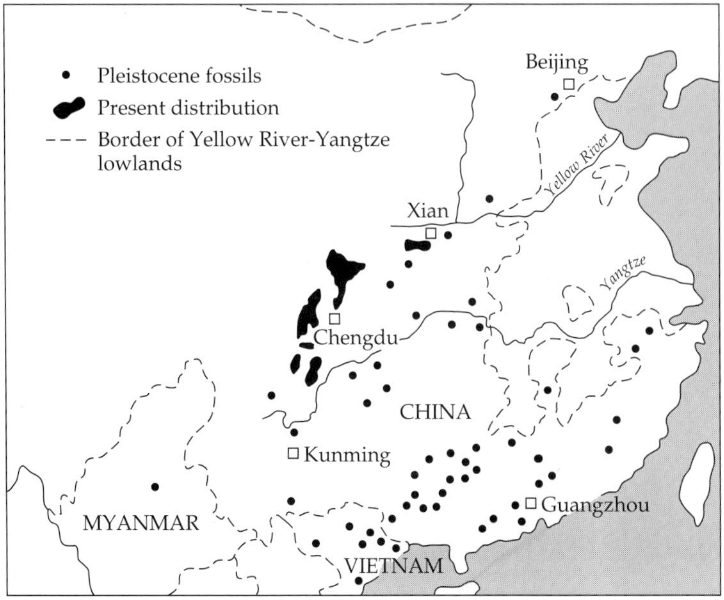

Pandas were once widely distributed in southern and eastern China, and even into Myanmar (Burma) and Vietnam. They are now restricted to a few areas near the cities of Chengdu and Xian. (After Schaller 1993.)

In the United States alone, about 50 million cats are kept as pets, 70 times more than the world's total of zoo animals.

A current goal of most major zoos is to establish viable, long-term captive breeding populations of rare and endangered animals. Zoos, working with affiliated universities, government wildlife departments, and conservation organizations, are the logical choice for the development of captive populations of these species because they have the needed knowledge and experience in animal care, veterinary medicine, animal behavior, reproductive biology, and genetics. Only relatively few of the rare mammal species kept by zoos currently have self-sustaining captive populations (Ralls and Ballou 1983). In the United States, zoos have self-maintaining populations of about 100 species, only a small percentage of the number of species on display. Zoos still collect much of their stock from wild populations. To remedy this situation, zoos and affiliated conservation organizations have embarked on a major effort to build facilities and develop the technology necessary to establish breeding colonies of rare and endangered animals, and to develop the new methods and programs needed to reintroduce species in the wild (Dresser 1988; Hutchins et al. 1996). Some of these facilities are highly specialized, such as that run by the International Crane Foundation in Wisconsin, which is attempting to establish captive breeding colonies of all crane species.

For common animals, such as the raccoon and the white-tailed deer, there is no need to establish breeding colonies, since individuals of these common species can be readily obtained from the wild. The real need is for zoos to establish populations of rare species that can no longer be readily captured in the wild, such as the orangutan, Chinese alligator, and snow leopard (Figure 14.3). Colonies in zoos may represent many species' only chance of survival—even short-term survival—if their nat-

Figure 14.3 Snow leopards (*Panthera uncia*) reproduce well in captivity. Maintaining breeding colonies of these animals can reduce the zoos' need to capture individuals from the declining wild population. Since 1974, the majority of snow leopards in zoos have been born in captivity (white bars) and fewer animals were caught in the wild (dark bars). (After Bloomqvist 1995.)

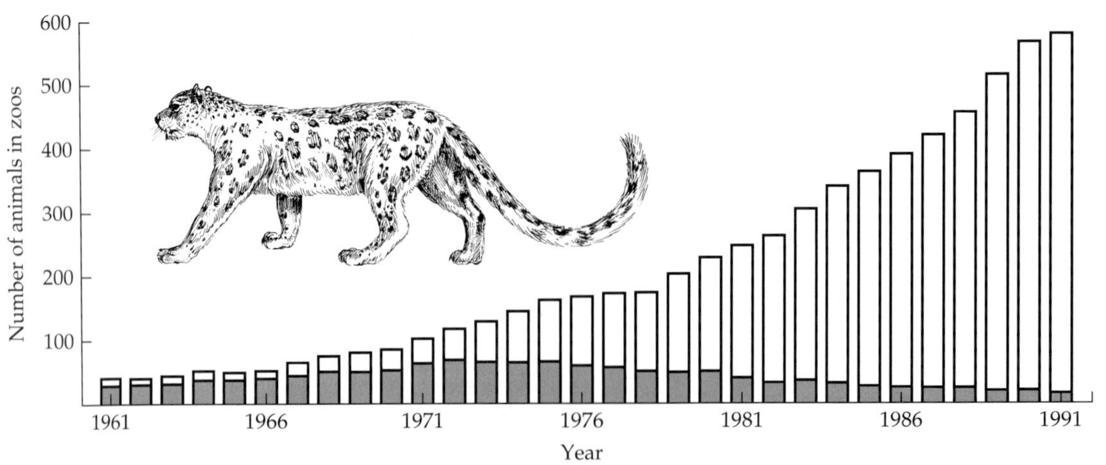

ural environments are too severely damaged or threatened by human activity. If a species goes extinct in the wild, captive breeding colonies can be a source of individuals to reestablish natural populations. If a concerted effort were made to establish breeding colonies of 100 to 150 individuals per mammal species, then about 2000 species could be maintained in captivity, with that number declining to around 1000 species if colony size was increased to 500 individuals. Zoos could establish breeding colonies of even more species if they directed more of their efforts to smaller-bodied species such as insects, amphibians, and reptiles that are less expensive to maintain in large numbers than large-bodied mammals such as giant pandas, elephants, and rhinos (Balmford et al. 1996).

The success of captive breeding programs has been enhanced by efforts to collect and disseminate knowledge about rare and endangered species. The Species Survival Commission's Conservation Breeding Specialist Group, a division of the IUCN (the International Union for the Conservation of Nature and Natural Resources), and affiliated organizations, such as the American Zoo and Aquarium Association, provide zoos with the necessary information for proper care and handling of these species, as well as updates on the status and behavior of animals in the wild (Wiese and Hutchins 1994). This includes data on nutritional requirements, anesthetic techniques to immobilize animals and reduce stress during transport and medical procedures, optimal housing conditions, and vaccinations and antibiotics to prevent the spread of disease.

Some rare species do not adapt or reproduce well in captivity. New techniques are being developed to maintain and enhance the low reproductive rates of these species (Kleiman et al. 1996). Some of these come directly from human and veterinary medicine, while others are novel methods for particular species. **Cross-fostering**, for example, can increase the reproductive success of certain species. If animal mothers are unable to raise their own young, foster parents from another species can sometimes raise their offspring. Many bird species, such as the bald eagle, normally lay only one clutch of eggs per year, but if the clutch of eggs is removed by biologists, the mother bird will lay and raise a second clutch of eggs. If the first clutch of eggs is given to another bird of a related species, two clutches of eggs will be produced per year for each rare female. This technique, known informally as "double-clutching," potentially doubles the number of offspring one female can produce.

Another aid to reproduction, similar to cross-fostering, is **artificial incubation**. If the mother does not adequately care for her offspring, or if the offspring are readily attacked by predators, parasites, or disease, humans may care for them during their vulnerable early stages. This approach has been tried extensively with sea turtles, birds, fishes, and amphibians: Eggs are collected and placed in ideal hatching conditions; the hatchlings are protected and fed during their vulnerable early stages; and the young are then released into the wild or raised in captivity. This approach is sometimes called a "Head Start" program.

Individuals of some animal species lose interest in mating while in captivity, and a zoo may have only one or a few individuals of a rare species such as the giant panda. In these circumstances, **artificial insemination** can be used when an isolated female animal comes into breeding condition, either on her own or after being chemically induced. Sperm can be collected from suitable males, stored until needed at low temperatures, and then used for artificial insemination with a receptive female. While artificial insemination is done routinely with many domesticated animal species, the exact techniques of sperm collection, sperm storage, recognition of female receptivity, and sperm delivery have to be worked out separately for each species in a conservation breeding program.

Figure 14.4 This bongo calf (*Tragelaphus euryceros*, an endangered species) was produced by embryo transfer using an eland (*Taurotagus oryxi*) as a surrogate mother at the Cincinnati Zoo Center for Reproduction of Endangered Wildlife. (Photograph © The Cincinnati Zoo.)

Embryo transfer has been accomplished successfully in a few rare animals such as the bongo, gaur, and Przewalski's horse. Superovulation, or production of multiple eggs, is induced using fertility drugs, and the extra eggs are collected, fertilized with sperm, and surgically implanted into surrogate mothers, sometimes using related common species. The surrogate mother will carry the offspring to term and then give birth (Figure 14.4) (Dresser 1988). In the future this technology may be used to increase the reproductive output of rare species.

Cutting edge medical and veterinary technology has the potential to develop innovative approaches for some species that are difficult to breed in captivity. These include cloning individuals from single cells (when only one or a few individuals remain), cross-species hybridization (when the remaining members of a species cannot breed among themselves), induced hibernation and diapause as a way of maintaining dormant populations, and biochemical and surgical sexing of animals that have no external sex differences. One of the most unusual and controversial techniques involves freezing eggs, sperm, embryos, and other tissue of species on the verge of extinction in the hope that these can be used to reestablish the species at some time in the future. The rapidly developing technology of cloning could possibly allow numerous individuals to be produced from these living cells. Many of these techniques are currently enormously expensive and must be worked out separately for each species. In any case, "frozen zoos" are no substitute for in situ and ex situ conservation that preserves ecological relationships and behaviors.

Managers of captive breeding programs are more careful now than in the past to avoid genetic problems when assigning mates (Figure 14.5). A careful analysis of zoo breeding records for 44 mammalian species including 16 ungulates, 16 primates, and 12 small mammals revealed that juvenile mortality was higher when closely related animals mated (such as fathers mating with their daughters) than among the offspring of unrelated animals (Ralls et al. 1988; Ebenhard 1995). "It was like re-inventing the wheel," Ballou stated (in Tangley 1988). "Anyone who has taken an introductory genetics course knows about the potential problems of inbreeding." As a result of such studies, North American zoos now use global computerized data bases to carefully track the genetic lineages of endangered captive animals to prevent pairing of related animals and avoid inbreeding depression as part of a species survival plan. One of the most important is the International Species Inventory System (ISIS), which provides information on 4200 kinds of animals at 395 zoological institutions in 39 countries.

Ex situ conservation efforts have been increasingly directed at saving endangered species of invertebrates as well. This is important because there are far more species of invertebrates than vertebrates, and many invertebrate species are restricted in distribution and declin-

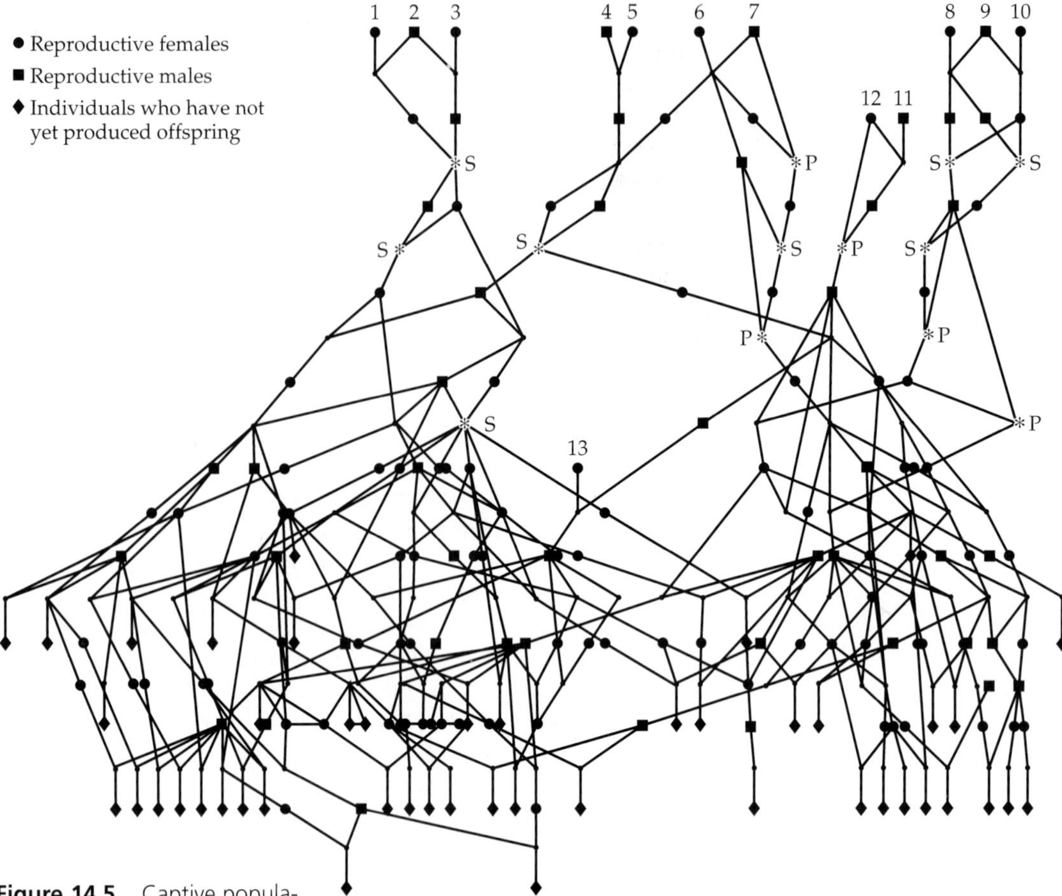

Figure 14.5 Captive populations often are extensively inbred, as illustrated by this pedigree of a captive group of Przewalski's horses. The 13 "founder" individuals are indicated with numbers. Matings among close relatives become common; some sibling matings (S) and parent–offspring matings (P) are highlighted with asterisks. (Modified from Thomas 1995.)

ing in numbers. One of the most striking examples is the partulid snails of the Pacific island of Moorea (Tudge 1992). All seven species of this snail family became extinct in the wild after a predatory snail was introduced to control an agricultural pest. Currently six of the seven partulid species survive only in a captive breeding program, with attempts being made to reintroduce the species into predator-free enclosures on Moorea.

Other important targets for ex situ conservation efforts are breeds of domestic animals on which human societies depend for animal protein, dairy products, leather, wool, agricultural labor, transportation, and recreation. Even though enormous populations of domestic animals exist (over 1 billion cattle and 1 billion sheep, for example), diverse and distinctive breeds of domestic animals adapted to local conditions are rapidly dying out as traditional agricultural practices are abandoned and intensive, high-yield agriculture is emphasized. For example, out of 3831 breeds of ass, water buffalo, cattle, goat, horse, pig, and sheep that existed in this century, 16% have already become extinct and an additional 15% are rare and in danger of extinction (Hall and Ruane 1993). Preservation of the genetic variation for characteristics such as disease resistance, drought tolerance, general health, and meat production represented by these breeds is crucial to animal breeding programs (Figure 14.6). Governments and conservation organizations are maintaining secure populations of some of these local breeds and developing frozen collections of sperm and embryos for later use. However, much more needs to be done to protect this global resource needed for healthy and productive domestic animals.

Ex situ techniques provide technological solutions to problems caused by human activities. Often the cheapest solution and the one most likely to succeed is protection of the species and its habitat in the wild so that it can recover naturally. When this solution is not possible, artificial methods are available to support those species that will become extinct without human intervention. When scientists consider these methods, they face a series of ethical questions that need to be addressed (Norton et al. 1995). First, how necessary and how effective are these methods for a particular species? Is it better for the last few individuals of a species to live out their days in the wild or to breed a captive population that may be unable to readapt to wild conditions? Second, does a population of a rare species that has been raised in captivity and does not know how to survive in its natural environment

Figure 14.6 Soay sheep are a relict breed of sheep living in the St. Kilda Islands, off the coast of Scotland. Soays retain characteristics of the first sheep brought to Britain more than 5000 years ago; some of these characteristics may be valuable for low-maintenance animal husbandry in the future: small size (25–36 kg); robust health; and the ability to shed their fleece. (Photograph by Stephen J. G. Hall.)

really represent a victory for the species? Third, are species held in captivity for their own benefit or the economic benefit of zoos?

Even when the answers to these questions indicate a need for ex situ management, it is not always feasible to create ex situ populations of rare animal species. A species may have been so severely reduced in numbers that there is low breeding success and high infant mortality due to inbreeding depression. Certain animals, particularly marine mammals, are so large or require such specialized environments that the facilities for maintaining and handling them are prohibitively expensive. Many invertebrates have complex life cycles in which their diet changes as they grow and in which their environmental needs vary in subtle ways. Many of these species are impossible to raise given our present knowledge. Finally, certain species are simply difficult to breed, despite the best efforts of scientists. Two prime examples of this are the giant panda (see Box 25) and the Sumatran rhino; neither species reproduces well in captivity, despite considerable effort by some of the best scientists to find effective methods.

Aquaria

Public aquaria have traditionally been oriented toward the display of unusual and attractive fish, sometimes supplemented with exhibits and performances of seals, dolphins, and other marine mammals. However, as concern for the environment has increased, conservation has developed into a major educational theme in aquaria. The need is great, since thousands of fish species are threatened with extinction. In North America alone, 24 species are known to have gone extinct since the arrival of European settlers, and 63 species are now classified as endangered (Williams and Nowak 1993). The rich fauna of the Mississippi basin and the unique desert pupfish of the southwestern United States are in particular danger. Extinctions of fishes are occurring worldwide in places such as the African Great Lakes and the Andean lakes. Already 15 of the 18 endemic fishes in Lake Lanao in the Philippines are extinct (Kornfield and Carpenter 1984). Freshwater mollusks are also a priority for protection because of their vulnerability to changes caused by water pollution and dams.

In response to this threat to aquatic species, ichthyologists, marine mammalogists, and coral reef experts who work for public aquaria are increasingly linking up with colleagues in marine research institutes, government fisheries departments, and conservation organizations to develop programs for the conservation of rich natural communities and species of special concern. Currently approximately 600,000 individual fish are maintained in aquaria, with most of these obtained from the wild. Major efforts are being made to develop breeding techniques so that rare species can be maintained in aquaria without fur-

out by botanical gardens discover new species and determine the distribution and status of known species, while nature reserves are maintained in more than 250 botanical gardens and serve as important conservation areas in their own right. In addition, botanical gardens are able to educate an estimated 150 million visitors per year about conservation issues (IUCN/WWF 1989). As stated by Ashton (1984):

> Botanic gardens have an opportunity, indeed an obligation which is open to them alone, to bridge between the traditional concerns of systematic biology and the returning needs of agriculture, forestry and medicine for the exploration and conservation of biological diversity.

The conservation of endangered species is becoming one of the major goals of botanical gardens as well as zoos. In the United States, conservation efforts by a network of 19 botanical gardens are being coordinated by the Center for Plant Conservation based at the Missouri Botanical Garden (Falk 1991). While most plant species occur in the tropics, the United States has 3000 species that are threatened in some way, and perhaps 700 of these species are in danger of going extinct within 5 to 10 years. More than 450 of the threatened species are now being grown in cultivation in these botanical gardens. Their ultimate goal is the reintroduction of these species into the wild.

The Botanical Gardens Conservation Secretariat (BGCS) of IUCN attempts to coordinate conservation efforts by the world's botanical gardens. Priorities of this program involve creating a worldwide data base to coordinate collecting activity and identify important species that are underrepresented or absent from living collections. Most botanical gardens are located in the temperate zone, even though most of the world's plant species are found in the tropics. A number of major gardens do exist in places such as Singapore, Sri Lanka, Java, and Colombia, but establishing new botanical gardens in the tropics should be a priority for the international community, along with training local plant taxonomists, geneticists, and horticulturalists to fill staff positions.

Seed Banks

Botanical gardens and research institutes have developed **seed banks**—collections of seeds from the wild and from cultivated plants. Seed banks have generally focused on the approximately 100 plant species that make up over 90% of human food consumption, but are devoting more and more attention to a wider range of species that may be threatened with extinction or loss of genetic variability.

Seeds of most plant species can be stored in cold, dry conditions in seed banks for long periods of time and then later germinated to produce new plants (Figure 14.9) (Eberhard et al. 1991). At low tempera-

(A)

(C)

(B)

(D)

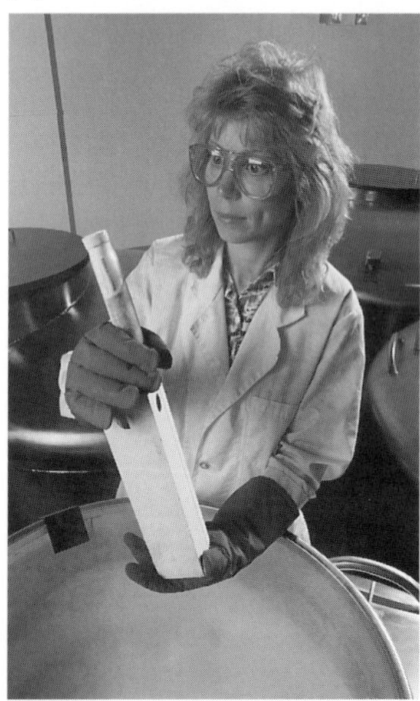

Figure 14.9 (A) The National Seed Storage Facility in Fort Collins, Colorado. (B) Seeds of many plant varieties are sorted, cataloged, and stored. Detailed labels describe the plant's characteristics and the place and date of collection. (C) At the National Seed Storage Facility some seeds are stored in hermetically sealed packets at –20°C. (D) Seeds are also stored in liquid nitrogen at –196°C. (Photographs courtesy of the U.S. Department of Agriculture.)

tures, a seed's metabolism slows down and the food reserves of the embryo are maintained. This property is extremely valuable for ex situ conservation efforts since seeds of large numbers of rare species can be stored in a small space with minimal supervision and at a low cost.

The United States Department of Agriculture (USDA) National Seed Storage Laboratory (NSSL) at Fort Collins, Colorado, stores some seeds in conditions as low as –196°C. The NSSL is part of the U.S. National Genetic Resource Program, which stores 450,000 seed samples from 8000 species. More than 50 other major seed banks exist in the world, many of them in developing countries. The focus of most of these facilities is on preserving the genetic variation needed for breeding purposes in crop species. While seed banks have great potential for conserving species, they have certain problems as well (Hamilton 1994). If power supplies fail or equipment breaks down, an entire frozen collection may be damaged. Even seeds in storage gradually lose their ability to germinate, after energetic reserves are exhausted and harmful mutations are accumulated. Old seed supplies simply may not germinate. To overcome the gradual deterioration of quality, samples must be regenerated periodically by germinating seeds, growing new plants to maturity, controlling pollination, and storing new samples. The testing and rejuvenation of seed samples can be a formidable task for seed banks with large collections. Renewing seed vigor in species that have large individual plants and delayed maturity, such as trees, may be extremely expensive and time-consuming.

Approximately 15% of the world's plant species have recalcitrant seeds that either lack dormancy or do not tolerate low-temperature storage conditions and consequently cannot be stored in seed banks. Seeds of these species must germinate right away or die. Species with recalcitrant seeds are much more common in tropical forests than in the temperate zone, and the seeds of many economically important tropical fruit trees, timber trees, and plantation crops such as cocoa, rubber, and Asian dipterocarp trees cannot be stored. Intensive investigations are underway to find ways of storing recalcitrant seeds; one possibility may be storing the embryo after removing the surrounding seed coat, endosperm, and other tissues. Plant species can be maintained in tissue culture in controlled conditions or propagated by cuttings from a parent plant, though these processes are usually more expensive than growing plants from seeds in most cases (Figure 14.10).

Agricultural Seed Banks

Seed banks have been embraced by the international agricultural community as an effective resource for preserving the genetic variability that exists in agricultural crops. Often resistance to particular diseases and pests is found in only one variety of a crop, known as a **landrace**, that is grown in only one small area of the world. Genetic variability is crucial to the agricultural industry's interest in maintaining and increasing the high productivity of modern crops and their ability to respond to changing environmental conditions such as acid rain, changing weather patterns, and soil erosion. Researchers are in a race against

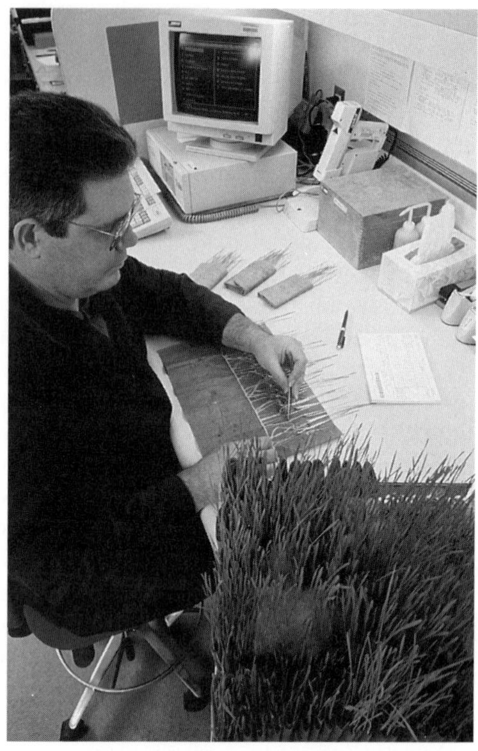

Figure 14.10 Cereal seedlings are checked for quality prior to their long-term cold storage. (Photograph courtesy of the U.S. Department of Agriculture.)

time to preserve genetic variability because traditional farmers throughout the world are abandoning their diverse local crop varieties in favor of standard, high-yielding varieties (Altieri and Anderson 1992). This worldwide phenomenon is illustrated by Sri Lankan farmers, who grew 2000 varieties of rice until the late 1950s when they switched over to five high-yielding varieties (Rhoades 1991). So far over 2 million collections of seeds have been acquired by agricultural seed banks (Box 26). Agricultural researchers have been combing the world for landraces of major food crops that can be stored and later hybridized with modern varieties in crop improvement programs. Many of the major food crops such as wheat, maize (corn), oats, and potatoes are well represented in seed banks, and other important crops such as rice, millet, and sorghum are being intensively collected (Plucknett et al. 1987).

The value of agricultural seed banks is illustrated in the following classic example. Rice crops in Africa were being devastated by grassy stunt virus strain 1. To find a solution to this problem, agricultural researchers grew wild and cultivated rice plants from thousands of seed samples obtained from collections around the world (Lin and Yuan 1980). One seed sample of wild rice from Gonda, Uttar Pradesh, India, was found to contain a gene for disease resistance. These wild plants were immediately incorporated into a major breeding program to transfer the gene for virus resistance into high-yielding varieties of rice. If the sample of wild rice had not been collected or had died out before being discovered, the future of rice cultivation in Africa would have been uncertain. All countries of the world benefit from breeding programs in the development of higher productivity of their crops.

Despite their obvious successes in collecting and storing material, agricultural seed banks are not wholly satisfactory. Collections are often poorly documented regarding the locality of collection and growing conditions. Many of the seeds are of unknown quality and may not germinate. Crops of regional significance as well as medicinal plants, fiber plants, and other useful plants are not as well represented in seed banks, nor are species with recalcitrant seeds, such as rubber, cacao, palms, and many tropical fruit trees, even though these are economically significant to tropical countries. One of the few ways to preserve genetic variation in these species is to establish special botanical gardens, known as clonal repositories or clonal orchards, which require considerable area and expense. In the past, root crops such as cassava (manioc), yams, and sweet potatoes had not been well represented in seed banks because they often do not form seeds. Though techniques are being developed to produce and store seeds of root crops, currently, these species are preserved by vegetative propagation in special gardens such as the International Potato Centre in Peru and the International Center for Tropical Agriculture in Colombia (Figure 14.11). This undertaking is crucial, as these root crops are very important in

Figure 14.11 The International Potato Centre maintains a living collection of 5000 samples of potatoes growing outdoors at its facility in Peru. (Photograph courtesy of the International Potato Centre.)

Box 26 Seed Savers and Crop Varieties

Preserving genetic diversity is a major concern for conservation biologists with good reason: even among populations that seem healthy, low genetic diversity can leave a population vulnerable to disease, a factor that holds potentially disastrous consequences for a threatened species. Many common crop plants, including the fruits and vegetables that most people eat regularly, are potentially threatened by low genetic diversity. The reason for this is simple: commercial farming tends to emphasize a few varieties that have high yield and appeal to consumer preferences for flavor, shape, size, and color. In doing so, many unique varieties of common crops have been ignored and are now relatively uncommon, even rare. Some varieties might have died out altogether, if not for the activities of ordinary gardeners and plant breeders belonging to a small Iowa-based organization, founded in 1975, called Seed Savers Exchange (SSE).

Seed Savers Exchange concentrates on preserving many little-known landrace varieties of crop plants from all over the world. This task is accomplished by the ingenious yet simple means of making these varieties available to individual gardeners and plant breeders—hobbyists who garden for their own pleasure or benefit, as well as various university agricultural programs and historic preservation societies—through newsletters and catalogs. In the 20 years of its existence, SSE has accumulated a list of some 1000 individual gardeners and plant breeders responsible for preserving over 12,000 different varieties of crop plants, which are offered in the SSE catalog to other growers. More than 65% of these varieties are offered by only one grower, demonstrating just how unusual many of these varieties have become (Cherfas 1996).

Many of these plants have long and fascinating histories, particularly the heirloom plants that can be traced back for centuries—even millennia—in their native habitat. Some are still linked to ongoing cultural traditions: Peruvian farmers in isolated Andean villages, for example, grow varieties of potatoes that may have been handed down from generation to generation since pre-Columbian times, yet remain completely unknown in nearby regions. Other plants may be interesting to look at, have medicinal properties, or be unusually colorful or flavorful. These reasons alone are sufficient rationale for most gardeners to want to obtain these varieties. For many gardeners, the opportunity to grow rare, unusual, and interesting plants is one of the great pleasures of gardening, and SSE is an excellent source of such plants.

Seed Savers Exchange works on a unique system: members pay a nominal fee in exchange for a catalog that describes the varieties available and provides the names of suppliers. The founders, Kent and Diane Whealy, run a farm in Iowa (appropriately called Heritage Farm) at which all of the different varieties are grown. They have enlisted amateur and professional growers to act as curators for specific crops. Curators may grow hundreds of varieties of melons, tomatoes, beans, or peppers, but they are specifically responsible for a smaller number of individual varieties. To assure that no crop is left out because of habitat or climate limitations, curators are located in different parts of the United States and in different climatic zones.

SSE makes a phenomenal number of interesting and unique plants available to ordinary gardeners. One curator in Iowa offers almost 200 different types of squash and 53 varieties of watermelon. And for those growers seeking a particular variety—perhaps one they remember from childhood, but for which they have no name—the "Plant Finder Service," appearing annually in the *Seed Savers Harvest Edition*, publishes growers' descriptions of the plants they want and appeals to the general membership for help finding them. In the near future, even more information will be made available through a television program planned for PBS called *Seed Time,* which will focus on heirloom plants.

The loss of the heirloom varieties that SSE hopes to protect could have serious consequences for the long-term sustainability of agriculture worldwide, because as the varieties die out, they take with them traits that may some day prove necessary to mainstream crops—the ability to adapt to environmental extremes of heat or cold, for example, or resistance to diseases and pests. These characteristics are of greatest interest to those concerned with the future of agriculture, because as more and more acreage is devoted to a few common varieties of crops, the genetic diversity of crop species declines, and, as

The Seed Savers Exchange produces the *Garden Seed Inventory*, an inventory of 245 seed catalogs and 6483 vegetable varieties. The headquarters of Seed Savers Exchange is the Heritage Farm in Iowa, where many unusual and hard-to-find vegetable varieties are grown. The screen boxes enclose particular varieties, and prevent cross-pollination between varieties.

has been observed many times in populations of threatened animal and plant species suffering from poor genetic diversity, devastating bouts of disease or attacks by pests become a serious risk. The Irish potato famine of 1845–1846, in which more than a million people starved to death, was the result of a blight on the all-important potato crop, most of which was composed of a single variety. Had potato farmers used even 1% of the more than 2000 potato varieties available, it is possible that a few varieties would have proven resistant to the disease; this might have alleviated (if not averted) some of the human suffering.

Despite the fact that all societies are dependent on agriculture, few of the wealthy industrial nations put significant resources into investigating the traits of the less common strains of ordinary crop plants. The United States Department of Agriculture, for example, operates its National Seed Storage Laboratory (NSSL) on an annual budget of around $30 million—a drop in the bucket by government standards, so little that it is not included as a separate line item when the budget is reviewed by Congress. This agency is so underfunded and ignored that it is likely to fail in its most important mission: preserving and cataloging the thousands of known varieties of crop plants and their wild relatives. The likelihood of failure increases as time passes for one simple reason: as seeds grow older, they lose their viability and die. Many of the seeds in the collection

Box 26 (continued)

are 20–40 years old, which means that as many as half of them might already have lost their viability and that the unique genetic makeup of those seeds is irretrievably lost. The only way to avoid seed deterioration is to periodically germinate and multiply the varieties, but low funding ensures that the enormous task of maintaining all varieties is physically impossible because of the small NSSL staff. This issue could lead to serious consequences: for example, researchers seeking strains of wheat resistant to the Russian aphid, an introduced pest, had to sort through 10,000 varieties of wheat and related cereals stored in the National Seed Storage Laboratory to find 2030 resistant varieties—a success rate of less than 0.3% after five years of searching. Had they waited a few years longer to begin the search, it is entirely possible that their rate of success would have been even lower as the older seeds lost their viability. Who can say what important traits may already have been lost?

Private organizations such as the Seed Savers Exchange—which recently went international in an attempt to preserve heirloom plants all over the world, especially in Eastern Europe—have filled in the gap to an extent. Turning the garden hobbyist's enthusiasm into a tool for conservation, this organization has managed to spread the word to an attentive worldwide audience of gardeners, breeders, and agricultural research and teaching institutions. Nevertheless, loss of crop varieties is a serious threat to world food supplies and should be recognized and addressed by world food organizations such as the United Nations Food and Agriculture Organization, as well as by governments' agricultural departments and ministries. For all their valiant efforts, organizations like Seed Savers Exchange/Seed Savers International are like the child who plugged the hole in the dike with his thumb: through quick thinking they have found a temporary solution, but unless the rest of the global village comes to their rescue, they will be unable to stop impending disaster.

the diet of people in developing tropical countries. An alternative method of conserving this genetic variability involves the in situ preservation of traditional agricultural practices (see Chapter 20).

One of the most important sources of genetic variation for use in breeding programs is the wild relatives of crop species. For example, more than 20 wild species of potatoes have been used in the development of modern potato varieties. However, only about 2% of the collections in agricultural seed banks come from wild relatives of crop plants (Hoyt 1988). Only the wild relatives of wheat and potatoes are well represented in seed banks. The majority of wild relatives for major crops such as rice and cassava still remain to be adequately collected.

Seed banks are coordinated by the Consultative Group on International Agricultural Research (CGIAR) and the International Board for Plant Genetic Resources (IBPGR) (Fuccilo et al. 1998). One of the largest seed banks, holding 60,000 rice collections, is maintained by the International Rice Research Institute (IRRI), an organization instrumental in the development of high-yielding, Green Revolution crop varieties. Other specialized seed collections are held by the International Maize and Wheat Improvement Center (Centro Internacional de Mejoramiento de Maiz y Trigo, or CIMMYT) in Mexico, with 12,000 samples of maize and 100,000 samples of wheat, and by the center for apples at the National Clonal Germplasm Repository in Geneva, New York.

ter 2). The most extensive information on genetic variation in plants comes from accumulated studies of allozyme variation in more than 400 species (Hamrick et al. 1991). These studies show that the most important factor in determining the total amount of genetic variation in a plant species is the geographical range of the species; widespread species have more than twice as much genetic variation as species of restricted range. Also, plant species have, on average, 78% of their genetic variability within populations and 22% of their variability among populations, though many species differ from these average values depending on their reproductive system and morphology. These data suggest strategies for protecting the gene pool of rare and endangered species by both in situ protection of carefully selected populations and a well-planned collection program for ex situ preservation.

Using information on patterns of genetic variation, the Center for Plant Conservation (1991) has developed a list of five seed sampling guidelines for conserving the genetic variability of endangered plant species that could be modified for other groups of species such as animals, fungi, and microorganisms:

1. The highest priority for collecting should be species that (a) are in danger of extinction—that is, species showing a rapid decline in number of individuals or number of populations; (b) are evolutionarily or taxonomically unique; (c) can be reintroduced into the wild; (d) have the potential to be preserved in ex situ situations; (e) have potential economic value for agriculture, medicine, forestry, or industry.

2. Samples should be collected from up to five populations per species to ensure a sampling of the genetic variability contained among populations. Where possible, populations should be selected to cover the geographical and environmental range of the species. All populations should be sampled for the 70% of endangered species that have five or fewer populations.

3. Samples should be collected from 10 to 50 individuals per population. Sampling fewer than 10 individuals may miss alleles that are common in the population. Sampling more than 50 individuals may not result in obtaining enough new alleles to justify the effort. In general, sample sizes should be at the high end of the range when the population appears to be phenotypically variable, the site is heterogeneous, and the plants are outcrossing.

4. The number of seeds (or cuttings, bulbs, etc.) collected per plant is determined by the viability of the species' seeds. If seed viability is high, then only a few seeds need to be collected per individual; if seed viability is low, then many seeds per individual have to be collected.

5. If individual plants of a species have a low reproductive output, collecting many seeds in one year may have a negative effect on the sampled populations. This is particularly true for annuals and other short-lived plants. In these cases, a better strategy would be to spread the collecting over several years.

The CPC (1991) concludes:

> Conservation collections are only as good as the diversity that they contain. Thus the forethought and methods that go into sampling procedures play a critical role in determining the ultimate quality of the collection, as well as its usability for purposes such as reintroduction and restoration. In the long run, the real significance of collections in biological conservation is their role in reinforcing the management and maintenance of natural populations. Collectors should view themselves not as 'preserving' static entities, but as providing a stepping-stone on the pathway to survival and evolution.

Conserving the Genetic Resources of Trees

Forestry is a huge, global industry that depends on the genetic variation found in trees for its long-term success (Ledig 1988; Rogers and Ledig 1996). As with crop plants, trees are genetically variable, with each population often adapted to local conditions of climate, soil, and pests (Figure 14.13). Seeds collected from one geographic area and planted elsewhere under different environmental conditions may not develop into vigorously growing trees. The success of a forestry program depends on establishing tree plantations from a good sample of seeds obtained from a suitable geographic location. For example, a plantation in a wet mountainous area requires seeds obtained from trees adapted to those conditions rather than to a dry lowland site. The results of seed selection may not be known till years or decades later when a poor initial seed sample results in slow-growing, misshapen, disease-ridden trees with poor wood quality. Relying on wild-collected seeds for establishing plantations has its drawbacks because selective logging often removes the superior trees and leaves the inferior ones behind.

To conserve genetic variation in tree species, foresters have used cuttings and families of closely related seeds to establish plantations of superior genetic varieties, called clone banks, for long-term maintenance and research of commercially important tree species (Ledig 1988). For loblolly pine (*Pinus taeda*) alone, 8000 clones are being grown in clone banks in the southeastern United States. Selected trees are used to establish seed orchards for producing commercial seed. Storage of seeds is difficult for many important genera of trees such as oaks (*Quercus*) and poplars (*Populus*). Even pine seeds cannot be stored indefinitely and must eventually be grown out as trees.

Preservation of areas where commercial tree species occur naturally

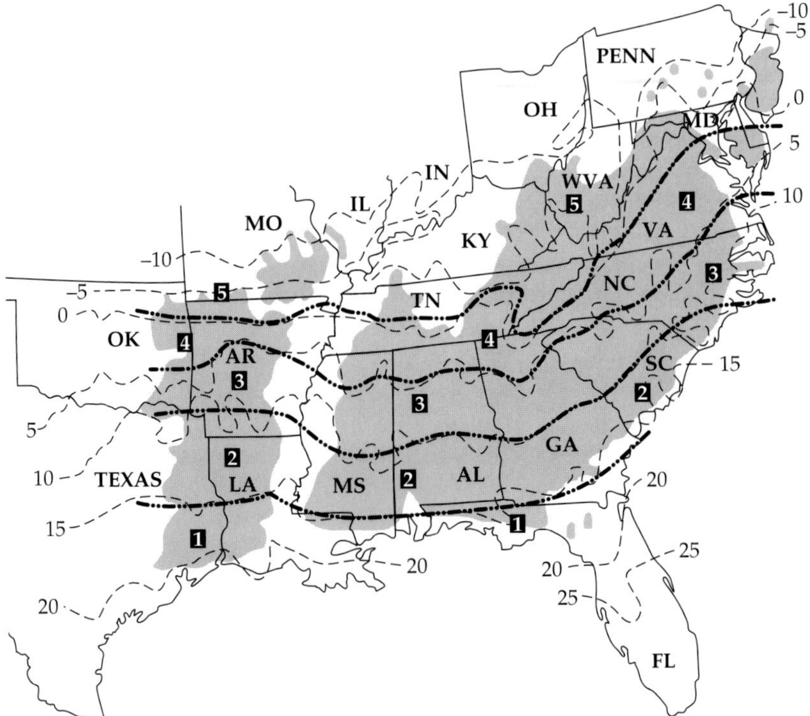

Figure 14.13 Five seed zones based on climate have been established for the shortleaf pine (*Pinus echinata*); seed zone boundaries are shown with heavy dashed lines. New tree plantations should be established using seeds from the same seed zone in order to have the best growth. The lighter dashed lines are minimum temperature isotherms defining areas with the same minimum temperature (given in °F); for example, in typical winters the temperature in southern Florida does not drop below 25°F. (From Rogers and Ledig 1996.)

is being considered as a way of protecting genetic variability. International cooperation is needed in forestry research and conservation because commercial species are often grown far from their countries of origin. For example, loblolly pine (*Pinus taeda*) and Monterey pine (*Pinus radiata*) from North America are planted on 5.8 million ha of land outside that continent. In New Zealand 1.3 million ha are planted in Monterey pine, making it a key element in the national economy. In Hungary, 19% of the forested area is planted in North American shipmast locust (*Robinia pseudoacacia* var. *rectissima*), because the species produces durable wood and grows on degraded, low-nutrient sites. These forest plantations far from home still depend on natural populations of the species to supply the genetic variability required for continued improvements and survival in a hostile environment.

Summary

1. Some species that are in danger of going extinct in the wild can be maintained in artificial conditions under human supervision; this is known as ex situ or off-site preservation. These captive colonies can be used later to reestablish species in the wild.

2. Zoos are developing self-maintaining populations of many rare vertebrates, often using modern techniques of veterinary medicine to increase their reproductive rates. Managers of zoos are developing breeding programs to maintain the genetic variability of species and prevent inbreeding depression.

3. Marine mammalogists, ichthyologists, and coral reef experts who work for public aquaria are developing breeding techniques and conservation programs for the protection and preservation of endangered fishes, marine mammals, and aquatic invertebrates. The preservation of coral reef species and marine mammals are important scientific problems that are also of great interest to the general public.

4. The world's 1500 botanical gardens and arboreta are now collecting rare and endangered species as a priority. The seeds of most species of plants can be stored for long periods of time under cold conditions in seed banks. Seed banks often specialize in the collection of major crop species, commercial timber species, and their close relatives in order to preserve material for genetic improvement programs.

For Discussion

1. What are the similarities and differences among the ex situ conservation methods used for plants, terrestrial animals, and aquatic species?

2. Would biological diversity be adequately protected if every species were raised in captivity? Is this possible? Practical? How would freezing a tissue sample of every species help to protect biological diversity? Again, is this possible and is it practical?

3. Are the arguments for preserving the genetic variability in domesticated species of animals and plants (and their close relatives) the same arguments we would put forward for saving endangered wild species?

4. How much of a zoo's, an aquarium's, or botanical garden's resources should be devoted for conservation efforts in order for the institution to announce that it is involved in conservation? What sort of conservation activities are appropriate for each institution? Visit such an institution and evaluate it for its conservation activities and efforts; use or modify some of the methods of Balmford et al. 1996.

Suggested Readings

Balmford, A., G. M. Mace and N. Leader-Williams. 1996. Designing the Ark: Setting priorities for captive breeding. *Conservation Biology* 10: 719–727. Zoos should focus more on smaller-bodied species that breed well in captivity and are cheaper to maintain.

Brush, S. B. and D. Stabinsky (eds.). 1996. *Valuing Local Knowledge: Indigenous People and Intellectual Property Rights.* Island Press, Washington, D.C. Case studies of how local people can gain economic benefits from the species they know and protect.

Diversity: A New Journal for the International Genetic Resources Community. 4905 Del Ray Avenue, Suite 401, Bethesda, MD 20814. Informative newsletter about current topics related to agricultural genetic resources. See also *Geneflow*, International Plant Genetic Resources Institute, Via delle Sette Chieses 142, 00145 Rome, Italy, and Agricultural Research, U.S. Department of Agriculture, Washington, D.C. 20250.

Frankel, O., A. Brown and J. Burdon. 1995. *The Conservation of Plants*. Cambridge University Press, Cambridge. A comprehensive advanced treatment.

Fuccilo, D., L. Sears and P. Stapleton. 1998. *Biodiversity in Trust: Conservation and Use of Plant Genetic Resources in CGIAR Centres*. Cambridge University Press, New York. A major international effort is being made to coordinate the conservation of plant genetic resources.

Given, D. R. 1995. *Principles and Practice of Plant Conservation*. Timber Press, Portland, OR. Good summary of plant conservation approaches.

Hamilton, M. B. 1994. Ex situ conservation of wild plant species: Time to reassess the genetic assumptions and implications of seed banks. *Conservation Biology* 8: 39–49. Will seed banks preserve a sufficient range of a species' genetic variation?

Kleiman, D. G., M. E. Allen, K. V. Thompson, and S. Lumpkin. 1996. *Wild Animals in Captivity: Principles and Techniques*. University of Chicago Press, Chicago. Leading experts give current information on a range of issues facing zoos.

Norton, B. G., M. Hutchins, E. F. Stevens and T. L. Maple. 1995. *Ethics on the Ark: Zoos, Animal Welfare, and Wildlife Conservation*. Smithsonian Institution Press, Washington, D.C. Vigorous examination of the ethical issues confronting modern zoos.

Olney, P. J. and F. A. Fisken (eds.). 1995. *1994 International Zoo Yearbook: Volume 34*. Zoological Society of London, London. Wide range of articles on animals in captivity; see other volumes in this series as well.

Philippart, J. C. 1995. Is captive breeding an effective solution for the preservation of endemic species? *Biological Conservation* 72: 281–295. Focus on rare and endangered fish species.

Plucknett, D. L., N. J. H. Smith, J. T. Williams and N. M. Anishetty. 1987. *Gene Banks and the World's Food*. Princeton University Press, Princeton, NJ. Gene banks are central to ensuring the security of the world's food supply and the continuing vitality of modern agriculture.

Rhoades, R. E. 1991. World's food supply at risk. *National Geographic* 179 (April): 74–105. A beautifully illustrated popular account of the decline of traditional agricultural varieties and the need for seed banks.

Robinson, M. H. 1992. Global change, the future of biodiversity and the future of zoos. *Biotropica* (special issue) 24: 345–352. This article focuses on the modern role of zoos in conservation and education.

Rogers, D. L. and F. T. Ledig. 1996. *The Status of Temperate North American Forest Genetic Resources*. U.S. Department of Agriculture Forest Service and Genetic Resources Conservation Program, University of California, Davis. Clearly written report on forest genetic resources.

Schaller, G. B. 1993. *The Last Panda*. University of Chicago Press, Chicago. A personal account of a conservation program set within a complex political and economic landscape.

Snyder, N. F. and six others. 1996. Limitations of captive breeding in endangered species recovery. *Conservation Biology* 10: 338–348. Captive breeding programs should be initiated only if a species cannot survive in the wild without them.

Tarpy, C. 1993. Zoos: Taking down the bars. *National Geographic* 184 (July): 2–37. A great article on the new role of zoos in animal species conservation.

Wiese, R. J. and M. Hutchins. 1994. *Species Survival Plans: Strategies for Wildlife Conservation*. American Zoo and Aquarium Association, Bethesda, MD. Beautifully illustrated guide to major conservation programs involving captive breeding; see also the *Annual Report on Conservation and Science*.

PART FIVE

Practical Applications

Gila trout

CHAPTER 15

Establishing Protected Areas

PROTECTING HABITATS that contain healthy, intact biological communities is the most effective way to preserve biological diversity. One could argue that it is ultimately the only way, because we have the resources and knowledge to maintain only a small minority of the world's species in captivity. A critical step in protecting biological communities is establishing legally designated protected areas that are governed by laws and rules that allow widely varying degrees of commercial resource use, traditional use by local people, and recreational use. Proponents of habitat preservation often must generate considerable political will and financial resources to ensure that, once established, the protected areas achieve their purposes.

Protected areas can be established in a variety of ways, but the two most common mechanisms are government action (often at a national level, but also regionally or locally) and purchases of land by private conservation organizations such as the Audubon Society and The Nature Conservancy (Box 27), or by private individuals. While legislation and land purchases by themselves will not ensure habitat preservation, they lay the groundwork. Partnerships among governments of developing countries in the tropics, international conservation organizations, multinational banks, and the governments of developed countries bring together funding, training, and scientific and management expertise to help tropical countries establish new national parks.

Protected areas also have been established by traditional societies wishing to maintain their way of life or just to preserve their land. National governments in many countries, including the United States, Canada, Colombia, and Malaysia, have recognized the rights of traditional societies, although in some cases recognition only follows conflict in the courts, in the press, and on the land. In many cases, assertion of local rights over traditional lands have involved violent confrontations with government authorities seeking to develop the land, sometimes with loss of life (Gadgil and Guha 1992; Western et al. 1994).

The IUCN System of Classification

Biological communities vary from a few that are virtually unaffected by human influence, such as communities found on the ocean floor or in the most remote parts of the Amazon rain forest, to those that are heavily modified by human activity, such as agricultural land, cities, and artificial ponds. Even in the most remote areas of the world, human influence is present in the forms of air pollution, rising carbon dioxide levels, and subsistence harvesting—yet in the most heavily modified human environments, remnants of the original biota may still exist and thrive. Habitats with intermediate levels of disturbance present some of the most interesting challenges and opportunities for conservation biology because they often cover large geographical areas. Considerable biological diversity may remain in selectively logged tropical forests, heavily fished oceans and seas, and grasslands grazed by domestic livestock (Western 1989; Redford 1992). When a conservation area is established, the right compromise must be found between protecting biological diversity and ecosystem function and satisfying the immediate and long-term needs of the local human community and the national government for resources.

When land is being considered for protection, decisions must be made during the planning process regarding how much human disturbance will be allowed. An existing protected area may require further protection if current human activities are damaging important aspects of biological diversity; alternatively, greater human activity may be

Box 27 Ecologists and Real Estate Experts Mingle at The Nature Conservancy

For nearly a century, nonprofit organizations such as the Sierra Club and the Audubon Society have sought to encourage the conservation of wild species and habitats. The number of these organizations has increased in recent decades at the local, national, and international levels. Of the many organizations that now fight to protect biological diversity, The Nature Conservancy (TNC) is set apart by a unique approach that applies the methods of private business to accomplish the conservation of rare species and habitats. Simply put, The Nature Conservancy either buys threatened habitat outright or shows landowners how managing their land for conservation can be as profitable as developing it.

Founded in 1951, The Nature Conservancy had more than 800,000 members by 1995. TNC is not as widely known as some conservation organizations, nor is it as vocal. TNC advocates a nonconfrontational, businesslike approach that contrasts with the methods of some high-profile, activist conservation groups such as Greenpeace and EarthFirst! (Grove 1988). Still, its methods have been quietly successful: in the United States alone, more than 3.2 million ha have been set aside through the work of TNC, much of which has eventually become state or national parks or wildlife refuges. Outside the United States, 42 million ha have been protected with their help.

The Nature Conservancy maintains a fund of over $160 million, created from private and corporate donations with which they can make direct land purchases when necessary. Through these methods, the organization has created the largest system of private natural areas and wildlife sanctuaries in the world. One such outstanding property is the 14 ha of land surrounding the shoals at Pendleton Island on Virginia's Clinch River (Stolzenburg 1992). These 300 meters of shoals have 45 species of freshwater mussels and may be among the richest localities for mussels in the world. The decision of TNC in 1984 to buy this small piece of land and get involved in cleaning up the Clinch River represents an important step in recognizing the importance of aquatic invertebrates to overall biological diversity.

The Nature Conservancy's approach is creative; like other land trust organizations, if TNC cannot purchase land outright for the protection of habitat, it offers alternatives to landowners that make conservation a financially attractive option. Such alternatives include enabling the landowner to obtain tax benefits in exchange for accepting legal restrictions or conservation easements preventing development. In other cases, the landowner can donate the land to TNC and retain lifetime occupancy, which in essence permits the owner to have a rent- and mortgage-free home and to receive a sizable tax deduction as well. TNC also seeks methods that allow the preserves it owns to support themselves financially. The cost of maintaining one South Dakota prairie preserve is partially defrayed by

Paul Todd of The Nature Conservancy (left) discusses the management of the Silver Creek Preserve in Idaho with neighboring rancher Bud Purdee. (Photograph © Martha Hodgkins-Green.)

Box 27 (continued)

maintaining a resident bison herd. Grazing by bison enhances biological diversity in these grasslands, provided the herd does not become too large; when the herd grows to a size at which overgrazing becomes a possibility, the excess animals are sold. The sale of bison brings roughly $25,000 annually to the preserve.

In addition, The Nature Conservancy supports and encourages efforts to identify populations of rare and endangered species and to manage biological diversity in the United States (The Nature Conservancy 1996). Often TNC sells at cost or donates land it has purchased to state governments or federal agencies that will protect the land. Some parcels of land are so valuable that they have been designated as national wildlife refuges by the government. TNC also promotes state-level conservation through Natural Heritage Programs in all 50 states, which generally are joint ventures between TNC and state governments (Jenkins 1996). The Nature Conservancy provides training and staff to inventory plant and animal populations in each state. The data collected are recorded in a computerized database located in each state and at TNC headquarters in Arlington, Virginia; with this data base, TNC biologists can keep track of the status of species and populations throughout the nation. When Natural Heritage Program biologists identify populations of species that are rare, unique, declining, or threatened, the state has information allowing it to make wise decisions.

The Nature Conservancy is distinguished from other conservation organizations by its businesslike approach. TNC generally refuses to bring lawsuits against projects encroaching on the habitat of endangered species, preferring to provide financial incentives to promote conservation. But the Conservancy's businesslike approach is successful largely because developers, who too often have no great love for environmentalists, respect and understand TNC's methods. The fundamental principle of TNC is, in essence, "Land conservation through private action." So far, the idea has proved to be sound.

appropriate and not harmful. In general, when greater amounts of human disturbance are permitted, a narrower scope of biodiversity is preserved. The International Union for the Conservation of Nature (IUCN) has developed a system of classification for protected areas that ranges from minimal to intensive allowed use of the habitat by humans (IUCN 1994):

I. *Strict nature reserves and wilderness areas.* These protect natural organisms and natural processes in an undisturbed state, in order to have representative examples of biological diversity for scientific study, education, environmental monitoring, and maintenance of genetic variation. Included are two subcategories: (Ia) primarily includes nature reserves, established for scientific research and monitoring; (Ib) primarily includes wilderness areas maintained for recreation, for subsistence economic activities, and to protect natural processes.

II. *National parks.* Large areas of outstanding scenic and natural beauty that are of national or international importance, maintained for scientific, educational, and recreational use; they usually are not used for commercial extraction of resources.

III. *National monuments and landmarks.* Smaller areas designed to preserve unique natural areas of special national interest.

IV. *Managed wildlife sanctuaries and nature reserves.* Similar to strict nature reserves, but some human manipulation may be necessary to maintain the characteristics of the community. Some controlled harvesting may be permitted.

V. *Protected land and seascapes.* Areas that embody the harmonious interaction of people and the environment through the traditional, nondestructive use of natural resources, while providing opportunities for tourism and recreation. Such areas may include grazing land, orchards, or fishing villages.

VI. *Managed resource protected areas.* These allow for the sustained production of natural resources, including water, wildlife, grazing for livestock, timber, tourism, and fishing, in a manner that ensures the preservation of biological diversity. These areas are often large and may include both modern and traditional uses of natural resources.

Of these categories, the first five can be defined as true **protected areas**, because their habitat is managed primarily for biological diversity. A stricter definition would include only the first four categories. Areas in the last category are not managed primarily for biological diversity, though this may be a secondary management goal. **Managed areas** can be particularly significant because they are often much larger in area than protected areas, because they still may contain many or even most of their original species, and because protected areas are often embedded in a matrix of managed areas.

Protected Areas

As of 1994, around 8600 protected areas had been designated worldwide, covering some 8 million* km^2 (Table 15.1) (IUCN 1994; WRI 1994). Although 8 million km^2 may seem impressive, it represents only about 6% of the Earth's total land surface. The world's largest park is in Greenland and covers 972,000 km^2, accounting for about 12% of the global area protected. Only 3% of the Earth's surface is strictly protected in scientific reserves and national parks. The measurements of protected areas in individual countries and on continents are only approximate because sometimes the laws protecting national parks and wildlife sanctuaries are not actually enforced, and sometimes sections of managed areas, which are not technically protected, are care-

*Uncertainty about the number and size of protected areas stems from the different standards used throughout the world and the degree of protection actually given to a designated area.

TABLE 15.1 **Protected and managed areas in the world's geographical regions**

	Protected areas (IUCN categories I–V)			Managed areas (IUCN category VI)		
Region	**Number of areas**	**Size (km^2)**	**Percent of land area**	**Number of areas**	**Size (km^2)**	**Percent of land area**
Africa	704	1,388,930	4.6	1,562	746,360	2.5
Asia[a]	2,181	1,211,610	4.4	1,149	306,290	1.1
North and Central America	1,752	2,632,500	11.7	243	161,470	0.7
South America	667	1,145,960	6.4	679	2,279,350	12.7
Europe	2,177	455,330	9.3	143	40,350	0.8
U.S.S.R. (former)	218	243,300	1.1	1	4,000	0
Oceania[b]	920	845,040	9.9	91	50,000	0.6
World[c]	8,619	7,922,660	5.9	3,868	3,588,480	2.7

Source: WRI 1994.
[a] Not including the former U.S.S.R.
[b] Australia, New Zealand, and the Pacific Islands.
[c] Includes only lands protected by national governments; does not include private or locally protected sites; also does not include Antarctica.

fully protected in practice. Examples of the latter are the sections within U.S. national forests designated as wilderness areas. The coverage of protected areas varies dramatically among countries; there are high proportions of land protection in Germany (25%), Austria (25%), and the United Kingdom (19%) and surprisingly low proportions in Russia (1.2%), Greece (0.8%), and Turkey (0.3%).

The momentum to establish protected areas has been increasing throughout the twentieth century and reached its peak in the 1970s and early 1980s (Figure 15.1). The drop-off during the 1980s reflects the lack of political will on the part of citizens and governments to designate more protected areas and the perception that enough land has already been protected. Protected areas will never cover a large percentage of the Earth's surface—perhaps 7%–10% or slightly more—due to the perceived needs of human society for natural resources. Many protected areas are located on land considered to be of little economic value. This limited area of protected habitat emphasizes the biological significance of the 10%–20% of the land that is managed for resource production. In the United States, the Forest Service and the Bureau of Land Management together manage 24% of the land (primarily for resource production), while in Costa Rica about 17% of the land is managed for timber production and as Indian reserves.

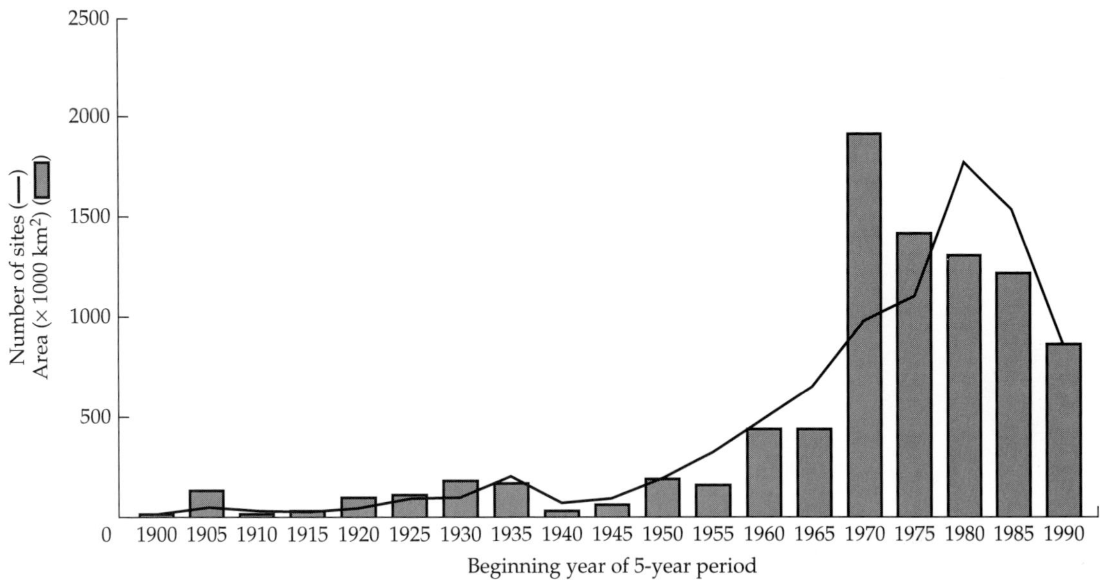

Figure 15.1 The solid line graphs the number of new protected areas; the bars indicate the area encompassed in new protected areas (in km^2) at 5-year intervals. (After McNeeley et al. 1994.)

Marine conservation has lagged behind terrestrial conservation efforts; even establishing priorities has proved difficult (Agardy 1997). Determining biogeographic provinces for the marine environment is much more difficult than for the terrestrial environment because boundaries between realms are less sharp, dispersal of larval and adult stages is more widespread, and the marine environment is less well known (Grassle 1991). Scientists have described 40 marine biogeographic provinces using a combination of the distribution of related marine animals (coastal, shelf, ocean) as well as physical properties that affect ecology and distribution (currents, temperature) (Hayden et al. 1984).

Urgent efforts are being made throughout the world to protect marine biological diversity in each one of these biogeographic provinces by establishing marine parks comparable to terrestrial parks (Kenchington and Agardy 1990), such as the Hol Chan Marine Reserve in Belize, which is proving invaluable to the rapidly growing ecotourism industry. The El Nido Marine Reserve along the coast of Palawan Island in the Philippines provides protection for the sea cow (also called the dugong), the hawksbill sea turtle, and the Ridley sea turtle. Over 1300 marine and coastal protected areas have been established worldwide, protecting about 800,000 km^2 (Agardy 1997). Accounting for half of the total are the three largest marine protected areas: the Great Barrier Reef Marine Park in Australia, the Galápagos Marine Park, and the Netherlands' North Sea Reserve. About one-fourth of the 300 internationally recognized biosphere reserves include coastal or estuarine habitats (Ray and Gregg

1991). Protection of the nursery grounds of commercial species and maintaining areas for recreational diving and fishing are among the main economic reasons for establishing these reserves. Unfortunately, many of these reserves only exist on the map and receive little protection from overharvesting and pollution. Regulating the harvesting of fish that migrate in international waters has proven to be very difficult, and water pollution can damage extensive coastal areas and enclosed seas. These problems need to be seriously addressed (Norse 1993).

The Effectiveness of Protected Areas

If protected areas cover only a small percentage of the total area of the world, how effectively can they preserve the world's species? Concentrations of species occur at particular places in the landscape: along elevational gradients, at places where different geological formations are juxtaposed, in areas that are geologically old, and at places that have an abundance of critical natural resources (e.g., streams and water holes in otherwise dry habitats; caves and hollow tree trunks that can be used by birds, bats, and other animals for nesting; salt licks that provide essential mineral nutrients) (Carroll 1992).

Often a landscape contains large expanses of a fairly uniform habitat type and only a few small areas of rare habitat types. Protecting biological diversity in this case probably will not depend so much on preserving large areas of the common habitat type as on including representatives of all the habitats in a system of protected areas. Recent conservation management plans for Sarawak on the northwest coast of Borneo have emphasized the need to distribute new national parks in order to cover all major vegetation types and biological communities (Kavanaugh et al. 1989). The following examples illustrate the potential effectiveness of protected areas of limited extent:

- Parks and wildlife sanctuaries cover only about 8% of Thailand but include 88% of its resident forest bird species (Rand 1985, reported in Reid and Miller 1989).
- The Indonesian government plans to protect populations of all native bird and primate species within its system of national parks and reserves. This goal is being accomplished by designating 10% of Indonesia's land as protected area.
- In most of the large tropical African countries, the majority of the native bird species have populations inside protected areas (Table 15.2). For example, Zaire has more than 1000 bird species, and 89% of them occur in the 3.9% of the land area under protection. Similarly, 85% of Kenya's birds are protected in only 5.4% of the land area included in parks (Sayer and Stuart 1988).
- The 30 major protected areas in tropical Africa collectively include 67 of the 70 species of kingfishers, bee-eaters, rollers, hoopoes, and

teristics of their vegetation, each of which supports unique biological communities—shows that the amount of protected area and the percentage of area protected vary considerably (Table 15.3). Based on the information in this table, probably the greatest priority for conservation would be to increase the area of protection for temperate grasslands and lake systems because these communities are limited in area and only a small percentage of their area is protected.

A total of 124 countries currently have protected areas. While it could be argued that all countries should have at least one national park, large countries with rich biotas and a variety of ecosystem types would obviously benefit from having many protected areas.

The 1982 IUCN Bali Action Plan recognizes the need to conserve ecosystems in its objective to establish a worldwide network of national parks and protected areas covering all terrestrial ecological regions. In this effort, regions throughout the world are being evaluated for the current percentage of area under protection, threats, conservation importance, and need for action. Reviews have been completed for the Indomalayan Realm (MacKinnon and MacKinnon 1986a; WCMC 1992), the Afrotropical Realm (MacKinnon and MacKinnon 1986b), and Oceania (Dahl 1986). This information is being used to classify countries on the basis of their conservation needs (Dingwall et al. 1994).

TABLE 15.3 ***The relative protection of 14 major biomes***

Biome type	Total area (km^2)	Number of protected areas	Area protected (km^2)	Percent of area protected
Tropical rain forests and moist forests	10,513,210	506	538,334	5.1
Tropical dry forests/woodlands	17,312,538	799	817,551	4.7
Tropical grasslands/savannahs	4,264,833	59	235,128	5.5
Subtropical/temperate rain forests/woodlands	3,930,979	899	366,297	9.3
Temperate broadleaf (deciduous) forests	11,216,660	1507	358,240	3.2
Temperate evergreen coniferous forests	3,757,144	776	177,584	4.7
Temperate grasslands	8,976,591	194	99,982	0.8
Warm deserts/semi-deserts	24,279,842	300	984,007	4.1
Cold deserts	9,250,252	136	364,720	3.9
Boreal forests and woodlands	15,682,817	429	487,227	3.1
Tundra (Arctic and alpine grasslands)	22,017,390	78	1,645,043	7.5
Island systems (e.g., Hawaii, Galápagos, etc.)	3,252,270	530	322,769	9.9
Lake systems (e.g., U.S. Great Lakes, African Great Lakes)	517,694	17	6,635	1.3
Mountain systems (e.g., Andes, Himalayas)	10,633,145	1277	852,494	8.0

Source: Data from IUCN 1994.

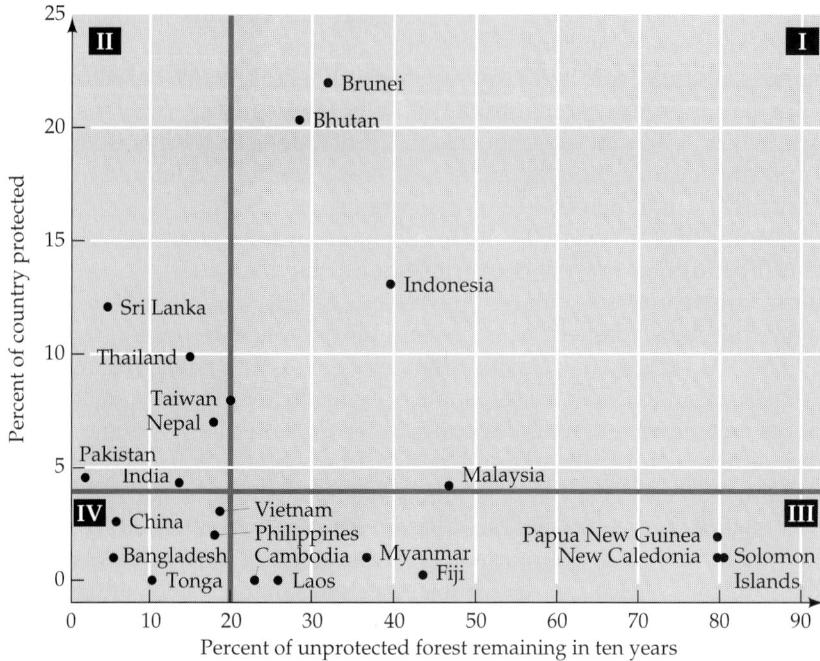

Figure 15.6 Distribution of Indo-Pacific countries based on (1) the percentage of their forests that are currently protected and (2) the percentage of unprotected forest predicted to remain intact in 10 years. The figure highlights countries with at least 20% forest cover but less than 4% of that protected; these are high-priority countries for establishing reserves. (After Dinerstein and Wikramanayake 1993.)

In a system developed by Dinerstein and Wikramanayake (1993), tropical Asian countries are classified into four categories on the basis of the percent of their currently protected rain forest and the percent of unprotected forest predicted still to be intact in 10 years (Figure 15.6). Category I countries (Brunei, Indonesia, Bhutan, and Malaysia) have protected large amounts of forest and will have remaining unprotected forests in the near future. The funding priority for these countries should be for park infrastructure, so that "paper parks" become real parks on the ground. Category II countries (Thailand, Sri Lanka, India, Nepal, and Pakistan) have many parks, but the remaining unprotected forest is disappearing rapidly. New parks need to be created before all of the unprotected forests and their associated species are eliminated. Category III countries (such as Papua New Guinea, Solomon Islands, and Laos) have a lot of forest but few protected areas, usually because of other national priorities and minimal financing from conservation organizations and developed countries. Funding the establishment of new parks would be a good investment. Category IV countries (Vietnam, Philippines, China, and Tonga) have little protected forest and little forest left to protect; the remaining unprotected areas are being degraded rapidly by human activities. Saving the remaining forest patches in these countries is an urgent conservation priority.

need prompt attention. These images can sometimes provide a dramatic illustration that current government policies are not working on the ground and need to be changed. This approach can highlight correlations among the abiotic and biotic elements of the landscape, help plan parks that include ecosystem diversity, and even suggest sites to search for rare species.

An ambitious attempt to apply GIS is the Eastside Ecosystem Management Project, which is charged with analyzing the ecosystem, biodiversity, and socioeconomic factors of the Columbia River Basin east of the Cascade Mountains (McLean 1995). One hundred specialists drawn from the U.S. Bureau of Land Management, the Forest Service, and other agencies are digitizing 10,000 maps covering 600,000 km^2 and including 100 layers of information. The goal is to produce a management plan that addresses the overall needs of the region: preserving endangered species such as the northern spotted owl, preserving salmon and trout fisheries, maintaining the timber industry, and allowing for local economic development.

International Approaches

In order to help establish priorities in conservation efforts, attempts have been made by the International Union for the Conservation of Nature (IUCN), the World Conservation Monitoring Centre, Birdlife International, and others to identify "hot spots" for preservation: key areas of the world that have great biological diversity, high levels of endemism, and are under immediate threat of species extinctions and habitat destruction (Figure 15.10; Table 15.4). Using these criteria for rain forest plants, Myers (1988a) identified 12 tropical hot spots that together include 14% of the world's plant species on only 0.2% of its total land surface. This analysis was later expanded (Myers 1991) to include 8 nonforest habitats—four in the tropics and four outside of the tropics in Mediterranean-type climates. One notable area is southern Africa, including South Africa, Lesotho, Swaziland, Namibia, and Botswana, which has 23,200 plant species, 80% of which are endemic to the region. Another valuable approach has been to identify 12 megadiversity countries that together contain 60%–70% of the world's biological diversity: Mexico, Colombia, Brazil, Peru, Ecuador, Zaire, Madagascar, Indonesia, Malaysia, India, China, and Australia (Table 15.5). These countries are possible targets for increased funding and conservation attention (Mittermeier 1988; Mittermeier and Werner 1990).

International priorities and global hot spots overlap considerably. There is general agreement on the need for increased conservation efforts and the establishment of additional protected areas in the following regions:

- *Latin America*: The coastal forests of Ecuador; the Atlantic coast forest of Brazil.

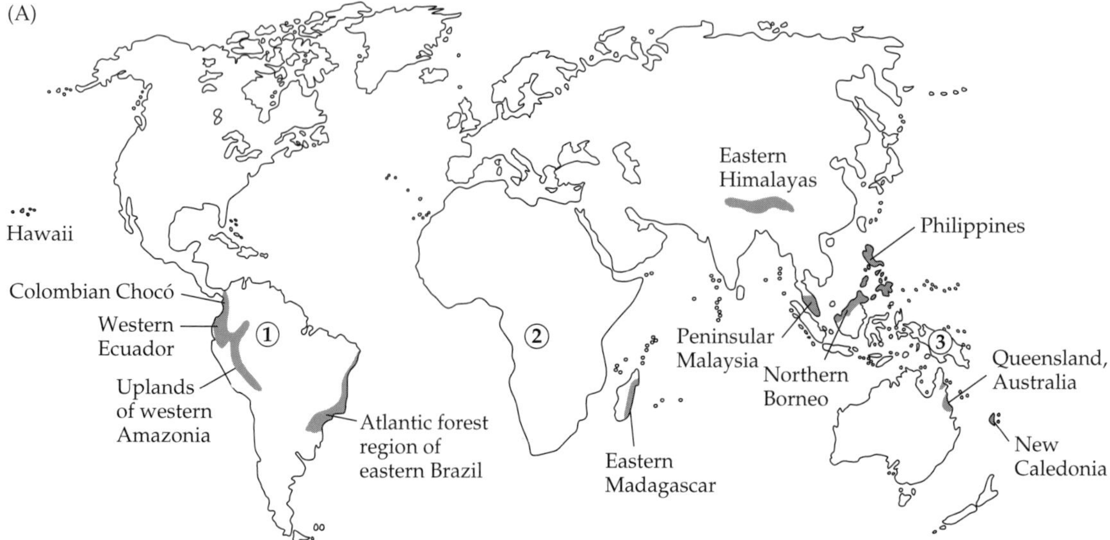

Figure 15.10 "Hot spots" of high endemism and significant threat of imminent extinctions. (A) Tropical rain forest hot spots, plus the Eastern Himalayas. The circled numbers indicate the only three remaining tropical rainforest wilderness areas of any extent. (B) Eight hot spots in other climatic ecosystems. (Data from Myers 1988, 1991.)

- *Africa*: The mountain forests of Tanzania and Kenya; the large lakes throughout the continent; the island of Madagascar.
- *Asia*: Southwestern Sri Lanka; the eastern Himalayas; Indochina (Myanmar, Thailand, Kampuchea, Laos, Vietnam, and southeastern China); the Philippines.
- *Oceania*: New Caledonia.

Additional priorities for conservation efforts include the eastern and southern Brazilian Amazon, the uplands of the western Amazon, Colombia, Cameroon, equatorial West Africa, the Sudanian zone, Borneo, Sulawesi, Peninsular Malaysia, Bangladesh/Bhutan, eastern Nepal, and Hawaii.

The hot spot approach is being further refined to include the percentage of each country that is now protected and the degree to which habitats within a country are predicted to remain intact in the near future (Dinerstein and Wikramanayake 1993). An assessment of governments' ability to establish and maintain parks once the funding is available needs to be done.

Wilderness Areas

Large blocks of land that have been minimally affected by human activity, that have a low human population density, and are not likely to be developed in the near future are perhaps the only places on Earth where large mammals can survive in the wild. These wilderness areas can remain as controls showing what natural communities are like with minimal human influence. For example, large protected areas of wilderness in the Chang Tang Reserve of the Tibetan Plateau will be

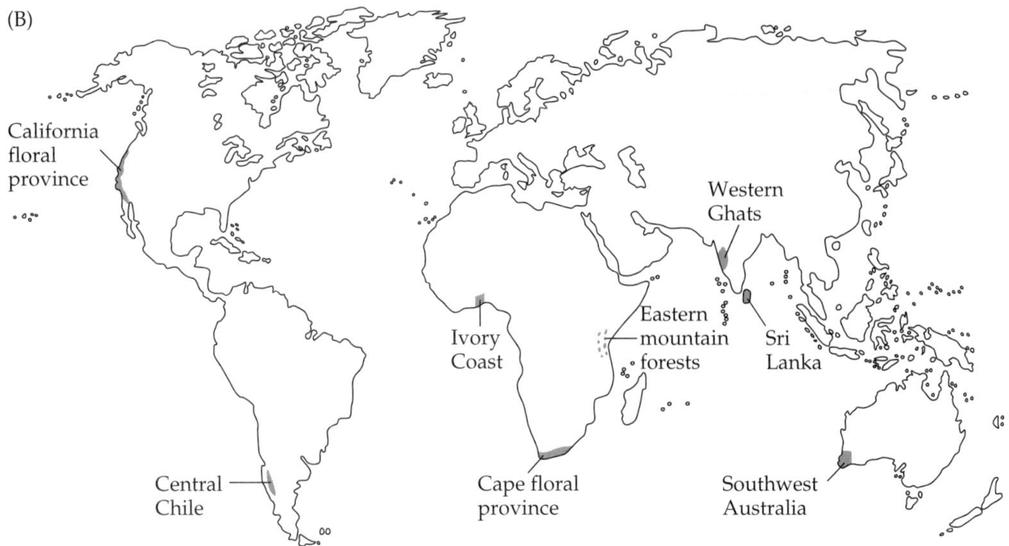

TABLE 15.4 **Numbers of endemic species in some "hot spot" areas**

Region	Area (km^2)	Vascular plants	Mammals	Reptiles	Amphibians
Upland western Amazonia	100,000	5000	—	—	ca. 70
Atlantic coastal Brazil	1,000,000	5000	40	92	168
Western Ecuador	27,000	2500	9	—	—
Colombian Chocó	100,000	2500	8	137	111
Philippines	250,000	3700	98	120	41
Northern Borneo	190,000	3500	42	69	47
Peninsular Malaysia	120,000	2400	4	25	7
Southwestern Australia	113,000	2830	10	25	22
Western Ghats (India)	50,000	1600	7	91	84
Madagascar	62,000	4900	86	234	142
Cape region (South Africa)	134,000	6000	16	43	23
California Floristic Province	324,000	2140	15	25	7
Central Chile	140,000	1450	—	—	—
New Caledonia	15,000	1400	2	21	0
Eastern Himalayas	340,000	3500	—	20	25

Source: Data from Myers 1988a; World Conservation and Monitoring Centre 1992.
Note: Original area of rain forest only is given for the tropical regions.

TABLE 15.5 **"Top ten" countries with the largest number of species of selected well-known groups of organisms**

Rank	Mammals	Birds	Amphibians	Reptiles	Swallowtail butterflies	Flowering plants[a]
1	Indonesia 515	Colombia 1721	Brazil 516	Mexico 717	Indonesia 121	Brazil 55,000
2	Mexico 449	Peru 1701	Colombia 407	Australia 686	China 99–104	Colombia 45,000
3	Brazil 428	Brazil 1622	Ecuador 358	Indonesia ca. 600	India 77	China 27,000
4	Zaire 409	Indonesia 1519	Mexico 282	Brazil 467	Brazil 74	Mexico 25,000
5	China 394	Ecuador 1447	Indonesia 270	India 453	Myanmar 68	Australia 23,000
6	Peru 361	Venezuela 1275	China 265	Colombia 383	Ecuador 64	S. Africa 21,000
7	Colombia 359	Bolivia ca. 1250	Peru 251	Ecuador 345	Colombia 59	Indonesia 20,000
8	India 350	India 1200	Zaire 216	Peru 297	Peru 58	Venezuela 20,000
9	Uganda 311	Malaysia ca. 1200	U.S.A. 205	Malaysia 294	Malaysia 55	Peru 20,000
10	Tanzania 310	China 1195	{Venezuela Australia} 197	{Thailand Papua New Guinea} 282	Mexico 52	U.S.S.R. (former) 20,000

Source: After Conservation International; data from numerous sources. Swallowtail data from Collins and Morris 1985. Data on flowering plants from Davis et al. 1986.

[a] Numbers of species given for flowering plants are estimates.

needed to preserve the remaining, declining populations of the wild yak (*Bos grunniens*) from hunting, habitat encroachment, and hybridization with domesticated yaks (Schaller and Wulin 1996). In the United States, proponents of the Wildlands Project are advocating the management of whole ecosystems to preserve viable populations of large carnivores such as grizzly bears, wolves, and large cats (Noss and Cooperrider 1994). Three large tropical wilderness areas also have been identified and established as conservation priorities (Figure 15.10A) (Conservation International 1990; Bryant et al. 1997):

- *South America*. One arc of wilderness containing rain forest, savannah, and mountains but few people runs through the southern Guianas, southern Venezuela, northern Brazil, Colombia, Ecuador, Peru, and Bolivia.

- *Africa.* A large area of equatorial Africa centered on the Zaire basin has a low population density and undisturbed habitat, including large portions of Gabon, the Republic of the Congo, and Zaire. Warfare and lack of government control prevents effective conservation activities in parts of the region.
- *New Guinea.* The island of New Guinea has the largest tracts of undisturbed forest in the Asian Pacific region despite the impacts of logging, mining, and transmigration programs. The eastern half of the island is the independent nation of Papua New Guinea, with 3.9 million people on 462,840 km^2 of land. The western half of the island, Irian Jaya, is a state of Indonesia and has a population of only 1.4 million people on 345,670 km^2. Large tracts of forest also occur on the island of Borneo, but logging, plantation agriculture, an expanding human population, and the development of a transportation network are rapidly reducing the area of undisturbed forest.

Centers of Diversity

Certain organisms are used as **biological diversity indicators** when specific data about whole communities are absent. Diversity in birds, for example, is considered a good indicator of the diversity of a community in some areas of the world. Several analyses have put this principle into practice, though it is also true that sometimes different groups of organisms will not correspond in their geographical patterns of diversity. In one case, Terborgh and Winter (1983) identified areas of Colombia and Ecuador that had the greatest concentrations of bird species and proposed that these areas should be made into protected areas. In another case, analysis of existing data bases revealed that the protection of sites with endangered plants in the United States also would protect many endangered animal species—on a relatively small amount of the total U.S. land area (Dobson et al. 1997).

This approach is now being expanded in a systematic way. The IUCN Plant Conservation Office in England is identifying and documenting about 250 global centers of plant diversity with large concentrations of species (WWF/IUCN 1997). The International Council for Bird Protection (ICBP) is identifying localities with large concentrations of birds that have restricted ranges, called Endemic Bird Areas (EBAs) (Stattersfield et al. 1998). To date, 218 localities containing 2451 restricted-range bird species have been identified (Figure 15.11). Many of these localities are islands and isolated mountain ranges that also have many endemic species of lizards, butterflies, and plants, and thus represent priorities for conservation. Further analysis has highlighted EBAs that contain no protected areas and require urgent conservation measures.

An innovative approach uses the detailed British bird census records to identify potential sites for new nature reserves (Williams et

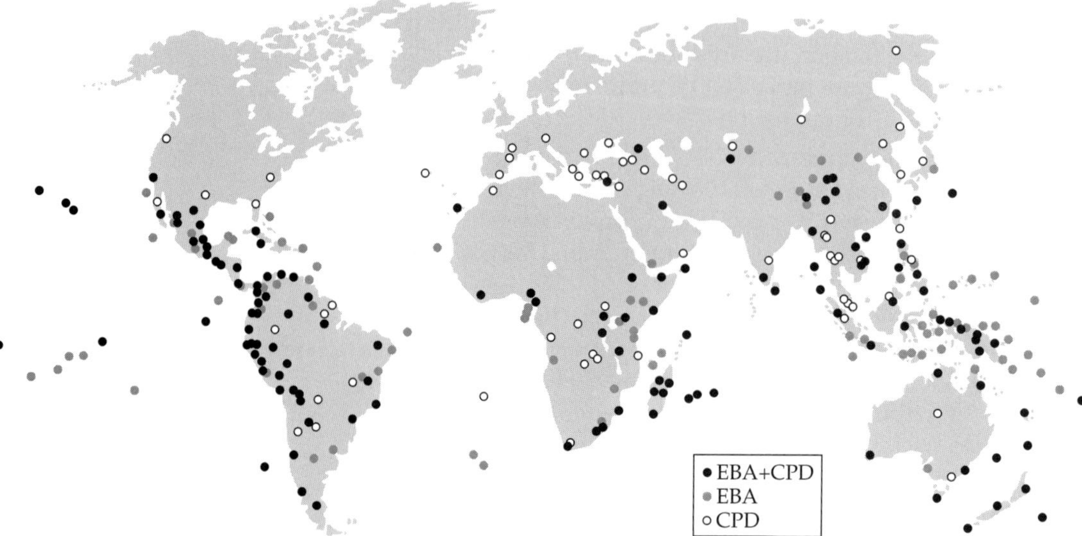

Figure 15.11 Two large projects have identified centers of diversity. Birdlife International has identified Endemic Bird Areas (EBAs) that include concentrations of restricted-range species; and the Centers of Plant Diversity Project (CPD) has identified high concentrations of restricted-range plant species. There is considerable overlap between the areas of species concentration, with many of the sites found in tropical areas. Many EBAs are also found on islands, and CPDs are sometimes found in more temperate and Mediterranean climates. (From Stattersfield et al. 1998.)

al. 1996). Using 170,098 documented breeding records of 218 species within 2827 10 km × 10 km census grid cells covering all of Britain, three possible reserve systems were analyzed for their ability to protect breeding sites for British birds in a network including 5% of the grid cells. These three systems were created to (1) protect hot spots of richness that contain the most species, (2) protect hot spots of rare species (narrowly distributed endemics), and (3) protect sets of **complementary areas** selected for the greatest combined number of species. The results of the analysis show that while selecting species hot spots results in the greatest number of bird species per grid cell, it misses 11% of Britain's rare bird species. In contrast, selecting for complementary areas protects all of the bird species and is probably the most effective conservation strategy. Complementary areas can be selected on the basis of additional species or representative habitats not currently protected. The advantage of this approach is that each additional protected area adds to the range of biological diversity protected.

Establishing Protected Areas with Limited Data

In many countries, the data bases needed to identify centers of diversity have not yet been assembled. In some cases, groups of biologists can be convened to pool their collective knowledge, identifying localities that should be protected (Hawksworth et al. 1997). Teams of biologists can be dispatched to poorly known areas to make an inventory of species. Where decisions on park boundaries have to be made quickly, biologists are being trained to make "Rapid Biodiversity Assessments" that involve making lists of species, checking for species of special concern, estimating the total number of species, and looking out for new species and features of special interest (Oliver and Beattie 1993).

In general, new protected areas should encompass biological communities that are rich in endemic species, that contain community types underrepresented in other protected areas, that support threatened species, and that contain resources of potential use to people, such as species of potential agricultural or medicinal use. However, such data typically do not exist. One way of circumventing the lack of data is to base decisions on general principles of ecology and conservation biology, as described more completely in Chapter 16. For example, Jared Diamond (1986) was asked by the Indonesian government to help design a national park system covering Irian Jaya, the western half of New Guinea (Figure 15.12). On the surface this seemed like an impossible task, since much of the region had never been surveyed biologically. However, Diamond was able to propose a series of reserves based on sound conservation principles. The principles include protecting elevational gradients that encompass diverse habitats, the need to have large parks to protect low-density species, the need to protect representative habitats in different climatic zones, and the need to protect individual biogeographic areas that have many endemic species.

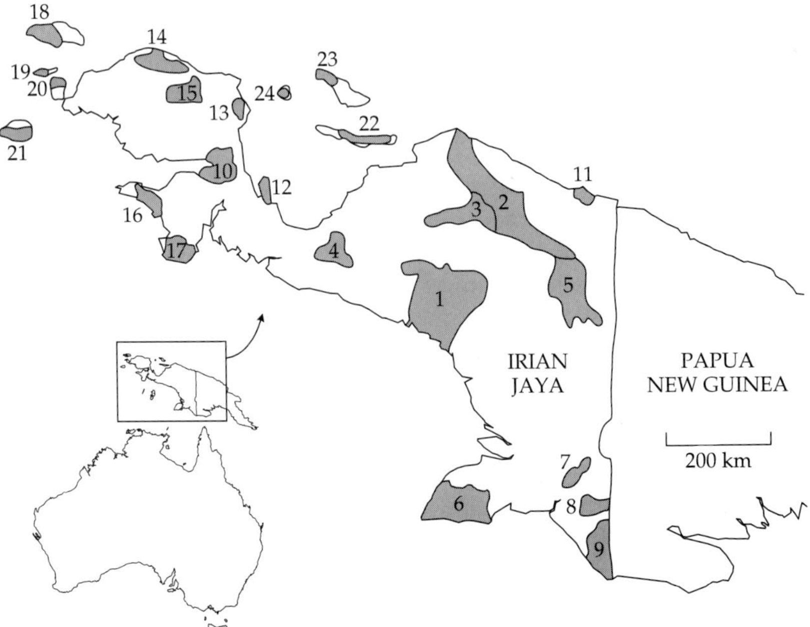

Figure 15.12 Reserves in Irian Jaya approved by the Indonesian government as of 1983. In addition to the 24 large reserves indicated, an additional 11 smaller reserves were established. Reserves were positioned to include major habitat types, centers of endemism, and islands. (From Diamond 1986.)

National Priorities

The international conservation community can help national and local governments establish guidelines and find opportunities to protect biological diversity, but in the end they must determine their own priorities. Many countries are in the process of doing so or have recently prepared National Environmental Action Plans, National Biodiversity Action Plans, or Tropical Forest Action Plans.

The Indonesian government has recently considered the need to balance the protection of its treasure trove of 15%–25% of the world's species against the requirements of its growing population of 185 million people. The Indonesian Biodiversity Action Plan calls for the expansion of its park system to include about 10% of the area of the country to protect all species in the wild. Additional priorities include strengthening park management, developing the support of local people for parks, securing stable funding for the parks, and developing new zoo and botanical garden facilities. Appropriate for a nation made up of 17,000 islands, plans are included to greatly increase the protection of marine and coastal waters, particularly mangroves.

Resources and personnel can be effectively directed to the most critical conservation problems worldwide once priorities are established. Prioritization should reduce the tendency of funding agencies, tropical scientists, and development officers to cluster together in a few politically stable, accessible countries with high-profile projects. The decision of the MacArthur Foundation, one of the largest private sources of funds for conservation activities, to concentrate on different areas of the world for several years at a time—a "moving spotlight" approach—is a valuable counter to the tendency to concentrate all resources on a few well-known places such as Costa Rica, Kenya, and Brazil.

The amount of money available to acquire and manage new national parks is increasing substantially as a result of the creation of the Global Environment Facility (GEF) at the 1992 Earth Summit. The GEF is providing $1.5 billion over three years for environmental projects and approximately one-third of these funds are allocated for biodiversity projects. Conservation biologists can play a valuable role in using their field experience to identify and recommend new areas suitable for preservation.

Park management, a subject covered in subsequent chapters, is of central importance in ensuring that a park actually fulfills its goals and is not just a "paper park" that is soon destroyed and degraded. Furthermore, biological communities inside a protected area are not immune to outside forces such as hunting, pollution, poverty, and war, which may threaten their existence. As Dasmann (1987) stated,

> The [U.S. National] Park Service is responsible for all resources within the park, but its authority ends at the park boundary. Air,

> water, wildlife, seeds, nutrients, [and] energy move in and out of the park, but once across the boundary some other agency assumes responsibility.

In many cases, this means that if issues outside park boundaries are not addressed, biological diversity will continue to decline within protected areas.

Summary

1. Protecting habitat is the most effective method for preserving biological diversity. Land can be purchased by governments, private organizations such as The Nature Conservancy, or private individuals. The extent of human impacts on protected habitats varies greatly, and compromises must be made between protecting biological diversity and satisfying human needs. Protected areas include nature reserves, national parks, wildlife sanctuaries, national monuments, and protected landscapes and seascapes. Considerable biological diversity may be present in unprotected multiple-use management areas.

2. About 6% of the Earth's surface is included in about 8600 protected areas. The total will probably never exceed 10% due to the perceived needs of human society for the use of natural resources. Yet in many countries 10%–20% of the land is managed for multiple-use resource production.

3. Well-selected protected areas can initially protect large numbers of species. However, the future of many of these species remains in doubt due to small population sizes, the inability of the protected area to supply all of the needed requirements of species, the tendency of many species to migrate, and threats from outside the protected area. To effectively preserve biological diversity, protected areas need to be large and well managed and to include examples of all biological communities.

4. Government agencies and conservation organizations are now setting priorities for establishing new protected areas based on the relative distinctiveness, endangerment, and utility of the species and biological communities occurring in a place. Natural Heritage Programs and IUCN specialist groups focus on establishing parks to protect endangered species and communities. International approaches involve identifying hot spots of large concentrations of bird and plant species. If these areas can be protected, then most of the world's biological diversity will be protected.

For Discussion

1. Obtain a map of a town, state, or nation that shows protected areas (such as nature reserves and parks) and multiple-use managed areas. Who is responsible for each parcel of land, and what is their purpose in managing it?

    a. Consider aquatic habitats in this region (ponds, marshes, streams, rivers, lakes, estuaries, coastal zones, etc.). Who is responsible for managing these environments, and how do they balance the need for protecting biological diversity with the needs of society for natural resources?

    b. If you could add protected areas to this region, where would you place them and why? Show their exact location, size, and shape and justify your choices.

2. Imagine that the only population of a rare and declining flamingo species lives along the shore of an isolated lake. This lake has numerous unique species of fish, crayfish, and insects. The lake and its shores are owned by a logging company that is planning to build a paper mill on the shore where the flamingos nest. This mill will seriously pollute the lake and destroy the food eaten by the flamingos. You have $1 million to spend on conservation in this area and the company is willing to sell the lake and its shores for $1 million. An effective flamingo conservation program involving captive breeding, release of new individuals into the population, habitat improvement, and natural history studies would cost $750,000. Is it better to buy the land and not devote the resources to helping the flamingo? Or would it be better to take care of the flamingo and allow the lake to be destroyed? Can you suggest other alternatives or possibilities?

Suggested Readings

Agardy, T. S. 1997. *Marine Protected Areas and Ocean Conservation.* R. G. Landes Company, Austin, Texas. A wide range of planning, design, and policy issues are discussed by a leading authority.

Crumpacker, D. W., S. W. Hodge, D. Friedley and W. P. Gregg, Jr. 1988. A preliminary assessment of the status of major terrestrial and wetland ecosystems on federal and Indian lands in the United States. *Conservation Biology* 2: 103–115. Comprehensive analysis of the gaps in the protection of U.S. biological communities.

Dinerstein, E. and E. D. Wikramanayake. 1993. Beyond hot spots: How to prioritize investments to conserve biodiversity in the Indo-Pacific region. *Conservation Biology* 7: 53–65. Large amounts of information and quantitative analysis.

Dingwall, P., J. Harrison and J. A. McNeely (eds.). 1994. *Protecting Nature: Regional Reviews of Protected Areas.* IUCN, Gland, Switzerland. Authoritative reports on current status of protected areas throughout the world.

Dobson, A. P., J. Rodriguez, W. M. Roberts and D. S. Wilcove. 1997. Geographic distribution of endangered species in the United States. *Science* 275: 550–554. A visually appealing perspective on where concentrations of endangered species occur.

International Union for the Conservation of Nature. 1994. *Guidelines for Protected Area Management Categories.* IUCN, Gland, Switzerland. Definitive work on protected areas. Also see other publications by the IUCN.

Johnson, N. 1995. *Biodiversity in the Balance: Approaches to Setting Geographic Conservation Priorities.* Biodiversity Support Program, World Wildlife Fund, Washington, D.C. Excellent overview of the approaches used to establish conservation priorities.

McLean, H. 1995. Smart maps: forestry's newest frontier. *American Forests* (March–April): 15–38. Introductory article listing major GIS projects.

Mittermeier R. A. and T. B. Werner. 1990. Wealth of plants and animals unites "megadiversity" countries. *Tropicus* 4(1): 1, 4–5. Twelve countries contain the majority of the world's plant and animal species.

Myers, N. 1991. The biodiversity challenge: Expanded "hot spots" analysis. *Environmentalist* 10: 243–256. Highlights centers of biodiversity.

The Nature Conservancy. 1996. *Designing a Geography of Hope: Guidelines for an Ecoregion-Based Conservation in The Nature Conservancy.* The Nature Conservancy, Arlington, VA. Clearly stated conservation philosophy for guiding land aquisition policy.

Oliver, I. and A. J. Beattie. 1993. A possible method for the rapid assessment of biodiversity. *Conservation Biology* 7: 562–568. Quick methods to assess biodiversity without being concerned with exact identification.

Scott, J. M. and B. Csuti. 1996. Gap analysis for biodiversity survey and maintenance. In *Biodiversity II: Understanding and Protecting our Biological Resources*, M. L. Reaka-Kudla, D. E. Wilson and E. O. Wilson (eds.), pp. 321–340. John Henry Press, Washington, D.C. Geographic Information Systems (GIS) represent an innovative approach to identifying gaps in conservation programs.

Stattersfield, A. J., M. J. Crosby, A. J. Long and D. C. Wege. 1998. *Endemic Bird Areas of the World: Priorities for Biodiversity Conservation*. Birdlife International, Cambridge. Highlights areas that need additional protection.

Williams, P. 1995. A comparison of richness hot spots, rarity hot spots, and complementary areas for conserving the diversity of British birds. *Conservation Biology* 10: 155–174. Elegant use of census data to pinpoint concentrations of rare species.

World Resources Institute. 1994. *World Resources 1994–95*. Oxford University Press, New York. Assessment of the world's natural resources and protected areas with numerous tables and summaries.

CHAPTER 16

Designing Protected Areas

THE SIZE AND PLACEMENT of protected areas throughout the world are often determined by the distribution of people, potential land values, the political efforts of conservation-minded citizens, and historical factors. In many cases, lands are set aside for conservation protection because they have no immediate commercial value, "the lands that nobody wanted" (Pressey 1994; Wallis deVries 1995). The largest parks usually occur in areas where few people live and where the land is considered unsuitable or too remote for agriculture, logging, urban development, or other human activities. Examples are the low heath forests on nutrient-poor soils at Bako National Park in Malaysia, the rugged, rocky mountain parks of Switzerland, the huge desert parks of the U.S. Southwest, and the 100 million ha of federal land in Alaska occupying tundra and mountains. Small conservation areas are common in large metropolitan areas and in densely settled and industrialized countries like England. Many of the conservation areas and parks in metropolitan areas of Europe and North America were formerly estates of wealthy citizens and royalty. In the U.S. Midwest, a number of the prairie nature reserves are old cemeteries, railroad rights-of-way, and other oddly shaped pieces with unusual histories.

Although parks and conservation areas often have been created in a haphazard fashion, depending on the availability of money and land, a considerable body of ecological literature has been developed addressing the most efficient way to design conservation areas to protect biological diversity (Game and Peterken 1984; Pressey et al. 1993; Shafer 1997). Some of the guidelines relate to the island biogeography model of MacArthur and Wilson (1967), described in Chapter 8. This approach makes the critical assumption, which is often invalid, that parks are habitat islands isolated by expanses of inhospitable terrain. Nevertheless, the guidelines developed from this research have proved to be of great interest to governments, corporations, and private landowners who are being urged or mandated to manage their properties both for the commercial production of natural resources and for biological diversity.

Key questions conservation biologists have addressed include:

1. How large must nature reserves be to protect species?
2. Is it better to have a single large reserve or many smaller reserves?
3. How many individuals of an endangered species must be protected in a reserve to prevent extinction?
4. What is the best shape for a nature reserve?
5. When several reserves are created, should they be close together or far apart, and should they be isolated from one another or connected by corridors?

Researchers working with island biogeography models have proposed some answers to these questions, but they are still being debated (Figure 16.1). Some scientists even question if these models, developed for islands in an ocean, are truly applicable to fragmented landscapes and systems of protected areas. The most thorough, critical look at this subject is *Nature Reserves: Island Theory and Conservation Practice* (Shafer 1990), in which models are examined in relation to empirical evidence and practical experience.

Reserve Size

An early debate occurred over whether species richness is maximized in one large nature reserve or in several smaller ones of an equal total area (Diamond 1975; Simberloff and Abele 1982; Soulé and Simberloff 1986); this is known in the literature as the SLOSS debate (*s*ingle *l*arge *o*r *s*everal *s*mall). For example, is it better to set aside one reserve of

small reserves account for 30%–40% of the protected area of the Netherlands (McNeely et al. 1994).

Bukit Timah Nature Reserve in Singapore is an excellent example of a small reserve providing long-term protection for numerous species. This 50-ha forest reserve represents 0.2% of the original forested area and has been isolated from other forests since 1860, yet it still protects 74% of the original flora, 72% of the original bird species, and 56% of the fish (Corlett and Turner 1996). In addition, small reserves located near populated areas make excellent conservation education and nature study centers that further the long-range goals of conservation biology by developing public awareness of important issues (Deardon 1995).

Reserve Design in South Africa

The issue of nature reserve size is highlighted by conservation efforts to protect threatened plant species of the flora in Cape Province of South Africa. The Cape is one of the most remarkable floristic regions in the world; it occupies only 90,000 km^2, about the same size as the U.S. state of Maine, but contains 8590 vascular plant species, the highest ratio of plant species to area of any temperate or subtropical region

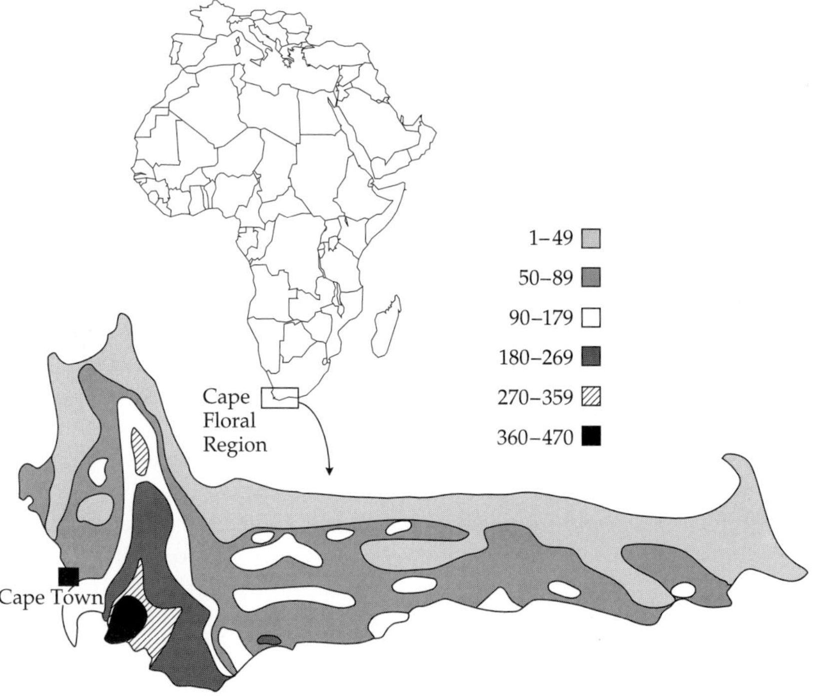

Figure 16.5 Species richness for flowering plants increases to an incredible level in the fynbos vegetation of the southwest corner of the Cape Floral Province in South Africa. The map shows the number of species in characteristic and endemic plant families, such as the Proteaceae, Ericaceae, and Restionacae. (From Rebelo and Siegfried 1990, based on Oliver et al. 1983.)

in the world (Figure 16.5). Furthermore, 68% of the species and five plant families are endemic to this small region. One reason for the high species diversity is the presence of five distinct vegetation types in the area, particularly the great species richness of the fynbos vegetation type (Rebelo and Siegfried 1990).

Unfortunately, this unique ecosystem is being reduced in area and damaged by agriculture, urban development, fire, and the invasion of exotic species. About 19% of the Cape flora—1621 species—are naturally rare or threatened by human activity (Hall et al. 1984). One of the most characteristic families of the Cape flora is the Proteaceae. Plants of this family are horticulturally important for their attractive flowers arranged in condensed, colorful heads. Fifty-three species of Proteaceae are restricted to only one or two populations; each population occupies an area of less than 5 km^2 and usually contains less than 1000 individuals. A proposed system of a few large parks of at least 100 km^2 in area would not protect most of these rare species. A better system would have many smaller, scattered reserves that would protect populations of individual rare species and unique habitat types (Tansley 1988). Such a system would be difficult, but not impossible, for reserve personnel to manage.

Effective Preservation of Species

Because population size is the best predictor of extinction probability (Terborgh and Winter 1980), reserves should be sufficient in area to preserve large populations of important species (rare and endangered species, keystone species, economically important species, etc.). Small populations may be vulnerable to extinction due to environmental fluctuations, demographic variation, inbreeding, and the loss of alleles, as described in Chapter 11. An isolated nature reserve that contains only four elephants will not have a self-perpetuating elephant population; an elephant population of 500 is far more likely to be self-perpetuating. The best evidence to date suggests that populations of at least several hundred reproductive individuals are needed to ensure the long-term viability of vertebrates, with several thousand individuals being a desirable goal (Lande 1995; see also Chapters 11 and 12). Having more than one population of a rare species within the nature reserve will increase the probability of survival for the species; if one population goes extinct, the species remains in the reserve and can potentially recolonize its former range.

While small populations of rare species in scattered isolated nature reserves may not be viable, several strategies exist to facilitate their survival. They can be managed as one metapopulation with efforts made to encourage natural migration between the nature reserves by maintaining connectivity. Occasionally individuals can be collected from one nature reserve and added to the breeding population of another. This may bolster the numbers at a site with a declining population. Also, if even a small number of individuals move between populations, the harmful genetic effects of small population size are dramatically reduced. Transporting individuals long distances between populations and transporting individuals between populations that appear to be genetically distinct should be done cautiously to avoid the spread of disease and outbreeding depression—the lowered survival rate and reproductive ability of offspring that follows from the breeding of individuals that are genetically far apart, such as sibling species or separate varieties (see Chapter 11).

A more difficult aspect of ensuring viable populations in reserves is dealing with the needs of wide-ranging species that cannot tolerate human disturbance. Ideally, a nature reserve should be large enough to include a viable population of the most wide-ranging species in it. Protection of the habitat of wide-ranging species, which are often large or conspicuous flagship species, or indicator species, will often provide adequate protection for the other species in the community. The large parks in eastern Africa managed for elephants, lions, and other large wildlife also protect numerous bird species. Extensive areas of pine habitat surrounding the Savannah River nuclear processing plant in South Carolina are being managed to protect the red-cockaded woodpecker (*Picoides borealis*), a species that needs large stands of mature longleaf pine trees (Figure 16.6). In the process, many endangered plant species are being protected as well.

The effective design of nature reserves requires a thorough knowledge of the natural history of important species and information on the distribution of biological communities. Feeding requirements, nesting behavior, daily and seasonal movement patterns, potential predators and competitors, and susceptibility to disease and pests all help determine an effective conservation strategy within nature reserves designed to include as many habitat requirements as possible for each species. A balance has to be struck between focusing on the needs of the flagship species to the exclusion of all other species and managing only for maximum species diversity, which could result in the loss of the flagship species that interest the general public.

Minimizing Edge and Fragmentation Effects

It is generally agreed that parks should be designed to minimize harmful edge effects. Round-shaped conservation areas minimize the edge-to-area ratio, and the center is farther from the edge than in other park shapes. Long, linear parks have the most edge, and all points in the park are close to the edge. Using these same arguments for parks with four straight sides, a square park is a better design than an elongated rectangle of the same area. These ideas have rarely, if ever, been implemented. Most parks have irregular shapes because land acquisition is typically a matter of opportunity rather than a matter of design.

As discussed in Chapter 9, internal fragmentation of reserves by

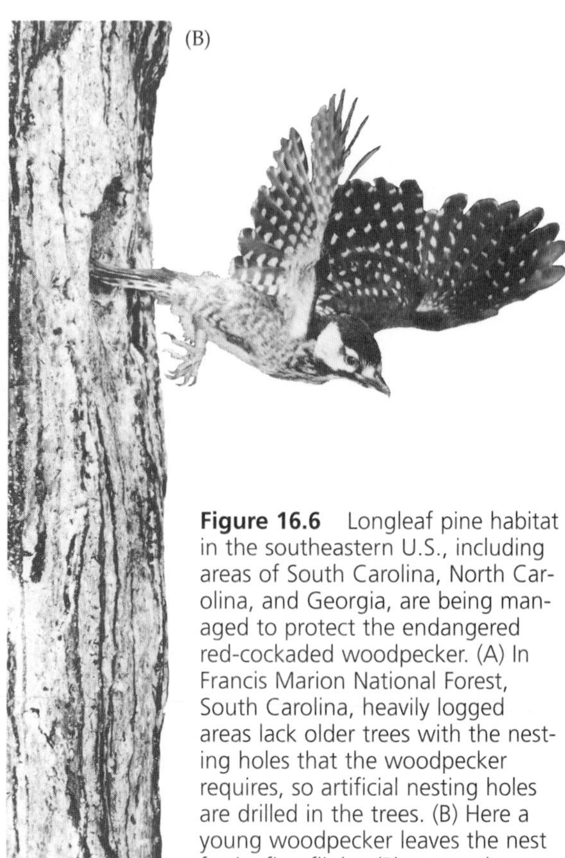

Figure 16.6 Longleaf pine habitat in the southeastern U.S., including areas of South Carolina, North Carolina, and Georgia, are being managed to protect the endangered red-cockaded woodpecker. (A) In Francis Marion National Forest, South Carolina, heavily logged areas lack older trees with the nesting holes that the woodpecker requires, so artificial nesting holes are drilled in the trees. (B) Here a young woodpecker leaves the nest for its first flight. (Photographs © Derrick Hamrick.)

roads, fences, farming, logging, and other human activities should be avoided as much as possible, because fragmentation often divides a large population into two or more smaller populations, each of which is more vulnerable to extinction than is the large population (Schonewald-Cox and Buechner 1992). Fragmentation also provides entry points for exotic species that may harm native species, creates more undesirable edge effects, and creates barriers to dispersal that reduce the probability of colonization of new sites and decrease the necessary gene flow for genetic variability.

The forces promoting fragmentation are powerful, because protected areas are often the only undeveloped land available for new projects such as agriculture, dams, and residential areas. This has been particularly true in densely settled areas such as Western Europe where undeveloped land is scarce and there is intense pressure for development (Wallis deVries 1995). In the eastern United States, many

Florida panther. Culverts and tunnels create passages under roads and railways and allow dispersal between habitat for lizards, amphibians, and mammals (Yanes et al. 1995). The Wildlands Project has a detailed plan that would link all large protected areas in the United States by habitat corridors, creating a system that would allow large and currently declining mammals to coexist with human society.

Corridors that facilitate natural patterns of migration will probably be the most successful at protecting species. For example, large grazing animals often migrate in regular patterns across a rangeland in search of water and the best vegetation. In seasonally dry savannah habitats, animals often migrate along the riparian forests that grow along streams and rivers (Spackman and Hughes 1995; Machtans et al. 1996). In mountainous areas, many bird and mammal species regularly migrate to higher elevations during the warmer months of the year. This principle was put into practice in Costa Rica to link two wildlife reserves, the Braulio Carillo National Park and La Selva Biological Station. A 7700-ha corridor of Costa Rican forest several kilometers wide, known as La Zona Protectora, was set aside to provide an elevational link that allows at least 35 species of birds to migrate between the two large conservation areas (Wilcove and May 1986).

As the global climate changes in the coming decade, many species will begin to migrate to higher elevations and to higher latitudes. Protecting expected migration routes—such as north–south river valleys, ridges, and coastlines—would be a useful precaution. Extending existing protected areas in the direction of anticipated species movements would help to maintain long-term populations.

Although the idea of corridors is intuitively appealing, there are some possible drawbacks (Simberloff et al. 1992). Corridors may facilitate the movement of pest species and disease; thus a single infestation could quickly spread to all of the connected nature reserves and cause the extinction of all populations of a rare species. Also, animals dispersing along corridors may be exposed to greater risks of predation, because human hunters as well as animal predators tend to concentrate on routes used by wildlife.

At present, empirical evidence supporting the value of corridors is very limited, despite a lot of enthusiasm for the idea (Rosenberg et al. 1997). The value of habitat corridors needs to be evaluated on a case-by-case basis. In general, maintaining existing corridors is probably worthwhile, because many of them are along watercourses that may be biologically important habitats themselves. When new parks are being carved out of large blocks of undeveloped land, incorporating corridors by leaving small clumps of original habitat between large conservation areas may facilitate movement in a "stepping-stone" process. Similarly, forest species are more likely to disperse through a matrix of recovering secondary forest than if the surrounding habitat is cleared farms and pastures. Corridors are most obviously needed along known migration routes. The abilities of different types of species to use corridors and intervening habitat areas to migrate between protected areas clearly needs to be assessed.

All of these theories of reserve design have been developed mainly with land animals and plants in mind. The applicability of these ideas to aquatic nature reserves, where dispersal mechanisms are largely unknown, requires further investigation. Protecting marine nature reserves requires particular attention to pollution control because of its subtle and widespread destructive effects. Steps in the right direction have been taken by the governments of islands such as the Turks and Caicos in the Caribbean: many individual islands have half or even more of their coastlines designated as marine parks. The entire island of Bonaire is a protected marine park, with ecotourism emerging as the leading industry.

Case Studies

Several case studies serve to illustrate the concept and practical applications of habitat corridors, and some of the difficulties involved in establishing and maintaining such protected pathways.

A PROPOSED WILDLIFE CORRIDOR IN TANZANIA In Tanzania, large herds of wildebeest, zebras, and other large animals migrate seasonally between Tarangire National Park and Lake Manyara National Park in search of food and water (Mwalyosi 1991). Lake Manyara National Park is notable for its scenic lake and rift escarpment and its high density and diversity of animal life attracted by the lush vegetation and reliable source of water. Because of its attractions and despite its small size, Lake Manyara National Park has the third largest number of visitors per year and the second highest amount of tourist revenue of any park in Tanzania. Managing wildlife in the area is a problem because the park is only 110 km^2 in size and is increasingly becoming surrounded by agricultural settlements. Originally the park was surrounded by the rough rangeland of the Masai Ecosystem, across which wildlife migrated freely. However, in the last few decades, the human population and their cattle have increased dramatically because irrigation has allowed farming to expand. Agricultural acreage in the vicinity of the park increased from 218 ha in 1957 to 1093 ha in 1980. While the total area is not great, some of the cultivated fields are within the traditional migratory routes of animals, resulting in damage to crops, killing of animals by farmers, and repeated conflicts between farmers and conservation authorities. If farmland continues to expand, this conflict will escalate.

To solve this problem, a proposal has been made to establish a defined migratory route between Tarangire National Park and Lake

Manyara National Park and to buy the adjacent farmland and return it to rangeland (Figure 16.8) (Mwalyosi 1991). If animals wander off their migratory routes and damage crops, farmers will be compensated for their losses from revenue paid by tourists. In this way, the value of preserving animals will be demonstrated to the people. In addition, barriers are being constructed to keep animals within the confines of the parks, and arrangements are being made with local people to allow them to continue to obtain the firewood, sand, and fish that they traditionally collected in the park.

CORRIDORS IN LOUISIANA WETLANDS The Tensas River basin in northeastern Louisiana originally contained one million hectares of flat, poorly drained forested land characteristic of the enormous Mississippi River floodplain (Gosselink et al. 1990). These floodplain forests

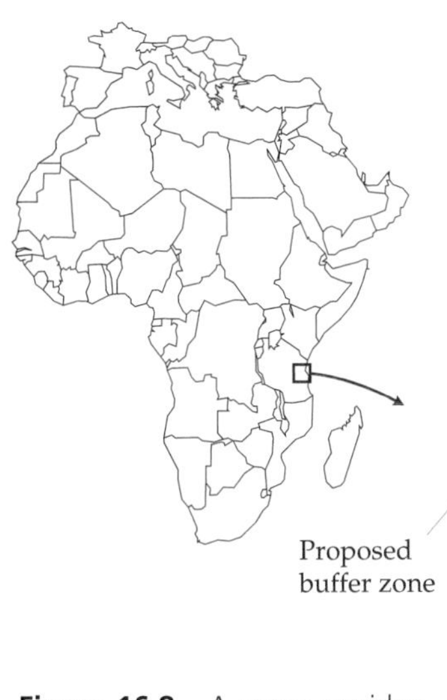

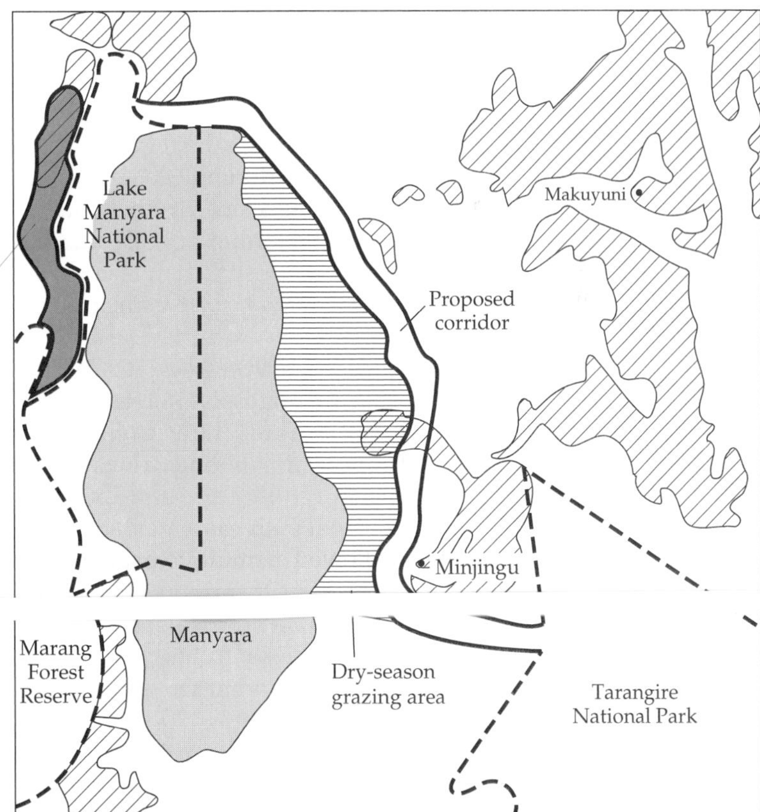

Figure 16.8 A game corridor has been proposed to allow game herds to migrate between Lake Manyara and Tarangire National Parks in northeastern Tanzania. Current cropland is indicated by diagonal hatching. The horizontally hatched area between the lake and the proposed corridor is an area used by tribespeople for dry-season grazing of their herds. A proposed "buffer zone" (dark gray) would allow additional areas for grazing. (From Mwalyosi 1991.)

are among the most productive in the United States for fish and wildlife and support large populations of migratory and resident birds. Large government flood control projects on the Mississippi River opened the land for development, and the Tensas River basin is now being fragmented by logging and conversion to agricultural fields for soybean, cotton, rice, and corn production. In 1957, 560,000 ha of forest remained, with the two largest blocks containing a total of 326,500 ha. By 1990, 157,000 ha remained, only 16% of the original forest, with four large patches (ranging in area from 10,00 to 30,000 ha) in protected areas and the remaining forest in smaller patches scattered throughout the basin. The Tensas River basin originally supported populations of the red wolf (*Canis rufus*), the Florida panther (*Felis concolor coryi*), and the ivory-billed woodpecker (*Campephilus principalis*), none of which are now found in the area; significant declines also have been observed in the total number of bird species and the abundance of one-third of forest-dependent bird species. Along with habitat destruction has come a decline in water quality, an increase in soil erosion, and flooding following heavy rainfall.

One strategy currently being pursued by The Nature Conservancy and government departments involves protecting the biological diversity of the Tensas River basin through acquiring and protecting a system of corridors that will link the separate forest blocks into larger units (Llewellyn et al. 1996). Adding 400 hectares of forest corridor would increase the size of the largest complex of connected forest from 50,000 ha to 100,000 ha. Adding 600 hectares of corridors in the western edge of the basin would link together several large fragments in the 3000 to 10,000 ha range, forming a 63,000-ha forest complex. These large forest blocks might be of sufficient size to protect some of the large wildlife species in the region, such as the black bear.

COMMUNITY BABOON SANCTUARY Corridors may be valuable at a small scale, linking isolated forest patches. Such an approach has been undertaken at the 47 km^2 Community Baboon Sanctuary (CBS) in Belize (Figure 16.9). Populations of black howler monkeys (*Alouatta pigra*) were declining because local landowners were clearing forest along the Belize River to create new agricultural land (Horwich and Lyon 1998), and the monkeys were unable to cross open fields between forest patches. As their food sources declined and their ability to move through the river forest became impaired, the monkey population underwent a serious decline. To reverse this trend, the 450 villagers living and owning land in the CBS agreed, in 1985, to maintain corridors of forest approximately 20 m wide along the watercourses and property boundaries. Forest corridors also are being established across large fields and between forest patches. Other components of the plan include protecting trees that provide food for the monkeys and build-

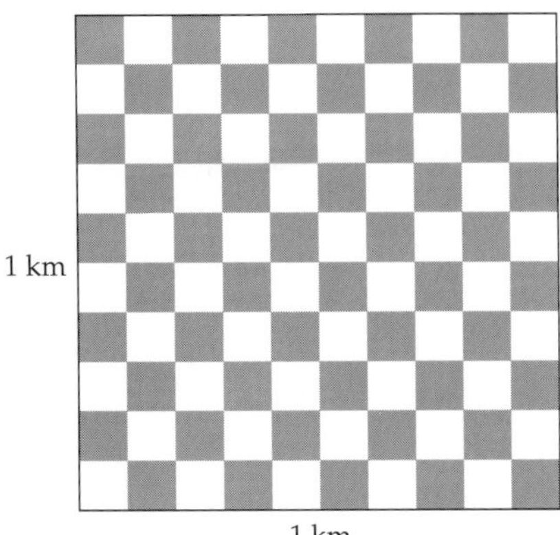

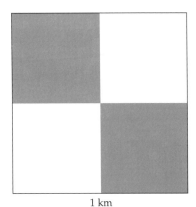

Figure 16.11 Two square nature nature reserves, each 100 ha in area (1 km on a side). They have equal areas of forest (shaded) and pasture (unshaded), but in very different size patches. Which landscape pattern benefits which species? This is a question managers will encounter.

A landscape of large patches and minimal edge effects is generally favored by conservation biologists; this pattern minimizes habitat disturbance and protects species that depend on old-growth vegetation. In contrast, wildlife managers interested in increasing species such as deer have observed that the overall abundance of certain birds and mammals is *greatest* at the edges of habitats, where foods from two habitat types are present, primary productivity (the amount of plant growth per year) is often high, and certain species from both communities live close together. Moreover, many animal species appear to be specialists on conditions at the edges of habitats.

To increase the number and diversity of animals, wildlife managers sometimes create the greatest amount of landscape variation possible within the confines of their game management unit (Yahner 1988). Fields and meadows are created and maintained, small thickets are encouraged, fruit trees and crops are planted on a small scale, small patches of forests are periodically cut, small ponds and dams are developed, and numerous trails and dirt roads meander across and along all of the patches. The result is a park transformed into a mass of edges where transition zones abound. In one old textbook on wildlife management, managers are advised to "develop as much edge as possible" because "wildlife is a product of the places where two habitats meet" (Yoakum and Dasmann 1971). This traditional approach is changing, as wildlife biologists include a broader set of goals to their management policies.

The conserv[illegible] goal of maintaining biological diversity is not just to include as many species as possible within small nature reserves, but to protect those species most in danger of extinction as a result of human activity. Small reserves broken up into many small habitat units within a compressed landscape may have a large number of species, but these are likely to be principally

Box 28 **National Wildlife Refuges**

When is protected land really protected? That question is being debated by managers of the National Wildlife Refuges (NWRs) scattered throughout the United States (Chadwick 1996). The first refuge was established in 1903, when President Theodore Roosevelt declared Pelican Island in Florida a protected area for birds. Since then more than 500 wildlife refuges have been established in every state and in many territories. National Wildlife Refuges differ from national parks in that they are specifically set aside to benefit native flora and fauna rather than humans. Yet pressure from hunters, oil companies, and other special interest groups has influenced Congress to allow uses that may ultimately be incompatible with wildlife protection.

In many cases, NWRs provide the only protected habit for endangered species: panthers prowl the Florida Panther NWR; desert bighorn sheep and the Sonoran pronghorn roam in Cabeza Prieta NWR in Arizona; Lake Wales Ridge NWR protects a unique Florida scrub ecosystem; and sea turtles nest on the sandy beaches of Culebra, a tiny island off the coast of Puerto Rico. Wildlife refuges also provide essential habitat for species that are not endangered. Refuges dotting the north–south flyways used by migratory birds provide vital stopover habitats and nesting grounds and host countless other species that are surviving well. In total, the NWR system protects 168 threatened or endangered species.

Yet 60% of all NWRs allow activities harmful to wildlife. Over half of the nation's refuges allow hunting on the grounds that permits and special stamps sold to hunters finance and maintain much of the NWR system; 207 NWRs also allow trapping. Additional moneys from the Land and Water Conservation Fund came with the primary mission to increase public space for recreation, rather than conservation. Some lands transferred from other federal organizations came with attendant drilling, mining, or grazing rights, which persisted under the National Wildlife Refuge title. The U.S. Fish and Wildlife Service, which is charged with managing the NWRs, must decide which activities are compatible with wildlife. Numerous Congressional committees have been unable to resolve this question. If trapping a thousand alligators every year in Sabine NWR is biologically sustainable, what about harvesting alligator eggs? If biologists ask ranchers to graze additional cattle to improve foraging conditions for geese in Merced NWR, why are grazing privileges being restricted in the Charles M. Russell NWR? Are the subsistence hunting and fishing privileges given to Yupik Eskimos substantially different from the hunting permits provided to duck hunters? Are power launches carrying birdwatchers different from boats towing water-skiers? Drawing the line is not easy, and shifting political winds make resolution more difficult. Whenever conservation ethics come up against business interests, any solution is bound to be imperfect.

Great blue herons nesting in the Tarpon Bay area of "Ding" Darling National Wildlife Refuge on Sanibel Island, Florida. (Photograph © 1998 Bob Sacha.)

the most difficult species to protect are rare species and wide-ranging species that require a large area.

3. Parks need to be designed to minimize harmful edge effects and, if possible, should contain an entire ecosystem. The tendency to fragment parks with roads, fences, and other human developments should be avoided, because they inhibit migration and facilitate the spread of exotic species, diseases, and other undesirable species. Whenever possible, government authorities and private owners should coordinate their activities and manage adjoining small parcels of land as one large unit.

4. Habitat corridors have been proposed to link isolated conservation areas. These corridors may allow the movement of animals between protected areas, which would facilitate gene flow as well as dispersal and colonization of new sites. The empirical evidence supporting the value of corridors is still limited. Habitat corridors will be most effective when they protect existing routes of migratory animals.

5. In the past, wildlife biologists advocated creating a mosaic of habitats with abundant edges. While this landscape design often increases the number of species and the overall abundance of animals, it may not favor some species of greatest conservation concern, which often occupy large blocks of undisturbed habitat.

For Discussion

1. The only known population of a rare shrub species exists in a 10 m × 10 m area in a 1-ha (100 m × 100 m) patch of metropolitan woodland. Should this woodland be established as a protected area or is it too small to protect the species? How would you make this determination? What suggestions could you make for designing and managing a park that would increase the chances of survival for this shrub species?

2. Obtain a map of a national park. How does the shape and location of this national park differ from the ideal design discussed in this chapter? What would it take to improve the design of the park and/or coordinate its management with surrounding landholders, so that it had a greater likelihood of preserving biodiversity?

3. Obtain a map of protected areas for a country or region. Consider how these protected areas could be linked by a system of habitat corridors. What would it accomplish? How much land would have to be acquired? How much would it cost? To complete this exercise, you might have to make many assumptions.

Suggested Readings

Chadwick, D. H. 1996. Sanctuary: U.S. National Wildlife Refuges. *National Geographic* 190 (April): 2–35. A beautifully illustrated article, written in popular style.

Cook, E. A. and H. N [illegible] 1994. *Landscape Planning and Ecological Networks*. El [illegible], Amsterdam. Conservation planning in a wide variety of ecosyster [illegible] ith many European examples.

Deardon, [illegible] 995. Park literacy and conservation. *Conservation Biology* 9: 1654– [illegible]. Excellent short essay on the role of protected areas as museums, zoos [illegible] aygrounds, cathedrals, reservoirs, laboratories, schoolrooms, and so c [illegible]

Diamond, J. M. 1975. The island dilemma: Lessons of modern biogeographic studies for the design of natural reserves. *Biological Conservation* 7: 129–146. An early attempt to apply the island biogeography model to nature reserve design.

Forman, R. T. 1995. *Land Mosaics: The Ecology of Landscapes and Regions*. Cambridge University Press, New York. Introductory textbook.

Game, M. and G. F. Peterken. 1984. Nature reserve selection strategies in the woodlands of Central Lincolnshire, England. *Biological Conservation* 29: 157–181. Practical guide to land acquisition decisions.

Hansson, L., L. Fahrig and G. Merrian (eds.). 1995. *Mosaic Landscapes and Ecological Processes*. Chapman and Hall, London. Clearly written chapters by leading authorities makes this a good resource for learning about landscape ecology.

Mann, C. C. and M. L. Plummer. 1995. Are wildlife corridors on the right path? *Science* 270: 1428–1430. Controversy erupts as conservation theory is applied to actual land management decisions.

Newmark, W. D. 1995. Extinction of mammal populations in Western North American national parks. *Conservation Biology* 9: 512–526. Extinction rates of mammal populations are lowest in large parks.

Pressey, R. L., C. J. Humphries, C. R. Margules, R. I. Vane-Wright and P. H. Williams. 1993. Beyond opportunism: Key principles for systematic reserve selection. *Trends in Ecology and Evolution* 8: 124–128. An alternative to the current haphazard approach to land acquisition.

Rosenberg, D. K., B. R. Noon and E. C. Meslow. 1997. Biological corridors: Form, function, and efficiency. *BioScience* 47: 677–687. Many experiments are evaluating corridors and will hopefully determine their value to conservation efforts.

Schwartz, M. W. 1997. *Conservation in Highly Fragmented Landscapes.* Chapman & Hall, New York. Designing and managing nature reserves, with a particular emphasis on the U.S. Midwest. See the excellent article by Shafer.

Shafer, C. L. 1990. *Nature Reserves: Island Theory and Conservation Practice*. Smithsonian Institution Press, Washington, D.C. A comprehensive, well-illustrated review of the theories of reserve design, which presents evidence and counter-evidence for particular theories.

Simberloff, D., J. A. Farr, J. Cox and D. W. Mehlman. 1992. Movement corridors: Conservation bargains or poor investments? *Conservation Biology* 6: 493–505. A critical examination of the conservation value of habitat corridors.

Wallis deVries, M. F. 1995. Large herbivores and the design of large-scale nature reserves in Western Europe. *Conservation Biology* 9: 25–33. Excellent review of the difficulties of conserving large herbivores in a densely settled, highly developed region; and strategies for designing better, larger protected areas.

CHAPTER 17

Managing Protected Areas

ONCE A PROTECTED AREA has been legally established, it often must be carefully managed if biological diversity is to be maintained. The conventional wisdom that nature knows best and that there is a balance of nature leads some people to believe that biodiversity is best served when there is no human intervention. The reality is often very different; in many cases humans have already modified the environment so much that the remaining species and communities need human intervention in order to survive. The world is littered with "paper parks" that have been created by government decree and then left to flounder. These parks have gradually—and sometimes rapidly—lost species, and their habitat quality has been degraded. In some countries, people do not hesitate to farm, log, mine, hunt, and fish in protected areas because government land is owned by everyone, anybody can take whatever they want, and nobody is willing to intervene. The crucial point is that parks must sometimes be actively managed to prevent deterioration (Sutherland and Hill 1995; Halvorson and Davis 1996). Park management decisions are made most effectively when information is provided by research and monitoring programs and funds are available to implement management plans.

It is also true that sometimes the best management involves doing nothing; management practices are sometimes ineffective or even detrimental. For example, active management to promote the abundance of a game species such as deer has frequently involved eliminating top predators, such as wolves and cougars; without predators to control them, game populations (and, incidentally, rodents) sometimes increase far beyond expectations. The result is overgrazing, habitat degradation, and a collapse of the animal and plant communities. Overenthusiastic park managers who remove fallen trees and underbrush to improve a park's appearance may unwittingly remove a critical resource needed by certain animal species for nesting and overwintering. Here, a clean park equals a biologically sterile park. In many parks, fire is part of the ecology of the area. Attempts to suppress fire completely are expensive and waste scarce management resources. They may eventually lead to loss of fire-dependent species and to massive, uncontrollable fires of unnatural intensity. Attempts to reduce the illegal poaching of black and white rhinos by cutting off their valuable horns have apparently resulted in the inability of adult rhinos to chase away predators, greatly increasing mortality of rhino calves (Cunningham and Berger 1997).

Many good examples of park management come from Britain, where there is a history of scientists and volunteers successfully monitoring and managing small reserves such as the Monks Wood and Castle Hill Nature Reserves (Goldsmith 1991; Peterken 1996). At these sites, the effects of different grazing methods (sheep vs. cattle, light vs. heavy grazing) on populations of wildflowers, butterflies, and birds are closely followed. In a symposium volume entitled *The Scientific Management of Animal and Plant Communities for Conservation* (Duffey and Watt 1971), Morris concluded that

> [t]here is no inherently right or wrong way to manage a nature reserve ... the aptness of any method of management must be related to the objects of management for any particular site. ... Only when objects of management have been formulated can results of scientific management be applied.

Small reserves, such as those found in long-settled areas and large cities, will generally require more active management than large reserves because they often are surrounded by an altered environment, have less interior habitat, and are more easily affected by exotic species and human activities. In large reserves, natural processes may continue without the need for active management; simply maintaining the park boundaries may be sufficient.

Many government agencies and conservation organizations have clearly articulated the protection of rare and endangered species as one of their top management priorities. These priorities are often outlined in mission statements, which allow managers to defend their actions. For example, at the Cape Cod National Seashore in Massachusetts, protecting tern and piping plover nesting habitat on beaches has been given priority over the use of the area by off-road vehicles and the "right" of sport fishermen to fish (Figure 17.1). A hands-off policy by park managers that did not restrict beach access by fishermen and vehicles would result in the rapid destruction of the shorebird colonies.

An important aspect of park management involves establishing a monitoring program on key components related to biological diversity such as the water level of ponds, the number of individuals of rare and endangered species, the density of herbs, shrubs, and trees, and the dates migratory animals arrive at and leave the park. The exact types of information gathered depend on the goals of park management (Sample 1994). Not only does monitoring allow managers to determine the health of the park, but it can suggest which management practices are working and which are not. With the right information, managers may be able to adjust park management practices to increase the chances of success.

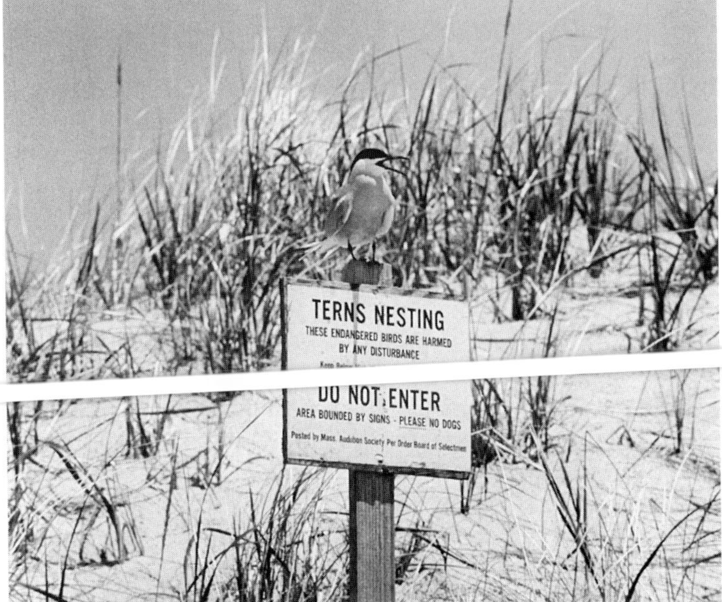

Figure 17.1 Tern nesting habitat in the Cape Cod National Seashore and at nearby beaches is extremely vulnerable to the "wear and tear" that is inevitable in a heavily visited recreation area. Public access to these areas may have to be restricted and the area patrolled by "tern wardens." (Photograph by David C. Twichell.)

In the case of an important wildflower species whose population inside a park is declining, a monitoring program needs to be established to determine the number and location of all plants, broken down by flowering and nonflowering individuals (see Chapters 11 and 12). Observations of the natural history of the species need to be made to determine the best growing conditions (Spellerberg 1994). This information can then be used to assess whether the habitat can be managed to increase the species' population size, perhaps by removing exotic, competing species. Perhaps additional populations of the species can be developed elsewhere in the park. It might be possible to augment the existing population by the release of individuals raised in captivity or through other techniques (see Chapter 13). Continued monitoring will reveal whether these programs are working.

One species that has been intensively monitored for decades is the giant cactus, or saguaro (*Carnegiea gigantea*), an icon of the desert landscape (McAuliffe 1996). In 1933, the Saguaro National Monument was established east of Tucson, Arizona, to protect this flagship species. Detailed observations, combined with precise photographic records (Figure 17.2), show that stands of saguaro are declining within the park. Investigations over an 80-year period suggest that adult cacti are damaged or killed by periods of subfreezing weather that occur about once a decade. The good news is that permanent research plots within the park have recorded the establishment of large numbers of young saguaro plants. These will be closely watched to see if new cactus forests appear in the next century.

Identifying and Dealing with Threats to Protected Areas

Management of protected areas must take into account factors that threaten the biological diversity and ecological health of the park. These include many of the threats detailed in Chapters 9 and 10, including exotic species, low population size among rare species, habitat destruction or degradation, and human use. In 1990, the World Conservation Monitoring Centre and UNESCO conducted a survey of 89 World Heritage sites to identify their management problems (WRI 1992). The responses showed a wide range of management problems as well as significant differences among continents (Table 17.1). Threats to protected areas were generally greatest in South America and least in Europe. The most serious management problems in Oceania were development and introduced species. Illegal wildlife harvesting, fire, grazing, and cultivation were major threats in both South America and Africa. Inadequate park management was a particular problem in developing countries in Africa, Asia, and South America. The greatest threats faced by parks in industrialized countries were internal and external threats associated with major economic developments such as mining, logging, agriculture, and water projects. Although these gen-

TABLE 17.1 (CONTINUED)

	Percent of sites reporting problems with:				
Continent	**Grazing and cultivation**	**Illegal wildlife harvesting**	**Fire, natural threats**	**Introduced species**	**Insufficient management[c]**
Africa	56	68	52	8	52
Asia	40	40	40	10	70
Europe	27	9	18	27	0
Oceania	40	10	40	60	10
South America	75	63	88	25	63
North and Central America	29	33	24	43	10

monarch is one of the most beautiful, well-known, and beloved butterfly species in North America. Monarchs that breed west of the Rockies migrate to overwintering sites spread 500 miles along the Pacific coast from Marin County, California, to Baja California (Weiss et al. 1991). These sites are forest groves located within 1 km of the ocean and characterized by moderate temperature and protection from the wind. Most of the monarch aggregations occur in forest groves dominated by the blue gum (*Eucalyptus globulus*), an exotic species introduced into California from Australia about a century ago (Figure 17.3). The flowers of the eucalyptus are an important winter nectar source for the monarchs. Protection of these butterfly sites from development has proved to be a controversial issue because the blue gum itself is an exotic species. Even though blue gum forests are important for monarchs, they are depauperate in other species of insects and small mammals. Blue gum forests also sometimes pose fire hazards because of the build-up of dead brush. The complexity of these issues creates a difficult problem for those responsible for deciding whether or not to protect blue gum forests.

Habitat Management

A park may have to be aggressively managed to ensure that original habitat types are maintained. Many species only occupy specific habitats and specific successional stages of that habitat. When land is set aside as a protected area, often the pattern of disturbance and human usage changes so markedly that many species previously found on the site fail to persist. Natural disturbances, including fires, grazing, and tree falls, are key elements in the ecosystem required for the presence of certain rare species. In small parks, the full range of successional stages may not be present at a site, and many species may be missing for this reason; for example, in an isolated park dominated by old-

Figure 17.3 In California, monarch butterflies aggregate in groves of blue gum eucalyptus trees. Should these trees be protected, despite the fact that they are an exotic species from Australia? (Photograph by Ken Lucas/Biological Photo Service.)

growth trees, species characteristic of the early successional herb and shrub stage may be missing (Figure 17.4). If this small park is swept entirely by a fire or a windstorm, the species characteristic of old-growth forest may be eliminated. In many isolated protected areas in metropolitan areas, frequent fires started by people, and other human disturbances, eliminate many of the late successional plant and animal species. However, early successional species may also be missing if they are not present in adjacent sites that serve as colonization sources.

Park managers sometimes must actively manage sites to ensure that all successional stages are present, so that species characteristic of each stage have a place to persist and thrive (Box 29). One common way to do this is to periodically set localized, controlled fires in grassland, shrublands, and forests to reinitiate the successional process. In some wildlife sanctuaries, grasslands and fields are maintained by mowing, shallow plowing, and keeping livestock in order to retain open habitat in the landscape. For example, many of the unique wildflowers of

CASE STUDY: TWO FENS The need for managing habitat to maintain populations of rare species is illustrated by the example of Crystal Fen in northern Maine, recognized for its numerous rare plant species (Jacobson et al. 1991). An apparent drying of this extensive fen (a type of wet meadow or marshland) and an increase in woody vegetation were attributed by some biologists to the construction of a railroad in 1893 and a drainage ditch in 1937; there was concern that the fen community might be lost. Subsequent studies using aerial photography, vegetation history, and dated fossil remains from peat layers collectively showed that the construction of the railroad bed had allowed the wetland to *expand* in area by impeding drainage. The fen also increased in area following fires started by cinder-producing locomotives. Today, the relatively large area of fen in which rare plants occur is primarily a product of human activity. The construction of the drainage ditch and the decrease in fires following the change to diesel-powered engines are allowing the vegetation to return to its original state. If the goal is to maintain the current extent of the fen and the populations of rare species, management practices involving periodic burning, removing woody plants, and manipulating drainage patterns are necessary.

Controlled disturbance is also necessary to maintain some species in English fens. The fen violet, *Viola persicifolia,* has declined rapidly in Europe, as its habitat of open, alkaline peaty areas such as fens have been drained and altered. In England, the species is known only sporadically from two sites in Cambridgeshire (Pullin and Woodell 1987). At Woodwalton Fen National Nature Reserve, the species had apparently disappeared, but it was found again after considerable soil disturbance caused by commercial digging of peat and scrub clearance. The ability of populations to reappear after several decades suggests that the species has long-lived seeds that germinate opportunistically when soil is brought to the surface after trees are blown over. A management policy involving removal of scrub and disturbance of soil appears to be necessary for the continued existence of the fen violet in England.

The type of controlled disturbance that provides optimal results can be determined through field experiments. For example, chalk grasslands in Britain require specific management measures to maintain a biologically rich community. Experiments have shown that the number of species, the particular species present, and the [illegible] abundance are determined by the management regime: whether the grassland is grazed, mowed, or burned; the time of year of the management; and whether the management is carried out continuously, annually, or rotationally (Morris 1971). Certain management regimes favor certain groups of species over others.

KEYSTONE RESOURCES In the same way that natural patterns of disturbance may need to be artificially maintained, it may be necessary to preserve or maintain **keystone resources.** These include sources of food, water, minerals, natural shelter, and so forth on which many species depend. For example, an artificial salt lick could be built in place of one that was destroyed, or artificial pools could be built in streambeds to provide replacement water supplies. Keystone resources and keystone species could conceivably be enhanced in managed conservation areas to increase the populations of species whose members have declined. For example, by planting native fruit trees, building an artificial pond, and providing salt licks, it might be possible to maintain vertebrate species in a smaller conservation area at higher densities than would be predicted based on studies of species distribution in undisturbed habitat. Artificial ponds not only provide needed habitat for attractive insects such as dragonflies, but are important centers of public education in urban areas (Steytler and Samways 1995). Another example is providing nesting boxes or drilling nesting holes in trees for birds as a substitute resource when there are few dead trees with nesting cavities (see Figure 16.6). In this way a viable population of a rare species could be established, whereas without such interventions the population size of the rare species might be too small to persist. In each case a balance must be struck between establishing nature reserves free from human influence and creating seminatural gardens in which the plants and animals are dependent on people.

Park Management and People

Human use of the landscape is a reality that must be dealt with in park design (Kramer et al. 1997). People have been a part of virtually all the world's ecosystems for thousands of years, and excluding humans from nature reserves could have unforeseen consequences. A savannah protected from fires set by people may change to forest, with a subsequent loss of the savannah species. When people who have traditionally used products from inside a nature reserve are suddenly refused access to the area, they suffer from the loss of basic resources that they need to stay alive, and they will understandably be angry, frustrated, and unlikely to support conservation.

The use of parks by local people and outside visitors must be a central part of any management plan, both in developed and developing countries (MacKinnon et al. 1992; Kothari et al. 1996). Many parks flourish or are destroyed depending on the degree of support, neglect, hostility, or exploitation they receive from the humans who use them. If the purpose of a protected area is explained to local residents and most residents agree with the objectives and respect the rules of the park, then the area may maintain its natural communities. In the most positive scenario, local people become involved in park management and planning, are trained and employed by the park authority, and benefit from the protection and regulation of activity within the park (Figure 17.6). At the other extreme, if there is a history of bad relations and distrust between local people and the government, or if the purpose of the park is not explained adequately, the local people may reject the park concept and ignore park regulations. In this eventuality, the local people will clash with park personnel to the detriment of the park.

There is now increasing recognition that involvement of local people is the crucial, missing element in many conservation management strategies. Top-down strategies, in which governments try to impose conservation plans, need to be integrated with bottom-up programs, in which villages and other local groups formulate and reach their own development goals (Clay 1991). As explained by Lewis (Lewis et al. 1990):

> If any lesson can be learned from past failures of conservation in Africa, it is that conservation implemented solely by government for the presumed benefit of its people will probably have limited success, especially in countries with weakened economies. Instead,

Figure 17.6 Local residents collect cane grass and thatching materials from Chitwan National Park in Nepal. Park officials weigh the bundles in order to keep the harvest at a sustainable level. (Photograph ©John F. Lehmkuhl.)

conservation for the people and by the people with a largely service and supervisory role delegated to the government could foster a more cooperative relationship between government and the residents living with the resource. This might reduce the costs of law enforcement and increase revenues available to other aspects of wildlife management, which could help support the needs of conservation as well as those of the immediate community. Such an approach would have the added advantage of restoring to local residents a greater sense of traditional ownership and responsibility for this resource.

The United Nations Educational, Scientific, and Cultural Organization (UNESCO) has pioneered this approach with its Man and the Biosphere (MAB) Program (Figure 17.7). This program has designated hundreds of Biosphere Reserves worldwide in an attempt to integrate human activities, research, and protection of the natural environment at a single location (Batisse 1997). The concept involves a core area in which biological communities and ecosystems are strictly protected, with a surrounding buffer zone in which nondestructive research is carried out and traditional human activities are carefully monitored for their impact on bio-

Figure 17.7 Past policies have attempted to protect natural areas by sealing them off from outside influences. Such policies may fail to recognize ecological and social forces that threaten the ecosystem. The Man and the Biosphere Program attempts to integrate the needs and cultures of local people in park planning and protection. (Poster from "Ecology in Action: An Exhibit," UNESCO, Paris, 1981.)

Opening conservation to man

Is the best way to protect a natural area to seal it off in a "closed jar" from the outside human world? Sooner or later such a policy can destroy the area it was intended to protect. Ecological and sociological pressures - both inside and outside - eventually may shatter the reserve.
Almost all natural areas have been modified by man: creating a reserve by excluding man can upset the ecological balance. Boundaries may not coincide with territorial areas and feeding grounds. Pressure builds up within the reserve. Jammed inside, some animals overbreed, others "eat themselves to starvation"
In some cases, nature reserves are created by excluding the local inhabitants from their traditional grazing and hunting areas. They have difficulty in accepting that these areas are only accessible to tourists. Gradually illicit hunting, grazing and cropping may encroach upon and eradicate the reserve.
MAB emphasizes man's partnership with nature. A reserve is open and interacts with its region. The local people can be its guardians.
It is not suggested that the traditional policy of conservation should be changed everywhere. Certainly some areas must remain untouched. But there are fewer and fewer natural areas left to conserve and certain reserves are being destroyed by these internal and external pressures. Opening conservation to man does not only apply to the Kenyan situation here but to many other countries. It may be a longer term solution.
The diagram (right) illustrates how a Kenyan specialist envisages integrating wildlife conservation, tourism and traditional land use through zonation into different use areas, research for rational management and participation of the local population. The term "biosphere reserve" was coined to identify reserves putting the "open" concept into practice.

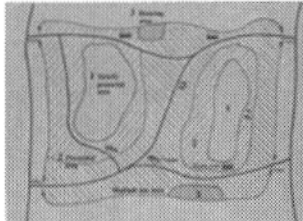

diversity. Then there is a transitional zone in which greater human impacts are allowed, including sustainable development.

The general principle of surrounding core conservation areas with buffer and transition zones in which some extraction of natural products occurs can have several desirable effects. First, the good will of local people will be maintained since they will continue to obtain their basic requirements from the natural environment. Second, certain desirable features of the landscape created by human use may be maintained, such as farms and gardens. Third, buffer zones create a transition between highly protected core conservation and human-dominated areas, which may facilitate animal movement (Figure 17.8).

Without a buffer zone, the effective area of the park may be greatly reduced by human activity (Lamprey 1974):

> In the experience of many African national park authorities, the presence of intensive settlement on the boundaries produces a *de facto* zone of 'limited conservation' inside the park, within which some poaching, tree-felling, grazing, grass burning, and other illicit activities may occur, necessitating constant policing.

Human populations will continue to increase dramatically in the coming decades, while resources such as firewood and wild meat will become harder to find. Managers of nature reserves in the developing world need to anticipate ever greater demand for use of the remaining patches of natural habitat.

Figure 17.8 The general pattern of an MAB reserve includes a core protected area surrounded by a buffer zone in which human activities are monitored and managed and research is carried out, and a transition zone of sustainable development and experimental research.

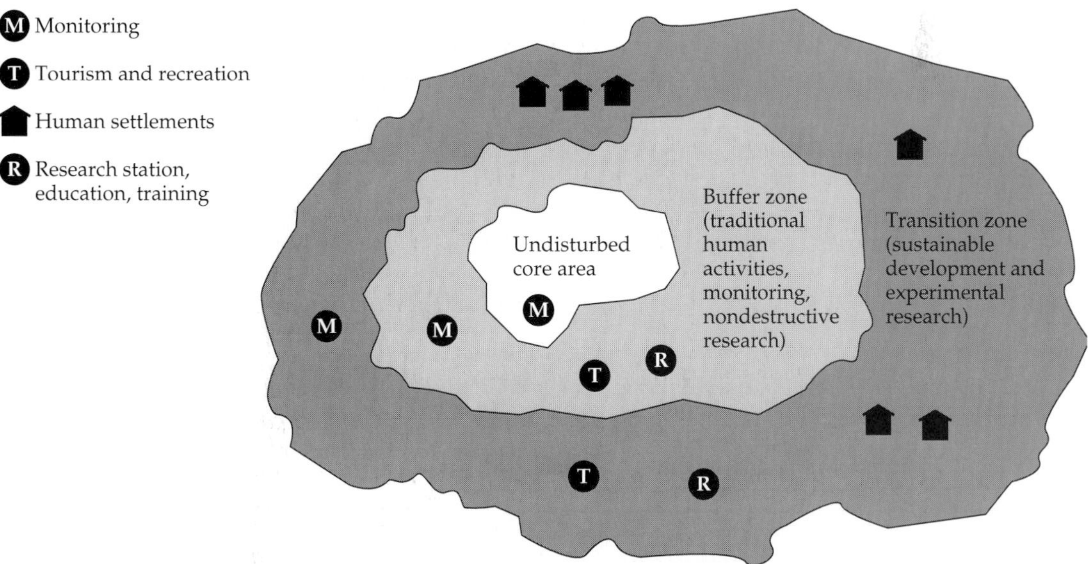

Regulating Activities Inside Protected Areas

If certain human activities that are incompatible with maintaining biological diversity within a protected area are allowed to continue, important elements of the biological communities eventually may be destroyed.

- *Commercial harvesting of fish and game.* Some regulated hunting and fishing may be acceptable for personal consumption and sport, as long as it is sustainable over time, but harvesting for commercial sale frequently leads to the elimination of species. Commercial hunting and fishing within a reserve, if it is allowed at all, must be carefully monitored by park officials to ensure that animal populations are not depleted. Regulated hunting may also be necessary to control exotic animals and herbivore populations in areas with reduced populations of carnivore species. Establishment of marine reserves with regulated fishing or areas in which fishing is prohibited has proved an effective way to rebuild and maintain populations of fish (Figure 17.9) (Salm and Clark 1984; Russ and Alcala 1996; Coblentz 1997).
- *Intensive harvesting of natural plant products.* Again, collection of natural plant products such as fruits, fibers, and resins for personal use may be acceptable, while commercial harvesting may be detrimental. Even personal collecting can be unacceptable in national parks with tens of thousands of visitors per year, and where the local human population is large in relation to the area of the park. Monitoring plant populations is needed to ensure that overharvesting does not occur.

Figure 17.9 Large reef fish had been overharvested at Apo Island in the Philippines and were rarely seen. (A) Location of the unfished reserve (shaded area) on the eastern side of the island, with fished (nonreserve) area on the west. The positions of six underwater census areas are shown for each site. (B) After the island was protected as a marine reserve, the number of fish observed increased substantially. (After Russ and Alcala 1996.)

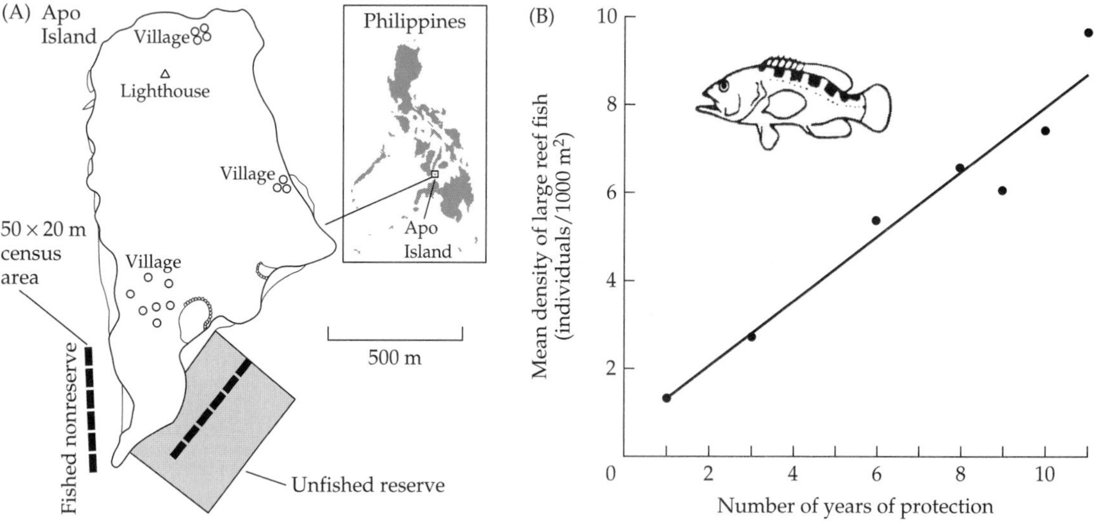

- *Illegal logging and farming*. These activities degrade the habitat and cause the elimination of species. Where these activities are large scale, commercial in nature, and controlled by outside interests, they must be eliminated if possible. However, when the logging and farming are being done by local people to supply their basic human needs, then stopping these activities becomes very difficult and could be counterproductive. Some regulated harvesting and farming may even be useful to maintain successional stages and to preserve traditional agricultural systems.
- *Fire.* Occasional fires set accidentally or deliberately by local people to open up habitats, to provide forage for livestock and wildlife, and to reduce undesirable species may help to create a variety of successional stages. Fires that are more frequent than would occur naturally can dry out a habitat, cause soil erosion, and eliminate many native species.
- *Recreational activities*. These popular activities, such as hiking off trails, camping outside designated areas, and riding motorcycles, off-road vehicles, and mountaineering bikes, can eliminate sensitive plants and animals from protected lands and must be controlled and restricted to specified areas by park managers. Even such activities as birdwatching must sometimes be curtailed (Box 30). In many heavily used parks, frequent traffic by hikers wearing heavy boots has degraded vegetation along trails. Redwood trees in California, for instance, are harmed when park visitors compress the soil too tightly by walking around the trunks.

Even in a well-regulated park, air pollution, acid rain, water pollution, global climate change, and the changing composition of atmospheric gases influence natural communities and cause some species to increase and others to decrease and be eliminated. Unfortunately, natural history studies show that invasive exotic species are likely to be the main beneficiary of an altered environment since they tend to be adaptable, efficient dispersers and able to tolerate disturbance. The ability of park managers to deal with these major, externally driven alterations in ecosystem processes is rather limited. Experiments are being conducted in which basic compounds such as lime are added to water bodies to prevent acidification; however, these measures will never take the place of needed environmental reforms to limit human production and consumption patterns.

ZONING A basic tool used by park managers to deal with a variety of conflicting demands on a protected area is **zoning**, which sets aside designated areas that permit or give priority to certain activities. Some areas of a forest may be designated for timber production, hunting, wildlife protection, or watershed maintenance. A marine reserve might

Box 30 Conservation Management of American Cranes

It is often the case in conservation biology that closely related species have completely different conservation needs. A classic illustration of this principle is the difference between two American crane species, the whooping crane (*Grus americana*) and the sandhill crane (*Grus canadensis*). Though these species are closely related, relatively small differences in their biology and behavioral patterns have determined disparate success for each population. Whereas most populations of sandhill cranes are well established and thriving, whooping cranes have only a small, unstable remnant population.

The overall population of sandhill cranes is estimated at well over 500,000 birds. This estimate is somewhat deceiving, since it hides the varying success of some subspecies of sandhill crane; for example, the lesser sandhill crane numbers in the hundreds of thousands, while only about 120 Mississippi sandhill cranes exist in the wild (Ellis et al. 1996). However, the majority of sandhill crane subspecies, whatever their population size, have responded well to conservation management, especially where habitat preservation guidelines and hunting restrictions have been effectively enforced.

In contrast, the total 1996 whooping crane population was estimated at 216 individuals in the wild and roughly the same number in captivity (J. C. Lewis, personal communication). While this total represents a substantial increase from the population's low point of 15 birds in 1942 (Johnsgaard 1991), whooping crane conservation efforts over the past four decades have not been entirely successful, despite their intensity and creativity. Although the rate of increase has been that expected in a healthy population, the very small founder population has limited the potential for growth. The survival of young from year to year has been highly variable (Dennis et al. 1991), and whooping cranes appear to have a ten-year cycle of population fluctuation superimposed on their long-term trend of population increase.

The contrast between sandhill cranes' positive response to comparatively limited conservation efforts and the failure of whooping cranes to rebound despite intensive efforts on their behalf raises an intriguing problem: Why should one species be successful while the other is not? In general, the answer lies in the response of each species to the presence of human disturbance in its favored habitat. Whooping cranes have a number of biological and behavioral attributes that make them much more sensitive than sandhill cranes to human disturbance. First, the reduction of wetlands due to agricultural development in the midwestern plains and prairies has affected whooping cranes more than sandhill cranes. Most of the historical nesting sites for whooping cranes are located in the midst of what is now prime agricultural and range land in the United States. Second, whooping cranes prefer large open expanses with excellent visibility for long distances. Most of these habitats are disappearing as wetlands and large midwestern waterways, such as the Platte River and tributaries of the Missouri River, are drained or diverted for agriculture. Sandhills prefer smaller wetlands, often bordered by grasslands or forest, which have remained more abundant. Third, whooping cranes apparently have a much lower rate of success in raising their young than sandhills; though both species typically lay two eggs per nest, whooping cranes are less likely to raise both chicks to maturity.

The migratory nature of the whooping crane also makes protection more difficult for wildlife managers. The nesting grounds in Wood Buffalo National Park in Canada are closed to the public and to low-flying aircraft during the sensitive nesting period. Maintaining marshes and sandbars along the migration routes is a constant element in the management plan for the species, involving a wide range of government and private landowners (Cannon 1996). However, mortality during migration, particularly from collision with power lines, is high. The restricted wintering distribution along the Texas coast also raises the risk of extinction. The whooping crane overwinters in the Arkansas National Wildlife Refuge, where lands have been set aside for its protection. However, the construction of the Gulf Intracoastal Waterway through the Arkansas NWR in the early 1940s has led to heavy barge traffic, much of it carrying petrochemical products. One accidental grounding could seriously impact the entire population of whooping

Above: Captive-born juvenile whooping cranes are taught foraging and flying skills by a person wearing a whooping crane costume. The cranes will eventually be released into the wild without ever seeing an "unmasked" human. (Photograph courtesy of the International Crane Foundation.)

Below: Regulation of boat traffic at the Arkansas National Wildlife Refuge is an important part of managing the refuge for whooping cranes. The wake of large boats can erode the marsh, and tour boats carrying birdwatchers can disturb the colony. (Photograph courtesy of the International Crane Foundation.)

cranes. River traffic has eroded the marsh away from the channel, resulting in significant loss of crane habitat. Tour boats also ply the channel, carrying birdwatchers and tourists eager to catch a glimpse of these spectacular birds but presenting the potential for disturbance (Lewis 1995).

This combination of factors inhibiting whooping crane reproductive success and survival requires conservation methods tailored to the specific needs of the species. Conservation methods used so far have been problematic: attempts to create a captive flock by raising chicks hatched from "second" eggs taken from whooping crane nests have not been successful. One strategy involved placing whooping crane eggs in sandhill crane nests to be raised by sandhill crane "foster parents." Though a number of whooping crane chicks were raised successfully by these substitute parents, none of those that reached maturity took mates or bred, possibly because of social or sexual imprinting on their foster parents (Mahan and Simmers 1992). The project was subsequently abandoned. Later attempts to rear chicks from "second" eggs using captive cranes or human surrogates have been more successful.

Forty-eight whooping cranes now exist in Florida as a result of the reintroduction of a nonmigratory flock begun in 1993, and plans are underway to reintroduce a migratory flock in the Canadian prairies during the next decade (J. C. Lewis, personal communication).

The prescription for species management appears to be straightforward in this case: protect and restore suitable habitat and continue to supplement wild populations with captive-raised birds. Habitat protection for a migratory animal is especially challenging, however, and conservation efforts also need to address the problem of reestablishing migratory routes. For now, though, the whooping crane seems to be saved from extinction. However, only continued management offers the potential for this species to be out of danger.

allow fishing in certain areas and strictly prohibit it in others; certain areas might be designated for surfing, water-skiing, and recreational diving, but these sports may be prohibited elsewhere. The challenge in zoning is to find a compromise that people are willing to accept and that provides for the long-term, sustainable use of natural resources.

Ningaloo Marine Park, located off the west coast of Australia, provides an example of multiple-use zoning implemented to meet a variety of demands. This park protects the world's largest fringing coral barrier reef, 250 km (156 miles) in length, including such notable species as dugongs (*Dugong dugong*), humpback whales (*Megaptera novaeangeliae*), and whale sharks (*Rhincodon typus*). More than 500 species of fish and 200 species of coral have been reported from the reef; this diversity is comparable to the well-known Great Barrier Reef off eastern Australia. The park has three primary zoning divisions: eight **sanctuary zones** in which human impact is minimized and only the viewing of marine life is permitted; seven **recreation zones** that can include swimming, boating, and recreational fishing; and one **general use zone** in which supervised commercial and recreational fishing is allowed.

Park Management Resources

For park management to be effective, there must be a sufficient number of well-equipped, motivated park personnel who are willing to carry out park policy. In many areas of the world, particularly in developing countries but also in developed countries, protected areas are understaffed and lack the equipment to patrol remote areas of the reserve. Without enough radios and vehicles, the park staff may be restricted to the vicinity of headquarters, unaware of what is happening in their own park. Management programs cannot be completed or even started in these circumstances.

This situation is illustrated by a comparison between the national parks of the United States and the Brazilian Amazon (Table 17.2) (Peres and Terborgh 1995). The United States employs 4,002 park rangers in contrast to 23 in Brazil, that is, approximately one ranger per every 82 km^2 of park in the U.S., in contrast to one ranger for every 6,053 km^2 of park in Brazil. Most of Brazil's parks lack even basic transportation, such as motorized boats, trucks, or jeeps; it is clearly impossible for Brazil's small park staff to adequately patrol large, rugged parks on foot or by canoe. A further irony of this unbalanced funding is that vast sums are spent on captive breeding and conservation programs by zoos and conservation organizations in the developed countries of the world while the biologically rich parks of so many developing countries are languishing for lack of resources. For instance, the San Diego Zoological Society, largely used for keeping exotic animals on display

TABLE 17.2 **Comparison of personnel and resources available for the protection of national parks and biological reserves in the Brazilian Amazon and the United States**

Feature	Brazilian Amazon	U.S.A.
Protected area (in km^2)	139,222	326,721
Number of park rangers	23	4,002
Total number of park personnel[a]	65	19,000
Park ranger-to-km^2 ratio	1:6,053	1:82
Percent of nature reserves with at least one:		
Park guard	31	100
Administrative building	45	100
Guard post	52	100
Motor vehicle	45	100

Source: After Peres and Terborgh 1995.
[a] Includes all office staff.

for the public, has an annual budget of $70 million, which is about the same as the combined wildlife conservation budgets of all African countries south of the Sahara.

Summary

1. Protected areas often must be managed to maintain biological diversity because the original conditions of the area have been altered by human activities. In some cases the best management involves doing nothing. Effective management begins with a clearly articulated statement of priorities. Monitoring can be used to determine whether management practices are working or need to be adjusted.

2. Parts of protected areas may have to be periodically burned, dug up, or otherwise disturbed by people to create the openings and successional stages that certain species need. Such management is crucial, for example, to some endangered butterfly species that need early successional food plants to complete their life cycle.

3. Keystone resources such as nesting sites and water holes often need to be preserved, restored, or even added to protected areas in order to maintain populations of some species.

4. Local residents and outside visitors are key elements in park management. It is often crucial to find a compromise between banning human use of park resources and allowing unlimited use that allows people to use park resources in a sustainable manner without harming biological diversity.

5. For park management to be effective, protected areas must have an adequate staff and resources. In many cases, personnel and resources are insufficient to accomplish management objectives.

For Discussion

1. Think about a national park or nature reserve you have visited. In what ways was it well run or poorly run? What were the goals of the park or reserve, and how could they be achieved through better management?

2. Imagine a public nature preserve in a metropolitan area that protects a number of endangered species. Would the nature preserve be more effectively run by a government agency, a group of scientists, the local residents living near the reserve, a nongovernmental environmental organization (NGO), or by a council made up of all of them? What are the advantages and disadvantages of each of these possibilities?

3. Can you think of special challenges in the management of aquatic preserves, such as coastal estuaries, islands, or freshwater lakes, that would not be faced by managers of terrestrial protected areas?

4. Imagine you are a park ranger at Yellowstone National Park during the great fires of 1988. How would you explain the ecologically beneficial role of fire in mature lodgepole pine forests while reassuring park visitors that their park is not being destroyed?

Suggested Readings

Cannon, J. R. 1996. Whooping crane recovery: A case study in public and private cooperation in the conservation of endangered species. *Conservation Biology* 10: 813–821. A wide range of private and public organizations have cooperated in the whooping crane management plan.

Cunningham, C. and J. Berger. 1997. *Horn of Darkness: Rhinos on the Edge.* Oxford University Press, New York. The emotional story of evaluating Namibia's rhino protection program and the resulting tangle with government officials.

Duffy, E. and A. S. Watt (eds.). 1971. *The Scientific Management of Animal and Plant Communities for Conservation.* Blackwell Scientific Publications, Oxford. Examples of intensive management of small conservation areas.

Halvorson, W. L. and G. E. Davis (eds.). 1996. *Science and Ecosystem Management in the National Parks.* University of Arizona Press, Tucson. Research, monitoring, and management are important in maintaining the health of protected areas.

Kothari, A., N. Singh and S. Suri (eds.). 1996. *People and Protected Areas: Toward Participatory Conservation in India.* Sage Publications, New Delhi. In India, rural poverty and the protection of biodiversity are being dealt with together.

Kramer, R., C. van Schaik and J. Johnson (eds.). 1997. *Last Stand: Protected Areas and Defense of Tropical Biodiversity.* Oxford University Press, New York. Many leading authorities question the current view that working with local people is the key to protecting biodiversity, arguing instead for a stronger emphasis on preservation.

MacKinnon, J., K. MacKinnon, G. Child and J. Thorsell. 1992. *Managing Protected Areas in the Tropics.* IUCN, Gland, Switzerland. An excellent introduction to management issues.

Peres, C. and J. W. Terborgh. 1995. Amazonian nature reserves: An analysis of the defensibility status of existing conservation units and design criteria for the future. *Conservation Biology* 9: 34–46. Critical evaluation of Brazil's protected area system, with many constructive suggestions.

Peterken, G. F. 1996. *Natural Woodland, Ecology and Conservation in Northern Temperate Regions*. Cambridge University Press, Cambridge. Authoritative description of natural processes and how they can be used in conservation management.

Pyne, S. J. 1997. *Fire in America: A Cultural History of Wildland and Rural Fire*. The University of Washington Press, Seattle. Fire is an important factor in shaping biological communities and is part of many modern management techniques.

Russ, G. R. and A. C. Alcala. 1996. Marine reserves: Rates and patterns of recovery and decline of large predatory fish. *Ecological Applications* 6: 947–961. Case study of islands in the Philippines shows increases in fish populations following the establishment of marine reserves. Contains an extensive bibliography on marine reserves.

Salm, R. and J. Clark. 1984. *Marine and Coastal Protected Areas: A Guide for Planners and Managers*. IUCN, Gland, Switzerland. Special methods are needed in these environments.

Sample, V. A. (ed.). 1994. *Remote Sensing in Ecosystem Management*. Island Press, Washington, D.C. Management of large areas is sometimes only possible using the broad geographical perspective provided by remote sensing.

Spellerberg, I. F. 1994. *Evaluation and Assessment for Conservation: Ecological Guidelines for Determining Priorities for Nature Conservation*. Chapman and Hall, London. Methods for developing a management plan for conservation areas.

Sutherland, W. J. and D. A. Hill. 1995. *Managing Habitats for Conservation*. Cambridge University Press, Cambridge. An active approach is needed to maintain species and communities.

Warren, M. S. 1990. The successful conservation of an endangered species, the Heath Fritillary Butterfly *Mellicta athalia*, in Britain. *Biological Conservation* 55: 37–56. Case study of management for species preservation.

CHAPTER 18

Outside Protected Areas

A CRUCIAL COMPONENT of conservation strategies must be the protection of biological diversity outside as well as inside protected areas. As Western (1989) says, "If we can't save nature outside protected areas, not much will survive inside." More than 90% of the world's land will remain outside of protected areas, according to even the most optimistic predictions. Most of these unprotected lands are not used intensively by humans and still harbor some of their original biota. Strategies for reconciling human needs and conservation interests in these unprotected areas are critical to the success of conservation plans (Gradwohl and Greenberg 1988; Western and Pearl 1989). Because most of the land area in most countries will never be protected, numerous rare species will inevitably occur outside these areas. In the United States, more than one-third of the species listed under the U.S. Endangered Species Act are found exclusively on private land, and most of the listed species are found predominantly on private land.

Relying on parks and reserves to protect biological diversity can create a "siege mentality" in which species inside the parks are rigorously protected while species outside can be rapidly exploited. McNeely (1989) remarks that

> [by] their very nature as legally established units of land management, national parks have boundaries. Yet nature knows no boundaries, and recent advances in conservation biology are showing that national parks are usually too small to effectively conserve the large mammals or trees that they are designed to preserve. The boundary post is too often also a psychological boundary, suggesting that since nature is taken care of by the national park, we can abuse the surrounding lands, isolating the national park as an 'island' of habitat which is subject to the usual increased threats that go with insularity.

The strategy of establishing large, new national parks to protect biological diversity and biosphere reserves to protect traditional societies has quickly been adopted by countries such as Brazil and Malaysia to deflect international criticisms of their intensive development policies. However, if the areas outside the parks are degraded, then the biological diversity within the protected areas will decline as well (Table 18.1), because many species migrate across park boundaries to access resources that the park itself cannot provide. In general, the smaller a protected area is, the more it is dependent on neighboring unprotected lands for the long-term maintenance of biological diversity. Also, the number of individuals of any one species contained within park

TABLE 18.1 ***The number of large herbivore species currently in some East African national parks, and the number expected to remain if areas outside the parks become unavailable to wildlife***

		Number of species in park	
National park	**Area (km^2)**	**Now**	**If areas outside parks exclude wildlife[a]**
Serengeti, Tanzania	14,504	31	30
Mara, Kenya	1,813	29	22
Meru, Kenya	1,021	26	20
Amboseli, Kenya	388	24	18
Samburu, Kenya	298	25	17
Nairobi, Kenya	114	21	11

Source: Data from Western and Ssemakulu 1981.

[a] Estimated number of species that will remain if areas outside the protected parks exclude wildlife due to agriculture, hunting, herding, or other human activities.

boundaries may be lower than the minimum viable population size. In these cases, new national parks may be bones thrown to the international conservation community; while they are answers to immediate criticism, they are not solutions to the long-term problem.

Case Studies

Three case studies of individual species illustrate the importance of land outside protected areas.

THE SNAIL KITE The snail kite (*Rostrhamus sociabilis*), or Everglades kite, is a rare bird species found in southern Florida; it is protected under the U.S. Endangered Species Act (Takegawa and Beissinger 1989; Graham 1990b; LaRoe et al. 1995). In recent years the number of snail kites has fluctuated between 300 and 800 individuals after reaching a low point of 256 birds in the 1960s. In most years, the kites feed on snails in the large wetlands located in Loxahatchee National Wildlife Refuge. In dry years, the kites are forced to leave the refuge for canals, flooded fields, and small permanent marshes, where they are vulnerable to shooting and accidents. These wetland habitats outside of the protected areas are rapidly being developed, posing a serious threat to the long-term survival of the snail kite. Long-term conservation of the snail kite depends on the preservation of these wetland habitats.

MOUNTAIN SHEEP Mountain sheep (*Ovis canadensis*) often occur in isolated populations in steep, open terrain surrounded by large areas of unsuitable habitat (Bleich et al. 1990). Since mountain sheep were considered to be slow colonizers of new habitat, past conservation efforts focused on the protection of known mountain sheep habitat and the release of sheep into areas that they previously occupied. However, studies using radio telemetry have revealed that mountain sheep often move well outside their normal territories and even show considerable ability to move across inhospitable terrain between mountain ranges. The isolated mountain sheep populations are really parts of a large metapopulation that occupies a much greater area (see Figure 12.8). These observations emphasize the need to protect not only the land occupied by mountain sheep but also habitat between populations that act as stepping-stones for dispersal, colonization, and gene flow.

THE FLORIDA PANTHER The Florida panther (*Felis concolor coryi*) is an endangered subspecies of puma in South Florida with probably no more than 50 individuals (Maehr 1990). This panther was designated the Florida state animal in 1982 and has since received a tremendous amount of government and research attention. Half of the present range of the panther is in private hands, and animals tracked with radio collars have all spent at least some of their time on private lands (Figure 18.1).

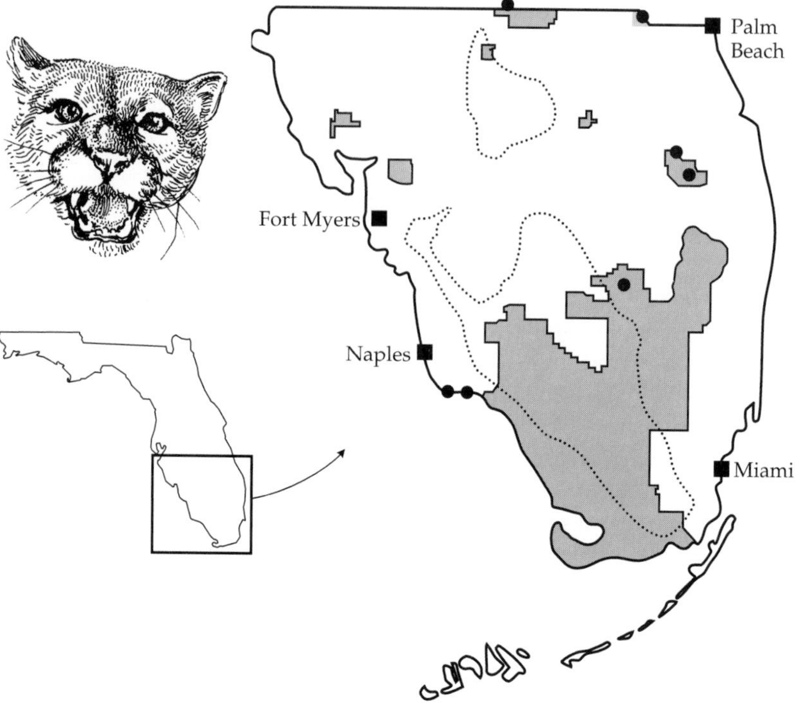

Figure 18.1 The Florida panther (*Felis concolor coryi*) is found on both public and private lands in South Florida. The dotted lines enclose areas known to be used by radio-collared panthers; the black dots represent sightings or other signs of uncollared panthers. Public lands are shaded. (After Maehr 1990.)

The importance of private lands is illustrated by the fact that private lands typically are on better soils that support more prey species, so that panthers spending most of their time on private lands have a better diet and are in better condition than panthers on public land. Acquiring the 400,000 ha of private land occupied by the panther would be financially and politically difficult. Even slowing down the pace of land development may be impractical. Two viable possibilities are educating private owners on the value of conservation, and paying willing landowners to practice management options that allow the continued existence of panthers—specifically, minimizing habitat fragmentation and maintaining preferred habitats of hardwood hammock forest, mixed hardwood swamp, and cypress swamp (Maehr and Cox 1995).

The Value of Unprotected Habitat

Strategies in which private landowners are educated about the need to protect rare species and biological communities are obviously the key to the long-term survival of many species. In many countries, government programs inform road builders and developers of the locations of rare species or threatened communities and help them modify their plans to avoid damage to the sites.

Native species often can continue to live in unprotected areas, especially when those areas are set aside or managed for some other purpose that is not harmful to the ecosystem. Forests that are selectively logged on a long cutting cycle or are farmed using traditional shifting cultivation by a small number of farmers may still contain a considerable percentage of the original biota (Poore and Sayer 1991; Thiollay 1992). In Malaysia, most bird species are still found in rain forests 25 years after selective logging, when undisturbed forest is available nearby to act as a source of colonists (Johns 1996).

In the United States, excellent examples of natural habitat occur on military reservations such as Fort Bragg in North Carolina, nuclear processing facilities such as the Savannah River site in South Carolina, and watersheds adjacent to metropolitan water supplies such as the Quabbin Reservoir in Massachusetts. Although dams, reservoirs, canals, dredging operations, port facilities, and coastal development destroy and damage aquatic communities, some species are capable of adapting to altered conditions, particularly if the water is not polluted. In estuaries and seas managed for commercial fisheries, many native species remain because commercial and noncommercial species alike require that the chemical and physical environment not be damaged.

Military reservations are particularly important habitats. Security zones surrounding government installations are some of the most outstanding natural areas in the world. The U.S. Department of Defense manages more than 10 million ha, much of it undeveloped, containing over 200 threatened and endangered species (Box 31). For example, the White Sands Missile Range in New Mexico is almost 1 million ha in area, about the same size as Yellowstone National Park. While certain sections of the reservation may be damaged by military activities, much of the habitat remains as an undeveloped buffer with restricted access.

Other areas that are not protected by law may retain species because the human population density and degree of utilization is typically very low. Border areas such as the demilitarized zone between North and South Korea often have an abundance of wildlife because they remain undeveloped and depopulated. Mountain areas, often too steep and inaccessible for development, are frequently managed by governments as valuable watersheds that produce a steady supply of water and prevent flooding; they also harbor important natural communities. Likewise, desert species may be at less risk than other unprotected communities because desert regions are considered marginal for human habitation and use. In many parts of the world, wealthy individuals have acquired large tracts of land for their personal estates and

Box 31 In Defense of Wildlife ... Send in the Marines!

The thump of mortar fire and the thudding of tank treads hardly seem compatible with wildlife conservation, yet some of the largest expanses of undeveloped land in the United States are on military reservations located throughout the nation. The U.S. Department of Defense controls more than 10 million hectares of land, nearly one-third the size of the 35 million hectares of national park lands owned by the National Park Service. Whereas national parks host millions of visitors a year, access to military bases is limited to military personnel and authorized visitors; because of these restrictions, much of the land remains in its natural state. Moreover, the land used for military exercises often is not used intensively; for instance, the Air Force uses only 1250 ha of its 44,000-ha base in Avon Park, Florida, and similar small fractions are used at other sites (Boice 1996; Cohn 1996). As a result, many military bases have become de facto refuges for wildlife. Endangered desert tortoises, manatees, red-cockaded woodpeckers, bald eagles, Atlantic white cedars, and the least Bell's vireo all have found safe havens on military lands.

Obviously, military reservations differ from true wildlife refuges in one important aspect: they are sites for significant disturbances caused by military exercises. While much of the land may be left undisturbed as a security zone, large parts of the otherwise undeveloped land may be used periodically for acclimating troops to potential combat environments. Many bases contain toxic waste dumps and high levels of chemical pollutants, and human disturbance in the form of bomb explosions, artillery practice, or the use of heavy vehicles can have a significant effect on the resident wildlife.

The passage of the Legacy Resource Management Program in 1991 by Congress allowed the military to place greater emphasis on environmentally sound practices by giving them funding for research and conservation programs (Jacobson and Marynowski 1997). Recent programs have ranged from helping individual species to restoring entire habitats. At the Naval Weapons Station at Charleston, South Carolina, Navy biologists have installed nest boxes and drilled holes in trees to provide future nest sites for the endangered red-cockaded woodpecker. Abandoned underground bunkers are being modified to provide habitat for bats. Construction of a pipeline in San Pedro, California,

The endangered Hawaiian stilt (*Himantopus mexicanus knudseni*) lives on exposed mudflats in Nu'upia Wildlife Management Area of the Hawaii Marine Corps Base. The Marine Corps periodically uses amphibious assault vehicles to break up exotic woody plants that threaten to cover the mudflats and exclude the stilt. (Photographs courtesy of the Department of Defense.)

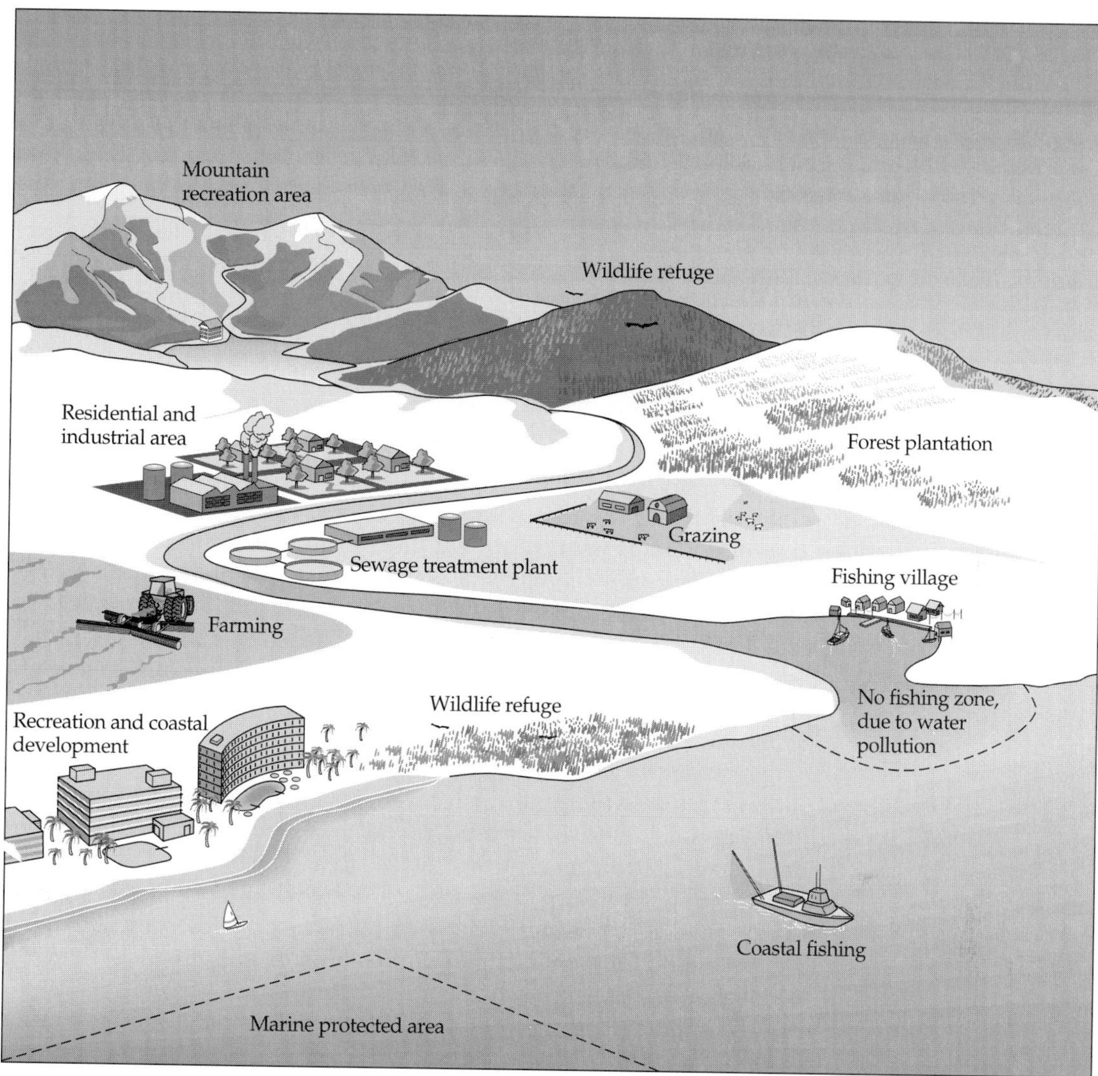

Figure 18.4 Ecosystem management involves joining together all of the stakeholders who receive benefits from and affect a large ecosystem. In this case, a watershed needs to be managed for a wide variety of purposes, many of which affect each other. (Modifed from Miller 1996.)

practice of conservation biology is being strongly embraced by government, business, and conservation groups.

Important themes in ecosystem management include:

- Seeking and understanding connections between all levels and scales in the ecosystem hierarchy, that is, from the individual organism to the species, to the community, and to the ecosystem.
- Ensuring viable populations of all species, representative examples of all biological communities and successional stages, and healthy ecosystem functions.

- Monitoring significant components of the ecosystem (numbers of individuals of significant species, vegetation cover, water quality, etc.), gathering the needed data, and then using the results to adjust management in an adaptive manner (sometimes referred to as **adaptive management**).
- Changing the rigid policies and practices of land management agencies, which often result in a piecemeal approach; instead, interagency cooperation and integration at the local, regional, national, and international levels, and cooperation and communication encouraged between public agencies and private organizations.
- Minimizing external threats to the ecosystem and maximizing sustainable benefits derived from it.
- Recognizing that humans are part of ecosystems and that human values influence management goals.

A recent survey found at least 619 ecosystem management projects in the United States with ecosystem preservation and restoration as their major goals (Yaffee et al. 1996). Most of them have started only since 1991. Land ownership is predominantly private for 41% of the projects, predominantly public for 31%, and mixed for 27%. Projects on private land predominated in the Northeast, Midwest, and Southeast, while projects on public land were more common in the Northwest and Southwest.

One example of ecosystem management is the Malpai Borderlands Group, a cooperative enterprise of ranchers and local landowners who promote collaboration between private landowners, government agencies, and conservation organizations such as The Nature Conservancy. The Group is working to develop a network of cooperation across nearly 400,000 ha of unique, rugged mountain and desert habitat along the Arizona and New Mexican border (Glenn 1997). This country of isolated mountains, or "sky islands," includes the Animas and Peloncillo Mountains. This is one of the richest biological areas in the United States, supporting Mexican jaguars, 265 species of birds, and 90 species of mammals (Figure 18.5). It includes 19 listed threatened and endangered species, and dozens of other rare and endemic species, such as the New Mexico ridge-nosed rattlesnake, the lesser long-nosed bat, and the Yaqui chub. The Malpai Borderlands Group is using controlled burning as a range management tool, reintroducing native grasses, applying innovative approaches to cattle grazing, incorporating scientific research into management plans, and taking action to avoid habitat fragmentation by using conservation easements to prevent residential development. Their goal is to create "a healthy, unfragmented landscape to support a diverse, flourishing community of human, plant and animal life in the Borderlands Region" (Yaffee et al. 1996).

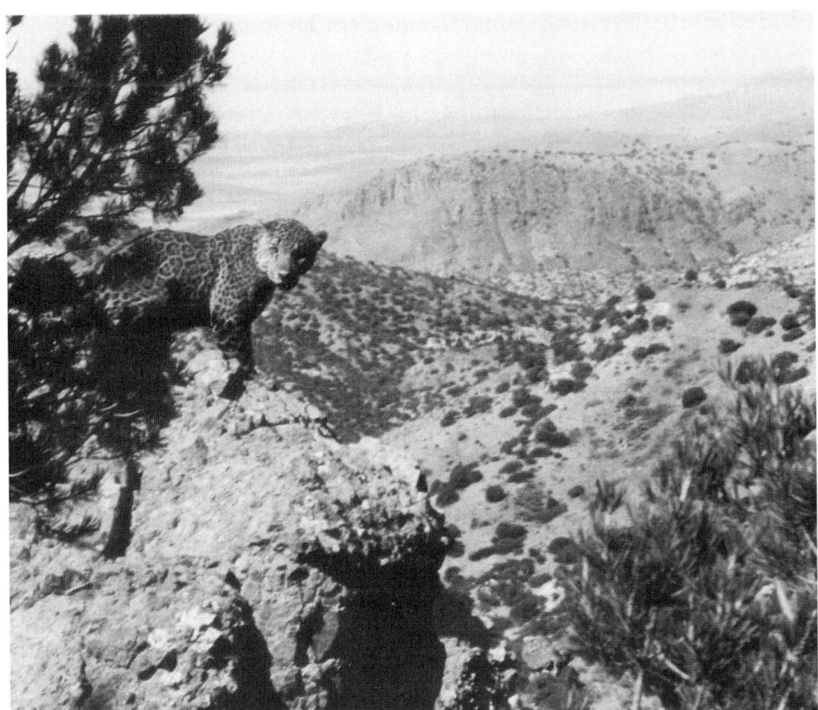

Figure 18.5 The Malpai Borderlands Group, encourages ecosystem management for 400,000 ha of desert and mountains in southern Arizona and New Mexico. Numerous rare and endangered species, including the Mexican jaguar (*Panthera onca*), are protected in the process. (Photograph by Warner Glenn, from *Eyes of Fire: Encounter with a Borderland Jaguar.*)

Ecosystem management is still in the early stages of development and many projects have experienced difficulties. A survey of 90 large projects in the United States revealed that the major threats to management goals were hydrologic alteration (changes in the water supply to the land), conversion to urban uses, and exotic species (Table 18.2). There were some striking differences among regions of the country: agricultural practices and pollution create major obstacles in the Southeast, forest management practices thwart goals in the Northwest, and grazing is particularly significant in the Southwest.

A logical extension of ecosystem management is **bioregional management**, which often focuses on a single large ecosystem such as the Caribbean Sea, the Great Barrier Reef of Australia, or a series of linked ecosystems such as the protected areas of Central America (Miller 1996). A bioregional approach is particularly appropriate where there is a single continuous, large ecosystem that crosses international boundaries. For the 16 countries that participate in the Mediterranean Action Plan, bioregional cooperation is absolutely necessary, because the enclosed Mediterranean Sea has weak tides that cannot quickly remove pollution resulting from deforestation and soil erosion, high human populations

TABLE 18.2 **Major management threats at 90 ecosystem management projects in the United States[a]**

Threat	All U.S.	Northeast	Southeast	Midwest	Northwest	Southwest
Hydrologic alteration	**42**	18	**54**	**41**	**57**	**47**
Land conversion to urban uses	**40**	**47**	**46**	33	**43**	37
Exotic species	38	35	23	29	**46**	**58**
Agricultural practices	34	18	**62**	**44**	13	32
Roads, other infrastructures	34	35	38	22	**50**	37
Disruption of fire regime	34	29	31	32	36	**42**
Nonpoint source pollution[b]	33	**41**	**64**	31	21	21
Grazing, range management	24	13	31	11	21	**47**
Timber, forest management	23	6	15	11	**71**	26

Source: Data from Yaffee et al. 1996.

[a] Values shown are the percent of management projects in each region that report specific threats as significant. The most significant values (above 40%) are shown in bold.

[b] This is pollution whose source cannot be exactly pinpointed (such as fertilizers and pesticides in water running off agricultural fields), as opposed to "point source pollution" from a specific and identifiable location (such as factory smokestacks or a sewage treatment plant).

along the coasts, and heavy oil tanker traffic (Figure 18.6). This combination of problems threatens the health of the entire Mediterranean ecosystem, including the sea, its surrounding lands, and its associated tourist and fishing industries. Cross-boundary management is also necessary because pollution from one country readily damages the water and beaches of neighboring countries. Participants in the plan agree to cooperate in monitoring and controlling pollution, carrying out research, and developing new pollution control methods.

Managed Coniferous Forests

The coniferous forests of the Pacific Northwest of the United States are managed for a variety of natural resources, but timber production traditionally has been considered the most important (Hansen et al. 1991, 1995; Halpern and Spies 1995). In this ecosystem, the issue of timber production versus the conservation of unique species—the northern spotted owl (*Strix occidentalis caurina*) and the marbled murrelet (*Brachyramphus marmoratus*)—has become a highly emotional and political debate billed as "owls versus jobs." Some environmentalists want to stop all cutting in old-growth forests, while many local citizens want the logging industry to continue current practices without outside interference. However, research on forest management techniques has indicated possible compromise solutions.

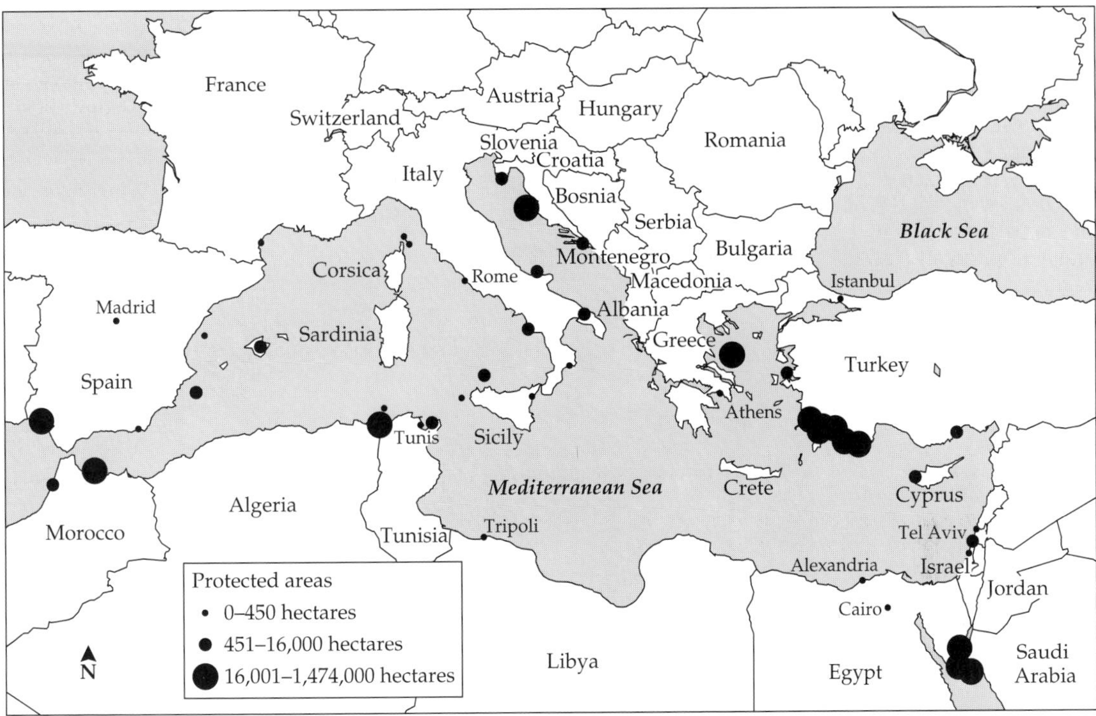

Figure 18.6 The countries participating in the Mediterranean Action Plan cooperate in monitoring and controlling pollution and coordinating their protected areas. Major protected areas along the coast are shown as dots. (From Miller 1996, after Kelleher 1995.)

Following fires, windstorms, or other disturbances, forests in the Pacific Northwest pass through four distinct successional stages:

1. The early successional stage (0–20 years), dominated by herbs and shrubs.
2. Young forest (20–80 years), characterized by vigorously growing trees.
3. Mature forest (80–200 years) with a declining growth rate and closed canopy.
4. Old-growth forest (more than 200 years), in which shade-tolerant conifers replace the dead and dying pioneer trees.

Old-growth forests (see Figure 17.5B) are periodically damaged by fire and windstorms, and the damaged patches return to the early successional stage. Despite the great difference in vegetation structure among these four stages, taxonomic studies have shown that there are relatively few differences in species composition and the number of species among them. Several species of bats and cavity-nesting birds, such as the northern spotted owl, however, are confined to old-growth forests. The reason for this similarity is that all of these forest types

Figure 18.7 Staggered harvesting of trees in managed forests of the Pacific Northwest produces a striking mosaic landscape of forest fragments. Within each patch, all vegetation is at the same successional stage. (Photograph by A. Levno.)

have at least a few old, large trees surviving, some dead standing trees, and fallen trees that remain after fires and storms. Certain insects, amphibians, fungi, and mosses may also need the moist, shady conditions and deep litter layer found only in old-growth forests. These resources are sufficient to support a complex community of plants and animals. However, current commercial logging practices remove the living and dead trees of all ages in order to maximize wood production, which reduces structural complexity in the next forest cycle. In managed forests of the Pacific Northwest, the practice of clear-cutting staggered patches of timber produces a landscape pattern that is a mosaic of forest fragments, with different tree ages across fragments and uniform ages within them (Figure 18.7).

Current research indicates that managed forests contain considerable biological diversity and suggests specific ways in which conifer forests can be managed to both produce timber and maintain a greater number of species. These lessons are being incorporated into the "new forestry" or "ecological forestry" advocated for the Pacific Northwest (Hansen et al. 1995; Kohm and Franklin 1997). This novel method essentially involves clear-cutting, but a low density of large live trees, standing dead trees, and some fallen trees are left to provide structural complexity and to serve as habitat for animal species in the next forest cycle (Figure 18.8). Forest fragmentation might also be reduced

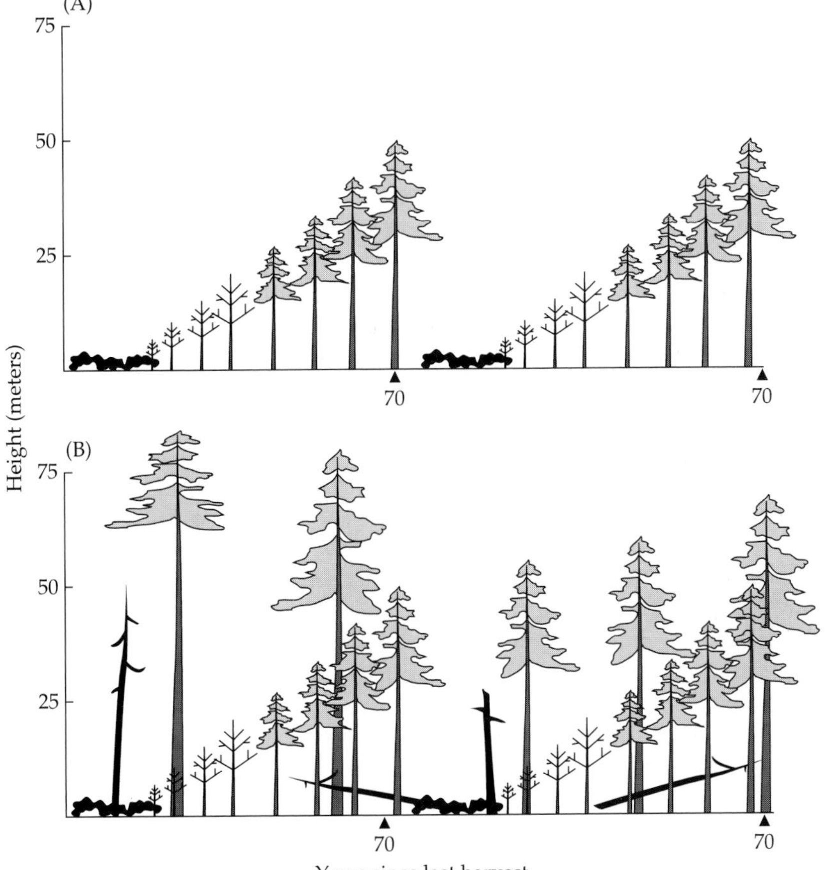

Figure 18.8 (A) The conventional clear-cutting illustrated in Figure 18.6 involves removing all trees from an area on a 70-year cycle, thus reducing the structural diversity of the forest. (B) Proposed new practices would better maintain structural diversity by leaving behind some old trees, standing dead trees, and fallen trees. (After Hansen et al. 1991.)

by harvesting in patterns that maintain forest in larger blocks. These alternative harvesting methods have policy and economic implications. If forests can be harvested in a way that allows all of the original species to be retained, then this would represent an improvement over current logging practices, at least from the perspective of conservation biology. However, ecological forestry requires a reduced harvest of timber at the time of cutting and a somewhat longer cutting cycle, resulting in a lower profit for the timber industry. Ecological forestry also fails to satisfy strict environmentalists who want to set aside large landscapes of old-growth forest as wilderness areas. They argue that the regions last "big trees" should not be cut down for economic reasons, even if this can be done without extinguishing species. United States citizens will have to decide what compromises can be made between preserving these forests and the human use of natural resources.

African Wildlife Outside Parks

East African countries such as Kenya are famous for the spectacular wildlife populations found in their national parks, which are the basis of a valuable ecotourist industry. Despite the fame of the parks, about three-fourths of Kenya's 2,000,000 large animals live in rangelands outside the parks' boundaries (Western 1989). The rangelands of Kenya occupy 700,000 km^2, or about 40% of the country. Among the well-known species found predominantly outside the parks are the giraffe (89%), the impala (72%), Grevy's zebra (99%), the oryx (73%), and the ostrich (92%). Only the rhinoceros, elephant, and wildebeest are found predominantly inside the parks; rhinos and elephants are concentrated in parks because poachers seeking ivory, horn, and hides have virtually eliminated external populations of these animals. The large herbivores found in the parks often graze seasonally outside them. Many of these species would be unable to persist in the parks if they were restricted within park boundaries due to fencing, poaching, and agricultural development.

Areas surrounding national parks are often used as rangeland for domestic cattle. It may seem intuitively obvious that the cattle compete for range, water, and vegetation; however, studies have shown that the main factor determining the productivity and number of Kenyan wildlife species is not competition from livestock but the amount of rainfall (Figure 18.9). The productivity of the rangelands, as measured by the weight of animals produced per km^2 per year, increases in a lin-

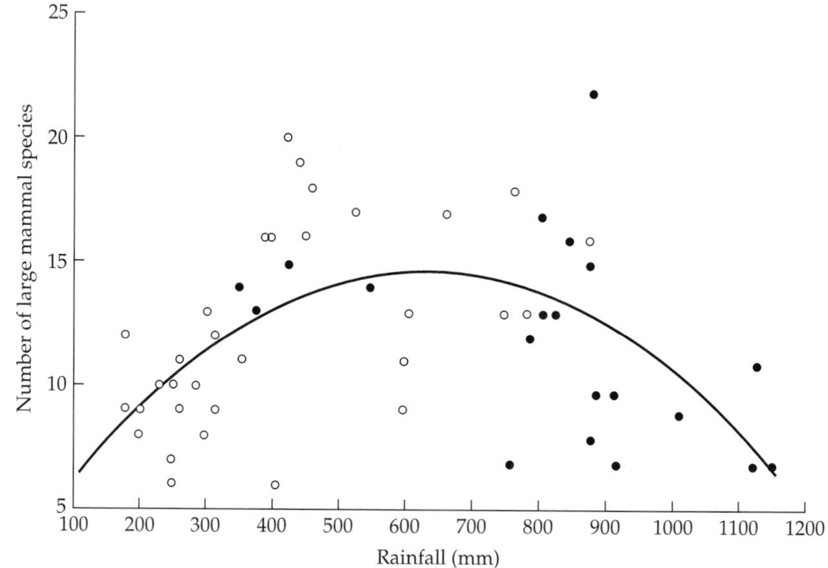

Figure 18.9 The number of large mammal species in East African ecosystems is apparently determined by annual rainfall, with the greatest number of species occurring in regions of intermediate rainfall. Ecosystems dominated by livestock (open circles) are no poorer in species than national parks, where livestock is banned (black circles). (After Western 1989.)

ear fashion with rainfall; the number of species on the land is highest with intermediate amounts of rainfall. The presence of livestock outside the parks does not affect the number of wildlife species present and has only a slight effect on productivity. It would appear that limited grazing of livestock may be compatible with wildlife conservation in some circumstances and that commercial range may extend the effective area of a wildlife preserve. Even in areas where there is commercial ranching, there appears to be little change in the types of wildlife species present. To support this point, Western (1989) has pointed out that human pastoralists, such as the Masai in Tanzania, have lived in East Africa for over 3000 years without even one large herbivore going extinct.

The continued existence of wild species on unprotected African lands appears to be attributable to a stable social structure and secure land tenure in the local human population. These tend to be characteristic of both traditional and highly developed societies. In these situations, control of resources is highly regulated by a recognized authority and current needs can be deferred to enhance future production of resources. Countries in which there is migration, poverty, unclear ownership of resources, and a breakdown of authority are likely to experience the greatest environmental deterioration and destruction of biological communities, because in these circumstances people must focus on their immediate needs with little concern for the future value of resources. In some unstable countries, there is an unregulated proliferation of guns in rural areas and an inability to control poaching. In a study of factors affecting the status of the African elephant, the most important were the extent of civilian disruptions and to a lesser extent the socioeconomic status of the people (Burrill et al. 1986). Elephant populations in stable countries were increasing by 2.5% per year, while in unstable countries they are declining by 16% per year. Literacy, annual income, and conservation measures also contribute to elephant increases.

In East Africa, a number of factors contribute to the persistence of wildlife in unprotected areas with substantial rural settlement (Western 1989). Many wildlife species are valued for their meat, so their presence on rangeland is encouraged. Private ranching in which wildlife and livestock are managed together is more profitable than managing livestock alone. Other wildlife species may be at very low numbers, or they are elusive and ignored by ranchers. Some areas containing wildlife are not used by people because of an inadequate water supply, warfare, disease, or inaccessibility. Here, wildlife can exist without interference. Some species such as elephants are tolerated since they open up woody vegetation for grassland and enhance the habitat for livestock. Finally, some species are protected by laws against hunting and trading, which are enforced by government agents; others persist simply because people enjoy them, finding them beautiful or amusing, and so tolerate their presence.

In Kenya and neighboring countries, there is now a movement to create a new government policy that allows rural communities and landowners to profit directly from the presence of large game animals (Baskin 1994). With assistance from international donor agencies, local ecotourist businesses, including hiking, photography, canoeing, and horseback safaris, are being established. When the land is adequately stocked with animals, trophy hunting is also allowed for high fees; sale of the meat and hide from hunting expeditions provides additional revenue.

Community-Based Wildlife Management in Zambia

In many areas of Africa, wildlife has declined dramatically during the last several decades, despite attempts by national governments to impose top-down conservation policies and to establish effective national parks. Local residents and conservation officers are now working together to increase the level of community involvement in national park wildlife management. One example of how community involvement might work in Africa comes from the ADMADE (Administrative Management Design for game management areas) program initiated to resolve conflicts in the Luangwa River Valley in eastern Zambia (Lewis 1995).

The Luangwa River Valley supports a world-famous concentration of wildlife and contains four national parks in which people are not allowed to live or hunt (Lewis et al. 1990). Surrounding the parks and occupying a much greater total area are game management areas in which tribal people live and in which hunting is allowed only with permits. However, hunting licenses were so expensive that licenses were taken out only by safari hunters, and local residents, who cannot afford them, were angry about a system that prevented them from obtaining the meat they needed to feed their families but permitted sport hunters to take trophies. From a national economic perspective, the single greatest revenue earner in game management areas is the license fees paid by foreign safari hunters—but less than 1% of this revenue was returned to the economy of the local villages. Not surprisingly, local residents came to resent the parks, the tourists, and the safaris. Chief Matama (quoted in Lewis et al. 1990) summarized the feelings of his people in a speech:

> Tourists come here to enjoy the lodges and to view the wildlife. Safari companies come here to kill animals and make money. We are forgotten.... Employment here is too low. Luangwa Lodge employs only about 4 people, and safari hunting employs no one. How can you ask us to cooperate with conservation when this is so?

As a consequence of these attitudes, illegal poaching of elephants, rhinos, and other animals increased dramatically during the 1970s and 1980s, and wildlife populations began to plummet. Personnel from the

National Parks and Wildlife Service (NPWS) were ineffective at stopping the poaching; since they were not from the local area, they were unwelcome in the villages, and they did not actively patrol the game management areas. Local people perceived NPWS personnel as acting only in the interests of the safari companies and having little regard for local concerns. Poaching at least gave them meat and the chance to make some money.

To remedy this deteriorating situation, an experimental program was initiated in 1987 in the Lupande Game Managment Area, which occupies 4849 km^2 in the Luangwa Valley and has 20,000 people. The key elements of the program are:

1. Local residents are hired and trained as scouts. These scouts are to remain in their own village areas to act as wildlife custodians.
2. The NPWS personnel live with the community, supervising the scouts, explaining the goals of the program to the villagers, and promoting community participation.
3. All workers hired in the program for construction of buildings, wildlife maintenance, and seasonal work come from the local villages.
4. Revenues are provided to the program by allowing safari companies to bid for hunting rights. Forty percent of this revenue is returned to local villages for community projects, and 60% is used for carrying out wildlife management. Additional revenue is provided by sustained-yield harvesting of hippos and commercial sale of meat, hides, and teeth.
5. Decisions on wildlife managment and employment practices are made following discussions with tribal chiefs and village leaders. Village leaders and community members themselves decide how best to spend the community development funds.

Nine years later, this community-based program appears to be sucessful at addressing many of the earlier problems of wildlife management. In 1988 the ADMADE program was extended throughout the entire country. The National Parks and Wildlife Service also set up the Institute for Community-Based Resource Management, where more than 500 village scouts have been trained and research is carried out. These village scouts patrol actively, catching poachers and seizing firearms; as a result illegal killing of elephants and black rhinos has declined in some areas by 90%. Local people have begun to appreciate the employment opportunities and revenue provided by the program. Poachers from outside the area are now being reported to the village scouts since they are now seen as a threat to a community resource. The income generated through regulated, sustainable safari hunting and tourism provides for most of the expenses of the program, although methods for payment are still being worked out. One of the

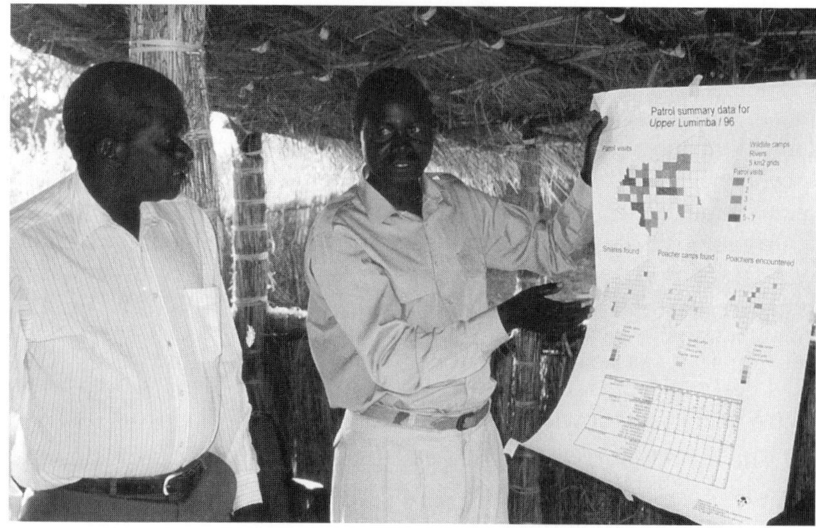

Figure 18.10 Community leaders in the ADMADE program use maps in their discussions on wildlife management. These maps are prepared using a Geographic Information Systems (GIS) analysis incorporating data collected by village scounts and licensed hunters. (Photograph courtesy of ADMADE, Zambia.)

most innovative features of this program involves collaboration with local leaders to develop Geographical Information System maps of their lands using data provided by village scouts, wildlife officers, and outside researchers (Figure 18.10). These maps can be used to show changes in wildlife density, animal migration routes, land use patterns, and income potential (Lewis 1995). Local leaders have used them to develop long-range management plans that represent the best compromise between national wildlife policy and the needs of the local people.

Since 1993, the revenues from wildlife-based industries in ADMADE areas have been growing at about 20% per year, and wildlife stocks and habitat are protected where the program is effectively administered. As a result of strong public support for ADMADE, the Zambian government has revised its Wildlife Act to give legal status to local communities as the rightful management authority for wildlife in game management areas. The ADMADE Program demonstrates how involving local people in wildlife management and revenue sharing offers a potentially effective way of reconciling conflicts.

Summary

1. Considerable biological diversity exists outside of protected areas, particularly in habitat managed for multiple-use resource extraction. Such unprotected habitats are vital for conservation because in all countries, protected areas account for only a small percentage of total area. Animal species living in protected areas often forage or migrate onto unprotected land where they are vulnerable to hunting, habitat loss, and other threats from humans. Govern-

ments are increasingly including the protection of endangered species as a priority on multiple-use land.

2. Government agencies, private conservation organizations, businesses, and private landowners are cooperating on a large scale to achieve conservation objectives and to sustainably use natural resources. Over 600 such ecosystem management projects are currently underway in the United States.

3. In temperate forest ecosystems, biological diversity can be enhanced if logging operations minimize fragmentation, and if some late-successional components, including living trees, standing dead trees, and fallen trees, are left. These trees are important resources for animal species, especially cavity-nesting birds.

4. In Africa, many of the characteristic large animals are found predominantly in rangeland outside the parks. Local people and landowners often maintain wildlife on their land for a variety of purposes; further incentives are being developed to encourage this practice.

For Discussion

1. Consider a national forest that has been used for decades for logging, hunting, and mining. If endangered plant species are discovered in this forest, should these activities be stopped? Can logging, hunting, and mining coexist with endangered species and, if so, how? If logging has to be stopped or scaled back, do logging companies or their employees deserve any compensation?

2. Imagine that you are informed by the government that the endangered Florida panther lives on a piece of land that you own and were planning to develop as a golf course. Are you happy, angry, confused, or proud? What are your options? What would be a fair compromise that would protect your rights, the rights of the public, and the rights of the panther?

3. Choose a large aquatic ecosystem that includes more than one country, such as the Black Sea, the Rhine River, the Caribbean, or the St. Lawrence River. What agencies or organizations have responsibility for ensuring the long-term health of the ecosystem? In what ways do they, or could they, cooperate in managing the area?

Suggested Readings

Boice, L. P. 1996. Endangered species management on U.S. Air Force lands. *Endangered Species Update* 13(9): 6–8. The U.S. military is getting involved in conservation; see other issues of the excellent magazine.

Christensen, N. L. and 12 others. 1996. The report of the Ecological Society of America committee on the scientific basis for ecosystem management. *Ecological Applications* 6: 665–691. Special issue of journal devoted to this topic, with many excellent articles.

Gradwohl, J. and R. Greenberg. 1988. Saving the Tropical Forest. EARTHSCAN Ltd., London. Innovative aproaches to protect tropical biodiversity.

Grumbine, R. E. 1994. What is ecosystem management? *Conservation Biology* 8: 27–38. Argues for a new philosophy to manage lands in a more integrated manner.

Hansen, A. J., T. A. Spies, F. J. Swanson and J. L. Ohmann. 1991. Conserving biodiversity in managed forests. *BioScience* 41: 382–392. New logging techniques can minimize the damage to biodiversity.

Holling, C. S. and G. K. Meffe. 1996. Command and control and the pathology of natural resource management. *Conservation Biology* 10: 328–337. The need for more flexible government agencies to retain natural ecosystem processes.

Kohm, K. and J. F. Franklin (eds.). 1997. *Creating a Forestry for the 21st Century: The Science of Ecosystem Management.* Island Press, Washington, D.C. U.S foresters are taking a broad, thoughtful view of forest management that includes biodiversity.

Miller, K. R. 1996. *Balancing the Scales: Guidelines for Increasing Biodiversity's Chances Through Bioregional Management.* World Resources Institute, Washington, D.C. Large ecosystems must be managed cooperatively by all affected countries and private organizations.

Noss, R. F. and A. Y. Cooperrider. 1994. *Saving Nature's Legacy: Restoring and Protecting Biodiversity*. Island Press, Washington, D.C. Practical advice on how to include the protection of biological diversity as a management objective.

Poore, D. and J. Sayer. 1991. *The Management of Tropical Moist Forest Lands.* IUCN, Gland, Switzerland. A comprehensive guide to management issues.

Szaro, R. C. and D. W. Johnston (eds.). 1996. *Biodiversity in Managed Landscapes: Theory and Practice*. Oxford University Press, New York. Leading authorities apply conservation biology principles to practical problems.

Western, D. and M. Pearl (eds.) 1989. *Conservation for the Twenty-First Century.* Oxford University Press, New York. Essays by leading authorities, many of which are related to conservation outside protected areas.

Yaffee, S. L. et al. 1996. *Ecosystem Management in the United States: An Assessment of Current Experience.* Island Press, Washington, D.C. Summary descriptions of 105 selected projects, along with listings and contact information for 619 projects. A great source of information.

CHAPTER 19

Restoration Ecology

DAMAGED AND DEGRADED ecosystems provide an important opportunity for conservation biologists to put research findings into practice by participating in the restoration of the original species and communities (Jordan et al. 1990; Daily 1995). Rebuilding damaged ecosystems has great potential for enlarging and enhancing the current system of protected areas. **Ecological restoration** is defined as "the process of intentionally altering a site to establish a defined, indigenous, historic ecosystem. The goal of this process is to emulate the structure, function, diversity, and dynamics of the specified ecosystem" (Society of Ecological Restoration 1991). **Restoration ecology** refers to research and scientific study that investigates methods of carrying out these restorations (Cairns and Heckman 1996). In many cases, businesses are required by law to restore habitats degraded by activities such as strip mining or water pollution.

Sometimes the activities that damaged biological communities were government practices such as dumping sewage into rivers and estuaries by municipalities or chemical pollution on military bases. Restoration efforts are sometimes part of the **mitigation** process in which a new site—often incorporating wetland communities—is created or rehabilitated as a substitute for a site destroyed by development (Zedler 1996). At other times, ecological processes such as annual floods and fires, which are disrupted by dams or levees and fire suppression, need to be restored.

Ecological restoration has its origins in older applied technologies that attempted to restore ecosystem functions or species of known economic value: wetland replication to prevent flooding, mine site reclamation to prevent soil erosion, range management of overgrazed lands to increase production of grasses, and tree planting on cleared land for timber and recreational values (Kusler and Kentula 1990; Urbanska et al. 1997). However, these technologies often produce only simplified biological communities or communities that cannot maintain themselves. With the emergence of a dynamic view of biological diversity as an important social concern, the reestablishment of the original species assemblages and communities has been included as a major goal in restoration plans. The input of conservation biologists is needed to make these efforts succeed.

Ecosystems can be radically changed by natural phenomena such as volcanic eruptions, hurricanes, and fires triggered by lightning, but they typically recover to their original biomass, community structure, and even a similar species composition through the process of **succession**. However, some ecosystems are so degraded by human activity that their ability to recover on their own is severely limited. The original plant species will not be able to grow at a site if the soil has been washed away by erosion. Recovery is particularly unlikely when the damaging agent is still present in the ecosystem. For example, restoration of degraded savannah woodlands in western Costa Rica and the western United States is not possible as long as the land continues to be overgrazed by introduced cattle; reduction of the grazing pressure is obviously the key starting point in these restoration efforts (Fleischner 1994).

Once the damaging agent is removed or controlled, the original communities may reestablish themselves by natural successional processes from remnant populations. However, recovery is unlikely when many of the original species have been eliminated over a large area, so that there is no source of colonists. For example, prairie species were eliminated from huge areas of the United States when the land was converted to agriculture. Even when an isolated patch of land is no longer cultivated, the original community does not become reestablished, because there is no source of seeds or colonizing animals of the original species. The site also may be dominated by exotic species, which often become established in disturbed areas. Recovery also is unlikely when the physical environment has been so altered that the original species can no longer survive there; examples include mine sites, where the restoration of natural communities may be delayed by decades or even centuries due to soil erosion and the heavy-metal toxicity and low nutrient status of remaining soil (Figure 19.1). Restoration in these habitats requires modification of the physical environment by adding soil, nutrients, and water, and by reintroducing species to the point where the natural process of succession and recovery can begin. These restored sites then need to be monitored for years, even decades, to determine how well management goals are being achieved and if further intervention is required.

In certain cases entirely new environments are created by human activity, such as reservoirs, canals, landfills, and industrial sites. If these sites are neglected, they often become dominated by exotic and weedy species, resulting in biological communities that are not useful to people, not typical of the surrounding areas, valueless from a conservation perspective, and aesthetically unappealing. If these sites are properly prepared and native species are reintroduced, native communities possibly can be restored. New habitat is often deliberately created as part of a mitigation process to compensate for habitats damaged or destroyed elsewhere. The goal of these and other restoration efforts often is to create new habitats that are comparable to existing **reference sites,** in terms of ecosystem functions or species composition

Figure 19.1 To speed the recovery of this devastated coal mine site in Wyoming, crews planted 120,000 shrubs. Mining sites often need a great deal of human help in order to recover even a semblance of biodiversity. (Photograph from Jordan et al. 1990.)

(White and Walker 1997; Rheinhardt 1996). Reference sites provide explicit goals for restoration, providing quantitative measures of the success of a project. Indeed, reference sites or conditions are central to the very concept of restoration, and to determine whether the goals of restoration projects are being achieved, both the restoration and the reference sites need to be monitored over time.

Restoration ecology provides theory and techniques to restore these various types of degraded ecosystems. Four main approaches are available in restoring biological communities and ecosystems (Figure 19.2) (Cairns 1986; Bradshaw 1990; Cairns and Heckman 1996):

1. *No action*, because restoration is too expensive, because previous attempts at restoration have failed, or because experience has shown that the ecosystem will recover on its own. The last approach is typical of old agricultural fields in eastern North America, which return to forest within a few decades after being abandoned for agriculture. Restored prairie wetlands often are not planted under the assumption that all species that can grow there eventually will become reestablished; however, this assumption may not be true (Galatowitsch and Van der Valk 1996).
2. *Replacement* of a degraded ecosystem with another productive type, sometimes called "habitat creation." For example, replacing

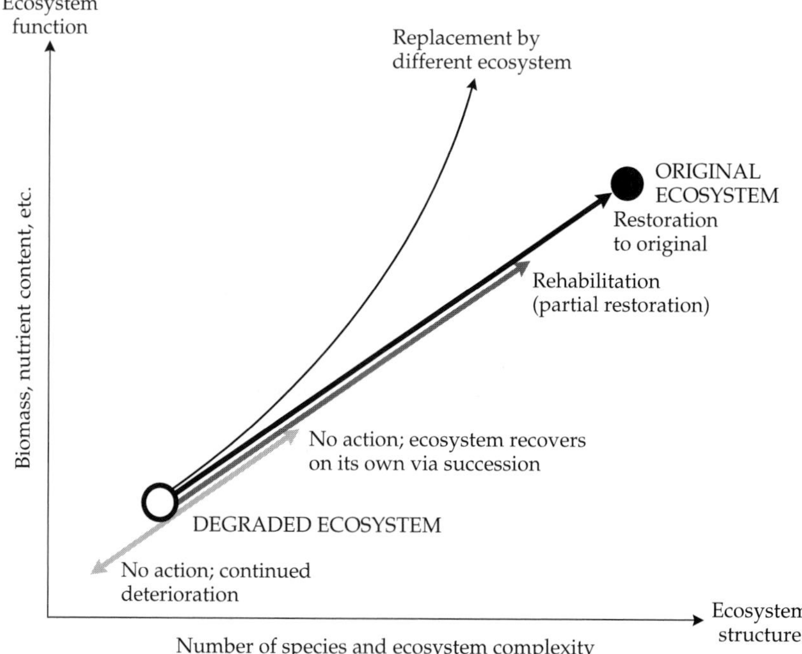

Figure 19.2 Degraded ecosystems have lost their structure (in terms of species and their interactions with the physical and biological environments) and their function (the accumulation of biomass, and soil, water, and nutrient processes). Decisions must be made as to whether the best course of action is to restore, rehabilitate, or replace the degraded site, or whether the best course is no action. (After Bradshaw 1990.)

a degraded forest area with a productive pasture. Replacement at least establishes a biological community on a site and restores ecological functions such as flood control and soil retention. In the future this new community might eventually come to incorporate a larger number of native species.

3. *Rehabilitation* of at least some of the ecosystem functions and some of the original species, such as replacing a degraded forest with a tree plantation or replanting a degraded grassland with a few species that can survive. Rehabilitation focuses on dominant species that are critical to ecosystem function, delaying action on the rare and less common species that are part of a complete restoration program.
4. *Restoration* of the area to its original species composition and structure by an active program of site modification and reintroduction of the original species. Restoration must first determine and reduce the source of ecological degradation. For example, a source of pollution must be controlled before a lake ecosystem can be restored. Natural ecological processes must be reestablished and allowed to heal the system.

Civil engineers and others involved in major projects deal with the restoration of degraded habitats in a practical, technical manner. Their goals are to find economical ways to permanently stabilize land surfaces, prevent soil erosion, make the site look better to neighbors and the general public, and if possible restore the productive value of the land (Daily 1995). Sewage treatment plants must be built as part of the restoration of lakes, rivers, and estuaries. To restore wetland communities needed for flood control and wildlife habitat, dams and channels may have to be altered to establish the original water flow patterns. Ecologists contribute to these restoration efforts by developing ways to restore the original communities in terms of species diversity, species composition, vegetation structure, and ecosystem function. To be practical, ecological restoration must also consider the speed of restoration, the cost, the reliability of results, and the ability of the final community to persist with little or no further maintenance. Practitioners of ecological restoration must have a clear grasp of how natural systems work and what methods of restoration are feasible (Clewell and Rieger 1997). Considerations of the cost and availability of seeds, when to water plants, how much fertilizer to add, and how to prepare the surface soil may become paramount in determining a project's success. Dealing with such practical details generally has not been attractive to academic biologists in the past, but these details must be considered in ecological restoration.

Restoration ecology is valuable to the science of ecology because it provides a test of how well we understand a biological community; the extent to which we can successfully reassemble a functioning community from its component parts demonstrates the depth of our knowledge, and points out deficiencies in our information. As Bradshaw (1990) has said, "Ecologists working in the field of ecosystem restoration are in the construction business, and like their engineering colleagues, can soon discover if their theory is correct by whether the airplane falls out of the sky, the bridge collapses, or the ecosystem fails to flourish." In this sense, restoration ecology can be viewed as an experimental methodology that complements existing programs of basic research on intact systems. In addition to its role as a conservation strategy, restoration ecology provides an opportunity to completely reassemble communities in different ways, to see how well they function, and to test ideas on a larger scale than would be possible otherwise (Diamond 1990; Gilpin 1990; Baldwin et al. 1994; Dobson 1997b).

Some of the most extensive work on restoration has been done on wetlands, including swamps and marshes (Galatowitsch and Van der Valk 1994; Holloway 1994; Zedler 1996). Wetlands are often filled in or damaged, because their importance in flood control, maintenance of water quality, and preservation of biological communities is either not known or not appreciated. More than half of the original wetlands in the United States have already been lost, and in heavily populated states such as California, over 90% have been lost (Cairns and Heckman 1996). Because of the current U.S. government policy of "no net loss of wetlands," large development projects that damage wetlands must repair them or create new wetlands to compensate for those damaged beyond repair (Box 32). The focus of these efforts has been on recreating the original hydrology of the area followed by planting native species. Experience has shown that such efforts to restore wetlands often do not closely match the biological communities or hydrological characteristics of reference sites. The subtleties of species composition, water movement, and soils, as well as the site history, are too difficult to match. However, the restored wetlands often do have some of the wetland plant species, they have some of the beneficial ecosystem characteristics such as flood control and pollution reduction, and they are often valuable for wildlife habitat. Further study and research of restoration methods may result in further improvement.

One high-profile case of restoration in the United States involved the Grand Canyon. Scientists were challenged to come up with exactly the right methodology to restore the Colorado River ecosystem where it flows through the Grand Canyon. The river had been drastically altered in 1963 by the construction of the Glen Canyon Dam and the filling in of Lake Powell. While the project did provide water and electricity throughout the region, less water flowed into the river. Most significantly, the loss of water greatly reduced the spring floods that once surged through the canyon, creating new beaches and habitat for the unique Grand Canyon fish species. Without the flooding to carry new sediment and scour the banks, beaches and banks were either worn away or became overgrown with woody vegetation, and introduced game fish began to replace native fish. To restore this crucial flooding event, the Bureau of Reclamation, after extended discussion among scientists and engineers, released an experimental flood of 900 million m^3 over the course of one week in March 1996 (Collier et al. 1997). The flood was effective in creating new beaches and habitat for native fish species. As a result of this success, more floods are planned for the future.

Highly visible restoration efforts are also taking place in many urban areas, reducing the intense human impact on ecosystems as well as enhancing the quality of life for city dwellers. Local citizen groups often welcome the opportunity to work with government agencies and conservation groups to restore degraded urban areas. Unattractive drainage canals in concrete culverts can be replaced by winding streams bordered with large rocks and planted with native wetland species. Vacant lots and neglected lands can be replanted with native shrubs, trees, and wildflowers. These efforts have the additional benefits of fostering neighborhood pride and creating a sense of community.

Restoring native communities to huge urban landfills presents one of the most unusual opportunities. In the United States, 150 million tons of trash are being buried in over 5000 active landfills each year. These eyesores can be the focus of conservation efforts. When they have reached their maximum capacity, these landfills are usually capped by sheets of plastic and layers of clay to prevent toxic chemicals and pollutants from seeping out. If these sites are left alone, they are often colonized by weedy, exotic species. However, planting native shrubs and trees attracts birds and mammals that will bring in and disperse the seeds of a wide range of native species.

Consider the ongoing restoration of the Fresh Kills landfill on Staten Island in New York City (Young 1995). The site occupies over 1000 ha, has a volume 25 times that of the Great Pyramid of Giza, and has garbage mounds as tall as the Statue of Liberty. Certain sections of the landfill have reached their maximum capacity and are now undergoing restoration. The project began by using bulldozers to contour the site, creating an appearance and drainage similar to natural coastal dunes. Next, 52,000 individuals of 18 species of trees and shrubs were planted to create distinctive native plant communities: an oak scrub forest, a pine-oak forest, and a low shrubland. Herbs were planted within these communities. Right away, the trees provided perching places for fruit-eating birds that brought seeds of many new species to the site. After just one year, seedlings of 32 additional woody plant species had appeared on the site. The site appears to be on its way to establishing a native ecosystem. Native birds of conservation interest such as ospreys, hawks, and egrets nest and feed there. However,

Box 32 **Easier Said Than Done: Restoring the Kissimmee River**

The Kissimmee River is a long, meandering river in central Florida that runs from Lake Kissimmee to Lake Okeechobee. Historically, its loops and bends created a mosaic of wetlands and floodplains that supported a highly diverse community of waterfowl, wading birds, fish, and other wildlife. The hydrology of the Kissimmee River is unique. The large number of headwater lakes, streams, and sloughs that drain into the Kissimmee River, combined with flat floodplains and low riverbanks, lead to frequent and prolonged flooding, and outstanding wildlife habitat.

But the annual floods that created such a unique ecosystem were not considered compatible with the rapid expansion of urban and agricultural development in the 1950s and 1960s. In response to the growing demand for flood protection, the Kissimmee River was channelized. The U.S. Army Corps of Engineers dug a 90-km long drainage canal, built levees, and regulated water flow from the feeder lakes. Two-thirds of the wetlands were drained, one-third of the river's natural channel was

The Kissimmee River Restoration project involves removing two water control structures (S-65B and S-65C) and backfilling the 37 km of canal between them. In the process, 72 km of continuous river channel will be restored, and floodwaters will cover the floodplain once again. (From South Florida Water Management District.)

destroyed, and much of the drained land was developed for agriculture. As the water flow was altered, oxygen concentrations in the water declined. An ecosystem that had been characterized by highly variable water levels and patchy, diverse habitats became a stable, homogeneous environment. The results were immediate: overwintering bird populations declined to 10% of their original size, habitat for game fish was degraded, and a diverse natural community of wading birds and fish was replaced by common and exotic species such as cattle egrets, gar, and bowfin (Toth 1996). The diversity and number of invertebrates also decreased. Intensive agriculture on former wetlands transported high levels of nutrients into the channelized river and eventually into Lake Okeechobee, accelerating the eutrophication process.

As the impact of the channelization became apparent, public pressure from conservation groups mounted to restore the Kissimmee River to its original state. Initial plans focused on restoring certain target species or functions of the river. Fishermen lobbied for restoration of the largemouth bass fishery. Residents clamored for improving water quality by restoring the filtering function of the wetlands. Hunters and birdwatchers focused on improving conditions for waterfowl. Ultimately, it became clear that efforts needed to focus on restoring the ecological integrity of the whole ecosystem, rather than on individual characteristics such as species abundance (Toth and Aumen 1994).

A demonstration project in 1984 used weirs to reestablish aspects of the hydrology of the area, including variable water flows and flooding. River water was directed into the former wetland, recreating marshland and reestablishing old river channels. Within one year, wetland plant communities responded positively to the treatments. Fish and bird populations increased dramatically in the flooded areas. This demonstration project and other restoration studies and modeling efforts provided evidence that the restoration of the Kissimmee River was technically feasible.

In 1992, the U.S. Congress authorized the restoration of the water flow pattern of the Kissimmee River, involving back-filling 37 km of canal, removing two water control structures, and re-carving 15 km of old river channel. In the process, 11,000 ha of wetland and 72 continuous km of the twisting river channel will be restored. To accomplish this, 35,000 ha of land will be acquired by the government. Important habitat will be provided for over 300 bird species, including the endangered bald eagle, snail kite, and wood stork. The project began in 1997 and is scheduled to run for 12 years. A major component of the project involves continuous ecological evaluation to determine the degree of success at each phase, and the opportunity for fine-tuning the plan along the way. The final project cost is estimated to be $435 million, shared equally between the federal government and the State of Florida. While this cost may seem enormous, the totality of ecosystem services provided by a healthy, restored Kissimmee River will also be of great value.

because the landfills contain toxic materials, there is some concern that the roots of large trees might break up the clay on top of the landfill, releasing polluted water into the surrounding environment.

Many efforts to restore ecological communities have focused on lakes, prairies, and forests. These environments have suffered severe alteration from human activities and are good candidates for restoration work, as described below.

Lakes

Limnologists involved in multibillion dollar efforts to restore lakes are already gaining valuable insights into community ecology and trophic structure that otherwise would not be possible (Welch and Cooke 1990;

MacKenzie 1996). One of the most common types of damage to lakes and ponds is cultural eutrophication caused by excess mineral nutrients produced by human activity. Signs of eutrophication include increases in the algae population (particularly surface scums of blue-green algae), lowered water clarity, lowered oxygen content of the water, fish kills, and an eventual increase in the growth of floating plants and other water weeds.

Attempts to restore eutrophic lakes have not only provided practical management information, but have also provided insight into the basic science of limnology (the study of the chemistry, biology, and physics of freshwater). In many lakes, reducing amounts of mineral nutrients entering the water through better sewage treatment or by diverting polluted water leads to reversal of the eutrophication process and restoration of the original conditions; this approach is known as bottom-up control. In other lakes, improvement does not occur, suggesting that the lake has internal mechanisms that are recycling excess nutrients from the sediment to the water column and keeping the nutrient levels artificially high.

One possible mechanism for the continual presence of excess nutrients in the water column involves fish species such as the carp (*Cyprinus carpio*) and the brown bullhead (*Ictalurus nebulosus*) that eat nutrient-rich organic matter on the lake bottom and then excrete these nutrients into the column. This hypothesis is supported by declines in phosphorus concentrations after carp populations are reduced in eutrophic lakes. The composition of the fish community also can affect the eutrophication process through predator–prey relationships. In some eutrophic lakes, planktonic invertebrates (such as the crustacean *Daphnia*) that eat algae are rapidly consumed by the fish, allowing the algae to grow unchecked. If predatory fish (which feed on other fish) are added to the lake, the populations of zooplankton-eating fish often drop, crustacean populations increase, the abundance of algae decreases, and water quality improves. Improvements in water quality achieved through manipulations of fish populations are referred to as top-down control, illustrating how restorationists can take advantage of natural processes of recovery and reestablishment of ecosystem dynamics in their work.

One of the most dramatic and expensive examples of lake restoration has been Lake Erie (Makarewicz and Bertram 1991). Lake Erie was the most polluted of the Great Lakes in the 1950s and 1960s, characterized by deteriorating water quality, extensive algal blooms, declining indigenous fish populations, the collapse of commercial fisheries, and oxygen depletion in deeper waters. To address this problem, the United States and Canadian governments have invested more than $7.5 billion since 1972 in wastewater treatment facilities, reducing the annual discharge of phosphorus into the lake from 15,260 tons in 1972 to 2449 tons in 1985. Once water quality began to improve in the mid-1970s and the 1980s, stocks of the native commercial walleye pike (*Stizostedion vitreum vitreum*), a predatory fish, began to increase on their own. Other predatory and game fish were added to the lake by state agencies. As a result, both bottom-up and top-down control agents worked to improve lake quality.

The 1980s saw continued improvement in Lake Erie water quality, as shown by lower concentrations of phosphorus, lower phytoplankton (algal) abundance, and a shift in the trophic community toward higher relative numbers of algal-feeding zooplankton and predatory fish, and lower numbers of zooplankton-feeding fish (Figure 19.3). There is even some evidence of improvement in oxygen levels at the lower depths of

Figure 19.3 Signs of recovery in Lake Erie. (A) Levels of phosphorus at the eastern and western ends of the lake. Phosphorus levels are lowered by treating the sewage and other human effluents that enter the lake. (B) Algal abundance. Algae flourish in the presence of phosphorus; algal blooms lower the water quality and eliminate other species. (C) Walleye pike abundance, as measured by the sport fishermen catch. Walleye are predatory fish that feed on zooplanktivorous fish such alewife and spottail shiners; adding walleye to the lake is one way to increase the population of crustaceans and other zooplankton, which in turn feed on the algae. (D) The abundance of alewife and shiners, measured by the catch per hour in Lake Erie fishing trawlers. When populations of these fish reach overly high levels, they decimate the zooplankton population; with fewer zooplankton to feed on them, algal blooms flourish even more. Alewife and shiner populations declined after the introduction of walleye and other predatory fish. (After Makarewicz and Bertram 1991.)

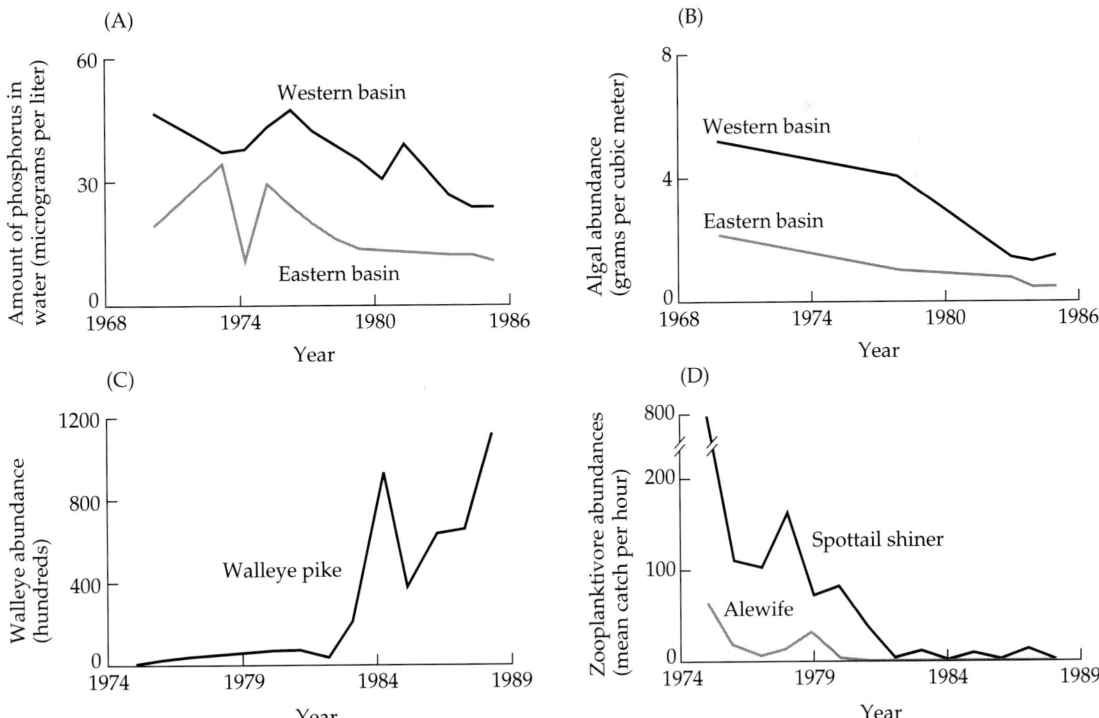

the lake. Even though the lake may never return to its original condition because of the large number of exotic species and altered water chemistry, the combination of bottom-up and top-down controls—and the investment of billions of dollars—has resulted in a significant degree of restoration in this large, highly managed ecosystem.

Prairies

Many small parcels of former agricultural land in North America have been restored as prairies. Because they are species-rich, have many beautiful wildflowers, and can be established within a few years, prairies represent ideal subjects for restoration work (Samson and Knopf 1996; Packard and Mutel 1997). Also, the technology used for prairie restoration is similar to that of gardening and agriculture and is well suited to incorporating volunteer labor. Of course, reestablishing the full range of plant species, soil structure, and invertebrates could take centuries, or may never occur.

Some of the most extensive research on the restoration of prairies has been carried out in Wisconsin, starting in the 1930s. A wide variety of techniques have been used in these prairie restoration attempts, but the basic method involves a site preparation of disking, burning, and raking, if prairie species are present, or of eliminating all vegetation by plowing or application of herbicides, if only exotics are present. Native plant species are then established by transplanting them in prairie sods obtained elsewhere, planting individuals grown from seed, or scattering prairie seed collected from the wild or from cultivated plants (Figure 19.4). The simplest method is gathering hay from a native prairie and sowing it on the prepared site. In summarizing five decades of Wisconsin experiments, Cottam (1990) observes:

> All of these methods work, but the success rate is highly variable and depends on the quantity of weeds present, the amount and timing of precipitation, the way the seeds are stratified, and a number of other variables both known and unknown. ... Native prairies are usually very heterogeneous, with masses of one species growing together in one place and other species growing together in another place. Why the plants distribute themselves as they do is not easily discerned, so at best a lot of guesswork and intuition goes into the actual planting of the species, and a large amount of background information increases the chance of success. There is room for error, however, because prairie plants generally have a broad range of tolerance. If they are established within their optimum habitat, the species will interact and ultimately sort themselves out into a reasonable approximation of a native prairie.

Prairie restoration projects are useful for educational and demonstration purposes in areas covered by agricultural landscapes and for their

(A)

(B)

Figure 19.4 (A) In the late 1930s, members of the Civilian Conservation Corps (one of the organizations created by President Franklin Roosevelt in order to boost employment during the Great Depression) participated in a University of Wisconsin project to restore the wild species of a Midwestern prairie. (B) The prairie as it looked 50 years later. (Photograph from the University of Wisconsin Arboretum and Archives.)

ability to excite the imagination of urban dwellers eager to be involved in conservation efforts. The Chicago metropolitan area is particularly well known for such projects. In concluding his essay, Cottam says, "Prairie restoration is an exciting and rewarding enterprise. It is full of surprises, fantastic successes, and abysmal failures. You learn a lot—usually more about what not to do than what to do. Success is seldom high, but prairie plants are resilient, and even a poor beginning will in time result in a beautiful prairie."

One of the most ambitious and controversial proposed restorations involves re-creating a short-grass prairie ecosystem, or "buffalo commons," on about 380,000 km^2 of the Plains states, from the Dakotas to Texas and from Wyoming to Nebraska (Popper and Popper 1991; Mathews 1992). This land is currently used for environmentally damaging and often unprofitable agriculture and grazing supported by government subsidies. The human population of this region is declining as farmers and townspeople go out of business and young people move away. From an ecological, sociological, and even an economic perspective, the best long-term use of much of the region might be as a restored prairie ecosystem. The human population of the region could stabilize around nondamaging core industries such as tourism, wildlife management, and low-level grazing by cattle and bison, leaving only the best lands in agriculture.

Restoration of Tropical Dry Forest in Costa Rica

Throughout the world, tropical forests are being degraded by logging, grazing, fire, shifting cultivation, and collection of fuelwood. These lands often become degraded to the point where they have few remaining trees and little value to the local human population. In order to reverse these disastrous trends, governments, local people, and private organizations are involved in planting hundreds of millions of tree seedlings per year to restore the forest cover.

An exciting experiment in restoration ecology is currently taking place in northwestern Costa Rica. The tropical dry forests of Central America have suffered from large-scale conversion to cattle ranches and farms. Cattle grazing, fire, and clearing have reduced this diverse community to a few fragments. Even in these fragments, exotic grasses and hunting pressure threaten remaining native species. This destruction has gone largely unnoticed as international scientific and public attention has focused on the more glamorous rain forests. To reverse this situation, U.S. ecologist Daniel Janzen has been working with Costa Rica's National Park Service and local people to restore 75,000 ha of land in the Guanacaste Conservation Area (Figure 19.5) (Allen 1988; Janzen 1988b). The plans for restoration of this area of marginal ranches, low-quality pastures, and forest fragments include planting native trees, controlling fires, and banning hunting. Livestock grazing is being reduced to levels necessary for controlling exotic grasses, which fuel fires and prevent the regeneration of native plant species. The goal is to eliminate exotic species and reestablish a forest ecosystem within the next 100 to 300 years. Already, native shrubs and saplings are becoming established on their own in the abandoned pastures, and they may soon outcompete the exotic species now that the original ecosystem processes are being restored.

(A)

(B)

(C)

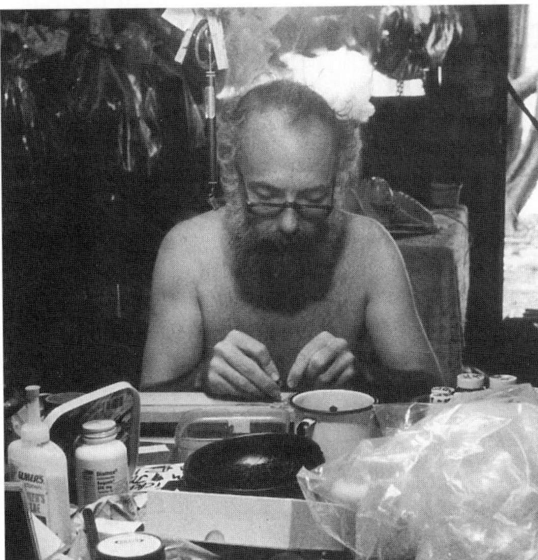

Figure 19.5 (A) The Guanacaste Conservation Area is an experiment in restoration ecology—an attempt to restore the devastated and fragmented tropical dry forest of Costa Rica. (B) Eight years of fire suppression allowed native trees and other species to become established once again, turning a barren grassland (left) into a young forest (right). (Photographs by C. R. Carroll.) (C) Daniel Janzen, an ecologist from the United States, is the driving force behind the restoration project in Guanacaste. Here he inspects moth specimens from the study area. (Photograph by William H. Allen.)

One innovative aspect of this restoration effort is the incorporation of local people into many aspects of park management and the intended role of the park in the cultural and educational lives of the people. Many of the farmers and ranchers living within the park borders were given the opportunity to be trained as park employees and to use their skills and knowledge of the area to develop the park. Those individuals showing initiative and ability are being trained as park managers and biologists. Almost 100 Costa Ricans are now working on various aspects of the project.

A key element in the restoration plan is what has been termed **biocultural restoration**, meaning that the park will serve as a center for teaching the 40,000 local residents about natural history and the principles of ecology and conservation. Janzen (quoted in Allen 1988) believes that, in rural areas such as Guanacaste, providing an opportunity for learning about nature can be one of the most valuable functions of national parks and restored areas:

> The public is starving for and responds immediately to presentations of complexity of all kinds—biology, music, literature, politics, education, et cetera. … The goal of biocultural restoration is to give back to people the understanding of the natural history around them that their grandparents had. These people are now just as culturally deprived as if they could no longer read, hear music, or see color.

To achieve this goal, educational and research programs have been designed to include local students at grade schools, high schools, and universities, as well as citizen groups. By educating the local community about natural history and teaching them the value of the park, there is hope that people will become advocates both locally and nationally for the conservation of natural resources. Janzen continues,

> The most practical outcome is that this program will begin to generate an ongoing populace that understands biology. In 20 to 40 years, these children will be running the park, the neighboring towns, the irrigation systems, the political systems. When someone comes along with a decision to be made about conservation, resource management, or anything else, you want that person to understand the biological processes that are behind that decision because he or she knew about them since grade school.

Funding for land purchases and park management comes from the Costa Rican government and donations from over 4000 individuals, institutions, and private international foundations. In the future, operating income to pay for the $1.2 million annual budget will increasingly come from fees paid by foreign and Costa Rican scientists working at the biological field stations. Also, the proximity of the park to the Pan American Highway makes it an ideal location for ecotourism. Employment in these expanding research, tourist, and educational facilities will provide a significant source of income for the local community, particularly for those who are interested in nature and education. A key element in the future success of the Guanacaste Conservation Area is that the plan for park development and management provides the proper integration of community needs and restoration needs in a way that satisfactorily fulfills both. Also, by having scientists involved in the design and implementation of the project, basic and applied information will be obtained that can be used to advance the science of restoration ecology.

In the final analysis, this restoration effort has been so successful and has attracted so much media attention in large part because a highly articulate, well-known individual—Daniel Janzen—committed all his time and resources to a cause in which he passionately believed.

His enthusiasm and vision have inspired many other people to join his cause. His example is a classic illustration of how a single individual or a small group of people can be a potent force for conservation.

The Fine Points of Restoration Ecology

Efforts to restore degraded terrestrial communities generally have emphasized the establishment of the original plant community. This emphasis is appropriate because the plant community typically contains the majority of the biomass and provides structure for the rest of the community. However, more attention needs to be devoted to the other major components of the community. Myccorhizal fungi (see Box 8 in Chapter 5) and bacteria play a vital role in soil decomposition and nutrient cycling; soil invertebrates are important in creating soil structure; herbivorous animals are important in reducing plant competition and maintaining species diversity; birds and insects are often essential pollinators; and many birds and mammals have vital functions as insect predators, soil diggers, and seed dispersers. Many of these non-plant species can be transferred to a restored site in sod samples, while large animals and above-ground invertebrates may have to be deliberately caught in sufficient numbers and then released onto restored sites to establish new populations. If an area is going to be destroyed and then restored later, as might occur during strip mining, the top layer of soil, which contains the majority of buried seeds, soil invertebrates, and other soil organisms can be carefully removed and stored for later use in restoration efforts (Urbanska et al. 1997). While this is a step in the right direction, many species will still be lost during this process and the community structure will be completely altered.

Restoration ecology will play an increasingly important role in the conservation of biological communities, if degraded lands can be restored to their original species composition and added to the limited existing area of protected conservation areas. Because degraded areas are unproductive and of little economic value, governments may be willing to restore them and increase their productive and conservation value. Restoration ecology is becoming one of the major growth areas in conservation biology, and has its own professional scientific society, the Society for Ecological Restoration, and journals, *Restoration Ecology* and *Restoration and Management Notes*. However, conservation biologists in this field must take care to ensure that restoration efforts are legitimate, rather than just a public-relations cover by environmentally damaging industrial corporations only interested in continuing business as usual (Falk and Olwell 1992; Holloway 1994; Zedler 1996). A 50-ha "demonstration" project in a highly visible location does not compensate for thousands or tens of thousands of hectares damaged elsewhere and should not be accepted as such by conservation biologists. The best long-term strategy still is to protect and manage biological communities where they are naturally found; only in these places can we be sure that the requirements for the long-term survival of all species are available.

Summary

1. Restoration ecology provides and investigates the methodology for reestablishing populations and whole communities in degraded, damaged, or even destroyed habitat. In many cases, these restoration efforts are required by law, particularly on mine sites. Rehabilitation of certain species or ecosystem functions may be an appropriate goal if complete restoration is impossible or too expensive. Establishment of new communities such as wetlands, forests, prairies, and lakes provides an opportunity to enhance biological diversity in habitats that have little other value. Restoration ecology not only has practical value in restoring the ecosystem functions and the natural appearance of a place; it also provides insight into community ecology by reassembling a community from its original species.

2. Restoration projects begin by eliminating or neutralizing the factors that prevent the system from recovering. Then some combination of site preparation, habitat management, and introduction of the original species gradually allows the community to regain the species and ecosystem characteristics of designated reference sites. Restoration efforts are usually concerned with the soil, plants, and hydrology of the site, but animals, symbiotic fungi, and bacteria also need to be included in restoration plans.

3. Most attempts to restore severely degraded habitat have had only limited success in restoring the original species composition and ecosystem function. Creating new habitat in one place to compensate for the destruction of a similar habitat elsewhere, known as mitigation, often will not be an effective conservation strategy; the best strategy is to protect populations and communities where they currently occur.

For Discussion

1. Restoration ecologists are becoming more successful at restoring biological communities. Does this mean that biological communities can be moved around the landscape and positioned in convenient places that do not inhibit further expansion of human activities?

2. How would you evaluate the success of a project that is currently restoring a biological community? What criteria and techniques would you use? How much time would you need to monitor the restored community?

3. What do you think are some of the easiest natural communities to restore? The most difficult?

4. Conservation efforts are particularly difficult in areas of Africa where there is an increasing human population, poverty, warfare, and environmental damage. Consider the plight of the mountain gorilla living in the Virunga Mountains of Africa. If it is not possible to protect this species in its native locality, why not use African plants to restore a degraded site in a more stable place, such as the mountains of Costa Rica, Mexico, or Puerto Rico, and then release a population of gorillas onto the site? This would create a protected community of African species in the New World. Is this feasible? What are the advantages and disadvantages of such a restoration approach?

Suggested Readings

Baldwin, A. D., J. de Luca and C. Pletsch (eds.). 1994. *Beyond Preservation: Restoring and Inventing Landscapes*. University of Minnesota Press, Minneapolis. Invigorating discussion of the philosophical basis of restoration ecology.

Cairns, J. and J. R. Heckman. 1996. Restoration ecology: The state of an emerging field. *Annual Review of Energy and the Environment* 21: 167–189. Excellent summary of the field.

Daily, G. C. 1995. Restoring value to the world's degraded lands. *Science* 269: 350–354. Restoration is expensive, but it can be an important long-term investment in the future.

Dobson, A. P., A. D. Bradshaw and A. J. M. Baker. 1997. Hopes for the future: restoration ecology and conservation biology. *Science* 277: 515–522. Overview of the field in a special edition of *Science* devoted to human impact on the planet.

Galatowitsch, S. M. and A. G. Van der Valk. 1996. *Restoring Prairie Wetlands: An Ecological Approach*. Iowa State University Press, Ames, IA. Practical guide on how to do it, and how to see whether it worked.

Holloway, M. 1994. Nurturing nature. *Scientific American* 270: 98–108. Overview of attempts to restore wetlands, and why they often do not succeed.

Janzen, D. H. 1988. Tropical ecological and biocultural restoration. *Science* 239:243–244. Unique integration of ecology and public education.

Jordan III, W. R., M. E. Gilpin and J. D. Aber (eds.). 1990. *Restoration Ecology: A Synthetic Approach to Ecological Research*. Cambridge University Press, Cambridge. Papers outlining case studies and general approaches to restoration ecology.

MacKenzie, S. H. 1996. *Integrated Resource Planning and Management: The Resource Approach in the Great Lakes Basin*. Island Press, Washington D.C. Half of the work in restoring ecosystems is the planning, legal, and administrative process.

Mathews, A. 1992. *Where the Buffalo Roam*. Grove Weidenfield, New York. Superb popular account of the controversial "buffalo commons" proposal.

Packard, S. and C. Mutel (eds.). 1997. *Tallgrass Prairie Restoration Handbook*. Island Press, Washington, D.C. A wide variety of prairie and savannah restoration projects are explored.

Restoration Ecology and *Restoration & Management Notes*. Check out these two journals to see what is really happening in the field. Available from the Society for Ecological Restoration, 1207 Seminole Highway, Suite B, Madison WI 53711.

Samson, F. B. and F. L. Knopf (eds.). 1996. *Prairie Conservation: Preserving America's Most Endangered Ecosystem*. Island Press, Washington D.C. So little remains of what was once a vast ecosystem.

Urbanska, K. M., N. R. Webb and P. J. Edwards (eds.). 1997. *Restoration Ecology and Sustainable Development*. Cambridge University Press, Cambridge. A collection of the latest case studies, with many European examples.

White, P. S. and J. L. Walker. 1997. Approximating nature's variation: selecting and using reference information in restoration ecology. *Restoration Ecology* 5: 338–349. Selecting reference sites is difficult because no two sites are exactly the same; see other excellent articles in this special edition of the journal.

Zedler, J. B. 1996. Ecological issues in wetland mitigation: An introduction to the forum. *Ecological Applications* 6: 33–37. A special issue of *Ecological Applications* provides excellent information on the creation of new wetlands.

PART SIX

Conservation and Human Societies

Mule deer

CHAPTER 20

Conservation and Sustainable Development at the Local and National Levels

MOST EFFORTS TO PRESERVE species and habitats rely on initiatives from concerned citizens, conservation organizations, and government officials. These actions may take many forms, but they begin with individual and group decisions to prevent the destruction of habitats and species in order to preserve something of perceived value (Figure 20.1). Governments and community organizations are often involved because the environment is perceived to be a public good, with public policy and public action directly determining optimal allocation of resources. As Peter Raven (in Tangley 1986), director of the Missouri Botanical Garden, remarked regarding the accelerated loss of biological diversity: "You can think about it on a worldwide basis, and then it becomes discouraging and insoluble, or you can think about it in terms of specific opportunities, seize those opportunities, and reduce the problem to a more manageable size."

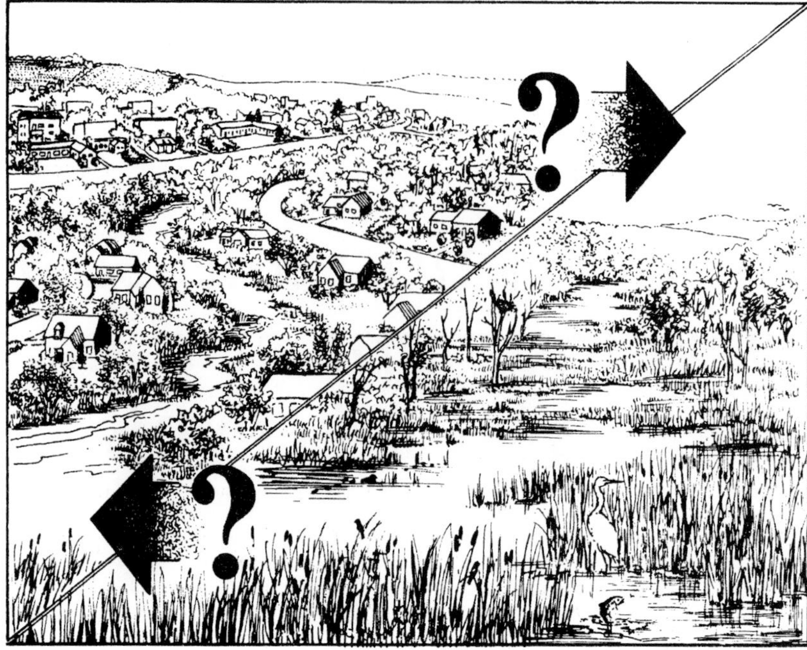

Figure 20.1 Decisions must be made concerning compromises between development to meet human needs and the preservation of the natural world. (From Gersh and Pickert 1991; drawing by Tamara Sayre.)

Efforts to preserve biological diversity, however, sometimes come into conflict with actual or perceived human needs. Increasingly, conservation biologists, policy makers, and land managers are recognizing the need for **sustainable development**—economic development that satisfies both present and future needs for resources and employment while minimizing its impact on biological diversity (Lubchenco et al. 1991). The concept of sustainable development has been applied in a variety of ways. As defined by some environmental economists, **economic development** implies improvements in organization but not necessarily increases in resource consumption and should be clearly distinguished from **economic growth**, that is, material increases in the amount of resources used. If sustainable development is to be a useful concept in conservation biology, it must emphasize improving current development and limiting growth. Investing in national park infrastructure to improve protection of biological diversity and provide revenue opportunities would be an example of movement toward sustainable development along these lines, as would implementation of less destructive logging and fishing practices.

Many large corporations, and the policy organizations that they fund, have misused the concept of sustainable development to "greenwash" their industrial activities without any change in practice (Willers 1994). Can a plan to establish a huge mining complex in the middle of a forest wilderness justifiably be called sustainable development simply because a small percentage of the land area is set aside as a park? Some conservation biologists have been portrayed as going to the opposite extreme, advocating that vast areas of the world should be kept off limits to all development and allowed to remain or return to wilderness (Mann and Plummer 1993). As with all controversies, informed scientists and citizens must study the issues closely and then make careful decisions that best reflect the genuine needs of human society and the protection of biological diversity.

Local Conservation

In modern societies, local (city and town) and regional (county, state, provincial) governments pass laws to provide effective protection for species and habitats (Gross et al. 1991; Press et al. 1996; Buck 1996). Laws are passed because citizens and political leaders feel that they represent the will of the majority and provide long-term benefits to the society. Conservation laws regulate activities that directly affect species and ecosystems. The most prominent of these laws govern when and where hunting and fishing can occur; the size, number, and species of animals that can be taken; and the types of weapons and traps and other equipment that can be used. Restrictions are enforced through licensing requirements and patrols by game wardens and police. In some settled and protected areas, hunting and fishing are banned entirely. Similar laws affect the harvesting of plants, seaweed, and shellfish. Related legislation includes prohibitions on trade in wild-collected animals and plants. Certification of origin of biological products may be required to ensure that wild populations are not illegally depleted. These restrictions have long applied to certain animals such as trout and deer, and plants of horticultural interest such as rhododendrons, azaleas, and cacti.

Laws that control the way in which land is used are another means of protecting biological diversity. These laws include restrictions on amount of land use or access, type of land use, and pollution generated. For example, vehicles and even people on foot may be restricted from habitats and resources that are sensitive to damage, such as bird-nesting areas, bogs, wildflower patches, and sources of drinking water. Uncontrolled fires may severely damage habitats, so practices contributing to accidental fires, such as campfires, are often rigidly controlled. Zoning laws sometimes prevent construction in sensitive areas such as barrier beaches and floodplains. Even where development is permitted, building permits increasingly are reviewed to ensure that damage is not done to endangered species or to wetlands. For major regional and national projects, environmental impact statements, which describe the damage that the project could cause, must be prepared. Governments regulate manufacturing, mining, transportation, waste disposal, and other human activities to prevent air and water pollution that can damage biological communities, natural resources, and human health.

Passage and enforcement of conservation-related laws on a local level can become an emotional experience that divides a community and even leads to violence (see Box 36 in Chapter 22). Conservationists must be able to convince the public that using a resource in an intelligent and sustainable manner creates the greatest long-term benefit for the society. The general public must be made to look beyond the immediate benefits that come with rapid and destructive exploitation. For example, towns often need to restrict development in watershed areas to protect water supplies; this may mean that houses and businesses are not built, and landowners may have to be compensated. Mountain bikes and hikers may need to be restricted to particular areas of parks to prevent damage to trail systems, wildflower populations, and fragile habitats; such restrictions limit popular recreational activities. The ability to negotiate, compromise, and explain positions, often using the best scientific evidence available, is an important quality in conservationists. A fervent belief in one's cause is not enough.

The rhetoric of conservation biology can also enter local debate in ways that may be inappropriate. Citizens seeking to resist any development near their own homes ("Not in my backyard!") may use conservation arguments to justify their objections. For example, a citizens' group in Boston attempted to support their objections to a new school on the basis that the cars dropping off students would create excess carbon dioxide and contribute to global warming. Though the argument had little basis in fact, the use of this rationale by the citizens' group was detrimental to conservation efforts in one respect: when conservation issues are misused in this manner, valid conservation initiatives suffer by association. Frivolous use of conservation arguments causes community leaders to take genuine conservation issues less seriously or to suspect the intentions of conservationists. Real concern for endangered species and habitats may be ridiculed as "hysteria" by policy makers or treated as a manifestation of a hidden political or business agenda.

One of the most powerful strategies to protect biological diversity at the local level is the designation of intact biological communities as nature reserves or conservation land. Governments often set aside public lands for various conservation purposes and to preserve future options. Government bodies buy land as local parks for recreation, conservation areas to maintain biological diversity, forests for timber production and other uses, and watersheds to protect water supplies. Wealthy individuals establish private estates for their own enjoyment. Businesses such as timber companies, electric companies, and cattle ranches may set aside parts of their land that are not suitable for utilization. Finally, private conservation organizations acquire land for preservation to protect biological diversity and places of historical, cultural, scenic, and educational value. In some cases, land is purchased outright, but land is often donated to conservation organizations by public-spirited citizens. Many of these citizens receive significant tax benefits from the government to encourage these land donations.

Land Trusts

In many countries, private conservation organizations are among the leaders in acquiring land for conservation (Elfring 1989; Dwyer and Hodge 1996). In the United States alone, over 800,000 ha of land are protected at a local level by **land trusts**, which are private, nonprofit corporations established to protect land and natural resources. At a national level, major organizations such as The Nature Conservancy and the Audubon Society have protected an additional 3 million ha.

Land trusts are particularly common in Europe. In the Netherlands about half of the protected areas are privately owned. In Britain, the National Trust has more than 2 million members and owns over 200,000 ha of land, much of it farmland, including 26 National Nature Reserves, 466 Sites of Special Scientific Interest, 355 properties of Outstanding National Beauty, and 40,000 archaeological sites (Figure 20.2). Among the many private land trusts in Britain, the most notable is the Royal Society for the Protection of Birds (RSPB), which has almost 900,000 members and manages 130 reserves with an area of 92,000 ha. A major emphasis of many of these reserves is nature conservation, often linked to school programs. The RSPB has an annual income of about 30 million pounds sterling and is active in bird conservation issues around the world.

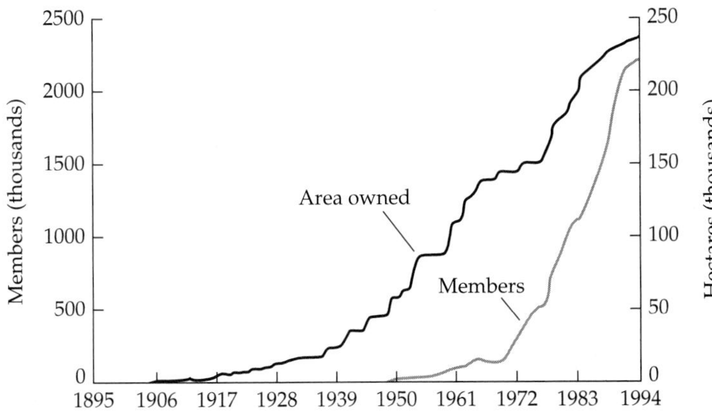

Figure 20.2 Membership in the British National Trust has been undergoing a dramatic increase, with a corresponding increase in land ownership. (Adapted from Dwyer and Hodge 1996.)

Jean Hocker (in Elfring 1989), executive director of the Land Trust Exchange, an association of land trust organizations, explains their purpose:

> Different land trusts may save different types of land for different reasons. Some preserve farmland to maintain economic opportunities for local farmers. Some preserve wildlife habitat to ensure the existence of an endangered species. Some protect land in watersheds to improve or maintain water quality. Whether biologic, economic, productive, aesthetic, spiritual, educational, or ethical, the reasons for protecting land are as diverse as the landscape itself.

To designate the variety of objectives, these organizations are collectively referred to as **CARTs**: Conservation, Amenity, and Recreation Trusts.

In addition to outright purchase of land, both governments and conservation organizations protect land through **conservation easements**. Landowners will often give up the right to develop, build on, or subdivide their property in exchange for a sum of money, a lower real estate tax, or some other tax benefit. For many landowners, accepting a conservation easement is an attractive option, because they receive a financial advantage while still owning their land, and they feel that they are assisting conservation objectives. Because of these considerations, many landowners will voluntarily accept conservation restrictions without compensation. Sometimes the government or conservation organization purchases the **development rights** to the land, compensating the landowner for not selling it to developers. Another option that land trusts and governments use is **limited development**, in which a landowner, a property developer, and a conservation organization reach a compromise allowing part of the land to be commercially developed while the remainder is protected by a conservation easement. Limited development projects are often successful because the developed lands typically have their value enhanced by being adjacent to conservation land. Limited development also allows the construction of necessary buildings for an expanding human society.

Local efforts by land trusts to protect land are sometimes criticized as being elitist because they remove land from productive use and often lower the revenue collected from land taxes. However, the loss of tax revenue from land acquired by a land trust is often offset by the increased value of property adjacent to the conservation area. In addition, nature reserves, national parks, wildlife refuges, and other protected areas generate revenue throughout the local economy, which benefits the community (Power 1991). Finally, by preserving important features of the landscape and natural communities, local nature reserves also preserve and enhance the cultural heritage of the local society, providing benefits for all.

National Legislatures

Throughout much of the modern world, national governments and national conservation organizations play a leading role in conservation activities. The establishment of national parks is a common conservation strategy. National parks are the single largest source of protected lands in many countries. For example, Costa Rica's national parks protect more than half a million hectares, or about 8% of the nation's land area (WRI 1992). Outside the parks, deforestation is proceeding rapidly, and soon the parks may represent the only undisturbed habitat and source of natural products such as timber in the whole country. The U.S. National Park system, with 369 sites, covers 35 million ha (Pritchard 1991).

National legislatures and governing agencies are the principal bodies setting standards that limit environmental pollution. Laws regulating aerial emissions, sewage treatment, waste dumping, and development of wetlands are often enacted to protect human health and resources such as drinking water, forests, and commercial and sport fisheries (Buck 1996). The effectiveness with which these laws are enforced shows a nation's determination to protect its citizens and natural resources (Tobin 1990). At the same time, these laws protect biological communities that would otherwise be destroyed by pollution. The air pollution that exacerbates human respiratory disease, kills commercial forests, and ruins drinking water also kills terrestrial and aquatic species.

National governments, through the control of their borders, ports, and commerce, can have a substantial effect on the protection of biological diversity. To protect forests and regulate their use, governments can ban logging, as was done in Thailand following disastrous flooding; restrict the export of logs, as was done in Indonesia; and even ban the import of forestry equipment. To prevent the exploitation of rare species, governments can restrict the possession of certain species and control all imports and exports of the species through laws such as the Convention on International Trade in Endangered Species (CITES) and the U.S. Endangered Species Act. For example, the export of ivory from the rare rhinoceros hornbill bird (*Buceros rhinoceros*), a valuable international commodity used for carving, is strictly controlled by the Malaysian government.

Finally, national governments can identify endangered species within their borders and take steps to conserve them, such as acquiring habitat for the species, controlling use of the species, developing a research program on the species, and implementing in situ and ex situ recovery plans.

The U.S. Endangered Species Act of 1973

In the United States, the principal conservation law protecting species is the Endangered Species Act of 1973. This legislation has been a model for other countries, though its implementation has often been controversial (Clark et al. 1994; Chadwick 1995). The Endangered Species Act was created by the U.S. Congress to "provide a means whereby the ecosystems upon which endangered species and threatened species depend may be conserved [and] to provide a program for the conservation of such species." Species are protected under the Act if they are on the official list of endangered and threatened species.

As defined by law, endangered species are those likely to become extinct as a result of human activities and natural causes in all or a major portion of their range, while threatened species are those likely to become endangered in the near future (Easter-Pilcher 1996). The Secretary of the Interior, acting through the U.S. Fish and Wildlife Service, and the Secretary of Commerce, acting through the National Marine Fisheries Service (NMFS), can add and remove species from the list based on information available to them. In addition, a recovery plan is required for each listed species. More than 1100 U.S. species have been added to the list, as well as around 550 endangered species from elsewhere in the world that may be imported into the United States.

The Act requires all U.S. government agencies to consult with the Fish and Wildlife Service and the NMFS to determine whether their activities will affect listed species and prohibits activities that will harm these species and their habitat. This feature is critical because much of the threat to species comes from logging, cattle grazing, and mining on federal lands. The law also prevents private individuals, businesses, and local governments from harming or "taking" listed species and damaging their habitat, and prohibits all trade in listed species. Private land is important to species recovery because around half of the listed species are found exclusively on private land (Dwyer et al. 1995; Wilcove et al. 1996). The feature of protecting habitats in effect uses listed species as indicator species to protect entire biological communities and the thousands of species that they contain.

An analysis of the U.S. Endangered Species Act shows a number of revealing trends. The great majority of species listed under the Act are plants and vertebrates, despite the fact that most species are insects and other invertebrates. More than 40% of the 300 mussel species found in the U.S. are extinct or in danger of extinction, yet only 56 species are listed under the Act (Stolzenburg 1992). Clearly, greater efforts must be made to study the lesser known and underappreciated invertebrate groups and extend listing to endangered species whenever necessary. Another study of species covered by the Act has shown that animals only have about 1000 remaining individuals at the time of listing and plants have fewer than 120 individuals remaining (Wilcove et al. 1993). Reduced populations of species may encounter the genetic and demographic problems associated with small population size that can prevent recovery. At the extreme were 39 species listed when they had 10 or fewer individuals remaining and a freshwater mussel that was listed when it had only a single remaining population that was not reproducing. Endangered species should be given protection under the Act before they decline to the point where recovery becomes difficult. An early listing of a declining species might allow it to recover and become a candidate for removal from the list more quickly.

In the two decades since its enactment, the Endangered Species Act has become increasingly important as a conservation tool. The Act has provided the legal basis for protecting some of the most well-known animal species in the United States, such as the grizzly bear, the bald eagle, the whooping crane, and the gray wolf. Because the law protects the ecosystems in which endangered species live, entire biological communities and thousands of species have in effect been covered at the same time (Carroll et al. 1996). It has also become a source of contention between conservation and business interests in the United States. The conservation opinion is expressed by Bill Reffalt of the Wilderness Society (in Horton 1992): "The Endangered Species Act is a safety net for species we've put in jeopardy while we get our act together to take care of the planet. Ultimately we've got to convince people that human progress running counter to the existence of species simply is not sustainable." The best long-term success for the legal protection of species is prevention of habitat loss that causes species to be endangered in the first place. This point is emphasized by Randall Snodgrass of the National Audubon Society: "If the Act is truly to prevent further species loss it's got to evolve into a next generation wildlife law instead of [an emergency] law that just recovers species from the brink."

The protection afforded to listed species is so strong that business interests and landowners often lobby strenuously against the listing of species in their area. At the extreme are landowners who destroy endangered species on their property to evade the provisions of the Act, a practice known as "shoot, shovel, and shut up." Such was the fate of half of the only known population of the St. Thomas Island prickly ash, which was destroyed in 1985 before it was added to the list of protected species (Mann and Plummer 1995). At present almost 4000 species are candidates under consideration for listing; while awaiting official decisions, some of these species have probably gone extinct. The reluctance to put species on the list is caused primarily by the restrictions it places on economic activity, but is also due to the difficulty of rehabilitating species to the point where they can be removed from the list, or "de-listed" (Tear et al. 1995). So far only 21 of more than 900 listed U.S. species have been de-listed, the most notable successes being the brown pelican and the American alligator (Figure 20.3). In 1994 the bald eagle was moved from the highly regulated "endangered" category to the less critical "threatened" category because its numbers had increased from 400 breeding pairs in the 1960s to the current 4000. Fifteen species were de-listed because they went extinct, because new populations

Figure 20.3 The American alligator is a conservation success story. It is one of only six species in the United States that has been de-listed under the Endangered Species Act; that is, it is judged no longer to be threatened or in need of strict protection. (Photograph by Brian Parker/ Tom Stack & Associates.)

were found, or because biologists decided that they were not truly distinct species. Overall, approximately one-third of the listed species are still declining in numbers, one-third are stable or increasing and, most surprisingly, one-third are of unknown status (Wilcove et al. 1996).

The difficulty of implementing recovery plans for so many species is often not primarily biological but, to a large extent, political, administrative, and ultimately financial. The U.S. Fish and Wildlife Service annually spends only around $113 million on activities related to the Act; most of these funds are used for land acquisition and legal expenses. One estimate suggests that over $4 billion would be needed to remove the threat of extinction from all listed species. The cost might be even higher now because of a U.S. Supreme Court ruling that recognizes the rights of private landowners to sue the government for financial compensation if species protection policies deprive a landowner of all economic use of the property. While funding for the Endangered Species Act has been growing steadily over the past 20 years, the number of species protected under the Act has been growing even faster. As a result, there is less money *per species* now than previously (Figure 20.4). The key to effective protection of species will probably involve working to a greater extent with private landowners. Specifically, the tax laws should be changed so that landowners can receive a tax deduction for maintaining habitats occupied by endangered species. Tax deductions should also apply to any restoration or management costs, such as weeding, controlled burning, establishing nest holes, and planting native species.

The economic implications of protecting listed species can be staggering. Pro-business groups have been formed that use environmental-sounding rhetoric to argue against the Endangered Species Act, promoting instead "wise use" of natural resources—in most cases, uses that prioritize human needs for jobs, raw materials, and economic development over the requirements of species or ecosystems. In an

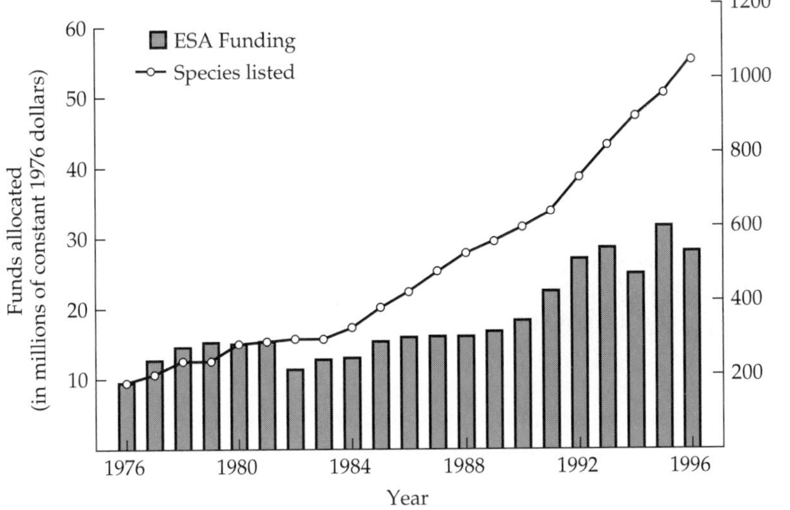

Figure 20.4 The number of species protected by the U.S. Endangered Species Act has been increasing at a faster rate than the funding available to protect these species (expressed in 1976 dollars). As a result, the money available per species is declining. (From Wilcove et al. 1996.)

attempt to find compromises between the economic interests of the country and conservation priorities, the Endangered Species Act was amended in 1978 to allow a cabinet-level committee, the so-called God Squad, to exclude certain populations of endangered species from protection. This issue is illustrated by the 2.8 million ha of old-growth forest in the Pacific Northwest, potentially worth billions of dollars, that have been designated as critical protected habitat for the northern spotted owl. Limitations on logging in this region, strongly advocated by environmental organizations, have been fiercely resisted by business and citizen groups in the region, as well as by many politicians. After years of negotiations, legal maneuvering, and political lobbying, a solution to this ongoing controversy still has not been found. Recognition that intact watersheds are needed to provide abundant clean water for residential and business use, to reduce the risk of flooding, and to maintain salmon populations and the valuable commercial and sport fisheries they support may eventually tip the balance toward the preservation of these forests.

Compromise Solutions

Concerns about the implications of the Endangered Species Act have often forced business organizations, conservation groups, and governments to develop compromises that reconcile both conservation and business interests (Clark et al. 1994; Hoffman et al. 1997). To provide a legal mechanism to achieve this goal, Congress amended the Endangered Species Act in 1982 to allow the design of **Habitat Conservation Plans** (HCPs). These plans are drawn up by the concerned parties—

developers, conservation groups, and local governments—and given final approval by the U.S. Fish and Wildlife Service. An HCP is a regional plan that allows development in designated areas and also protects remnants of biological communities or ecosystems that contain groups of actual or potentially endangered species (Noss et al. 1997). In one case, an innovative program in Riverside County, California, allows developers to build within the historic range of the endangered Stephen's kangaroo rat (*Dipodomys stephensi*) if they contribute to a fund that will be used to buy wildlife sanctuaries. Already, more than $25 million has been raised for the program, which has a goal of $100 million. In this case and others, the result is a compromise in which development proceeds but pays a higher cost to support conservation activities.

In 1991 the state of California passed the Natural Community Conservation Planning Act that emphasizes habitat conservation and the protection of species on a regional scale in a manner similar to HCPs. Natural Community Conservation Planning has been applied to the contentious issue of development in the coastal sage scrub of southern California (Atwood and Noss 1994). This area includes almost 100 rare, sensitive, threatened, or endangered plants and animals, most notably the coastal California gnatcatcher (*Polioptila californica californica*), protected under the U.S. Endangered Species Act, and the coastal cactus wren (*Campylorhynchus brunnecapillus sandiegensis*). As a result of agricultural development and more recent urban development, less than 20% of the original coastal sage scrub still exists, divided into small habitat fragments. The remaining habitat includes some of the country's most valuable land for real estate development. Without some regional plan, continuing development of the remaining scrub would almost certainly result in the extinction of the endangered coastal California gnatcatcher (Figure 20.5).

Rather than face the severe restrictions of the Endangered Species Act, a Natural Community Conservation Plan has been developed for the southern California region that includes 160,000 ha of habitat. Negotiating the plan has proved to be a challenge, considering that three-fourths of the habitat is privately owned and the planning area includes 50 cities and 5 counties; the largest public landowner—the U.S. Department of Defense—uses its portion of the land for military practice. The plan involves surveying and monitoring coastal sage scrub communities, in particular endangered bird species, with the goal of protecting permanent reserves in high-quality habitat. Some limited development will continue during this planning process, allowing regions within the plan to lose up to 5% of their lower-quality habitat. This development is being directed away from the areas likely to be designated as permanent reserves. While the plan is not perfect, it is at least an attempt to create the next generation of conservation planning: a multispecies, ecosystem, or community-based approach extending over a wide geographic region that includes many projects, landowners, and jurisdictions.

(A)

(B)

Figure 20.5 (A) In southern California, a Natural Community Conservation Plan has been established to protect the California gnatcatcher, shown here at a nest with its chicks. (B) Protecting large blocks of coastal sage scrub community from uncontrolled development and fragmentation is key to the plan. (Photographs by Robb Hirsch.)

Traditional Societies and Biological Diversity

Human activities are not automatically incompatible with biological diversity; there are a number of highly diverse communities existing in places where people have lived for many generations and used the resources of their environment in a sustainable manner. Local people practicing a traditional way of life in rural areas, with relatively little outside influence in terms of modern technology, are variously referred to as tribal people, indigenous people, native people, or traditional people (Dasmann 1991). Worldwide, there are approximately 250 million indigenous people in more than 70 countries, occupying 12% to 19% of the Earth's land surface (Redford and Mansour 1996). These established indigenous people are distinct from more recent settlers who may not be as concerned with the health of surrounding biological communities. Local people often have established local systems of rights to natural resources, which sometimes are recognized by their governments. In most areas of the world, local people are increasingly coming into contact with the modern world, resulting in changing belief systems (particularly among the younger members of society) and greater use of goods manufactured outside the community.

People have lived in nearly every terrestrial ecosystem of the world for thousands of years as hunters, fishermen, farmers, and gatherers. Even remote tropical rain forests that are designated as wilderness by governments and conservation groups often have a small, sparse human population. In fact, tropical areas of the world have had a long association with human societies, because the tropics have been free of glaciation and are particularly amenable to human settlement. The great biological diversity of the tropics has coexisted with human societies for thousands of years, and in most places humans did not substantially damage the biological diversity of their surroundings. Traditional societies utilizing innovative irrigation methods and a mixture of crops were often able to support relatively high human population densities without destroying the environment or the surrounding biological communities. For example, areas of the Maya lowlands in Mexico, Belize, Guatemala, and Honduras are lightly settled at present, with only about five people per km^2; the area is covered by forests and has many unique species and biological communities. However, at the height of Maya civilization, approximately 1200 years ago, the region had densities of up to 500 people per km^2 and the range of species apparently was maintained (Figure 20.6) (Gomez-Pompa and Kaus 1992). The low population densities among traditional societies of many Neotropical rain forest areas today are an

Figure 20.6 A thousand years ago, Maya farms and cities occupied a wide area of the Central American lowlands, with no apparent loss of species. Today the ruined cities are overgrown by tropical forests. (Photograph by R. Primack.)

tural prohibitions against cutting the forest along the Upper Río Negro, which they recognize as important to the maintenance of fish populations. The Tukano believe that these forests belong to the fish and cannot be cut by people. They have also designated extensive refuges for fish and permit fishing along less than 40% of the river margin. Chernela observes, "As fishermen dependent upon river systems, the Tukano are aware of the relationship between their environment and the life cycles of the fish, particularly the role played by the adjacent forest in providing nutrient sources that maintain vital fisheries."

Another example of a traditional conservation ethic is that of the Patzcuaro Indian communities of central Mexico (Toledo 1991). The resources of Lake Patzcuaro are regulated at the community level and shared equally. Because the community as a whole benefits from these restrictions, it has been able to resist outside influences that lead to the pollution and overfishing that have damaged many other nearby lakes.

Local people can also manage the environment to maintain biological diversity, as shown by the traditional agroecosystems and forests of the Huastec Indians of northeastern Mexico (Alcorn 1984). In addition to their permanent agricultural fields and swidden agriculture, the Huastec maintain managed forests (*te'lom*) on slopes, along watercourses, and in other areas that are either fragile or unsuitable for intensive agriculture (Figure 20.9). These forests contain more than 300 species of plants from which the people obtain food, wood, and other products. Species composition in the forest is altered in favor of useful species by planting and periodic selective weeding. These forest resources provide Huastec families with the means to survive the failure of their cultivated crops. Comparable examples of intensively managed village forests exist in traditional societies throughout the world (Oldfield and Alcorn 1991; Redford and Padoch 1992; Nepstad and Schwartzman 1992).

Local People and Their Governments

Park managers throughout the world frequently cite conflicts with local people as their most serious problem. In a survey of 98 national parks throughout the world, about half of the parks reported problems associated with the illegal collection of wildlife, removal of plant materials, poor relations with local people, and conflicting demands on park resources (Machlis and Tichnell 1985). In the developing world, local people typically obtain food, fuelwood, and building materials from their immediate environment. Without these products, some local people may not be able to survive. If the park provides overall benefits to local communities in terms of employment, revenue sharing, and regulated access to natural products, then the community may accept and support the park. However, when a new park is created, or if the boundaries of an existing park are rigidly enforced, people may be denied access to a resource that they have traditionally used or even

Figure 20.9 A Huastec Indian woman at a *te'lom*, an indigenous managed forest in northeastern Mexico. Here she collects sapote fruit (*Manilkara achras*) and cuttings of a frangipani tree (*Plumeria rubra*) for planting. (From Alcorn 1984; photograph by Janis Alcorn.)

protected. The common practice of disregarding the traditional rights and practices of local people in order to establish new conservation areas has been termed **ecocolonialism** because of its similarity to the historical abuses of native rights by colonial powers of past eras (Cox and Elmqvist 1993, 1997). Local people will often react antagonistically when their traditional rights are curtailed (Clay 1991; Poffenberger 1996). In order to survive, local people will violate the park boundaries, sometimes resulting in confrontations with park officers. In effect, the creation of a national park often turns local people into poachers, even though they have not changed their behavior. Even worse, if local people feel that the park and its resources no longer belong to them, but to an outside government, they may begin to exploit the resources of the park in a destructive manner.

An extreme example of such a conflict occurred in 1989, when angry members of the Bodo tribe in Assam, India, killed 12 employees of the Manas National Park and opened the area for farming and hunting (McNeely et al. 1990). The Bodos justified their action on the basis that they were reclaiming traditional lands that had been stolen from them by the British and not returned to them by the modern Indian government. The fact that Manas has been designated a World Heritage Site and contains endangered species such as the Indian rhinoceros and the pygmy hog was not relevant to the Bodos; the advantages of the national park were not apparent to them.

Local people sometimes take the lead in protecting biological diversity from destruction by outside influences such as mining and dam construction. The destruction of communal forests by government-sanctioned logging operations has been a frequent target of protests by traditional people throughout the world. In India, followers of the Chipko movement hug trees to prevent logging (Gadgil and Guha 1992). In Borneo, the Penans, a small tribe of hunter-gatherers, have attracted worldwide attention by their blockades of logging roads entering their traditional forests. In Thailand, Buddhist priests are working with villagers to protect communal forests and sacred groves from commercial logging operations (Figure 20.10). As stated by a Tambon leader in Thailand, "This is our community forest that was just put inside the new

Figure 20.10 Buddhist priests in Thailand offer prayers and blessings to protect communal forests and sacred groves from commercial logging operations. (Photograph by Project for Ecological Recovery, Bangkok.)

national park. No one consulted us. We protected this forest before the roads were put in. We set up a roadblock on the new road to stop the illegal logging. We caught the district police chief and arrested him for logging. We warned him not to come again" (Alcorn 1991).

Biological Diversity and Cultural Diversity

Biological and cultural diversity are often linked. Rugged tropical areas of the world, where the greatest concentrations of species are found, are frequently the areas where people have the greatest cultural and linguistic diversity (McNeely and Keeton 1995). The geographical isolation by mountain ranges and complex river systems that favors biological speciation also favors the differentiation of human cultures. The cultural diversity found in places such as Central Africa, Amazonia, New Guinea, and Southeast Asia is one of the most valuable resources of human civilization, providing unique insights into philosophy, religion, music, art, resource management, and psychology (Denslow and Padoch 1988). The protection of these traditional cultures within their natural environments provides the opportunity to achieve the dual objectives of protecting biological diversity and preserving cultural diversity. In the words of Toledo (1988):

> In a country that is characterized by the cultural diversity of its rural inhabitants, it is difficult to design a conservation policy without taking into account the cultural dimension; the profound relationship that has existed since time immemorial between *nature* and *culture* . . . Each species of plant, group of animals, type of soil and landscape nearly always has a corresponding linguistic expression, a category of knowledge, a practical use, a religious meaning, a role in ritual, an individual or collective vitality. To safeguard the natural heritage of the country without safeguarding the cultures which have given it feeling is to reduce nature to something beyond recognition, static, distant, nearly dead.

Cultural diversity is strongly linked to the genetic diversity of crop plants. In mountainous areas in particular, the inaccessible terrain often leads to the development of diverse tribes that develop local plant varieties known as **landraces**; these cultivars are adapted to the local climate, soils, and pests, and satisfy the tastes of the local people. The genetic variation in these landraces has global significance to modern agriculture for the improvement of crop species.

Individual landraces are typically named and have many identifying characteristics. For example, in the rugged Nuba mountains of Sudan, the Nuba people are divided into 62 distinct language groups and grow dozens of landraces of sesame that are identified with particular tribes and places (Bedigian 1991). These diverse landraces of sesame are starting to decline in importance, and their continued existence is in doubt as a cash economy displaces the traditional way of life.

INVOLVING TRADITIONAL SOCIETIES IN CONSERVATION EFFORTS In the developing world, a rigid separation between lands used by local people to obtain natural resources and strictly protected national parks is often impossible. Local people may live in protected areas or traditionally use the resources of the protected areas. Also, considerable biological diversity often occurs on traditionally managed land owned by local people. Many examples exist in which people are allowed to enter protected areas periodically to obtain natural products. In Biosphere Reserves, local people are allowed to use resources from designated buffer zones. In Chitwan National Park in Nepal, local people are allowed to collect canes and thatch (see Figure 17.6) (Lehmkuhl et al. 1988). Large game animals are harvested for meat in many African game reserves. Through compromise, the economic needs of local people are included in conservation management plans, to the benefit of both the people and the reserve. Such compromises, known as Integrated Conservation–Development Projects (ICDPs), are increasingly being regarded as one of the best conservation strategies (Wells and Brandon 1992; Alpert 1995; Primack et al. 1998). There are many strategies for integrating the protection of biological diversity, the customs of traditional societies, the genetic variation of traditional crops, and economic development that could be classified as Integrated Conservation–Development Projects (Caldecott 1996; Maser 1997).

BIOSPHERE RESERVES UNESCO's Man and the Biosphere Program (MAB), described in Chapter 17, includes among its goals the maintenance of "samples of varied and harmonious landscapes resulting from long-established land use patterns" (Batisse 1997). This program has been extremely successful: 327 Biosphere Reserves in 85 countries cover over 200 million ha (Figure 20.11). The MAB Program recognizes the role of people in shaping the natural landscape, as well as the need to find ways in which people can sustainably use natural resources without degrading the environment. The research framework, applied in its worldwide network of designated Biosphere Reserves, integrates natural science and social science research. It includes investigations of how biological communities respond to different human activities, how humans respond to changes in their natural environment, and how degraded ecosystems can be restored to their former condition.

One valuable example of a Biosphere Reserve is the Kuna Yala Indigenous Reserve on the northeast coast of Panama (Gregg 1991). In this protected area of 60,000 ha of tropical forest, 30,000 Kuna people in 60 villages practice traditional medicine, agriculture, and forestry, with documentation and research undertaken by scientists from outside institutions. The Kuna carefully regulate the levels of scientific research in the reserve, insist on local training and local guides accompanying the scientists, and require the payment of research fees and the presen-

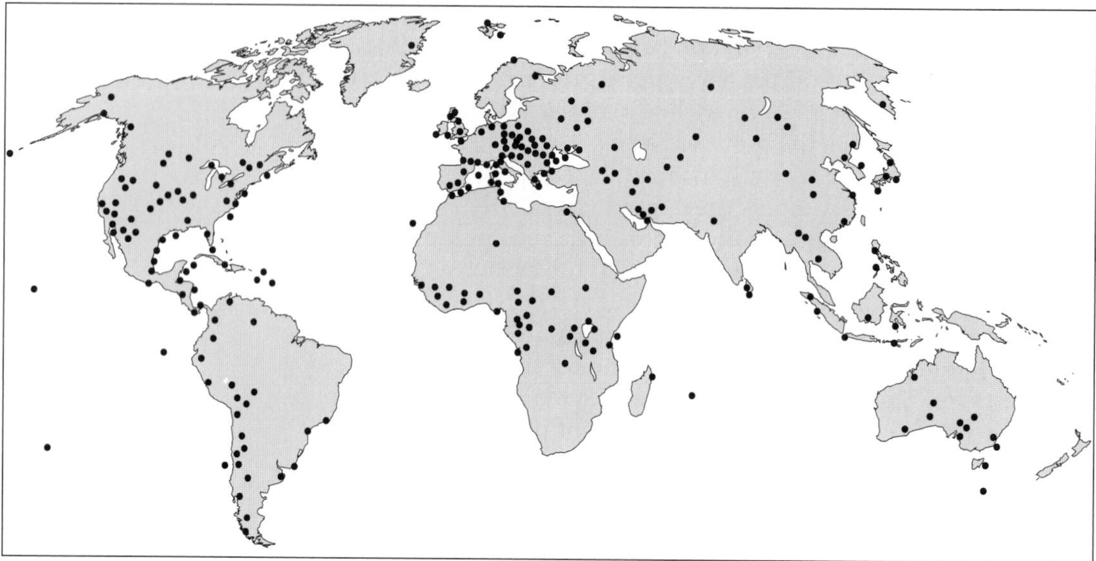

Figure 20.11 Locations of recognized Biosphere Reserves (dots). A lack of reserves is apparent in biologically important regions such as New Guinea, the Indian subcontinent, South Africa, and Amazonia. (Data from WCMC 1992.)

tation of reports before scientists leave the area. The Kuna even control the type and rate of economic development in the reserve and have their own paid, outside advisors. The level of empowerment of the Kuna is unusual, and it illustrates the potential for traditional people to take control of their destiny, way of life, and environment. However, as traditional conservation beliefs erode in the face of outside influences, younger Kuna are beginning to question the need to rigidly protect the reserve (Redford and Mansour 1996). Empowering traditional people is no guarantee that biodiversity will be preserved, particularly as traditions change or disappear.

IN SITU AGRICULTURAL CONSERVATION In many areas of the world, local farmers cultivating locally adapted varieties of crop plants can preserve genetic variability in these species. For example, there are thousands of distinct varieties of potatoes grown by Andean farmers in South America (Figure 20.12). Often these farmers will grow many varieties in one field to minimize the risk of crop failure and for the different uses of each variety. Similarly, traditional farmers in the Apo Kayan of Borneo may grow more than 50 varieties of rice. These local varieties often have unique genes for dealing with disease, nutrient deficiencies, pest resistance, drought tolerance, and other environmental variations (Cleveland et al. 1994). Moreover, these local varieties continue to evolve new genetic combinations, some of which may be effective in dealing with looming global environmental threats. However, farmers throughout the world are abandoning their traditional forms of agriculture with

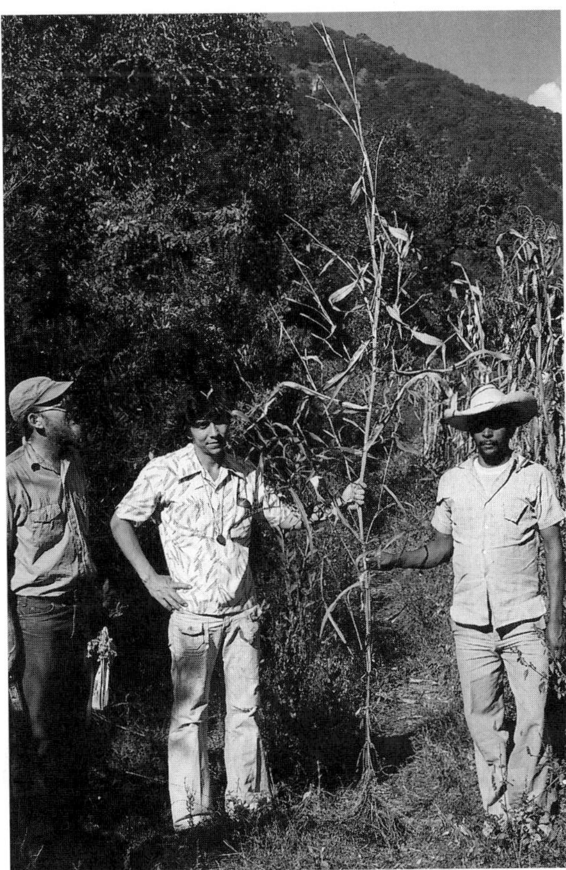

Figure 20.14 *Zea diploperennis* is a perennial relative of maize, shown here growing on the edge of a traditional maize field in the Sierra de Manantlán Biosphere Reserve in Mexico. An American scientist, a Mexican scientist, and a local farmer are among those involved in conservation efforts. (Photograph by Hugh Iltis.)

Countries have also established special reserves to conserve areas containing wild relatives of commercial crops. Species reserves protect the wild relatives of wheat, oats, and barley in Israel, and 127 such reserves were created in the former Soviet Union.

EXTRACTIVE RESERVES In many areas of the world, people have extracted products from natural communities for decades and even centuries. The sale and barter of these natural products are a major part of their livelihood, and the right to continue collecting natural products from the surrounding countryside is an important concern of local people (Box 33) (Western et al. 1994). The establishment of national parks that exclude the traditional collection of products will meet with as much resistance from the local community as will a land-grab that involves exploitation of the natural resources and their conversion to other uses.

The Brazilian government is trying to address the legitimate demands of local citizens through a new type of protected area known

Box 33 People-Friendly Conservation in the Hills of Southwest India

There is no question that human activities play an overwhelming role in the decline of many species and habitats. All too often, however, conservation activists forget that human beings are among the potential victims of the worldwide biological diversity crisis. Some rural societies have already been affected by the decline of leaves, fruits, roots, and other nontimber forest products (NTFPs) traditionally harvested for household use and for sale in local markets. For some of these people, natural products represent a crucial subset of their income, and some may be essential for food preparation, medicines, or rituals. In many cases, external political or economic pressures have damaged or destroyed the social mechanisms that traditionally prevented overuse of a particular resource so that many NTFPs that were once harvested in a sustainable manner are now becoming depleted. As forests shrink in size and become degraded through increased pressure on both timber and nontimber resources, it is uncertain whether NTFP collection is sustainable in particular areas—if not, alternative sources of income and supplies must be found to support rural families. Yet few efforts have been made to document and monitor the harvesting methods and amounts of different NTFPs taken, a vital first step in determining sustainable harvesting levels (Peters 1994).

An important case study is underway in the Biligiri Rangaswamy Temple (BRT) Sanctuary in southwestern India. This hilly, forested area contains species from both the Western and Eastern Ghats mountain chains and is known for the density and diversity of its wildlife (Bawa et al. 1998). The inhabitants of the BRT forests, the Soliga people, are the remaining members of an ancient tribe that has survived in this remote area. The Soligas lived in the region for centuries as shifting cultivators but became sedentary agriculturists during the past century as a result of efforts by first the British colonial government and later the national government to curtail shifting cultivation and preserve the forest. Since the 540-km^2 BRT Sanctuary was established in 1974, shifting cultivation has been completely banned; instead, many of the Soligas farm small pieces of land (1–2 ha) and collect NTFPs for their own use and for sale through government-sponsored cooperatives. At present, some 4500 Soligas occupy 25 settlements within and around the sanctuary.

A study of NTFP harvesting by the Soligas has been underway since 1993, involving researchers from both India and the United States. The format and goals of this study are a significant departure from the commonplace conservation methodology, which tends to focus first upon a species, habitat, or ecosystem. Although the primary goal of the study is the conservation of biological resources in the BRT forest, the study is uncommon in that it approaches the problem from a sociological and economic perspective rather than with a strictly biological slant. Most conservationists would agree that conservation efforts cannot succeed if they do not make some provision for the people who depend on a threatened resource, but it is unusual for the people to be the principal focus of a biological conservation project.

The project began by using extensive surveys to determine whether NTFPs truly play a vital role in

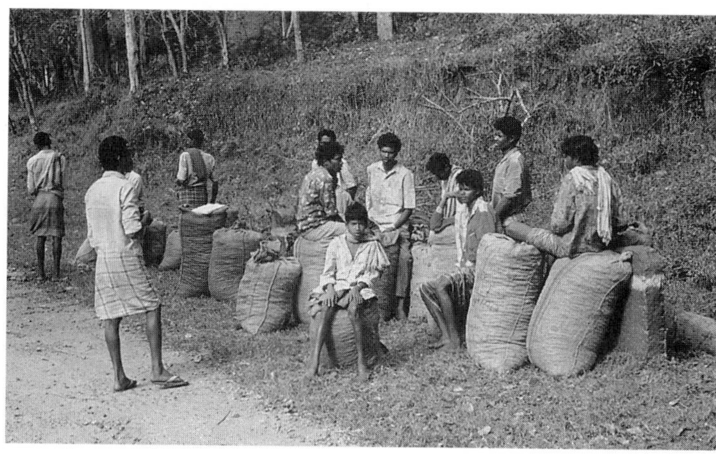

Soliga villagers collect nontimber forest products from the nature sanctuary.

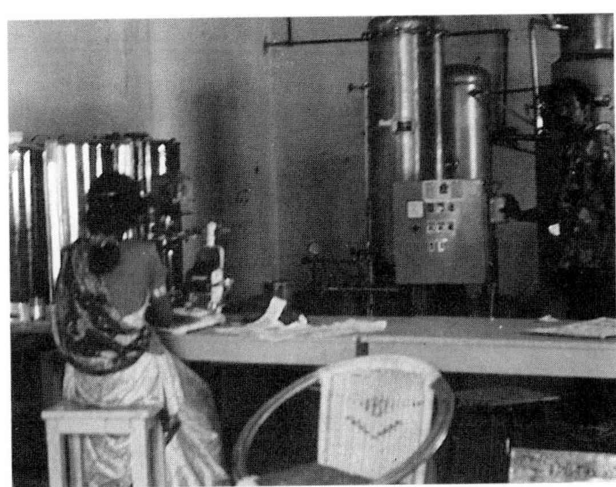

A local worker processes honey in a factory established in the village.

A display of Soliga products in a village store.

the Soliga household economy (Hegde et al. 1996). Nontimber forest products constitute as much as 50% of an average Soliga household's annual income, but the study found that commonplace NTFP extraction practices are neither sustainable nor efficient, nor do they produce maximum benefits for the Soligas, even though many local products have great potential market value. The BRT forests contain a number of edible and medicinal plant species, many of which the Soligas regularly collect for home use and for sale. Other natural products such as honey provide supplemental income, although they can be difficult to collect—honey collectors in particular risk not only bee stings but also more serious injuries related to falls from the large trees where the bees nest.

Moreover, because there is open access to these unregulated resources, collection of NTFPs often occurs at the wrong time of year to promote regeneration, or is done using methods that damage the resource. In the case of honey collection, for instance, collection from a nest ideally should take place after bee larvae have matured to the point when they will not suffer from the loss of the honey. If the honey is collected too soon in the bees' growth cycle, the larvae may die, and fewer bees in the hive mean that less honey is produced—and the resource begins a slow downward spiral of depletion. Such problems have also been seen in certain plant resources. Medicinal plants have been overharvested near the villages so that people must go ever farther to find plants to collect. Tree species with edible or medicinal fruits have been so intensively collected that there are few saplings or young trees to provide the next generation when the older trees die.

A further problem is that local people sell raw materials through the government-controlled cooperatives, although the greatest amount of profit comes only after the product is processed and marketed. Thus, the Soligas do not receive the greatest possible return from the forest products they harvest and can only increase their income by collecting greater amounts of raw materials.

In response to these concerns, researchers have begun to create enterprises that improve the Soligas' ability to make a living from forest products without overharvesting them. The idea behind this project is simple: if the Soligas process the raw materials themselves, they can eliminate the middlemen between them and the consumers. The Soligas can obtain further income by marketing and selling the products directly in nearby towns and cities. By doing this, they can earn a much higher rate per unit of raw materials they harvest and therefore will need to harvest less to make ends meet.

Several enterprises are already underway. The first involves collecting and processing honey from both wild and domestic apiaries. This honey is sold directly to consumers using the Soligas' own

Box 33 (continued)

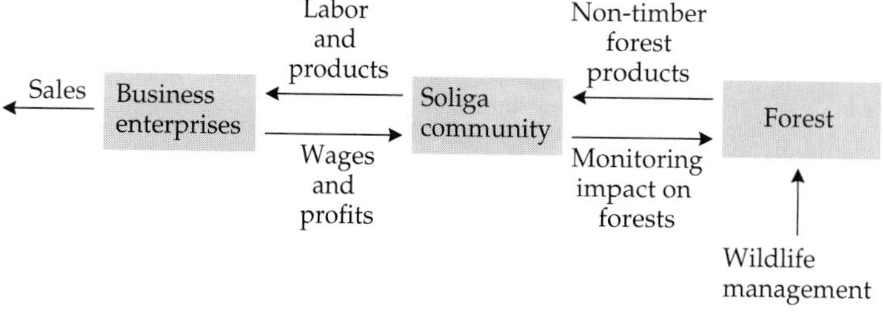

A simple model of the Biligiri Rangaswamy Hills project. (Modified from Bawa et al. 1998.)

brand name (*Prakruti*, which means "nature"). The second project produces jams and pickles for sale, using the fruits of forest species. A third activity produces and markets herbal medicines using both wild herbs collected from the forest and herbs cultivated in gardens.

Finally, the Soligas and researchers have joined forces to develop a management team that monitors the forests and the financial well-being of the enterprises. In other words, the Soligas are assuming responsibility for the long-term maintenance of the resource base as well as the functioning of the factories. When monitoring reveals that a particular NTFP is being depleted, harvesting levels can be reduced until the resource base recovers. As the economic ventures started by this program gain momentum, hopefully more and more of the local residents will find that conserving forest resources is in their best interest. Those concerned with the conservation of species and habitat could ask for nothing more.

as an **extractive reserve**, in which settled people collect natural products such as rubber, resins, and Brazil nuts in a way that minimizes damage to the forest ecosystem (Murrieta and Rueda 1995). Such areas, composed of about 3 million ha, guarantee the ability of local people to continue their way of life against possible conversion of the land to cattle ranching and farming. At the same time, the government protection afforded to the local population also serves to protect the biological diversity of the area because the ecosystem remains basically intact (Nepstad and Schwartzman 1992).

Extractive reserves appear to be appropriate to the Amazon rain forests, where about 68,000 rubbber tapper families live. The rubber tappers live at a density of only about one family per 300–500 ha, of which they clear a few hectares for growing food. Commercial rubber tapping has been going on in the Amazon for over 100 years, and rubber-tapping areas presently occupy 4%–7% of the Amazon area. The efforts of Chico Mendes and his subsequent assassination in 1988 drew worldwide attention to the plight of the rubber tappers (see Box 36 in Chapter 22). In response to both local and international concern, the Brazilian government established extractive reserves in rubber-tapping areas. The reserves make sense because the rubber collection system appears to be economically viable. The rubber tappers themselves have a strong vested interest against habitat destruction because it also would destroy their livelihood. The real challenge for the rubber tappers and their Brazilian and international allies is to develop other natural products that can be collected and sold at a good market price (Clay 1991), perhaps even at a premium as "rain forest products."

The Brazilian experiment has indicated that extractive reserves are a possible mechanism to preserve biological diversity, but has also shown a number of limitations (Browder 1990). First, these reserves occupy only a small percentage of the Amazon; conservation efforts aimed at protecting the Amazon really need to concentrate on reducing the rates of deforestation caused by ranching and farming activities, which already occupy 24% of the northern Amazon region. Second, extractive reserves provide occupations for only a tiny percentage of the millions of Brazilians who need a livelihood. Third, populations of large animals in extractive reserves are often substantially reduced due to subsistence hunting. Finally, rubber tappers may be forced to cut down their forests and change over to farming and ranching if the market for their product fails.

Zimbabwe, in southeastern Africa, is aggressively applying community development and sustainable harvesting strategies in its efforts to preserve wildlife populations. The government of Zimbabwe has developed a series of innovative programs for generating income from wildlife that is used to run wildlife programs and provide clear benefits to local people (Taylor and Dunstone 1996). Much of the funding to support, develop, and administer these programs comes from foreign governments. The U.S. Agency for International Development subsidizes CAMPFIRE (Communal Area Management Programme For Indigenous Resources), in which local communities working with the government sell sport hunting rights to safari companies. Revenue is also generated through the sale of live animals and ecotourism.

Programs involving the controlled harvesting of wildlife appear to result in far greater densities of animals, including elephants, crocodiles, ostriches, and buffaloes, and greater benefits to local people. As a result, uncontrolled subsistence harvesting and poaching have declined as people realized the benefits of joining the program. Approximately 82,000 households with 600,000 people participate in CAMPFIRE to manage 1 million ha. The program generates Z$10 million per year in revenue, more than 50% of which is returned to the people for both personal income and building needed community infrastructure such as school rooms or grinding mills. Within villages, people are involved in protecting the wildlife and the habitat it occupies because they know it is the key to maintaining the long-term income of the village. At a village meeting, during which wildlife revenues were being distributed, one leader stated, "This money comes to you from your wildlife. It is your money. The decision is yours. You cannot wait for the government. You can develop your community according to how you decide." Despite the apparent success of this program, questions have been raised by animal rights organizations as to why the U.S. government is subsidizing a program that depends on the desires of wealthy safari hunters to kill animals. Is this really a good example of conservation? Also, it is unknown how long the program would persist if the substantial subsidies provided by foreign governments were reduced or withdrawn.

COMMUNITY-BASED INITIATIVES In many cases, local people already protect biological communities such as forests, wildlife, rivers, and coastal waters in the vicinity of their homes. Such protection is often enforced by village elders with justification based on religious and traditional beliefs. Governments and conservation organizations can assist local conservation initiatives by providing legal title to traditional lands, access to scientific expertise, and financial assistance to develop needed infrastructure. One example is the Baboon Sanctuary in eastern Belize, created by a collective agreement among a group of villages to maintain the forest habitat required by the local population of black howler monkeys (see Figure 16.9) (Horwich and Lyon 1998). Ecotourists visiting the sanctuary pay a fee to the village organization, and additional payments are made if they stay overnight and eat meals with a local family. Conservation biologists working at the site have provided training for local nature guides, a body of scientific information on the wildlife, funds for a local natural history museum, and business training for the village leaders.

In the Pacific islands of Samoa, much of the rain forest land is under collective ownership by groups of indigenous people (Cox and Elmqvist 1991; Cox 1997). Villagers are under increasing pressure to sell logs from their forests to pay for schools and other necessities. Despite this situation, the local people have a strong desire to preserve the land because of the forest's religious and cultural significance, as well as its value for medicinal plants and other products. A variety of solutions were developed to meet these conflicting needs: in American, or Eastern, Samoa, the U.S. government agreed to lease forest and coastal land from the villages to establish a new national park. In this case, the villages retained ownership of the land and traditional hunting and collecting rights. Also, village elders were assigned places on the park advisory board. In Western Samoa, international conservation organizations and various donors agreed to build schools, medical clinics, and other public works projects that the villages needed in exchange for stopping all commercial logging. Thus, each dollar donated did double service, both protecting the forest and providing humanitarian aid to the villages.

Living with Biodiversity

A key element in the success of many of the projects discussed in the preceding section was the ability to build on and work with stable, flexible local institutions. Conservation initiatives involving recent immigrants or impoverished, disorganized local people are generally more difficult. While working with local people may be a desirable goal, in some cases this simply is not possible. Excluding people from protected areas and rigorously patrolling the boundaries is sometimes the only way to preserve biological diversity (Kramer et al. 1997).

The catchphrase "Think globally, act locally," is a true measure of how conservation must work. In the preceding examples, one factor is consistently true: whether they are supporting conservation activities or opposing them, ordinary people with no strong feelings about conservation are more likely to respond to issues that affect their day-to-day lives. If people learn that a species or habitat to which they are accustomed to having access might be taken away from them because of pressures to develop the land (or to conserve a species), they may feel compelled to take direct action. This feeling can be a double-edged sword; when harm to the environment is viewed by local inhabitants as a threat to their well-being, it can be used to the advantage of conservation, but it is often the case that conservation activities are perceived as threatening the local way of life or obstructing the community from beneficial economic development. The challenge for conservation biologists is to energize local people in support of conservation while recognizing and addressing the objections of those who oppose it.

Summary

1. Legal efforts to protect biodiversity occur at the local, regional, and national levels, and regulate activities affecting both privately and publicly owned lands. These laws limit pollution, curtail or ban certain types of development, and set rules for hunting and other recreational activities—all with the aim of preserving biodiversity and protecting human health. Governments and private land trusts may buy land for conservation purposes or acquire conservation easements and development rights for future protection.

2. National governments can protect biodiversity by establishing national parks, controlling imports and exports at their borders, and creating regulations for air and water pollution. The most effective law in the United States for protecting species is the Endangered Species Act of 1973. The protection afforded under the law is so strong that pro-business and development groups are often forced to work with biologists to develop compromises that protect species and allow some development.

3. Local people practicing traditional ways of life are found in every terrestrial ecosystem. Often the present composition of plants and animals in a biological community has been influenced by the activities of these residents. Some tra-

ditional societies have strong conservation ethics and management practices that are compatible with the protection of biological diversity. Working with local people sometimes provides the opportunity to achieve the dual objectives of protecting biological diversity and preserving cultural diversity.

4. Local residents and outside visitors are key elements in park management. Protected areas may flourish or be destroyed, depending on how local people view them. A crucial element is often finding a compromise between the extremes of banning all human use of park resources and allowing unlimited use. Initiatives that allow people to use park resources in a sustainable manner without harming biological diversity are sometimes called Integrated Conservation–Development Projects. Examples include: biosphere reserves, allowing limited harvesting of resources and in situ conservation of local landraces of food crops.

For Discussion

1. Apply the concepts of *development* and *growth* to aspects of the economy that you know about. Are there industries showing or at least approaching sustainable development? Are there industries or aspects of the economy that are clearly not sustainable? Are development and growth always linked, or can there be growth without development, or development without growth? Consider industries such as logging, mining, education, road building, home construction, and nature tourism.

2. What are the roles of government agencies, private conservation organizations, businesses, community groups, and individuals in the conservation of biological diversity? Can they work together, or are their interests necessarily opposed to each other?

3. Imagine that a new tribe of hunting-and-gathering people is discovered in a remote area of the Amazon that has previously been designated for logging and mining. The area is also found to contain numerous species new to science. Should the project go forward as planned and the people be given whatever employment they are suited for? Should the area be closed to all exploitation, and the people and new species allowed to live undisturbed? Should the tribe be contacted by social workers, educated in special schools, and eventually incorporated into modern society? Can you think of a possible compromise that would integrate conservation and development? In such a case, who should decide what actions should be taken?

4. CAMPFIRE involves a rural area in Africa generating income through safari hunting, nature photography, and wildlife viewing. Elephants are hunted in this program despite the fact that they are a protected species under the Convention on International Trade in Endangered Species. What ethical, economic, political, ecological, and social issues are raised by this high-profile program?

Suggested Readings

Alcorn, J. B. 1993. Indigenous peoples and conservation. *Conservation Biology* 7: 424–426. This article and others in the same issue explore different perceptions of indigenous people.

Alpert, P. 1995. Applying ecological research at integrated conservation and development projects. *Ecological Applications* 5: 857–860. One of several valuable articles on community management of tropical forests and wildlife, in a special issue on ICDPs.

Batisse, M. 1997. Biosphere reserves: A challenge for biodiversity conservation and regional development. *Environment* 39(5): 7–15, 31–35. History and accomplishments of this important program.

Buck, S. J. 1996. *Understanding Environmental Administration and Law*. Island Press, Washington, D.C. How environmental law is made and how it is applied in practice.

Caldecott, J. 1996. *Designing Conservation Projects*. Cambridge University Press, Cambridge. Practical advice on setting up conservation projects, from initial concept to implementation. Includes development options and case studies.

Carrol, C. R. et al. 1996. Strengthening the use of science in achieving the goals of the Endangered Species Act: An assessment by the Ecological Society of America. *Ecological Applications* 6: 1–11. Scientific principles of conservation biology need to be incorporated into the Endangered Species Act.

Clark, T. W., R. P. Reading and A. L. Clarke. 1994. *Endangered Species Recovery: Finding the Lessons, Improving the Process*. Island Press, Washington, D.C. Administrative and political considerations are surprisingly important in the conservation of many high-profile species.

Cox, P. A. 1997. *Nafanua: Saving the Samoan Rain Forest*. W. H. Freeman, New York. Exciting and beautiful account of a scientist's efforts to save a forest and help a village.

Dwyer, J. C. and I. D. Hodge. 1996. *Countryside in Trust: Land Management by Conservation, Recreation and Amenity Organisations*. John Wiley and Sons, Chichester. Description of the enormous growth of land trusts in Britain.

Gomez-Pompa, A. and A. Kaus. 1992. Taming the wilderness myth. *BioScience* 42: 271–279. Traditional people often have their own approaches to preserving biodiversity.

Hoffman, A. J., M. H. Bazerman and S. L. Yaffee. 1997. Balancing business interests and endangered species protection. *Sloan Management Review* 39 (1): 59–73. Business and conservation groups can sometimes work together for mutual benefit.

Mann, C. C. and M. Plummer. 1995. Is Endangered Species Act in Danger? *Science* 267: 1256–1258. Critical evaluation of the Endangered Species Act.

Maser, C. 1997. *Sustainable Community Development: Principles and Practices*. Imaginative look at principles of sustainability, drawing on a wide range of examples from around the world.

McNeeley, J. A. and W. S. Keeton. 1995. The interaction between biological and cultural diversity. In *Cultural Landscapes of Universal Value*, B. von Droste, H. Plachter, G. Fisher and M. Rossler (eds). Gustav Fischer Verlag, New York, pp. 25–37. Excellent essay with many examples.

Murrieta, J. R. and R. P. Rueda. 1995. *Extractive Reserves*. 1995. IUCN Forest Conservation Programme. IUCN Publications, Cambridge. Technical studies on methodology and production; see other IUCN publications.

Noss, R. F., M. A. O'Connell and D. D. Murphy. 1997. *The Science of Conservation Planning: Habitat Conservation under the Endangered Species Act*. Island Press, Washington, D.C. Scientific research and principles need to have a more important role in conservation planning.

Press, D., D. F. Doak and P. Steinberg. 1996. The role of local government in the conservation of rare species. *Conservation Biology* 10: 1538–1548. Action at the local level is often the appropriate scale for protecting small populations of rare species and particular sites of special interest.

Primack, R., D. Bray, H. Galletti, and I. Ponciano (eds.) 1998. *Timber, Tourists and Temples: Conservation and Development in the Maya Forest of Belize, Guatemala, and Mexico*. Island Press, Washington, D.C. Intricate social, political, and economic factors affect conservation issues in this important region.

Redford, K. H. and J. A. Mansour (eds.). 1996. *Traditional Peoples and Biodiversity Conservation in Large Tropical Landscapes.* The Nature Conservancy, Arlington, VA. Eight case studies, with strong emphasis on how indigenous people can work with conservation biologists to protect biological diversity.

Tear, T. H., J. M. Scott, P. H. Hayward and B. Griffith. 1995. Recovery plans and the Endangered Species Act: Are criticisms supported by the data? *Conservation Biology* 9: 182–195. Recovery plans for many listed endangered species should have information on species abundance and population dynamics as well as assessments of public attitudes and other social and economic factors.

Western, D. 1997. *In the Dust of Kilimanjaro.* Island Press, Washington, D.C. The Director of the Kenya Wildlife Service provides a personal view of the need for integration of people and wildlife on the African landscape.

Western, D., R. M. Wright and S. C. Strum (eds.). 1994. *Natural Connections: Perspectives in Community-Based Conservation.* Island Press, Washington, D.C. Strong collection of case studies focusing on rural communities.

Wilcove, D., M. J. Bean, R. Bonnie and M. McMillan. 1996. *Rebuilding the Ark: Toward a More Effective Endangered Species Act for Private Land.* Environmental Defense Fund, Washington, D.C. Better management of private lands are crucial to the protection of endangered species, because that is where most of them are found.

CHAPTER 21

An International Approach to Conservation and Sustainable Development

BIOLOGICAL DIVERSITY is concentrated in the tropical countries of the developing world, most of which are relatively poor and experiencing rapid rates of population growth, development, and habitat destruction. The developed countries of the world (including the United States, Canada, Japan, Australia, and many of the European nations) require the biological diversity of the tropics to supply genetic material and natural products for agriculture, medicine, and industry. The general public is also anxious to preserve appealing species such as elephants, lions, and whales, which are interesting to see in zoos and nature reserves, read about, and watch on television. Developing countries are often willing to preserve biological diversity, but they may be unable to pay for the habitat preservation, research, and management required for the task. How can countries work together to preserve biological diversity?

The protection of biological diversity is a topic that must be addressed at multiple levels of government. While the major control mechanisms that presently exist in the world are based within individual countries, international agreements are increasingly being used to protect species and habitats. International cooperation is an absolute requirement for several reasons. First, species migrate across international borders. Conservation efforts must protect species at all points in their ranges; efforts in one country will be ineffective if critical habitats are destroyed in a second country to which an animal migrates. For example, efforts to protect migratory bird species in northern Europe will not work if the birds' overwintering habitat in Africa is destroyed. Efforts to protect whales in U.S. coastal waters will not be effective if these species are killed or harmed in international waters. Species are particularly vulnerable when they are migrating, as they may be more conspicuous, more tired, or more desperately in need of food and water.

Second, international trade in biological products is commonplace. A strong demand for a product in a wealthy country can result in the overexploitation of the species by a poor country to supply this demand. When wealthy people are willing to pay high prices for exotic pets and esoteric wildlife products such as tiger bones, rhino horn, and bear gallbladders, poachers or poor, desperate people will take or kill even the very last animal to obtain this income. To prevent overexploitation, there is a need for education, economic alternatives for the people involved, and control and management of the trade at both the points of export and import.

Third, the benefits of biological diversity are of international importance. The community of nations is helped by the species and varieties that can be used in agriculture, medicine, and industry, the ecosystems that help regulate climate, and the national parks and biosphere reserves of international scientific and tourist value. Wealthy countries of the temperate zone that benefit from tropical biological diversity need to be willing to help the less wealthy countries of the world that preserve it.

Finally, many problems of environmental pollution that threaten ecosystems are international in scope and require international cooperation. Such threats include atmospheric pollution and acid rain; the pollution of lakes, rivers, and oceans; global climate change; and ozone depletion. Consider the river Danube, which flows through Germany, Austria, Slovakia, Hungary, the former Yugoslavia, Bulgaria, and Romania before emptying into the Black Sea—another international body of water. Only countries working together can solve these problems.

Agreements for Protecting Species

The single most important treaty protecting species at an international level is the **Convention on International Trade in Endangered Species** (CITES), established in 1973 in association with the **United Nations**

Environmental Program (UNEP) (Wijnstekers 1992; Hemley 1994). The treaty has currently been ratified by more than 120 countries. CITES, headquartered in Switzerland, establishes lists (known as Appendices) of species for which international trade is to be controlled or monitored. Member countries agree to restrict trade in and destructive exploitation of these species. Appendix I includes approximately 675 animals and plants for which commercial trade is prohibited. Appendix II includes about 3700 animals and 21,000 plants whose international trade is regulated and monitored. For plants, Appendices I and II cover important horticultural species such as orchids, cycads, cacti, carnivorous plants, and tree ferns; timber species and wild-collected seeds are increasingly being considered for regulation as well. For animals, closely regulated groups include parrots, large cat species, whales, sea turtles, birds of prey, rhinos, bears, and primates. Species collected for the pet, zoo, and aquarium trades and species harvested for their fur, skin, or other commercial products also are closely monitored.

International treaties such as CITES are implemented when a country signing the treaties passes laws to enforce them. Once CITES laws are passed within a country, police, customs inspectors, wildlife officers, and other government agents can arrest and prosecute individuals possessing or trading in CITES-listed species and seize the products or organisms involved (Figure 21.1). In one case in Florida, an individual was sentenced to 13 months in jail for attempting to smuggle an orangutan into the United States. The CITES secretariat periodically sends out bulletins aimed at publicizing specific illegal activities. In recent years these bulletins have even suggested that *all* wildlife trade with countries such

Figure 21.1 In August of 1995 Belgian customs inspectors seized an enormous shipment of contraband wildlife items. The haul contained many items banned by the CITES treaty, including monkey skulls, stuffed specimens of rare bird species, and tiger pelts. Parts from over 2000 individual animals were identified in the shipment. (AP Photo/Pierre Thielemans.)

as Italy and Thailand be temporarily halted because of their unwillingness to restrict the illegal export of wildlife from their territory.

Member countries are required to establish their own management and scientific authorities to implement their CITES obligations. Technical advice is often provided by nongovernment organizations such as the **International Union for the Conservation of Nature** (IUCN) Wildlife Trade Specialist Group, the **World Wildlife Fund** (WWF) **TRAFFIC network**, and the **World Conservation Monitoring Centre** (WCMC) Wildlife Trade Monitoring Unit. CITES is particularly active in encouraging cooperation among countries as well as conservation efforts by development agencies. The treaty has been instrumental in restricting the trade in certain endangered wildlife species; its most notable success has been a global ban on the ivory trade, which was causing severe declines in African elephant populations (Box 34).

Another key treaty is the Convention on Conservation of Migratory Species of Wild Animals, often referred to as the Bonn Convention, signed in 1979, with a primary focus on bird species. This convention serves as an important complement to CITES by encouraging international efforts to conserve bird species that migrate across international borders and by emphasizing regional approaches to research, management, and hunting regulations. The problem with this convention is that only 36 countries have signed it and its budget is very limited. It also does not cover other migratory species, such as marine mammals and fish. Other important international agreements that protect species include the following:

- Convention on Conservation of Antarctic Marine Living Resources
- International Convention for the Regulation of Whaling, which established the International Whaling Commission
- International Convention for the Protection of Birds and the Benelux Convention on the Hunting and Protection of Birds
- Convention on Fishing and Conservation of Living Resources in the Baltic Sea and the Belts
- Miscellaneous agreements protecting specific groups of animals, such as prawns, lobsters, crabs, fur seals, Antarctic seals, salmon, and vicuña

A weakness of all these international treaties is that any nation's participation is voluntary and countries can withdraw from the convention to pursue their own interests when they find the conditions of compliance too difficult (French 1994). This flaw was highlighted when several countries walked out on the International Whaling Commission because of its ban on whale hunting. Persuasion and public pressure are the principal means used to induce countries to enforce treaty provisions and prosecute violators, though funding through treaty organizations can also help.

Box 34 **The War for the Elephant: Is the Armistice Over?**

Conservationists must occasionally take radical steps to save an overexploited species from extinction. For those concerned with the fate of the African elephant (*Loxodonta africana*) in the 1970s and 1980s, the measures employed to preserve the species sometimes amounted to actual warfare. Park rangers who wanted to prevent the elephant's extinction had to protect the animals with drawn weapons. At the center of the conflict was the demand for elephant ivory, which grew rapidly during the 1970s and early 1980s because of the rising buying power of East Asian consumers. Over 800 tons of ivory were required annually to meet market demands (Jones 1990). In 1989, before the worldwide trade was halted, raw ivory sold for as much as $120 per pound ($55 per kg), with poachers getting only $6 of that price per pound ($2.70 per kg). Most elephant poaching was not done by impoverished small-time hunters, but by organized bands of poachers. The poachers carried automatic weapons, including AK-47 assault rifles—more than sufficient firepower to take down an entire family group of elephants and certainly enough to withstand any group of wildlife officials trying to prevent them from poaching. Frequently, the bands had ties to military or government forces, and they did not hesitate to cross national borders in pursuit of elephant herds. In some cases, the poachers were the same people whose job it was to protect the animals: the game wardens themselves.

Under these circumstances it is hardly surprising that the total elephant population on the African continent dropped from 1.3 million in the late 1970s to under 600,000 by the late 1980s. Poaching accounted for 60% of elephant mortality in Kenya's Tsavo ecosystem during the late 1970s and probably increased to 80–90% in the 1980s as the price of ivory rose in world markets. Even these numbers are not entirely indicative of the extent of the slaughter, since a significant portion of the remaining elephants are part of the large, well-protected herds of Zimbabwe, Botswana, South Africa, Malawi, and Namibia. East Africa's population was decimated: Kenya lost an estimated 85% of its elephant herd, Uganda nearly 90%—some 150,000 animals in less than a decade. Kenya's president, Daniel arap Moi, decided that drastic action was required to stop the illegal killing of elephants. In 1989, he appointed world-famous paleoanthropologist Richard Leakey to head the new, semiautonomous Kenya Wildlife Service. Arap Moi and Leakey instituted a harsh policy toward poachers: patrols of game wardens would aggressively search for and arrest poachers. Game wardens were supplied with military rifles and instructed to shoot back if the poachers resisted arrest. This new policy, combined with other incen-

Elephant tusks confiscated from poachers are kept under heavily armed guard in Kenya. Although they could be a source of revenue, the Kenyan government's resolve to stop the illegal ivory trade has led them to destroy ivory rather than put it on the market. (Photograph by Chris Johns/ National Geographic Image Collection.)

Box 34 (continued)

tives, including higher pay, increased the commitment of game wardens to their job.

At the same time, the East African countries joined together to ask the member nations of CITES to halt ivory imports. Under the existing system, the ivory trade was officially regulated by the CITES treaty, and each country allocated a specified maximum export quota. The reality was that countries that had reached their quota freely passed additional ivory to neighboring countries, where it was reexported with official permits. It has been estimated that more than 80% of the ivory being exported from Africa came from elephants killed by poachers (Dobson and Poole 1992). When the ban was finally instituted in 1989, the price of ivory dropped dramatically, and so did the rate of poaching. At that point the ivory ban imposed by CITES represented a last-ditch effort to end poaching of elephants. Without these measures and without the harsh penalties imposed by national governments, there literally would be no elephants left in East Africa today.

The damage done to the East African elephant herds by three decades of unrestricted hunting is more than a matter of mere numbers. First, elephants are social animals with complex behaviors that are taught to younger elephants by their elders (Poole 1996). Because the poachers selectively killed the elephants with the largest tusks—in other words, the older elephants, generally between 25 and 60 years of age—the transmission of knowledge from mature animals to the next generation has been disrupted. The remaining population of elephants is essentially composed of young animals in their teens or twenties that lack the experience to know where food and water may be available in times of drought. In addition, male elephants under normal circumstances rarely breed before age 30; adult male elephants, prized by poachers for their large tusks, are now virtually nonexistent in much of Africa.

Second, elephants have a profound impact upon the development of microhabitats on which many other animals depend. Elephants strip leaves, knock down trees, and trample brush as they feed, opening up habitat for other kinds of vegetation. The elephants' foraging patterns initiate succession phases in the West and Central African rain forest and the East African bush, opening up areas for grazing animals such as gazelle, zebra, and wildebeest, and, in West and Central Africa, encouraging the growth of vegetation favored by gorillas. With fewer elephants available to perform this service, less open habitat is created, and the other species suffer as a consequence, including those that, like the gorilla, are already hard-pressed by habitat destruction. Finally, elephants learn to avoid areas where the herd has suffered heavy poaching losses. This restriction on the elephants' range comes on top of habitat loss due to human activities, another major factor in elephant population decline (Caughley and Gunn 1996). Game wardens in several countries have observed that the elephants tend to cluster near park headquarters, where they are safest from poaching gangs. The concentration of elephants in these small areas strains the capacity of the region to support the population.

The efforts to save the elephant have had a significant, positive impact. The ivory ban appears to have worked—the price of ivory dropped precipitously, and poaching became much less attractive. Furthermore, efforts to hire, train, and supply a military-style cadre of dedicated park rangers have created a deterrent to further poaching. Yet even after all of these efforts, the elephant is not entirely safe; countries in southern Africa with stable elephant herds have been granted a partial lifting of the trade ban on the strength of their claim that the sale of elephant products provides financial support for their successful elephant management programs. Herds in Zimbabwe, Botswana, and South Africa are protected from hunting and provided with water; as a result, the herds are so healthy that they require annual culling to prevent habitat damage. The wildlife managers in these countries can justifiably assert that elephants are in no danger of becoming extinct on a local scale. But in other parts of Africa, wildlife officers and conservation biologists are bracing for the impact of the partially lifted ban. Will the measures designed to prevent poaching work? Or will the slaughter that has so badly damaged many elephant populations in East Africa be renewed—this time killing the few remaining elephant families? Only time can tell for certain, but the eyes of many people concerned with the fate of these majestic animals will be watching closely.

Agreements for Habitat Protection

Habitat conventions at the international level complement species conventions by emphasizing unique ecosystem features that need to be protected. Within these habitats, multitudes of individual species can be protected. Three of the most important are the **Convention on Wetlands of International Importance Especially as Waterfowl Habitat** (or the Ramsar Convention on Wetlands), the **Convention Concerning the Protection of the World Cultural and Natural Heritage** (or the World Heritage Convention), and the **UNESCO Man and the Biosphere Program** (or the Biosphere Reserves Program). Countries designating protected areas under these conventions voluntarily agree to administer them under the terms of the conventions; countries do not give up sovereignty over these areas to an international body but retain full control over them.

The Ramsar Convention on Wetlands was established in 1971 to halt the continued destruction of wetlands, particularly those which support migratory waterfowl, and to recognize the ecological, scientific, economic, cultural, and recreational values of wetlands (Kusler and Kentula 1990; Hails 1996). The Ramsar Convention covers freshwater, estuarine, and coastal marine habitats, and includes more than 844 sites with a total area of more than 54 million ha (Figure 21.2). The 94 countries that have signed the Ramsar Convention agree to conserve and protect their wetland resources and designate for conservation purposes at least one wetland site of international significance.

Figure 21.2 Izunuma is a Ramsar-listed wetland in Japan. Rice paddies, roads, and buildings come right up to the edge of the lake. More than 25,000 geese overwinter on the lake and feed in the rice paddies. (Photograph by M. Kunimoto.)

The World Heritage Convention is associated with UNESCO, IUCN, and the International Council on Monuments and Sites (von Droste et al. 1995). This convention has received unusually wide support, with 109 countries participating. The goal of the convention is to protect cultural and natural areas of international significance through its World Heritage Site Program. The convention is unusual because it emphasizes the cultural as well as biological significance of natural areas and recognizes that the world community has an obligation to support the sites financially. Limited funding for World Heritage Sites comes from a special World Heritage Fund, which also supplies technical assistance. As with the Ramsar Convention, this convention seeks to give international support to protected areas that are established initially by national legislation. The 100 World Heritage Sites include some of the world's premier conservation areas (Figure 21.3): Serengeti National Park in Tanzania, Sinharaja Forest Reserve in Sri Lanka, Iguaçu in Brazil, Manu National Park in Peru, the Queensland Rain Forest of Australia, and Great Smoky Mountains National Park in the United States, to name a few.

UNESCO's Man and the Biosphere Program (MAB) began in 1971. Biosphere reserves are designed to be models demonstrating the compatibility of conservation efforts and sustainable development for the benefit of local people, as described in Chapter 20. As of 1996, a total of

(A)

(B)

Figure 21.3 World Heritage Sites include some of the most revered and well known conservation areas in the world. (A) Iguaçu Falls, Iguaçu National Park, Brazil. (B) Starfish thrive in the clear waters off Kanawa Island, one of the islands of Komodo National Park, Indonesia. (Photographs © Joshua Schachter of IUCN.)

329 reserves had been created in more than 83 countries, covering more than 1.7 million km^2, and including 44 reserves in the United States (see Figure 20.11). Although they are not required to be protected areas, biosphere reserves are sometimes managed as a special category of protected area by countries such as Mexico and Guatemala.

These three conventions establish an overarching consensus regarding appropriate conservation of protected areas and certain habitat types. More limited international agreements protect unique ecosystems and habitats in particular regions, including the Western Hemisphere, the Antarctic biota, the South Pacific, Africa, the Caribbean, and European Union (World Resources Institute 1994). Other international agreements have been ratified to prevent or limit pollution that poses regional and international threats to the environment. The Convention on Long-Range Trans-Boundary Air Pollution in the European Region recognizes the role that long-range transport of air pollution plays in acid rain, lake acidification, and forest dieback. The Convention on the Protection of the Ozone Layer was signed in 1985 to regulate and phase out the use of chlorofluorocarbons, which have been linked to the destruction of the ozone layer and a resulting increase in the levels of harmful ultraviolet light.

Marine pollution is another key area of concern because of the extensive areas of international waters not under national control and the ease with which pollutants released in one area can spread to another area. Agreements covering marine pollution include the Convention on the Prevention of Marine Pollution by Dumping of Wastes and Other Matters, the Convention on the Law of the Sea, and the Regional Seas Program of the United Nations Environmental Program (UNEP). Regional agreements cover the northeastern Atlantic, the Baltic, and other specific locations, particularly in the North Atlantic region.

Earth Summit 1992

Protecting the environment is ultimately a global task. Despite continued destruction of key resources and ecosystems, significant strides have been made in adopting a global approach to sound environmental management. One of the most significant hallmarks of this progress was the international conferences held for 12 days in June 1992 in Rio de Janeiro, Brazil. Known officially as the United Nations Conference on Environment and Development (UNCED), and unofficially as the Earth Summit or the Rio Summit, the conference brought together representatives from 178 countries, including heads of state, leaders of the United Nations, and major nongovernment and conservation organizations. Their purpose was to discuss ways of combining increased protection of the environment with more effective economic development in less wealthy countries, often referred to as **sustainable devel-**

opment (United Nations 1993a,b). The conference was successful in heightening awareness of the seriousness of the environmental crisis and placing the issue at the center of world attention. A noteworthy feature of the conference was the clear linkage established between the protection of the environment and the need to alleviate Third World poverty through increased levels of financial assistance from wealthier countries. While the wealthy countries of the world have the resources to provide for their citizens and protect the environment, for many of the poor countries, the immediate use of natural resources is the key to raising the standard of living of an impoverished population. At the Earth Summit, the wealthy countries collectively agreed that they would assist the poor countries of the world in protecting the global environment and especially tropical biodiversity.

The central achievement of the Earth Summit was the willingness of the participants to work together on long-term goals, as stated by UNCED Secretary-General Maurice F. Strong (quoted in Haas et al. 1992):

> The Earth Summit is not an end in itself, but a new beginning. The measures you agree on here will be but the first steps on a new pathway to our common future. Thus, the results of this conference will ultimately depend on the credibility and effectiveness of its follow-up.

In addition to initiating many new projects, conference participants discussed, and most eventually signed, five major documents:

- *The Rio Declaration.* This nonbinding Declaration provides general principles to guide the actions of both wealthy and poor nations on issues of the environment and development. The right of nations to utilize their own resources for economic and social development is recognized, as long as the environments of other nations are not harmed in the process. The Declaration affirms the "polluter pays" principle, in which companies and governments take financial responsibility for the environmental damage that they cause. As stated in the Declaration, "States shall cooperate in a spirit of global partnership to conserve, protect, and restore the health and integrity of the earth's ecosystem. In view of the different contributions to global environmental degradation, states have common, but differentiated responsibilities."
- *Convention on Climate Change.* This agreement requires industrialized countries to reduce their emissions of carbon dioxide and other greenhouse gases and to make regular reports on their progress. While specific emission limits were not decided upon, the convention states that greenhouse gases should be stabilized at levels that will not interfere with the Earth's climate. The U.S., the world's major user of fossil fuels, initially resisted the provisions of this convention, along with China and the oil-producing states of the Middle East.

- *Convention on Biodiversity.* The Convention on Biodiversity has three objectives: protecting biological diversity, using it sustainably, and sharing the benefits of new products made with wild and domestic species (Glowka et al. 1994; Raustiala and Victor 1996). While the first two objectives are straightforward, the last point recognizes that developing countries should receive fair compensation for the use made of species collected within their borders. The Convention also recognizes that indigenous people should share in the benefits derived from biological diversity, particularly when they have contributed their own local knowledge of species. In the past, industrialized countries often developed new crops, medicines, and biotechnology products based on tropical species without returning any of the new information, new products, or profits to the developing country in which the wild species was originally found. Developing international intellectual property rights laws that fairly share the financial benefits of biological diversity is proving to be a major challenge to the convention, with some progress and some roadblocks still to overcome (Posey 1996). The treaty has been ratified by almost 170 nations so far, but the United States Congress has delayed ratifying the treaty, in part because of perceived restrictions on its enormous biotechnology industry.
- *Statement on Forest Principles.* An agreement on the management of forests proved to be difficult to negotiate, with strong differences of opinion between tropical and temperate countries. The resulting nonbinding agreement calls for the sustainable management of forests, but does not impose conditions to ensure that this occurs. Protection of forests will most likely come from individual governments, local communities, private companies, and conservation organizations rather than from a single, all-encompassing agreement.
- *Agenda 21.* This 800-page document is an innovative attempt to describe in a comprehensive manner the policies needed for environmentally sound development. Agenda 21 links the environment with other development issues that are often considered separately, such as child welfare, poverty, gender issues, technology transfer, and the unequal division of wealth. Plans of action are described to address problems of the atmosphere, land degradation and desertification, mountain development, agriculture and rural development, deforestation, aquatic environments, and pollution. Financial, institutional, technological, and legal mechanisms for implementing these action plans are also described. The United States has responded to Agenda 21 by issuing a report, "America: A New Consensus for Prosperity, Opportunity, and a Healthy Environment for the Future," that outlines how the goal of sustainability could be applied to the United States (Olson 1996).

The most contentious issue was deciding how to fund the Earth Summit programs, particularly the Convention on Biodiversity and Agenda 21. The cost of these programs was estimated to be about $600 billion per year, of which $125 billion was to come from the developed countries as overseas development assistance (ODA). Because existing levels of ODA amount to $60 billion per year for all activities, this means that implementing these international conventions would require a several-fold increase of the present foreign aid commitment. This increase in funding was not agreed to by the developed countries, struggling to balance budgets and pay for domestic programs. As an alternative proposal, the Group of 77, a group of developing countries, suggested that industrialized countries increase their level of foreign assistance to 0.7% of their Gross National Product by the year 2000, roughly doubling their level of assistance. While the richer countries agreed in principle to this figure, no schedule was set to meet the target date. Of 21 donor countries, only five countries have reached the specified target levels in terms of percentage of Gross National Product donated: Norway (1.4%), Denmark (0.96%), Sweden (0.92%), the Netherlands (0.88%), and Finland (0.76%), with the United States notably lagging behind at 0.2%.

The frustration of the developing countries was eloquently summarized by Dr. Mahathir bin Mohamed, Prime Minister of Malaysia:

> The poor countries of the world have been told to preserve their forests and other genetic resources on the off chance that at some future date something is discovered which might prove useful to humanity. But now they are told that the rich will not agree to compensate the poor for their sacrifices, arguing that the diversity of genes stored and safeguarded by the poor are of no value until the rich, through their superior intelligence, release the potential within.

A major new source of funds for conservation and environmental activities related to the Convention on Biological Diversity is the **Global Environment Facility** (GEF), created in 1991 by the World Bank in cooperation with the United Nations Development Program (UNDP) and the United Nations Environmental Program (UNEP). Most of the funds for the program were authorized and the projects approved by the time the Earth Summit convened in June 1992. The GEF was established as a three-year pilot program with a budget of over $850 million to be used for funding projects relating to climate change, biodiversity, international waters, and ozone depletion. Examples of projects sponsored by the GEF are the following:

- *Zimbabwe.* Wildlife Management and Environmental Conservation Project to support local communities in obtaining greater economic value from wildlife.
- *Ghana.* Conservation of coastal wetlands critical to birds migrating

along the East Atlantic Flyway through better design of sewage treatment facilities and support of sustainable community projects.

- *Turkey.* Creating crop management zones and forest gene resource zones to conserve traditional varieties and wild ancestors of grain, legume, and fruit tree species that are vital to the maintenance of modern agriculture.
- *Brazil.* Changes in land reform policy and tax subsidies are being developed to protect the remaining fragments of Brazil's Atlantic Forest.

Recent evaluations of the GEF and the convention on Biological Diversity judged the first round of projects to be a mixed success. On the positive side, the GEF provided increased funding for conservation and biodiversity projects, reviewing biodiversity-related legislation, transferring conservation information, planning national biodiversity strategies, identifying and protecting important ecosystems and habitats, and enhancing the capacity to carry out biodiversity projects (Keohane and Levy 1996). However, the lack of participation by community groups and government leaders was identified as a major problem (Bowles and Prickett 1994; UNDP/UNEP/World Bank 1994). An additional problem was the mismatch of large-scale funding over short periods with the long-term needs of poor countries.

Many environmental projects supported by international aid do not provide lasting solutions to the problems because of failure to deal with the "3 Cs"; environmental aid will be effective when applied to situations in which both donors and recipients have a genuine *concern* to solve the problems (Do key people really want the project to be successful, or are they just pocketing the money?), when mutually satisfactory and enforceable *contracts* for the project can be agreed on (Will the work actually be done once the money is given out?), and where there is the *capacity* to undertake the project in terms of institutions, personnel, and infrastructure (Do people have the skills to do the work, and do they have the necessary resources, such as vehicles, research equipment, buildings, and libraries, to carry out the work?). Despite these problems, the first round of projects was considered to be sufficiently successful to recommend a second round of funding. Hopefully, the second round of projects will deal with the issues raised by the first round.

Considering that the Earth Summit provided a moment when the world's leaders and public attention were focused on environmental issues and there was maximum pressure to get something accomplished, the inability of the major industrial countries to allocate enough funds to implement the five conference agreements has been disappointing. However, the fact remains that two important agreements—the Convention on Biological Diversity and the Convention on Climate—were ratified by many countries and have formed the basis

Figure 21.4 World leaders met in 1997 for "Rio +5," a follow-up of the Earth Summit. In Rio de Janeiro, Mikhail Gorbachev, the former president of the Soviet Union, addresses a forum that includes prominent political and environmental leaders. (Photograph by Hiromi Kobori.)

for many specific actions on the part of governments and conservation organizations. Follow-up meetings through 1997 have indicated a willingness on the part of governments to continue the discussion (Figure 21.4). The most notable success has been the international agreement, reached at Kyoto in December of 1997, to reduce global greenhouse gas emissions to below 1990 levels.

Funding

How are funds allocated to international conservation projects? When a conservation need is identified, such as protecting a species, establishing a nature reserve, or training park personnel, this often initiates a complex process of project design, proposal writing, fundraising, and implementation that involves different types of conservation organizations. Conservation foundations (e.g., the MacArthur Foundation), international organizations (e.g. the Global Environment Facility), and government agencies (e.g., U.S. Agency for International Development) often provide money for conservation programs through direct grants to the institutions that implement the projects (e.g., Colorado State University, Missouri Botanical Garden, the governments of developing countries). In some cases, foundations and government agencies give money to major conservation **nongovernment organizations** (NGOs) (e.g., World Wildlife Fund, the Wildlife Conservation Society), which in turn provide grants and technical assistance to local conservation organizations. The major international conservation organizations are often active in establishing, strengthening, and funding local nongovernment organizations as well as government programs in the developing world that can run conservation programs. From the perspective of an international conservation organization like the World Wildlife Fund, working with local organizations in developing countries is an effective strategy because it trains and supports groups of citizens within the country, who can then be advocates for conservation for years to come.

A common pattern is that an active local conservation program in a developing country will have funding from one or more conservation foundations and foreign governments, scientific links to international conservation NGOs, and affiliations with local and overseas research institutions. In such a manner, the world conservation community is knit together through networks of money, expertise, and mutual interests. The Program for Belize (PFB) is a good example of this. At first glance the PFB is a Belizean organization, staffed by Belizean personnel, with the main purpose of managing a Belizean conservation facility, the Rio Bravo Conservation and Management Area. However, the PFB has an extensive network of research, institutional, and financial connections to government agencies (e.g., the U.S. Agency for International Development) and private organizations (e.g., the Manomet Observatory, and the Audubon Society in Massachusetts) in other countries.

International Funding and Sustainable Development

Increasingly, groups in the developed countries are realizing that if they want to preserve biological diversity in species-rich but cash-poor countries, they cannot simply provide advice: a financial commitment is also required. Institutions within the United States represent some of the largest sources of financial assistance. The aid these organizations provide is substantial: in 1991, a total of 1410 projects receiving aid from U.S. institutions were identified in 102 developing countries, accounting for a total investment of $105 million (Abramovitz 1991, 1994). The predominant sources of funds were U.S. government agencies ($70 million) such as the Agency for International Development and the National Science Foundation, charitable foundations ($20 million) such as the MacArthur Foundation, Mellon Foundation, W. Alton Jones Foundation, and Pew Charitable Trusts, and nongovernment organizations ($10 million) such as the World Wildlife Fund, Conservation International, and The Nature Conservancy. Conservation investments by large foundations increased sevenfold between 1987 and 1991, and government funding tripled during this period, demonstrating that tropical conservation has clearly been targeted as a funding priority (Figure 21.5). These projects were carried out by government agencies (e.g., U.S. Fish and Wildlife Service, the Peace Corps),

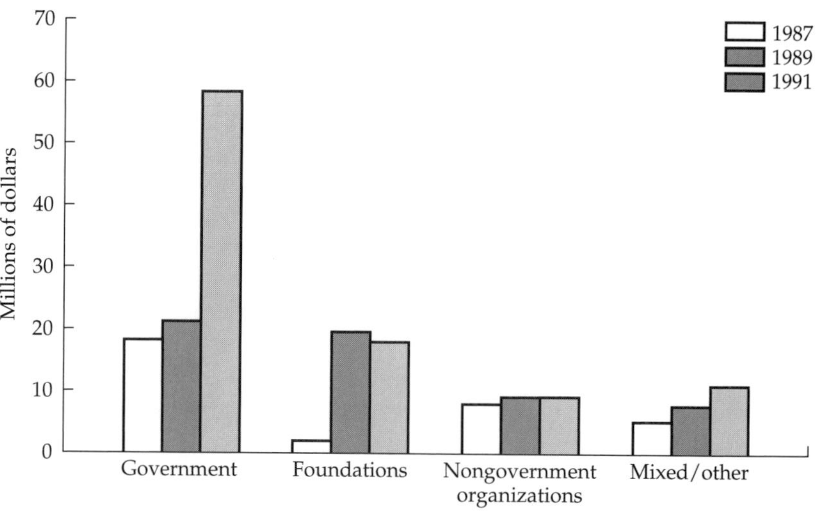

Figure 21.5 Funding from United States sources for biodiversity research and conservation efforts in developing countries, by type of funding organization: organizations and divisions of the U.S. government; charitable foundations and trusts; nongovernment organizations such as the World Wildlife Fund; and funding from multiple sources or from miscellaneous institutions (such as universities, zoos, and museums). (From Abramovitz 1994.)

nongovernment organizations (e.g., the Wildlife Conservation Society, World Wildlife Fund), museums (e.g., Field Museum of Natural History, the Smithsonian Institution), botanical gardens (e.g., Missouri Botanical Garden, New York Botanical Garden), zoos, and universities.

In allocation of funds, the major activities receiving U.S. funds were research (38%), site and species management (25%), institutional strengthening (15%), policy planning and analysis (11%), and education (8%). The projects funded by U.S. institutions were overwhelmingly concentrated in Latin America and the Caribbean, which received 54% of the funds (Abramovitz 1994). Funding was much lower in other regions of the world, with only four countries in Africa (Botswana, Kenya, Madagascar, and Tanzania) and five in Asia (Bhutan, India, Indonesia, the Philippines, and Thailand) receiving more than $1 million per year (Table 21.1).

Less than 1% of the $11 billion spent each year by the U.S. government in foreign assistance funds biodiversity protection. Within the U.S., the leading government agency providing economic and humanitarian aid is the Agency for International Development (AID), which has a budget of over $5 billion per year. With programs and missions in about 60 developing countries, AID is a dominant presence in foreign assistance activities. To reflect growing environmental concerns, the U.S. Congress amended the Foreign Assistance Act in 1983 to make the conservation of biological diversity and the protection of endangered species an integral part of AID foreign assistance activities. The amendment requires AID to spend money each year on biodiversity projects, in particular supporting local conservation efforts,

TABLE 5.1 **U.S. funding for tropical biodiversity conservation in 1991**

Country	1991 funding ($U.S.)[a]	Land area (× 1000 ha)	Dollars per 1000 ha
Brazil	9,278,761	851,197	11
Mexico	7,948,514	195,820	41
Philippines	6,405,862	30,000	214
Costa Rica	5,079,758	5,110	994
Ecuador	4,576,125	28,356	161
Indonesia	3,260,962	190,457	17
Peru	2,397,939	128,522	19
Paraguay	2,357,722	40,675	58
Botswana	2,250,500	58,173	39
Madagascar	1,723,960	58,704	29
Tanzania	1,666,323	94,509	18
Jamaica	1,547,087	1,099	1,408
Belize	1,368,468	2,296	596
Bolivia	1,318,753	109,858	12
Kenya	1,293,816	58,037	22
Bhutan	1,272,220	4,700	271
Chile	1,127,156	75,695	15
India	1,084,009	328,726	3
Thailand	1,090,956	51,312	21

Source: Funding data from World Resources Institute Biodiversity Projects Database, in Abramovitz 1994.

[a] Table includes those countries that received more than $1,000,000.

education, and ecosystem protection. To provide guidance for this effort, a panel of government and nongovernment representatives was convened to formulate an official U.S. policy on biodiversity, released as the *U.S. Strategy on the Conservation of Biological Diversity: An Interagency Task Force Report to Congress* (AID 1985).

While funding levels for conservation in developing countries are increasing substantially each year, the amount of money being spent is still inadequate to protect the great storehouse of biological riches needed for the long-term prosperity of human societies. In comparison with the billions of dollars allocated to other large U.S. science projects, such as the Human Genome Project and the space program, the $105 million per year being spent by U.S. institutions on biological diversity remains meager.

National Environmental Funds

An increasingly important mechanism used to provide secure, long-term support for conservation activities in developing countries are national environmental funds (NEFs). NEFs are typically set up as conservation trust funds or foundations in which a board of trustees—composed of representatives of the host government, conservation organizations, and donor agencies—allocates the annual income (interest and dividends) from an endowment to support inadequately funded government departments, as well as nongovernment conservation organizations and activities. NEFs have been established in more than 20 countries with funds contributed by the United States government and by major organizations such as the World Bank and the World Wildlife Fund (IUCN/TNC/WWF 1994; Mitikin and Osgood 1994).

One important early example of an NEF, the Bhutan Trust Fund for Environmental Conservation (BTF), was established in 1991 by the government of Bhutan in cooperation with the United Nations Development Program and the World Wildlife Fund. The BTF has already received about $14 million out of its goal of $20 million, with the Global Environment Facility being the largest donor. Activities include surveying the rich biological resources of this eastern Himalayan country, training foresters, ecologists, and other environmental professionals, promoting environmental education, establishing and managing protected areas, and designing and implementing integrated conservation development projects. Other trust funds supported by the Global Environment Facility are for Peru ($4 million), Uganda ($5 million), and the Eastern Carpathian region (Poland, Slovakia, and Ukraine, $0.6 million).

Debt-for-Nature Swaps

Many countries in the developing world have accumulated huge international debts. Collectively, these countries owe about $1.3 trillion to international financial institutions, which represents 44% of their collective Gross National Products (Dogsé and von Droste 1990). This money was borrowed in the hope of stimulating economic development, which would generate the income necessary to pay off the loans (Gullison and Losos 1993). However, low prices for the exports of developing countries, high fuel costs, mismanagement of projects, and overpopulation have combined to make repayment of these loans difficult or impossible for many countries. Some developing countries have rescheduled their loan payments, unilaterally reduced payments, or even stopped making their payments. As a result, the commercial banks that hold these debts are selling the debts at a steep discount on the international secondary debt market. For example, Brazilian debt has traded for about 22% of its face value, Costa Rican for 14%–18%, and Peruvian for as little as 5%. In Peru's case this would mean that a $1 million loan owed to a bank could be purchased for $50,000 on the international secondary debt market.

Using a creative approach, this Third World debt is being used as a vehicle for financing projects to protect biological diversity, so-called

debt-for-nature swaps. These swaps appear to offer great opportunities to help all participants, they have great public relations appeal, and they are relatively simple in theory.

In a debt-for-nature swap, a nongovernment conservation organization (NGO) in the developed world, such as Conservation International, cooperates with the government of a debtor country, such as Bolivia, in developing a proposal involving an environmental activity. This activity could involve land acquisition for conservation purposes, park management, development of park facilities, conservation education, or sustainable development projects. The international NGO negotiates with a local NGO or local government agency that is willing to actually implement the environmental program. The international NGO then finds a bank that has a loan from the debtor country that it is willing to donate or sell the loan to the NGO at a large discount. This debt must be for an amount and of a form that is acceptable to the debtor country. After the international NGO has acquired the loan, the loan is returned to the debtor country so that no more payments have to be made on the debt. In exchange, the debtor country agrees to supply a certain amount of local currency for the agreed-on conservation activities, often by issuing bonds that pay a fixed annual amount for the project.

In other swaps, governments of developed countries owed money directly by developing countries may decide to cancel a certain percentage of the debt if the developing country will agree to contribute to a national environmental fund or other conservation activity. Such programs have converted debt valued at $1 billion for conservation and sustainable development activities in Colombia, Poland, Madagascar, and a dozen other countries. The total amount of debt involved in debt-for-nature swaps is only about 0.1% of Third World debt, so their overall effect in reducing indebtedness has been minimal so far.

Costa Rica has taken the lead in debt swaps. Outside conservation organizations have spent $12 million to purchase more than $79 million of foreign debt, which has then been exchanged for $42 million in bonds for use in conservation activities at La Amistad Biosphere Reserve, Braulio Carillo National Park, Corcovado National Park, Guanacaste National Park, Tortuguero National Park, and Monteverde Cloud Forest, a private reserve. The interest on the bonds is used to establish a fund administered by the Costa Rican government and several local NGOs, including the Costa Rican Parks Foundation. This money has been used to acquire land for parks, to develop and institute a plan for managing these reserves, and to establish projects in sustainable development. Even in Costa Rica, which has had the majority of debt swap agreements, only 5% of its international debt has been released by these agreements, and the underlying causes of deforestation and loss of diversity have not been eliminated.

Debt-for-nature swaps have been primarily undertaken by Latin American countries which have large debts. However, innovative conservation efforts are also needed in African and South Asian countries, which are even poorer and have less international debt. Also, with the breakup of the Soviet Union, it has become apparent that the resulting countries have massive environmental problems that require international expertise and financial support. Debt-for-nature swap agreements might be an important funding mechanism here.

While debt-for-nature swaps have great potential advantages, they present a number of potential limitations to both the donor and the recipient (Patterson 1990). Debt swaps will not necessarily change the underlying problems that led to environmental degradation in the first place. Farmers still need land to farm, timber industries continue to log, and cash-hungry developing countries still have a motivation to exploit the environment for profit. Also, spending money on conservation programs might divert money from other necessary domestic programs such as medical care and schools. In addition, protection of nature reserves can be economically burdensome to financially strapped governments. If the overall government budget is increased to pay for conservation activities, it might contribute to inflation. There is also the public perception that land is being "sold" to foreign concerns. If the public feels that their government is giving up control of the country to foreign governments or organizations, the people will be more likely to ignore regulations and encroach on protected lands.

Despite these concerns, debt-for-nature swaps appear to be one of the most innovative mechanisms for encouraging conservation activities in the developing world. Now that these swaps have proved feasible in countries like Costa Rica, other countries and organizations are encouraged to try them. Debt swaps are now being incorporated into major foreign assistance programs such as the Enterprise for the Americas and are influencing the establishment of new funding mechanisms such as the Global Environment Facility.

Marine Environments

Innovative funding such as national environment funds and debt-for-nature swaps are particularly needed for marine protected areas, which have lagged behind terrestrial protected areas in conservation efforts (Hooten and Hatziolos 1995). The ease with which the marine environment can be polluted, the high value of seashore real estate, and the open access to marine resources mean that such protected areas will require special attention. Funding to establish low-impact ecotourism facilities and restricted fishing zones are among the possibilities that need to be examined and given trial funding in the immediate future.

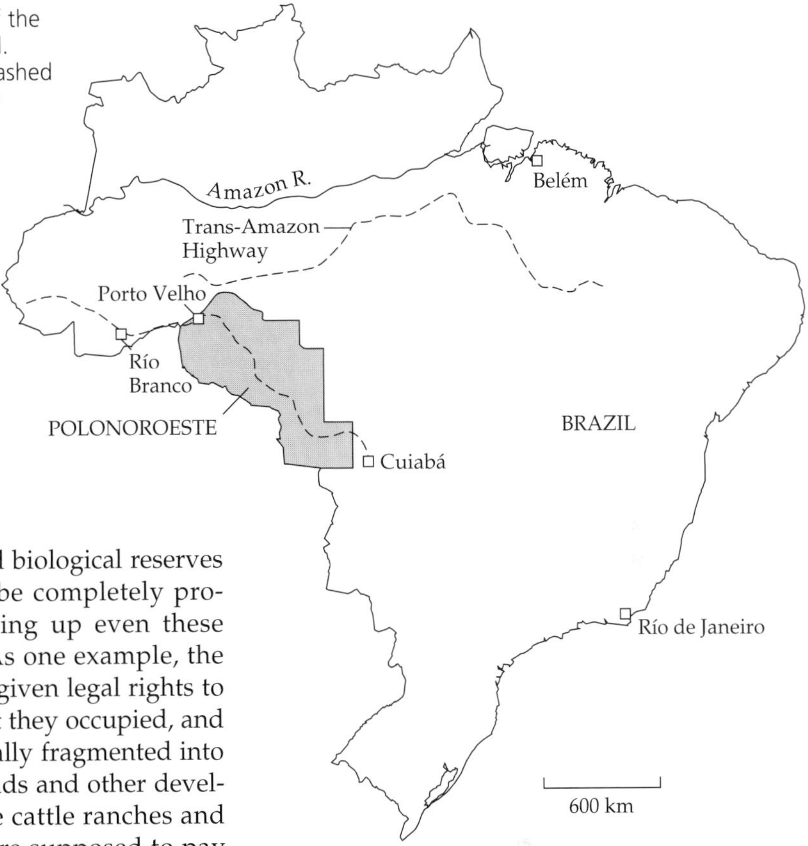

Figure 21.6 The location of the Polonoroeste project in Brazil. Highways are indicated by dashed lines. (From Fearnside 1987.)

Amerindian reserves and biological reserves that were supposed to be completely protected, effectively opening up even these areas to deforestation. As one example, the Ianomãmi Indians were given legal rights to only 30% of the land that they occupied, and this holding was eventually fragmented into 19 separate pieces by roads and other developments. In general, the cattle ranches and tree plantations that were supposed to pay for the loans have failed after colonists abandoned their plots, resulting in the increased indebtedness of the Brazilian government. The overall result has been environmental devastation with minor, fleeting economic benefits. Despite this lack of environmental safeguards, the World Bank continues to fund road construction in Rondonia (Kapur et al. 1997). Massive forest destruction in Rondonia and elsewhere in Brazil has continued through the 1990s, with particularly high rates of clearing and forest fires in 1997.

Dam Projects

A major class of projects financed by MDBs are dam and irrigation systems that provide water to agricultural activities and generate hydroelectric power (Goodland 1990). While dams provide important benefits, these projects destroy free, wild rivers and often damage large aquatic ecosystems by changing water depth and current patterns, increasing sedimentation, and creating barriers to dispersal. As a result of these changes, many species are no longer able to survive in the altered environment (Box 35).

Box 35 How Much Will the Three Gorges Dam Really Cost?

On the surface, it sounds like a great idea: build a dam to control flooding, improve navigation, and provide clean hydroelectric power to millions of people. The Yangtze River is one of the largest rivers in the world, running from the Tibetan plateau through China and emptying into the East China Sea. A series of floods in 1954 killed more than 30,000 people, and flooding in 1991 claimed at least another 3000 victims (Edmonds 1992). The area is economically depressed and per capita income is low. In 1992, the Chinese government gave final approval to build a dam downriver of the Three Gorges area of the Yangtze River in central China, with the aims of improving navigation, protecting approximately 10 million people from floods, and generating electricity for industrial development. Construction of the main dams has already begun. It is estimated that the electricity generated by the dam will reduce coal consumption (the primary source of electricity) by 30–50 million tons each year, significantly reducing air pollution (Jingling 1993). Slower currents and a more stable water flow would also improve shipping.

Yet the costs of building the dam are high—over US$30 billion. Substantial funding will come from government-sponsored finance agencies such as Germany's Hermes Guarantee and Japan's Export-Import Bank. And as the reservoir behind the dam fills, it will flood low-lying areas, necessitating the resettlement of entire villages, towns, and cities—over a million people in all (Chau 1995). The long, narrow reservoir will stretch across more than 400 km of the Yangtze valley, from Yichang westward to Chongqing, China's largest city. Temples, pagodas, and other important cultural sites will be submerged by up to 100 m of water. The Yangtze River basin also contains a freshwater fishery that provides two-thirds of the country's catch and agricultural lands that yield 40% of the country's crops—much of which will be affected by the dam. The dam's effect on natural communities is also likely to be profound and detrimental.

Previous water projects involving human resettlement have been less than successful. Often people are resettled in areas so far from their original homes that they have had trouble adjusting. To

A photograph of the dam under construction gives a sense of the magnitude of the undertaking. (Photograph © 1998 Bob Sacha.)

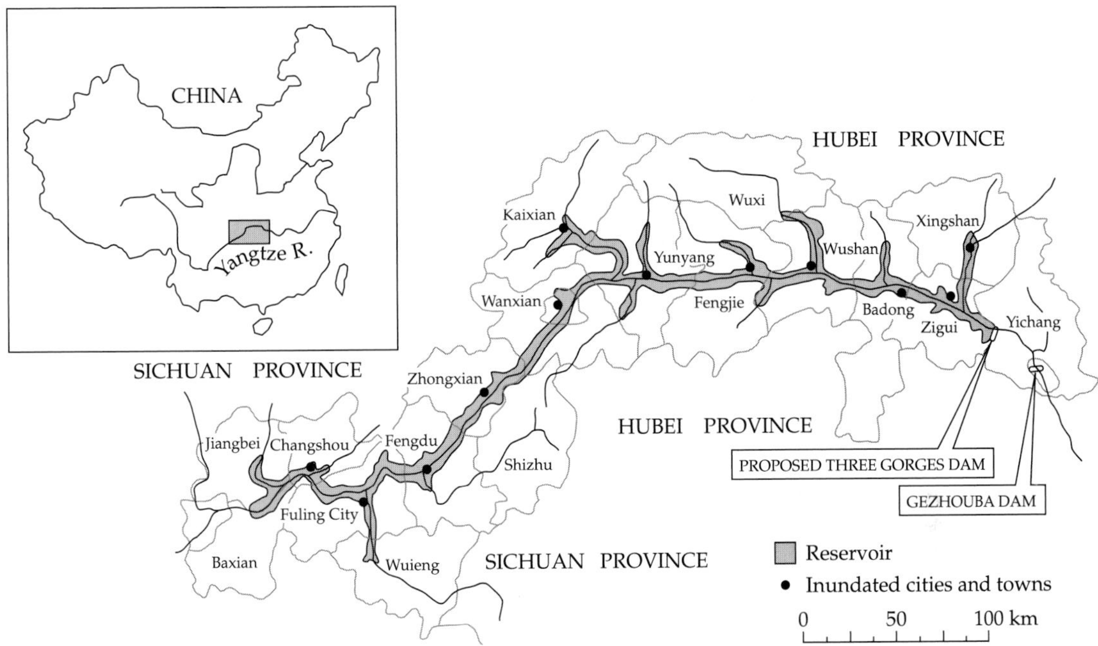

The Three Gorges Dam will flood a 400-km stretch of the Yangtze River Valley in central China. Because the terrain comprises gorges, ravines, and mountain slopes, the resulting reservoir will be narrow and deep. (After Chau 1995.)

avoid this problem, the plan is to move people uphill from their current location. However, those uphill sites that are not already in use are typically steep, covered with thin, infertile soil, and lack sufficient water for agriculture. It is estimated that five times the present farmlands will be needed to yield the same amount of food. As steep hillsides are deforested, erosion will accelerate, increasing the buildup of silt behind the dam.

Dams have a fairly predictable impact on the environment. They block the movement of nutrients downriver, slow water flow, and decrease variations in the water level. Slower currents decrease oxygen levels and decrease the ability of the river to flush out pollutants. As the hydrology changes, so does the composition of the plant and animal communities. With the construction of the Three Gorges Dam, the rare Chinese sturgeon (*Acipenser sinensis*) probably will be unable to swim up the Yangtze River to spawn. The endangered Chinese river dolphin (*Lipotes vexillifer*), a species with only about 300 individuals left, moves up and down the river with rising and falling water levels and may have difficulty moving in conditions of stable water levels. Countless other species will be affected as well.

Some of these concerns have been addressed by the dam's planners. Millions of dollars have been spent to terrace steep slopes for agriculture, and large tracts of uncultivated land on the margins of the areas to be flooded have been set aside for relocation efforts. Electricity provided by the dam should reduce deforestation caused by collection of fuelwood. Reforestation efforts have been planned to reduce erosion and deposition of silt in the river. Little is known, however, about how suitable marginal lands are for farming, how fast silt will build up behind the dam, or how endangered species in the drainage basin will adapt to the altered hydrology. Perhaps the best emblem of the Three Gorges Dam is the endangered Siberian crane (*Grus leucogeranus*), symbolic of well-being among the Chinese, that feeds in shallow waters along the Yangtze River basin. Changing water levels may affect its survival—and the prosperity of the Chinese people as well.

Ironically, the destruction of biological diversity may be a key to the failures of some of the large international dam projects that have devastated tropical rain forests. The loss of plant cover on the slopes above water projects often results in soil erosion and siltation, with resulting loss of efficiency, higher maintenance costs, and damage to irrigation systems and dams. Protecting the forests and other natural vegetation in the watersheds is now widely recognized as an important and relatively inexpensive way to ensure the efficiency and longevity of these water projects, while at the same time preserving large areas of natural habitat (Figure 21.7). In one study of irrigation projects in Indonesia, it was found that the cost of protecting watersheds ranged only from 1%–10% of the total cost of the project, in contrast to an estimated 30%–40% drop in efficiency due to siltation if the forests were not protected (MacKinnon 1983). One of the most successful examples of an effective environmental investment was the $1.2 million irrigation sector loan by the World Bank to assist in the development and protection of Dumoga-Bone National Park in northern Sulawesi, Indonesia (McNeely 1987). A 278,700-ha primary rain forest, which included the catchment area on the slopes above a $60 million irrigation project financed by the World Bank, was converted into a national park (Figure 21.8). In this particular case, the World Bank was able to protect its original investment through less than 2% of the project's cost and create a significant new national park in the process.

Figure 21.7 A hydroelectric dam on the Volta River in Ghana. The watersheds around such dams must be protected if the dams are to operate efficiently. (Photograph courtesy of FAO.)

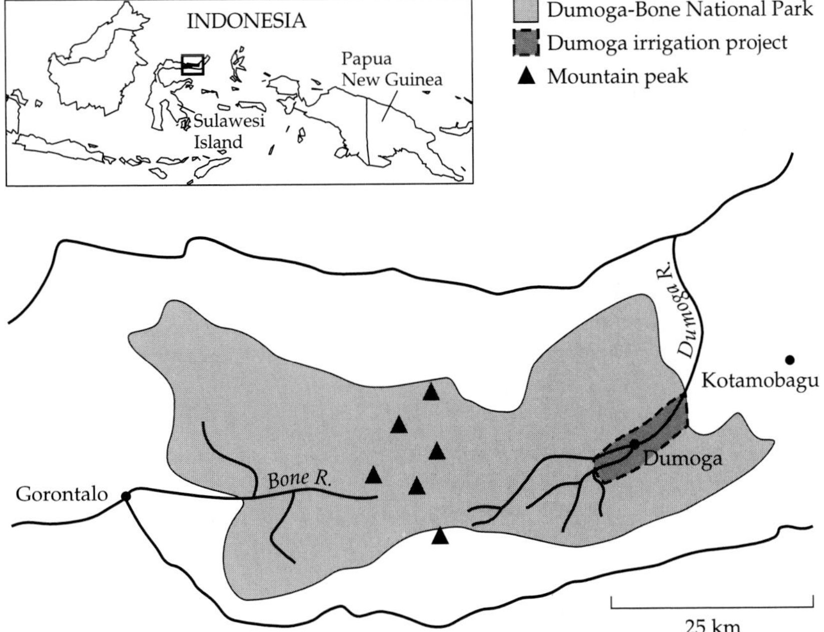

Figure 21.8 The Dumoga-Bone National Park on the northern arm of Sulawesi Island, Indonesia, protects the watershed above the Dumoga Irrigation Project. (After Wells and Brandon 1992.)

Changing the Funding Process

Why are big projects approved? If many of the large international development projects are so economically unsuccessful and environmentally harmful, why do host countries want them and why do the MDBs agree to finance them? Projects are often funded because economists make overly optimistic predictions on production schedules and prices of commodities, and minimize potential problems. Surveys and pilot studies are not undertaken or their results are disregarded; comparable projects elsewhere are not evaluated. The environmental costs of projects are often ignored or minimized, since these variables are considered external to economic analysis (see Chapters 4 and 5). However, an accurate model of a project such as a large dam would include all of its benefits and costs, including the effects of soil erosion, the loss of biological diversity, the impact of water pollution on the health and diet of local people, and the loss of income associated with the destruction of renewable resources.

Host governments often want large projects to proceed regardless of unfavorable reviews since the projects provide temporary jobs, economic prosperity, and some release from social tensions for the duration of the project. Local business leaders, especially those with close links to the government, endorse the projects because they can make large profits on project contracts. Industrialized countries that support the banks encourage these loans to stabilize governments in host countries that are friendly to their interests, but which may lack popular support. Bank officials themselves want to make big loans because that is their reason for being, and they continue to make loans for projects that experience should tell them are not economically profitable or environmentally sound.

How could the multilateral development banks operate more responsibly? First, they should stop environmentally destructive projects. This step would require the banks to develop economic cost–benefit models for development projects that include the environmental and ecological effects of projects. Also, banks need to encourage open public discussions from all groups in a country before projects are implemented (Goodland 1992). The MDBs are moving in this direction by allowing public examination, independent evaluations, and discussions of environmental impact reports by local organizations affected by projects being considered for funding.

Because the MDBs are primarily financed by the governments of the major developed countries such as the United States, Japan, Germany, Italy, the United Kingdom, France, and Canada, the policies of the MDBs can be scrutinized by the elected representatives of the MDB member countries, the national media, and conservation organizations. As some of the ill-conceived projects of the World Bank have been publicly criticized in the U.S. Congress and elsewhere, the World Bank has reacted by requiring new projects to be more environmentally responsible, hiring ecological and environmental staff to review new and ongoing projects, conducting more thorough environmental analyses, and adopting a management policy called "new environmentalism" that recognizes the linkages between economic development and environmental sustainability (Steer 1996).

This new environmentalism recognizes that there is a high environmental cost of inappropriate economic policies, reducing poverty is often crucial to protecting the environment, and economic growth must incorporate environmental values. To implement this policy, the World Bank has dramatically increased its lending in the area of environmental management. As of 1996, the Bank has environmental investments of $11.5 billion for 153 projects in 62 countries; 8% of its recent investments have been for environmental projects (Figure 21.9). This increased environmental investment has attracted another $14.5 billion from other sources, bringing the total investment to $26 billion. The projects are heavily oriented toward pollution abatement and control, but also include funding for biodiversity conservation, forest management, and the conservation of natural resources.

For the remaining 92% of its recent investments, the World Bank now requires environmental impact assessments as well as careful review by its environmental staff. Many conservation organizations remain skepti-

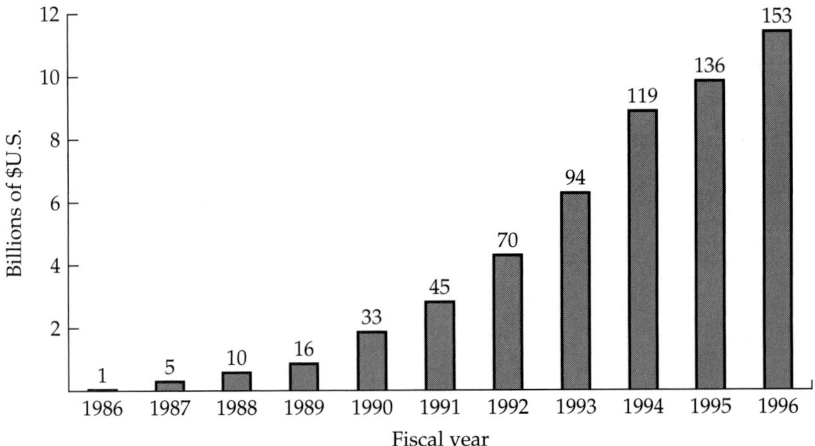

Figure 21.9 The value of environmental projects currently being funded by the World Bank. Numbers of projects are given above the bars. (After Steer 1996.)

cal that the World Bank will apply this new environmentalism policy to the bulk of its investments as time goes on. Careful scrutiny of its actions in the future is required, particularly the lending done by the affiliated International Finance Corporation and import-export banks, which lend to the private sector. Watching the funding decisions of the MDBs rather than their speeches and reports is crucial, as they have proven to be extremely effective at public relations.

Giant development projects in remote areas seem to fascinate both the MDBs and the governments of developing countries. One such project to watch is the mammoth Hidrovia Project in South America, in which the Paraguay-Parana River would be dredged and channeled so that large ships could carry cargo from Buenos Aires on the Argentina coast 3000 km north into Bolivia, Paraguay, and Brazil (Eckstrom 1996). This river system drains the Pantanal in South America, the world's largest wetland, covering nearly 200,000 square kilometers in southwestern Brazil, eastern Bolivia, and northeastern Paraguay—an area larger than England, Wales, and the Netherlands combined. The wetland is like a vast, unspoiled, version of the U.S. Everglades, fabulously rich in endangered wildlife such as jaguars, tapirs, maned wolves, and giant otters. Environmentalists believe the Hidrovia project will completely alter the hydrology of the area, submerging some areas, drying out others, and leading to an enormous loss of biological diversity. In Argentina, unprecedented flooding downriver could result. The final cost of the project is estimated to be $1 billion, with three times that much in added maintenance costs over the next 25 years. The preliminary engineering and environmental impact study will cost $10.5 million, sponsored by the Inter-American Bank and the UNDP. The area is also being surveyed for the placement of a natural gas pipeline from Bolivia to the coast of Brazil.

It remains to be seen whether the MDBs will actually act in a more responsible manner, or if they are just adapting their rhetoric to the political climate. It is also true that the MDBs have no enforcement authority; once the money is handed over, countries can choose to ignore the environmental provisions in an agreement, despite local and international protests. One of the MDB's few effective options is to cancel further funding for these projects and delay new projects. As Rich (1990) points out:

> Real reform in the MDBs will not occur without steady and increased political pressure. What has been won so far is an unprecedented and undeniable place for citizen activism, the only force that can bring accountability to the agencies controlling the international development agenda. But the fact that the World Bank and the IDB have undertaken some bureaucratic reforms does not mean that environmentalists can assume that their case is won, or even that their ideas will get a sympathetic hearing. New posts have been created in the past without disrupting 'business as usual.' Environmentalists should remember that for any bank or bureaucracy, let alone the MDBs, nothing is cheaper than words.

There are two recent cases in which the MDBs showed their mettle with regard to environmental degradation. In Papua New Guinea, the World Bank refused to provide development loans until the government carried out a number of measures that would ensure more prudent forest management practices. In Cambodia, a related international bank, the International Monetary Fund, withheld a loan until the government showed similar willingness to address serious problems related to its timber industry. These are hopeful examples of the ability of the MDBs to foster responsible use of the globe's resources.

Conclusion

The need for increased funding for biodiversity remains great at local, national, and international levels. At present, about \$4 billion is spent each year in the budgets of protected areas, yet \$17 billion would be required for managing the world's biological diversity adequately (WCMC 1992; Heywood 1995). While \$17 billion sounds like an enormous amount of money, it is small relative to the \$245 billion spent each year on agricultural subsidies and the \$1 trillion spent on military defense. Certainly the world's priorities could be modestly adjusted, giving more resources to the protection of biological diversity. Instead of the United States rushing forward in a race against itself to produce the next generation of fighter aircraft, missiles, and other weapons systems, what about spending what it takes to protect biological diversity? Instead of the world's affluent consumers buying the latest round of consumer luxuries and electronic gadgets to replace things that still work, what about contributing more money to conservation organizations and causes?

Summary

1. International agreements and conventions that protect biological diversity are needed because species migrate across borders, because there is an international trade in biological products, because the benefits of biological diversity are of international importance, and because the threats to diversity are often international in scope and require international cooperation. The Convention on International Trade in Endangered Species (CITES) was enacted to prevent destructive trade in endangered species. CITES prohibits trade in some species and regulates and monitors trade in others. Other international agreements protect habitat such as the Ramsar Convention on Wetlands, the World Heritage Convention, and the UNESCO Biosphere Reserves Program.

2. Five major environmental documents were signed at the 1992 Earth Summit, the most important being the Convention on Biodiversity and the Convention on Global Climate Change. Funds to implement the provisions of these treaties are being provided by the Global Environment Facility, a $1 billion fund administered by the World Bank.

3. Conservation groups and governments in developed countries are increasing funding to protect biological diversity in developing tropical countries. Funding by U.S. government agencies for conservation projects in developing countries tripled between 1987 and 1991, with private foundations increasing their funding sevenfold. While the increased levels of funding are welcome, the amount of money is still inadequate to deal with the loss of biological diversity that is taking place.

4. Innovative approaches are being developed to finance the preservation of biodiversity. One approach involves setting up national environmental funds in which the annual income from an endowment is used to finance conservation activities. A second approach involves debt-for-nature swaps in which the foreign debt obligations of a government are canceled in exchange for the government providing increased conservation funding.

5. International development banks, including the World Bank, have often funded massive projects in developing countries that cause widespread environmental damage. The World Bank is now attempting to be more environmentally responsible in its lending policies.

For Discussion

1. Imagine that Brazil, Indonesia, China, or Canada builds an expensive dam that will take decades to pay back its costs, or may never pay back its costs. Who are the winners and who are the losers? Consider the local people who had to move, newly arrived settlers, construction companies, timber companies, local banks, international banks, the urban poor, government leaders, environmental organizations, and anyone else that you think will be affected. Consider also the animals and plants that lived in the watershed before the dam was built. Can they survive in the same region? Can they migrate to another place?

2. In what ways are poverty and the conservation of biological diversity linked? Should these problems be attacked together or separately?

3. How do national governments decide on an acceptable amount of money to spend on protecting biological diversity? How much money should a particular country spend on protecting biological diversity? Can you calculate an amount? What are the most cost-effective measures governments can take to protect biological diversity?

4. Suppose a species was discovered in Peru that could potentially cure a major disease affecting millions of people if it was developed properly. If the government of Peru did not show interest in protecting this wonderful species, what could the international community do to protect the species and to fairly compensate the country for doing so? Come up with a variety of offers, suggestions, or alternatives that could be used to convince the government and people of Peru to protect the species.

Suggested Readings

Abramovitz, J. N. 1994. *Trends in Biodiversity Investments: U.S.-Based Funding for Research and Conservation in Developing Countries, 1987–1991.* World Resources Institute, Washington, D.C. Unique presentation on biodiversity funding, with a list of projects, research institutions, and funding sources.

Bowles, I. A. and G. T. Prickett. 1994. *Reframing the Green Window: An Analysis of the GEF Pilot Phase Approach to Biodiversity and Global Warming and Recommendations for the Operational Phase.* Conservation International and Natural Resource Defense Council, Washington, D.C. Analysis of the Global Environment Facility, with suggestions on improvement.

Chau, K. 1995. The Three Gorges project of China: Resettlement prospects and problems. *Ambio* 24: 98–102. The consequences of massive-scale development. Take note of this excellent journal on the human environment.

Dogsé, P. and B. von Droste. 1990. *Debt-for-Nature Exchanges and Biosphere Reserves.* UNESCO, Paris. Excellent summary of debt-for-nature swaps, including case histories.

Eckstrom, C. K. 1996. A wilderness of water: Pantanal. *Audubon* 98(2): 54–65. An enormous South American wetland is on the verge of development. What can be protected? See other articles in this beautiful magazine.

Glowka, L., F. Burhenne-Guilman and H. Synge. 1994. *A Guide to the Convention on Biological Diversity.* IUCN, Gland, Switzerland. Explanation of the Convention, along with background material.

Hails, A. J. (ed.). 1996. *Wetlands, Biodiversity, and the Ramsar Convention: The Role of the Convention on Wetlands in the Conservation and Wise Use of Biodiversity.* Ramsar Convention Bureau, Gland, Switzerland. Overview of the convention with many featured examples.

Hemley, G. (ed.). 1994. *International Wildlife Trade: A CITES Sourcebook.* Island Press, Washington, D.C. Wildlife trade is an enormous business, and many species are highlighted.

Hooten, A. J. and M. E. Hatziolos (eds.). 1995. *Sustainable Financing Mechanisms for Coral Reef Conservation. Environmentally Sustainable Development Proceedings Series No. 9.* The World Bank, Washington, D.C. Excellent short essays by leading experts.

Kapur, D., J. P. Lewis and R. Webb (eds.). 1997. *The World Bank: Its First Half-Century.* The Brookings Institute, Washington, D.C. Thorough, critical examination of the World Bank's lending policies.

Keohanne, R. O. and M. A. Levy (eds.). 1996. *Institutions for Environmental Aid: Pitfalls and Promises.* MIT Press, Cambridge, MA. Giving money often does not solve the problem.

Olson, M. H. 1996. Charting a course for sustainability. *Environment* 38 (4): 10–15, 30–36. President's Council on Sustainable Development presents U.S. response to Agenda 21.

Poole, A. 1996. *Coming of Age with Elephants: A Memoir.* Hyperion, New York. Personal account of how studies of elephants in Kenya led to involvement in their protection.

Posey, D. A. 1996. Protecting indigenous peoples' rights to biodiversity. *Environment* 38 (8): 6–9, 37–45. Innovative new methods are being developed to compensate local people for the biological diversity that they protect and about which they have information.

Rabinowitz, A. 1995. Helping a species go extinct: The Sumatran rhino in Borneo. *Conservation Biology* 9: 482–488. Spending money on high-profile projects sometimes hides an unwillingness to tackle tough problems on the ground.

Raustiala, K. and D. G. Victor. 1996. Biodiversity since Rio: The future of the Convention on Biological Diversity. *Environment* 38(4): 16–26, 37–45. Excellent article describing efforts to negotiate a working convention.

TRAFFIC USA. World Wildlife Fund, Washington, D.C. TRAFFIC USA is an informative newsletter covering the international trade in wildlife and wildlife products, with an emphasis on CITES activities.

von Droste, B., H. Plachter and M. Rossler (eds.). 1995. *Cultural Landscapes of Universal Value.* Gustav Fischer Verlag, New York. The current status of World Heritage sites.

tected biological resources in their agriculture, industry, research programs, zoos, aquaria, botanical gardens, and educational systems. Related economic and social problems must be resolved at the same time, particularly those relating to poverty and war. Reducing or forgiving foreign debt payments, debt-for-nature swaps, and environmental trust funds may be additional mechanisms to achieve these goals. Individual citizens can donate money and participate in organizations that further advance these conservation goals.

Problem: Economic analyses often paint a falsely encouraging picture of development projects that are environmentally damaging.

Response: New types of cost-benefit analyses must be developed and used that include environmental and human costs such as soil erosion, water pollution, loss of natural products, loss of traditional knowledge with potential economic value, loss of tourist potential, loss of species of possible future value, and loss of places to live. In particular, the effects of large projects on local people typically have been ignored in economic analyses and should be given more attention. Environmental impact analyses also need to include comparative studies of similar projects completed elsewhere and the probabilities and costs of possible worst-case scenarios.

Problem: Ecosystem services do not receive the recognition they deserve in economic decision-making.

Response: Economic activities should be linked with the maintenance of ecosystem services through fees, penalties, and land acquisition. The "polluter pays" principle must be adopted, in which polluters pay for cleaning up the environmental damage their activities have caused. Factories and human settlements must become morally and financially responsible for pollution that they cause. A step in this direction is the recent initiative by electric power companies to plant trees in the tropics to absorb the excess carbon dioxide that their factories produce. As further examples, hydroelectric projects and dam projects need to be linked to watershed protection and acquisition. Coastal fishing industries, local human settlements, and conservation organizations must join together to protect coastal wetlands, mangroves, and estuaries; these ecosystems are important feeding grounds and nurseries for commercial species and provide a wide range of other environmental services (Figure 22.1).

Problem: Much of the destruction of the world's biological diversity is caused by people who are desperately poor and simply trying to survive.

Response: Conservation biologists need to work with charitable and humanitarian organizations to assist local people in organizing and developing sustainable economic activities that do not damage biolog-

Figure 22.1 Throughout the world, biological communities are severely threatened by the full range of human activities. Here, in the Seychelles Islands off the East African coast, excessive development, water pollution, land reclamation, erosion, and overexploitation of resources threaten the rich diversity of marine life and need to be dealt with immediately in a Coastal Zone Management Plan. (Photograph by O. Lindén.)

ical diversity. Integrated conservation-development projects (ICDPs) represent one approach. Foreign assistance programs need to be carefully planned to help alleviate rural poverty, rather than primarily benefiting urban elites, as they often do. Because the funds of conservationists are limited and problems are urgent, conservation efforts should be concentrated on people who are affecting areas of major biological importance. Conservation biologists and organizations are increasing their participation in programs promoting smaller families. Reducing human population growth should be closely linked to efforts aimed at improving economic opportunities and halting environmental degradation (Dasgupta 1995).

Problem: Decisions on land conversion and the establishment of protected areas are often made by central governments with little input from people and local organizations in the region being affected. Consequently, local people sometimes feel alienated from conservation projects and do not support them.

Response: Local people have to believe that they will benefit from the conservation project and that their involvement is important. To achieve this goal, environmental impact statements and other project information should be publicly available to encourage open discussion at all steps of a project. Local people should be provided with whatever assistance they may need in order to understand and evaluate the implications of the project being presented to them. Decision-making mechanisms should be established to promote joint management and ecosystem management that ensure that the rights and responsibilities for management of conservation projects and other protected areas are shared between government agencies, conservation organizations, local communities, and businesses (Western et al. 1994). In some cases, a regional plan such as a habitat conservation plan or a natural community conservation plan may have to be developed that reconciles the needs for some development and loss of habitat with the need to protect species and representative examples of the biological community.

Problem: Revenues, business activities, and scientific research associated with national parks and other protected areas do not directly benefit surrounding communities.

Response: Whenever possible, local people should be trained and employed in parks as a way of utilizing local knowledge and providing local income. Also, a portion of park revenues can be used to fund local community projects such as schools, clinics, roads, cultural activities, sports programs and facilities, and community businesses—an infrastructure that benefits a whole village or region. Conservation biologists working in national parks should periodically explain the purpose and results of their work to nearby communities and school groups, and listen to what the local people have to say.

Problem: National parks and conservation areas often have inadequate budgets to pay for conservation activities. Revenues that they collect are often returned to government treasuries.

Response: Increased funds for park management can often be raised by charging tourists, scientists, and other visitors higher rates for admission, lodging, or meals that reflect the actual cost of maintaining the area. Concessions selling goods and services may be required to contribute a percentage of their income to the park's operation. Making sure that these revenues and profits remain at the park and in the surrounding area is important. Also, zoos and conservation organizations in the developed world can make direct financial contributions to conservation efforts in developing countries.

Problem: People cut down tropical forests and graze rangelands to establish title to the land, even when lands are not suitable for agriculture or intensive resource extraction. Timber companies that lease forests and ranchers that rent rangeland from the government often damage the land and reduce its productive capacity in pursuit of short-term profits.

Response: Change the laws so that people can obtain titles and leases to harvest selected trees and use rangelands only as long as the health of the biological community is maintained (Davis and Wali 1994). Tax subsidies that encourage the overexploitation of natural resources should be eliminated; instead, tax subsidies should be provided for land management that enhances conservation efforts (Losos et al. 1995; Wilcove et al. 1996).

Problem: In many countries, governments are inefficient and bound by excessive regulation and consequently are slow and ineffective at protecting biological communities.

Response: Local nongovernment conservation organizations and citizen groups are often the most effective agents for dealing with conservation issues. Individual citizens need to learn about local environmental issues, communicate that information, and take action when necessary. Local conservation organizations should be encouraged and supported politically, scientifically, and financially. New foundations should be started by individuals, organizations, and businesses to support conservation efforts financially.

Problem: Many businesses, banks, and governments are uninterested in and unresponsive to conservation issues.

Response: Lobbying efforts may be effective at changing the policies of institutions that want to avoid bad publicity. Petitions, rallies, letter-writing campaigns, press releases, and economic boycotts all have their place when reasonable requests for change are ignored (Figure 22.2; Box 36). The key point is that conservationists have to be realistic and have a long-term perspective. But unrealistic demands for immediate

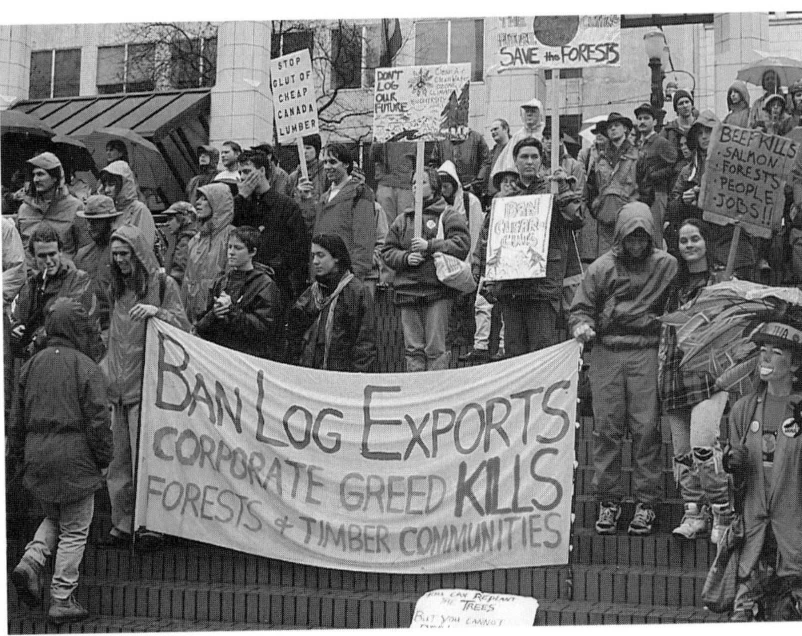

Figure 22.2 Demonstrations such as this protest against the extensive logging of old-growth forests in the Pacific Northwest can focus media attention on environmental problems that the society needs to deal with. (Photograph by Michael Graybill and Jan Hodder/Biological Photo Service.)

Box 36 Environmental Activism Confronts the Opposition

The past decade has witnessed a tremendous increase in popular awareness of environmental issues (Gore 1992). Many conservation organizations such as the Sierra Club, the World Wildlife Fund, and The Nature Conservancy, to name only a few, have gained hundreds of thousands of new members. Greenpeace, one of the most active organizations in protesting environmental destruction, had approximately 3.5 million members in 1994 and annual donations of $145 million (Motavalli 1995). The surge in environmental awareness, however, has recently triggered a disturbing backlash from those industries, business interests, labor organizations, and even some governments that resent and fear any restrictions on the exploitation of natural resources (Ehrlich and Ehrlich 1996; Kurlansky 1996). Conservation of natural resources may be linked, in some peoples' minds, to a loss in profits and job opportunities. When people fear losing their jobs or businesses because of conservation measures, they feel anger toward environmental activists, particularly in a slow economy. Incidents of intimidation, threats, and physical harassment, sometimes frighteningly violent, have been reported worldwide by environmental activists.

Perhaps the best-known violent incident occurred in 1988, when Chico Mendes, a Brazilian activist organizing rubber tappers to resist the encroachment of cattle ranching and logging in the Amazon rain forest, was assassinated by ranchers. Mendes's martyrdom created a worldwide uproar and focused global attention upon the destruction of the rain forest. The conviction of the rancher who allegedly ordered the murder was an initial victory for Mendes's supporters; before this incident, large landowners, loggers, and miners could—and did—act with impunity against activists, labor leaders, native people, and anyone else who stood in the way of the exploitation of Brazil's forests (Toufexis 1992). The victory, however, was short-lived; the conviction was overturned on appeal. Moreover, many other activists in Brazil have been beaten or killed, both before and since Mendes's death. Activists claim that hit lists circulate openly among developers, loggers,

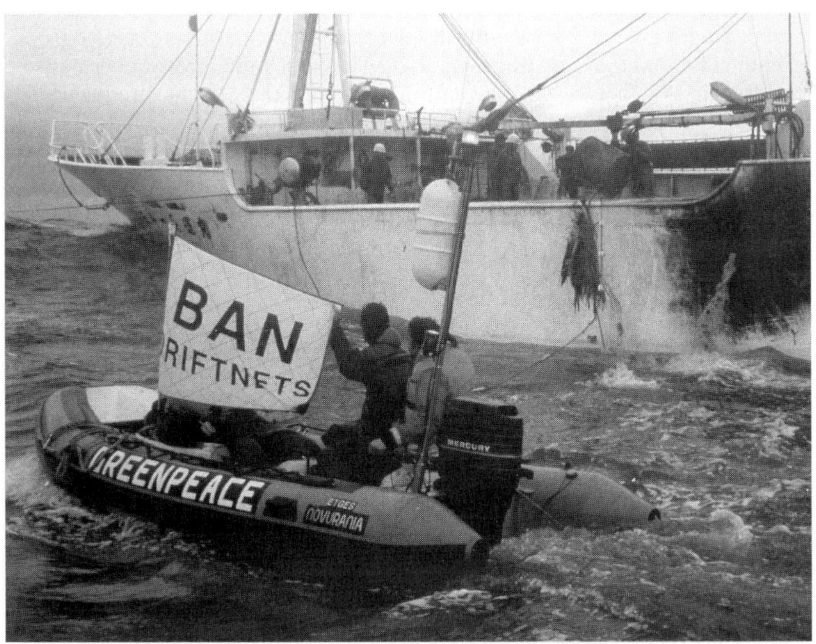

Greenpeace ships have attracted global media attention during high-profile confrontations with ships involved in illegal fishing and whaling operations, or activities considered by them to be immoral. (Photograph courtesy of Greenpeace.)

Box 36 (continued)

and ranchers, groups whom the government often seems unwilling to control.

Environmentalists in many countries often face arrest and abuse at the hands of their own governments. People who protest destructive activities have been branded as subversives, traitors, or foreign agents for fighting against government policies that promote unrestricted development at the expense of the environment. Based upon these and other charges, some activists have been interrogated, jailed, beaten, and tortured. In 1995, nine environmental activists were hanged in Nigeria after a secret trial; they were members of the Ogoni tribe, whose land is being destroyed by a massive oil production operation sanctioned by the Nigerian government. Such incidents occur even in countries considered progressive with regard to conservation.

The persecution and injustices faced by environmentalists are most commonly found in developing nations, but such problems are by no means limited to just these places. Individual activists fighting against industrial pollution and destruction of important biological communities in North America and Europe have also been victims of persecution, ranging from arson to assault to attempted murder. On occasion, authorities responsible for investigating the crimes have responded with either indifference or overt antagonism toward the victims. In a famous incident, French government agents were convicted in the 1985 bombing in New Zealand of the Greenpeace flagship *Rainbow Warrior*, in which a crew member died. The ship was being readied to leave for the South Pacific to protest the French nuclear weapons testing program. When the French resumed testing in 1995, Greenpeace ships again headed into the target zone, challenging French Navy ships. Groups such as the Sea Shepherd Society sometimes deliberately provoke a confrontation by damaging the nets and ships of illegal fishing and whaling operations.

Activists interested in protecting the environment and biological diversity are joining the entire spectrum of organizations, from mainstream political parties to hard-line confrontational groups. Environmental activists are attempting to persuade or, if that fails, to force society to accept the limitations that must be imposed on human consumption if the biosphere is to survive. Business organizations and conservative elements in the labor movement are increasingly lobbying and forming action groups to counter conservation groups. In an interesting twist, these prodevelopment groups often use environmental rhetoric to argue for the "wise use" of natural resources.

Unfortunately, open discussion can give way to anger, confrontation, and intimidation, in some cases resulting in violence. Conservation biologists must help to develop innovative approaches that inform, educate, and organize diverse groups of people to find solutions to environmental problems and to de-fuse the tensions and violence that plague many societies.

change sometimes also have value in eliciting realistic counterproposals from previously unresponsive institutions. In many situations, radical environmental groups such as Greenpeace and EarthFirst! dominate media attention with dramatic, publicity-grabbing actions, while mainstream conservation organizations such as The Nature Conservancy, Conservation International, the Environmental Defense Fund, and the World Wildlife Fund follow behind to negotiate a compromise.

The Role of Conservation Biologists

Conservation biology differs from many other scientific disciplines in that it plays an active role in the preservation of biological diversity in all its forms: species, genetic variability, biological communities, and ecosystem functions (Barry and Oelschlaeger 1996). Members of the diverse disciplines that contribute to conservation biology share the common goal of protecting biological diversity. Ideally, their different conservation perspectives and wide range of experiences should lead to an inclusive atmosphere that permits people with diverse interests to find common ground (Norton 1991).

The ideas and theories of conservation biology are increasingly being incorporated into decisions about park management and species protection. At the same time, botanical gardens, museums, nature centers, zoos, national parks, and aquaria are reorienting their programs to meet the challenges of protecting biological diversity. The need for large parks and the need to protect large populations of endangered species are two particular topics that have received widespread attention in both academic and popular literature. The vulnerability of small populations to local extinction, even when they are carefully protected and managed, and the alarming rates of species extinction and destruction of unique biological communities worldwide have also been highly publicized. As a result of this publicity, the need to protect biological diversity is entering political debate and has been targeted as a priority for government conservation programs.

One of the most serious challenges facing conservation biology is reconciling the needs of local people and the need to preserve biological diversity (Western et al. 1994, 1997). How can poor people, particularly in the developing world but also in rural areas of developed countries, be convinced to respect nature reserves and biological diversity when they are desperate to obtain the food, wood, and other natural products that they need for their daily survival? Park managers in particular need to find compromises, such as the concepts of biosphere reserves and integrated conservation-development projects, that allow people to obtain the natural resources that they need to support their families and yet not damage the natural communities of the park. At national and international levels, the world's resources must be distributed more fairly to end the inequalities that exist today. Effective programs must be established to stabilize the world's human population. At the same time, the destruction of natural resources by industries must be halted, so that the short-term quest for profits does not lead to a long-term ecological catastrophe (Goodland 1992). Management strategies to preserve biological diversity also need to be developed for the 95% of the terrestrial environment that will remain outside of protected areas, as well as for the vast, largely unexplored marine environment.

If these challenges are to be met successfully, conservation biologists must take on several active roles. They must become more effective *educators* in the public forum as well as in the classroom (Box 37). Conservation biologists need to educate as broad a range of people as possible about the problems that stem from loss of biological diversity (Collett and Karakashain 1996). Conservation biologists often teach college students and write technical papers addressing these issues,

Box 37 **Two Who Made a Difference**

At its heart, conservation biology is rooted in a love of the natural world. Those who feel this way may express this love in many different ways: by planting gardens, enjoying parks, studying biology, or taking action to protect species and ecosystems. In any of these cases, it is not necessary to become a professional biologist to have a powerful impact on behalf of biological conservation. In fact, two highly respected individuals who contributed greatly to conservation were not biologists: Gerald Durrell, an animal lover who devoted much of his life to protecting endangered species, and Jacques Cousteau, a self-taught oceanographer and inventor who became a world-renowned spokesman for protection of the world's oceans. Both of these men were passionately interested in the natural world, but more important, both communicated their passion to millions of people around the world through their writings and films.

Gerald Durrell (1925–1995) began by collecting animals and working in a zoo as a young boy. As an adult he became concerned about the animals that enchanted him—and he loved them all, even the "small uglies," as he called the many odd and unattractive creatures such as snakes and scorpions that most people find repugnant. Durrell became convinced that direct action was necessary to prevent extinction of many species. Using his inheritance, Durrell made numerous expeditions in the late 1940s and 1950s to Africa, South America, Madagascar, and other locales rich in unusual and exotic animals. When his money ran out, Durrell wrote popular accounts of his travels, such as *A Zoo in My Luggage*, and eventually was able to use book royalties to finance his dream: a 15-ha zoo in Jersey, England, which had as its main objective the promotion of wildlife conservation worldwide. As part of this goal, Durrell started captive-breeding programs for many endangered species, organized special expeditions to rescue endangered species, and established programs to collect data on threatened species. Some of these endeavors were ahead of their time: for example, Durrell was unflaggingly critical of zoos that did not concern themselves with proper diet or living conditions for their charges. Most zookeepers of the day (Durrell's zoo opened in 1959) were more concerned with creating an exhibit that visitors would enjoy rather than with making life healthy for the animals on display—and many animals did not thrive under such conditions. Durrell's own zoo was designed to be sensitive to the needs of the animals, not the visitors, an innovation that many professionals considered eccentric at the time. Yet modern zoos worldwide now imitate his "eccentric" policy, creating miniature ecosystems that house their occupants in conditions that approximate their natural homes. The zoo also established a program to train wildlife biologists from developing countries who would become advocates for conservation, modern-day Noahs, upon their return. Most important, however, the zoo, Durrell's popular books, and his appearances on radio and television shows—including several series broadcast worldwide—provided a pulpit for him to express his unwavering love of nature. His numerous books helped to introduce ordinary people to the wonders of a natural world far beyond their homes, and the Jersey zoo gave visitors a real-life glimpse of the animals he loved and strove to protect.

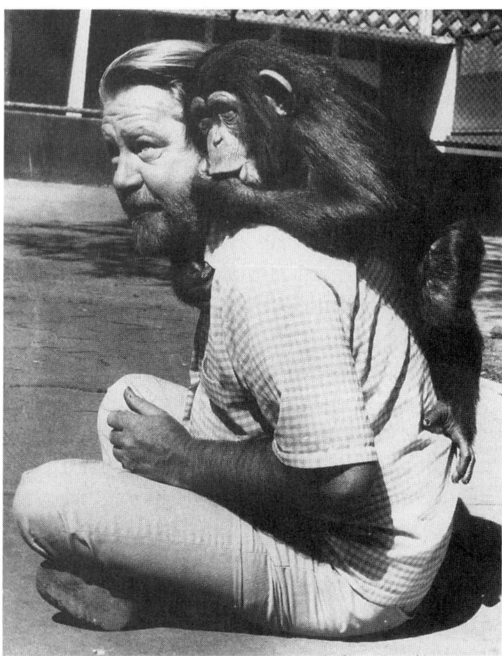

Gerald Durrell (1925–1995)

Jacques Cousteau (1910–1997), an inventor and filmmaker, likewise translated his enormous talents into popular media presentations to promote conservation. At his death, Cousteau, age 87, was a world-renowned advocate for protection of ocean species. Many who read his obituaries probably were surprised to discover that he had no formal education in oceanography or marine biology; in fact, Cousteau's initial training was as a pilot in the French Navy. Forced to quit flying in 1933 after a serious accident, Cousteau rehabilitated from his injuries by swimming in the Mediterranean Sea—and there took the first steps toward opening the oceans to the popular imagination. Part of Cousteau's recovery time was spent collaborating on the invention of equipment crucial to underwater exploration: water-tight goggles, underwater cameras, and most important, the Aqua-lung, a self-contained underwater breathing apparatus ("scuba") now used commonly all over the world. These inventions led Cousteau to begin the endeavors for which he is most famous: a series of expeditions aboard his ship, *Calypso*, that documented the oceans' wonders on film. From the mid-1950s through the 1960s, Cousteau's films and later television show were critically acclaimed and highly popular, and their success helped to fund more challenging explorations of the deep sea.

Jacques Yves Cousteau (1910–1997)

As the years passed, however, Cousteau could see that marine species were in trouble from pollution and overexploitation. Many of the places that he had visited previously and captured on film—particularly those in the Mediterranean—had become degraded and ugly. The native animals had mostly disappeared. Responding to this challenge, in 1974 he founded the nonprofit Cousteau Society to support and publicize marine conservation (Marden 1998). Outspoken and pragmatic, Cousteau was not always politically adept: aside from his wife, he never allowed women to be crew members on the *Calypso*, he was occasionally criticized for harming marine animals or "staging" encounters with sea creatures in order to get good footage, and he always refused to place the welfare of ocean animals above that of people. But he worked tirelessly to promote ocean conservation until his death, and his accomplishments are beyond measure. People who have even a passing knowledge of undersea life owe much of that knowledge to Jacques Cousteau. He made underwater exploration possible—both directly, by inventing equipment that made diving easy and inexpensive, and indirectly, by inspiring a new generation of oceanographers and marine biologists through his films. Just as important, he made the oceans accessible without destroying their mystery. Any person who dons scuba gear, who sees for him or herself the mysteries of marine life, who plays with an octopus or swims among schools of fish might pretend to be Jacques Cousteau for a little while. But Cousteau's greatest gift was to bring the same sense of excitement and thrill to people who never ventured within ten miles of the ocean, much less climbed into a wetsuit with an airtank, mask, and flippers.

Durrell and Cousteau eventually may be remembered as two of the most widely publicized and influential individuals in the history of conservation. Their careers spanned the twentieth century; their writings and films are a legacy that have touched (and will continue to touch) millions of people. That neither man had formal training is no flaw; on the contrary, it is a valuable lesson to people from all walks of life to know that anyone with sufficient passion for knowledge can turn a simple love of nature into a message of inspiration.

but they reach only a limited audience in this way; conservation biologists need to reach a wider range of people through speaking in villages, elementary and secondary schools, parks, and neighborhood gatherings. Also, the themes of conservation need to be even more widely incorporated into public discussions. Conservation biologists must spend more of their time writing articles and editorials for newspapers and magazines, as well as speaking on radio, television, and other mass media. Remember that only a few hundred or a few thousand people read most scientific papers. In contrast, millions of adults saw the movies *Gorillas in the Mist, Medicine Man,* and *The Emerald Forest,* and tens of millions of children have watched *Captain Planet, Kratt's Creatures, Ferngully,* and *Seibert the Seal,* all of which have very powerful conservation themes.

The efforts of Merlin Tuttle and Bat Conservation International (BCI) illustrate how public attitudes toward even unpopular species can be changed. BCI has campaigned throughout the United States and the world to educate people on the importance of bats in ecosystem health, emphasizing their roles as insect eaters, pollinators, and seed dispersers. A valuable part of this effort has involved producing bat photographs and films of exceptional beauty. In Austin, Texas, Tuttle intervened when citizens petitioned the city government to exterminate the hundreds of thousands of Mexican freetail bats (*Tadarida brasiliensis*) that lived under a downtown bridge. He was able to convince people that the bats controlled noxious insect populations over a wide area, eating many thousands of insects every night. The Austin campaign proved so successful that not only did the city government decide to protect the bats, but now citizens and tourists gather each evening to watch the clouds of bats emerge from their roosts (Figure 22.3). The bats have become a source of civic pride.

Conservation biologists must also become *politically active.* Involvement in the political process allows conservation biologists to influence the passage of new laws to support the preservation of biological diversity or to argue against legislation that would prove harmful to species or ecosystems (Grumbine 1993; 1994). An important first step in this process is joining conservation organizations or mainstream political parties to gain strength by working in a group and to learn more about the issues (although there is also room for people who prefer to work by themselves). Recent difficulties in getting the U.S. Congress to reauthorize the Endangered Species Act dramatically illustrate the need for greater political activism. Though much of the political process is time-consuming and tedious, it is often the only way to accomplish major conservation goals such as acquiring new land for reserves or preventing overexploitation of old-growth forests. Conservation biologists need to master the language and methods of the legal process and form effective alliances with environmental lawyers, citizen groups, and politicians.

Figure 22.3 Citizens and tourists gather in the evening to watch bats emerge from their roosts on the underside of a bridge in Austin, Texas. (Photograph by Merlin Tuttle, Bat Conservation International.)

Conservation biologists need to become *organizers* within the biological community. Many professional biologists in universities, museums, high schools, and government agencies concentrate their energies on the specialized needs of their professional niche. They may feel that their institutions want them to concentrate on "pure science" and "not get involved in politics." These people may not realize that the world's biological diversity is under imminent threat of destruction, and their contributions are urgently needed to save it (Huenneke 1995). Or they may imagine themselves to be too busy or unimportant to get involved in the struggle. By stimulating interest in this problem among their colleagues, conservation biologists can increase the ranks of trained professional advocates fighting the destruction of natural resources; these professional biologists may also find their involvement to be personally and professionally beneficial, as their new interests may result in heightened scientific creativity and more inspired teaching.

Conservation biologists need to become *motivators* convincing a range of people to support conservation efforts. At a local level, conservation programs have to be created and presented in ways that provide incentives for local people to support them. Local people need to be shown that protecting the environment not only saves species and biological communities, but also improves the long-term health of their families and their own economic well-being (Edwards 1994; Cesario 1996). Discussions, education, and publicity need to be a major part of any such program. Careful attention must be devoted in particular to convincing business leaders and politicians to support conservation efforts. Many of these people will support conservation efforts when they are presented in the right way; sometimes conservation is perceived to have good publicity value, or supporting it is perceived to be better than a confrontation that may otherwise result. National leaders may be among the most difficult people to convince, since they must respond to a diversity of interests; however, whether it is by reason, sentiment, or career self-interest, once converted to the conservation perspective, these leaders may be in a position to make a major contribution to the cause.

Finally, and most important, conservation biologists need to become effective *managers* and *practitioners* of conservation projects (Bohlen 1993). They must be willing to find out what is really happening, to get their hands dirty, to talk with local people, to knock on doors, and to take risks. Conservation biologists must learn everything they can about the species and communities that they are trying to protect and then make that knowledge available to others. If conservation biologists are willing to put their ideas into practice, and to work with park managers, land-use planners, politicians, and local people, then progress will follow. Getting the right mix of models, new theories, innovative approaches, and practical examples will be the key to the success of the discipline. Once this balance is found, conservation biologists working with an energized citizenry will be in a position to protect the world's biological diversity during this unprecedented era of change.

Summary

1. There are major problems involved in protecting biological diversity; to address these problems, many changes must be made in policies and practices. These changes must occur at local, national, and international levels and require action on the part of individuals, conservation organizations, and governments.

2. Conservation biologists must demonstrate the validity of the theories and approaches of this new discipline and actively work with all components of society to protect and restore biological diversity.

For Discussion

1. Is conservation biology fundamentally different from other branches of biology such as physiology, genetics, or cell biology? Does conservation biology have underlying assumptions that are distinct from other fields of biology?

2. As a result of studying conservation biology, have you decided to change your lifestyle or your level of political activity? Do you think you can make a difference in the world, and if so, in what way?

Suggested Readings and Key Source Material

Barry, D. and M. Oelschlaeger. 1996. A science for survival: Values for conservation biology. *Conservation Biology* 10: 905–911. This excellent article and others, in a special section of this issue, assert that conservation biology includes advocacy for the protection of biological diversity as an important part of the discipline.

Bohlen, J. T. 1993. *For the Wild Places: Profiles in Conservation.* Island Press, Washington, D.C. Patricia Chapple Wright, David Western, George Archibold, Louis Diego Gomez and Rick Steiner have made major accomplishments in conservation.

Brown, L. R., C. Flavin and H. French. 1997. *State of the World 1997: A Worldwatch Institute Report on Progress Toward a Sustainable Society.* W. W. Norton, New York. Thorough analyses of the issues of most pressing importance. See other Worldwatch publications as well.

Collett, J. and S. Karakashain (eds.). 1996. *Greening the College Curriculum: A Guide to Environmental Teaching in the Liberal Arts.* Island Press. Washington, D.C. Environmental and conservation issues can be a theme unifying many university courses and programs of study.

Conservation Biology. The cutting-edge journal in the field. Browsing back issues is well worthwhile. Excellent articles can also be found in the journals *BioScience, Biological Conservation, Ecological Applications, Ambio, Environmental Conservation, Audubon,* and *National Geographic.*

Erlich, A. H. and P. R. Erlich. 1996. *Betrayal of Science and Reason: How Anti-Environmental Rhetoric Threatens Our Future.* Island Press, Washington, D.C. Environmental arguments are being criticized and countered by strong arguments from groups favoring development.

Giono, J. 1989. *The Man Who Planted Trees.* Collins Dove, Melbourne, Australia. Simple, beautiful story about how one person can make a change in society.

Gore, A. 1992. *Earth in the Balance: Ecology and the Human Spirit.* Houghton Mifflin, New York. The U.S. vice president passionately and intelligently argues the need to give greater effort to environmental protection.

Grumbine, R. E. 1993. *Ghost Bears: Exploring the Biodiversity Crisis.* Island Press, Washington, D.C. This popular book weaves together elements of conservation biology, law, policy, and activism.

Grumbine, R. E. (ed.). 1994. *Environmental Policy and Biodiversity.* Island Press, Washington, D.C. Conservation can occur when societies have the political will to act.

Heywood, V. H. (ed.). 1995. *Global Biodiversity Assessment.* Cambridge University Press, Cambridge. The most complete single source of information on biological diversity.

Huenneke, L. F. 1995. Involving academic scientists in conservation research: Perspectives of a plant ecologist. *Ecological Applications* 5: 205–214. Academic scientists need to involve themselves in practical problems and the political process.

Jacobson, S. K., E. Vaughan and S. W. Miller. 1995. New directions in conservation biology: Graduate programs. *Conservation Biology* 9: 5–17. Descriptions of 51 U.S. graduate programs with lists of faculty.

Kurlansky, M. 1996. Oil, toil and tyranny. *Audubon* 98 (2): 128. Large companies will only protect the environment when they are pressured to do so.

Losos E., J. Haynes, A. Phillips and C. Alkiere. 1995. Taxpayer-subsidized resource extraction harms species. *BioScience* 45: 446–455. Many of the threats to species occur during resource extraction on government lands.

Marden, L. 1998. Jacques Yves-Costeau. *National Geographic* (February): 70–89. A short biography with great photographs in a special issue on exploration.

Meffe, G. K. and C. R. Carroll. 1997. *Principles of Conservation Biology*, Second Edition. Sinauer Associates, Sunderland, MA. Excellent advanced textbook.

Middleton, S. and D. Littschwager. 1994. *Witness: Endangered Species of North America.* Chronicle Books. Superb photographs; also watch this team on discussion-provoking video: *America's Endangered Species: Don't Say Good-Bye.* National Geographic Video. 1997. Directed by Robert Kenner.

Motavelli, J. 1995. In harm's way. *E: The Environmental Magazine* 6(6): 28–37. Forcefully written article about Greenpeace's activist approach.

Myers, N. 1996. *Ultimate Security: The Environmental Basis of Political Stability.* Island Press, Washington, D.C. Wars and civil disturbances are increasingly caused for environmental reasons; protecting the environment is crucial to providing global security.

Pachlke, R. (ed.). 1995. *Conservation and Environmentalism: An Encyclopedia.* Garland Publishing, New York. Resource for finding out more about particular topics.

Polunin, N. and L. M. Curme. 1997. *World Who Is Who and Does What in Environment and Conservation.* St. Martin's Press, New York. A broad listing of people, projects, and activities.

Rabinowitz, A. 1995. Helping a species go extinct: The Sumatran rhino in Borneo. *Conservation Biology* 9: 482-488. Spending money on high-profile projects sometimes hides an unwillingness to tackle tough problems on the ground.

Wilson, E. O. 1992. *The Diversity of Life.* Belknap Press, Cambridge, MA. The best popular book on the biodiversity crisis, eminently suitable to recommend or give to interested people.

Wilson, E. O. 1994. *Naturalist.* Island Press, Washington, D. C. A deep appreciation of natural history was the starting point for this important conservation biologist.

WRI/IUCN/UNEP. 1992. *Global Biodiversity Strategy: Guidelines for Action to Save, Study and Use Earth's Biotic Wealth Sustainably and Equitably.* World Resources Institute, Washington, D.C. Current views on needed policy changes, with a long list of key people in the field.

APPENDIX

Selected Environmental Organizations and Sources of Information

The best single reference on conservation activities is the *Conservation Directory*, updated each year by the National Wildlife Federation, 1400 Sixteenth Street N.W., Washington, D.C. 20036. This directory lists thousands of local, national, and international conservation organizations, conservation publications, and leaders in the field of conservation. Other publications of interest include *The New Complete Guide to Environmental Careers* (1993), published by Island Press, 1718 Connecticut Avenue N.W., Washington, D.C. 20009, *Environmental Profiles: A Global Guide to Projects and People* (1993), published by Garland Publishing, 717 Fifth Avenue, New York, N.Y. 10022, and *World's Who's Who and Does What in Environment and Conservation* (1997), by N. Polunin and L. M. Curme, published by St. Martins Press, New York.

The following is a list of some major organizations and resources.

American Zoo and Aquarium Association
7970-D Old Georgetown Road
Bethesda, MD 20814 U.S.A.
www.aza.org
Preservation and propagation of captive wildlife.

BirdLife International
Wellbrook Court
Girton Road
Cambridge CB3 0NA, United Kingdom
Formerly known as International Council for Bird Preservation. Determines conservation status and priorities for birds throughout the world.

Center for Marine Conservation
1725 DeSales Street N.W., Suite 600
Washington, D.C. 20036 U.S.A.
www.cmc-ocean.org
Focus on marine wildlife and ocean and coastal habitats.

Center for Plant Conservation and Missouri Botanical Garden
P.O. Box 299
St. Louis, MO 63166-0299 U.S.A.
www.mobot.org
Major centers for worldwide plant conservation activities.

CITES Secretariat, UNEP
15 Chemin des Anemones
Case Postale 356
1219 Chatelaine
Geneva, Switzerland
Regulates trade in endangered species.

Conservation International
2501 M Street N.W., Suite 200
Washington, D.C. 20037 U.S.A.
www.conservation.org
Active in conservation efforts and working for sustainable development.

Earthwatch Institute
680 Mt. Auburn Street
P.O. Box 9104
Watertown, MA 02272 U.S.A.
gaia.earthwatch.org
Clearinghouse for international projects in which volunteers can work with scientists.

Environmental Data Research Institute
1655 Elmwood Avenue, Suite 225
Rochester, N.Y. 14620-3426 U.S.A.
Publishes *Environmental Granting Foundations*, a comprehensive guide to funding sources.

Environmental Defense Fund
257 Park Avenue South
New York, N.Y. 10010 U.S.A.
www.edf.org
Involved in scientific, legal, and economic issues.

Friends of the Earth
1025 Vermont Avenue N.W., Suite 300
Washington, D.C. 20005-6303 U.S.A.
www.essential.org/FOE/FOE.html
International environmental organization working to improve public policy.

Greenpeace, U.S.A., Inc.
1436 "U" Street N.W.
Washington, D.C. 20009 U.S.A.
www.greenpeace.org
www.greenpeaceusa.org
Activist organization, known for grassroots efforts and dramatic protests against environmental damage.

Institute for Economic Botany and New York Botanical Gardens
Bronx, N.Y. 10458 U.S.A.
Research and conservation programs involving plants that are useful to people.

International Union for the Conservation of Nature and Natural Resources (IUCN)
Avenue de Mont Blanc
CH-1196 Gland, Switzerland
www.iucn.org
Also known as the World Conservation Union (WCU). This is the premier coordinating body for international conservation efforts. Produces directories of specialists who are knowledgeable about captive breeding programs and other aspects of conservation.

National Audubon Society
700 Broadway
New York, N.Y. 10003 U.S.A.
www.audubon.org
Extensive program, including wildlife conservation, public education, research, and political lobbying.

National Wildlife Federation
8925 Leesburg Pike
Vienna, VA 22184
www.nwf.org
Advocates for wildlife conservation. Publishes the *Conservation Directory*, as well as the outstanding children's publications *Ranger Rick* and *Your Big Backyard*.

Natural Resources Defense Council, Inc.
40 West Twentieth Street
New York, N.Y. 10011 U.S.A.
www.nrdc.org
Uses legal and scientific methods to monitor and influence government actions and legislation.

The Nature Conservancy
1815 North Lynn Street
Arlington, VA 22209 U.S.A.
www.tnc.org
Emphasis on land preservation. Maintains extensive records on rare species distribution in the Americas, particularly North America.

Rainforest Action Network
221 Pine Street, Suite 500
San Francisco, CA 94104 U.S.A.
www.ran.org/ran
Works actively for rain forest conservation.

Ramsar Convention Bureau
Rue Mauverney 28
CH-1196 Gland, Switzerland
www.iucn.org/themes/ramsar/
Promotes international conservation of wetlands.

Royal Botanical Gardens, Kew
Richmond
Surrey TW9 3AB, United Kingdom
www.rbgkew.org.uk
The famous "Kew Gardens" are home to a leading botanical research institute.

Sierra Club
85 Second Street, Second Floor
San Francisco, CA 94105-3441 U.S.A.
www.sierraclub.org

Leading advocate for the preservation of wilderness and open space.

Smithsonian Institution and National Zoological Park
1000 Jefferson Drive S.W.
Washington, D.C. 20560 U.S.A.
www.si.edu/organiza/museums/zoo/nzphome.htm
The National Zoo and the nearby U.S. National Museum of Natural History represent a vast resource of literature, biological materials, and skilled people.

Society for Conservation Biology
c/o Blackwell Scientific Publications, Inc.
350 Main Street
Malden, MA 02148 U.S.A.
Leading scientific society for the field. Develops and publicizes new ideas and scientific results through the journal *Conservation Biology*.

Student Conservation Association
Box 550
Charlestown, NJ 03603 U.S.A.
www.sca-inc.org/advance/text/home.htm
Places volunteers with conservation organizations and public agencies.

United Nations Development Programme (UNDP)
U.N. Plaza
New York, N.Y. 10017 U.S.A.
Funds and coordinates international economic development activities, particularly those that use natural resources in a responsible way.

United Nations Environment Programme (UNEP)
P.O. Box 30552
Nairobi, Kenya
or
1899 "F" Street N.W.
Washington, D.C. 20006 U.S.A.
www.unep.ch
International program of research and management relating to major environmental problems.

United States Fish and Wildlife Service
Washington, D.C. 20240 U.S.A.
www.fws.gov
The leading U.S. government agency in the conservation of endangered species, with a vast research and management network. Major activities also take place within other federal government units, such as the National Marine Fisheries Service and the U.S. Forest Service. The Agency for International Development is active in many developing nations. Individual state governments have comparable units, with National Heritage programs being especially relevant. The *Conservation Directory* shows how these units are organized.

The Wilderness Society
900 Seventeenth Street N.W.
Washington, D.C. 20006-2598 U.S.A.
www.tws.org
Organization devoted to preserving wilderness and wildlife.

Wildlife Conservation Society and New York Zoological Society
2300 Southern Boulevard
Bronx, N.Y. 10460 U.S.A
www.wcs.org
Leaders in wildlife conservation and research.

World Bank
1818 "H" Street N.W.
Washington, D.C. 20433 U.S.A.
A multinational bank involved in economic development; increasingly concerned with environmental issues.

World Conservation Monitoring Centre
219 Huntingdon Road
Cambridge CB3 0DL, United Kingdom
www.wcmc.org.uk
Monitors global wildlife trade, the status of endangered species, natural resource use, and protected areas.

World Resources Institute (WRI)
1709 New York Avenue N.W.
Washington, D.C. 20006 U.S.A.
www.wri.org
Research center producing excellent papers on environmental, conservation, and development topics.

World Wildlife Fund (WWF)
1250 Twenty-Fourth Street N.W.
Washington, D.C. 20037 U.S.A.
www.wwf.org
Also known as the Worldwide Fund for Nature. Major conservation organization, with branches throughout the world. Active both in research and in the management of national parks.

Xerces Society
4828 Southeast Hawthorne Boulevard
Portland, OR 97215 U.S.A.
www.xerces.org/home.htm
Focuses on the conservation of insects and other invertebrates.

Zoological Society of London
Regents Park
London NW1 4RY, United Kingdom
Center for worldwide activities to preserve nature.

Bibliography

Abram, D. 1996. *The Spell of the Sensuous: Perceptions and Language in a More-Than-Human World*. Pantheon Books, New York.

Abramovitz, J. N. 1991. *Investing in Biological Diversity: U.S. Research and Conservation Efforts in Developing Countries*. World Resources Institute, Washington, D.C.

Abramovitz, J. N. 1994. *Trends in Biodiversity Investments: U.S.-Based Funding for Research and Conservation in Developing Countries, 1987–1991*. World Resources Institute, Washington, D.C.

Adams, D. and M. Carwardine. *Last Chance to See*. 1990. Harmony Books, New York.

Agardy, T. S. 1997. *Marine Protected Areas and Ocean Conservation*. R. G. Landes Company, Austin, TX.

Aguirre, A. A. and E. E. Starkey. 1994. Wildlife disease in U.S. National Parks: Historical and coevolutionary perspectives. *Conservation Biology* 8: 654–661.

AID (Agency for International Development). 1985. *U.S. Strategy on the Conservation of Biological Diversity: An Interagency Task Force Report to Congress*. U.S. Government Printing Office, Washington, D.C.

Akçakaya, H. R. 1990. Bald ibis *Geronticus eremita* population in Turkey: An evaluation of the captive breeding project for reintroduction. *Biological Conservation* 51: 225–237.

Akçakaya, H. R. 1994. RAMAS/GIS: *Linking Landscape Data with Population Viability Analysis* (*Version 1.0*). Applied Biomathematics, Setauket, NY.

Akçakaya, H. R., M. A. Burgman and L. R. Ginzburg. 1997. *Applied Population Ecology: Using RAMAS Ecolab*. Applied Biomathematics, Setauket, NY.

Alcock, J. 1993. *Animal Behavior: An Evolutionary Approach*, 5th ed. Sinauer Associates, Sunderland, MA.

Alcorn, J. B. 1984. Development policy, forests and peasant farms: Reflections on Huastec-managed forests' contributions to commercial production and resource conservation. *Economic Botany* 38: 389–406.

Alcorn, J. B. 1991. Ethics, economies and conservation. *In* M. L. Oldfield and J. B. Alcorn (eds.), *Biodiversity: Culture, Conservation and Ecodevelopment*, pp. 317–349. Westview Press, Boulder, CO.

Alcorn, J. B. 1993. Indigenous peoples and conservation. *Conservation Biology* 7: 424–426.

Allan, T. and A. Warren (eds.). 1993. *Deserts, the Encroaching Wilderness: A World Conservation Atlas*. Oxford University Press, London.

Allen, C., R. S. Lutz and S. Demarais. 1995. Red imported fire ant impacts on Northern Bobwhite populations. *Ecological Applications* 5: 632–638.

Allen, W. H. 1988. Biocultural restoration of a tropical forest: Architects of Costa Rica's emerging Guanacaste National Park plan to make it an integral part of local culture. *BioScience* 38: 156–161.

Allendorf, F. W. and C. Servheen. 1986. Genetics and the conservation of grizzly bears. *Trends in Ecology and Evolution* 1: 88–89.

Allendorf, F. W. and R. F. Leary. 1986. Heterozygosity and fitness in natural populations of animals. *In* M. E. Soulé (ed.), *Conservation Biology: The Science of Scarcity and Diversity*, pp. 57–76. Sinauer Associates, Sunderland, MA.

Alpert, P. 1995. Applying ecological research at integrated conservation and development projects. *Ecological Applications* 5: 857–861.

Altaba, C. R. 1990. The last known population of the freshwater mussel *Margaritifera auricularia* (Bivalvia, Unionoida): A conservation priority. *Biological Conservation* 52: 271–286.

Altieri, M. A. and M. K. Anderson. 1992. Peasant farming systems, agricultural modernization and the conservation of crop genetic resources in Latin America. *In* P. L. Fiedler and S. K. Jain (eds.), *Conservation Biology: The Theory and Practice of Nature Conservation, Preservation and Management*, pp. 49–64. Chapman and Hall, New York.

Alverson, W. S., W. Kuhlmann and D. M. Waller. 1994. *Wild Forests: Conservation Biology and Public Policy*. Island Press, Washington, D.C.

Ames, M. H. 1991. Saving some cetaceans may require breeding in captivity. BioScience 41: 746–749.

Anderson, A. B. (ed.). 1990. *Alternatives to Deforestation*. Columbia University Press, New York.

Andreae, C. 1995. Australian botanist unveil 'new-old' tree. *The Christian Science Monitor*. January 4, 1995. p. 12.

Angel, M. V. 1993. Biodiversity of the pelagic ocean. *Conservation Biology* 7: 760–772.

Antonovics, J. 1976. The nature of limits to natural selection. *Annals of the Missouri Botanical Garden* 63: 224–247.

Arita, H. T., J. G. Robinson and K. H. Redford. 1990. Rarity in Neotropical forest mammals and its ecological correlates. *Conservation Biology* 4: 181–192.

Armbruster, P. and R. Lande. 1993. A population viability analysis for African elephant (*Loxodonta africana*): How big should reserves be? *Conservation Biology* 7: 602–610.

Arrow, K., B. Bolin, R. Costanza, P. Dasgupta, C. Folke, et al. 1995. Economic growth, carrying capacity and the environment. *Science* 268: 520–522.

Ashley, M. V., D. J. Melnick and D. Western. 1990. Conservation genetics of the black rhinoceros (*Diceros bicornis*). I. Evidence from the mitochondrial DNA of three populations. *Conservation Biology* 4: 71–77.

Ashton, P. S. 1984. Botanic gardens and experimental grounds. *In* V. H. Heywood and S. M. Moore (eds.), *Current Concepts in Plant Taxonomy*, pp. 39–48. Academic Press, London.

Askins, R. A. 1995. Hostile landscapes and the decline of migratory songbirds. *Science* 267: 1956–1957.

Atwood, J. L. and R. F. Noss. 1994. Gnatcatchers and Development: A "Train Wreck" Avoided? *illahee* 10 (2): 123–130.

Avise, J. C. and J. L. Hamrick (eds.). 1996. *Conservation Genetics: Case Histories from Nature*. Chapman and Hall, New York.

Baker, C. S. and S. R. Palumbi. 1994. Which whales are hunted? A molecular genetic approach to monitoring whaling. *Science* 265: 1538–1539.

Baldwin, A. D., J. de Luca and C. Pletsch (eds.). 1994. *Beyond Preservation: Restoring and Inventing Landscapes*. University of Minnesota Press, Minneapolis, MN.

Balick, M. J. and P. A. Cox. 1996. *Plants, People and Culture: The Science of Ethnobotany*. Scientific American Library, New York.

Balick, M. J., E. Elisabetsky and S. A. Laird (eds.). 1996. *Medicinal Resources of the Tropical Forest: Biodiversity and Its Importance to Human Health*. Columbia University Press, New York.

Ballou, J. D. 1995. *Golden Lion Tamarin Global Masterplan Report*, 8.

Balmford, A. 1996. Extinction filters and current resilience: The significance of past selection pressures for conservation biology. *Trends in Ecology and Evolution* 11: 193–196.

Balmford, A. and A. Long. 1994. Avian endemism and forest loss. *Nature* 372: 623–624.

Balmford, A., G. M. Mace and N. Leader-Williams. 1996. Designing the ark: Setting priorities for captive breeding. *Conservation Biology* 10: 719–728.

Baltz, D. M. 1991. Introduced fishes in marine systems and inland seas. *Biological Conservation* 56: 151–177.

Barbier, E. B. 1993. Valuation of environmental resources and impacts in developing countries. *In* R. K. Turner (ed.), *Sustainable Environmental Economics and Management*, pp. 319–337. Belhaven Press, New York.

Barbier, E. B., J. C. Burgess and C. Folke. 1994. *Paradise Lost? The Ecological Economics of Biodiversity*. Earthscan Publications, London.

Barinaga, M. 1995. New study provides some good news for fisheries. *Science* 269: 1043.

Barrett, S. C. H. and J. R. Kohn. 1991. Genetic and evolutionary consequences of small population size in plants: Implications for conservation. *In* D. A. Falk and K. E. Holsinger (eds.), *Genetics and Conservation of Rare Plants*, pp. 3–30. Oxford University Press, New York.

Barry, D. and M. Oelschlaeger. 1996. A science for survival: Values for conservation biology. *Conservation Biology* 10: 905–911.

Bartley, D., M. Bagley, G. Gall and B. Bentley. 1992. Use of linkage disequilibrium data to estimate effective size of hatchery and natural fish populations. *Conservation Biology* 6: 365–375.

Baskin, Y. 1994. There's a new wildlife policy in Kenya: Use it or lose it. *Science* 265: 733–734.

Baskin, Y. 1997. *The Work of Nature: How the Diversity of Life Sustains Us*. Island Press, Washington, D.C.

Batisse, M. 1997. A challenge for biodiversity conservation and regional development. *Environment* 39(5): 7–33.

Bawa, K. S. 1990. Plant-pollinator interactions in tropical rainforests. *Annual Review of Ecology and Systematics* 21: 399–422.

Bawa, K. S. 1992. Mating systems, genetic differentiation and speciation in tropical rain forest plants. *Biotropica* (special issue) 24: 250–255.

Bawa, K. S. and S. Dayanandan. 1997. Socioeconomic factors and tropical deforestation. *Nature* 386: 562–563.

Bawa, K. S., S. Lele, K. S. Murali, and B. Ganesan. 1998. Extraction of non-timber forest products in Biligiri Rangan Hills, India: Monitoring of a community-based project. *In* K. Saterson, R. Margolis, and N. Salafsky (eds.), *Measuring Conservation Impact: Proceedings from a Symposium at the 1996 Joint Meeting of the Society for Conservation Biology and the Ecological Society of America, Providence, RI*. Biodiversity Support Program, Washington, D.C.

Bawa, K. S. and A. Markham. 1995. Climate change and tropical forests. *Trends in Ecology and Evolution* 10: 348–349.

Bawa, K. S. and S. Menon. 1997. Biodiversity monitoring: The missing ingredients. *Trends in Ecology and Evolution* 12: 42.

Bazzaz, F. A. and E. D. Fajer. 1992. Plant life in a CO_2–rich world. *Scientific American* 266: 68–74.

Beard, J. 1991. Bug detectives crack the tough cases. *Science* 254: 1580–81.

Beccaloni, G. W. and K. J. Gaston. 1995. Predicting the species richness of neotropical forest butterflies: Ithomiinae (*Lepidoptera nymphalidae*) as indicators. *Biological Conservation* 71: 77–86.

Beck, B. B. and A. F. Martins. 1995. *Golden Lion Tamarin Reintroduction Annual Report*, 7.

Beck, B. B., L. G. Rapport, M. R. Stanley Price and A. C. Wilson. 1994. Reintroduction of captive-born animals. *In* P. J. Olney, G. M. Mace and A. T. C. Feistner (eds.), *Creative Conservation: Interactive Management of Wild and Captive Animals*, pp. 265–286. Chapman and Hall, London.

Bedigian, D. 1991. Genetic diversity of traditional sesame cultivars and cultural diversity in Sudan. *In* M. L. Oldfield and J. B. Alcorn (eds.), *Biodiversity: Culture, Conservation and Ecodevelopment*, pp. 25–36. Westview Press, Boulder, CO.

Beebee, T. J. C. 1996. *Ecology and Conservation of Amphibians*. Chapman and Hall, London.

Beebee, T. J. C., et al. 1990. Decline of the Natterjack Toad *Bufo calamita* in Britain: Palaeoecological, documentary and experimental evidence for breeding site acidification. *Biological Conservation* 53: 1–20.

Béland, P. 1996. The beluga whales of the St. Lawrence River. *Scientific American* 274: 74–81.

Benz, B. F., L. R. Sánchez-Velásquez and F. J. Santana Michel. 1990. Ecology and ethnobotany of *Zea diploperennis*: Preliminary investigations. *Maydica* 35: 85–98.

Berger, J. 1990. Persistence of different-sized populations: An empirical assessment of rapid extinctions in bighorn sheep. *Conservation Biology* 4: 91–98.

Bibby, C. J. et al. 1992. *Putting Biodiversity on the Map: Priority Areas for Global Conservation*. International Council for Bird Preservation, Cambridge.

Bierregaard, R. O., T. E. Lovejoy, V. Kapos, A. A. Dos Santos and R. W. Hutchings. 1992. The biological dynamics of tropical rainforest fragments. *BioScience* 42: 859–866.

Billington, H. L. 1991. Effect of population size on genetic variation in a dioecious conifer. *Conservation Biology* 5: 115–119.

Birdlife International. 1997. *Climate Change and Wildlife*. Conference Proceedings.

Birkeland, C. (ed). 1997. *The Life and Death of Coral Reefs*. Chapman and Hall, New York.

Blaustein, A. R. 1994. Chicken little or Nero's fiddle? A perspective on declining amphibian populations. *Herpetologica* 50: 85–97.

Blaustein, A. R. and D. B. Wake. 1995. The puzzle of declining amphibian populations. *Scientific American* 272 (4): 52–57.

Bleich, V. C., J. D. Wehausen and S. A. Holl. 1990. Desert-dwelling mountain sheep: Conservation implications of a naturally fragmented distribution. *Conservation Biology* 4: 383–389.

Bodmer, R. E., J. F. Eisenberg and K. H. Redford. 1997. Hunting and the likelihood of extinction of Amazonian mammals. *Conservation Biology* 11: 460–466.

Boersma, P. D. 1996. Marine conservation: Protecting the exploited commons. *Society for Conservation Biology Newsletter* 3 (4): 1.

Bohlen, J. T. 1993. *For the Wild Places: Profiles in Conservation*. Island Press, Washington, D.C.

Boice, L. P. 1996. Endangered species management on U.S. Air Force lands. *Endangered Species Update* 13 (9): 6–7.

Bonnell, M. L. and R. K. Selander. 1974. Elephant seals: Genetic variation and near-extinction. *Science* 184: 908–909.

Bormann, F. H. 1976. An inseparable linkage: Conservation of natural ecosystems and conservation of fossil energy. *BioScience* 26: 759.

Boucher, G. and P. J. D. Lambshead. 1995. Ecological biodiversity of marine nematodes in samples from temperate, tropical and deep-sea regions. *Conservation Biology* 9: 1594–1605.

Bowles, I. A. and G. T. Prickett. 1994. *Reframing the Green Window: An Analysis of the GEF Pilot Phase Approach to Biodiversity and Global Warming and Recommendations for the Operational Phase*. Conservation International/National Resources Defense Council, Washington, D.C.

Bowles, M. L. and C. J. Whelan. 1994. *Restoration of Endangered Species: Conceptual Issues, Planning and Implementation*. Cambridge University Press, Cambridge.

Boyce, M. S. 1992. Population viability analysis. *Annual Review of Ecology and Systematics* 23: 481–506.

Bradshaw, A. D. 1990. The reclamation of derelict land and the ecology of ecosystems. *In* W. R. Jordan III, M. E. Gilpin and J. D. Aber (eds.), *Restoration Ecology: A Synthetic Approach to Ecological Research*, pp. 53–74. Cambridge University Press, Cambridge.

Breman, H. 1992. Desertification control, the West African case: Prevention is better than cure. *Biotropica* (special issue) 24: 328–334.

Brenan, J. P. M. 1978. Some aspects of the phytogeography of tropical Africa. *Annals of the Missouri Botanical Garden*. 65: 437–478.

Briggs, J. C. 1995. *Global Biogeography*. Elsevier, Amsterdam.

Briscoe, D. A., J. M. Malpica, A. Robertson, G. J. Smith, R. Frankham, R. G. Banks and J. S. F. Barker. 1992. Rapid loss of genetic variation in large captive populations of Drosophila flies: Implications for the genetic management of captive populations. *Conservation Biology* 6: 416–425.

Brooks, T. M., S. L. Pimm and N. J. Collar. Deforestation predicts the number of threatened birds in insular Southeast Asia. *Conservation Biology* 11: 382–394.

Brooks, T., A. Balmford. 1996. Atlantic forest extinctions. *Nature* 380: 115.

Browder, J. O. 1990. Extractive reserves will not save the tropics. *BioScience* 40: 626.

Brown, B. E. and J. C. Ogden. 1993. Coral bleaching. *Scientific American* 268: 64–70.

Brown, G. M. 1993. The economic value of elephants. *In* E. B. Barbier (ed.), *Economics and Ecology: New Frontiers in Sustainable Development*. Chapman and Hall, London.

Brown, L. R., C. Flavin and H. French. 1997. *State of the World 1997: A Worldwatch Institute Report on Progress Toward a Sustainable Society*. W. W. Norton, New York.

Brownlow, C. A. 1996. Molecular taxonomy and the conservation of the red wolf and other endangered carnivores. *Conservation Biology* 10: 390–396.

Brush, S. B. and D. Stabinsky (eds.). 1996. *Valuing Local Knowledge: Indigenous People and Intellectual Property Rights*. Island Press, Washington, D.C.

Bryant, D., D. Nelson and L. Tangley. 1997. *The Last Frontier Forests: Ecosystems and Economies on the Edge*. World Resources Institute, Washington, D.C.

Buchmann, S. L. and G. P. Nabhan. 1996. *The Forgotten Pollinators*. Island Press, Washington, D.C.

Buck, S. J. 1996. *Understanding Environmental Administration and Law*. Island Press, Washington, D.C.

Burbidge, A. A. and N. L. McKenzie. 1989. Patterns in the modern decline of Western Australia's vertebrate fauna: Causes and conservation implications. *Biological Conservation* 50: 143–198.

Burgman, M. A., S. Ferson and H. R. Akcakaya. 1993. *Risk Assessment in Conservation Biology*. Chapman and Hall, London.

Burks, D. C. (ed.). 1994. *Place of the Wild: A Wildlands Anthology*. Island Press/Shearwater, Washington, D.C.

Burrill, A., I. Douglas-Hamilton and J. Mackinnon. 1986. Protected areas as refuges for elephants. *In* J. Mackinnon and K. Mackinnon (eds.), *Protected Areas Systems Review of the Afrotropical Realm.* IUCN, Gland, Switzerland.

Bustamante, R. H. and J. C. Castilla. 1990. Impact of human exploitation on populations of the intertidal southern bull-kelp *Durvilae antartica* (Phaeophyta, Durvileales) in Central Chile. *Biological Conservation* 52: 205–220.

Butman, C. A., J. T. Carlton and S. R. Palumbi. 1995. Whaling effects on deep-sea biodiversity. *Conservation Biology* 9: 462–465.

Buzas, M. A. and S. J. Culver. 1991. Species diversity and dispersal of benthic Foraminifera. *BioScience* 41: 483–489.

Cade, T. J., J. H. Endersone, C. G. Thelander and C. M. White (eds.). 1998. *Peregrine Falcon Populations: Their Management and Recovery.* The Peregrine Fund, Boise, ID.

Cairns, J. and J. R. Heckman. 1996. Restoration ecology: The state of an emerging field. *Annual Review of Energy and the Environment* 21: 167–189.

Cairns, J., Jr. 1986. Restoration, reclamation and regeneration of degraded or destroyed ecosystems. *In* M. E. Soulé (ed.), *Conservation Biology: The Science of Scarcity and Diversity*, pp. 153–181. Sinauer Associates, Sunderland, MA

Caldecott, J. 1988. *Hunting and Wildlife Management in Sarawak.* IUCN, Gland, Switzerland.

Caldecott, J. 1996. *Designing Conservation Projects.* Cambridge University Press, Cambridge.

Caldwell, L. 1985. Science will not save the biosphere but politics might. *Environmental Conservation* 12: 195–197.

Callicott, J. B. 1990. Whither conservation ethics? *Conservation Biology* 4: 15–20.

Callicott, J. B. 1994. *Earth's Insights: A Multicultural Survey of Ecological Ethics from the Mediterranean Basin to the Australian Outback.* University of California Press, Berkeley, CA.

Callicott, J. B. and R. T. Ames. 1989. *Nature in Asian Traditions of Thought: Essays in Environmental Philosophy.* State University of New York Press, Albany.

Campbell, S. 1980. Is reintroduction a realistic goal? *In* M. E. Soulé and B. A. Wilcox (eds.). *Conservation Biology: An Evolutionary-Ecological Perspective*, pp. 263–269. Sinauer Associates, Sunderland, MA.

Canby, T. Y. 1993. Bacteria: Teaching old bugs new tricks. *National Geographic* 184 (2): 36–60.

Cannon, J. R. 1996. Whooping Crane recovery: A case study in public and private cooperation in the conservation of endangered species. *Conservation Biology* 10: 813–822.

Carlton, J. T. and J. B. Geller. 1993. Ecological roulette: the global transport of nonindigenous marine organisms. *Science* 261: 78–82.

Caro, T. M. and M. K. Laurenson. 1994. Ecological and genetic factors in conservation: A cautionary tale. *Science* 263: 485–486.

Carrol, C. R. et al. 1996. Strengthening the use of science in achieving the goals of the Endangered Species Act: An assessement by the Ecological Society of America. *Ecological Applications* 6: 1–12.

Carroll, C. R. 1992. Ecological management of sensitive natural areas. *In* P. L. Fiedler and S. K. Jain (eds.), *Conservation Biology: The Theory and Practice of Nature Conservation, Preservation and Management*, pp. 347–372. Chapman and Hall, New York.

Carson, H. L. 1983. The genetics of the founder effect. *In* C. M. Schonewald-Cox, S. M. Chambers, B. MacBryde and L. Thomas (eds.), *Genetics and Conservation: A Reference for Managing Wild Animal and Plant Populations*, pp. 189–200. Benjamin/Cummings, Menlo Park, CA.

Carson, R. 1962. *Silent Spring.* Reprinted 1982 by Penguin, Harmondsworth, UK.

Carte, B. K. 1996. Biomedical potential of marine natural products: Marine organisms are yielding novel molecules for use in basic research and medical applications. *BioScience* 46: 271–286.

Caswell, H. 1989. *Matrix Population Models: Construction, Analysis and Interpretation.* Sinauer Associates, Inc., Sunderland, MA.

Caughley, G. and A. Gunn. 1996. *Conservation Biology in Theory and Practice.* Blackwell Science, Malden, MA.

Caulfield, C. 1985. *In the Rainforest.* Alfred A. Knopf, New York.

Ceballos-Lascuráin, H. (ed.) 1993. *Tourism and Protected Areas.* IUCN, Gland, Switzerland.

Center for Plant Conservation. 1991. Genetic sampling guidelines for conservation collections of endangered plants. *In* D. A. Falk and K. E. Holsinger (eds.), *Genetics and Conservation of Rare Plants*, pp. 224–238. Oxford University Press, New York.

Chadwick, D. H. 1993. The American prairie: Roots of the sky. *National Geographic* 184: 90–119.

Chadwick, D. H. 1995. The Endangered Species Act. *National Geographic* 187: 2–41.

Charlesworth, D. and B. Charlesworth. 1987. Inbreeding depression and its evolutionary consequences. *Annual Review of Ecology and Systematics* 18: 237–268.

Chase, A. 1986. *Playing God in Yellowstone: The Destruction of America's First National Park.* Atlantic Monthly Press, Boston, MA.

Chau, K. C. 1995. The Three Gorges Project of China: Resettlement prospects and problems. *Ambio* 24: 98–102.

Cheke, A. S. and J. F. Dahl. 1981. The status of bats on western Indian Ocean islands with special reference to *Pteropus. Mammalia* 45: 205–238.

Cherfas, J. 1991. Disappearing mushrooms: Another mass extinction? *Science* 254: 1458.

Cherfas, J. 1993. Backgarden biodiversity. *Conservation Biology* 7: 6–7.

Cherfas, J. 1996. Forbidden fruit and vegetables. *Plant Talk* 5: 17–19.

Chernela, J. 1987. Endangered ideologies: Tukano fishing taboos. *Cultural Survival Quarterly* 11: 50–52.

Chester, C. C. 1996. Controversy over the Yellowstone's biological resources. *Environment* 38 (6): 10–15, 34–36.

Chichilnisky, G. 1996. The economic value of Earth's resources. *Trends in Ecology and Evolution* 11: 135–140.

Christensen, N. L. et al. 1996. The report of the Ecological Society of America Committee on the Scientific Basis for Ecosystem Management. *Ecological Applications* 6: 665–692.

Church, R. L., D. M. Stoms and F. W. Davis. 1996. Reserve selection as a maximal covering location problem. *Biological Conservation* 76: 105–112.

Clark, C. 1992. Empirical evidence for the effect of tropical deforestation on climatic change. *Environmental Conservation* 19: 39–47.

Clark, T. W., R. P. Reading and A. L. Clark (eds.). 1994. *Endangered Species Recovery: Finding the Lessons, Improving the Process*. Island Press, Washington, D.C.

Clark, W. C. 1989. Managing planet Earth. *Scientific American* 261: 47–54.

Clay, J. 1991. Cultural survival and conservation: Lessons from the past twenty years. *In* M. L. Oldfield and J. B. Alcorn (eds.), *Biodiversity: Culture, Conservation and Ecodevelopment*, pp. 248–273. Westview Press, Boulder, CO.

Clemmons, J. R. and R. Buchholz (eds.). 1997. *Behavioral Approaches to Conservation in the Wild*. Cambridge University Press, New York.

Cleveland, D. A., D. Soleri and S. E. Smith. 1994. Do folk crop varieties have a role in sustainable agriculture? *BioScience* 44: 740–751.

Clewell, A. and J. Rieger. 1997. What practitioners need from restoration ecologists. *Restoration Ecology* 5: 350–354.

Coblentz, B. E. 1990. Exotic organisms: A dilemma for conservation biology. *Conservation Biology* 4: 261–265.

Coblentz, B. E. 1997. Subsistence consumption of coral reef fish suggests non-sustainable extraction. *Conservation Biology* 11: 559–561.

Cohn, J. P. 1991. New focus on wildlife health. *BioScience* 41: 448–450.

Cohn, J. P. 1996. New defenders of wildlife. *BioScience* 46: 11–14.

Collar, N. J., M. J. Cosby and A. J. Sattersfield. 1994. *Birds to Watch: The World List of Threatened Birds*. Birdlife Conservation Series No. 4. Birdlife International, Cambridge, United Kingdom.

Collett, J. and S. Karakashain (eds.). 1996. *Greening the College Curriculum: A Guide to Environmental Teaching in the Liberal Arts*. Island Press, Washington, D.C.

Collier, M. P, R. H. Webb and E. D. Andrews. 1997. Experimental flooding in Grand Canyon. *Scientific American* 276: 82–89.

Collins, N. M. and M. G. Morris. 1985. *Threatened Swallowtail Butterflies of the World*. IUCN, Gland, Switzerland.

Colwell, R. K. 1986. Community biology and sexual selection: Lessons from hummingbird flower mites. *In* T. J. Case and J. Diamond (eds.) *Ecological Communities*, pp. 406–424. Harper and Row Publishers, New York.

Commoner, B. 1971. *The Closing Circle*. Alfred A. Knopf, New York.

Conant, S. 1988. Saving endangered species by translocation. *BioScience* 38: 254–257.

Condit, R., S. P. Hubbel and R. B. Foster. 1992. Short-term dynamics of a Neotropical forest. *BioScience* 42: 822–828.

Connell, J. H. and E. Orias. 1964. The ecological regulation of species diversity. *American Naturalist* 98: 399–404.

Connor, E. F. and E. D. McCoy. 1979. The statistics and biology of the species-area relationship. *American Naturalist* 13: 791–833.

Conservation International. 1990. *The Rain Forest Imperative*. Conservation International, Washington, D.C.

Conway, W. G. 1988. Can technology aid species preservation? *In* E. O. Wilson and F. M. Peter (eds.), *Biodiversity*, pp. 199–208. Sinauer Associates, Sunderland, MA.

Cook, E. A. and N. H. van Lier. (eds.). 1994. *Landscape Planning and Ecological Networks*. Elsevier, Amsterdam.

Corlett, R. T. and I. M. Turner. 1996. The conservation value of small, isolated fragments of lowland tropical rain forest. *Trends in Ecology and Evolution* 11: 330–333.

Costanza, R., O. Segurea and J. Martinez-Alier. 1996. *Getting down to Earth: Practical Applications of Ecological Economics*. Island Press, Washington, D.C.

Costanza, R., R. d'Arge, R. de Groot, S. Farber and nine others. 1997. The value of the world's ecosystem services and natural capital. *Nature* 387: 253–260.

Cottam, G. 1990. Community dynamics on an artifical prairie. *In* W. R. Jordan III, M. E. Gilpin and J. D. Aber (eds.), *Restoration Ecology: A Synthetic Approach to Ecological Research*, pp. 257–270. Cambridge University Press, Cambridge.

Cowling, R. M., P. W. Rundel, B. B. Lamont, M. K. Arroyo and M. Arianoutsou. 1996. Plant diversity in mediterranean-climate regions. *Trends in Ecology and Evolution* 11: 362–366.

Cox, G. W. 1993. *Conservation Ecology*. W. C. Brown, Dubuque, IA.

Cox, P. A. 1997. *Nafanua: Saving the Samoan Rain Forest*. W. H. Freeman, New York.

Cox, P. A. and M. J. Balick. 1994. The ethnobotanical approach to drug discovery. *Scientific American* 270: 82–87.

Cox, P. A. and T. Elmqvist. 1991. Indigenous control of tropical rainforest reserves: An alternative strategy for conservation. *Ambio* 20: 317–321.

Cox, P. A. and T. Elmqvist. 1993. Ecocolonialism and indigenous knowledge systems: Village controlled rainforest preserves in Samoa. *Pacific Conservation Biology* 1: 6–13.

Cox, P. A. and T. Elmqvist. 1997. Ecocolonialism and indigenous-controlled rainforest preserves in Samoa. *Ambio* 26: 84–89.

Cox, P. A., T. Elmqvist, D. Pierson and W. E. Rainey. 1991. Flying foxes as strong interactors in South Pacific island ecosystems: A conservation hypothesis. *Conservation Biology* 5: 448–454.

Cree, A., C. H. Daugherty and J. M. Hay. 1995. Reproduction of a rare New Zealand reptile, the tuatara *(Sphenodon punctatus)*, on rat-free and rat-inhabited islands. *Conservation Biology* 9: 373–384.

Crow, J. F. and N. E. Morton. 1955. Measurement of gene frequency drift in small populations. *Evolution* 9: 202–214.

Crumpacker, D. W., S. W. Hodge, D. Friedley and W. P. Gregg, Jr. 1988. A preliminary assessment of the status of major terrestrial and wetland ecosystems on federal and Indian lands in the United States. *Conservation Biology* 2: 103–115.

Cullota, E. 1995. Many suspects to blame in Madagascar extinctions. *Science* 268: 156–1569.

Cully, A. 1996. Knowlton's cactus (*Pediocactus knowltonii*) reintroduction. *In* D. A. Falk , C. Miller and M. Olwell (eds.), *Restoring Diversity: Strategies for Reintroduction of Endangered Plants*. Island Press, Washington, D.C.

Cunningham, C. and J. Berger. 1997. *Horn of Darkness: Rhinos on the Edge*. Oxford University Press, New York.

Curio, E. 1996. Conservation needs ethology. *Trends in Ecology and Evolution* 11: 260–263.

Currie, D. J. 1991. Energy and large-scale patterns of animal- and plant-species richness. *American Naturalist* 137: 27–49.

Curtis, J. T. 1956. A prairie continuum in Wisconsin. *Ecology* 36: 558–566.

Dahl, A. L. 1986. *Review of the Protected Areas System in Oceania*. IUCN/UNEP, Gland, Switzerland.

Daily, G. C. (ed.). 1997. *Nature's Services: Societal Dependence on Ecosystem Services*. Island Press, Washington, D.C.

Daily, G. C. 1995. Restoring value to the world's degraded lands. *Science* 269: 350–354.

Dallmeier, F. (ed.) 1992. *Long-Term Monitoring of Biological Diversity in Tropical Forest Areas*. MAB Digest No. 11. UNESCO, Paris.

Daly, H. E. and J. B. Cobb, Jr. 1989. *For the Common Good: Redirecting the Economy Toward Community, the Environment and a Sustainable Future*. Beacon Press, Boston MA

Darling, J. D. 1988. Working with whales. *National Geographic* 174: 886–908.

Darwin, C. R. 1859. *On the Origin of Species*. John Murray, London.

Darwin, C. R. 1868. *The Variation of Animals and Plants Under Domestication*. Orange Judd and Company, New York.

Darwin, C. R. 1876. *The Effects of Cross and Self Fertilization in the Vegetable Kingdom*. John Murray, London.

Dasgupta, P. S. 1995. Population, poverty and the local environment. *Scientific American* 272: 40–45.

Dasmann, R. F. 1987. World parks, people and land use. *In* R. Hermann and T. B. Craig (eds.), *Conference on Science in National Parks: The Fourth Triennial Conference on Research in National Parks and Equivalent Reserves*, pp. 122–127. The George Wright Society and the U.S. National Parks Service.

Dasmann, R. F. 1991. The importance of cultural and biological diversity. *In* M. L. Oldfield and J. B. Alcorn (eds.), *Biodiversity: Culture, Conservation and Ecodevelopment*, pp. 7–15. Westview Press, Boulder, CO.

Dasmann, R. F., J. P. Milton and P. H. Freeman. 1973. *Ecological Principles for Economic Development*. John Wiley & Sons, London.

Daugherty, C. H., A. Cree, J. M. Hay and M. B. Thompson. 1990. Neglected taxonomy and continuing extinctions of tuatara (*Sphenodon*). *Science*. 347: 177–179.

Davis, M. B. and C. Zabinski. 1992. Changes in geographical range resulting from greenhouse warming: Effects on biodiversity in forests. *In* R. Peters and T. E. Lovejoy. (eds.), *Global Warming and Biological Diversity*, pp. 297–308. Yale University Press, New Haven, CT.

Davis, S. D. et al. 1986. *Plants In Danger: What Do We Know?* IUCN, Gland, Switzerland.

Davis, S. H. and A. Wali. 1994. Indigenous land tenure and tropical forest management in Latin America. *Ambio* 23: 485–490.

Davis, W. 1995. *One River: Explorations and Discoveries in the Amazon Rainforest*. Simon & Schuster, New York.

Deardon, P. 1995. Park literacy and conservation. *Conservation Biology* 9: 1654–1656.

Decker, D. J., M. E. Krasny, G. R. Goff, C. R. Smith and D. W. Gross (eds.). 1991. *Challenges in the Conservation of Biological Resources: A Practitioner's Guide*. Westview Press, Boulder, CO.

Del Tredici, P. 1991. Ginkgos and people: A thousand years of interaction. *Arnoldia* 51: 2–15.

DeMauro, M. M. 1993. Relationship of breeding system to rarity in the lakeside daisy (*Hymenoxys acaulis* var. *glabra*). *Conservation Biology* 7: 542–550.

Dennis, B., P. L. Munholland and J. M. Scott. 1991. Estimation of growth and extinction parameters for endangered species. *Ecological Monographs* 61: 115–143.

Denslow, J. S. and C. Padoch, (eds.). 1988. *People of the Tropical Rain Forest*. University of California Press, Berkeley, CA.

Devall, B. and G. Sessions. 1985. *Deep Ecology: Living as if Nature Mattered*. Gibbs Smith Publisher, Salt Lake City, UT.

Diamond, A. W. 1985. The selection of critical areas and current conservation efforts in tropical forest birds. *In* A. W. Diamond and T. E. Lovejoy (eds.), *Conservation of Tropical Forest Birds*, pp. 33–48. Technical Publication No. 4, International Council for Bird Preservation, Cambridge, UK.

Diamond, J. M. 1975. The island dilemma: Lessons of modern biogeographic studies for the design of natural reserves. *Biological Conservation* 7: 129–146.

Diamond, J. M. 1984. "Normal" extinctions of isolated populations. *In* M. H. Nitecki, (ed.), *Extinctions*, pp. 191–245. University of Chicago Press, Chicago.

Diamond, J. M. 1987. Extant unless proven extinct? Or, extinct unless proven extant? *Conservation Biology* 1: 77–81.

Diamond, J. M. 1988a. Factors controlling species diversity: Overview and synthesis. *Annals of the Missouri Botanical Gardens* 75: 117–129.

Diamond, J. M. 1988b. Red books or green lists? *Nature* 332: 304–305.

Diamond, J. M. 1990. Reflections on goals and on the relationship between theory and practice. *In* W. R. Jordan III, M. E. Gilpin and J. D. Aber. (eds.), *Restoration Ecology: A Synthetic Approach to Ecological Research*, pp. 329–336. Cambridge University Press, Cambridge.

Diamond, J. M. The design of a nature reserve system for Indonesian New Guinea. *In* M. E. Soulé (ed.), *Conservation Biology: The Science of Scarcity and Diversity*, pp. 485–503. Sinauer Associates, Sunderland, MA.

Diamond, J. M., K. D. Bishop and S. van Balen. 1987. Bird survival in an isolated Java woodland: Island or mirror? *Conservation Biology* 4: 417–422.

Didham, R. K. 1996. Insects in fragmented forests: A functional approach. *Trends in Evolution and Ecology* 11: 255–260.

Dietz, J. M., L. A. Dietz and E. Y. Nagagata. 1994. The effective use of flagship species for conservation of biodiversity: The example of lion tamarins in Brazil. *In* P. J. S. Olney, G. M. Mace and A. T. C. Feistner (eds.), *Creative Conservation: Interactive Manangement of Wild and Captive Animals*, Chapman and Hall, London.

Dinerstein, E. and E. D. Wikramanayake. 1993. Beyond hotspots: How to prioritize investments to conserve biodiversity in the Indo-Pacific region. *Conservation Biology* 7: 53–65.

Dinerstein, E. and G. F. McCracken. 1990. Endangered greater one-horned rhinoceros carry high levels of genetic variation. *Conservation Biology* 4: 417–422.

Dingwall, P., J. Harrison and J. A. McNeely (eds.). 1994. *Protecting Nature: Regional Reviews of Protected Areas*. IUCN Publications, Gland, Switzerland.

Doak, D. F. and L. S. Mills. 1994. A useful role for theory in conservation. *Ecology* 75: 615–626.

Dobson, A. 1995. Biodiversity and human health. *Trends in Ecology and Evolution* 10: 390–392.

Dobson, A. P. and J. H. Poole. 1992. Ivory: Why the ban must stay! *Conservation Biology* 6: 149–151.

Dobson, A. P., A. D. Bradshaw and A. J. M. Baker. 1997b. Hopes for the future: Restoration ecology and conservation biology. *Science* 277: 515–522.

Dobson, A. P., J. P. Rodriguez, W. M. Roberts and D. S. Wilcove. 1997a. Geographic distribution of endangered species in the United States. *Science* 275: 550–554.

Docherty, D. E. and R. I. Romaine. 1983. Inclusion body disease of cranes: A serological follow-up to the 1978 die-off. *Avian Diseases* 27: 830–835.

Dodd, C. K. and R. A. Seigel. 1991. Relocation, repatriation and translocation of amphibians and reptiles: Are they conservation strategies that work? *Herpetologica* 47: 336–350.

Dodd, C. K., Jr. 1990. Effects of habitat fragmentation on a stream-dwelling species, the flattened musk turtle *Stenotherus depressus*. *Biological Conservation* 54: 33–45.

Dogsé, P. and B. von Droste. 1990. *Debt-For-Nature Exchanges and Biosphere Reserves*. UNESCO, Paris.

Donázar, J. A. and C. Fernández. 1990. Population trends of the griffon vulture *Gyps fulvus* in Northern Spain between 1969 and 1989 in relation to conservation measures. *Biological Conservation* 53: 83–91.

Dowling, T. E. and M. R. Childs. 1992. Impact of hybridization on a threatened trout of the southwestern United States. *Conservation Biology* 6: 355–364.

Downing, T. E., S. B. Hecht, H. A. Pearson and C. Garcia-Downing. 1992. *Development or Destruction: The Conversion of Tropical Forest into Pasture in Latin America*. Westview Press, Boulder, CO.

Drake, J. A., et al. (eds.). 1989. *Biological Invasions: A Global Perspective*. SCOPE Report No. 37. John Wiley, New York.

Drayton, B. and R. Primack. 1996. Plant species lost in an isolated conservation area in metropolitan Boston from 1894 to 1993. *Conservation Biology* 10: 30–40.

Dregné, H. E. 1983. *Desertification of Arid Lands*. Academic Press, New York.

Dresser, B. L. 1988. Cryobiology, embryo transfer and artificial insemination in ex situ animal conservation programs. *In* E. O. Wilson and F. M. Peter (eds.) *Biodiversity*, pp. 296–308. National Academy Press, Washington, D.C.

Drost, C. A. and G. M. Fellers. 1996. Collapse of a regional frog fauna in the Yosemite Area of the California Sierra Nevada, USA. *Conservation Biology* 10: 414–426.

Duffus, D. A. and P. Dearden. 1990. Non-consumptive wildlife-oriented recreation: A conceptual framework. *Biological Conservation* 53: 213–231.

Duffy, E. and A. S. Watts (eds.). 1971. *The Scientific Management of Animal and Plant Communities for Conservation*. Blackwell Scientific Publications, Oxford.

Dufour, D. L. 1990. Use of tropical rainforest by native Amazonians. *BioScience* 40: 652–659.

Dugan, P. (ed.). 1993. *Wetlands in Danger: A World Conservation Atlas*. Oxford University Press, New York.

Dwyer, J. C. and I. D. Hodge. 1996. *Countryside in Trust: Land Management by Conservation, Recreation and Amenity Organizations*. John Wiley and Sons, Chichester, UK.

Dwyer, L. E., D. D. Murphy and P. R. Ehrlich. 1995. Property rights case law and the challenge to the Endangered Species Act. *Conservation Biology* 9: 725–742.

Eales, S. 1992. *Earthtoons: The First Book of Ecohumor*. Warner Books, New York.

Easter-Pilcher, A. 1996. Implementing the Endangered Species Act: Assessing the listing of species as endangered or threatened. *BioScience* 46: 355–363.

Ebenhard, T. 1995. Conservation breeding as a tool for saving animal species from extinction. *Trends in Ecology and Evolution* 10: 438–443.

Eberhardt, L. L. and J. M. Thomas. 1991. Designing environmental field studies. *Ecological Monographs* 61: 53–73.

Echelle, A. A. and A. F. Echelle. 1997. Genetic introgression of endemic taxa by non-natives: a case study with Leon Springs pupfish and sheepshead minnow. *Conservation Biology* 11: 153–161.

Eckstrom, C. K. 1996. A wilderness of water: Pantanal. *Audubon* 98(2): 54–65.

Edmonds, R. L. 1991. The Sanxia (Three Gorges) project: The environmental argument surrounding China's super dam. *Global Ecology and Biogeography Letters* 1: 105–125.

Edwards, M. 1994. Pollution in the former USSR: Lethal legacy. *National Geographic* 186(8): 70–99.

Edwards, P. J., R. M. May and N. R. Webb (eds.). 1994. *Large-scale Ecology and Conservation Biology*. Blackwell Scientific Publications, Oxford.

Ehrenfeld, D. W. 1970. *Biological Conservation*. Holt, Rinehart and Winston, New York.

Ehrenfeld, D. W. 1978. *The Arrogance of Humanism*. Oxford University Press, New York.

Ehrenfeld, D. W. 1989. Hard times for diversity. *In* D. Western and M. Pearl (eds.), *Conservation for the Twenty-first Century*, pp. 247–250. Oxford University Press, New York.

Ehrlich, A. H. and P. R. Ehrlich. 1996. *Betrayal of Science and Reason: How Anti-Environmental Rhetoric Threatens Our Future*. Island Press, Washington, D.C.

Ehrlich, P. R. and A. H. Ehrlich. 1968. *The Population Bomb*. Amereon, Mattituck, NY.

Ehrlich, P. R. and A. H. Ehrlich. 1981. *Extinction: The Causes and Consequences of the Disappearance of Species*. Random House, New York.

Ehrlich, P. R. and D. D. Murphy. 1987. Conservation lessons from long-term studies of checkerspot butterflies. *Conservation Biology* 1: 122–131.

Ehrlich, P. R. and H. A. Mooney. 1983. Extinction, substitution and ecosystem services. *BioScience* 33: 248–254.

Ehrlich, P. R. and P. H. Raven. 1964. Butterflies and plants: A study in coevolution. *Evolution* 18: 586–608.

Eisner, T. 1991. Chemical prospecting: A proposal for action. *In* F. H. Bormann and S. R. Kellert (eds.), *Ecology, Economics, Ethics: The Broken Circle*, pp. 196–202. Yale University Press, New Haven, CT.

Eisner, T. and E. A. Beiring. 1994. Biotic exploration fund: Protecting biodiversity through chemical prospecting. *BioScience* 44: 95–98.

Elfring, C. 1989. Preserving land through local land trusts. *BioScience* 39: 71–74.

Elliot, R. 1992. Intrinsic value, environmental obligation and naturalness. *The Monist* 75: 138–160.

Ellis, D. H., G. F. Gee and C. M. Mirande (eds.). 1996. *Cranes: Their Biology, Husbandry and Conservation*. Hancock House Publishers, Blaine, WA.

Ellis, R. 1992. Whale kill begins anew. *Audubon* 94: 20–22.

Ellstrand, N. C. 1992. Gene flow by pollen: Implications for plant conservation genetics. *Oikos* 63: 77–86.

Ellstrand, N. C. and D. R. Elam. 1993. Population genetic consequences of small population size: Implications for plant conservation. *Annual Review of Ecology and Systematics* 24: 217–242.

Elton, C. S. 1958. *The Ecology of Invasions*. John Wiley, New York.

Emerson, R. W. 1836. *Nature*. James Monroe and Co., Boston, MA.

Enderson, J. H., et al. 1995. Population changes in North American peregrines. *Transactions of the 60th North American Wildlife and Natural Resource Conference*, 142–161.

Erdelon, W. 1988. Forest ecosystems and nature conservation in Sri Lanka. *Biological Conservation* 43: 115–135.

Erwin, T. L. 1982. Tropical forests: Their richness in Coleoptera and other arthropod species. *Coleopterists Bulletin*. 36: 74–75.

Erwin, T. L. 1983. Beetles and other insects of tropical forest canopies at Manaus, Brazil, sampled by insecticidal fogging. *In* S. L. Sutton, T. C. Whitmore and A. C. Chadwick (eds.), *Tropical Rain Forest: Ecology and Management*, pp. 59–75. Blackwell Scientific Publications, Edinburgh.

Essen, P. 1994. Tree mortality patterns after experimental fragmentation of an old-growth conifer forest. *Biological Conservation* 68: 19–28.

Estes, J. A. 1996. The influence of large, mobile predators in aquatic food webs: Examples from sea otters and kelp forests. *In* S. P. R. Greenstreet and M. L. Tasker (eds.), *Aquatic Predators and their Prey*, pp. 65–72. Fishing News Books, Blackwell Scientific Publications, Malden, MA.

Estes, J. A. and D. O. Duggins. 1995. Sea otters and kelp forests in Alaska: Generality and variation in a community ecological paradigm. *Ecological Monographs* 65: 75–100.

Etter, R. J. and J. F. Grassle. 1992. Patterns of species diversity in the deep sea as a function of sediment particle size diversity. *Nature* 360: 575–578.

Eudey, A. A. 1987. *Action Plan for Asian Primate Conservation: 1987–1991*. IUCN Species Survival Commission Primate Specialist Group, IUCN, Gland, Switzerland.

Faith, D. P. 1994. Phylogenetic diversity: A general framework for the prediction of future diversity. *In* P. L. Forey, C. J. Humphries and R. I. Vane-Wright (eds.), *Systematics and Conservation Evaluation*. Oxford University Press, New York.

Falk, D. A. 1991. Joining biological and economic models for conserving plant genetic diversity. *In* D. A. Falk and K. E. Holsinger (eds.), *Genetics and Conservation of Rare Plants*, pp. 209–224. Oxford University Press, New York.

Falk, D. A. and K. E. Holsinger (eds.). 1991. *Genetics and Conservation of Rare Plants*. Oxford University Press, New York.

Falk, D. A. and P. Olwell. 1992. Scientific and policy considerations in restoration and reintroduction of endangered species. *Rhodora* 94: 287–315.

Falk, D. A., C. I. Millar and M. Olwell (eds.). 1996. *Restoring Diversity: Strategies for Reintroduction of Endangered Plants*. Island Press, Washington, D.C.

Farnsworth, E. J. and J. Rosovsky. 1993. The ethics of ecological field experimentation. *Conservation Biology* 7: 463–472.

Farnsworth, N. R. 1988. Screening plants for new medicines. *In* E. O. Wilson and F. M. Peter (eds.), *Biodiversity*, pp. 83–97. National Academy Press, Washington, D.C.

Fearnside, P. M. 1987. Deforestation and international economic development projects in Brazilian Amazonia. *Conservation Biology* 1: 214–221.

Fearnside, P. M. 1990. Predominant land uses in Brazilian Amazonia. *In* A. Anderson (ed.), *Alternatives to Deforestation: Steps Toward Sustainable Use of the Amazon Rain Forest*, pp. 233–251. Columbia University Press, Irvington, NY.

Fearnside, P. M. 1996. Brazil. *In* C. S. Harcourt and J. A. Sayer (eds.), *The Conservation Atlas of Tropical Forests: The Americas*. Simon and Schuster, New York.

Fearnside, P. M. and J. Ferraz. 1995. A conservation gap analysis of Brazil's Amazonian vegetation. *Conservation Biology* 9: 1134–1148.

Ferry, L. 1995. *The New Ecological Order*. University of Chicago Press, Chicago.

Fillon, F. L., A. Jacquemot and R. Reid. 1985. *The Importance of Wildlife to Canadians*. Canadian Wildlife Service, Ottawa.

Fischer, A. G. 1960. Latitudinal variations in organic diversity. *Evolution* 14: 64–81.

Fischer, H. 1995. *Wolf Wars: The Remarkable Inside Story of the Restoration of Wolves to Yellowstone*. Falcon Press, Helena, MT.

Fitzgerald, S. 1989. *International Wildlife Trade: Whose Business Is It?* World Wildlife Fund, Washington, D.C.

Fitzgibbon, C. D., H. Mogaka and J. H. Fanshawe. 1995. Subsistence hunting in Arabuko-Sokoke Forest, Kenya and its effects on mammal populations. *Conservation Biology* 9: 1116–1127.

Flather, C. H. and J. R. Sauer. 1996. Using landscape ecology to test hypotheses about large-scale abundance patterns in migratory birds. *Ecology* 77: 28–35.

Fleischner, T. L. 1994. Ecological costs of livestock grazing in western North America. *Conservation Biology* 8: 629–644.

Foose, T. J. 1983. The relevance of captive populations to the conservation of biotic diversity. *In* C. M. Schonewald-Cox, S. M. Chambers, B. MacBryde and L. Thomas (eds.). *Genetics and Conservation*, pp. 374–401. Benjamin/Cummings, Menlo Park, CA.

Forman, R. T. 1995. *Land Mosaics: The Ecology of Landscapes and Regions*. Cambridge University Press, New York.

Forman, R. T. and M. Godron. 1981. Patches and structural components for a landscape ecology. *BioScience* 31: 733–740.

Forrester, D. J. 1971. Bighorn sheep lungworm-pneumonia complex. *In* J. W. Davis and R. C. Anderson (eds.). *Parasitic Diseases of Wild Mammals*, pp. 158–173. Iowa State University Press, Ames, IA.

Fossey, D. 1990. *Gorillas in the Mist*. Houghton Mifflin, Boston.

Fox, J., P. Yonzon and N. Podger. 1996. Mapping conflicts between biodiversity and human needs in Langtang National Park. *Conservation Biology* 10: 562–569.

Frankel, O., A. Brown and J. Burdon. 1995. *The Conservation of Plants*. Cambridge University Press, Cambridge.

Frankham, R. 1996. Relationships of genetic variation to population size in wildlife. *Conservation Biology* 10: 1500–1508.

Franklin, I. R. 1980. Evolutionary change in small populations. *In* M. E. Soulé and B. A. Wilcox (eds.). *Conservation Biology: An Evolutionary-Ecological Perspective*, pp. 135–149. Sinauer, Sunderland, MA.

Frazer, N. B. 1992. Sea turtle conservation and halfway technology. *Conservation Biology* 6: 179–184.

Fredrickson, J. K. and T. C. Onstatt. 1996. Microbes deep inside Earth. *Scientific American* 275: 68–73.

Freeland, W. J. and W. J. Boulton. 1992. Coevolution of food webs: Parasites, predators and plant secondary compounds. *Biotropica* (Special Issue) 24: 309–327.

Freese, C. H. (ed.). 1997. *Harvesting Wild Species: Implications for Biodiversity Conservation*. Johns Hopkins University Press, Baltimore, MD.

French, H. F. 1994. Making environmental treaties work. *Scientific American* 271: 94–97.

Fricke, H. and K. Hissmann. 1990. Natural habitat of the coelocanths. *Nature* 346: 323–324.

Fuccilo, D., L. Sears and P. Stapleton. 1998. *Biodiversity in Trust: Conservation and Use of Plant Genetic Resources in CGIAR Centres*. Cambride University Press, New York.

Fujita, M. S. and M. D. Tuttle. 1991. Flying foxes (Chiroptera: Pteropodidae): Threatened animals of key ecological and economic importance. *Conservation Biology* 5: 455–463.

Fuller, R. J., R. D. Gregory, D. W. Gibbons, J. H. Marchant, et al. 1995. Population declines and range contractions among lowland farmland birds in Britain. *Conservation Biology* 9: 1425–1441.

Funch, P. and R. Kristensen. 1995. Cycliophora is a new phylum with affinities to Entoprocta and Ectoprocta (*Symbion pandora*). *Nature* 378: 711–714.

Futuyma, D. J. 1995. *Science on Trial: The Case for Evolution*. Revised Edition. Sinauer Associates, Sunderland, MA.

Futuyma, D. J. 1998. *Evolutionary Biology*, 3rd Edition. Sinauer Associates, Sunderland, MA.

Gadgil, M. and R. Guha. 1992. *This Fissured Land: An Ecological History of India*. Oxford University Press, Oxford.

Gage, J. D. and P. A. Tyler. 1991. *Deep-Sea Biology: A Natural History of Organisms at the Deep Seafloor*. Cambridge University Press, Cambridge.

Galatowitsch, S. M. and A. G. Van der Valk. 1996. *Restoring Prairie Wetlands: An Ecological Approach*. Iowa State University Press, Ames, IA.

Galdikas, B. 1995. *Reflections of Eden: My Years with the Orangutans of Borneo*. Little Brown, Boston.

Game, M. and G. F. Peterken. 1984. Nature reserve selection strategies in the woodlands of Central Lincolnshire, England. *Biological Conservation* 29: 157–181.

Gaston, K. J. 1991. The magnitude of global insect species richness. *Conservation Biology* 5: 283–296.

Gaston, K. J. 1994. Spatial patterns of species description: How is our knowledge of the global insect fauna growing? *Biological Conservation* 67: 37–40.

Gates, D. M. 1993. *Climate Change and Its Biological Consequences*. Sinauer Associates, Sunderland, MA.

Gentry, A. H. 1986. Endemism in tropical versus temperate plant communities. *In* M. E. Soulé (ed.), *Conservation Biology: The Science of Scarcity and Diversity*, pp. 153–181. Sinauer Associates, Sunderland, MA.
Gerrodette, T. and W. G. Gilmartin. 1990. Demographic consequences of changing pupping and hauling sites of the Hawaiian monk seal. *Conservation Biology* 4: 423–430.
Gersh, J. and R. Pickert. 1991. Land-use modeling: Accommodating growth while conserving biological resources in Dutchess County, New York. *In* D. J. Decker, M. E. Krasnyk, G. R. Goff, C. R. Smith and D. W. Gross (eds.), *Challenges in the Conservation of Biological Resources: A Practitioner's Guide*, pp. 233–242. Westview Press, Boulder, CO.
Gibbons, A. 1992. Conservation biology in the fast lane. *Science*. 255: 20–22.
Giese, M. 1996. Effects of human activity on adelie penguin *Pygoscelis adeliae* breeding success. *Biological Conservation* 75: 157–164.
Gigon, A., R. Langenauer, C. Meier and B. Nienergelt. 1998. Blue Lists of the successfully stabilized or promoted animal and plant species of the Red Lists. Methods and application in northern Switzerland. *Verhöff. Geobot. Inst.* ETH, Zürich.
Gilbert, G. S. and S. P. Hubbell. 1996. Plant diseases and the conservation of tropical forests. *BioScience* 46: 98–106.
Gilpin, M. E. 1990. Experimental community assembly: Competition, community structure and the order of species introductions. *In* W. R. Jordan III, M. E. Gilpin and J. D. Aber (eds.), *Restoration Ecology: A Synthetic Approach to Ecological Research*, pp. 151–161. Cambridge University Press, Cambridge.
Gilpin M. and I. Hanski. 1991. *Metapopulation dynamics: Empirical and Theoretical Investigations.* Academic Press, New York.
Gilpin, M. E. and M. E. Soulé. 1986. Minimum viable populations: Processes of species extinction. *In* M. E. Soulé (ed.), *Conservation Biology: The Science of Scarcity and Diversity*, pp. 19–34. Sinauer Associates, Sunderland, MA.
Giono, J. 1989. *The Man Who Planted Trees*. Collins Dove, Melbourne , Australia.
Giovannoni, S. J., T. B. Britschgi, C. L. Moyer and K. G. Field. 1990. Genetic diversity in Sargasso Sea bacterioplankton. *Nature* 345: 60–63.
Gipps, J. H. W. (ed.). 1991. *Beyond Captive Breeding: Reintroducing Endangered Species Through Captive Breeding*. Zoological Society of London Symposia, No. 62. Clarendon Press, Oxford.
Girdner, B. 1992. The condor will soar anew: Zoo program brings California birds back from the brink of extinction. *The Boston Globe*. January 6, 1992.
Gittleman, J. L. 1994. Are the pandas successful specialists or evolutionary failures? *BioScience* 44: 456–464.
Given, D. R. 1995. *Principles and Practice of Plant Conservation*. Timber Press, Portland, OR.
Glenn, W. 1997. A model for cooperative land management: The Malpai Borderlands Group. *Society for Conservation Biology Newsletter* 4 (2): 1–2.
Glowka, L., F. Burhenne-Guilman and H. Synge. 1994. *A Guide to the Convention on Biological Diversity.* IUCN, Gland, Switzerland.
Godoy, R. A., R. Lubowski and A. Markandya. 1993. A method for the economic valuation of non-timber tropical forest products. *Economic Botany* 47: 220–233.
Goerck, J. M. 1997. Patterns of rarity in the birds of the Atlantic forest of Brazil. *Conservation Biology* 11: 112–118.
Goldingay, R. and H. Possingham. 1995. Area requirements for viable populations of the Australian gliding marsupial (*Petaurus australis*). *Biological Conservation* 73: 161–167.
Goldman, B. and F. H. Talbot. 1976. Aspects of the ecology of coral reef fishes. *In* O. A. Jones and R. Endean (eds.), *Biology and Geology of Coral Reefs*, Vol. 3, pp. 125–154 . Academic Press, New York.
Goldschmidt, T. 1996. *Darwin's Dreampond: Drama in Lake Victoria*. MIT Press, Cambridge, MA.
Goldsmith, B. (ed.). 1991. *Monitoring for Conservation and Ecology*. Chapman and Hall, New York.
Gomez-Pompa, A. and A. Kaus. 1992. Taming the wilderness myth. *BioScience* 42: 271–279.
Gomez-Pompa, A. and A. Kaus. 1988. Conservation by traditional cultures in the tropics. *In* V. Martin (ed.), *For the Conservation of Earth*. Fulcrum Inc., Golden, CO.
Goodland, R. J. A. 1990. The World Bank's new environmental policy for dams and reservoirs. *Water Resources Development* 6: 226–239.
Goodland, R. J. A. 1992. Environmental priorities for financing institutions. *Environmental Conservation* 19: 9–22.
Gore, A. 1992. *Earth in the Balance: Ecology and the Human Spirit*. Houghton Mifflin, New York.
Gosselink, J. G. et al. 1990. Landscape conservation in a forested wetland watershed. *BioScience* 40: 588–600.
Gotelli, N. J. 1995. *A Primer of Ecology*. Sinauer Associates, Sunderland, MA.
Grabherr, G., M. Dottfried and H. Pauli. 1994. Climate effects on mountain plants. *Nature* 369: 448.
Gradwohl, J. and R. Greenberg. 1988. *Saving the Tropical Forest*. EARTHSCAN Ltd., London.
Graham, F. 1990. Kite vs. stork. *Audubon* 92: 104–111.
Grant, P. R. and B. R. Grant. 1992. Darwin's finches: Genetically effective population sizes. *Ecology* 73: 766–784.
Grant, P. R. and B. R. Grant. 1997. The rarest of Darwin's finches. Conservation Biology11: 119–126.
Grassle, J. F. 1985. Hydrothermal vent animals: Distribution and biology. *Science* 229: 713–717.
Grassle, J. F. 1991. Deep-sea benthic biodiversity. *BioScience* 41: 464–469.
Grassle, J. F., P. Lasserre, A. D. McIntyre and G. C. Ray. 1991. Marine biodiversity and ecosystem function. *Biology International*. Special Issue 23: i-iv, 1–19.
Green, B. H. 1989. Conservation in cultural landscapes. *In* D. Western and M. Pearl (eds.), *Conservation for the Twenty-First Century*, pp. 182–198. Oxford University Press, New York.

Green, G. N. and R. W. Sussman. 1990. Deforestation history of the eastern rain forests of Madagascar from satellite images. *Science* 248: 212–215.

Gregg, W. P., Jr. 1991. MAB Biosphere Reserves and conservation of traditional land use systems. *In* M. L. Oldfield and J. B. Alcorn (eds.), *Biodiversity: Culture, Conservation and Ecodevelopment* , pp. 274–294. Westview Press, Boulder, CO.

Greuter, W. 1995. Extinction in Mediterranean areas. *In* J. H. Lawton and R. M. May. *Extinction Rates*. pp. 88–97. Oxford University Press, Oxford.

Griffith, B., J. M. Scott, J. W. Carpenter and C. Reed. 1989. Translocation as a species conservation tool: Status and strategy. *Science* 245: 477–480.

Grifo, F. and J. Rosenthal (eds.). 1997. *Biodiversity and Human Health*. Island Press, Washington, D.C.

Grigg, R. W. and D. Epp. 1989. Critical depth for the survival of coral islands: Effects on the Hawaiian archipelago. *Science* 243: 638–641.

Groom, M. J. and N. Schumaker. 1993. Evaluating landscape change: Patterns of worldwide deforestation and local fragmentation. *In* P. M. Kareiva, J. G. Kingsolver and R. B. Huey (eds.), *Biotic Interactions and Global Change*, pp. 24–44. Sinauer Associates, Sunderland, MA.

Gross, D. W., B. T. Wilkins, R. R. Quinn and A. E. Zepp. 1991. Local land protection and planning efforts. *In* D. J. Decker, M. E. Krasny, G. R. Goff, C. R. Smith and D. W. Gross (eds.), *Challenges in the Conservation of Biological Resources: A Practitioner's Guide*, pp. 355–366 . Westview Press, Boulder, CO.

Grove, N. 1988. Quietly conserving nature. *National Geographic* 174 (1): 818–844.

Grove, R. H. 1990. Colonial conservation, ecological hegemony and popular resistence: Towards a global sysnthesis. *In* J. M. MacKenzie (ed.), *Imperialism and the Natural World*. University of Manchester Press, Manchester.

Grove, R. H. 1992. Origins of Western environmentalism. *Scientific American* 267: 42–47.

Grumbine, E. R. 1993. *Ghost Bears: Exploring the Biodiversity Crisis*. Island Press, Washington, D.C.

Grumbine, E. R. 1994a. What is ecosystem management? *Conservation Biology* 8: 27–38.

Grumbine, E. R. 1994b. *Environmental Policy and Biodiversity*. Island Press, Washington, D.C.

Guerrant, E. O. 1992. Genetic and demographic considerations in the sampling and reintroduction of rare plants. *In* P. L. Fiedler and S. K. Jain (eds.), *Conservation Biology: The Theory and Practice of Nature Conservation, Preservation and Management*, pp. 321–344. Chapman and Hall, New York.

Guerrant, E. O. and B. M. Pavlik. 1998. Reintroduction of rare plants: Genetics, demography and the role of *ex-situ* conservation methods. *In* P. L. Fiedler and P. M. Kareiva (eds.), *Conservation Biology: For the Coming Decade*. Chapman and Hall, New York.

Gullison, R. E. and E. C. Losos. 1993. The role of foreign debt in deforestation in Latin America. *Conservation Biology* 7: 140–147.

Gupta, T. A. and A. Guleria. 1982. *Non-wood Forest Products from India*. IBH Publishing Co., New Delhi.

Guzman, H. M. 1991. Restoration of coral reefs in Pacific Costa Rica. *Conservation Biology* 5: 189–195.

Haas, P. M., M. A. Levy and E. A. Parson. 1992. Appraising the Earth Summit: How should we judge UNCED's success? *Environment* 34 (8): 7–35.

Hafernik, J. E., Jr. 1992. Threats to invertebrate biodiversity: Implications for conservation strategies. *In* P. L. Fiedler and S. K. Jain (eds.), *Conservation Biology: The Theory and Practice of Nature Conservation, Preservation and Management* pp. 171–195. Chapman and Hall, New York.

Hails, A. J. (ed.). 1996. *Wetlands, Biodiversity and the Ramsar Convention: The Role of the Convention on Wetlands in the Conservation and Wise Use of Biodiversity*. Ramsar Convention Bureau, Gland, Switzerland.

Hair, J. D. 1988. The economics of conserving wetlands: A widening circle. Paper presented at Workshop in Economics, IUCN General Assembly, 4–5 February 1988, Costa Rica.

Hair, J. D. and G. A. Pomerantz. 1987. The educational value of wildlife. *In* D. J. Decker and G. R. Goff (eds.). *Valuing Wildlife: Economic and Social Perspectives*, pp. 197–207. Westview Press, Boulder, CO.

Hall, A. V., B. de Winter, S. P. Fourie and T. H. Arnold. 1984. Threatened plants in Southern Africa. *Biological Conservation* 28: 5–20.

Hall, S. J. G. and J. Ruane. 1993. Livestock breeds and their conservation: A global overview. *Conservation Biology* 7: 815–826.

Halpern, C. B. and T. A. Spies. 1995. Plant diversity in natural and managed forests of the Pacific Northwest. *Ecological Applications* 5: 913–935.

Halvorson, W. L. and G. E. Davis (eds.). 1996. *Science and Ecosystem Management in the National Parks*. University of Arizona, Tucson.

Hamilton, M. B. 1994. Ex situ conservation of wild plant species: Time to reassess the genetic assumptions and implications of seed banks. *Conservation Biology* 8: 39–49.

Hammond, P. M. 1992. Species Inventory. *In* WCMC, *Global Diversity: Status of the Earth's Living Resources*. pp. 17–39. Chapman and Hall, London.

Hamrick, J. L., M. J. W. Godt, D. A. Murawski and M. D. Loveless. 1991. Correlations between species traits and allozyme diversity: Implications for conservation biology. *In* D. A. Falk and K. E. Holsinger (eds.), *Genetics and Conservation of Rare Plants*, pp. 75–86. Oxford University Press, New York.

Hamrick, J. L., Y. B. Linhart and J. B. Mitton. 1979. Relationships between life history characteristics and electrophoretically detectable genetic variation in plants. *Annual Review of Ecology and Systematics* 10: 173–200.

Hanley, N. and C. Spash. 1994. *Cost-Benefit Analysis and the Environment*. Edward Elgar Publishing, Cheltenham, UK.

Hansen, A. J., S. L. Garman, J. F. Weigand, D. L. Urban, W. C. McComb and M. G. Raphael. 1995. Alternative silvicultural regimes in the Pacific Northwest: Simulations of ecological and economic effects. *Ecological Applications* 5: 535–555.

Hansen, A. J., T. A. Spies, F. J. Swanson and J. L. Ohmann. 1991. Conserving biodiversity in managed forests. *BioScience* 41: 382–392.

Hanski, I. and M. Gilpin. 1991. Metapopulation dynamics: Brief history and conceptual domain. *Biological Journal of the Linnean Society* 42: 3–16.

Hanski, I., A. Moilanen and M. Gyllenberg. 1996. Minimum viable metapopulation size. *American Naturalist* 147: 527–541.

Hanski, I. and D. Simberloff. 1997. The metapopulation approach, its history, conceptual domain and application to conservation. *In* I. Hanski and D. Simberloff (eds.), *Metapopulation Biology*, pp. 5–26. Academic Press, Inc., San Diego, CA.

Hansson, L., L. Fahrig and G. Merriam (eds.). 1995. *Mosaic Landscapes and Ecological Processes.* Chapman and Hall, London.

Harcourt, A. H. 1995. Population viability estimates: Theory and practice for a wild gorilla population. *Conservation Biology* 9: 134–142.

Hardin, G. 1968. The tragedy of the commons. *Science* 162: 1243–1248.

Hardin, G. 1985. *Filters Against Folly: How to Survive Despite Economists, Ecologists and the Merely Eloquent.* Viking Press, New York.

Hardin, G. 1993. *Living Within Limits: Ecology, Economics and Population Taboos.* Oxford University Press, New York.

Hargrove, E. C. (ed.). 1986. *Religion and the Environmental Crisis.* University of Georgia Press, Athens, GA.

Hargrove, E. C. 1989. *Foundations of Environmental Ethics.* Prentice-Hall, Englewood Cliffs, NJ.

Harper, J. L. 1977. *Population Biology of Plants.* Academic Press, New York.

Harrison, J. L. 1968. The effect of forest clearance on small mammals. *In Conservation in Tropical Southeast Asia.* IUCN, Morges, Switzerland.

Harte, J. and R. Shaw. 1995. Shifting dominance within a montane vegetation community: Results of a climate-warming experiment. *Science* 267: 876–879.

Hartell, K. E. 1992. Non-native fishes known from Massachusetts fresh waters. *Occasional Reports of the Museum of Comparative Zoology Fish Department* 2: 1–9.

Hausfater, G. and K. Kennedy. 1986. Dian Fossey (1932–1985). *American Anthropologist* 88: 965–956.

Hawksworth, D. L. 1990. The long-term effects of air pollutants on lichen communities in Europe and North America. *In* G. M. Woodwell (ed.), *The Earth in Transition: Patterns and Processes of Biotic Impoverishment*, pp. 45–64. Cambridge University Press, Cambridge.

Hawksworth, D. L. 1991. *The Biodiversity of Microorganisms and Invertebrates: Its role in Sustainable Agriculture.* CAB International, Wallingford, UK.

Hawksworth, D. L. and J. M. Richie (eds.). 1993. *Biodiversity and Biosystematic Priorities: Microorganisms and Invertebrates.* CAB International, Wallingford, England.

Hawksworth, D. L., P. M. Kirk and S. D. Clark (eds.). 1997. *Biodiversity Information.* Oxford University Press, New York.

Hayden, B. P., G. C. Ray and R. Dolan. 1984. Classification of coastal and marine environments. *Environmental Conservation* 11: 199–207.

Hedgpeth, J. W. 1993. Foreign invaders. *Science* 261: 34–35.

Hedrick, P. W., D. Hedgecock and S. Hamelberg. 1995. Effective population size in winter-run Chinook Salmon. *Conservation Biology* 9: 615–625.

Hegde, R., S. Suryaprakash, L. Achoth and K. S. Bawa. 1996. Extraction of non-timber forest products in the forests of Biligiri Rangan Hills, India. *Economic Botany* 50: 243–251.

Hellawell, J. M. 1986. *Biological Indicators of Freshwater Pollution and Environmental Management.* Elsevier Applied Science Publisher, London.

Hemley, G. (ed.). 1994. *International Wildlife Trade: A CITES Sourcebook.* Island Press, Washington, D.C.

Hendrickson, D. A. and J. E. Brooks. 1991. Transplanting short-lived fishes in North American deserts: Review, assessment and recommendations. *In* W. L. Minckley and J. E. Deacon (eds.), *Battle Against Extinction: Native Fish Management in the American West.* University of Arizona Press, Tuscon.

Herren, H. R. and P. Neunschwander. 1991. Biological control of cassava pests in Africa. *Annual Review of Entomology* 36: 257–283.

Heschel, M. S. and K. N. Paige. 1995. Inbreeding depression, environmental stress and population size variation in Scarlet Gilia (*Ipomopsis aggregata*). *Conservation Biology* 9: 126–133.

Heyer, W. R., M. A. Donnelly, R. W. McDiarmid, L. -A. C. Hayek and M. S. Foster (eds.). 1994. *Measuring and Monitoring Biological Diversity: Standard Methods for Amphibians.* Smithsonian Institution Press, Washington, D.C.

Heywood, V. H. (ed.). 1995. *Global Biodiversity and Assessment*, Cambridge University Press, New York.

Heywood, V. H., G. M. Mace, R. M. May and S. N. Stuart. 1994. Uncertainties in extinction rates. *Nature* 368: 105.

Hiers, J. K. and J. P. Evans. 1997. Effects of anthracnose on dogwood mortality and forest composition of the Cumberland Plateau (U.S.A.). *Conservation Biology* 11: 1430–1435.

Hill, C. J. 1995. Linear strips of rain forest vegetation as potential dispersal corridors for rain forest insects. *Conservation Biology* 9: 1559–1566.

Hinrichsen, D. 1987. The forest decline enigma. *BioScience* 37: 542–546.

Hochberg, M. E., J. Clobert and R. Barbault (eds.). 1996. *Aspects of the Genesis and Maintenance of Biological Diversity.* Oxford University Press, Oxford.

Hodgson, G. and J. A. Dixon. 1988. Logging versus fisheries and tourism in Palawan. *East-West Environmental Policy Institute Occasional Paper No. 7.* East-West Center, Honolulu.

Hodgson, J. G. 1986. Commonness and rarity in plants with special reference to the Sheffield flora. Part I. The identity, distribution and habitat characteristics of the common and rare species. Part III. Taxonomic and evolutionary aspects. *Biological Conservation* 36: 199–252, 275–296.

Hoffman, A. J., M. H. Bazerman and S. L. Yaffee 1997. Balancing business interests and endangered species protection. *Sloan Management Review* 39 (1): 59–73.

Hofman, R. J. 1995. The changing focus of marine mammal conservation. *Trends in Ecology and Evolution* 10: 462–465.

Holl, K. D., G. C. Daily and P. R. Ehrlich. 1995. Knowledge and perceptions in Costa Rica regarding environment, population and biodiversity issues. *Conservation Biology* 9: 1548–1558.

Holling, C. S. and G. K. Meffe. 1996. Command and control and the pathology of natural resource management. *Conservation Biology* 10: 328–338.

Holloway, M. 1994. Nurturing nature. *Scientific American* 270: 98–108.

Homer-Dixon. T. F., J. H. Boutwell and G. W. Rathjens. 1993. Environmental change and violent conflict. *Scientific American* 268: 38–45.

Hooten, A. J. and M. E. Hatziolos (eds.). 1995. *Sustainable Financing Mechanisms for Coral Reef Conservation. Environmentally Sustainable Development Proceedings Series No. 9.* The World Bank, Washington, D.C.

Hornocker, M. G. 1992. Learning to live with mountain lions. *National Geographic* 182 (7): 52–65.

Horton, T. 1992. The Endangered Species Act: Too tough, too weak, or too late? *Audubon* 94: 68–74.

Horwich, R. H. and J. Lyon. 1998. Community-based development as a conservation tool: The Community Baboon Sanctuary and the Gales Point Manatee Reserve. *In* R. B. Primack, D. Bray, H. A. Galletti and I. Ponciano (eds.), *Timber, Tourists and Temples: Conservation and Development in the Maya Forest of Belize, Guatemala, and Mexico*, pp. 343–364. Island Press, Washington, D.C.

Hourigan, T. F. and E. S. Reese. 1987. Mid-ocean isolation and the evolution of Hawaiian Reef fishes. *Trends in Ecology and Evolution* 2: 187–191.

Howarth, F. G. 1990. Hawaiian terrestrial arthropods: An overview. *Bishop Museum Occasional Papers* 30: 4–26.

Howe, H. F. 1984. Implications of seed dispersal by animals for tropical reserve management. *Biological Conservation* 30: 261–281.

Huenneke, L. F. 1995. Involving academic scientists in conservation research: Perspectives of a plant ecologist. *Ecological Applications* 5: 209–214.

Hughes, T. P. 1994. Catastrophes, phase shifts and large-scale degradation of a Caribbean coral reef. *Science* 265: 1547–1551.

Huston, M. A. 1994. *Biological Diversity: The Coexistence of Species on Changing Landscapes.* Cambridge University Press, Cambridge.

Hutchings, M. J. 1987. The population biology of the early spider orchid, *Ophrys sphegodes* Mill. I. A demographic study from 1975–1984. *Journal of Ecology* 75: 711–727.

Hutchins, M. and W. G. Conway. 1995. Beyond Noah's Ark: The evolving role of modern zoological parks and aquariums in field conservation. *International Zoo Yearbook* 34: 117–130.

Iltis, H. H. 1988. Serendipity in the exploration of biodiversity: What good are weedy tomatoes? *In* E. O. Wilson and F. M. Peter (eds.), *Biodiversity*, pp. 98–105. National Academy Press, Washington, D.C.

Intergovernmental Panel on Climate Change (IPCC). 1996. *Climate Change 1995: The Science of Climate Change.* World Meteorological Organization and United Nations Environmental Program.

IUCN. 1990. *The IUCN Red Data Book.* IUCN, Gland, Switzerland.

IUCN. 1994a. *Guidelines for Protected Area Management Categories.* IUCN, Gland, Switzerland.

IUCN. 1994a. *IUCN Red List Categories.* IUCN, Gland, Switzerland.

IUCN. 1996. *1996 IUCN Red List of Threatened Animals.* IUCN, Gland, Switzerland.

IUCN/TNC/WWF. 1994. *Report of the First Global Forum on Environmental Funds.* IUCN, Gland, Switzerland.

IUCN/UNEP. 1986a. *Review of the Protected Areas System in the Indo-Malayan Realm.* IUCN, Gland, Switzerland.

IUCN/UNEP. 1986b. *Review of the Protected Areas System in the Afrotropical Realm.* IUCN, Gland, Switzerland.

IUCN/UNEP. 1988. *Coral Reefs of the World.* 3 Volumes. IUCN, Gland, Switzerland.

IUCN/UNEP/WWF. 1991. *Caring for the Earth: A Strategy for Sustainable Living.* Gland, Switzerland.

IUCN/WWF. 1989. *The Botanic Gardens Conservation Strategy.* IUCN, Gland, Switzerland.

Jacobson, G. L., Jr., H. Almquist-Jacobson and J. C. Winne. 1991. Conservation of rare plant habitat: Insights from the recent history of vegetation and fire at Crystal Fen, northern Maine, USA. *Biological Conservation* 57: 287–314.

Jacobson, S. K. and S. Marynowski. 1997. Public attitudes and knowledge about ecosystem managment of Department of Defense lands in Florida. *Conservation Biology* 11: 770–778.

Jacobson, S. K., E. Vaughan and S. W. Miller. 1995. New directions in conservation biology: Graduate programs. *Conservation Biology* 9: 5–17.

Jaffe, M. 1994. *And No Birds Sing.* Simon and Schuster, New York, NY.

James, F. C., C. E. McCulloch and D. A. Wiedenfeld. 1996. New approaches to the analysis of population trends in land birds. *Ecology* 77: 13–27.

Jannasch, H. W. and M. J. Motti. 1985. Geomicrobiology of deep-sea hydrothermal vents. *Science* 229: 717–720.

Janzen, D. H. 1986. The eternal external threat. *In* M. Soulé (ed.), *Conservation Biology: The Science of Scarcity and Diversity*, pp. 286–303. Sinauer Associates, Sunderland, MA.

Janzen, D. H. 1988a. Tropical dry forests: The most endangered major tropical ecosystem. *In* E. O. Wilson and F. M. Peter (eds.), *Biodiversity.* National Academy Press, Washington, D.C.

Janzen, D. H. 1988b. Tropical ecological and biocultural restoration. *Science* 239: 243–244.

Jenkins, R. E. 1996. Natural Heritage Data Center Network: Managing information for managing biodiversity. *In* R. C. Szaro and D. W. Johnston (eds.), *Biodiversity in Managed Landscapes: Theory and Practice*, pp. 176–192. Oxford University Press, New York.

Jiménez, J. A., K. A. Hughes, G. Alaks, L. Graham and R. C. Lacy. 1994. An experimental study of inbreeding depression in a natural habitat. *Science* 266: 271–273.

Jingling, T. 1993. The features of of the Three Gorges Reservoir. *In* S. Luk and J. Whitney (eds.), *Megaproject: A Case Study of China's Three Gorges Project*. Armonk, New York.

Johannes, R. E. 1978. Traditional marine conservation methods in Oceania and their demise. *Annual Review of Ecology and Systematics* 9: 49–64.

Johns, A. D. 1996. Bird population persistence in Sabahan logging concessions. *Biological Conservation* 75: 3–10.

Johnsgaard, P. A. 1991. *Crane music: A Natural History of American Cranes*. Smithsonian Institution Press, Washington, D.C.

Johnson, N. 1995. *Biodiversity in the Balance: Approaches to Setting Geographic Conservation Priorities*. Biodiversity Support Program, World Wildlife Fund, Washington, D.C.

Johnson, N. and B. Cabarle. 1993. *Surviving the Cut: Natural Forest Management in the Humid Tropics*. WRI, Washington, D.C.

Joklik, W., B. Moss and B. Fields. 1993. Why the smallpox virus stocks should not be destroyed. *Science* 262: 1225–1226.

Jones, H. L. and J. M. Diamond. 1976. Short-time-base studies of turnover in breeding birds of the California Channel Islands. *Condor* 76: 526–549.

Jones, R. F. 1990. Farewell to Africa. *Audubon* 92: 1547–1551.

Jordan, W. R., III, M. E. Gilpin and J. D. Aber (eds.). 1990. *Restoration Ecology: A Synthetic Approach to Ecological Research*. Cambridge University Press, Cambridge.

Kapur, D., J. P. Lewis and R. Webb (eds.). 1997. *The World Bank: Its First Half-Century*. The Brookings Institute, Washington, D.C.

Kaufman, L. 1992. Catastrophic change in a species-rich freshwater ecosystem: Lessons from Lake Victoria. *BioScience* 42: 846–858.

Kaufman, L. and A. S. Cohen. 1993. The great lakes of Africa. *Conservation Biology* 7: 632–633.

Kaufman, L. and K. Mallory (eds.). 1993. *The Last Extinction*. 2nd edition. The MIT Press (in cooperation with the New England Aquarium), Cambridge, MA.

Kavanaugh M., A. A. Rahim and C. J. Hails. 1989. *Rainforest Conservation in Sarawak: An International Policy for WWF*. WWF Malaysia, Kuala Lumpur.

Keller, L. F., P. Arcese, J. N. M. Smith, W. M. Hochachka and S. C. Stearns. 1994. Selection against inbred song sparrows during a natural population bottleneck. *Nature* 372: 356–357.

Kellert, S. R. 1996. *The Value of Life: Biological Diversity and Human Society*. Island Press/Shearwater Books, Washington, D.C.

Kellert, S. R. and E. O. Wilson (eds.). 1993. *The Biophilia Hypothesis*. Island Press, Washington, D.C.

Kelly, P. K. 1994. *Thinking Green: Essays on Environmentalism, Feminism and Nonviolence*. Parallax Press, Berkeley, CA.

Kenchington, R. A. and M. T. Agardy. 1990. Achieving marine conservation through biosphere reserve planning and management. *Environmental Conservation* 17: 39–44.

Kendrick, R. 1995. Diminishing returns. *National Geographic* 188 (5): 2–37.

Keohanne, R. O. and M. A. Levy (eds.). 1996. *Institutions for Environmental Aid: Pitfalls and Promises*. MIT Press, Cambridge, MA.

Kiew, R. 1991. *The State of Nature Conservation in Malaysia*. Malayan Nature Society, Kuala Lumpur.

Kimmins, J. P. 1987. *Forest Ecology*. Macmillan, New York.

Kimura, M. and J. F. Crow. 1963. The measurement of effective population numbers. *Evolution* 17: 279–288.

Kinnaird, M. F. and T. G. O'Brien. 1991. Viable populations for an endangered forest primate, the Tana River crested mangabey (*Cercocebus galeritus galeritus*). *Conservation Biology* 5: 203–213.

Kleiman, D. G. 1989. Reintroduction of captive mammals for conservation. *BioScience* 39: 152–161.

Kleiman, D. G., M. E. Allen, K. V. Thompson and S. Lumpkin. 1996. *Wild Animals in Captivity: Principles and Techniques*. University of Chicago Press, Chicago.

Klein, B. C. 1989. Effects of forest fragmentation on dung and carrion beetle communities in central Amazonia. *Ecology* 70: 1715–1725.

Klein, M. L., S. R. Humphrey and H. F. Percival. 1995. Effects of ecotourism on distribution of waterbirds in wildlife refuge. *Conservation Biology* 9: 1454–1465.

Knight, R. R. and L. L. Eberhardt. 1985. Population dynamics of Yellowstone grizzly bears. *Ecology* 66: 323–334.

Kohm, K. and J. F. Franklin (eds.). 1997. *Creating a Forestry for the 21st Century: The Science of Ecosystem Management*. Island Press, Washington, D.C.

Koopowitz, H., A. D. Thornhill and M. Andersen. 1994. A general stochastic model for the prediction of biodiversity losses based on habitat conversion. *Conservation Biology* 8: 425–438.

Kornfield, I. and K. E. Carpenter. 1984. Cyprinids of Lake Lanao, Philippines: Taxonomic validity, evolutionary rates and speciation scenarios. *In* A. A. Echelle and I. Kornfield (eds.), *Evolution of Species Flocks*, pp. 69–84. University of Maine Press, Orono, ME.

Kothari, A., N. Singh and S. Suri (eds.). 1996. *People and Protected Areas: Toward Participatory Conservation in India*. Sage Publications, New Delhi.

Kozol, A. et al. 1994. Genetic variation in the endangered burying beetle *Nicrophorus americanus* (Coleoptera: Silphidae). *Annals of the Entomological Society of America* 87: 928–935.

Kramer, R., C. van Shaik and J. Johnson (eds.). 1997. *Last Stand: Protected Areas and Defense of Tropical Biodiversity*. Oxford University Press, New York.

Kraus, S. D. 1990. Rates and potential cause of mortality in North Atlantic right whales (*Eubalaena glacialis*). *Marine Mammal Science* 6: 278–291.

Kremen, C., A. M. Merenlender and D. D. Murphy. 1994. Ecological monitoring: A vital need for integrated conservation and development programs in the tropics. *Conservation Biology* 8: 388–397.

Kricher, J. 1998. *A Neotropical Companion*. Princeton University Press, Princeton, NJ.

Krishnan, R., J. M. Harris and N. R. Goodman (eds.). 1995. *A Survey of Ecological Economics*. Island Press, Washington, D.C.

Kristensen, R. M. 1983. Loricifera, a new phylum with Aschelminthes characters from the meiobenthos. *Zeitschrift fur Zoologische Systematik* 21: 163–180.

Küchler, A. W. 1964. *Potential Natural Vegetation of the Conterminous United States*. Special Publication Number 36, American Geographical Society, New York.

Kummer, D. M. and B. L. Turner III. 1994. The human causes of deforestation in Southeast Asia. *BioScience* 44: 323.

Kurlansky, M. 1996. Oil, toil and tyranny. *Audubon* 98 (2): 128.

Kushmaro, A., M. Fine and E. Rosenberg. 1996. Bacterial infection and coral bleaching. *Nature* 380: 396.

Kusler, J. A. and M. E. Kentula (eds.). 1990. *Wetland Creation and Restoration: The Status of the Science*. Island Press, Washington, D.C.

Lacy, R. C. 1987. Loss of genetic diversity from managed populations: Interacting effects of drift, mutation, immigration, selection and population subdivision. *Conservation Biology* 1: 143–158.

Lacy, R. C. and D. B. Lindenmayer. 1995. A simulation study of the impacts of population subdivision on the mountain brushtail possum *Trichosurus caninus* Ogilby (Phalangeridae: Marsupialia), in south-eastern Australia: Loss of genetic variation within and between subpopulations. *Biological Conservation* 73: 131–142.

Lambert, F. 1991. The conservation of fig-eating birds in Malaysia. *Biological Conservation* 58: 31–40.

Lamprey, H. F. 1974. Management of flora and fauna in national parks. *In* H. Elliot (ed.), *Second World Conference on National Parks*, pp. 237–248. IUCN, Morges, Switzerland.

Lande, R. 1988. Genetics and demography in biological conservation. *Science* 241: 1455–1460.

Lande, R. 1995. Mutation and conservation. *Conservation Biology* 9: 782–792.

Lande, R. and G. F. Barrowclough. 1987. Effective population size, genetic variation and their use in population management. *In* M. E. Soulé (ed.), *Viable Populations for Management*, pp. 87–124. Cambridge University Press, Cambridge.

Lasiak, T. 1991. The susceptibility and/or resilience of rocky littoral molluscs to stock depletion by the indigenous coastal people of Transkei, southern Africa. *Biological Conservation* 56: 245–264.

Laurance, W. F. 1991a. Ecological correlates of extinction proneness in Australian tropical rain forest mammals. *Conservation Biology* 5: 79–89.

Laurance, W. F. 1991b. Edge effects in tropical forest fragments: Application of a model for the design of nature reserves. *Biological Conservation* 57: 205–219.

Laurance, W. F. 1994. Rainforest fragmentation and the structure of small mammal communities in tropical Queensland. *Biological Conservation* 69: 23–32.

Laurance, W. F. and R. O. Bierregaard, Jr. (eds.). 1997. *Tropical Forest Remnants: Ecology, Management and Conservation of Fragmented Communities*. The University of Chicago Press, Chicago.

Laurance, W. F., K. R. McDonald and R. Speare. 1996. Epidemic disease and the catastrophic decline of Australian rain forest frogs. *Conservation Biology* 10: 406–414.

Lawton, J. H. and R. M. May (eds.). 1995. *Extinction Rates*. Oxford University Press, Oxford.

Leader-Williams, N. 1990. Black rhinos and African elephants: Lessons for conservation funding. *Oryx* 24: 23–29.

Leakey, R. and R. Lewin. 1996. *The Sixth Extinction: Patterns of Life and the Future of Humankind*. Doubleday, Anchor, New York.

Ledig, F. T. 1988. The conservation of diversity in forest trees. *BioScience* 38: 471–479.

Lee, K. 1996. The source and locus of intrinsic value. *Environmental Ethics* 18: 297–308.

Lehmkuhl, J. F., R. K. Upreti and U. R. Sharma. 1988. National parks and local development: Grasses and people in Royal Chitwan National Park, Nepal. *Environmental Conservation* 15: 143–148.

Leighton, M. and N. Wirawan. 1986. Catastrophic drought and fire in Borneo tropical rain forest associated with the 1982–1983 El Niño southern oscillation event. *In* G. T. Prance (ed.), *Tropical Rain Forests and World Atmosphere*, pp. 75–102. Westview Press, Boulder, CO.

Lemonick, M. D. 1997. Under attack: It's humans, not sharks, who are nature's most fearsome predators. *Time* 150: 59–64.

Leopold, A. 1939a. A biotic view of land. *Journal of Forestry* 37: 113–116.

Leopold, A. 1939b. The farmer as a conservationist. *American Forests* 45: 294–299, 316, 323.

Leopold, A. 1949. *A Sand County Almanac and Sketches Here and There*. Oxford University Press, New York.

Leopold, A. 1953. *Round River*. Oxford University Press, Oxford.

Lesica, P. and F. W. Allendorf. 1992. Are small populations of plants worth preserving? *Conservation Biology* 6: 135–139.

Levin, S. A. 1996. Economic growth and environmental quality. *Ecological Applications* 6: 12.

Lewis, D. M. 1995. Importance of GIS to community-based management of wildlife: Lessons from Zambia. *Ecological Applications* 5: 861–872.

Lewis, D. M., G. B. Kaweche and A. Mwenya. 1990. Wildlife conservation outside protected areas—lessons from an experiment in Zambia. *Conservation Biology* 4: 171–180.

Likens, G. E. 1991. Toxic winds: Whose responsibility? *In* F. H. Bormann and S. R. Kellert (eds.), *Ecology, Economics, Ethics: The Broken Circle*, pp. 136–152. Yale University Press, New Haven, CT.

Lin, S. C. and L. P. Yuan. 1980. Hybrid rice breeding in China. *International Rice Research Institute, Innovative Approaches to Rice Breeding*. Manila, Philippines.

Lindberg, K. 1991. *Policies for Maximizing Nature Tourism's Ecological and Economic Benefits*. World Resources Institute, Washington, D.C.

Linden, E. 1994. Ancient creature in a lost world. *Time* (June): 52–54.

Lindenmayer, D. B. and R. C. Lacy. 1995. Metapopulation viability of arboreal marsupials in fragmented old-growth forests: Comparison among species. *Ecological Applications* 5: 183–199.

Line, L. 1993. Silence of the songbirds. *National Geographic* 183(6): 68–91.

Lipske, M. 1991. Big hopes for bold beasts: Can grizzlies and wolves be reintroduced safely into old haunts? *National Wildlife* 29: 44–53.

Llewellyn, D. W., G. P. Shaffer, N. J. Craig, L. Creasman, et al. 1996. A decision-support system for prioritizing restoration sites on the Mississippi River alluvial plain. *Conservation Biology* 7: 1446–1456.

Lloyd, B. D and R. G. Powlesland. 1994. The decline of kakapo *Strigops habroptilus* and attempts at conservation by translocation. *Biological Conservation* 69: 75–85.

Loehle, G. and B. Li. 1996. Habitat destruction and the extinction debt revisited. *Ecological Applications* 6: 665–692.

Loeschcke, V., J. Tomiuk and S. K. Jain (eds.). 1994. *Conservation Genetics*. Birkhauser Verlag, Basel, Switzerland.

Loope, L. L. 1995. Strategies for long-term protection of biological diversity in rainforests of Haleakala National Park and East Maui, Hawaii. *Endangered Species Update* 12 (6): 1–5.

Loope, L. L., O. Hamann and C. P. Stone. 1988. Comparative conservation biology of oceanic archipelagoes: Hawaii and the Galápagos. *BioScience* 38: 272–282.

Losos, E., J. Haynes, A. Phillips and C. Alkiere. 1995. Taxpayer-subsidized resource extraction harms species. *BioScience* 45: 446–455.

Lovejoy, T. E., R. O. Bierregaard, Jr., A. B. Rylands et al. 1986. Edge and other effects of isolation on Amazon forest fragments. *In* M. E. Soulé (ed.), *Conservation Biology: The Science of Scarcity and Diversity*, pp. 257–285. Sinauer Associates, Sunderland, MA.

Lovelock, J. 1988. *The Ages of Gaia*. W. W. Norton, New York.

Lubchenco, J., et al. 1991. The sustainable biosphere initiative: An ecological research agenda. *Ecology* 72: 371–412.

Ludwig, D. 1993. Environmental sustainability: Magic, science and religion in natural resource management. *Ecological Applications* 3: 555–558.

Ludwig, D., R. Hilborn and C. Walters. 1993. Uncertainty, resource exploitation and conservation: Lessons from history. *Science* 260: 17, 36.

Luper-Foy, S. 1992. Justice and natural resources. *Environmental Values* 1: 47–64.

Lutz, R. A. and R. M. Haymon. 1994. Rebirth of a deep-sea vent. *National Geographic* 186 (5): 114–126.

Lynch, J. F. and D. F. Whigham. 1984. Effects of forest fragmentation on breeding bird communities in Maryland, USA. *Biological Conservation* 28: 287–324.

MacArthur, R. H. and E. O. Wilson. 1967. *The Theory of Island Biogeography*. Princeton University Press, Princeton, NJ.

MacDonald, D. W. 1996. Dangerous liaisons and disease. *Nature* 379: 400.

Mace, G. M. 1994. Classifying threatened species: means and ends. *Phil. Tran. Royal Soc. Lond. B* 344: 91–97.

Mace, G. M. 1995. Classification of threatened species and its role in conservation planning. *In* J. H. Lawton and R. M. May (eds.), *Extinction Rates*, pp. 131–146. Oxford University Press, Oxford.

Mace, G. M. and R. Lande. 1991. Assessing extinction threats: Towards a reevaluation of IUCN threatened species categories. *Conservation Biology* 5: 148–157.

Machlis, G. E. and D. L. Tichnell. 1985. *The State of the World's Parks: An International Assessment of Resource Management, Policy and Research*. Westview Press, Boulder, CO.

Machtans, G. S., M. Villard and S. J. Hannon. 1996. Use of riparian buffer strips as movement corridors by forest birds. *Conservation Biology* 7: 1366–1380.

MacKenzie, J. J. and M. T. El-Ashry. 1988. *Ill-Winds: Airborne Pollutions's Toll on Trees and Crops*. World Resources Institute, Washington, D.C.

MacKenzie, S. H. 1996. *Integrated Resource Planning and Management: The Resource Approach in the Great Lakes Basin*. Island Press, Washington, D.C.

MacKinnon, J. 1983. *Irrigation and watershed protection in Indonesia*. Report to IBRD Regional Office, Jakarta.

MacKinnon, J. and K. MacKinnon. 1986a. *Review of the Protected Areas System in the Indo-Malayan Realm*. IUCN/UNEP, Gland, Switzerland.

MacKinnon, J. and K. MacKinnon. 1986b. *Review of the Protected Areas System in the Afro-tropical Realm*. IUCN/UNEP, Gland, Switzerland.

MacKinnon, J., K. MacKinnon, G. Child and J. Thorsell. 1992. *Managing Protected Areas in the Tropics*. IUCN, Gland, Switzerland.

Mader, H. J. 1984. Animal habitat isolation by roads and agricultural fields. *Biological Conservation* 29: 81–96.

Madsen, T., B. Stille and R. Shine. 1996. Inbreeding depression in an isolated population of adders *Vipera berus*. *Biological Conservation* 75: 113–118.

Maehr, D. S. 1990. The Florida panther and private lands. *Conservation Biology* 4: 167–170.

Maehr, D. S. and J. A. Cox. 1995. Landscape features and panthers in Florida. *Conservation Biology* 9: 1008–1020.

Magnuson, J. J. 1990. Long-term ecological research and the invisible present. *BioScience* 40: 495–501.

Mahan, T. A. and B. S. Simmers. 1992. Social preference of four cross-foster reared Sandhill Cranes. *Proceedings North American Crane Workshop* 6: 43–49.

Makarewicz, J. C. and P. Bertram. 1991. Evidence for the restoration of the Lake Erie ecosystem. *BioScience* 41: 216–223.

Maltby, E. 1988. Wetland resources and future prospects: An international perspective. *In* J. Zelazny and J. S. Feierabend (eds.), *Wetlands: Increasing Our Wetland Resources*, pp. 3–14. National Wildlife Federation, Washington, D.C.

Mangel, M. and C. Tier. 1994. Four facts every conservation biologist should know about persistence. *Ecology* 75: 607–614.

Manire, C. A. and S. H. Gruber. 1990. Many sharks may be headed towards extinction. *Conservation Biology* 4: 10–11.

Mann, C. C. and M. L. Plummer. 1993. The high cost of biodiversity. *Science* 260: 1868–1871.

Mann, C. C. and M. L. Plummer. 1995a. Is Endangered Species Act in danger? *Science* 267: 1256–1258.

Mann, C. C. and M. L. Plummer. 1995b. Are wildlife corridors on the right path? *Science* 270: 1428–1430.

Marden, L. 1998. Master of the deep: Jacques Yves-Costeau. *National Geographic* 193(2): 70–79.

Mares, M. A. 1992. Neotropical mammals and the myth of Amazonian biodiversity. *Science* 255: 976–979.

Marsh, G. P. 1864. *Man and Nature; or, Physical Geography as Modified by Human Action*. Reprinted in 1965, D. Lowenthal (ed.), Harvard University Press, Cambridge, MA.

Martin, P. S. and R. G. Klein (eds.) 1984. *Quaternary Extinctions: A Prehistoric Revolution*. University of Arizona Press, Tucson, AZ.

Maser, C. 1997. *Sustainable Community Development: Principles and Practices*. St. Lucie Press, Delray Beach, FL.

Mathews, A. 1992. *Where the Buffalo Roam*. Grove Weidenfeld, New York.

Matthiessen, P. 1959. *Wildlife in America*. Viking Press, New York.

Mauchamp, A. 1997. Threats from alien plant species in the Galapagos Islands. *Conservation Biology* 11: 260–263.

May, R. M. 1988. Conservation and disease. *Conservation Biology* 2: 28–30.

May, R. M. 1992. How many species inhabit the Earth? *Scientific American* 267: 42–48.

Mayr, E. 1991. *One Long Argument: Charles Darwin and the Genesis of Modern Evolutionary Thought*. Harvard University Press, Cambridge.

McAuliffe, J. R. 1996. Saguaro cactus dynamics. *In* W. Halvorson and G. Davis (eds.), *Science and Ecosystem Management in the National Parks*, pp. 96–131. University of Arizona Press, Tucson.

McCallum, H. and A. Dobson. 1995. Detecting disease and parasite threats to endangered species and ecosystems. *Trends in Ecology and Evolution* 10: 190–194.

McCloskey, J. M. and H. Spalding. 1989. A reconnaissance-level inventory of the amount of wilderness remaining in the world. *Ambio* 18: 221–227.

McCullough, D. R. (ed.). 1996. *Metapopulations and Wildlife Conservation*. Island Press, Washington, D.C.

McGoodwin, J. R. 1990. *Crisis in the World's Fisheries: People, Problems and Politics*. Stanford University Press, Stanford, CA.

McKibben, B. 1996. What good is a forest? *Audubon* 98 (3): 54–65.

McLachlan, J. A. and S. F. Arnold. 1996. Environmental estrogens. *American Scientist* 84: 452–461.

McLaren, B. E. and R. O. Peterson. 1994. Wolves, moose and tree rings on Isle Royale. *Science* 266: 1555–1558.

McLaughlin, A. 1993. *Regarding Nature: Industrialism and Deep Ecology*. State University of New York Press, Albany.

McLean, H. E. 1995. Smart maps: Forestry's newest frontier. *American Forests* (March/April): 13–21.

McNaughton, S. J. 1989. Ecosystems and conservation in the twenty-first century. *In* D. Western and M. Pearl (eds.), *Conservation for the Twenty-first Century*, pp. 109–120. Oxford University Press, New York.

McNeely, J. A. 1987. How dams and wildlife can coexist: Natural habitats, agriculture and major water resource development projects in tropical Asia. *Conservation Biology* 1: 228–238.

McNeely, J. A. 1988. *Economics and Biological Diversity: Developing and Using Economic Incentives to Conserve Biological Resources*. IUCN, Gland, Switzerland.

McNeely, J. A. 1989. Protected areas and human ecology: How national parks can contribute to sustaining societies of the twenty-first century. *In* D. Western and M. Pearl (eds.), *Conservation for the Twenty-first Century*, pp. 150–165. Oxford University Press, New York.

McNeely, J. A. and W. S. Keeton. 1995. The interaction between biological and cultural diversity. *In* B. von Droste, H. Plachter, G. Fisher and M. Rossler (eds.), *Cultural Landscapes of Universal Value*, pp. 25–37. Gustav Fischer Verlag, New York.

McNeely, J. A., et al. 1990. *Conserving the World's Biological Diversity*. IUCN, World Resources Institute, CI, WWF-US, the World Bank, Gland, Switzerland and Washington, D.C.

McNeely, J. A., J. Harrison, P. Dingwall (eds.). 1994. *Protecting Nature: Regional Reviews of Protected Areas*. IUCN, Cambridge.

McPhee, J. 1971. *Encounters with the Archdruid*. Farrar, Straus and Giroux, New York.

Medina, E. and O. Huber. 1992. The role of biodiversity in the function of savannah ecosystems. *In* O. T. Solbrig, H. M. van Emden and P. G. W. J. van Oordt (eds.), *Biodiversity and Global Change*, pp. 139–158. International Union of Biological Sciences, Paris.

Meffe, G. K. and C. R. Carroll. 1997. *Principles of Conservation Biology*, Second Edition. Sinauer Associates, Sunderland, MA.

Meffe, G. K., A. H. Ehrlich and D. Ehrenfeld. 1993. Human population control: The missing agenda. *Conservation Biology* 7: 1–3.

Menges, E. S. 1986. Predicting the future of rare plant populations: Demographic monitoring and modeling. *Natural Areas Journal* 6: 13–25.

Menges, E. S. 1990. Population viability analysis for an endangered plant. *Conservation Biology* 4: 52–62.

Menges, E. S. 1992. Stochastic modeling of extinction in plant populations. *In* P. L. Fiedler and S. K. Jain (eds.), *Conservation Biology: The Theory and Practice of Nature Conservation, Preservation and Management* , pp. 253–275. Chapman and Hall, New York.

Meyer, W. B. 1996. *Human Impact on the Earth*. Cambridge University Press, Cambridge.

Meyer, W. B. and B. L. Turner II. 1994. *Changes in Land Use and Land Cover: A Global Perspective*. Cambridge University Press, New York.

Mickleburgh, S. P., P. A. Racey and A. M. Hutson. 1992. *Old World Fruit Bats*. IUCN, Gland, Switzerland.
Miller, B., R. P. Reading and S. Forrest. 1996. *Prairie Night: Black-Footed Ferret and the Recovery of Endangered Species*. Smithsonian Institution Press, Washington, D.C.
Miller, K. R. 1996. *Balancing the Scales: Guidelines for Increasing Biodiversity's Chances Through Bioregional Management*. World Resources Institute, Washington, D.C.
Miller, P. 1995. Crusading for chimps and humans: Jane Goodall. *National Geographic* 188: 102.
Mills, E. L., H. H. Leach, J. T. Carlton and C. L. Secor. 1994. Exotic species and the integrity of the Great Lakes. *BioScience* 44: 666–676.
Mills, L. S. and F. W. Allendorf. 1996. The one-migrant-per-generation rule in conservation and management. *Conservation Biology* 10: 1509–1518.
Milton, S. J., W. R. J. Dean, M. A. du Plessis and W. R. Siegfried. 1994. A conceptual model of arid rangeland degradation. *BioScience* 44: 70–76.
Minckley, W. L. 1995. Translocation as a tool for conserving imperiled fishes: Experiences in western United States. *Biological Conservation* 72: 297–309.
Mitchell, J. G. 1992. Our disappearing wetlands. *National Geographic* 182 (10): 3–45.
Mitchell, J. G. 1994. Our national parks. *National Geographic* 186 (4): 2–55.
Mitikin, K. and D. Osgood. 1994. *Issues and Options in the Design of Global Environment Facility-Supported Trust Funds for Biodiverisity Conservation*. World Bank, Washington, D.C.
Mittermeier, R. A. 1988. Primate diversity and the tropical forest: Case studies from Brazil and Madagascar and the importance of the megadiversity countries. *In* E. O. Wilson and F. M. Peter (eds.), *Biodiversity*, pp. 145–154. National Academy Press, Washington, D.C.
Mittermeier, R. A. and T. B. Werner. 1990. Wealth of plants and animals unites "megadiversity" countries. *Tropicus* 4: 1, 4–5.
Mlot, C. 1992. Botanists sue Forest Service to preserve biodiversity. *Science* 257: 1618–1619.
Moffat, M. W. 1994. *The High Frontier: Exploring the Tropical Rainforest Canopy*. Harvard University Press, Cambridge, MA.
Mohsin, A. K. M. and M. A. Ambak. 1983. *Freshwater Fishes of Peninsular Malaysia*. University Pertanian Malaysia Press, Kuala Lumpur, Malaysia.
Moiseenko, T. 1994. Acidification and critical loads for surface waters: Kola, northern Russia. *Ambio* 23: 418–424.
Moore, N. 1987. *The Bird of Time: Science and the Politics of Nature Conservation*. Cambridge University Press, Cambridge.
Morales, J. C., P. M. Andau, J. Supriatna, Z.-Z. Zainuddin, and D. J. Melnick. 1997. Mitochondrial DNA variability and conservation genetics of the Sumatran rhinoceros. *Conservation Biology* 11: 539–543.
Morell, V. 1986. Dian Fossey: Field science and death in Africa. *Science 86* 7: 17–21.
Morell, V. 1993. Primatology: Called 'trimates,' three bold women shaped their field (Dian Fossey, Jane Goodall and Birute Galdikas). *Science* 260: 420–425.
Morell, V. 1994. Serengeti's big cats going to the dogs. *Science* 264: 23.
Morell, V. 1996. New mammals discovered by biology's new explorers. *Science* 273: 1491.
Morris, M. G. 1971. The management of grassland for the conservation of invertebrate animals. *In* E. Duffey and A. S. Watt (eds.), *The Scientific Management of Animal and Plant Communities for Conservation*, pp. 527–552. Blackwell Scientific Publications, London.
Mosquin, T., P. G. Whiting and D. E. McAllister. 1995. *Canada's Biodiversity: The Value of Life, Its Status, Economic Benefits, Conservation Costs and Unmet Needs*. Canadian Museum of Nature, Ottawa.
Motavelli, J. 1995. In harms's way. *E: The Environmental Magazine* 6(6): 28–37.
Mowat, F. 1984. *Sea of Slaughter*. McClelland and Stewart, Toronto.
Moyle, P. B. 1995. Conservation of native freshwater fishes in the Mediterranean-type climate of California, USA: A review. *Biological Conservation* 72: 271–279.
Moyle, P. B. and R. A. Leidy. 1992. Loss of biodiversity in aquatic ecosystems: Evidence from fish faunas. *In* P. L. Fiedler and S. K. Jain (eds.), *Conservation Biology: The Theory and Practice of Nature Conservation, Preservation and Management*, pp. 127–169. Chapman and Hall, New York.
Muir, J. 1901. *Our National Parks*. Houghton Mifflin, Boston, MA.
Muir, J. 1916. *A Thousand Mile Walk to the Gulf*. Houghton Mifflin, Boston, MA.
Munn, C. A. 1992. Macaw biology and ecotourism or "when a bird in the bush is worth two in the hand". *In* S. R. Beissinger and N. F. R. Snyder (eds.), *New World Parrots in Crisis*. Smithsonian Institution Press, Washington, D.C.
Munn, C. A. 1994. Macaws: Winged rainbows. *National Geographic* 185: 118–140.
Murphy, D. D., D. E. Freas and S. B. Weiss. 1990. An environment-metapopulation approach to population viability analysis for a threatened invertebrate. *Conservation Biology* 4: 41–51.
Murphy, P. G. and A. E. Lugo. 1986. Ecology of tropical dry forest. *Annual Review of Ecology and Systematics* 17: 67–88.
Murrieta, J. R. and R. P. Rueda. 1995. *Extractive Reserves*. 1995 IUCN Forest Conservation Programme. IUCN Publications, Cambridge.
Mustart, P, J. Juritz, C. Makua, S. W. Van der Merwe and N. Wessels. 1995. Restoration of the clanwilliam cedar *Widdringtonia cedarbergensis*: The importance of monitoring seedlings planted in the cederberg, South Africa. *Biological Conservation* 72: 73–76.
Mwalyosi, R. B. 1991. Ecological evaluation for wildlife corridors and buffer zones for Lake Manyara National Park, Tanzania and its immediate environment. *Biological Conservation* 57: 171–186.
Myers, F. W. and A. Anderson. 1992. Microbes from 20,000 feet under the sea. *Science* 255: 28–29.

Myers, J. G. 1934. The arthropod fauna of a rice-ship, trading from Burma to the West-Indies. *Journal of Animal Ecology* 3: 146–149.

Myers, K. 1986. Introduced vertebrates in Australia, with emphasis on mammals. *In* R. H. Grove and J. J. Burdon (eds.), *Ecology of Biological Invasions*, pp. 120–136. Cambridge University Press, Cambridge.

Myers, N. 1979. *The Sinking Ark: A New Look at the Problem of Disappearing Species*. Pergamon, New York.

Myers, N. 1980. *Conversion of Tropical Moist Forests*. National Academy of Sciences, Washington, D.C.

Myers, N. 1983. *A Wealth of Wild Species*. Westview Press, Boulder, CO.

Myers, N. 1984. *The Primary Source: Tropical Forests and Our Future*. Norton, New York.

Myers, N. 1986. Tropical deforestation and a mega-extinction spasm. *In* M. E. Soulé, (ed.), *Conservation Biology: The Science of Scarcity and Diversity*, pp. 394–409. Sinauer Associates, Sunderland, MA.

Myers, N. 1987. The extinction spasm impending: Synergisms at work. *Conservation Biology* 1: 14–21.

Myers, N. 1988a. Threatened biotas: "Hotspots" in tropical forests. *Environmentalist* 8: 1–20.

Myers, N. 1988b. Tropical forests: Much more than stocks of wood. *Journal of Tropical Ecology* 4: 209–221.

Myers, N. 1991a. The biodiversity challenge: Expanded "hotspots" analysis. *Environmentalist* 10: 243–256.

Myers, N. 1991b. Tropical deforestation: The latest situation. *BioScience* 41: 282.

Myers, N. 1993. Sharing the earth with whales. *In* L. Kaufman and K. Mallory (eds.), *The Last Extinction*, pp. 179–194. MIT Press, Cambridge, MA.

Myers, N. 1996. *Ultimate Security: The Environmental Basis of Political Stability*. Island Press, Washington, D.C.

Myneni, R. B., C. D. Keeling, C. J. Tucker, G. Asrar and R. R. Nemani. 1997. Increased plant growth in the northern high latitudes from 1981 to 1991. *Nature* 386: 698–702.

Nabhan, G. P. 1985. Native crop diversity in Aridoamerica: Conservation of regional gene pools. *Economic Botany* 39: 387–399.

Nabhan, G. P. 1989. *Enduring Seeds: Native American Agriculture and Wild Plant Conservation*. North Point Press, San Francisco.

Naess, A. 1986. Intrinsic value: Will the defenders of nature please rise? *In* M. E. Soulé (ed.), *Conservation Biology: The Science of Scarcity and Diversity*, pp. 153–181. Sinauer Associates, Sunderland, MA.

Naess, A. 1989. *Ecology, Community and Lifestyle*. Cambridge University Press, Cambridge.

Nash, R. 1982. *Wilderness and the American Mind*. Yale University Press, New Haven, CT.

Nash, R. 1990. *American Environmentalism: Readings in Conservation Biology*. McGraw-Hill, New York.

Nash, S. 1991. What price nature? *BioScience* 41: 677–680.

National Research Council. 1996. *Ecologically Based Pest Management: New Solutions for a New Century*. National Academy Press, Washington, D.C.

Nei, M., T. Maruyama and R. Chakraborty. 1975. The bottleneck effect and genetic variability in populations. *Evolution* 29: 1–10.

Nepstad, D. C. and S. Schwartzman (eds.). 1992. *Non-Timber Products from Tropical Forests: Evaluation of a Conservation and Development Strategy*. The New York Botanical Garden, Bronx, NY.

Netherlands National Committee for IUCN/Steering Group for World Conservation Strategy. 1988. *The Netherlands and the World Ecology: Towards a National Conservation Strategy in and by the Netherlands*. Netherlands National Committee, Amsterdam.

Newmark, W. D. 1995. Extinction of mammal populations in western North American national parks. *Conservation Biology* 9: 512–527.

Newton, I. 1994. The role of nest sites in limiting the numbers of hole-nesting birds: A review. *Biological Conservation* 70: 265–276.

Nickel, J. W. and E. Viola. 1994. Integrating environmentalism and human rights. *Environmental Ethics* 16: 265–273.

Niemelå, J., D. Langor and J. R. Spence. 1993. Effects of clear cut harvesting on boreal ground-beetle assemblages (Coleoptera: Carabidae) in Western Canada. *Conservation Biology* 7: 551–561.

Nilsson, S. G., U. Arup, R. Baranowski and S. Ekman. 1995. Tree-dependent lichens and beetles as indicators in conservation forests. *Conservation Biology* 9: 1208–1216.

Nobre, C. A., P. J. Sellers and J. Shukla. 1991. Amazonian deforestation and regional climate change. *Journal of Climate* 4: 957–988.

Norse, E. A. (ed.). 1993. *Global Marine Biological Diversity: A Strategy for Building Conservation into Decision Making*. Island Press, Washington, D.C.

Norse, E. A. et al. 1986. *Conserving Biological Diversity in Our National Forests*. The Wilderness Society, Washington, D.C.

Norton, B. G. 1991. *Toward Unity Among Environmentalists*. Oxford University Press, New York.

Norton, B. G., M. Hutchins, E. F. Stevens and T. L. Maple. 1995. *Ethics on the Ark: Zoos, Animal Welfare and Wildlife Conservation*. Smithsonian Institution Press, Washington, D.C.

Noss, R. F. 1992. Essay: Issues of scale in conservation biology. *In* P. L. Fiedler and S. K. Jain (eds.). *Conservation Biology: The Theory and Practice of Nature Conservation, Preservation and Management*, pp. 239–250. Chapman and Hall, New York.

Noss, R. F. and A. Y Cooperrider. 1994. *Saving Nature's Legacy: Protecting and Restoring Biodiversity*. Island Press, Washington, D.C.

Noss, R. F., M. A. O'Connell and D. D. Murphy. 1997. *The Science of Conservation Planning: Habitat Conservation Under the Endangered Species Act*. Island Press, Washington, D.C.

Nunney, L. and D. R. Elam. 1994. Estimating the effective population size of conserved populations. *Conservation Biology* 8: 175–184.

O'Brien, S. J. and J. F. Evermann. 1988. Interactive influence of infectious disease and genetic diversity in natural populations. *Trends in Ecology and Evolution* 3: 254–259.

Odum, E. P. 1997. *Ecology: A Bridge Between Science and Society*. Sinauer Associates, Sunderland, MA.

Oelschlaeger, M. 1994. *Caring for Creation: An Ecumenical Approach to the Environmental Crisis.* Yale University Press, New Haven, CT.

Office of Technology Assessment of the U.S. Congress (OTA). 1987. *Technologies to Maintain Biological Diversity*. OTA-F-330. U.S. Government Printing Office, Washington, D.C.

Office of Technology Assessment of the U.S. Congress (OTA). 1993. *Report Brief.* U.S. Government Printing Office, Pittsburgh.

Oldfield, M. L. and Alcorn, J. B. (eds.). 1991. *Biodiversity: Culture, Conservation and Ecodevelopment.* Westview Press, Boulder, CO.

Oliver, I. and A. J. Beattie. 1993. A possible method for the rapid assessment of biodiversity. *Conservation Biology* 7: 562–568.

Oliver, I. and A. J. Beattie. 1996. Invertebrae morphospecies as surrogates for species: A case study. *Conservation Biology* 10: 99–110.

Olney, P. J. S. and P. Ellis (eds.). 1995. *1994 International Zoo Yearbook,* vol. 35. Zoological Society of London.

Olney, P. J. S., G. M. Mace and A. T. C. Feistner (eds.). 1994. *Creative Conservation: Interactive Management of Wild and Captive Animals.* Chapman and Hall, London.

Olson, M. H. 1996. Charting a course for sustainability. *Environment* 38 (4): 10–15, 30–36.

Olson, S. L. 1989. Extinction on islands: Man as a catastrophe. *In* M. Pearl and D. Western (eds.), *Conservation Biology for the Twenty-first Century*, pp. 50–53. Oxford University Press, Oxford.

Orians, G. H. 1995. Conservation biology. *In* W. K. Purves, G. H. Orians and H. C. Heller, *Life: The Science of Biology*, 4th Edition, pp. 1176–1195. Sinauer Associates, Sunderland, MA.

Orr, D. W. 1994. *Ecological Literacy: Education and the Transition to a Postmodern World.* State University of New York Press, Albany.

Osborn, F. 1948. *Our Plundered Planet.* Little, Brown, Boston.

Pace, F. 1991. The Klamath corridors: Preserving biodiversity in the Klamath National Forest. *In* W. E. Hudson (ed.), *Landscape Linkages and Biodiversity*, pp. 105–116. Island Press, Washington, D.C.

Packard, S. and C. Mutel (eds.). 1997. *Tallgrass Prairie Restoration Handbook.* Island Press, Washington, D.C.

Packer, C. 1992. Captives in the wild. *National Geographic* 181 (4): 122–136.

Packer, C., A. E. Pusey, H. Rowley, D. A. Gilbert, J. Martenson and S. J. O'Brien. 1991. Case study of a population bottleneck: Lions of the Ngorongoro Crater. *Conservation Biology* 5: 219–230

Paine, R. T. 1966. Food web complexity and species diversity. *American Naturalist* 100: 65–75.

Palmer, M. E. 1987. A critical look at rare plant monitoring in the United States. *Biological Conservation* 39: 113–127.

Panayotou, T. and P. S. Ashton. 1992. *Not by Timber Alone: Economics and Ecology for Sustaining Tropical Forests.* Island Press, Washington, D.C.

Panwar, H. S. 1987. Project Tiger: The reserves, the tigers and their future. *In* R. L. Tilson and U.S. Seal (eds.). *Tigers of the World: The Biology, Biopolitics, Management and Conservation of an Endangered Species*, pp. 100–117. Noyes Publications, Park Ridge, NJ.

Parfit, M. 1995. Diminishing returns: Exploiting the ocean's bounty. *National Geographic* 188 (5): 2–56.

Parikh, J. and K. Parikh. 1991. *Consumption Patterns: The Driving Force of Environmental Stress.* UNCED, Geneva, Switzerland.

Parkes, R. J., B. A. Cragg, S. J. Bale, et al. 1994. Deep bacterial biosphere in Pacific Ocean sediments. *Nature* 371: 410–413.

Paton, P. W. C. 1994. The effect of edge on avian nest success: How strong is the evidence? *Conservation Biology* 8: 17–26.

Patterson, A. 1990. Debt for nature swaps and the need for alternatives. *Environment* 32: 5–32.

Pearson, D. L. and F. Cassola. 1992. World-wide species richness patterns of tiger beetles (Coleoptera: Cicindelidae): Indicator taxon for biodiversity and conservation studies. *Conservation Biology* 6: 376–391.

Pechmann, J. H. K., D. E. Scott, R. D. Semlitsch, et al. 1991. Declining amphibian populations: The problems of separating human impacts from natural fluctuations. *Science* 253: 892–895.

Peluso, N. L. 1992. The Ironwood problem: The (mis)management and development of an extractive rain forest product. *Conservation Biology* 6: 210–219.

Peres, C. A. and J. W. Terborgh. 1995. Amazonian nature reserves: An analysis of the defensibility status of existing conservation units and design criteria for the future. *Conservation Biology* 9: 34–46.

Perfecto, I., R. A. Rice, R. Greenberg, and M. E. Van der Voort. 1996. Shade coffee: A disappearing refuge for biodiversity. *BioScience* 46: 598–608.

Perlman, D. and G. Adelson. 1997. *Biodiversity: Exploring Values and Priorities in Conservation.* Blackwell Scientific Publications, Cambridge, MA.

Perrings, C. 1995. Economic values of biodiversity. *In* V. H. Heywood (ed.), *Global Biodiversity Assessment*, pp. 823–914. Cambridge University Press, Cambridge.

Peterken, G. F. 1994. *Woodland Conservation and Management,* 2nd ed. Chapman and Hall, London.

Peterken, G. F. 1996. *Natural Woodland, Ecology and Conservation in Northern Temperate Regions.* Cambridge University Press, Cambridge.

Peters, C. M. 1994. *Sustainable Harvest of Non-timber Plant Resources in Tropical Moist Forest: An Ecological Primer.* Biodiversity Support Program, Washington, D.C.

Peters, C. M., A. H. Gentry and R. Mendelsohn. 1989. Valuation of a tropical forest in Peruvian Amazonia. *Nature* 339: 655–656.

Peters, R. L. and T. E. Lovejoy (eds.). 1992. *Global Warming and Biological Diversity.* Yale University Press, Boulder, CO.

Philippart, J. C. 1995. Is captive breeding an effective solution for the preservation of endemic species? *Biological Conservation* 72: 281–295.

Phillips, K. 1990. Where have all the frogs and toads gone? *BioScience* 40: 422–424.

Phillips, M. K. 1990 and V. G. Henry. 1992. Comments on red wolf taxonomy. *Conservation Biology* 6: 596–599.

Pianka, E. 1966. Latitudinal gradients in species diversity: A review of the concepts. *American Naturalist* 100: 33–46.

Pimental, D., C. Harvey, P. Resosudarmo, K. Sinclair, et al. 1995. Environmental and economic costs of soil erosion and conservation benefits. *Science* 267: 1117–1121.

Pimental, D., C. Wilson, C. McCullum, et al. 1997. Economic and environmental benefits of diversity. *BioScience* 47: 747–757.

Pimm, S. L. 1991. *The Balance of Nature?* University of Chicago Press, Chicago.

Pimm, S. L., H. L. Jones and J. Diamond. 1988. On the risk of extinction. *American Naturalist* 132: 757–785.

Pimm, S. L., M. P. Moulton, and L. J. Justice. 1995. Bird extinction in the Central Pacific. *In* J. H. Lawton and R. M. May (eds.), *Extinction Rates*, pp. 75–87. Oxford University Press, Oxford.

Pinchot, G. 1947. *Breaking New Ground.* Harcourt, Brace, New York.

Plotkin, M. J. 1993. *Tales of a Shaman's Apprentice.* Viking/Penguin, New York.

Plucknett, D. L., N. J. H. Smith, J. T. Williams and N. M. Anishetty. 1987. *Gene Banks and the World's Food.* Princeton University Press, Princeton, NJ.

Poffenberger, M. (ed.). 1990. *Keepers of the Forest.* Kumarian, West Hartford, CT.

Polunin, N. and L. M. Curme. 1997. *World Who Is Who and Does What in Environment and Conservation.* St. Martin's Press, New York.

Poole, J. 1996. *Coming of Age with Elephants: A Memoir.* Hyperion, New York.

Poore, D. and J. Sayer. 1991. *The Management of Tropical Moist Forest Lands.* IUCN, Gland, Switzerland.

Popper, F. J. and D. E. Popper. 1991. The reinvention of the American frontier. *Amicus Journal* (Summer): 4–7.

Porteous, P. L. 1992. Eagles on the rise. *National Geographic* 182 (11): 42–55.

Porter, S. D. and D. A. Savignano. 1990. Invasion of polygyne fire ants decimates native ants and disrupts arthropod communities. *Ecology* 71: 2095–2106.

Posey, D. A. 1992. Traditional knowledge, conservation and "the rain forest harvest". *In* M. Plotkin and L. Famolare (eds.), *Sustainable Harvest and Marketing of Rain Forest Products*, pp. 46–50. Island Press, Washington, D.C.

Posey, D. A. 1996. Protecting indigenous peoples' rights to biodiversity. *Environment* 38 (8): 6–9, 37–45.

Poten, C. J. 1991. A shameful harvest: America's illegal wildlife trade. *National Geographic* 180 (9): 106–132.

Powell, A. N. and F. J. Cuthbert. 1993. Augmenting small populations of plovers: An assessment of cross-fostering and captive-rearing. *Conservation Biology* 7: 160–168.

Power, M. E., D. Tilman, J. A. Estes, B. A. Menge, et al. 1996. Challenges in the quest for keystones. *BioScience* 46: 609–620.

Power, T. M. 1991. Ecosystem preservation and the economy in the Greater Yellowstone area. *Conservation Biology* 5: 395–404.

Prance, G. T., W. Balée, B. M. Boom and R. L. Carneiro. 1987. Quantitative ethnobotany and the case for conservation in Amazonia. *Conservation Biology* 1: 296–310.

Prendergast, J., R. M. Quinn, J. H. Lawton, B. C. Eversham and D. W. Gibbons. 1993. Rare species, the coincidence of diversity hotspots and conservation strategies. *Nature* 365: 335–337.

Prescott-Allen, C. and R. Prescott-Allen. 1986. *The First Resource: Wild Species in the North American Economy.* Yale University Press, New Haven, CT.

Press, D., D. F. Doak and P. Steinberg. 1996. The role of local government in the conservation of rare species. *Conservation Biology* 10: 1538–1548.

Pressey, R. L. 1994. Ad hoc reservations: Forward or backward steps in developing representative reserve systems. *Conservation Biology* 8: 662–668.

Pressey, R. L., C. J. Humphries, C. R. Margules, R. I. Vane-Wright and P. H. Williams. 1993. Beyond opportunism: Key principles for systematic reserve selection. *Trends in Ecology and Evolution* 8: 124–128.

Price, P. W. 1992. The resource-based organization of communities. *Biotropica* (Special Issue) 24: 273–282.

Primack, R. B. 1988. Forestry in Fujian province (People's Republic of China) during the Cultural Revolution. *Arnoldia* 48: 26–29.

Primack, R. B. 1992. Tropical community dynamics and conservation biology. *BioScience* 42: 818–820.

Primack, R. B. 1996. Lessons from ecological theory: Dispersal, establishment and population structure. *In* D. A. Falk, C. I. Millar and M. Olwell (eds.), *Restoring Diversity: Strategies for Reintroduction of Endangered Plants.* Island Press, Washington, D.C.

Primack, R. B. and B. Drayton. 1997. The experimental ecology of reintroduction. *Plant Talk* 11 (Oct.): 25–28.

Primack, R. B. and P. Hall. 1992. Biodiversity and forest change in Malaysian Borneo. *BioScience* 42: 829–837.

Primack, R. B. and T. Lovejoy (eds.). 1995. *Ecology, Conservation and Management of Southeast Asian Rainforests.* Yale University Press, New Haven, CT.

Primack, R. B. and S. L. Miao. 1992. Dispersal can limit local plant distribution. *Conservation Biology* 6: 513–519.

Primack, R. B., D. Bray, H. Galetti and J. Ponciano (eds.). 1998. *Timber, Tourists and Temples: Conservation and Development in the Maya Forest of Belize, Guatemala and Mexico.* Island Press, Washington, D.C.

Primack, R. B., E. Hendry and P. Del Tredici. 1986. Current status of *Magnolia virginiana* in Massachusetts. *Rhodora* 88: 357–365.

Pritchard, P. C. 1991. "The best idea America ever had": The National Parks service turns 75. *National Geographic* 180: 36–59.

Pullin, A. S. and S. R. J. Woodell. 1987. Response of the fen violet, *Viola persicifolia* Schreber, to different management regimes at Woodwalton Fen National Nature Reserve, Cambridgeshire, England. *Biological Conservation* 41: 203–217.

Pyne, S. J. 1997. *Fire in America: A Cultural Hisotry of Wildland and Rural Fire.* The University of Washington Press, Seattle.

Quammen, D. 1996. *The Song of the Dodo: Island Biogeography in an Age of Extinctions*. Scribner, New York.

Quinn, R. M., J. H. Lawton, B. C. Eversham and S. N. Wood. 1994. The biogeography of scarce vascular plants in Britain with respect to habitat preference, dispersal ability and reproductive biology. *Biological Conservation* 70: 149–157.

Rabinowitz, A. 1993. *Wildlife Field Research and Conservation Training Manual*. International Wildlife Conservation Park, New York.

Rabinowitz, A. 1995. Helping a species go extinct: The Sumatran rhino in Borneo. *Conservation Biology* 9: 482–488.

Rabinowitz, D., S. Cairns and T. Dillon. 1986. Seven forms of rarity and their frequency in the flora of the British Isles. *In* M. E. Soulé (ed.), *Conservation Biology: The Science of Scarcity and Diversity*, pp. 182–204. Sinauer Associates, Sunderland, MA.

Radmer, R. J. 1996. Algal diversity and commercial algal products: New and valuable products from diverse algae may soon increase the already large market for algal products. *BioScience* 46: 263–270.

Ralls, K. and J. Ballou. 1983. Extinction: Lessons from zoos. *In* C. M. Schonewald-Cox, S. M. Chambers, B. MacBryde and L. Thomas (eds.), *Genetics and Conservation: A Reference for Managing Wild Animal and Plant Populations*, pp. 164–184. Benjamin/Cummings, Menlo Park, CA.

Ralls, K. and R. L. Brownell. 1989. Protected species: Research permits and the value of basic research. *BioScience* 39: 394–396.

Ralls, K., J. D. Ballou and A. Templeton. 1988. Estimates of lethal equivalents and the cost of inbreeding in mammals. *Conservation Biology* 2: 185–193.

Ralls, K., P. H. Harvey and A. M. Lyles. 1986. Inbreeding in natural populations of birds and mammals. *In* M. Soule (ed.), *Conservation Biology: The Science of Scarcity and Diversity*, pp. 35–56. Sinauer Associates, Sunderland, MA.

Rauh, W. 1979. Problems of biological conservation in Madagascar. *In* D. Bramwell (ed.), *Plants and Islands*, pp. 405–421. Academic Press, New York.

Raup, D. M. 1979. Size of the Permo-Triassic bottleneck and its evolutionary implications. *Science* 206: 217–218.

Raup, D. M. 1992. *Extinction: Bad Genes or Bad Luck?* Norton, New York.

Raustiala, K. and D. G. Victor. 1996. Biodiversity since Rio: The future of the Convention on Biological Diversity. *Environment* 38 (4): 16–26, 37–45.

Raven, P. H. 1981. Research in botanical gardens. *Bot. Jahrb. Syst.* 102: 53–72.

Raven, P. H. and E. O. Wilson. 1992. A fifty-year plan for biodiversity surveys. *Science* 258: 1099–1100.

Ravenscroft, N. O. M. 1990. The ecology and conservation of the silver-studded blue butterfly *Plejebus argus* L. on the sandlings of East Anglia, England. *Biological Conservation* 53: 21–36.

Ray, G. C. and W. P. Gregg, Jr. 1991. Establishing biosphere reserves for coastal barrier ecosystems. *BioScience* 41: 301–309.

Ray, G. C., J. F. Grassle and contributors. 1991. Marine biological diversity. *BioScience* 41: 453–465.

Reading, R. P. and S. R. Kellert. 1993. Attitudes toward a proposed reintroduction of black-footed ferrets (*Mustela nigripes*). *Conservation Biology* 7: 569–580.

Reaka-Kudla, M. L., D. W. Wilson and E. O. Wilson (eds.). 1996. *Biodiversity II: Understanding and Protecting our Natural Resources*. National Academy Press, Washington, D.C.

Real, L. A. 1996. Sustainability and the ecology of infectious disease: Diseases and their pathogenic agents must be viewed as important parts of any ecosystem management strategy. *BioScience* 46: 88–96.

Rebelo, A. G. and W. R. Siegfried. 1990. Protection of fynbos vegetation: Ideal and real-world options. *Biological Conservation* 54: 15–31.

Redford, K. H. 1992. The empty forest. *BioScience* 42: 412–422.

Redford, K. H. and C. Padoch (eds.). 1992. *Conservation of Neotropical Rainforests: Working from Traditional Resource Use*. Columbia University Press, Irvington, NY.

Redford, K. H. and J. A. Mansour (eds.). 1996. *Traditional Peoples and Biodiversity Conservation in Large Tropical Landscapes*. The Nature Conservancy, Arlington, VA.

Reed, R. A., J. Johnson-Barnard and W. L. Baker. 1996. Contribution of roads to forest fragmentation in the Rocky Mountains. *Conservation Biology* 10: 1098–1107.

Regan, T. 1992. Does environmental ethics rest on a mistake? *The Monist* 75: 161–182.

Reid, V. W., S. A. Laird, R. G. Elmez et al. (eds.). 1993. *Biodiversity Prospecting*. World Resources Institute, Washington, D.C.

Reid, W. V. 1992. The United States needs a national biodiversity policy. *Issues and Ideas Brief*. World Resources Institute, Washington, D.C.

Reid, W. V. and K. R. Miller. 1989. *Keeping Options Alive: The Scientific Basis for Conserving Biodiversity*. World Resources Institute, Washington, D.C.

Reinartz, J. A. 1995. Planting state-listed endangered and threatened plants. *Conservation Biology* 9: 771–781.

Reinthal, P. N. and M. L. J. Stiassny. 1991. The freshwater fishes of Madagascar: A study of endangered fauna with recommendations for a conservation strategy. *Conservation Biology* 5: 231–243.

Repetto, R. 1990a. Deforestation in the tropics. *Scientific American* 262: 36–42.

Repetto, R. 1990b. *Promoting Environmentally Sound Economic Progress: What the North Can Do*. World Resources Institute, Washington, D.C.

Repetto, R. 1992. Accounting for environmental assets. *Scientific American* 266 (June): 94–100.

Rex, M. A. 1997. An oblique slant on deep-sea biodiversity. *Nature* 385: 577–590.

Rheinhardt, R. 1996. The role of reference wetlands in functional assessment and mitigation. *Ecological Applications* 6: 69–76.

Rhoades, R. E. 1991. World's food supply at risk. *National Geographic* 179 (April): 74–105.

Rich, B. 1990. Multilateral development banks and tropical deforestation. *In* S. Head and R. Heinzman (eds.), *Lessons from the Rainforest*. Sierra Club Books, San Francisco.

Rich, B. 1994. *Mortgaging the Earth*. Beacon Press, Boston.

Rich, T. C. G. and E. R. Woodruff. 1996. Changes in the vascular plant floras of England and Scotland between 1930–1960 and 1987–1988: The BSBI monitoring scheme. *Biological Conservation* 75: 217–229.

Richter-Dyn, N. and N. S. Goel. 1972. On the extinction of a colonizing species. *Population Biology* 3: 406–433.

Ricklefs, R. E. 1994. *The Economy of Nature*, 3rd Edition. W. H. Freeman and Co., New York.

Robinson, M. H. 1992. Global change, the future of biodiversity and the future of zoos. *Biotropica* (Special Issue) 24: 345–352.

Robinson, S. K., F. R. Thompson III, T. M. Donovan, D. R. Whitehead, and J. Faaborg. 1995. Regional forest fragmentation and the nesting success of migratory birds. *Science* 267: 1987–1990.

Rogers, D. L. and F. T. Ledig. 1996. *The Status of Temperate North American Forest Genetic Resources*. U.S. Department of Agriculture Forest Service and Genetic Resources Conservation Program, University of California, Davis.

Rojas, M. 1992. The species problem and conservation: What are we protecting? *Conservation Biology* 6: 170–178.

Rolston, H. III. 1987. On behalf of bioexuberance. *Garden* 11: 2–4, 31–32.

Rolston, H. III. 1988. *Environmental Ethics: Values In and Duties To the Natural World.* Temple University Press, Philadelphia.

Rolston, H. III. 1989. *Philosophy Gone Wild: Essays on Environmental Ethics*. Prometheus Books, Buffalo, NY.

Rolston, H. III. 1994. *Conserving Natural Value*. Columbia University Press, New York.

Rolston, H. III. 1995. Duties to Endangered Species. *In* W. A. Nierenberg (ed.), *Encyclopedia of Environmental Biology*. Harcourt/Academic Press, San Diego.

Rosenberg, D. K., B. R. Noon and E. C. Meslow. 1997. Biological corridors: Form, function and efficiency. *BioScience* 47: 677–687.

Ruckelshaus, W. D. 1989. Toward a sustainable world. *Scientific American* 261 (September): 166–175.

Rudel, T. and J. Roper. 1996. Regional patterns and historical trends in tropical deforestation, 1976–1990: A qualitative comparative analysis. *Ambio* 25: 166–170.

Ruggiero, L. F., G. D. Hayward and J. R. Squires. 1994. Viability analysis in biological evaluations: Concepts of population viability analysis, biological population and ecological scale. *Conservation Biology* 8: 364–368.

Russ, G. R. and A. C. Alcala. 1996. Marine reserves: Rates and patterns of recovery and decline of large predatory fish. *Ecological Applications* 6: 947–962.

Safina, C. 1993. Bluefin tuna in the West Atlantic: Negligent management and the making of an endangered species. *Conservation Biology* 7: 229–234.

Sagoff, M. 1990. *The Economy of Earth: Philosophy, Law and the Environment*. Cambridge University Press, Cambridge.

Salm, R. and J. Clark. 1984. *Marine and Coastal Protected Areas: A Guide for Planners and Managers*. IUCN, Gland, Switzerland.

Salwasser, H., C. M. Schonewald-Cox and R. Baker. 1987. The role of interagency cooperation in managing for viable populations. *In* M. E. Soulé (ed.), *Viable Populations for Conservation*, pp. 159–173. Cambridge University Press, Cambridge.

Sample, V. A. 1994. *Remote Sensing and GIS in Ecosystem Management*. Island Press, Washington, D.C.

Samson, F. B. and F. L. Knopf (eds.). 1996. *Prairie Conservation: Preserving America's Most Endangered Ecosystem*. Island Press, Washington, D.C.

Samways, M. J. 1994. *Insect Conservation Biology*. Chapman and Hall, London.

Santos, T and J. L. Telleria. 1994. Influence of forest fragmentation on seed consumption and dispersal of Spanish juniper *Juniperus thurifera*. *Biological Conservation* 70: 129–134.

Savidge, J. A., 1987. Extinction of an island forest avifauna by an introduced snake. *Ecology* 68: 660–668.

Sawhill, J. C. 1996. Conservation science comes of age. *Nature Conservancy* Jan/Feb: 5–9.

Sayer, J. A. and S. Stuart. 1988. Biological diversity and tropical forests. *Environmental Conservation* 15: 193–194.

Sayer, J. A. and T. C. Whitmore. 1991. Tropical moist forests: Destruction and species extinction. *Biological Conservation* 55: 199–213.

Schaller, G. B. 1993. *The Last Panda*. University of Chicago Press, Chicago.

Schaller, G. B. and L. Wulin. 1996. Distribution, status and conservation of wild yak *Bos grunniens*. *Biological Conservation* 76: 1–8.

Scheiner, S. M. and J. M. Rey-Benayas. 1994. Global patterns of plant diversity. *Evolutionary Ecology* 8: 331–347.

Schelhas, J. and R. Greenberg (eds.). 1996. *Forest Patches in Tropical Landscapes*. Island Press, Washington, D.C.

Schemske, D. W., B. C. Husband, M. H. Ruckelshaus, et al. 1994. Evaluating approaches to the conservation of rare and endangered plants. *Ecology* 75: 584–606.

Schmidt, K. 1997. Life on the brink. *Earth* (April): 26–33.

Schneider, D. 1995. Down and out in the Gulf of Mexico. *Scientific American* 272: 29.

Schneider, S. H. 1989. The changing climate. *Scientific American* 261 (September): 70–79.

Schonewald-Cox, C. M. 1983. Conclusions: Guidelines to management: A beginning attempt. *In* C. M. Schonewald-Cox, S. M. Chambers, B. MacBryde and L. Thomas (eds.), *Genetics and Conservation: A Reference for Managing Wild Animal and Plant Populations*, pp. 414–445. Benjamin/Cummings, Menlo Park, CA.

Schonewald-Cox, C. M. and M. Buechner. 1992. Park protection and public roads. *In* P. L. Fiedler and S. K. Jain (eds.), *Conservation Biology: The Theory and Practice of Nature Conservation, Preservation and Management*, pp. 373–396. Chapman and Hall, New York.

Schultes, R. E. and R. F. Raffauf. 1990. *The Healing Forest: Medicinal and Toxic Plants of the Northwest Amazonia*. Dioscorides Press, Portland.

Schwartz, M. W. 1997. *Conservation in Highly Fragmented Landscapes*. Chapman & Hall, New York.

Scott, J. M. and B. Csuti. 1996. Gap analysis for biodiversity survey and maintenance. *In* M. L. Reaka-Kudla, D. E. Wilson and E. O. Wilson (eds.), *Biodiversity II: Understanding and Protecting our Biological Resources*, pp. 321–340. John Henry Press, Washington, D.C.

Scott, J. M., B. Csuti and F. Davis. 1991. Gap analysis: An application of Geographic Information Systems for wildlife species. *In* D. J. Decker, M. E. Krasny, G. R. Goff, C. R. Smith and D. W. Gross (eds.), *Challenges in the Conservation of Biological Resources: A Practitioner's Guide*, pp. 167–179. Westview Press, Boulder, CO.

Scott, J. M., C. B. Kepler, C. van Riper III and S. I. Fefer. 1988. Conservation of Hawaii's vanishing avifauna. *BioScience* 38: 232–253.

Scott, M. E. 1988. The impact of infection and disease on animal populations: Implications for conservation biology. *Conservation Biology* 2: 40–56.

Sessions, G. 1987. The deep ecology movement: A review. *Environmental Review* 11: 105–125.

Shafer, C. L. 1990. *Nature Reserves: Island Theory and Conservation Practice.* Smithsonian Institution Press, Washington, D.C.

Shafer, C. L. 1995. Values and shortcomings of small reserves. *BioScience* 45: 80–88.

Shafer, C. L. 1997. Terrestrial nature reserve design at the urban/rural interface. *In* M. W. Schwartz (ed.), *Conservation in Highly Fragmented Landscapes*, pp. 345–378. Chapman and Hall, New York.

Shaffer, M. L. 1981. Minimum population sizes for species conservation. *BioScience* 31: 131–134.

Shaffer, M. L. 1991. Population viability analysis. *In* D. J. Decker, M. E. Krasny, G. R. Goff, C. R. Smith and D. W. Gross (eds.), *Challenges in the Conservation of Biological Resources: A Practitioner's Guide*, pp. 107–118. Westview Press, Boulder, CO.

Shi, D. E. 1985. *The Simple Life: Plain Living and High Thinking.* Oxford University Press, New York.

Shulman, S. 1986. Seeds of controversy. *BioScience* 36: 647–651.

Simberloff, D. S. 1986. Are we on the verge of a mass extinction in tropical rainforests? *In* D. K. Elliott (ed.), *Dynamics of Extinction*, pp. 165–180. John Wiley & Sons, New York.

Simberloff, D. S. 1988. The contribution of population and community biology to conservation science. *Annual Review of Ecology and Systematics* 19: 473–511.

Simberloff, D. S. 1992. Do species-area curves predict extinction in fragmented forest? *In* T. C. Whitmore and J. A. Sayer (eds.), *Tropical Deforestation and Species Extinction*. pp. 75–89. Chapman and Hall, London.

Simberloff, D. S. and L. G. Abele. 1982. Refuge design and island biogeographic theory: Effects of fragmentation. *American Naturalist* 120: 41–50.

Simberloff, D. S. and N. Gotelli. 1984. Effects of insularization on plant species richness in the prairie-forest ecotone. *Biological Conservation* 29: 27–46.

Simberloff, D. S., J. A. Farr, J. Cox and D. W. Mehlman. 1992. Movement corridors: Conservation bargains or poor investments? *Conservation Biology* 6: 493–505.

Simberloff, D. S., D. C. Schmitz and T. C. Brown. (eds.). 1997. *Strangers in Paradise: Impact and Management of Nonindigenous Species in Florida.* Island Press, Washington, D.C.

Simmons, R. E. 1996. Population declines, variable breeding areas and management options for flamingos in Southern Africa. *Conservation Biology* 10: 504–515.

Singer, P. 1979. Not for humans only. *In* K. E. Goodpaster and K. M. Sayre (eds.), *Ethics and Problems of the Twenty-first Century*, pp. 191–206. University of Notre Dame, Notre Dame, IN.

Sjoåsen, T. 1996. Survivorship of captive-bred and wild-caught reintroduced European otters *Lutra lutra* in Sweden. *Biological Conservation* 76: 161–165.

Smith, A. 1909. *An Inquiry into the Nature and Causes of the Wealth of Nations.* Bullock, J. L. (ed.), P. F. Collier & Sons, New York.

Smith, F. D. M., R. M. May, R. Pellew, T. H. Johnson and K. R. Walter. 1993. How much do we know about the current extinction rate? *Trends in Ecology and Evolution* 8: 375–378.

Snyder, N. F., S. R. Derrickson, S. R. Beissinger, J. W. Wiley, et al. 1996. Limitations of captive breeding in endangered species recovery. *Conservation Biology* 10: 338–349.

Society for Ecological Restoration. 1991. Program and abstracts, 3rd Annual Conference, Orlando, FL. 18–23 May 1991.

Sokolow, R. 1992. America's first food writer. *Natural History* 101: 68–71.

Soulé, M. (ed.). 1986. *Conservation Biology: The Science of Scarcity and Diversity.* Sinauer Associates, Sunderland, MA.

Soulé, M. (ed.). 1987. *Viable Populations for Conservation.* Cambridge University Press, Cambridge, UK.

Soulé, M. 1985. What is conservation biology? *BioScience* 35: 727–734.

Soulé, M. 1990. The onslaught of alien species and other challenges in the coming decades. *Conservation Biology* 4: 233–239.

Soulé, M. and D. Simberloff. 1986. What do genetics and ecology tell us about the design of nature reserves? *Biological Conservation* 35: 19–40.

Soulé, M. E. 1980. Thresholds for survival: Maintaining fitness and evolutionary potential. *In* M. E. Soulé and B. A. Wilcox (eds.), *Conservation Biology: An Evolutionary-Ecological Perspective*, pp. 151–170. Sinauer Associates, Sunderland, MA.

Southgate, D. and H. L. Clark. 1993. Can conservation projects save biodiversity in South America? *Ambio* 22: 163–166.

Spackman, S. C. and J. W. Hughes. 1995. Assessment of minimum stream corridor width for biological conservation: Species richness and distribution along mid-order streams in Vermont, USA. *Biological Conservation* 71: 325–332.

Spalton, A. 1993. A brief history of the reintroduction of the Arabian oryx (*Oryx leucoryx*) into Oman 1980–1992. *In* P. J. S. Olney and P. Ellis (eds.), *1992 International Zoo Yearbook*, Vol 32, pp. 81–90. BPCC Wheatons, Exeter, U.K.

Sparrow, H. R., T. D. Sisk, P. R. Ehrlich and D. D. Murphy. 1994. Techniques and guidelines for monitoring neotropical butterflies. *Conservation Biology* 8: 800–809.

Species Survival Commission. 1990. *Membership Directory*. IUCN, Gland, Switzerland.

Spellerberg, I. F. 1994. *Evaluation and Assessment for Conservation: Ecological Guidelines for Determining Priorities for Nature Conservation*. Chapman and Hall, London.

Spencer, C. N., B. R. McClelland and J. A. Stanford. 1991. Shrimp stocking, salmon collapse and eagle displacement. *BioScience* 41: 14–21.

Standley, L. A. 1992. Taxonomic issues in rare species protection. *Rhodora* 94: 218–242.

Stanley, T. 1995. Ecosystem management and the arrogance of humanism. *Conservation Biology* 9: 254–262.

Stanley-Price, M. R. 1989. *Animal Re-introductions: The Arabian Oryx in Oman*. Cambridge University Press, Cambridge.

Stattersfield, A. J., M. J. Crosby, A. J. Long and D. C. Wege. 1996. *Endemic Bird Areas of the World: Priorities for Biodiversity Conservation*. Birdlife International, Cambridge.

Steer, A. 1996. Ten principles of the New Environmentalism. *Finance and Development* 33 (4): 4–7.

Stehli, F. G. and J. W. Wells. 1971. Diversity and age patterns in hermatypic corals. *Systematic Zoology* 20: 115–125.

Stein, B. A. and S. R. Flack. 1997. *Species Report Card: The State of U.S. Plants and Animals*. The Nature Conservancy, Arlington, VA.

Stevens, J. 1993. Winning the war against mealybugs. *Technology Review* 96: 17–18.

Steytler, N. S. and M. J. Samways. 1995. Biotope selection by adult male dragonflies (Odonata) at an artificial lake created for insect conservation in South Africa. *Biological Conservation* 72: 381–386.

Stolzenburg, W. 1992. The mussels' message. *Nature Conservancy* 42: 16–23.

Stone, C. P. and L. L. Loope. 1996. Alien species in Hawaiian national parks. *In* W. L. Halvorson and G. E. Davis (eds.), *Science and Ecosystem Management in the National Parks*. The University of Arizona Press, Tuscon.

Stuart, S. N. 1987. Why we need action plans. *Species*. Newsletter #8 of the IUCN Species Survival Commission, February, 1987. Gland, Switzerland.

Sutherland, W. J. and D. A. Hill. 1995. *Managing Habitats for Conservation*. Cambridge University Press, Cambridge.

Swanson, F. J. and R. E. Sparks. 1990. Long-term ecological research and the invisible place. *BioScience* 40: 502–508.

Swengel, A. B. 1996. Effects of fire and hay management on abundance of prairie butterflies. *Biological Conservation* 76: 73–85.

Szafer, W. 1968. The ure-ox, extinct in Europe since the seventeenth century: An attempt at conservation that failed. *Biological Conservation* 1: 45–47.

Szaro, R. C. and D. W. Johnston (eds.). 1996. *Biodiversity in Managed Landscapes: Theory and Practice*. Oxford University Press, New York.

Takacs, D. 1996. *The Idea of Biodiversity*. The Johns Hopkins University Press, Baltimore.

Takegawa, J. E. and S. R. Beissinger. 1989. Cyclic drought, dispersal and the conservation of the snail kite in Florida: Lessons in the critical habitat. *Conservation Biology* 3: 302–311.

Tamarin, R. H. 1996. *Prinicples of Genetics*, 5th ed. Wm. C. Brown, Dubuque, IA.

Tangley, L. 1986. Saving tropical forests. *BioScience* 36: 4–15.

Tangley, L. 1988. Research priorities for conservation. *BioScience* 38: 444–448.

Tangley, L. 1996. Ground rules emerge for marine bioprospectors: Developers of natural products juggle potential profits and fairness. *BioScience* 46: 246–249.

Tansley, S. A. 1988. The status of threatened Proteaceae in the Cape flora, South Africa and the implications for their conservation. *Biological Conservation* 43: 227–239.

Tarpy, C. 1993. Zoos: Taking down the bars. *National Geographic* 184 (July): 2–37.

Tattersall, I. 1993. Madagascar's lemurs. *Scientific American* 268: 110–117.

Taubes, G. 1992. A dubious battle to save the Kemp's Ridley sea turtle. *Science* 256: 614–616.

Taylor, P. 1986. *Respect for Nature*. Princeton University Press, Princeton.

Taylor, V. J. and N. Dunstone (eds.). 1996. *The Exploitation of Mammal Populations*. Chapman and Hall, London.

Tear, T. H., J. M. Scott, P. H. Hayward and B. Griffith. 1995. Status and prospects for success of the Endangered Species Act: A look at recovery plans. *Science* 262: 976–977.

Temple, S. A. 1990. The nasty necessity: Eradicating exotics. *Conservation Biology* 4: 113–115.

Temple, S. A. 1991. Conservation biology: New goals and new partners for managers of biological resources. *In* D. J. Decker et al. (eds.), *Challenges in the Conservation of Biological Resources: A Practitioner's Guide*, pp. 45–54. Westview Press, Boulder, CO.

Templeton, A. R. 1986. Coadaptation and outbreeding depression. *In* M. E. Soulé (ed.), *Conservation Biology: The Science of Scarcity and Diversity*, pp. 105–116. Sinauer Associates, Sunderland, MA.

Terborgh, J. 1974. Preservation of natural diversity: The problem of extinction prone species. *BioScience* 24: 715–722.

Terborgh, J. 1976. Island biogeography and conservation: Strategy and limitations. *Science* 193: 1029–1030.

Terborgh, J. 1986. Keystone plant resources in the tropical forest. *In* M. E. Soulé (ed.), *Conservation Biology: The Science of Scarcity and Diversity*, pp. 330–344. Sinauer Associates, Sunderland, MA.

Terborgh, J. 1989. *Where Have All the Birds Gone?: Essays on the Biology and Conservation of Birds That Migrate to the American Tropics*. Princeton University Press, Princeton NJ.

Terborgh, J. 1992a. Why American songbirds are vanishing. *Scientific American* 264: 98–104.

Terborgh, J. 1992b. Maintenance of diversity in tropical forests. *Biotropica* (Special Issue) 24: 283–292.

Terborgh, J. and B. Winter. 1983. A method for siting parks and reserves with special reference to Columbia and Ecuador. *Biological Conservation* 27: 45–58.

The Nature Conservancy. 1996. *Designing a Geography of Hope: Guidelines for Ecoregion-Based Conservation in The Nature Conservancy*. The Nature Conservancy, Arlington, VA.

Thiollay, J. M. 1989. Area requirements for the conservation of rainforest raptors and game birds in French Guiana. *Conservation Biology* 3: 128–137.

Thiollay, J. M. 1992. Influence of selective logging on bird species diversity in a Guianan rain forest. *Conservation Biology* 6: 47–63.

Thomas, A. 1995. Genotypic inference with the Gibbs sampler. *In* J. Ballou, M. Gilpin and T. J. Foose (eds.), *Population Management for Survival and Recovery*. Columbia University Press, New York.

Thomas, C. D. 1990. What do real population dynamics tell us about minimum viable population sizes? *Conservation Biology* 4: 324–327.

Thomas, C. D. 1995. Ecology and conservation of butterfly metapopulations in the fragmented British landscape. *In* A. S. Pullin (ed.), *Ecology and Conservation of Butterflies*. Chapman and Hall, London.

Thomas, C. D. and J. C. G. Abery. 1995. Estimating rates of butterfly decline from distribution maps: The effect of scale. *Biological Conservation* 73: 59–65.

Thomas, D. W. 1982. The ecology of an African savannah fruit bat community: Resource partitioning and role in seed dispersal. Ph. D. Dissertation, University of Aberdeen, Scotland.

Thomas, K. S. 1991. *Living Fossil: The Story of the Coelocanth*. Norton, New York.

Thomashow, M. 1996. *Ecological Identity: Becoming a Reflective Environmentalist*. MIT Press, Cambridge.

Thoreau, H. D. 1863. *Excursions*. Ticknor and Fields, Boston, MA.

Thoreau, H. D. 1971. *Walden*. Princeton University Press, Princeton.

Thorne, E. T. and E. S. Williams. 1988. Disease and endangered species: The black-footed ferret as a recent example. *Conservation Biology* 2: 66–74.

Thornhill, N. W. (ed.). 1993. *The Natural History of Inbreeding and Outbreeding*. University of Chicago Press, Chicago, IL.

Tilman, D., D. Wedin, J. Knops. 1996. Productivity and sustainability influenced by biodiversity in grassland ecosystems. *Nature* 379: 718–720.

Tilman, D., R. M. May, C. L. Lehman and M. A. Nowak. 1994. Habitat destruction and the extinction debt. *Nature* 371: 65.

Tobin, R. 1990. *The Expendable Future: U.S. Politics and the Protection of Biological Diversity*. Duke University Press, Durham, NC.

Toledo, V. M. 1988. La diversidad biológica de México. *Ciencia y Desarollo*. Conacyt, México City.

Toledo, V. M. 1991. Patzcuaro's lesson: Nature, production and culture in an indigenous region of Mexico. *In* M. L. Oldfield and J. B. Alcorn (eds.), *Biodiversity: Culture, Conservation and Ecodevelopment*, pp. 147–171. Westview Press, Boulder, CO.

Toth, L. A. 1996. Restoring the hydrogeomorphology of the channelized Kissimmee River. *In* A. Brookes and F. D. Shields, Jr. (eds.), *River Channel Restoration: Guiding Principles for Sustainable Projects*. John Wiley and Sons, Chichester, England.

Toth, L. A. and N. G. Aumen. 1994. Integration of multiple issues in environmental restoration and resource enhancement in south central Florida. *In* J. Cairns, Jr., T. V. Crawford and H. Salwasser (eds.), *Implementing Integrated Environmental Management*. Virginia Polytechnic Institute and State University, Blacksburg, VA.

Toufexis, A. 1992. A new endangered species: Human protectors of the planet put their lives on the line. *Time* 139(17): 48–50.

Travis, J. 1993. Invader threatens Black, Azov Seas. *Science* 262: 1336–1337.

Tudge, C. 1992. Last stand for society snails. *New Scientist* 135: 25–29.

Tuljapurkar, S. and H. Caswell (eds.). 1997. *Structured-Population Models and Marine, Terrestrial and Freshwater Systems*. International Thompson Publishing, Florence, KY.

Tunnicliffe, V. 1992. Hydrothermal-vent communities of the deep sea. *American Scientist* 80: 336–349.

Turner, I. M, K. S. Chua, J. S. Y. Ong., B. C. Soong and H. T. W. Tan. 1996. A century of plant species loss from an isolated fragment of lowland tropical rain forest. *Conservation Biology* 10: 1229–1245.

U.S. Fish and Wildlife Service. 1995. *California Condor Recovery Plan*, third revision. p. 62, Portland, Oregon.

U.S. Office of Technology Assessment. 1987. *Technologies to Maintain Biological Diversity*. U.S. Government Printing Office, Washington, D.C.

UNDP/UNEP/World Bank. 1994. *Global Environment Facility: Independent Evaluation of the Pilot Phase*. The World Bank, Washington, D.C.

United Nations. 1993a. *Agenda 21: Rio Declaration and Forest Principles*. Post-Rio Edition. United Nations Publications, New York.

United Nations. 1993b. *The Global Partnership for Environment and Development*. United Nations Publications, New York.

Urbanska, K. M., N. R. Webb and P. J. Edwards (eds.). 1997. *Restoration Ecology and Sustainable Development*. Cambridge University Press, Cambridge.

Usher, M. B. 1991. Scientific requirements of a monitoring programme. *In* B. Goldsmith (ed.), *Monitoring for Conservation and Ecology*, pp. 15–32. Chapman and Hall, New York.

Van Driesche, R. G. and T. J. Bellows. 1996. *Biological Control*. Chapman and Hall, New York.

Van Swaay, C. A. M. 1990. An assessment of the changes in butterfly abundance in the Netherlands during the twentieth century. *Biological Conservation* 52: 287–302.

Van de Veer, D. and C. Pierce. 1994. *The Environmental Ethics and Policy Book: Philosophy, Ecology, Economics*. Wadsworth Publishing Company, Belmont, CA.

Vane-Wright, R. I., C. R. Smith and I. J. Kitching. 1994. A scientific basis for establishing networks of protected areas. *In* P. L. Forey, C. J. Humphries and R. I. Vane-Wright (eds.), *Systematics and Conservation Evaluation.* Oxford University Press, New York.

Verboom, J., A. Schotman, P. Opdam and J. A. J. Metz. 1991. European nuthatch metapopulations in a fragmented agricultural landscape. *Oikos* 61: 149–156.

Vernon, J. E. N. 1986. *Corals of Australia and the Indopacific.* Angus and Robertson, London.

Vincent, A. 1994. The improbable seahorse. *National Geographic* 186 (4): 37–52.

Vincent, A. C. J. and H. J. Hall. 1996. The threatened status of marine fishes. *Trends in Ecology and Evolution* 11: 360–361.

Vitousek, P. M. 1994. Beyond global warming: ecology and global change. *Ecology* 75: 1861–1876.

Vitousek, P. M., C. M. D'Antonio, L. L. Loope and R. Westerbrooks. 1996. Biological invasions as global environmental change. *American Scientist* 84: 468–478.

Volk, T. 1997. *Gaia's Body: A Physiology of the Earth.* Copernicus Press, New York.

von Droste, B., H. Plachter and M. Rossler (eds.). 1995. *Cultural Landscapes of Universal Value.* Gustav Fischer Verlag, New York.

Waller, G. (ed.). 1996. *Sealife: A Guide to Marine Environment.* Smithsonian Institution Press, Washington, D.C.

Wallis deVries, M. F. 1995. Large herbivores and the design of large-scale nature reserves in Western Europe. *Conservation Biology* 9: 25–33.

Waples, R. S. and D. J. Teel. 1990. Conservation genetics of Pacific salmon. I. Temporal changes in allele frequency. *Conservation Biology* 4: 144–156.

Ward, D. M., R. Weller and M. M. Bateson. 1990. 16 rRNA sequences reveal numerous uncultured microorganisms in a natural community. *Nature* 345: 63–65.

Ward, G. C. 1992. India's wildlife dilemma. *National Geographic* 181: 2–29.

Warren, K. J. (ed.). 1996. *Ecological Feminist Philosophies.* Indiana University Press, Bloomington.

Warren, M. S. 1991. The successful conservation of an endangered species, the Heath Fritillary butterfly *Mellicta athalia,* in Britain. *Biological Conservation* 55: 37–56.

Waters, T. 1992. Sympathy for the devil. *Discover* 13: 62.

Wayne, R. K., et al. 1991. Conservation genetics of the endangered Isle Royale gray wolf. *Conservation Biology* 5: 41–51.

WCED (World Commission on Environment and Development). 1987. *Our Common Future.* Oxford University Press, Oxford.

Weber, P. D. 1993. Reviving coral reefs. *In* L. R. Brown (ed.), *State of the World 1993.* Norton, New York.

Webster, D. 1997. The looting and smuggling and fencing and hoarding of impossibly precious feathered and scaly wild things. *The New York Times Magazine,* February 16, 1997, pp. 26–33, 48–49, 53, 61.

Weiss, S. B., et al. 1991. Forest canopy structure at overwintering monarch butterfly sites: Measurements with hemispherical photography. *Conservation Biology* 5: 165–175.

Welch, E. B. and G. D. Cooke. 1990. Lakes. *In* W. R. Jordan III, M. E. Gilpin and J. D. Aber (eds.), *Restoration Ecology: A Synthetic Approach to Ecological Research,* pp. 109–129. Cambridge University Press, Cambridge.

Wells, M. and K. Brandon. 1992. *People and Parks: Linking Protected Area Management with Local Communities.* The World Bank/WWF/USAID, Washington, D.C.

Wells, M. P. and K. Brandon. 1993. The principles and practices of buffer zones and local participation in biodiversity conservation. *Ambio* 22: 157–172.

Wells, S. and N. Hanna. 1992. *The Greenpeace Book on Coral Reefs.* Greenpeace, Washington, D.C.

Western, D. 1989. Conservation without parks: Wildlife in the rural landscape. *In* D. Western and M. Pearl (eds.), *Conservation for the Twenty-first Century,* pp. 158–165. Oxford University Press, New York.

Western, D. 1997. *In the Dust of Kilimanjaro.* Island Press, Washington, D.C.

Western, D. and J. Ssemakula. 1981. The future of the savannah ecosystem: Ecological islands or faunal enclaves? *African Journal of Ecology* 19: 7–19.

Western, D. and M. Pearl (eds.). 1989. *Conservation for the Twenty-First Century.* Oxford University Press, New York.

Western, D. and W. Henry. 1979. Economics and conservation in Third World national parks. *BioScience* 29: 414–418.

Western, D., R. M. Wright and S. C. Strum (eds.). 1994. *Natural Connections: Perspectives in Community-Based Conservation.* Island Press, Washington, D.C.

Whelan, T. (ed.). 1991. *Nature Tourism: Managing for the Environment.* Island Press, Washington, D.C.

Whitcomb, R. F., C. S. Robbins, J. F. Lynch, B. L. Whitcomb, M. K. Klimkiewicz and D. Bystrak. 1981. Effects of forest fragmentation on avifauna of the eastern deciduous forest. *In* R. L. Burgess and D. M. Sharpe (eds.), *Forest Island Dynamics in Man-Dominated Landscapes,* pp. 125–205. Springer-Verlag, New York.

White, P. S. 1996. Spatial and biological scales in reintroduction. *In* D. A. Falk, C. I. Millar and M. Olwell (eds.), *Restoring Diversity: Strategies for Reintroduction of Endangered Plants.* Island Press, Washington, D.C.

White, P. S. and J. L. Walker. 1997. Approximating nature's variation: Selecting and using reference information in restoration ecology. *Restoration Ecology* 5: 338–349.

Whitmore, T. C. 1990. *An Introduction to Tropical Rain Forests.* Clarendon Press, Oxford.

Whitmore, T. C. and J. A. Sayer. 1992. *Tropical Deforestation and Species Extinction.* Chapman and Hall, London.

Whitten, A. J. 1987. Indonesia's transmigration program and its role in the loss of tropical rain forests. *Conservation Biology* 1: 239–246.

Whitten, A. J., K. D. Bishop, S. V. Nash and L. Clayton. 1987. One or more extinctions from Sulawesi, Indonesia? *Conservation Biology* 1: 42–48.

Wiese, R. J. and M. Hutchins. 1994. *Species Survival Plans: Strategies for Wildlife Conservation.* American Zoo and Aquarium Association, Bethesda, MD.

Wijnstekers, W. 1992 *The Evolution of CITES*. CITES Secretariat, Geneva, Switzerland.

Wilcove, D. S. and R. M. May. 1986. National park boundaries and ecological realities. *Nature* 324: 206–207.

Wilcove, D. S., C. H. McLellan and A. P. Dobson. 1986. Habitat fragmentation in the temperate zone. *In* M. E. Soulé (ed.), *Conservation Biology: The Science of Scarcity and Diversity*, pp. 237–256. Sinauer Associates, Sunderland, MA.

Wilcove, D. S., M. McMillan and K. C. Winston. 1993. What exactly is an endangered species? An analysis of the U.S. Endangered Species List: 1985–1991. *Conservation Biology* 7: 87–93.

Wilcove, D., M. J. Bean, R. Bonnie and M. McMillan. 1996. *Rebuilding the Ark: Toward a More Effective Endangered Species Act for Private Land*. Environmental Defense Fund, Washington, D.C.

Wilkes, G. 1991. *In situ* conservation of agricultural systems. *In* M. L. Oldfield and J. B. Alcorn (eds.), *Biodiversity: Culture, Conservation and Ecodevelopment*, pp. 86–101. Westview Press, Boulder, CO.

Willers, B. 1994. Sustainable development: A New World deception. *Conservation Biology* 8: 1146–1148.

Williams, J. D. and R. M. Nowak. 1993. Vanishing species in our own backyard: Extinct fish and wildlife of the United States and Canada. *In* L. Kaufman and K. Mallory (eds.), *The Last Extinction*, pp. 107–140. MIT Press, Cambridge, MA.

Williams, P. H. 1994. Measuring more of biodiversity: Can higher-taxon richness predict wholesale species richness? *Biological Conservation* 67: 211–217.

Williams, P., D. Gibbons, C. Margules., A. Rebelo, et al. 1996. A comparison of richness hotspots, rarity hotspots and complementary areas for conserving the diversity of British birds. *Conservation Biology* 10: 155–174.

Wilson, D. E. and R. F. Cole. 1998. *Measuring and Monitoring Biological Diversity: Standard Methods for Mammals*. Smithsonian Institution Press, Washington, D.C.

Wilson, E. O. 1984. *Biophilia*. Harvard University Press, Cambridge, MA.

Wilson, E. O. 1987. The little things that run the world: The importance and conservation of invertebrates. *Conservation Biology* 1: 344–346.

Wilson, E. O. 1989. Threats to biodiversity. *Scientific American* 261: 108–116.

Wilson, E. O. 1991. Rain forest canopy: The high frontier. *National Geographic* 180: 78–107.

Wilson, E. O. 1992. *The Diversity of Life*. The Belknap Press of Harvard University Press, Cambridge, MA.

Wilson, E. O. 1994. *Naturalist*. Island Press, Washington, D.C.

Wilson, E. O. and F. M. Peter (eds.). 1988. *Biodiversity*. National Academy Press, Washington, D.C.

Woinarski, J. C. Z. and O. Price. 1996. Application of a taxon priority system for conservation planning by selecting areas which are most distinct from environments already reserved. *Biological Conservation* 76: 147–159.

Wolf, C. M., B. Griffith, C. Reed and S. A. Temple. 1996. Avian and mammalian translocations: Update and reanalysis of 1987 survey data. *Conservation Biology* 10: 1142–1155.

Wolkomir, R. 1995. California sea otters. *National Geographic* 187 (6): 42–61

World Commission on Environment and Development (WCED). 1987. *Our Common Future*. Oxford University Press, Oxford.

World Conservation Monitoring Centre. 1992. *Global Biodiversity: Status of the Earth's Living Resources*. Compiled by the World Conservation Monitoring Centre, Cambridge and Chapman and Hall, London.

World Resources Institute. 1994. *World Resources 1994–1995: A Guide to the Global Environment*. Oxford University Press, New York. See also other years.

World Wildlife Fund for Nature (WWF). 1989. *The Importance of Biological Diversity*. WWF, Gland, Switzerland.

WRI/IUCN/UNEP. 1992. *Global Biodiversity Strategy: Guidelines for Action to Save, Study and Use Earth's Biotic Wealth Sustainably and Equitably*. World Resources Institute, Washington, D.C.

Wright, R. G., J. G. MacCracken and J. Hall. 1994. An ecological evaluation of proposed new conservation areas in Idaho: Evaluating proposed Idaho national parks. *Conservation Biology* 8: 207–216

Wright, S. 1931. Evolution in Mendelian populations. *Genetics* 16: 97–159.

WWF/IUCN. 1997. *Centres of Plant Diversity: A guide and strategy for their conservation, 3: North America, Middle America, South America, Caribbean Islands*. Cambridge, UK.

Yaffee, S. L. et al. 1996. *Ecosystem Management in the United States: An Assessment of Current Experience*. Island Press, Washington, D.C.

Yahner, R. H. 1988. Changes in wildlife communities near edges. *Conservation Biology* 2: 333–339.

Yoakum, J. and W. P. Dasmann. 1971. Habitat manipulation practices. *In* R. H. Giles (ed.), *Wildlife Management Techniques*, pp. 173–231. The Wildlife Society, Washington, D.C.

Yonzon, P. B. and M. L. Hunter, Jr. 1991. Cheese, tourists and red pandas in the Nepal Himalayas. *Conservation Biology* 5: 196–202.

Young, R. A, D. J. P. Swift, T. L. Clarke, G. R. Harvey and P. R. Betzer. 1985. Dispersal pathways for particle-associated pollutants. *Science* 229: 431–435.

Young, T. P. 1994. Natural die-offs of large mammals: Implications for conservation. *Conservation Biology* 8: 410–418.

Young, W. 1995. A dump no more. *American Forests* 101: 58–59.

Zedler, J. B. 1996. Ecological issues in wetland mitigation: An introduction to the forum. *Ecological Applications* 6: 33–37.

Zonneveld, I. S. and R. T. Forman (eds.). 1990. *Changing Landscapes: An Ecological Perspective*. Springer-Verlag, New York.

Index

About the Author

Richard B. Primack is a Professor in the Biology Department at Boston University and Associate Director of the Environmental Studies Program. He received his B.A. at Harvard University in 1972 and his Ph.D. at Duke University in 1976 with Janis Antonovics. He completed postdoctoral fellowships at the University of Canterbury (with David Lloyd) and Harvard University (with Peter Ashton). The first edition of *Essentials of Conservation Biology* (1993) was also published in Chinese and German, and *A Primer of Conservation Biology* (1995) has been translated into Japanese and Indonesian. His other books include *A Field Guide to Poisonous Plants and Mushrooms of North America* (with Charles K. Levy); *A Forester's Guide to the Moraceae of Sarawak*; *Ecology, Conservation and Management of Southeast Asian Rainforests* (edited with Thomas Lovejoy); and *Timber, Tourists, and Temples: Conservation and Development in the Maya Forest of Belize, Guatemala and Mexico* (edited with David Bray, Hugo Galletti and Ismael Ponciano).

Dr. Primack's research interests include rare plant conservation and restoration; the ecology, conservation, and management of tropical forests in Southeast Asia and Central America; conservation biology education; and the natural history of orchids. He is the book review editor for the journal *Conservation Biology* and is Vice-Chair of the Tropical Ecosystems Directorate of the U.S. Man and the Biosphere Program.

About the Book

Editor: Andrew D. Sinauer

Project Editor: Carol J. Wigg

Copy Editor: Nancy G. Lucas

Production Manager: Christopher Small

Book Design and Production: Jefferson Johnson

Cover Design: Nina Dudley

Cover Manufacture: Henry N. Sawyer Company

Book Manufacture: Courier Companies, Inc.